Practical Boat Buying

4th edition

by the editors of

Practical Sailor

Belvoir Publications, Inc.

75 Holly Hill Lane
Greenwich, CT 06830

Library of Congress Cataloging in Publication Data

Practical Sailor

    Practical Boat Buying, 4th edition

    1. Boating, sailboat evaluation
    1. Title

© 1996 Belvoir Publications, Inc.
ISBN-1-879620-41-3

Contents - Vol. 2

Head-to-Head Comparisons

Buying Guide: Boats

Buying Guide: Gear

Morgan 34

A handsome shoal-draft keel/centerboarder well-suited to cruising the Keys or the Chesapeake.

In the late 1960s and early 1970s, the names Charley Morgan and Ted Irwin were practically synonymous with Florida boatbuilding. Charley Morgan was definitely one of the designers and builders that shaped the early and middle years of fiberglass sailboat building.

Morgan designs from that period run the gamut from cruising houseboats—the Out Island series—to the 12 meter sloop *Heritage,* the 1970 America's Cup defense candidate that Morgan designed, built, and skippered.

But before *Heritage*, before the Out Island series, Charley Morgan designed cruiser/racers to the CCA rule. His successful one-off boats were typified by *Paper Tiger, Sabre*, and *Maredea*. Early Morgan-designed production boats included the Columbia 40 and the Columbia 31.

In 1962, Morgan Yacht went into business to build the 28' Tiger Cub. In 1965, the company really got rolling, building the Morgan 26, the 36, and the 42. In 1966 the Morgan 34 was added to the line. It stayed in production until the 1972 model year, when it was phased out in preference to the Morgan 35, a slightly larger, faster boat which fit a little better into the new IOR racing rule.

The Morgan 34 is a typical late CCA-rule centerboarder. Charley Morgan specialized in this type of boat, which was favored under the rating rule and well-adapted to life in the shoal waters of the Florida coast and the Bahamas.

By today's standards, the Morgan 34 is a small boat, comparable in accommodations to a lot of 30-footers. When the boat was designed, she was as big as most other boats of her overall length.

In profile, the boat has a sweeping, moderately concave sheer. The ends of the boat are beautifully balanced: the bow profile is a slight convex curve,

Specifications

LOA	34' 0"
LWL	24' 9"
Beam	10' 0"
Draft	3' 3"/7' 9" (board up/down)
Displacement	12,500 lbs.
Ballast	5,000 lbs.

the overhanging counter aft is slightly concave. Esthetically, hull shapes of this period from the best designers are still hard to beat.

Sailing Performance

With a typical PHRF rating of 189, the Morgan 34 is not as fast as some of the more competitive cruiser/racers of the same vintage, such as the Tartan 34. With just a little more sail area than the Tartan 34, the Morgan 34 is about 1,300 pounds heavier.

Most owners rate the boat as about the same speed both upwind and downwind as boats of similar size and type. At the same time, the boat's performance is at least as good as a lot of more modern "pure" cruisers of the same length.

The rig is a simple, fairly low aspect ratio mast-head sloop, using a slightly-tapered aluminum spar,

Owners' Comments

"The boat has been safe and stable in some miserable dusters in Vineyard Sound. We replaced the Atomic 4 with a Universal diesel, and now the boat is a bit underpowered.

"It's built like a brick outhouse: solid. The mast sits on a steel plate which is slowly rusting away.

"I'd suggest the following: replace the wooden spreaders; replace the vermiculite icebox insulation, which packs down and is inefficient; install a seacock on the side galley drain line, since the sink goes below the water when heeled over."

—1969 model in New York

"The boat is faster than a Swiftsure 33 or Seabreeeze 35, slower than a Pearson 33 or Pearson 35. It has a large turning radius under power, and poor controllability in reverse.

"Failures have been a rotten wooden spreader (replaced before it failed), several centerboard pennants, a crack along the rudderpost, and the straps on the tiller fitting. The centerboard lifting arrangement is a Charley Morgan "go-fast" design, and is very prone to failure. It is the weakest link in this lovely boat."

—1968 model in North Carolina

"I would look for a pre-1970 model. Later boats have a great deal of molded-in furniture. Earlier boats have built-up interiors. Prior to hull #250, centerboards were bronze, which is a plus.

"The only second-class areas of construction are in the interior. The Formica looks bleak but it was a big advertising feature in 1967. The head doors are particle board, which swells up and comes apart when it gets wet.

"The hatches are not as watertight as modern ones. Ours drip when heavy spray comes over the cabintop. The lazarette and cockpit locker lids leak, too.

"The boat is sound and well-constructed. The shoal draft is a very attractive feature."

—1967 model in Ohio

"The boat has a classic exterior, a below-average interior. There's too much plastic and fake wood. The side galley layout is not the greatest. I'd look for a boat with the aft galley, which is much more practical.

"Overall, it's a well-built and well-balanced boat that endured over a year of cruising full time with four living aboard. At no time did we question the boat's integrity."

—1969 model in New York

stepped through to the keel.

Although there are double lower shrouds, the forward lowers are almost in line with the center of the mast, with the after lowers well behind the mast. On a lighter, more modern rig, this shroud arrangement would just about require a babystay, but on the stiff masts of the late 1960s, it would be essentially superfluous.

Early boats in the series have wooden spreaders. Unless well cared for, they can rot. For some reason, wooden spreaders on aluminum masts tend to get ignored more than the same spreaders on wooden masts.

The boom is a round aluminum extrusion equipped with roller reefing. Roller reefing is tedious, inefficient, and usually results in a poorly-shaped sail. If we were to buy a Morgan 34 for cruising, the first thing we'd do would be to buy a modern boom equipped with internal slab reefing.

Shroud chainplates are located right at the edge of the deck, so inboard genoa tracks would just about be a waste of time. The spreaders are short enough that you can sheet the genoa just inside the lifelines when hard on the wind.

Just about every piece of sailhandling equipment you'd normally expect on a cruiser/racer was an option on this boat. You may find extremely long genoa tracks—some boats originally carried 170% genoas, which were lightly penalized under the CCA rule—or you may find very short genoa tracks. Likewise, turning blocks, spinnaker gear, and internal halyards were all options.

The original jib sheet winches were Merriman or South Coast #5s. Compared to modern winches, they are slow and lack power. For anything other than casual daysailing, you'll want to upgrade to modern two-speed self-tailing winches for the genoa.

At the aft end of the cockpit, there is an old-fashioned flat mainsheet traveler track. Although this isn't a bad arrangement for a cruising boat, it would be tempting, while replacing the boom, to install a modern recirculating ball traveler. You could then keep the boat on her feet a little better close reaching in a breeze by simply easing the traveler car to leeward without slacking the mainsheet.

With the standard tiller, the mainsheet location is a bit of a problem, since the helmsman sits almost at the forward end of the cockpit. This is fine for racing, when the helmsman does nothing but steer, but it is awkward for shorthanded cruising.

Like a lot of boats with low aspect mainsails, the

Morgan 34 tends to develop weather helm quite quickly as the breeze builds. Despite a 40% ballast/displacement ratio, the boat is not particularly stiff. She is narrow, and the shoal draft keeps the vertical center of gravity quite high.

The boat is quite easy to balance under sail in moderate conditions, thanks to a narrow undistorted hull, a long keel with the rudder well aft, and a centerboard. Owners report that on wheel-steered boats, you can tighten down the brake and the boat will sail itself indefinitely upwind.

Engine

Standard engine in the Morgan 34 was the Atomic 4 or the Palmer M-60, both gasoline engines. Perkins 4-107 and Westerbeke 4-107 engines were $2,000 options.

If you can buy a used boat cheaply enough and plan to keep it for a few years, it would be a natural candidate for installation of one of Universal's new drop-in Atomic 4 diesel replacements. However, since a new diesel would cost about 25% of the total value of the boat, such an upgrade is not something to be taken lightly.

With the side-galley interior with quarterberths aft, engine access for minor service is reasonable through panels in the quarterberths.

Engine access is less straightforward with the aft galley arrangement, requiring removing the companionway steps just to get to the front end of the engine.

Almost unanimously, owners in our survey state that the boat is next to impossible to back down under power in any predictable direction. With a solid two-bladed prop in an aperture, reverse efficiency is minimal with no prop wash over the rudder.

A 26-gallon Monel fuel tank was standard. Monel, an alloy of copper and nickel, is one of the few tank materials that serves equally well for gasoline, diesel oil, or water. It is prohibitively expensive, and is therefore rarely used for tanks in modern production boats. You may also find a Morgan 34 with another, optional, 15-gallon fuel tank.

Construction

In the late 60s and early 70s, Morgans were of pretty average stock boat quality. Glasswork is heavy, solid, and unsophisticated.

The construction is a combination of good features, coupled with corners cut to keep the price down.

Through hull fittings are recessed flush to the hull—good for light air performance—yet gate valve shutoffs were standard. Believe it or not, you could buy bronze seacocks as options for about $5 to $25 each! That's what we call cutting corners.

Lead ballast is installed inside the hull shell. The

There were a few different interior arrangements offered. This one is our least favorite: we prefer a more conventional aft galley layout.

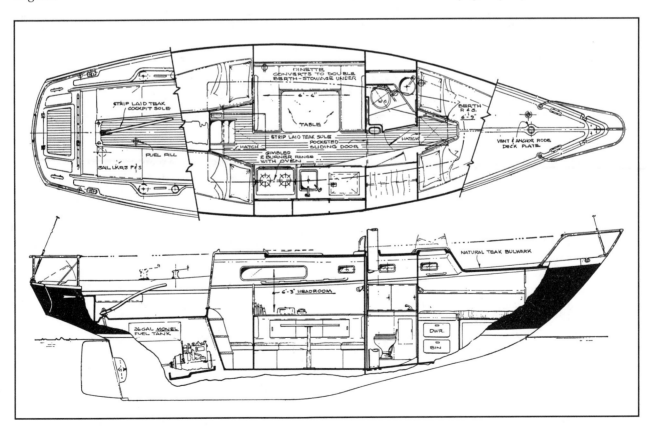

classic drawback to inside ballast is the vulnerability of the hull shell to damage in a grounding.

The cockpit is very large, larger than desirable for offshore sailing. In addition, there is a low sill between the cockpit and the main cabin, rather than a bridgedeck. You can block off the bottom of the companionway by leaving the lower dropboard in place, but this is not as safe an arrangement as a bridgedeck. Cockpit scuppers are smaller than we would want for offshore sailing.

Molded fiberglass hatches are in most cases more watertight than badly designed or maintained wooden hatches, but they are almost never as good as a modern metal-framed hatch. They're simply too flexible. When the seals get old, you tend to dog the hatch tighter and tighter, further compressing the seals and putting uneven pressure on the hatch cover. The result is almost always leaking. Leaking hatches may seem like a small problem, but they are like a splinter in your finger: the pain and nuisance are all out of proportion to the item inflicting the injury.

Like many centerboards, the Morgan 34's can be a problem. The original board was a bronze plate weighing about 250 pounds. When fully extended, the bronze board is heavy enough to add slightly to the boat's stability. Later boats have an airfoil fiberglass board of almost neutral bouyancy. There's a lot less wear and tear on the wire pennant with the glass board.

You may find a Morgan 34 that has been owner-finished from a hull or kit. Sailing Kit Kraft was a division of Morgan, and you could buy most of the Morgan designs in almost any stage of completion from the bare hull on up.

A kit-built boat can be a mixed blessing. If you find a boat that was finished by a skilled craftsman, it could be a better boat than a factory-assembled version. On the other hand, it could also be a disaster. Since the quality control of a kit boat is monitored only by the person building it, an extremely careful survey is required.

No matter how well executed it may be, an owner-completed kit boat rarely sells for more than a factory-finished version of the same boat. Most buyers would rather have a boat with a known pedigree, even if the pedigree is pretty average.

There's a decent amount of exterior teak on this boat, including the cockpit coamings, toerail, grabrails on the cabin, drop boards, hatch trim, and cockpit sole. Check the bedding and fastening of the cockpit coamings carefully. If you want to varnish coamings that have been either oiled or neglected, it may be necessary to remove and rebed them.

Exterior appearance of older boats such as the Morgan 34 is greatly improved by varnishing the teak trim. It particularly spiffs up boats with the faded gelcoat that is almost inevitable after 20 years of use.

The standard Morgan 34 was a pretty basic boat. There were single lifelines, a single battery. There was no sea hood over the main hatch, and no electric bilge pump. Most boats left the factory with a fair number of options, but you may not find a lot of things that would be standard today.

In general, the construction and design of the Morgan 34 are suited to fairly serious coastal cruising. We would not consider the boat for offshore

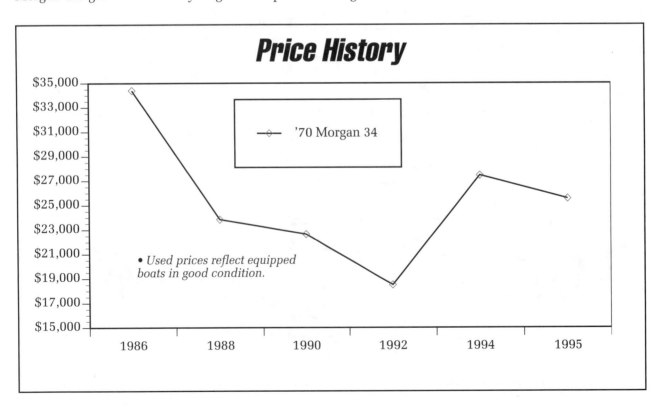

Price History

— ◇ — '70 Morgan 34

• *Used prices reflect equipped boats in good condition.*

passagemaking without improving cockpit scuppers, companionway and hatch sealing, cockpit locker sealing, and bilge pumps.

Interior

The Morgan 34 dates from the heyday of woodgrained Formica interiors. Woodgrained mica bulkheads are even more lifeless than oiled teak bulkheads. However, mica makes a pretty decent painting base if it is thoroughly sanded so that all traces of gloss are removed. Freshly-painted white bulkheads with varnished trim would make a world of difference in the interior appearance of this boat.

The interior trim on a lot of Morgan 34s is walnut, which is a pretty drab wood, even when varnished. For an extra $400 or so you could get teak trim. Unvarnished teak and walnut are very similar in appearance, although walnut is usually a bit darker.

The forward cabin contains the normal V-berths, with a drawer and bin below on each side. A stainless steel water tank fills most of the space under the forward berths. The standard tank holds 30 gallons, but many boats have the optional 60-gallon tank.

A fiberglass hatch provides fair-weather ventilation for the forward cabin. A double-opening hatch was optional, as were opening ports in place of the standard fixed ports. Below the hatch, headroom is just over 6'.

The head compartment on the port side is quite cramped when the door is closed. However, it almost doubles in size if you close off the forward cabin with the dual-purpose head door, then close the sliding pocket door that separates the forward passageway from the main cabin.

Unfortunately, this pocket door is particle board, and it is likely to be a mushy mess, since any leaks around the mast drip right onto the door. "Waterproof" particle board found its way into a lot of boats in the 1960s and early 1970s. It shouldn't have.

A shower installation was optional, and added about $800 to the base price of the boat for a pressure system, sump, pump and water heater. It is a desirable option if you plan on cruising.

You will find three different main cabin layouts. All were available as no-extra-cost options.

In the most common layout, the galley occupies the starboard side of the main cabin, with a dinette opposite. This arrangment was fairly common in the late 1960s and early 1970s. You either love this galley/dinette arrangement or you hate it. Having spent a fair amount of time sailing offshore with a similar layout, we can say unequivocally that we hate it.

With the modern U-shaped galley, the cook can stand in one place and reach everything by simply turning around. With a linear galley, the cook has to take several steps to move from the icebox to the stove. This is fine when the boat is tied to the dock, but offshore it means that there's no way the cook can wedge himself or herself in a single secure location while preparing meals.

A dinette also presents problems under way. Offshore, the most secure way to eat is to sit on the leeward settee, holding your plate in your lap. Unless there is a settee opposite the dinette, half the time you'll be sitting on the uphill side of the boat while you're trying to eat. This may be good for weight distribution while racing, but it's not very secure. We've seen more than a few bowls of beef stew go flying from the windward to the leeward side of the main cabin when the boat took a knockdown.

Two different aft galley arrangements were options. In one, the dinette is retained, with a settee opposite. In the other, the dinette is replaced by a settee and pilot berth.

Choosing between these two is purely a matter of taste. The pilot berth layout gives three sea berths in the main cabin. On the other hand, the dinette table can be lowered to form a double berth.

The aft galley is larger than the side galley. To port, there is a gimballed stove, a large dry well, and outboard lockers. A sink, icebox, and other lockers are located on the starboard side.

Reduced access to the engine is the only disadvantage we see to the aft galley layout.

In common with a lot of boats of this period, the electrical panel is inadequate for the amount of goodies that are likely to have been installed in the boat over its life. The panel is also located in the worst possible place—directly under the companionway hatch.

With the aft galley, a good location for the electrical panel would be outboard of the sink tucked under the side deck. In all likelihood, you're going to sacrifice that galley storage space to install navigation electronics anyway, since the top of the icebox is the only reasonable space to use as the chart table. That's right, there's no nav station in this boat: we're talking the late 1960s, when a boat with a radio, a depthsounder, and a knotmeter was heavily equipped with electronics.

There is reasonable storage space throughout the boat. Space under the settees is not taken up by tankage.

Headroom is 6' 3" on centerline throughout the main cabin, falling off to about 6' at the outboard edge of the cabin trunk. All the berths are at least 6' 6" long, and they are proportioned for normal-sized human beings.

Decor in the main cabin is decidedly drab, between woodgrain laminate bulkheads and a sterile white fiberglass overhead liner. The original upholstery was vinyl, completing the low-maintenance theme. Paint, varnish, and nice fabric cushions would make a Cinderella of an interior that is reasonably roomy, laid out well, and uncluttered.

Ventilation in the main cabin isn't great. There's no overhead ventilation hatch, although there's room to install one. Once again, the stock two small fixed ports may have been replaced with optional opening ports—a plus, but a small one.

A single long oval fixed port on either side of the main cabin gives the boat a very dated look. It would be tempting to remove the aluminum-framed port and replace it with a differently-shaped smoked polycarbonate window mounted on the outside of the cabin trunk and bolted through. We'd make a number of different patterns out of black construction paper and overlay them on the outside until we found a pleasing shape. You'd be surprised at how this would dress up appearance.

Conclusions

The Morgan 34 is similar in design and concept to the more-popular Tartan 34, which dates from the same period. By comparison, the Tartan 34 is lighter, faster, and has less wetted surface, since it lacks the Morgan's full keel. As a rule, we prefer the Tartan 34's construction details, although Morgan owners report somewhat less gelcoat crazing and deck delamination.

In 1970, the Morgan 34 and the Tartan 34 were almost identical in price. Today, however, the same Tartan 34 will cost about 20% more than the Morgan 34. Part of that difference in price stems from the fact that the Tartan 34 is less dated in appearance, design, and finishing detail.

If you want a keel/centerboarder for cruising in shoal waters such as the Bahamas, the Gulf of Mexico, or the Chesapeake, but don't want to spend the money for the Tartan 34, a Morgan 34 is a good alternative. With effort and money, you can upgrade the Morgan 34 quite a bit. As always, however, you should compare the dollars and amount of time invested before getting involved with a boat that dates from a period when the aesthetics of hull design were light years ahead of the nitty gritty of detailing and interior design. • **PS**

O'Day 34

An all-around family boat with a highly livable interior, but mediocre workmanship.

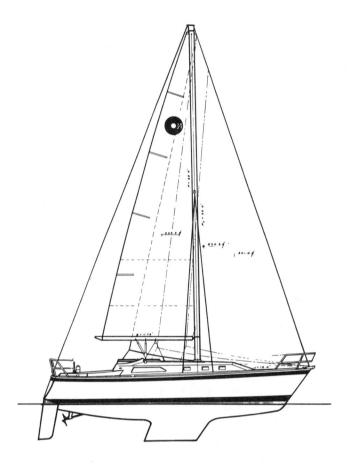

For many years O'Day was the builder of small boats. Founded by former Olympic champion, George O'Day, the company made its name with boats such as the International Tempest, International 505, Flying Dutchman, Madner, Rhodes 19, and the 16' 9" Daysailer. During the trailer-sailer revolution of the 1970s, O'Day added a series of retractable keel boats, most notably the O'Day 22 and 23. The O'Day 27, with a fixed keel, was queen of the nest. In 1975 a 32-footer was added, a 39-footer in 1982, and the largest boat the company was to build, the O'Day 40, in 1985.

One of the first American builders to pick up on Euro-styling, O'Day almost saved itself from ruin with the introduction in 1986 of the 272, and in the years immediately following, the 302 and 322. Unfortunately, these popular boats weren't enough, and O'Day went on the auction block. Pearson Yachts picked up some of the molds from Lear Siegler, the conglomerate that had bought it in turn from Bangor Punta, but Pearson, too, fell to the auctioneer's gavel not long after.

The Design

The O'Day 34 was built between 1981 and 1984. It was the 11th design the company commissioned from C. Raymond Hunt Associates. At the time, the principal designer at Hunt was John Deknatel.

It's always interesting to read the magazine ads and sales brochures hyping older boats. For example, the O'Day 34 brochure uses such phrases as, "Traditional lines. Contemporary style." "A luxuriously comfortable and practical offshore cruiser. " And, "The high performance sailing machine."

We'd agree most with the first quotation. The proportions of the boat are nicely balanced between topsides and cabin, and the raked bow and reverse

Specifications

LOA	34' 0"
LWL	28' 9"
Beam	11' 3"
Draft (shoal/deep)	4' 5"/5' 7"
Displacement	11,500 lbs.
Ballast (shoal/deep)	4,650/4,600 lbs.
Sail area	524 sq. ft.

transom work pretty well together. Calling the O'Day 34 an "offshore cruiser" and "high performance sailing machine" is stretching it a bit, however. We have always felt that O'Day's strong suit was the building of wholesome, all-around family boats.

The O'Day 34 is no exception. There is nothing radical about it: 40 percent ballast-to-displacement ratio, displacement-to-length ratio of 216, and a sensible sloop rig in terms of both design and sail area.

There is a not-so-old saying that it's much less expensive to build a boat that sits *on top* of the water than one that sits *in* the water. Boats that sit on the water have so-called flat bottoms with bolt-on keels. There isn't much beneath the cabin sole but space to collect condensation. Tanks and machinery are usu-

Owners' Comments

"Floor could be thicker; will flex under heavy weight. Make sure the cast iron keel has been properly maintained (i.e., primed, painted, etc.)."
1982 model in Massachusetts

"Significantly faster on port tack than on starboard tack; weight placement is uneven. My wife and I have found the O'Day 34 to be an ideal cruising boat. We previously had a Tartan 30 and quite frankly find the quality and amenities of the O'Day to be every bit as good. Rig needs careful tuning to achieve optimum performance. Motoring at anything over six knots is somewhat noisy and probably taxing the engine a bit. Boat becomes tender in a blow (over 30 knots)."
1973 model in Rhode Island

"Not a light air boat. Must be *something* she can't handle, but I have not found it yet. Very stiff."
1971 model in Virginia

ally located beneath the furniture or aft around the engine.

The keel of the O'Day 34 is modest, with a flat run on the bottom that will help it sit on a cradle. The hull fairs into a small skeg as it approaches the rudder, which is located as far aft as the designer could get it. Also note that with this type of underbody the propeller shaft is angled sharply downward, which is not ideal for achieving maximum thrust.

The interior plan speaks for itself as it is straightforward, practical, and thanks to 11' 3" of beam, reasonably spacious as well.

Construction

The hull of the O'Day 34 is constructed of solid fiberglass, while the deck is cored with balsa. The rudder is foam-cored fiberglass. A flange on the deck mold turns down over the hull, where it is mechanically fastened, glassed over inside and covered on the outside by a vinyl gunwale guard.

Company literature says the keel is lead, though several readers told us theirs are cast iron, a discrepancy we can't explain.

A distinguishing feature of production fiberglass boats in what might he called the modem era has been the increasing sophistication of the molds. Nowhere is this more evident than in the design and execution of interior pans (you can't really call them "liners"). These pans are carefully engineered to not only form the foundations of nearly all furniture, but also to take the place of stringers and some bulkheads by supporting the hull structure in key areas. The "unified grid pan" of the O'Day 34 is well done, with cutouts to provide decent access to most parts of the hull. Fiberglass floors support the keel. The inboard shrouds are anchored to the pan by means of Navtec chainplate rods. This method of building works well, but the pan must be strongly bonded to

The drop-leaf table on centerline seems to work well, despite the odd complaint. It features a storage well in its center, a handy feature. We like the U-shaped galley and separate nav station. The headroom is six-foot plus, and there's separate access to the head from the forward cabin.

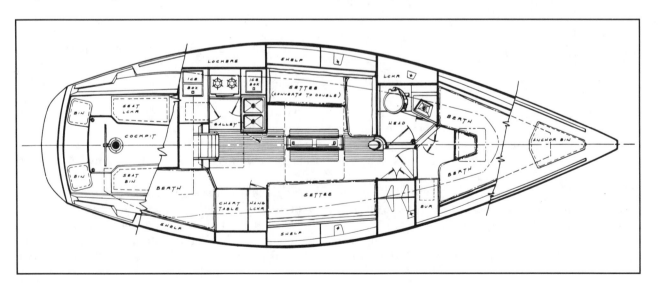

the hull, without causing hard spots, and this can can be difficult to ascertain, even by a professional surveyor.

According to the brochure, major bulkheads are bonded to the hull, bolted to the pan and screwed to the headliner. All wooden components are solid teak or teak-faced plywood.

The O'Day 34 was mass produced and built to a price. Owners' comments range from, "She's survived groundings, rocks and hurricanes, " to "Worst finish I have seen. Entire surface of boat has pinholes in gelcoat." Most disturbing are the several remarks referring to fastenings and supports, such as, "Reinforcement is missing in key areas."

We have received numerous complaints about the gelcoat, including porosity, voids, and stress cracking.

One reader said his rudder delaminated due to leakage, and that the replacement rudder blistered after three days.

Owners give at best fair ratings to the woodwork and cosmetics.

The Isomat spar and rig received generally high ratings with no failures reported.

Like most production boats built in large quantities, the O'Day 34 was never intended as a long-distance cruising boat, nor an offshore racer—the beef simply isn't there. It is, however, a good coastal cruiser that may be raced in local club regattas under the PHRF.

Performance

Owners rate speed upwind and off the wind between good and above average, with numerous caveats. The PHRF rating of the O'Day 34 with standard keel is about 147, with the shoal draft model rating a few seconds per mile slower. Some owners indicate ratings as much as 12 seconds faster, but these do not appear in our master listing.

The boat tracks fairly well upwind, but owners are not as fond of its handling off the wind, which is a little surprising given the extreme aft location of the rudder. However, compared to a full keel boat, most fin keelers will seem a bit skittish.

The vast majority of owners say the boat is very stable, even the shoal keel models. A large number also say the boat has a bothersome weather helm. One said he raked the mast forward and eliminated the problem. Another said it takes 18 knots of wind with full mainsail and 150-percent genoa to put the rail in the water. As would be expected of this design, it doesn't balance well at extreme angles of heel. Flat bottom boats like to sail on their bottoms, not on their sides, at which attitude their water planes become asymmetrical and their spade rudders tend to stall.

Under power, the O'Day 34 performs reasonably well with its three-cylinder, 21-hp. Universal diesel (30-gallon aluminum fuel tank). Power is cited as adequate only. Most owners say it backs down well. "First sailboat I've owned that (almost) backs in a straight line! " wrote a Wisconsin reader.

Interior

As suggested earlier, we don't have a lot to say about the interior, as the plan is quite conventional. We do note that it does have a nice, snug, U-shaped galley, which gives the cook his or her own private space to work. And there is a separate navigation area, as well as a wet locker.

Headroom is 6' 2" in the main cabin, lowering to 6' 1/2" forward. The V-berth measures 6' 7" by 6' 6". The settees are 6' 6" long and the quarter berth is 6' 5".

The galley is all twos, with twin sinks, twin iceboxes, and space for a two-burner stove. A propane stove with oven was optional. The water supply is contained in two tanks totaling 50 gallons.

The head has a 15-gallon holding tank standard, and an optional shower with hot and cold pressure-water system.

Owners give the interior generally high marks for livability and comfort. As seems the trend with this boat, however, such ratings are not without qualifications. One owner said, "Layout of settees and table is poor for any sitting position." More commonly, a Port Jefferson, New York owner called it "Superbly designed, inside and out. It feels like a much bigger boat."

Conclusion

The O'Day 34 does have its fans. Most owners like their boats, though most also have a few gripes, typically minor stuff that can be fixed or upgraded without a great deal of expense. We worry more about reports of deck and rudder delamination, and the absence of reinforcements in such areas as the bow. An owner in Tierre Verde, FIorida, sums it up well, saying, "Do not buy this boat if you want an offshore cruiser. Do buy this boat if you want a with-everything daysailer, a lake or bay or coastal cruiser. For the right purpose it's a great buy!"

This is a great boat for some people—fairly fast, most of the amenities for comfortable cruising, and nice looking. For those looking for a more solid, long-range cruiser, the O'Day 34 comes up short on several counts. The spade rudder, especially on the shoal keel version where it is essentially the same depth, is vulnerable. Complaints about delamination and inadequate reinforcements worry us, too. We don't know if our conclusions are justified, but we've always felt that O'Day was best at building smaller boats, and that their boats over 30 feet were just too "all-around" to excel at anything. Unless we found one at a price we couldn't refuse, we'd look for a 34 with more quality, like the Sabre 34. • **PS**

Irwin Citation 34

A mainstream coastal cruiser from an economy builder still managing to survive.

Irwin Yachts has been in operation for 27 years, one of the true old-timers in the fiberglass sail boat business. When we talked to them regarding the Irwin 34, they had just weathered the roughest storm of their history, having settled with their creditors and recovered from Chapter 11, when many other companies in similar situations were folding.

Irwin's recovery was marked by the start of a new production 50-foot cruiser. The new boat, like all the boats throughout the company's history, was designed by Ted Irwin, who has served continuously as CEO of the company as well as chief designer. In this respect, Irwin is like Catalina Yachts, whose CEO and chief designer Frank Butler is second only to Irwin in business longevity.

Like Catalina, Irwin has generally aimed at the economy end of the sailboat spectrum. However, unlike Catalina, Irwin Yachts has built a great variety of sailboats, 47 different models before their latest 50-footer—all sailboats, all larger than 20', from all-out race machines to full-tilt cruisers. Among American companies, only Pearson comes close to Irwin in the variety of cruising sailboats produced over the last quarter of a century.

The Irwin 34 is in many respects a typical Irwin boat. It was originally called the "Citation 34," which was meant to indicate that it was more of a plush cruiser than the race-oriented Irwins at the time, but more of a racer than the larger cruisers.

According to the company, 305 Irwin 34s were built in the production run, from 1978 to 1985, a moderate but successful model for the era. Near the end of its production, the boat was advertised as the Irwin 34 rather than the Citation 34. There were no major changes in the boat from beginning to end, just the details and equipment that are typical of any long production run.

Specifications

LOA	34' 3"
LWL	27' 4"
Beam	11' 3"
Draft	4' 0"/5' 4" (cb/keel)
Displacement	11,500 lbs.
Ballast	4,100 lbs.
Sail area	538 sq. ft.

Owners report mixed feelings in dealing with the company. Irwin dealers got good marks, though there are a few complaints about "incompetents and crooks." The main objection over the years has been about slow response from the company, especially regarding warranty claims on new boats and getting basic information on older models. However, long-term owners report that the company seems to have ups and downs in customer service.

Design and Construction

In design, the 34 looks like a cross between the old 1960s beamy CCA centerboarder and the mid-70s IOR racer, a combination that results in a moderate design and hence a healthy coastal cruiser. The bow has a distinctive concave curve, typical of many

Owners' Comments

"The hull is good, but the fittings seem to be borderline. It has the best layout I have seen in a 34, but I would not buy another one because the exterior finish is so poor."

—1980 model in the Chesapeake

"For a liveaboard, the boat offers the best price/size factor. A lot of little problems, though: gate valves are sealed with 3M-5200, making installation of seacocks very difficult. Tanks utilize excessive under-bunk space, Irwin's own wheel pedestal creates problems in mounting instruments, and the wheel is too large for the cockpit. It needs a self-tailing mainsheet winch and the sheet winches should be mounted further aft. Head lighting is terrible."

—1984 model in Galveston Bay

"There is little I can complain about, but I don't have the confidence I should in a boat this size. The fiberglass work is not, or doesn't seem to be of high quality. The mast also seems light, but I've had no problems."

—1980 model on Long Island Sound

"Don't hesitate—buy it. It's a great boat. I think it is built a little light for distance cruising. For the way I use it, it fits my needs."

—1982 model in Massachusetts

"This is a good boat for the money—fine for coastal cruising in fair weather. Irwin could spend more time on details."

—1981 model in Massachusetts

"The Irwin 34 is a 'price' boat, but after looking at the Sabre 34, Aloha 10.4, Baba 30, Pearson 34, O'Day 34, Cal 35, Catalina 36, and others, I feel that this is a better boat, and it was $10,000-$15,000 cheaper than any of the above."

—1983 model in Texas

"The boat needs to come with an owner's manual, including wiring and plumbing diagrams."

—1983 model on Lake of the Ozarks

"I had many problems, especially leaks which I had to fix, but I would buy another as it is a very good value and sails well for shoal draft."

—1982 model in Louisiana

"The Citation 34 is a well-designed and fast sailboat. More attention to details would make it watertight below decks and afford some badly needed privacy (a must in a boat designed to sleep six!). There is an obvious shortage of locker space, particularly a wet locker."

—1979 model in Lake Erie

"I had nine pages of warranty claims. Water and fuel tanks leaked; all ports leaked; all hatches leaked, the sump pump didn't work, the starboard chainplate wasn't installed properly, the shaft strut failed, all stanchions leaked, the teak finish-work below was not completed, gelcoat voids everywhere, traveller leaked, etc. etc. The words 'quality control' cannot be used with the word Irwin when describing production."

—1978 model in Florida

Irwin designs, and a flattish sheer, with a molded-in cove stripe to make the sheerline appear a bit higher in the bow. The stern sections have the peculiar tuck-up typical of IOR boats of the era. The trunk cabin is traditional looking and fairly low. Overall, we think the boat is an attractive example of the modern racer-cruiser.

Underwater, the hull is beamy and saucer shaped. The centerline of the hull aft of the keel forms a shallow fence which runs back to form a skeg in front of the spade rudder. Though the boat was available with a deep fin keel, drawing 5' 4", the centerboard model was far more popular. Company literature advertises a shoal draft keel as standard, with the fin and centerboard as options, but we have never seen a shoal-draft model and none of the owners in our surveys had the shoal-draft version. Brochures show the shallow-draft keel as identical in outline to the

centerboard model but with no board installed.

The centerboard lifts into a shallow stub keel, and the pennant is a Dacron rope; it runs to the deck through a tube which forms a grab rail at the front edge of the galley. We examined three used 34s, and the two centerboard models each had badly chafed centerboard pennants needing replacement.

Other than the chafe problem, the centerboard version of the boat is probably to be preferred if you have a choice. Unlike some boats which are designed for a fin and compromised with a centerboard, the hull shape looks well matched to the board, and few designers have as much experience with centerboards as Ted Irwin.

The hull is a conventional lay-up of mat and woven roving. The deck is a conventional balsa core sandwich.

The three boats we examined all had decent gelcoat

and exterior finish, but owners in our surveys report an inordinate incidence of gelcoat problems, including patches coming off, large voids, and excessive crazing. One boat we looked at had quite a few repaired spots in the deck molding, and we suspect most of the gelcoat problems were new boat problems. Once fixed, they should not be a major concern for the used boat buyer.

With regard to other elements of construction, quality is on the poor side. In fact, the three boats we examined were serious contenders in our own used-boat search but were finally rejected because we didn't like many details of the way the boats were built. For example, two of the boats we looked at clearly had a history of deck leaks at the portlights and a variety of fittings. The interior is generally well finished with teak-faced plywood and an interior liner, but the ceiling and liner made it very difficult to get at the inside of the hull and deck to trace or fix the leaks. It was clear that the previous owners had little luck in stopping the leaks. Further, the hull-to-deck joint is fastened with sheet metal screws rather than bolts. The screws are installed both vertically, from the top of the aluminum toe rail, and horizontally, from the side of the toe rail. Through-bolting is preferable.

More importantly, on the boat we were most interested in, it was evident that the hull-to-deck joint was leaking, at best a nuisance, at worst a major repair job. Though we couldn't examine most of the joint because of the interior joinerwork, we did find one spot where the deck molding actually did not overlap the hull flange. You could see the underside of the toerail from inside the boat.

On one boat, the deck cleats were fastened only with sheet metal screws, and on all the boats, the bow and stern pulpits were only screwed down rather than through-bolted.

There were several details—cheap through-hull valves, no washers on chainplate bolts—which were relatively easy to correct, but they put us off the boat.

Obviously, Irwin believes these construction details are adequate, but we consider them very minimal or problematic—something we would feel compelled to correct.

In contrast to the details, the basic fiberglass work seemed solid and good on all the boats we examined.

Interior

The interior of the 34 is generally well done, good production-line work with teak veneer and plastic. Some of the details of the cabinetry were a little sloppy on the boats we examined, but all in all the interior of the boat, when new, was undoubtedly a strong selling point.

There are three good berths—a V-berth double and a quarter berth. The quarter berth will be just a little tight, especially at the foot, for a large, tall man. The settee is usable as a single berth (it's a very comfortable settee), and the dinette opposite is convertible to a small double. The head is of good size, and the galley is well arranged in a sort of wrap-around U. There's a good electrical panel at the aft side of the galley. The nav station is set at an angle, with the table a bit small though adequate.

The Irwin 34 came with seven opening ports as well as forward and midship hatches, so ventilation should be good.

Stowage below is minimal, since tankage occupies space below the berths—a shortcoming of the modern hull shape. Tankage is adequate on the boat—30 gallons fuel, 80 gallons water, and a big holding tank for the head—a rarity on production boats of this size.

There's little bilge in the boat, which can cause problems when you take water inside the hull. This showed up in the discolored and delaminated teak/

The Irwin 34's interior has a fairly straightforward layout, but with a number of angled bulkheads to add interest. The sink is near the centerline to facilitate draining on either tack.

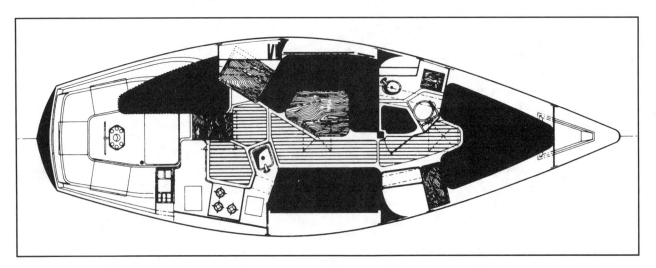

holly plywood on the cabin sole of two of the boats at which we looked.

Original standard equipment is quite complete and modern—hot/cold pressure water, shower, propane stove, 4" cushions, AC and DC electrical systems, and so on, meaning that little upgrading should be necessary, assuming the boat has been well kept.

Overall, the interior seems very desirable for a couple cruising or a couple with one or two children. There are no privacy doors for the forward cabin, so two couples will have to be (or become) intimate while cruising.

On Deck

The deck is conventional but well done for working the boat. There's a deck-opening anchor locker forward, wide side decks, and a good big cockpit with a small ice/beer locker, two lazarettes, and a propane tank locker.

A wheel was standard on the boat. A nice feature is that a portion of the cockpit sole is removable for superior engine access, the best we have seen on a boat this size. Cockpit drains are also large, another rarity on production boats.

The companionway opening is large, with just a small lip/step above the cockpit sole. While not desirable in an offshore boat, this is okay in a coastal cruiser and makes for easy access to the interior. Most owners will want to arrange a way to secure the lowest companionway drop board, so it can be left in place during rough conditions.

The mainsheet traveler is on the cabin top, just ahead of the companionway. While this is a conve-nient location, the boats we looked at had exceptionally unsightly dodgers because the multi-part mainsheet was somewhat in the way.

Performance

The boat came with a Yanmar 15, which generally gets good reports from owners, though some think the boat is a bit underpowered. A 20-hp Yanmar was available as an option, and this would be desirable if a buyer were choosing between otherwise similar boats; the 20-hp model would be smoother running as well as more powerful.

The boat we sailed handled adequately under power, though some owners report it difficult to back up straight. Most of the 34s had solid props, and the performance-oriented sailor will want to upgrade to a folding or feathering prop so the boat's sailing ability isn't hurt.

The boat has a big rig, well balanced between mainsail and jib, and as you can expect from Ted Irwin's design board, it is a good sailing boat. With a PHRF rating around 160, it is slightly slower than other cruiser/racers of that era, like the C & C 34, but it will make good passages, especially off the wind.

Many owners report that they consider the boat quite tender, especially the centerboard model, but we found the boat to be reasonably stiff, with lots of initial stability from the beamy hull. We didn't sail the boat in heavy air, but we suspect an early reef would be desirable. Cruisers will find that it works well to sail the boat under roller-furling jib alone.

Early boats may have the DynaFurl roller which came as an option from Irwin, and buyers may want

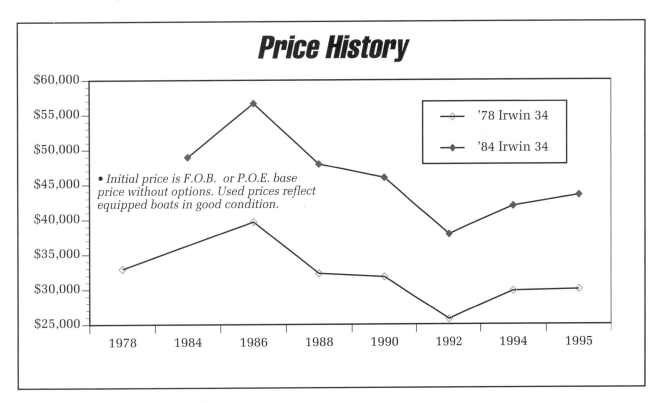

Price History

• Initial price is F.O.B. or P.O.E. base price without options. Used prices reflect equipped boats in good condition.

Legend: ’78 Irwin 34, ’84 Irwin 34

to factor in a replacement in their price figuring. The boats are generally of an age where the original sails are still aboard and, for all practical purposes, best used as drop cloths. Though the boat was advertised as a "club racer," we saw no used 34s with spinnakers or any spinnaker gear, so a chute and related gear may also have to be purchased to complete a sail inventory.

Standard winches on the boat were minimal, and an upgrade will be desirable if the original owner didn't buy the optional package when the boat was new.

The rig is adequate, the only problem reported by owners being paint problems on the mast, perhaps from a poor priming job on the aluminum. The mast of one boat we looked at had been re-painted.

Conclusions

It is an excellent design, a wholesome all-around racer/cruiser with shallow draft that would serve a family's needs as a coastal cruiser, at a reasonable cost.

Unfortunately, the Irwin 34 suffers from some corner-cutting: details of construction which are cheap or shoddy, such as using only screws to secure the hull-to-deck joint.

Realistically, those details should not hamper the boat's use in normal conditions as a coastal cruiser, but are substandard compared to many other boats available. We generally would not recommend the boat to anyone contemplating ocean passages, unless considerable basic upgrading had been completed.

But for a coastal cruiser, for an owner who likes to do some upgrading, the boat is a handsome, well-thought-out design, with a good interior, well-equipped. In today's market, it offers a lot of basic boat, especially if bought at the right price. • **PS**

Hunter 34

Like other Hunters, the 34 bears the stamp of a mass-produced boat—but she's better than older Hunters.

When the Hunter 34 was introduced in late 1982, it was the second of the "modern" generation of Hunters, the first being the rather remarkable Hunter 54. The Hunter company has been strongly identified with the long-distance singlehanded racing of its president, Warren Luhrs. Although Luhrs has not been particularly successful in his racing, his own boats have been innovative, and the concepts of innovation and high-tech have to some degree rubbed off on Hunter's production boats.

Hunter has always gone after the entry-level cruising boat owner, and has traditionally pushed its "Cruise Pac" concept—a boat delivered equipped down to the life jackets, and ready to go. This certainly reduces the amount of decision making required by inexperienced boat owners, and has been a successful marketing strategy. For more experienced sailors who would rather choose their own gear, the Cruise Pac idea is not necessarily a plus.

In just over three years, over 800 Hunter 34s were built. For the 1986 model year, the 34 was phased out in favor of the even more Eurostyled Legend 35.

A number of Hunter 34 owners responding to our survey moved up from smaller boats in the Hunter line—exactly what every builder would like to see happen. All reported that the Hunter 34 was light-years ahead in both design and workmanship compared to earlier models.

Because the Hunter 34 was only in production for a few years, few changes were made between model years. You are therefore less likely to find major upgrades on older boats than you would find on a boat that has been in production for a long time.

Sailing Performance

The Hunter 34 is a fast boat, particularly in light air. This is due almost entirely to her huge rig, which

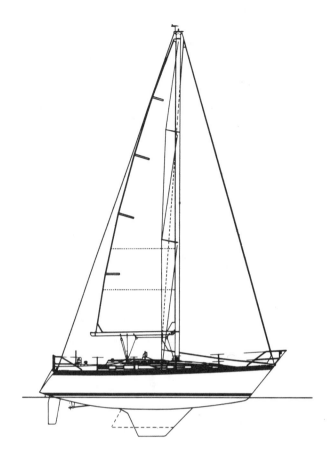

Specifications

LOA .... 34' 5"
LWL .... 28' 3"
Beam .... 11' 7"
Draft .... 4' 3"/5' 6" (shoal/std)
Displacement .... 11,820 lbs.
Ballast .... 5,000 lbs.
Sail area .... 577 sq. ft.

towers over 51' above the waterline. Owners report that in winds of from seven to 12 knots, the boat is practically unbeatable in club racing. The typical PHRF rating of 135 for the deep keel boat is faster than most other cruiser/racers of her size.

There is a price to be paid for that speed, however. A number of owners responding to our survey report that the original Hunter 34 is a very tippy boat, in either the deep keel or shoal draft version. In winds of 15 knots true or more, it's time to reef the main when going upwind. In fact, the boat's lack of stability is the single most commonly criticized aspect of the Hunter 34's performance in our survey. One owner was considering cutting several feet off his mast. Others have stepped down from 150% headsails to 135% or smaller overlaps.

Normally, you would expect a boat with a 42% ballast/displacement ratio to be stiff. The keel of the deep-draft Hunter 34, however, has most of its weight and volume up high, while the shoal draft keel, even with its extra 220 pounds of ballast, still has a fairly high vertical center of gravity. This just goes to show that you can't judge a boat's stability by its ballast/displacement ratio—you've got to know how far down that weight is, too.

Models late in the production run had more ballast. The 1985 Hunter 34 brochure shows about 450 pounds more ballast than in the 1983 model. For cruising, the additional ballast would be a real plus. For club racing with a full crew, the lighter boats could be sailed faster.

Using headsails smaller than 150% on the Hunter 34 would be a good idea, particularly if you couple them with a modern roller furling system. A 135% jib can more effectively be reduced to 110% than a 150% genoa can be reefed to 120%. Since the boat is sensitive to sail area, a good headsail roller furling system is a must, in our opinion.

According to several owners, the Hunter 34 carries substantial weather helm in anything more than very light air. This may in part be due to the boat's tenderness. As boats with wide sterns and narrow bows heel, the waterplane becomes substantially asymmetrical, which can give the boat a pronounced tendency to head up.

This weather helm may be exacerbated by an original rudder design that some owners report was both too small and too weak for the boat. Several owners reported cracking of the original rudders, which Hunter replaced with a larger, stronger, "high performance" rudder. Unfortunately, in some cases Hunter only paid part of the replacement costs; owners were stuck with the rest. We wouldn't want a Hunter 34 without the high performance rudder. The better rudder was standard equipment on 1984 and 1985 models.

The complex B&R rig, with its swept-back spreaders and diamond shrouds, is also a headache for some owners. There's a lot of rigging for a novice to adjust, and according to our survey, the dealers who commissioned the boats were not necessarily more capable of adjusting the rig than the owners.

One problem with the B&R rig is that, on any point of sail freer than a broad reach, the mainsail will fetch up on the spreaders and shrouds. You can apply patches to keep the spreaders from poking holes in the mainsail, but we think the shrouds are likely to chafe on the sail almost from head to foot when running, no matter what you do.

In addition, the lack of either forward lower shrouds, baby stay, or inner forestay means that if the headstay goes, the rig may follow before you can do anything to prevent it. One owner in our survey reported losing his rig when the roller furling headstay failed. Most new sailors have enough trouble tuning a simple, single-spreader rig with double lower shrouds. The multi-spreader, multi-shroud B&R rig may seem incomprehensible to them, and they may never be able to tune the rig for good performance.

The boat is very fast upwind, but only average in speed off the wind. With a spinnaker, downwind performance would be greatly improved. The high aspect ratio mainsail simply doesn't project enough area for efficient downwind sailing, particularly since you can't square the boom to the mast due to the swept-back spreaders.

Engine

Most Hunter 34s are equipped with the Yanmar 3GMF, a three-cylinder, fresh water cooled diesel that puts out about 22.5 hp. This is an excellent engine, although early versions, according to some owners in our survey, were plagued by vibration.

Some of the first Hunter 34s were equipped with the Westerbeke 21 diesel. In our opinion, the Yanmar is a much more desirable engine. For boats to be used in salt water, check to make sure that the engine is fresh water cooled, rather than raw water cooled. Some early versions of this engine lacked fresh water cooling, and they will not last as long when used in salt water.

Access to the engine for service is good. The Yanmar is more than adequate power for the boat, and she should cruise under power at 5 1/2 knots or more without any trouble. The fuel capacity of 25 gallons should give a range of about 275 miles.

Construction

Hunters are mass-produced boats at the low end of the price scale. The Hunter 34 was the first "small" Hunter to be built with a molded hull liner. A molded liner can add considerable strength to a single-skin boat, and the use of integral molded furniture components can greatly speed assembly. Assembly is the right word, too: these boats are assembled, rather than built.

The original tooling for a hull liner is quite expensive. It is therefore only practical on a boat that is expected to have a fairly large production run.

Not everything about the Hunter 34's hull liner is a plus, however. According to several owners, any leakage from the stuffing box can be trapped between the liner and the hull, never draining to the bilge. This could not only smell bad after a while, but could possibly cause problems in a cold climate if trapped water freezes without room to expand. The pre-assembly technique common with liners also means that many systems are installed in ways that can make them difficult to service after the hull, deck, and liner are put together.

Hunter quality control is criticized by some owners in our survey. Complaints include chafed hoses, raw edges, systems hooked up improperly, and leaking ports and hatches. In our opinion, that's a quality control problem, pure and simple, and it can be a maintenance headache for owners. One owner reported a leaking hull-to-deck joint. When he checked it, he found that many of the bolts had apparently never been torqued down when the hull and deck were joined. We don't think the boat should have left the factory in that condition.

On the positive side, owners of Hunter 34s who had owned older Hunters report that in general the construction details of the 34 are superior to those of older boats.

Do not expect to find a lot of fancy teak joinerwork on the Hunter 34. Some owners complain that both the interior and exterior teak trim is poorly fitted and poorly finished. Obviously, you could do a lot to improve this if you wanted to—as some owners have—but don't expect a dramatic increase in the value of the boat for your efforts.

The iron keels of the Hunter 34s can also be a maintenance headache. Some owners say the keels did not come from the factory with adequate protection to avoid rusting—which is almost impossible to prevent with an iron keel. Other owners report that the keel-to-hull seam cracks open, allowing salt water into the joint—which results in more rust. This is a cosmetic problem now, but we think it could over time become a structural problem.

The deck molding has been a source of trouble on some boats. The molded non-skid isn't very non-skid when it gets wet. There are also a number of reports of gelcoat flaws in the deck, including voids and blistering. At least one owner reports that the outer deck laminate in his cockpit has separated from the wood core.

Several owners complain that some molded deck components—cockpit locker covers, anchor well covers—are simply too light, and tend to crack.

Interior

The Hunter 34 was one of the first boats under 35' to offer a tri-cabin layout, and this interior design is frequently cited as a primary reason for buying the boat. Now, of course, it is common for boats this size to have three cabins.

The only real complaint voiced about the interior of the Hunter 34 is the narrowness of the foot of the forward V-berth. Despite being pushed far forward in the hull, the forward cabin feels big due to the long cabin trunk, which extends clear to the anchor well, giving extra headroom over the berth. Standing headroom in the forward cabin drops off to less than 6' due to the sloping cabin trunk.

Just aft of the forward cabin is a full-width head. This makes a lot of sense in a boat this size, since the combination of head and passageway would make for both a cramped head and a narrow passageway.

According to some owner surveys, the plumbing for the toilet leaves a lot to be desired. They report that the holding tank system smells, apparently due to porous hoses and a poor vent design.

Instead of the more common U-shaped dinette, the Hunter 34 has a rather old-fashioned dinette with athwartships seating. This certainly makes it easier to convert the dinette to a double berth, but it means that you can seat a maximum of four at the table for dinner. On the port side, the head of the settee berth is used as the seat for the chart table—a design compromise, since that settee is one of only two potential sea berths on the boat.

This was one of the first boats in its size range to offer a three-cabin interior, and overall it works well. Owners cite the interior as one of the boat's major selling points.

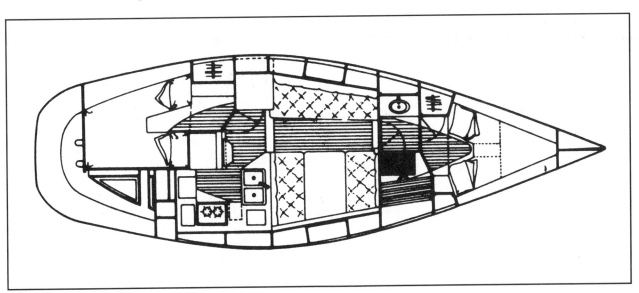

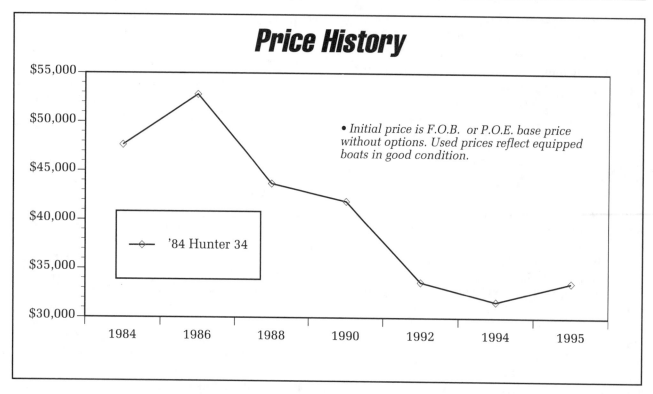

Price History

• Initial price is F.O.B. or P.O.E. base price without options. Used prices reflect equipped boats in good condition.

—◇— '84 Hunter 34

Original specifications call for a two-burner kerosene stove. Kerosene never caught on as a cooking fuel in this country, partly because it is so difficult to get high-grade kerosene here. Propane or CNG would be far better choices for cooking fuel, since low-grade kerosene is a dirty fuel, and alcohol is expensive, inefficient, and in our opinion, dangerous.

As you would expect on a boat this size, the aft cabin is pretty small, with limited standing area. Despite the fact that the double berth is mostly under the cockpit, there is adequate headroom over it due to the fact that the cockpit is quite shallow.

The privacy of the tri-cabin layout is very important for a family with children, or owners that like to cruise with another couple. The single fixed berth in the main cabin means that the boat will sleep only five without making up the dinette. "Only" five is a pretty good number in a boat this size, and the most important thing is that it sleeps five in a reasonable level of comfort. All in all, the interior of the Hunter 34 is well thought out and livable.

Conclusions

The general design and finish of the Hunter 34 are far ahead of older boats by the company. The Eurostyling of the deck and interior were pretty unusual when the boat first came out, but fairly typical of boats built five years after the Hunter 34 was introduced.

Nevertheless, this is still a mass-produced boat with what some owners consider mediocre quality control and finishing details. It is a fast sailer, but may be so tippy that it discourages some novices. You should definitely sail the boat before you buy it. The B&R rig may also scare off some new sailors.

Because of the problems with the deck molding, a used Hunter 34 should be carefully and professionally surveyed before purchase.

If you want a fast, modern small coastal cruiser with maximum room at minimum cost, a Hunter 34 would be a good choice. But remember that you're buying a mass-produced boat, and it's not realisitic to expect custom quality at this price. **• PS**

Tartan 34

There are a lot of shortcomings to the 34. But she's well designed and well built, and the price is right.

It may be hard to believe, but it's been about 25 years since Olin Stephens designed the breakthrough 12 meter sloop *Intrepid*. Just a year later, he designed the Tartan 34, a keel/centerboard, CCA racer/cruiser, for Douglass & McLeod Plastics, the company that became Tartan Marine.

The CCA was a true racer/cruiser rule. Heavy displacement was encouraged, and keel/centerboarders were treated more than fairly, as the success of designs such as S&S's *Finisterre* shows. Even top racing boats had real interiors—enclosed heads, permanent berths, usable galleys. You could buy a boat like the Tartan 34, and given good sails and sailing skills, you could actually be reasonably competitive on the race course. And then a couple could take their racing boat cruising, without a crew.

This was no "golden age" of yacht design, however. Interiors were unimaginative and fairly cramped. Galleys were small, and few boats had such amenities as hot water, gas cooking, refrigeration, and showers—things that are taken for granted today. Navigation stations were rudimentary. Sailhandling gear, by modern standards, was almost a joke. There were no self-tailing winches, few hydraulic rig controls, and roller-reefing headsail systems were primitive. Mylar and Kevlar were off in the future, loran was expensive and hard to use.

Yet some boats from this period, for all their "shortcomings" by modern standards, are classics in the truest sense: the Bermuda 40, the Luders 33, the Bristol 40, the Cal 40. And the Tartan 34.

More than 500 Tartan 34s were built between 1968 and 1978. By 1978 the CCA rule was long gone, PHRF racing was beginning to surge, and the MHS (now IMS) was in its infancy. The Tartan 34 had passed from a racer/cruiser to a cruiser, not because the boat had changed, but because sailboat racing

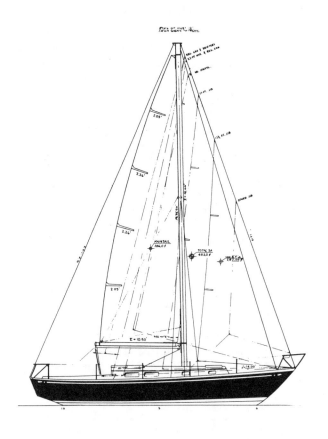

Specifications

LOA	34' 5"
LWL	25' 0"
Beam	10' 2"
Draft	3' 11"/8' 4" (board up/down)
Displacement	11,200 lbs.
Ballast	5,000 lbs.
Sail area	483 sq. ft.

had changed. The Tartan 34 was succeeded by the larger, more modern Tartan 37, a boat of exactly the same concept.

The boats are widely distributed in this country, but there are large concentrations along the North Atlantic coast, the Chesapeake, and in the Great Lakes. You'll find them wherever the water is shallow.

Read this and weep: in 1970, a Tartan 34, complete with sails, cost about $22,000. By 1975, the price had gone all the way up to $29,000. Today, equipped with more modern equipment, the boat would cost $100,000 to build.

Sailing Performance

The Tartan 34's PHRF rating of about 168 to 174 is

Owners' Comments

"Gelcoat on deck and cabin trunk is a bit thin and shows air pockets. Check for stress cracks in deck and forward cabin trunk corners, also wear between centerboard and centerboard axle.

"Check through hull fittings. Ours has brass pipe nipples and gate valves which have failed, but all in all we have a good vessel which sails very well."

—1971 model in Vermont

"I've really come to appreciate the traditional lines and the teak, although it's a pain to keep the teak looking good. Storage space is awkward and not all usable without difficulty.

"The large cockpit is great for daysailing with guests. We'd like a shower in the head. We added a wheel. Watch the placement: it should be between the icebox hatch and the cockpit locker, well forward.

"I wasn't in love with the boat when I bought her, but I've come to appreciate her quality, performance, and livability while adjusting to her few shortcomings."

—1972 model in Maryland

"The stainless steel water tank and icebox liner were poorly soldered, with cold joints. This is a great-sailing, forgiving boat for those who like a relatively fast traditional boat. You need to like teak and enjoy caring for it to keep the boat looking its best."

—1972 model in Pennsylvania

"The centerboard operating mechanism has broken twice, and the boom was shortened excessively in response to the IOR rule.

"Never crank the centerboard when there is any pressure or resistance on the board. This is a solid, attractive cruising boat."

—1975 model in Pennsylvania

"We've had problems with the deck gelcoat since day one, otherwise she has been a trouble-free boat. Other Tartans have had similar gelcoat problems.

"I would recommend the boat. She is a good sailing boat and an excellent value compared to new boats of her size."

—1976 model in New Jersey

"The icebox should be insulated better. The centerboard mechanism is unusually susceptible to damage. I've probably been further in a Tartan 34 than anyone: the Virgins, the Dominican Republic, Haiti, Puerto Rico, the Bahamas."

—1974 model in Florida

"The head is too small. The chart table is awful. Electrical switches are in a bad location. We shifted the traveler to the cabin top—much better.

"Overall it's a great boat, all boats being compromises of sorts. Engine location cannot be praised enough. Keep the tiller."

—1972 model in Rhode Island

comparable to more modern fast cruisers of similar displacement, such as the Nonsuch 30 and Pearson 31. The boat is significantly slower, however, than newer cruiser/racers of similar length but lighter displacement, like the C&C 33.

Like most centerboarders, the Tartan 34 is quite a bit faster downwind than upwind, and the boat can be run downwind more effectively than a fin-keeler. For example, in only 16 knots of true wind, optimum jibe angle is 173°—about 5° lower than the typical modern fin-keel boat.

Because of her shoal draft, the boat's center of gravity is fairly high. Righting moment at 1° is about 630 ft/lbs—some 20% less than a modern fin-keel cruiser/racer of the same displacement. This means that the Tartan 34 is initially more tender than a more modern deep-keel boat.

As first built, specifications called for 4,600 pounds of ballast. That was increased to 5,000 pounds on later models, although the boat's displacement is not listed by the builder as having increased with the addition of the ballast. We're not sure where the 400 pounds of displacement went.

The boat originally had a mainsail aspect ratio of about 2 1/2:1, with a mainsail foot measurement of 13'. The mainsheet on this model leads awkwardly to a cockpit-spanning traveler just above the tiller, well aft of the helmsman. An end-of-boom lead was essential because of the old-fashioned roller-reefing boom. This traveler location really breaks up the cockpit.

Although a tiller was standard, you will find wheel steering on many boats. Owners report no particular problems with either tiller or wheel. In both cases, the helmsman sits at the forward end of the cockpit.

With the introduction of the IOR, mainsail area was penalized relative to headsail area, and the main boom of the Tartan 34 was shortened by about 2 1/2'. This allowed placement of the traveler at the aft end of the bridgedeck, a far better location for trimming the main, which was still equipped with a roller-reefing boom.

Neither the base of the foretriangle nor the height of the rig was increased to offset the loss of mainsail area. According to some owners, the loss of about 35 square feet of sail area can be felt in light-air conditions. At the same time, shortening the foot of the mainsail did a lot to reduce the weather helm the boat carries when reaching in heavy air. Some boats with the shorter boom have made up the missing sail area by increasing jib overlap from 150% to 170%, but this lowers the aspect ratio of the sail, costing some efficiency.

We would recommend a compromise on boats with the roller-reefing boom. When the time comes to buy a new mainsail, get a new boom equipped with internal slab reefing, internal outhaul, and stoppers at the inboard end of the boom. If it's not already there, install a modern traveler on the bridgedeck. Instead of going with either the short or long mainsail foot, compromise on one of about 12'. A modern, deep-section boom would not require that the mainsheet load be spread out over the boom. You could sheet to a single point over the traveler, about 2' inboard of the end of the boom.

A major advantage of a centerboard is that the lead (the difference in fore-and-aft location between the center of lateral resistance of the hull and the center of effort of the sailplan) can be shifted as the balance of the boat changes. Tartan 34 owners report using the board to ease the helm when reaching in heavy conditions.

Like almost all S&S designs, the Tartan 34 is a good all-around sailing boat without significant bad habits. Owners who race the boat say that she should be sailed on her feet: at an angle of heel of over 20°, the boat starts to slow down and make leeway. USYRU's velocity prediction program disagrees, saying that the boat should be sailed at higher angles of heel upwind and reaching in wind velocities of 14 knots or more.

Since the boat is relatively narrow, the position of the chainplates at the deck edge is not a serious handicap for upwind performance. With single spreaders and double lower shrouds, the rig is about as simple and sturdy as you get. A yawl rig was optional, but most boats are sloops.

Engine

Like other auxiliaries of its era, most Tartan 34s are powered by the Atomic 4 gasoline engine. Beginning in 1975, the Farymann R-30-M diesel was an option. Either engine is adequate power for the boat, but it is not overpowered by any stretch of the imagination. The Atomic 4 is a smoother and quieter engine.

Those Atomic 4s are starting to get old. On a boat you plan to keep for more than a few years, the expense of switching over to a diesel can be justified. The Universal Model 25 is a drop-in replacement for the Atomic 4 in many cases, but check carefully to make sure there is enough room, since the Atomic 4 is one of the world's smallest four-cylinder engines.

The engine location under the port main cabin settee is a big plus, with one exception: since it's in the bilge, it is vulnerable in the case of hull flooding. Almost everything else about the installation is good. The engine weight is just aft of the longitudinal center of bouyancy, where its effect on trim and pitching moment is negligible. By disassembling the settee, you have complete access to the engine for servicing and repairs, and you'll be sitting in the middle of the main cabin, rather than crunched up under the cockpit. The shaft is short, minimizing vibration. There is no external prop strut to cause alignment problems, create drag, and possibly come loose from the hull.

The interior is utterly traditional, with all the bad features that go along with such a layout. One unusual feature is the cork cabin sole, which may be good for traction and insulation, but it gets dirty.

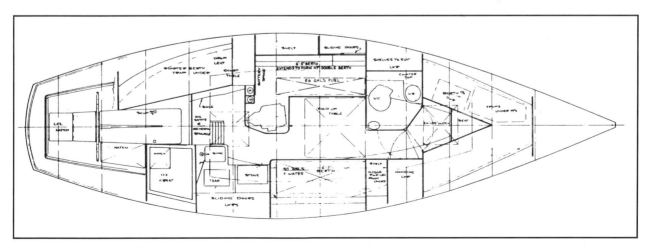

At the same time, clearance between the prop and the hull is minimal, so you can't go to a much bigger engine and prop. Because the prop is located far forward, the boat is difficult to back down in a straight line, and prop efficiency is reduced because the prop is partially hidden behind the trailing edge of the keel to reduce drag.

Some boats that race have replaced the orginal solid prop with a folding one, but if you mark the shaft so that you know when the prop is lined up with the back of the keel, the drag of the solid prop should be virtually indistinguishable from that of a folding prop. For best performance under both sail and power, we would choose a feathering prop if we had money to burn.

Original drawings show a 21-gallon gas tank located under the cockpit. Later boats have a 26-gallon fuel tank under the port settee in the main cabin, where the weight of fuel will have minimal effect on trim and pitching.

Construction

Tartan is a good builder, and the basic construction of the Tartan 34 is sound. There are, however, some age-related problems that show up repeatedly on our owners' surveys. The most common of these is gelcoat cracking and crazing of the deck molding, particularly in the area of the foredeck and forward end of the cabin trunk.

A related problem that some owners mention is delamination of the balsa-cored deck. Modern end-grain balsa coring is pre-sealed with resin by the manufacturer to prevent resin starvation when the core is actually glassed to the deck. A cored deck depends on its solid sandwich construction for rigidity. If there are spots where the core and deck are not completely bonded, the deck will yield in this area. This is what is referred to as a "soft" deck. As the deck flexes, the relatively brittle bond between the core and its fiberglass skin can fail, so that the "soft" areas grow. This is very common in older glass boats.

A very careful survey of the deck should be conducted when purchasing a Tartan 34. This will include tapping every square inch of the deck with a plastic mallet to locate voids or areas of delamination. Minor areas of delamination can be repaired by injecting epoxy resin through holes in the upper deck skin. Large areas of delamination may be cause for rejection of the boat, or a major price reduction.

Another frequently-mentioned problem with the Tartan 34 is the centerboard and its operating mechanism. Unlike many centerboards, this one secures positively in whatever position you set it—it won't freely pivot upward if you hit a rock. Centerboard groundings are extremely common, as it's very easy to forget that the board is down.

One construction detail on a boat of the general quality of the Tartan 34 is disturbing. On early boats, through hull fittings consist of brass pipe nipples glassed into the hull, with gate valves on the inside. This is acceptable on a boat used only in fresh water, since there won't be any galvanic corrosion. In salt water, however, this is an unacceptable installation. Brass pipe contains a lot of zinc, and it will disappear from the pipe nipples and gate valves just like your

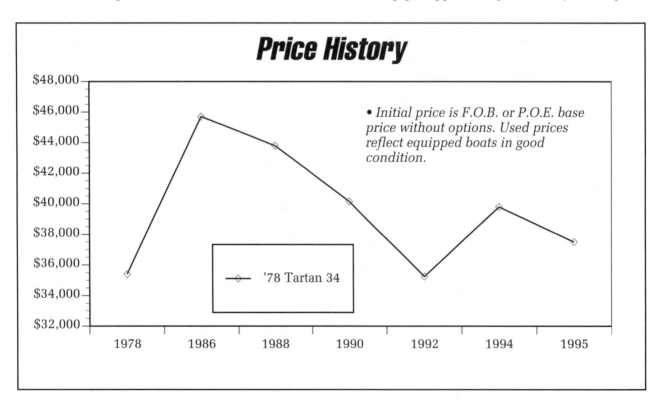

shaft zincs corrode away. Due to the age of the boats, these fittings should be immediately replaced with proper through hull fittings and seacocks, either of bronze or reinforced plastic.

Many deck fittings are chrome-plated bronze, and particularly on boats used in salt water, the chrome is likely to be pitted and peeling. Fortunately, this is a cosmetic problem, and you can get the stuff replated if you really want it to look good.

According to owner reports, the Tartan 34 has had an average number of cases of bottom blistering. That's pretty good for boats of this vintage.

There's a lot of exterior teak on the boat, including teak cockpit coamings, forward hatch frame, handrails, and a high teak toerail. On some boats we have looked at the toerail is kept varnished, but it isn't easy to keep varnish on a piece of teak that periodically gets dipped underwater.

The electrical system is pretty primitive, with a 30-amp alternator, fuses instead of circuit breakers, minimal lighting.

Over the years, most of these boats have added gear such as navigation electronics, more lights, pumps, and probably a second battery. We would carefully examine the electrical system, since pigtailing additional equipment onto a basic system can result in horrible installations.

Interior

If you want three-cabin interiors and condo-like space, you're not going to like the interior of the Tartan 34. This is not a floating motor home. It is a sailboat, and it has an interior layout that is as traditional as they get.

There is no pleasure-dome owner's cabin, shower stall, or gourmet galley. Even the nav station is rudimentary—a drop-leaf table at the head of the quarterberth.

There are fixed berths for five in the original arrangement, and the port settee extends to form a double. In later boats, lockers outboard of the port settee were replaced with a pilot berth. This may be a better arrangement for racing, but you don't need that many berths for cruising.

We wouldn't want to spend more than a weekend on the boat with more than four adults, and we wouldn't cruise for a week or more with more than two adults and two well-behaved children. But then we wouldn't do that on many boats less than 40'.

On the plus side, all the berths are long, including a 7' quarterberth. Even the forward V-berths are wide enough at the foot for big people.

Good headroom is carried all the way forward: 6' 2" in the forward cabin, a little more aft.

The cabin sole is pretty much level throughout the boat, except in front of the galley dresser and quarterberth.

The cabin sole is cork, an unusual feature. Cork is a good natural insulator, and provides great traction underfoot. It does, however, absorb dirt and grease, and it's difficult to keep clean.

Interior finish is typical of boats of this period: pretty drab, pretty basic. There are no fancy curved moldings and rounded laminated door frames. The original finish in early boats is painted plywood bulkheads with oiled teak trim. You can dress this up a lot by varnishing the wood trim. On later boats, the main bulkheads are teak-faced plywood, while the rest of the flat surfaces are white laminate.

There is a drop-leaf main cabin table, covered with wood-grained plastic laminate. Whoever invented wood-grained plastic laminate should be consigned to an eternity of varnishing splintery fir plywood with a foam brush on a foggy day. We'd rather see an acre of white Formica than a square foot of wood-grained plastic laminate, no matter how "real" it looks.

Because the fuel tank, water tanks, and engine are located under the main cabin settees, there's no storage space in these areas. Storage space in the rest of the boat is good, although hanging space for clothes is limited.

Water capacity is 36 gallons. This is inadequate for a boat that will cruise for more than a week with two people.

Like most boats from this period, the galley is small, consisting of a two-burner alcohol stove, an icebox with mediocre insulation, and a single sink. Original specifications called for a stove with no oven. Many boats by now have been upgraded to more modern cooking facilities—a must if you plan any real cruising.

The icebox is large, tucked under the starboard cockpit seat, and accessible from both the galley and the cockpit. It is difficult to reach into the box from the galley, since you have to stretch over the sink, and it has a vertical door rather than a horizontal hatch.

Conclusions

Given the shortcomings of boats such as the Tartan 34, why would you want one? There are lots of reasons. The boat is well-designed and well-built. With modern sailhandling equipment, two people can easily manage the sailing, and the boat will be reasonably fast.

The boat is seaworthy, the type of boat we'd choose for cruising someplace like the Bahamas. With minor upgrading, she is suited to reasonable offshore cruising.

Oh, yes, don't forget. This is a good-looking boat, a real classic. With freshly-painted topsides and varnished teak, she'll still turn heads anywhere. And that means a lot to a real sailor. • **PS**

Beneteau First 345

The marks of mass production on this flashy sloop, though masked, are still evident.

Can a boat be all things to all people? Last year in Rhode Island, two sailors who had differing ideas about what a sailboat should be went shopping for one to go partners on. One was mainly interested in performance and wanted a speedy club racer with sufficient amenities for one or two couples.

The second, with a wife and small child, was looking for more of a cruising boat, one that was stiff and stable but with excellent accommodations below. They settled on a Beneteau First 345, and at the end of their first sailing season both were satisfied with their choice.

History

Beneteau is far and away the most successful sailboat builder in the world right now. Its closest rival is another French company, Jeanneau, and in the United States only Catalina and Hunter match the kind of mass market appeal that Beneteau has enjoyed during the last half-decade. With 30 models available and annual sales last year of more than $70 million, Beneteau clearly is doing something right. Prior to the slowdown of recent years, Beneteau was cranking out 5,000 boats annually, about 400 of which were built in the U.S.

The company was founded by Andre Benjamin Beneteau in 1884 in the Atlantic coast town of Croix-de-Vie as a builder of wooden fishing boats. In the mid-60s at the instigation of Andre's granddaughter, Annette Roux, the firm took its first tentative dip into recreational boating waters with a small yacht called, appropriately, the Halibut.

By 1974, Beneteau had captured 11 percent of the French sailboat market, but it wasn't until the mid-1980s, when the strong U.S. dollar sent Americans searching overseas for bargains, that the company,

Specifications

LOA	34' 6"
LWL	28' 8"
Beam	11' 6"
Draft	6' 4"
Displacement	12,600 lbs.
Ballast	4,651 lbs.
Sail area	690 sq. ft. (with genoa)

along with other European builders, began making serious inroads into the U.S. sailboat market. Today, with Roux as chief executive officer, Beneteau exports 60 percent of its boats, primarily to the United States and Australia.

A favorable currency exchange may have initially attracted American buyers to French boats, but a blend of high style and performance gave them an increasing share of the market. Both Beneteau and Jeanneau had to overcome what Michael Lecholop, Beneteau's U.S. vice president for sales, called a misperception about their quality created by the strong dollar.

The exchange, he said, made the boats appear to be much cheaper than they actually were. Eventually, Beneteau gained a reputation for producing a

Owners' Comments

"Best sailing boat I've ever been on. Maneuverability excellent. Speed under power marginal."
—1987 model in Georgia

"We lose pointing ability due to shoal draft keel. Out in rough stuff, the boat holds up well. Heels rather easily. Cockpit is wet. No real place to put a dodger."
—1985 model in Vermont

"Our boat sails so beautifully. It's a stiff boat and it points high. It's heavy-duty."
—1984 model in Massachusetts

"Put two coats of varnish on the teak down below, don't buy the French sails."
—1985 model in Illinois

"Would prefer that the traveler not be across the companionway."
—1984 model in Virginia

boat of reasonable quality at a reasonable price—with the added plus of performance. In 1987, Beneteau felt confident enough of its U.S. sales to build its own plant in Marion, South Carolina. The firm, which had sales of $22 million last year in this country, is third in the American market behind Catalina and Hunter. In terms of quality, Lecholop said Beneteau considers its competition to be Tartan and the now-defunct Pearson.

Design

The Beneteau First 345 was designed as a moderate displacement racer/cruiser, and much of its popularity has been because of its success in blending the two functions. In fact, it could be said that the First is a racing boat that contains a cruising interior. The architect is Jean Berret, a Frenchman noted for his cruising and racing designs (he designed the 1985 Admiral's Cup winner, *Phoenix*, a Beneteau one-tonner).

At 12,600 pounds displacement the 345 is not overbuilt by any means but still substantially heavier than, for example, the Farr 34 (8,176 lbs.) or the J/35 (10,000 lbs.). On the other hand, it's significantly lighter than a full-keel 34-footer like the Mason 34 (14,020 lbs.) yet carries 690 square feet of sail compared to 602 square feet on the Mason.

The First has a PHRF rating of 120 in four of the largest national fleets (slightly higher in several other fleets), making it reasonably quick—faster by 20 seconds per mile than both the Tartan and Pearson 34, and faster than the Cal 34 and Catalina 34.

Within the Beneteau model line, the First series represents the performance-oriented designs, while the Evasion and the newer Oceanis are geared more for cruising. The fin keel and spade rudder of the 345, coupled with a shallow bottom, have minimal wetted surface. The keel comes in either a deep (6' 4") or shoal draft (4' 10") version. The boat is masthead-rigged and equipped with running backstays in addition to a permanent backstay, and carries as a norm a mainsail of 258 square feet (roughly) and a genoa of about 431 square feet. The running backstays apparently are necessary to help stabilize the tall stick when going to windward in heavy weather, but they will be a nuisance to the leisurely cruising couple.

The deck is clean and easy to move about, including the side decks leading forward. The cockpit is deep, roomy and protected by its coamings and wide side decks.

The First came with either a cruising or a racing package. In the racing version, the mast is a foot taller, a tiller replaces the wheel and the mainsheet traveler is positioned across the rear of the bridgedeck rather than across the cabin top. Unless you are adamant about having a wheel, the racing version seems to make the most sense because of easier access to the traveler. The 345 was in production from 1984 until 1988. More than 500 were sold—all but about 20 built in France.

Construction

French-built boats once bore the reputation of good design-poor quality. The French, their American counterparts would say, lacked modern, temperature-controlled facilities and often turned out suspect laminates. We're not sure what the old Beneteau facilities were like, but visitors to their newer plants tell a different story. Jono Billings of Jamestown Boat Yard in Rhode Island, an authorized Beneteau repair yard, called the South Carolina plant "the most modern I've seen. It's clean, there's very little smell and it's really well organized."

Jono Billings' repair work raises another issue about Beneteaus—their reputation for hull blistering. He said that one series of boats was made with a defective catalyst that resulted in a high rate of blistering. The company won a lawsuit against the resin maker and offers free repairs on all affected boats. According to Benetau, the catalyst problem affected several models between 1983 and 1985.

According to our own survey, Beneteau's overall

blistering record is high-average, about on a par with Pearson Yachts and C & C. The newer Beneteaus, that feature a blister barrier in the gelcoat, come with a limited 10-year warranty.

With six manufacturing plants, there's no mistaking that a Beneteau is a mass-produced boat with all the signs—interior liners, molded-in berths, lots of veneer, etc. But the result is a surprisingly well-constructed boat. Hulls are made of uncored reinforced fiberglass, laid up in alternating layers of chopped strand, omnidirectional mat and woven roving saturated with polyester resin. The hull is reinforced by interior stringers, structural bulkheads and by the interior fiberglass liner and pan.

Deck, cabin top and cockpit are a single glass molding, with built-in nonskid surfaces where appropriate. The deck is balsa-cored, and the 1985 model we looked at exhibited some exposed core material visible from within the chain locker that had been saturated with water, according to a recent marine survey. That trouble spot could herald further deck delamination, the surveyor concluded.

The hull-deck joint is a standard inward flange arrangement fastened with 3M 5200 sealant and further strengthened by the aluminum toe rail, which is riveted to the hull. The boats, according to Lecholop, are rated for offshore work under Bureau Veritas standards, the French equivalent of Lloyd's of London. Still, we prefer through-bolts to rivets; even if strength isn't the issue, bolts greatly facilitate future repairs.

The Isomat spar is keel-stepped. The keel, which is cast iron rather than lead, is secured to the hull by means of a laminated plate integral with the hull. The keel bolts, visible in the shallow bilge, appeared to be rusty despite a coating of some flexible compound. The rudder is fiberglass with a stainless steel stock (here again, the surveyor found excessive moisture, indicating potential future problems).

One problem with foreign-made boats is that all components may not meet U.S. standards. On the 1985 boat, the surveyor, A.D. Robbins and Co. of Dover, New Hampshire, found that the gate valve shutoff fixtures for the galley sink drain and engine seawater intake apparently were not of marine-grade copper alloys and thus corrosion prone and subject to failure. All other fixtures were bronze or stainless steel and satisfactory.

Performance

On an early October Saturday, with a moderately strong southeasterly wind blowing, *Godzilla* (nee *Witch of the Waves*) moved smartly out of Narragansett Bay on a close reach toward Brenton Reef tower. Sail consisted of an unreefed main of undetermined French make and a 140-percent roller furling jib from Ulmer-Kolius. The 345 is powerful and fast, and easily cut through the waves and over a cross swell coming in from the Atlantic. According to on-board instruments, the boat was moving along at close to its 7.1-knot hull speed on the reach— about normal for the conditions, the owners said. Switching to a beat, in 18 knots apparent, the boat naturally slowed (here, the crew attached the running backstays). On a run back toward the bay, *Godzilla* sped along at close to seven knots.

With its fin keel and fairly light ballast, the 345 reacted to gusts but was easily controlled. The regular crew felt the helm was nicely balanced, but we detected a tendency to round up in gusts. Some owners responding to our questionnaire also cited annoying weather helm.

The spade rudder, while requiring some working, made for fast tacking and quick response to the tiller. The owner of a 1987 model with a cutter rig reported excellent heavy-weather performance under staysail and reefed main. With a sloop rig, the boat flattens out when reefed before 20 knots. We've heard con-

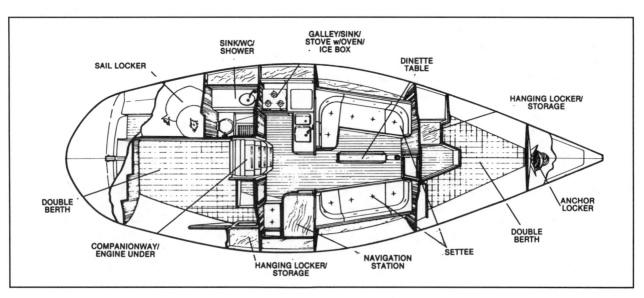

flicting opinions about the shoal draft version's pointing ability; based on our sail, the deep keel is close-winded.

The most common complaint in our questionnaires was the boat's poor speed and maneuverability under power. "Strong helm to fight when under power," wrote one, whose boat was powered by the standard Volvo 2002. "My only complaint is that under power the boat's performance is marginal," another said. The owners of *Godzilla,* which was powered by a 28-h.p. three-stroke Volvo 2003, had no such complaints. (Engine access from three sides, via the aft cabin and behind the companionway steps, is excellent.)

The cockpit is roomy and comfortable with sufficient freeboard and beam to keep things dry from whatever spray was sent up by the bow. The outboard sides of the coamings, over which the crew can hike out, are patterned with nonskid—a nice touch and "something you won't find on a cruising boat," said a racer in the crew.

Shrouds and lead blocks are inboard, allowing narrower sheeting angles. It is difficult, however, for the helmsman to reach the bridgedeck-mounted mainsheet traveler. Raise the jib, and you have a boat that's best sailed by two.

Clearly the boat is better set up for racing than short-handed cruising. Jibs are trimmed on #43 Lewmar winches retrofitted with cheap rubber collars that serve as a form of self-tailing. In reality, the setup was cumbersome and difficult to release under load; replacing them with genuine self-tailing gear is a priority of the owners.

Interior

The interior of the 345 is neat, functional and roomy. The layout, in typical Euro-style, has an aft cabin, dual settees in the saloon and a surprisingly roomy double V-berth forward. The aft cabin, to starboard, is a little cramped vertically, especially the berth under the cockpit—okay for sleeping but not much else. (One couple mitigates this by sleeping athwartships.) Another owner found it the perfect enclosed playpen for his toddler. The 345 comes in a second configuration, with two tiny quarter cabins and the head forward of the main cabin. This version is favored by the charter trade, but the single aft cabin seems preferable for ordinary cruising.

Aft and to port is the head. Both owners liked the location for its privacy and convenience. Like most enclosed heads on a boat this size, the compartment is a little small and could use a grabrail. The head is equipped with a Brydon marine toilet, fitted with a Y-valve leading to a holding tank.

Gray water from the shower is led forward to a bilge sump behind the mast step. Fresh water was contained in two tanks under the settees, totaling about 100 gallons. Some boats have rigid tanks; *Godzilla* has a flexible, bladder-type tank that seemed in good condition. Its light weight is another concession to performance, and it won't last as long as a quality rigid tank.

The L-shaped galley is forward of the head and equipped with a three-burner propane Electrolux stove. Refrigeration is an icebox. To starboard, there is a good-sized chart table, a bit cramped for head-

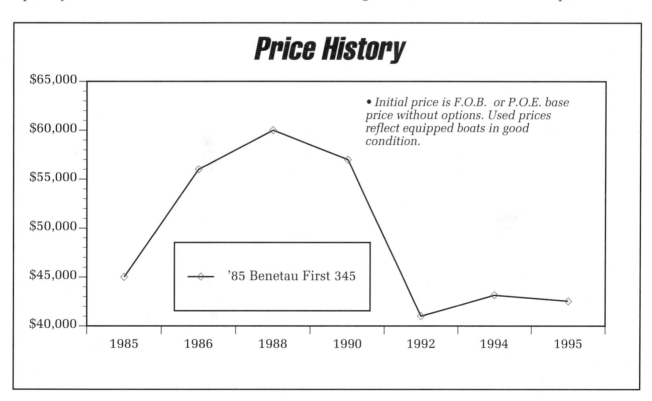

Price History

• Initial price is F.O.B. or P.O.E. base price without options. Used prices reflect equipped boats in good condition.

'85 Benetau First 345

room on the outboard side for anyone over 5' 10". The main saloon is spacious, the double settees comfortable (one reader praised the quality of French foam). The amidships table contains Beneteau's trademark wine rack plus additional storage space in the legs; beneath it is another trademark—the small bilge cover that converts to a dustpan. Headroom is more than six feet. Storage is ample and inconspicuous throughout.

It's almost impossible to find the inside of the hull because of the liner, the liberal use of teak veneer, and padding on the upper bulkheads and ceiling. The overall appearance is pleasant, not gaudy, and the padding is functional as well as aesthetic. Nevertheless, we'd hate to search for the source of a serious leak beneath all the interior decoration.

In the original Benetau First series, the settees and bunks were covered in subdued fabrics—green in this instance; the newer First S-series have the unusual Philippe Starck interiors with dark wood bulkheads and lots of silver and stainless steel, which Lecholop said "you either hate or love, but you won't forget."

The forward V-berth cabin, apparently the sleeping spot of choice for most 345 owners, is spacious, comfortable and private. There's a hanging closet to port, drawers to starboard and lots of natural light from a translucent hatch.

Natural lighting in the main cabin is supplied by side ports covered outside with a sporty, one-piece smoked Plexiglas panel. This is an inexpensive way to manufacture portlights, and it is stylish, but of course they cannot be made to open and the absence of frames often makes for an unfinished look. There is a double overhead sliding hatch that also serves as a spinnaker launching area. Several owners complained that the overhead fluorescent lighting is too dim.

Conclusions

Satisfied Beneteau 345 owners list style and performance as their motivation for selecting this model. They also refer to good value for the money. We'd have to agree on all points. You can get a Beneteau for under $50,000—in the low forties for an older model, which is somewhat more than a Hunter 34 but slightly less than a comparable Tartan. The boat sails exceptionally well, and the interior is pleasant and accommodating. It's not a Swan or a Sabre, but it is a reasonably well-put-together production boat that sells for a fair price.

The boat's strong point is definitely its performance. The deep narrow fin keel and spade rudder, plus shallow bilges, running backstays and flexible water tank make it unsuitable for long-term cruising. We worry too about the riveted toerail, maintenance on the iron keel and gate valves—all indicators of less than top quality construction. **• PS**

Catalina 34

From America's largest sailboat builder, this all-around design represents a good value.

It doesn't take a lot of brains to see that Catalina is doing something right that a lot of other sailboat makers aren't. They're the largest sailboat builder in the country, and a terrible year for them would be Valhalla for almost every other manufacturer. With more than 1,000 built in seven years, the Catalina 34 has to be in the running as the most successful production boat of the 1980s.

Equipment

When we went aboard the Catalina 34 at the 1990 Chicago Boat Show, we were first impressed by the equipment. Whereas many of the 1970s Catalinas came with what we considered second-rate hardware and gear that mandated owner upgrading, the 34, like the other contemporary Catalinas, is well equipped.

Self-tailing primary winches are standard and adequately sized; sail-handling hardware is all good; brand-names abound everywhere—stove, opening ports, pressure-water pump, head. It's all the same or similar to what you'd find on 34' boats costing $30,000 more.

The list of standard equipment is complete enough that you could conceivably sail the boat away with no options, a far cry from the old-fashioned method of selling a base boat with no lifelines, bilge pumps, or cushions aboard.

The 1990 boat we looked at carried a base price of $58,895, which included a main and 110% jib, mainsail cover, two-burner stove with oven, hot & cold pressure-water system, two batteries, 110-volt shore power system, boarding ladder, and lots of other equipment.

With electronics and other factory options (including a Hood furler and a microwave oven), the boat had a price of $75,999, and the dealer was

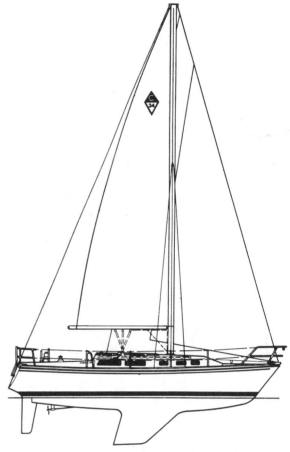

Specifications

LOA	34' 6"
LWL	29' 10"
Beam	11' 9"
Draft	5' 7"/3' 10" (fin/wing keel)
Displacement	11,950 lbs.
Ballast	5,000 lbs.
Sail area	528 sq. ft.

talking "special show price" to a serious customer on board. The only really essential pieces of equipment not on the boat were a couple of anchors, life jackets, flares, and a bell.

Design

Except for the old Catalina 38 (which was not a Frank Butler design), all the Catalinas have a similar conservatively modern look—fin keel and spade rudder, short overhangs, and a flattish sheerline. The distinctive cabin house and diamond-shaped sail emblem help identify a Catalina.

The hull of the 34 is modern, with full sections to provide lots of room below. It seems more refined than the Catalina 27, 30, and 36, which is probably why we prefer the 34. Like the other Catalinas, the 34

Owners' Comments

"Overall, the boat is good. It does what it was designed for well and with good value for the money. It needs some upgrading for any offshore work."

—New Hampshire owner

"I have been extremely pleased with the performance and quality of my 34. Have used it for three seasons with only minor problems—all of them easily corrected by myself."

—Michigan owner

"This is an excellent coastal cruiser built to a low sales price. I feel that basic safety is not compromised, but you do notice some quality problems in the teak and a few gelcoat cracks at corners where the mold was not completely filled. The interior space is excellent, but it does reduce storage space somewhat."

—Connecticut owner

"Blocks used on the mainsheet traveller suck. The ports leak (but have been changed to another manufacturer on newer boats)."

—Southern California owner

"Overall, a pretty good boat for the area we sail in and for the money. It's only average quality. There are much better quality boats out there, but you will pay 10% to 20% more for the same size. My wife says the galley is only fair."

—Detroit owner

"This boat far exceeds other boats of the same size in livability, especially since it costs substantially less than the Pearson, Tartan, and Island Packet. We looked at the Hunter, and it does not compare to the Catalina in quality of material and workmanship."

—New Jersey owner

"I'm not happy with the wing keel. I ordered the boom vang—it does not include the shackle. There were other small nickel and dime things."

—Rhode Island owner

combines a long waterline, a moderate to light displacement, and a large sail area to ensure good sailing performance.

The interior design is in the European mode, the first of the Catalinas to have the head aft by the companionway. Unlike European boats such as the Beneteau or Jeanneau in the same size range, however, the Catalina is very full forward, with a big V-berth cabin and a big dinette and settee ahead of the L-shaped galley and the nav station.

The aft cabin will be the principal cabin for most owners. It has a sizable athwartship berth. There's a seating area between the berth and the galley, though we're not sure how usable it would be.

According to our owner survey, the interior is the most praised aspect of the 34, with comments like "most room for the money" appearing in a majority of reports. It's always been a strong selling point with all the Catalinas—they're hard to beat for sheer interior volume.

There are several aspects of the Catalina design we don't like, such as the huge companionway hatches and molded furniture "pans" that limit stowage and access to the hull. But overall we cannot take serious objection to any important aspect of the design. They are wholesome but plain boats.

Performance Under Sail and Power

We sailed the 34 for only one afternoon, on Lake Michigan, and found the boat to be a good performer.

It was a puffy day, so the boat was occasionally overcanvased and developed a strong weather helm (due in part to a poorly shaped mainsail). Even with a good main, we suspect that cruisers will want to take an early reef as the wind builds; in fact, if we owned the boat we'd experiment with sailing it extensively under roller jib alone.

The 34 sailed well on all points of sail, but it seemed a bit sluggish off the wind without a downwind sail.

With a PHRF rating around 144, she is about in the middle of the speed range for contemporary boats her size, considerably slower than the J/35 but significantly faster than the Crealock 34.

We'd call her sailing ability respectable, good enough to make smart cruising passages and quick enough to sail to her handicap rating on the race course.

The 34 we sailed had the standard 5' 7" draft fin keel, but the boat also is available with a wing keel option, drawing 3' 10". Owner reports in our boat surveys give decidedly mixed reviews to the wing, some condemning it as only a "flopper-stopper" and not an efficient foil at all, and others praising its seaworthiness and the good ride it gives in waves. Unless we were desperate for the shallow draft, we'd be inclined to go with the standard fin rather than the wing.

Standard power is a three-cylinder Universal 25 diesel which we found adequate. However, owners again report mixed feelings about the engine. A few thought the boat was underpowered, a few said they wished they'd bought the three-bladed "cruising" prop, which is a popular option.

The boat does come with a four-cylinder Universal 35 diesel as an option, and this may be desirable for the cruiser as it gives more power.

To get better performance under power, we'd opt for the bigger diesel rather than the three-bladed solid prop, which would hurt sailing performance. In fact, we wouldn't consider even a two-bladed fixed prop on this boat, since it would degrade one of the Catalina 34's best qualities—her sailing performance.

Construction

Layup, laminates, balsa core and other construction details are conventional. The boat is generally well-engineered and well-executed. It is certainly adequate for typical coastal cruising, weekending, and daysailing.

If good engineering means doing a good job of adapting means to ends, or materials to functions, then the Catalina 34 is well-engineered.

True, we don't like the feel of the foredeck, which seems a little spongy compared to the teak-over-glass decks of our old Cheoy Lee. But we know a 1972 Catalina 27 well, and its foredeck has the same feel now that it had when new. It has served well and, we must conclude, was engineered and built as planned. We suspect the foredeck of the Catalina 34 will hold up for 20 years as well.

We don't like the way the interior liner flexes either, or the way it hides most of the inside of the hull, but it holds up and it performs the cosmetic function for which it was intended.

The chainplates seem small when we compare them to the half-inch stainless plates on our Carter 36. But we've never heard of a Catalina's chainplates failing, and they're undoubtedly up to the job. Good engineering.

Some boats are overbuilt, which can be expensive—a waste of money for an American coastal sailor who has no plans to sail in the Southern Ocean. Worse is to build a boat no better than the Catalina 34 and charge $30,000 more.

Conclusion

The Catalina 34 is a successful, all-around design from a hugely successful company. Because Catalina sells so many boats and runs an efficient manufacturing facility, its boats typically sell for less than other brands of comparable size.

This fact, plus the great number of used Catalinas on the market, mean that a buyer can be quite selective.

We do not recommend the Catalina 34 for extended offshore cruising, at least not without making some modifications to the companionway, upgrading the rigging, and possibly stiffening areas of the hull.

But the boat was neither designed, constructed, nor intended for such use. Indeed, most owners do not need such a boat. For the majority of American family sailors, the Catalina 34 will satisfy their needs just fine. • **PS**

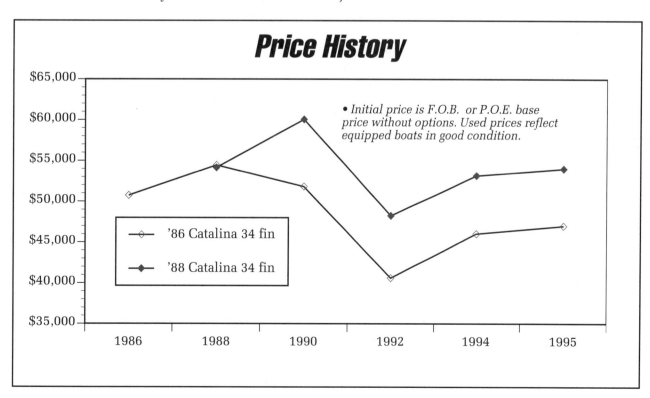

Price History

• *Initial price is F.O.B. or P.O.E. base price without options. Used prices reflect equipped boats in good condition.*

Legend:
- '86 Catalina 34 fin
- '88 Catalina 34 fin

The J/34c

An expensive coastal cruiser that has a single strong suit—sailing performance.

In 1985, J Boats first tested the cruising market with the J/40. They followed up in 1986 with the J/28. In 1987, they introduced yet another cruiser, the J/34c. Twenty-five were sold in the first production year. The last was built in 1990. The designation "c" was added to distinguish the boat from the J/34, an IOR design that failed both on the race course and in the sales room.

Like all the J/cruisers, the J/34c is an example of what happens when a group of "gung-ho" racers designs a cruising boat. Racers are obsessed with how a boat sails, how it feels. They know that ease of handling is essential for enjoyable sailing, and they know that this is as dependent on hardware choice and layout as it is on design.

For a racer, going below is something you do when you're too tired to sail anymore. This isn't to say that the J/34c is poorly laid out belowdecks. It's just that her strong points are abovedecks.

In appearance, the J/34c looks much like her sister J/cruisers. She has a fixed shoal draft keel, a straight sheer, and a slotted Goiot aluminum toerail. Her waterline, at 30', is long. It leaves her little overhang for appearance.

Although she has modest freeboard and cabin house profile (headroom below is barely 6'), she will still seem a little "squarish" for traditionalists. To enhance her appearance, a boat can be ordered with a 4" high teak toerail that tapers as it runs aft.

As a rule, the J Boat line is expensive. The 34c was no exception. Base price in 1989 was almost $100,000. With basic sails and electronics, and options like propane, shore power, vinyl overhead panels, varnished interior, swim ladder, dodger, roller furling, refrigeration, and spinnaker gear, the price could approach $130,000.

This puts the J/34c at the upper end of the price

Specifications

LOA	34' 6"
LWL	30' 0"
Beam	11' 1"
Draft	4' 11"
Displacement	10,000 lbs.
Ballast	4,500 lbs.
Sail area	712 sq. ft.

range for boats of her size. By comparison, the Hunter 33.5, while admittedly of lesser quality, had a 1989 base price of only $55,000. The Crealock 34, of similar quality to the J/34c, also had a similar $100,000 base price.

Hull and Deck

To support their claims of superior construction, Tillotson-Pearson had all of their larger boats, including the J/34c, ABS (American Bureau of Shipping) certified. Similar to a Lloyds certification, this proves that each boat has been built to certain standards and inspected by an independent surveyor at various stages of construction.

ABS has three levels of certification: hull plan approval, hull certification, and A-1 classification

which includes hull, power, electrical and plumbing systems. An ABS-certified boat is fitted with a bronze plaque. Any builder can claim he builds to ABS standards; without the plaque it is only a claim. ABS inspection and A-1 classification added about $2,000 to the cost of the J/34c.

Like all J Boats, the 34c is constructed of fiberglass and polyester resin, and cored with balsa. Standard, uncoated Baltek balsa is used, but the balsa sheets are sprayed with quick-catalyzed polyester before being laid in the mold. This helps seal the balsa end grain and avoid dry spots in the layup. This is an important step, because the laminate is not vacuum-bagged, as would be done on a custom boat.

A barrier layer of vinylester resin between the gelcoat and the first lamination prevents blistering, says the builder. The hull is warranted against blistering for 10 years.

Much of the laminate is of unidirectional cloth. Unlike typical fiberglass cloth, which is woven, unidirectional cloth is constructed by stitching sheets of unidirectional fibers together, typically at 90° or 45° angles. Without the "crimp" caused by having to weave the fibers around each other, the finished laminate is stronger.

The hull-to-deck joint is Tillotson-Pearson's standard, seaworthy, inward-turned hull flange with the deck and toerail through-bolted and bonded with 3M 5200 polyurethane adhesive.

All of the deck fittings are also bedded with 5200.

Superb hardware and good deck layout have resulted in a boat that is very easy to handle. On top of that, she is faster than most coastal cruisers her size.

The holes drilled for deck fastenings are counter-sunk to further improve the bond and reduce gelcoat crazing. This should ensure a watertight deck. The only drawback is that 5200 is such a powerful adhesive that later removal of hardware for repair or replacement is difficult.

The only molded interior components are the hull stringers, the icebox and the head. The rest of the interior is constructed of lauan teak-faced marine plywood and installed piece by piece.

When an interior is installed this way, you can use more fiberglass tabbing to attach it to the hull. This gives you the potential for a hull which will remain stiffer longer. With a one-piece molded interior, you must set the interior on putty and rely on spot tabbing.

All of the structural interior components in the J/34c are tabbed on both sides, for most of their length, with fiberglass cloth. The small, non-structural components are tabbed on one side with fiberglass mat. Except for the fact that no fillet is used to spread the loads on the tabbing, this is a good method.

Rig

Unlike many builders who have gone to less expensive spars from mass-production manufacturers like

Isomat, J Boats still equips its boats with more expensive rigs from Hall Spars.

The J/34c has a masthead double spreader rig, with speaders swept back 10°. Sweeping the spreaders aft gives the mast fore and aft stability, at the sacrifice of being able to adjust the bend easily. Running backstays are not needed to stabilize the mast.

Sweepback also requires the spreader bases to accept more of the shroud load. It should be no problem, as Hall uses a patented through-mast spreader bar, which incorporates tangs for the lower and intermediate shrouds. The spreaders fit over the bar, resulting in a clean, strong low-windage attachment.

Sweepback does hinder dead downwind performance slightly, because you cannot let the mainsail out as far. And it increases chafe on a fully-battened mainsail. We think the advantages outweigh these small drawbacks.

The mast is tapered and painted with Awlgrip. It is not anodized. The only mechanically fastened hardware items are the halyard exit plates and the spinnaker track. That's good, because like most production masts, the fittings are not bedded when installed. The gooseneck, vang fittings, cranes and halyard boxes are all welded on before the spar is painted.

Rod rigging is used, and the tangs are flush-mounted. Halyards are internal, but the spinnaker halyard turning blocks are hung from a masthead crane—a more seaworthy, traditional approach than the internal sheaves found on racing boats.

The boom has a powerful 6:1 outhaul with a recessed Teflon-lined track. A Hall Quik Vang is standard, and is a very convenient way to adjust boom vang tension. A Navtec hydraulic backstay adjuster is optional. The mast also has a single folding step to enable shorter crewmembers to climb up and attach the main halyard shackle. There are two reef lines, led internally. They cleat on deck-mounted clutch stoppers, a far more convenient system than gooseneck-mounted stoppers. A continuous system, made up of one line through the leech and the luff, would make reefing even simpler.

Engine and Mechanical Systems

The J/34c is powered by a 28 hp Volvo 2003 diesel engine. Being three-cylinder, it is relatively quiet. Engine access is good, but you have to get at it through a number of hatches because the engine is tucked well under the cockpit floor. There are two hatches next to the quarterberth and a single hatch in the cockpit sail locker, as well as the removable companionway ladder.

An aluminum fuel tank holds 26 gallons, which is adequate for coastal cruising.

Wiring and plumbing are done to ABS specifications. However, there is an exposed junction box in the head, where it is likely to get wet whenever someone takes a shower.

The head is equipped with a Raritan PH-2 toilet, and an 18-gallon holding tank with a Y-valve for overboard discharge. The toilet has a ceramic bowl and pumps with a lever handle, which is convenient, but the shut-off valve is operated with a knob instead of a lever. It's hard to dog down because it's often wet from overspray from the pump.

The boat we looked at had optional vinyl cabin overhead panels, held in place by strips of teak. The panels hide the wiring and deck fastenings, yet drop easily for access because they are held in place with un-bunged screws.

Standard water tank is 45 gallons, plenty for coastal cruising; an additional 35-gallon tank was optional. Hot and cold pressure water are standard. On the boat we sailed there was no overflow vent for

The interior is optimized for a couple or small family. Good features include a pair of doors in the main bulkhead, one of which leads to the head, the other to the forward cabin.

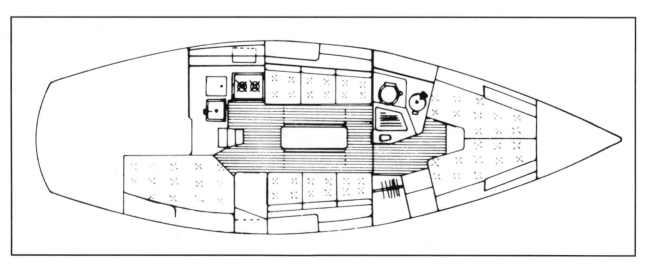

the water tank. Because the tank is plastic, when it is overfilled it expands and can damage the settee in which it is housed.

Propane cooking was an expensive option, but we recommend it over the alcohol alternative. A compartment aft of the cockpit holds two propane bottles, enough to last a summer of weekend sailing. The propane stove is a Force 10, two-burner gimbaled stove with oven.

Handling Under Power

The Volvo engine provides more than enough power. In flat water, the engine we used easily pushed the boat to hull speed, which was nearly 7 knots. A Martec folding prop is standard.

Edson wheel steering is standard, and includes a 40" diameter destroyer wheel. Combined with a balanced rudder and Harken roller rudder bearings, the J/34c is effortless to steer.

The boat is also equipped with an emergency tiller that can be quickly snapped onto the rudder post through a small hatch under the helmsman's seat. This is a good safety measure.

A 5" Ritchie compass is pedestal-mounted in a binnacle. It can only be read from behind the wheel. While this is fine for powering, it is difficult to use when the helmsman will be sitting to weather while sailing. Throttle and shift controls are also mounted on the steering pedestal.

Handling Under Sail

This is the J/34c's strong point, what sets her apart from the run-of-the-mill coastal cruiser. Her ease of handling is probably more a result of her deck layout and hardware than her design.

She is advertised as fast and smooth riding because of her long waterline. True, long waterlines have a higher potential hull speed. They can also make for a smoother ride when combined with short overhangs such as those on the J/34c. Short overhangs cut down on pitching by eliminating parasitic weight in the ends of the boat.

However, if not accompanied by a proportional increase in sail area, lengthening the waterline can detract from light air speed. The boat we sailed did seem to bog down in winds under 5 knots. It only had a 135% genoa. We'd recommend a 150% genoa, but the boat also seemed to be a bit on the tender side when the breeze increased to 12 knots. Remember that this is a shoal draft cruiser.

The J/34c's 30' waterline is long—perhaps too long. The leeward stern quarter was almost 5" under water when close reaching in a 6-8 knot breeze. Short overhangs may make it easier to climb up a stern ladder if thrown overboard, but if the bustle is insufficient to keep the stern from "digging" a hole in the water, speed can suffer.

This isn't to say that the J/34c is slow. In fact, she should be considered a performance cruiser, faster than a majority of cruisers her size. But like most boats, she isn't as perfect as the advertising suggests.

Her advertising also touts her large steering wheel and Harken rudder bearings. True, her steering is tight, quick to respond and frictionless. But like many modern designs, we'd have to say her rudder is overbalanced. A "balanced" rudder has the rudder

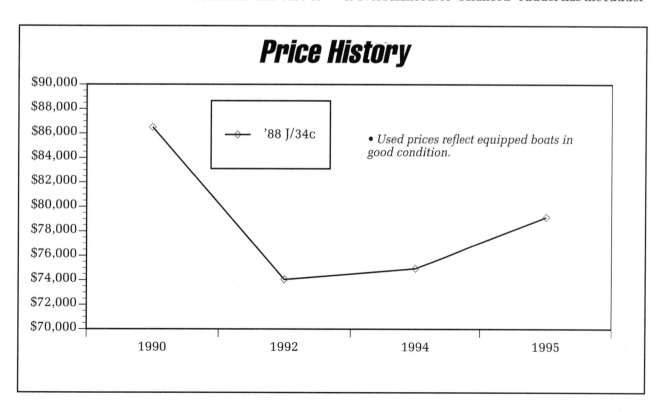

Price History

Legend: ◇ '88 J/34c

• *Used prices reflect equipped boats in good condition.*

post placed somewhere near the center of the rudder blade. The more "balanced," the less helm, or "feel" a boat has.

With the J/34c, there is no helm at all—if you leave the helm, while sailing upwind or reaching, she goes straight. If you start a turn while powering, the wheel won't return to center unless you bring it back. Some sailors like this type of effortless steering, but we think that with roller rudder bearings and a large steering wheel, you are not going to tire your arm with a little bit of weather helm.

The J/34c is equipped with what the Johnstones call a "UFO" keel. It is a shoal draft keel with a conventional leading edge sweepback, the bottom ending in a flattened bulb. Unlike a winged keel, it shouldn't snag lobster pots and weeds.

When run aground, however, the UFO keel will still be more difficult to free than a conventional keel. The Johnstones report that the UFO keel is about seven to nine seconds per mile slower than a conventional keel upwind, but neither slower nor faster when reaching or running—a reasonable trade-off for those who need shoal draft. But for those who sail in deep water, it would be better if there were a deep draft option.

On Decks

The deck layout of the J/34c is what makes her a joy to sail, especially if you're at the wheel. The boat is laid out for shorthanded cruising—singlehanded or doublehanded. The cockpit is designed for sailing, not for sitting at anchor. There is a disproportionate amount of space given to the helmsman.

The boat has a T-shaped cockpit, similar to that on the J/40. The coaming stops just forward of the steering pedestal. This gives the helmsman plenty of space for comfortable sitting on the deck on both sides of the wheel. Because you can sit to weather without discomfort, visibility is improved when sailing.

There is a raised seat, incorporating a horseshoe life ring as a cushion, aft of the wheel. But it's a long reach from the seat to the wheel. A short person would be inclined to steer with his or her toes.

A Harken traveler is located just in front of the steering pedestal. True, you do have to step over it to go forward from the helm, and the mainsheet can hook on the pedestal during a jibe, but the convenience when trimming sails makes it worth it.

The J/34c has a proportionally large mainsail and small genoa. This makes tacking easier, and sailing under mainsail alone possible. However, the size of the mainsail demands that you pay more attention to sail trim. The person best suited to judge that is the helmsman.

The traveler car has a 4:1 purchase, led to cam cleats at each end facing the helmsman. The mainsheet is double-ended, led to two Barient 22 self-tailing winchs, one on each side of the traveler, in easy reach of the helmsman.

Genoa winches, Barient 27 self-tailers, are also in reach of the helmsman, so he can adjust trim or cast off the sheet during a tack. There is a small price for the convenient proximity of these winches—on some points of sail the winch handles cannot be turned through 360°. All winches are adequately sized for the job.

The coaming forms nicely angled seatbacks in the foward half of the cockpit. The aft face of the wide molded coaming faces the helmsman, and is a good location for instrument readouts.

There is a huge cockpit locker to port. The single entry hatch is comprised of the seat and coaming. Because it is so big and heavy, it must be secured to the lifelines before you enter the locker. If the lid fell on you, you'd know it. The locker is large enough to hold a deflated dinghy, outboard, sails, plus other gear.

Stanchion bases are aluminum castings, which we never completely trust. These lock securely onto the aluminum toerail. Stainless steel stanchion bases are provided with the teak toerail option. On the standard boat there is no teak to maintain, save the cabin house handrails.

Reefs and halyards are led through quality Lewmar Spinlock clutch stoppers to Barient 21 self-tailers on the cabin house.

The anchor roller chock is not designed for any particular size or brand of ground tackle. Therefore, the anchor we used had to be secured with extra line to hold it in place while sailing. It would be better to design the chock for one anchor and make that anchor standard equipment.

A hawsepipe leads to a shallow, level compartment, so the anchor rode tends to pile up directly below it, obstructing the deck opening. With this system you should dry the rode on deck before stowing to prevent mildew.

Later boats are equipped with a conventional molded anchor locker.

A locker for a backup, Danforth-type anchor is an option. It holds the anchor vertically in a well just foward of the chainplates. While it saves the hassle of stowing the backup anchor belowdecks, it also constricts the space in the already small hanging locker in the forward cabin.

Belowdecks

This is a simple, old-fashioned interior with a few innovative twists. It is optimized for one couple or small family cruising. It isn't jammed full of undersized berths, nor is the 43"-wide quarterberth intended as a double berth.

There are two doors in the main bulkhead, one on

each side of the mast. One door opens into a large forward stateroom, the other into the head. You can also get access to the head from the forward stateroom. This is preferable to walking through the head to get to the forward stateroom, which is a more typical layout on a boat this size.

The V-berth in the forward stateroom is over 6' wide at the head and almost 3' wide at the foot, with enough headroom to sit up and read at night. The cushions are 4" foam, comfortable enough to sleep on your side without bruising your shoulders.

The stateroom also has bookshelves, a small dresser with drawers, and good ventilation through two hatches and one port. There are no cowl vents, however, so you may suffer during a rainy night when everything must be closed.

Lockers under the V-berth extend to the bottom of the boat. Although there are limber holes between lockers to drain water from the anchor compartment into the bilge, the holes are not flush with the hull, so water will not drain completely.

The holding tank is also under the V-berth. It would have to be flushed clean and stored without deodorant to make its smell unnoticeable. Access to the seacocks is through a door under the V-berth.

All of the interior is teak-faced plywood trimmed in teak. Hull ceiling is teak battens. On the standard boat the interior teak is oiled; varnish is an option. Joinerwork is of average quality. The cabin sole is varnished teak and holly. J Boats stopped using light-colored ash belowdecks after the J/36, because that wood turns black when it gets wet.

The head has less than 6' of headroom. Ventilation is good—one hatch and one port. The molded shower sump drains into the bilge. Most surfaces in the head drain well, but spilled water collects on the sink countertop. Full-length mirrors on the inside of both head doors give the user the illusion of spaciousness.

There are handrails on the cabin overhead. Unlike many boats, glued-in marine carpet or vinyl are not used on the overhead or the ceiling. Instead, gelcoat or vinyl drop panels are used. This is a good feature, as it gives you access to deck fastenings without major disassembly.

The cabin house and cockpit ports all open, giving good ventilation in fair weather. Some are so large you can stick your head through them. The first 25 boats had Bomar ports with only three dogs per port. The ports could distort and leak and the dogs could shear off if overtightened. In later boats a Bomar port with six dogs is used.

A Lewmar foward hatch is articulated so it can be opened to preset positions. It can be operated from above or belowdecks, but locked only from below.

Galley and icebox are a bit small. Stowage for dishes and silverware is under the companionway, in a compartment which allows them to drain and dry. As with most of the cabin stowage, galley stowage is behind sliding doors.

The sink is deep—so deep that we suspect it might gather a little water when heeled severely on starboard tack. The stove is covered by a counter which slides back for access to the burners.

The cabin table is large, if a bit wobbly on its tube-in-socket legs. It has utensil stowage in the center and fiddles on the edges.

There is a small nav station, using a cabin berth for a seat. It is adequate for weekend cruising, but not long-distance sailing.

Conclusions

The J/34c is a sailor's boat, and a well-to-do sailor, we might add, if he is to afford her hefty price tag. She's a weekend and coastal cruiser, not a blue water cruiser. She is comfortable for one couple with a kid or two, but not two couples. Because she handles so easily she should make an enjoyable beer can racer.

There are few boats that are better built. But there are a number of boats with equal or superior interiors for equal or less money.

You won't find many cruisers with the quality of hardware that is found on the J/34c. And you probably won't find any that are as easy to sail short-handed.

The boat is fast compared to cruisers of her size, but not as fast as the manufacturers would have you believe. That's typically the case with manufacturer hype.

No new boat is ever a good investment. They all depreciate with alarming speed. However, if the boat is well-promoted, and the builder is respected, as is the case with the J/34c, you can be assured of a reasonable resale value.

Is she worth it? If you plan to leave the boat at the dock and use it as a second home, certainly not. If you plan to sail her with regularity, maybe. It depends on how important the little details that make sailing fun are to you. • **PS**

Contest 35S

This well-executed Dutch cruiser offers performance suitable for coastal and offshore sailing.

Conyplex, builder of the Contest 35S, is an established company that was a pioneer in fiberglass boat construction. In 1958, it began work on fiberglass Flying Dutchmans, and two years later introduced the Contest 25, its first cruiser. More than 5,000 boats have been built since, with about 600 of these being exported to the U.S. through Van Breems Holland Yachts of Westport, Connecticut.

The Contest 35S is a new design, introduced in 1988 to replace the earlier Contest 35.

Martinus Van Breems, who also invented and markets the Dutchman mainsail containment system, brought hull #22 of the Contest 35S to Newport, Rhode Island for *Practical Sailor* to test. This gave us a good opportunity to crawl through the boat and sail it in a variety of wind conditions.

Design

All Contest sailboats are designed by Dick Zaal, who for years was Conyplex's in-house designer. Each displays certain trademarks: high freeboard, wooden rubrails, and low cabin profiles.

The Contest 35S conforms to the traditional Zaal style. The molded cockpit coaming that continues the line of the cabin all the way aft is certainly distinctive. It provides very comfortable back support, though the affect on appearance is not all that attractive, creating as it does a feeling of greater mass high and aft than one is accustomed to seeing on aft cockpit boats.

The hull form is powerful, with relatively full sections compared to many modern racer/cruisers. The moderate displacement-to-length ratio of 249 gives it reasonable speed for a cruising boat while retaining the ability to carry the amount of stores that are necessary for living aboard and short-term cruising.

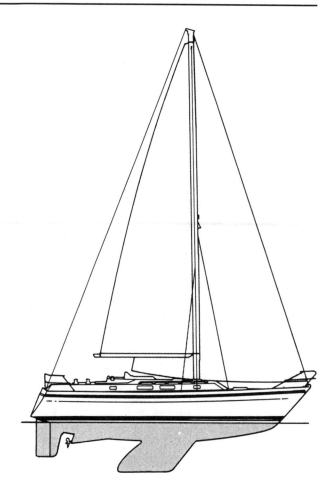

Specifications

LOA	34' 7"
LWL	28' 7"
Beam	11' 2"
Draft	5' 9"/4' 5" (std/wing keel)
Displacement	13,040 lbs.
Ballast	5,513 lbs.
Sail area	586 sq. ft.

Two keels are available. The standard keel is a cruising fin in which the foot is longer than the root (the section that attaches to the hull); the wing keel, which we tested, was developed in tank tests at the Marin Institute in the Netherlands and saves 1' 4" in draft.

The propeller shaft exits through a solid log rather than a strut, and though this increases wetted surface area somewhat, it is strong and also marginally improves directional stability. The rudder is hung on a full skeg—a smart feature on a cruising boat, providing that the skeg is well attached to the hull.

The rig is a conventional masthead sloop with double spreaders, high-aspect mainsail and the ability to carry large genoas. The boat we sailed had a fully battened main equipped with the Dutchman

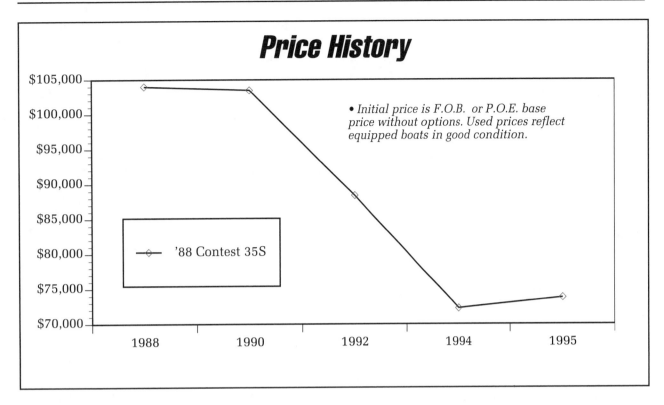

Price History

• *Initial price is F.O.B. or P.O.E. base price without options. Used prices reflect equipped boats in good condition.*

◇ '88 Contest 35S

system, and Profurl furling gear on the headsail. These two devices make a boat of this size about as easy to sail as is possible.

Construction

Because Contest boats are cruisers, built without too much concern for weight, there is nothing exotic about their construction. The hull and deck structure of the 35S is built of chopped strand mat, cloth and woven roving, cored with end-grain balsa.

The pros and cons of balsa coring are debated endlessly. It is an excellent material for using in sandwich with fiberglass, creating a strong, lightweight structure. The likelihood of it absorbing water is problematical and not of immediate concern in a new boat. However, whereas the racing boat must, by necessity, incorporate weight-saving materials and construction techniques, there is no reason the slower cruising boat should compromise itself for weight. We like a single skin fiberglass hull for cruising, if for no other reason than it's easier to repair than a cored hull. If you're trying to patch a hole on the beach of some Third World country, or even in a Caribbean boatyard, you'll appreciate working with solid fiberglass.

Conyplex assembles the hull and deck before building the interior; the opposite is the usual practice. The joint is glassed over with at least seven layers of cloth and also through-bolted. This is an extremely strong hull-to-deck joint that should never leak. By raising the deck a few inches above the joint, the joint, covered by a teak rubrail and stainless steel strip, is less vulnerable to damage from collision with pilings and other boats. This is a superb configuration, though again the raised deck increases apparent freeboard.

Another feature of the Contest that we like is the all-wood, built-up interior. All furniture is marine grade plywood fiberglassed to the hull—no molded fiberglass pans that are cold, noisy and may prohibit access to some parts of the hull. A further advantage of wood is the ability to customize it later; fiberglass simply doesn't allow as much flexibility to change interior plans. Then again, for the price of a Contest, you expect an all-wood interior.

Hardwood stringers and floors are fiberglassed to the hull to increase the rigidity of the structure; in a mass production boat these might be incorporated into the fiberglass pan or liner, along with furniture foundations.

Each Contest is delivered with a Lloyd's certificate, which means it has been constructed under the specific rules of that agency, and under the watchful eye of its inspectors. This costs the builder extra money—about $800—which is passed along to the buyer, but if you're looking for a quality boat to own a long time, it's probably worth it.

Interior

The layout of the Contest 35S is straightforward, with a few unexpected wrinkles.

The companionway hatch slides into a nice seahood, and though a small opening offers safety offshore, the shallow depth of the hatch and the orientation of the ladder make the trip below a little tight—one is careful not to hit his head. The forward

V-berths are 6' 7" long with shelves port and starboard. The hull is covered with an upholstery fabric; given the finely crafted joinerwork throughout this boat, we expected to find a wood ceiling in the bows, but were not overly disappointed as the fabric insulates moisture and sound, is pleasant to the touch, and does save weight over wood. Headroom here is 5' 11".

The saloon features a 6' 6" settee to port and an L-shaped settee to starboard, both of which will make good sea berths when fitted with lee cloths. Headroom in the saloon ranges from 6' 3" aft down to 6' 1-1/2" forward.

The navigation station is the right size for this boat, with enough space to spread charts folded once. Opposite is the galley, which we thought was a bit on the small side. There isn't much counter space for food preparation and even Martinus admitted that the icebox is small by U.S. standards.

The head is aft and to port, under the bridge deck. There is an access door to the double berth stateroom under the cockpit, giving each person his or her own side to get out of bed. The wet locker aft of the head is difficult to access; Martinus said the company was looking at other uses of this space, possibly a freezer.

The matte finish varnishing of the teak is nicely done. Dutch tiles around the galley are a Van Breems trademark. There are numerous stowage compartments, which are always appreciated. We were again surprised that the hull inside many of these compartments was merely spray painted—we expected wood or at least fabric, and we can only speculate that even top-end builders must sometimes find places to save costs. Overall, however, the Contest 35S is beautifully finished with much attention to detail.

Performance

We sailed the 35S in a variety of wind conditions ranging from light to moderate. The first thing we noticed was how well balanced it was under mainsail and #2 furling genoa. Hard on the wind, it was possible to take our hands off the Whitlock wheel; there was little tendency to round up.

A little weather helm, of course, is actually desirable, as it functions not only as a safety feature (allowing the boat to round up and spill wind in a strong gust), but also helps the helmsman develop feel for the optimum angle off the wind.

This observation was corroborated by tests of the boat reported in the British magazine *Yachting Monthly*, in which the author wrote, "If there is a criticism, it is that she was a little reticent about telling the helmsman when she was precisely in the groove."

Other than this, the boat tracked nicely and easily, remaining under control at all times. We found it a pleasure to steer, tacking through about 85 degrees and making about seven knots on a reach in 12 to 15 knots of wind, and about six knots beating in relatively calm bay waters.

Diesel auxiliary power is a 28-hp. Volvo diesel, which is well-insulated and equipped with a flexible drive coupling to minimize vibration. While running, it was quiet and smooth, a real pleasure for motoring and/or motor sailing. Our boat had a three-bladed prop, which didn't help sailing performance, but made backing out of slips a thoroughly manageable process.

Conclusion

To our mind, the Contest 35S is not an exciting boat in terms of looks or performance. Rather it is a solid, well-built, conservative cruiser that is tastefully appointed for comfortable living aboard. It is an able sailer that should carry a crew safely to most any place they wish to go. The Dutch are known for quality workmanship, and the Contest 35S is no exception.   • **PS**

The only real criticisms we have of the interior layout are a too-small icebox and an inaccessible hanging locker.

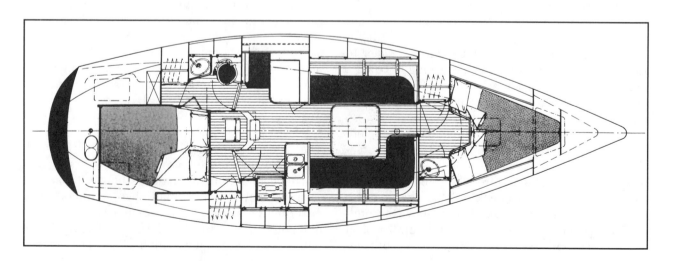

Ericson 35

A good step-up boat for a family on a tight budget; she may not be lavishly equipped, but she sails well.

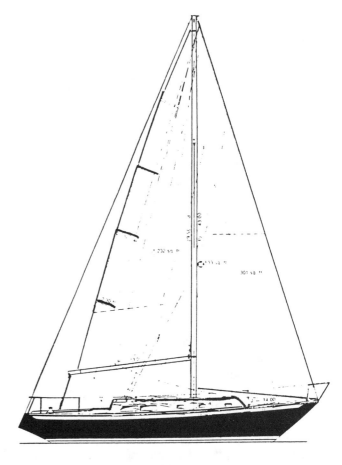

Ericson Yachts has gotten a lot of mileage out of 35-footers over the years. Way back when in 1965, the first Ericson 35 was a typical CCA cruising boat, with a long keel and attached rudder. In 1969, the Ericson 35-2 was introduced. A Bruce King design—as was the original 35—the 35-2 was an up-to-date racer/cruiser, with swept-back moderate fin keel, pronounced bustle, and semi-balanced shallow spade rudder.

The 35-2 stayed in production until 1982, when it was replaced by the 35-3, a larger, more modern boat. The 35-2 was a very successful design—about 600 were built over 13 years. She was not an IOR (International Offshore Rule) design, but the boat rated reasonably well under the new rule, and raced competitively at the local level.

Early IOR boats were little different from their late-CCA predecessors. It took designers several years to develop the types of ill-tempered boats that we now think of as IOR designs. This allowed wholesome production boats such as the Ericson 35 to be reasonably competitive at the local level.

The 35-2 is a good-looking boat. She has a very strong sheerline, powerful forward but not overly springy aft. The stern is hollow in profile, and the stem profile is just convex enough to look like a straight line.

The deckhouse is low in profile, despite the relatively low freeboard of the boat. Aesthetically, the only thing you can quibble with is the overly wide transom, which is fortunately not very high. A lot of current boats, of course, have transoms as wide as the Ericson 35's, and they practically drag the bottom of the transom in the water. The temptation to use these ugly modern rear ends as billboards has proven overwhelming, resulting in a whole new industry in the last decade: transom art. In comparison to many

Specifications

LOA	34' 8"
LWL	25' 10"
Beam	10' 0"
Draft	4' 11"
Displacement	11,600 lbs.
Ballast	5,000 lbs.

of today's production boats, the 35-2's transom looks positively dainty.

Sailing Performance

With a typical PHRF rating of 150 to 156, the Ericson 35-2's performance is respectable, but the boat is no hot rod. She's about the same speed as a Ranger 33.

You need to put the concept of speed into perspective. Despite a lot of "harumpfing" about the poor sailing qualities of modern boats, the fact is that the average fin-keel production cruiser/racer built today is faster—a lot faster—than good boats designed 20 years ago, such as the Ericson 35-2. Appendages and rigs are more efficient, wider beam gives greater sail-carrying ability in a breeze, and hull shapes are frequently more refined, as long as they're not overly influenced by the rating rules.

The newer Ericson 35-3, a slightly larger boat—she's closer to 36' than 35'—is about 30 seconds per mile faster than the 35-2. Same designer and builder, same concept; faster, more modern boat.

At the same time, an older production racer/cruiser such as the Ericson 35-2 is likely to be a lot faster than today's straight "cruising" boat. The Crealock 37, for example, is about 20 seconds per mile slower than the Ericson 35-2. "Fast" and "slow" are pretty relative concepts, particularly when you're moving at a slow jogging pace.

Despite a 43% ballast/displacement ratio, the 35-2 is not a particularly stiff boat. Owners give the boat average marks for stability, frequently commenting that stability is not a problem as long as sail is reduced appropriately. Frankly, this is true on almost any reasonably high-performance boat. We'd shy away from any boat that claims to be able to carry full sail upwind in 20 knots of breeze: the boat is likely to be grossly underpowered in light air.

The "average" stability stems from relatively narrow beam and relatively shoal draft, and is certainly not a major concern. We would recommend that you make a real effort to stow heavy equipment as low in the boat as possible—the boat's vertical center of gravity is somewhere around the height of the tops of the settees. You should also set up the boat so that she can be reefed as easily as possible.

You'll find both tiller and wheel steering on the 35-2. The cockpit is divided into two sections by a full-depth fiberglass bridgedeck which carries the mainsheet traveler. On wheel-steered models, the helmsman steers from the aft cockpit, and the sail handlers work from the forward cockpit. In tiller-steered boats, the helmsman sits toward the forward end of the main cockpit.

For best weight distribution, the forward helmsman's position is better, but it's tough to keep sheet tenders and the helmsman out of each other's way if they're both in that forward cockpit. When racing tiller-steered boats, the mainsheet tender will sit in the aft cockpit.

The aft-mounted wheel does clean up the forward cockpit nicely, giving you very good lounging space.

Several owners have added 400 pounds or so of additional ballast, and report that it makes the boat slightly stiffer without noticeably slowing her down in light air. There is plenty of room in the keel shell to add some extra ballast if you want, but we'd live with the boat for awhile before increasing the ballasting. At the same time, we certainly wouldn't remove ballast that had been added, as long as the boat trims to her lines fore and aft.

As designed, the main boom is very high off the deck, and has a pronounced droop at its after end. This is purely a device to reduce rated sail area for racing. Most boats never had droopy-clewed mains built, and we wouldn't recommend one. Unfortunately, the high boom can make it really awkward for a very short crew member to furl the sail or hook up the main halyard.

Some 35-2s we have seen have no main boom topping lift. Instead, a short length of wire is seized to the backstay, and hooked into the end of the main boom. This is totally unseamanlike, and potentially very dangerous. This system should be removed immediately from any boat, and replaced either with a permanently-attached topping lift, or a fixed vang such as the Hall Quik Vang.

The double spreader rig—unusual on a boat this small when the 35-2 was introduced—allows for fair tight sheeting angles, particularly when you add in the narrow beam of the boat. The spar section itself is quite rugged—not something you can bend very easily. You wouldn't want to bend the rig much in any case, since the mast is deck-stepped.

This is a good all-around sailing boat, with no particular quirks either upwind or downwind. The boat is not as fast on any point of sail as a newer, more racing-oriented design, but she's a good, solid sailer.

Several owners mention substantial weather helm when reaching in heavy air, but there are few boats that don't suffer from this. Ease the traveler down, flatten the main, and the helm should be reduced.

Construction

The Ericson 35-2 has an uncored hull built in a split mold. The two halves of the hull are glassed together with 11 laminations of mat and roving. There's nothing wrong with building a hull in two halves as long as the joint is adequately reinforced, and this is the proper way to do it. Nevertheless, you should carefully examine the hull centerline on the outside of any boat you are considering, checking for cracks.

Several owners in our survey report that leaking shroud chainplates have caused significant rot in the main bulkhead. Keeping chainplates watertight is a constant battle, particularly on a boat that is sailed hard. Problems should show up in the form of discoloration or delamination of the main bulkhead where the chainplates pierce the deck.

Because this is one of those problems that can cause hidden damage, we would think twice about buying a boat that showed a significant amount of chainplate leakage. Unfortunately, the damage may be hidden under covering fascia at the edge of the bulkhead in the main cabin, so some disassembly and probing may be required.

The chainplates are stainless steel straps, with integral welded caps designed to be bedded to the deck. If the bolts holding the chainplates to the bulkheads are snugged up tight, and if the caps are thoroughly bedded in either polyurethane or polysulfide, you should be able to keep the chainplates dry. However, it may require a one-time disassembly and removal of the chainplates to properly bed and install them. Running a bead of compound around the edge of the chainplate caps won't do the job.

The ballast is a lead casting dropped into the molded fiberglass keel. Examine the leading edge and bottom of the keel carefully for signs of hard grounding which may have damaged the keel shell.

Early 35-2s are equipped with gate valves on through hull fittings, rather than seacocks. Gate valves should immediately be replaced with more conventional tapered plug seacocks or ball valve seacocks, which can be firmly attached to the hull. Depending on the strength of the stem of the through hull fitting to support the shutoff valve—as you do with gate valves—is a risky proposition. We've seen plenty of through hull stems break off when you're trying to open a stuck valve. You can end up with the valve in your hand and a big hole in the hull, which is a bit of a problem if your boat happens to be in the water at the time.

Headsail sheet winches are mounted on fiberglass islands that are part of the deck molding. One owner reports that the plywood reinforcement in the top of the winch islands has rotted, the result of an improperly bedded winch. Plywood is frequently used by builders to add compression strength to laminates under hardware. No builder we know of takes the time to seal the core that is exposed when you drill for through-fastenings, so bedding is required.

Ericson 35-2 owners report an average incidence of hull blistering: about 30% have at least some hull blisters. Owners of two boats in our survey said their hulls were badly blistered.

Engine

Up until 1973, you could get any engine you wanted in the Ericson 35-2 as long as it was the Atomic 4 gasoline engine. After that a variety of diesels were offered as options until 1978, when a switch to diesels was made throughout the sailboat industry.

The most common diesel used in the boat in the mid-70s was the Westerbeke 4-91, a heavy 25-horse engine. But you'll also see Volvo, Yanmar, and Universal diesels, as well as the Westerbeke Pilot 20.

There are two different engine placements. In early models, the Atomic 4 is tucked under the aft end of the dinette, in the main cabin. Owners give this installation high marks for engine accessibility, and it keeps the weight in the middle of the boat.

Boats with the two-settee main cabin have the engine mounted aft, under the companionway. The engine is far less accessible in this location.

Watch out for terneplate steel fuel tanks on older boats. These are a potential fire hazard, as they are very susceptible to rust-out. The fuel capacity of 22.5 gallons is adequate for any of the standard engines.

Several owners report having incorrectly-propped engines, although it is not clear whether these are original engines or replacements. With either the Atomic 4 or any of the optional diesels, the boat should do at least 5 1/2 knots under power in calm seas at normal cruising revs. Don't count on using the stock 12 x 6 prop with anything but the Atomic 4. Likewise, the standard 3/4" shaft is a little small in diameter for any engine bigger than the Atomic 4.

The original engine exhaust is a water jacket system, fabricated of steel. Pinholes eventually develop between the walls of jacketed systems. These can allow water back into the engine. We'd recommend replacing water jacket systems with a simple, modern waterlift.

Interior

Despite the narrow beam, the Ericson 35-2 has a reasonably roomy, well thought out interior. Actually, it has two somewhat different interiors.

While not innovative, the interior arrangement is roomy and well thought out. In an unusual practice for sailboats, there was no attempt to cram too many berths into the boat.

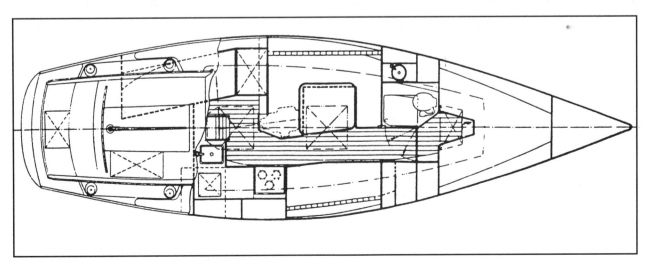

Interior decor changed significantly over the years. Early boats have mahogany interiors: varnished mahogany bulkheads, mahogany trim, mahogany hull ceiling. Very late boats have the all-teak interiors that became the fashion by the late 70s.

The all-teak interior is very dark, although rich-looking. The best thing to do with the teak interior is to varnish it. Use matte-finish varnish for veneered surfaces such as bulkheads, and high-gloss varnish on all solid wood. Of course, this is a lot of work.

The main reason that builders went to teak interiors is that they save a fortune in finishing time and money. The higher cost of teak is more than offset by the time savings. To properly varnish the interior of this boat would take about 200 hours, while a coat of oil could be applied in two working days.

The mahogany interior of older 35-2s is substantially lighter in color then the teak interior. There is also more contrast between the face veneer of the plywood bulkheads and the darker color of the solid mahogany trim. The mahogany must be kept well-varnished; an oil finish will not provide adequate protection for the mahogany surface.

If you're tired of dark wood interiors, it would be fairly easy to paint out the varnished mahogany ply interior. Simply sand the surface to remove all trace of gloss, then paint with a low-luster finish such as Interlux #221 Cabin Enamel. Leave the solid wood trim varnished for a nice contrast.

Painting out teak veneer surfaces is more of a problem, since the teak is likely to be oiled. Paint adheres poorly to teak in the best conditions, and very poorly to oiled teak.

All models have a conventional forward cabin: V-berths, storage shelves over, drawers and bins below. The 25-gallon stainless steel water tank is also mounted under the berth. This is an inadequate water supply for a boat with five berths that is to be used for anything more than weekend cruising. Several owners report adding additional tanks. Don't add them up forward, as it would change the trim of the boat.

Thanks to fine forward sections, the foot of the V-berth is extremely narrow. Several owners have built inserts to turn these berths into a double, but the job is complicated by a cutout at the head of the starboard berth, a feature designed to add elbow room.

In port in good weather, ventilation in the forward cabin is good, thanks to an opening overhead hatch. In rain, it's not so good: no cowl vents.

Older boats have padded vinyl hull liners forward; newer boats have teak ceiling strips.

The head compartment is reasonably roomy, and has good storage. There's a cabinet under the sink, and a locker outboard. There's also a large, tall locker next to the toilet, to which the forward lower shroud chainplate is bolted. Check for signs of leaking around this chainplate.

Ventilation in the head leaves a lot to be desired, but could be improved by a larger cowl vent and a small overhead hatch.

A shower sump was standard, but not all boats were equipped with pressure water. If you install a shower, don't forget to provide a sump pump. You don't want your shower to drain directly into the bilge.

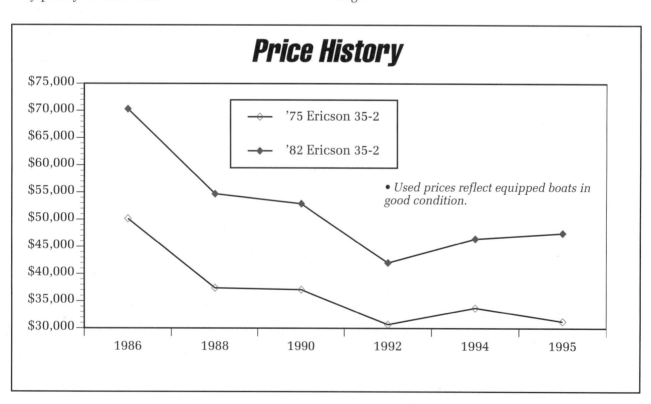

Price History

- '75 Ericson 35-2
- '82 Ericson 35-2

• *Used prices reflect equipped boats in good condition.*

Both main cabin layouts are roomy and comfortable. Bruce King and Ericson wisely decided not to try to get a pilot berth into a relatively narrow boat, opting for more elbow room and a little storage outboard of the settees.

A settee stretches along the starboard side of the main cabin. The settee is pushed fairly far forward to get more room in the aft galley. A cutout in the starboard forward bulkhead provides a footwell, making the settee long enough to use as a berth. There is a narrow shelf behind the settee—a good place to store books.

In the two-settee layout, there's a drop-leaf table just off centerline, allowing comfortable dinner seating for four on the two settees.

The dinette layout has both plusses and minuses. The fixed table can be lowered to form a big double berth, but in our experience, this type of arrangement is a nuisance. You need a big cushion to fit over the table, and that cushion has to be stowed somewhere when it's not in use. The multiple cushions required to create the dinette double never seem to fit together quite right, resulting in a berth that is big enough, but rarely comfortable.

In addition, the offset dinette table is too far away to allow use of the starboard settee for dining, so the dinette is it as far as company for dinner goes. It seats four in reasonable comfort, but as in most dinettes, you end up playing footsie with your dinner partners a lot of the time, which may or may not be a bad idea.

In the dinette layout, the engine is shoe-horned under the aft seat. This was fine with the Atomic 4, but it's hard to fit a diesel in the same space.

It's also pretty hard to effectively sound isolate an engine mounted in the middle of the main cabin, but modern insulation materials can help a lot.

Ericson owners are divided on the merits of the two main cabin arrangements. The midships engine is easier to service, but you sacrfice a lot of walking-around room in the main cabin. Look at both layouts before making a decision.

The aft half of the main cabin is virtually identical in both interiors. To port, there is a good-sized chart table, with enough space outboard to mount a reasonable array of goodies. The huge quarterberth forms the seat for the nav station.

To starboard is an L-shaped galley. Considering the vintage of the boat, the galley is quite good. There's room for a three-burner gimbaled stove with oven (though you'll find only alcohol stoves unless someone's done a retrofit). Aft of the stove is a decent working surface, with big drawers below. A single deep sink is mounted in the counter just below the companionway, with a big locker beneath.

The icebox is tucked back into a corner, but it's reasonably accessible, if a little small for extended cruising.

Both the battery selector switch and the electrical panel are mounted on the bulkhead aft of the galley. That puts them close to the battery, but the nav station would be a more logical location for electrical system management.

Main cabin ventilation is provided by a big overhead hatch, but there's no provision for ventilation in bad weather.

Surprisingly, the cabin sole throughout the boat is the molded fiberglass floor pan, with teak ply inserts. Compared to the finish in the rest of the boat, this is an unattractive detail, smacking of cost-cutting.

Finish in general is of good production boat quality. Detailing is only average.

The interior of the 35-2 is not in any way innovative, but it is roomy, decently finished, and well thought out. There has been no attempt to cram in a superfluous number of berths—if you ignore the dinette double—and there is reasonable privacy for a family.

Conclusions

The Ericson 35-2 is a wholesome family cruising boat. She sails well, and has enough exterior teak trim to look nice if you want to go to the trouble to keep it up. The Ericson molded fiberglass toerail is not particularly attractive, but it's a lot less maintenance than a teak toerail.

These were not lavishly-equipped boats. A lot of things that we take for granted today—multiple batteries, hot and cold water, a shower, self-tailing winches, double lifelines—were either optional or not available, particularly on early models. Some production shortcuts on older boats—steel fuel tanks, gate valves, small water tank—should be corrected at once, if they haven't already been replaced.

Since a lot of these boats have been raced, you may find a 35-2 with up-to-date sailhandling equipment, bigger winches, and good sails. Because of big differences in age, engine, equipment, and condition, prices range from bargain-basement to close to new-boat prices for entry-level boats of the same size.

This would be a good boat to move up to for a family with two children and a tight budget. The boat sails well enough to do a little club racing if you're so inclined, and it's the type of boat that serves as a reasonable teaching platform for older kids interesting in racing bigger boats. Unlike many modern cruisers, she's not a clunky sailing houseboat.

The relatively shoal draft will allow you to get into places inaccesssible to boats with a deep fin keel, making the boat suitable for areas such as Florida, the Chesapeake, and the Gulf of Mexico. With a little thoughtful upgrading and after a careful survey, you could do some limited offshore sailing—trips like Florida to the Bahamas—while you develop confidence in the boat, and in yourself. **• PS**

Alberg 35

This classic dates from the early days of fiberglass boatbuilding. Though aged, she has her good points.

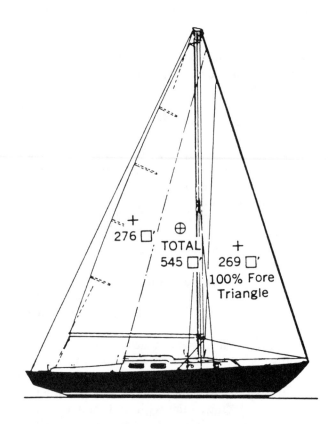

The year 1961 may not seem so long ago to those of us over 40, but believe it or not, it was pretty close to the dawn of big-time fiberglass sailboat building. Only a year before that, Hinckley stopped building production wooden sailboats. Two years earlier, in 1959, Pearson built the first Triton, the boat that was the prototype of the inexpensive small family fiberglass cruising sailboat. The Triton's big selling point was a low-maintenance hull that meant that Mom and Pop and the kids didn't have to spend all spring in the boatyard getting the boat ready for the summer.

These days, when getting the family sailboat ready in the spring may mean little more than a weekend spent washing and waxing the topsides, plus a quick coat of paint on the bottom, it's hard to remember that owning a boat some thirty years ago usually meant work—and a lot of it—or money, and a lot of that, too.

In 1961, Pearson added the 34' 9" Alberg 35 to its expanding sailboat line. The Alberg 35 was a fixture in the Pearson line until 1967. In 1968, the boat was replaced by the Shaw-designed Pearson 35, a slightly larger, more modern boat in keeping with the increasing demands of the market. During six years of production, over 250 Alberg 35s were built.

It's very tempting to call every good-looking, successful boat from the 1960s a classic. Well, the Alberg 35 is good-looking and was successful; we think it deserves to be called a classic. The boat has a handsome sheer, flattish for her day but old-fashioned and springy compared to current boats. She has a low, rounded cabin trunk with slightly raised doghouse, and just about perfectly balanced long overhangs both forward and aft.

Compared to more modern 35-footers, the Alberg 35 is narrow, short on the waterline and cramped.

Specifications

LOA	34' 9"
LWL	24' 0"
Beam	9' 8"
Draft	5' 2"
Displacement	12,600 lbs.
Ballast	5,300 lbs.
Sail area	545/583 (sloop/yawl)

The typical 35' cruiser/racer of the '90s is 4' longer on the waterline and more than a foot wider.

Sailing Performance

The term cruiser/racer was just entering the jargon in 1961. The Pearson sales brochure from 1967 calls the Alberg 35 a "proven ocean racer, cruiser." Note the term "ocean." The Alberg 35 was the smallest boat in the Pearson line to which that word was attached, unlike many builders who push anything with lifelines and a self-bailing cockpit as a "blue-water cruiser."

While the Alberg 35 had moderate success as a racer, the boat was—and still is—a cruising boat.

By current standards, the Alberg 35 is a slow boat for her length overall, with a typical PHRF rating of

Owners' Comments

"New, lighter hulls are clearly faster, but this is an excellent sea boat. Delamination has required considerable re-coring of deck. Gelcoat was seriously pitted when I bought her. Be prepared, until the wind gets up to 15 knots, to see all newer designs leave you far behind."

—1962 model in ME

"Leaks at stanchions can rot balsa core. Solid fiberglass hull looks good, cabin trunk shows small craze lines at curves. Because of the age of this boat, which I've owned for over 20 years, I've replaced items subject to wear or failure such as sails, halyards, sheaves, spreaders, turnbuckles, engine, lights, pumps and electronics. The boat has performed well in the Atlantic and has been incredibly dependable."

—1962 model in MD

"The boat has poor initial stability due to narrow beam, good ultimate stability. Original joinery and trim are primitive, but solid. Glass work is simple, fair, solid. Forward cabin is roomier than needed. My water and fuel tanks failed, causing major surgery. Wooden rudder was rebuilt and sheathed in polypropylene. An Alberg 35 is a pretty, solid, inexpensive, able sailer. The deficiencies are manageable."

—1962 model in MA

"Did Honolulu to Tahiti nonstop in 23 days. Boat is very seakindly. I took this boat on an 8,000-mile cruise through the Pacific. It is an excellent vessel for cruising. I added a pilothouse and heavier rigging, converted to diesel, added radar, an Aires steering vane and a galley freezer."

—1962 model in HI

"Spartan interior, inconvenient galley, cockpit too big for offshore. Berth size adequate, very plain interior, uncomfortable sitting, inconvenient table, no good navigation area. Good storage. Forefoot of keel easily damaged during dry storage. I bought this boat for beautiful lines, full keel, stability and price."

—1962 model in CT

"Reverse under power is a disaster—control is always in question. The boat is 25 years old and needs a lot of cosmetic work. It is solid, a good sailer, has handled our stupidities, and in general is a joy to own. It's not the fastest boat on the block. It's easy to sail, a little old-fashioned, but I'd recommend it without qualification."

—1963 model in MA

"New rig with bowsprit allows me to balance helm and walk away from the wheel for 30 minutes at a time. Deck gelcoat is in poor condition with small craze lines and very dull finish. Boat seems almost indestructible."

—1965 model in NJ

"Interiors nowadays are better designed, but in all other respects the Alberg 35 is an excellent compromise of essential qualities: speed, seaworthiness, looks, comfort, and cost."

—1967 model in IN

198. By way of comparison, her replacement, the Pearson 35, rates about 174, and the Ericson 35-2 about 150.

But Alberg 35s take to sea pretty well. The narrow, deep hull form makes for a very good range of positive stability—about 135°—and an easy motion in a seaway. Owners consider the boat slightly slower to slightly faster than other boats of similar size and type.

Unlike modern boats with wide beam and firm bilges, the narrow, slack Alberg 35 heels very quickly, despite a 42% ballast/displacement ratio. But narrow boats sail fairly efficiently at fairly steep heel angles. A modern boat such as the J/35 sails best upwind in 15 knots of true breeze at a 23° angle of heel, while a boat like the Alberg 35 will be sailing at close to a 30° angle in the same conditions.

With a rudder set well forward, it can take a lot of helm to keep the boat on course when reaching in a breeze. This isn't helped at all by the large, relatively low aspect ratio mainsail. At the same time, owners report that the boat tracks well, a quality missing in many newer boats.

The Alberg 35 was built both as a sloop and a yawl. Yawls were popular under the CCA (Cruising Club of America) Rule because mizzen and mizzen staysail area was lightly taxed. The yawl is not a bad rig for shorthanded cruising, since the mizzen can be used to help balance the boat, and is particularly useful in anchoring and weighing anchor under sail. From a performance and handling point of view on a boat this size, however, the yawl rig has few if any advantages. We would look for the sloop rig if we were shopping for an Alberg 35.

The mast is stepped on deck, over the doorway to the forward cabin. This requires substantial reinforcement of the bulkhead. Several owners in our survey report that the coring in the deck under the mast has crushed, allowing the top of the cabin to compress.

Both the sloop and yawl rigs have simple, fairly heavy aluminum masts. A varnished spruce roller-reefing main boom was standard. If we were buying an Alberg 35, we'd forget the roller reefing and set the boat up for slab reefing. In our experience, a roller-reefed mainsail is usually so baggy as to be useless for upwind sailing.

Several owners in our survey have added bowsprits to their boats, converting them to cutter rigs with yankee and staysail. This improves the boat's balance, as well as making sail combinations more flexible for cruising.

The cockpit is long and quite large, with plenty of room for daysailing hordes. Cockpit coamings are teak, and really look nice when varnished. The standard tiller takes up a lot of cockpit space, but most boats we've looked at have the optional pedestal wheel steering.

Big port and starboard cockpit lockers have poor locking arrangements, and drain straight to the bilge. Give a lot of thought to what will happen if the boat is pooped by a following sea, then go to work at improving hatch sealing and fastening.

Sail handling equipment on these boats is likely to be primitive. The old Merriman #5 genoa winches and #2 mainsheet and jib halyard winches date from the time when trimming and setting sails was expected to be a lot of work. We'd replace them all with modern, powerful self-tailing winches if anything other than daysailing is contemplated.

Likewise, there was originally no mainsheet traveler. On a narrow boat like this with the mainsheet led aft, there really isn't that much advantage to a traveler—it simply operates over too small a range of the boom's arc to offer much benefit.

If the mainsheet were re-led so that you could put a traveler on the bridgedeck, just in front of the steering pedestal, a traveler would be worthwhile. This, of course, would mean getting rid of the roller-reefing main, but in our opinion that's a good idea, anyway.

Wheel steering was an option, but you'll find it on a lot of Alberg 35s. We'd consider it a plus.

Engine

All Alberg 35s were powered by the ubiquitous Atomic 4 gasoline engine. If you're thinking about keeping an Alberg 35 for five or more years, the time has come to think about replacing the engine—preferably with a diesel.

Of course, a lot of owners have already retrofitted their boats with diesels, but the installations will obviously vary dramatically in quality.

Fortunately, Universal Motors has a diesel engine that is literally a bolt-in replacement for the Atomic 4. It's the Mini 4, and it will fit the same engine beds, has the same shaft alignment and same length as the Atomic 4, is slightly lighter, and is only 1" higher. There is room to squeeze new diesel into the engine box under the companionway.

Like most boats with the rudder mounted well forward and the prop fitted in an aperture, the Alberg 35 backs down poorly. This is simply a fact of life, so you have to get used to it. Steering ahead, the boat handles fine. The Atomic 4 is perfectly adequate power, giving a cruising speed of about 6 knots in calm water.

Construction

A lot of Alberg 35s are used for offshore cruising. Plain, rugged construction is one reason why. The hull is a heavy, uncored layup, not particularly stiff or strong for its weight, but easy to repair and relatively foolproof.

Rudder construction is a holdover from the days of wooden boats. It consists of a wooden rudder blade bolted to a heavy bronze rod, formed to the shape of the aft edge of the prop aperture. The rudder of any Alberg 35 should be examined carefully, not because this type of construction is poor, but simply because the rudders are getting old. The rudders may have been damaged in groundings, or the stock bolts may be corroded.

One advantage of rudder construction is that it is very easy to change the rudder design. If we had an Alberg 35, we would get rid of the original barn-door rudder blade and replace it with a more modern design with a straight trailing edge and more area near the bottom of the rudder.

This *Constellation*-type profile became pretty much standard with the last long-keel CCA boats designed before the *Intrepid*-type skeg and rudder of the late 1960s. The bottom of the new rudder could be angled up slightly to reduce the chance of damage in groundings.

Two aspects of the boat's construction have caused some problems for owners. The ballast casting is a single chunk of lead which is dropped into the hollow fiberglass keel molding.

Along the bottom of the keel, some boats have a void between the lead casting and the fiberglass shell, making the shell vulnerable to damage in groundings or even when hauling and launching the boat.

A surveyor should carefully evaluate this area for voids by sounding with a mallet. Voids can be fairly easily filled by injecting epoxy resin into the cavity.

The other problem could be more difficult to

solve. Decks of early boats like the Alberg 35 were frequently built using edge-grain rather than end-grain balsa. Edge-grain lacks the stiffness or compression strength of a modern end-grain balsa sandwich. Flexing of decks cored this way can break the bond between the fiberglass skins and balsa core. If the deck feels mushy, it is probably at least partially delaminated.

Repair—assuming the core is dry—involves drilling an extensive network of holes through the deck skin and core, being careful to reach but not penetrate the inner skin. Epoxy resin is then injected in each hole until it runs out of adjacent holes. The deck should be braced upward from below and weighted down from above until the resin cures.

This method works well with small areas of delamination, but is a tedious job in larger areas. At best, you end up with a deck sandwich that is somewhat stronger than the original that failed.

Major refinishing of the deck will then be required. Extensive deck "softness" is cause for rejecting any boat, regardless of age.

You will find a variety of tankage arrangements in boats of different vintages. According to one owner, early boats have galvanized fuel and water tanks, which will eventually rust through. Another owner had a huge built-in fiberglass fuel tank forward, which developed a leak and was replaced by a monel tank in the same location. Design specifications for late boats in the production run call for an integral fiberglass water tank of 48 gallons capacity located in the bilge under the main cabin sole, plus a 23-gallon monel fuel tank under the cockpit sole.

The advantage of the monel fuel tank is that it will not have to be replaced if a diesel engine is installed: simply flush it thoroughly with diesel fuel to remove any traces of gasoline, and you're in business. Monel is absolutely the best material for either fuel or water tanks, but it is prohibitively expensive.

Like most sailboats this old, you may find extensive gelcoat crazing and fading on both the hull and deck. This is a cosmetic problem up to the point where crazing allows water to migrate into the laminate, at which time it can become a structural problem. If the gelcoat has begun to buckle and peel, it's best to avoid the boat unless you're looking for a boat at a rock-bottom price for offshore sailing. Cosmetic repair of superficial crazing is labor-intensive, involving sanding, multiple coats of high-build epoxy primer, and complete refinishing, preferably with polyurethane. To have this done professionally would be prohibitively expensive.

The deck gear, standing rigging, and spars on these boats are getting old. Many of the boats have high mileage, since a large percentage are used for long-distance offshore cruising. Be prepared to do relatively simple jobs like removing and rebedding stanchions and deck fittings, installing backing plates, and replacing a lot of rigging. Sails more than five years old—other than storm sails that have seen little or no use—are candidates for replacement.

Interior

Because the Alberg 35 is narrow, it will seem cramped to those used to the condo-like interiors of modern 35-footers. The arrangement, though, is pretty good.

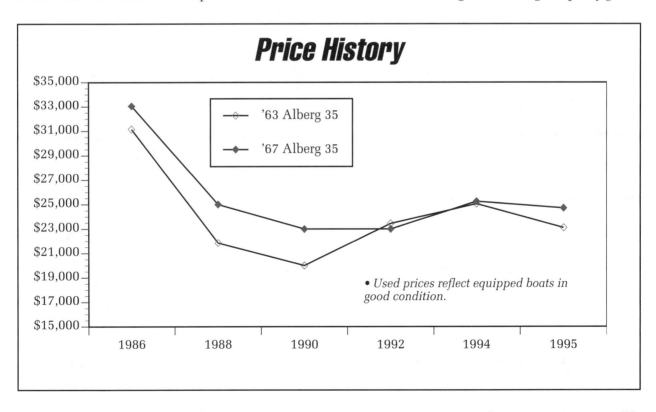

Used prices reflect equipped boats in good condition.

Two interiors were built: one is the "traditional interior #1" of practically every boat built in the last 50 years, the other is "dinette arrangement #1," which became popular when people started looking for more workable galleys about 20 years ago.

Both boats have large forward cabins, with V-berths, a hanging locker, a bureau and drawers under the berths. This is one reason the boat appeals to a lot of minimum-budget livaboards. The forward cabin can be a real owners' stateroom, even though it lacks a double berth. If you were handy, you could rip out the V-berths and build a good-sized diagonal double along either side of the cabin, building in additional storage opposite. The cabin is large enough that this wouldn't totally destroy standing space.

There are two bronze-framed opening ports and a hatch for ventilation in the forward cabin.

The head is aft of the forward cabin, and runs the full width of the boat—a good arrangement on a boat this narrow. With the doors to the main cabin and forward cabin shut, this gives a head compartment with a lot of elbow room. For daysailing, you only need to shut the door to the main cabin to get privacy—no worse than shutting the head door on any boat.

Ventilation is provided in the head via two opening ports plus a pair of cowl vents in Dorade boxes.

The Alberg 35 was one of the first boats of this size to be built with standard hot and cold pressure water, plus a shower. It was a big selling point back then; now it is taken for granted on a 35' boat.

The main cabin will have either the conventional arrangement of settee berths on each side with a fold-down table between, or the galley along one side with a U-shaped dinette opposite.

The dinette arrangement is a decidedly mixed blessing. By lowering the dining table, the dinette converts to a double berth. The original stove well in the dinette arrangement was big enough for a three-burner gimballed stove with oven, while the conventional aft galley has the rinky-dink two-burner alcohol stove that was standard equipment on most boats for many years.

With the dinette, there are two quarterberths aft which extend under the cockpit, and they are reasonable sea berths. In the conventional arrangement you would use the main cabin settees as sea berths, which is also fine.

Quarterberths can be stuffy in tropical climates, and they tend to end up as inefficient catch-all spaces for anything that is too big or awkward to stow in lockers or drawers.

But the aft galley is no prize. Galley counters are quite low due to the boat's low freeboard. There is a small single sink, plus the aforementioned instrument of torture in place of a stove, and an icebox whose top must perform double duty as galley work

space and a rudimentary chart table. With the dinette arrangement, the dining table will probably double as the nav station, although we'd be tempted to sacrifice one of the quarterberths to build in storage space plus a usable stand-up nav station.

It's no wonder that at least one owner reports tearing out the entire aft galley and starting from scratch.

Ventilation in the main cabin is non-existent, except for the main companionway hatch. Because of the step in cabin profile, fitting a ventilation hatch over this cabin is tricky, but it can be done.

Interior decor is very "period," and the early 1960s were perhaps the nadir of interior design in sailboats. "Low maintenance" fever was at its peak, and wood-grain plastic laminate ran rampant.

Fortunately, this is nothing that a little painting can't cure, or if you're really handy, you can laminate nice, clean, solid-color Formica over the old stuff on the counters and bulkheads, then varnish the wood trim. The improvement in interior appearance and apparent space would be amazing.

Conclusions

We've presented a pretty intimidating list of drawbacks to the Alberg 35. Now let's look at the positive side. This is a sturdy, ruggedly-built boat whose design and construction are suited for serious offshore sailing, with the caveat that you go through the boat from one end to the other, replacing every piece of gear that's tired, reinforcing and repairing as necessary.

There are not too many boats that you can buy for this kind of money and then head off to Tahiti in reasonable security.

It's a tinkerer's dream. You may not be ready to build a boat from scratch, but you can do modifications on the Alberg 35 to your heart's content without going broke or destroying your investment.

The boat is really good-looking, especially compared to a lot of modern high-sided tubs. If you're a fanatic, you can clean up, paint and refinish the boat to look almost as good as a Hinckley Pilot—almost.

Some Alberg 35s have been meticulously maintained, and are in beautiful condition. Some of them have been beat to pieces by other owners going cruising on the cheap. We'd look for a nice one, or one that had only cosmetic problems. The trick is figuring out which problems are only cosmetic.

A livaboard couple can be comfortable on this boat, having much more elbow room than on a smaller modern "live aboard" cruiser for which you'd pay more money.

You want a decent-sized boat for serious cruising, while spending about the same money as you would for a new 27-footer? Consider the Alberg 35. Buy it, and be off for warmer places.   • **PS**

Island Packet Cat

For those in the market for a trawler or motorsailer, this cat offers good performance under sail.

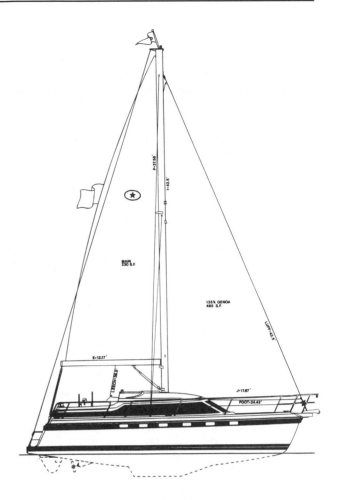

At a traditionalist sailor's first glance, the new Packet Cat 35-foot catamaran appears to be a bold but expensive, and not particularly attractive, departure from the monohull designs in the Island Packet Yachts line. The new cat is boxier, less sleek, and (to our eyes) less salty-looking than any of the Packet Cat monohulls, which range in length from 29 to 44 feet. The same thing applies in a comparison with several competitors' cruising multihulls; clearly, learning to love a multihull requires a different aesthetic.

But none of this is a problem for naval architect-designer-builder Bob Johnson, as we learned when he spent a couple of hours with us just before our test sail. During our interview he explained. "I didn't design this boat for the traditional sailor. Instead, I focused on the people who say sailing is too complicated, who want to relax, who don't want to work while sailing. The families and the women love it. And the price is not a sensitive issue with buyers, who tend to be fairly knowledgeable, analytical types." Johnson added that many Packet Cat buyers previously owned powerboats.

As for the aesthetics of the design, Johnson has a ready answer: "A lot of it is in the eye of the beholder; we call it the green-blue thing. You may say: 'I hate green; if it was blue, I'd love this boat.' We can't do anything about that. It's a question of individual perception. "

First impressions aside, how did we like the boat? Frankly, it started to grow on us even before we left the dock on our first sail.

Design

The first word that usually comes to mind when a monohull sailor thinks about catamarans is "fast."

Specifications

LOA	35' 0"
LWL	31' 0"
Beam	15' 0"
Draft	2' 6"
Displacement	12,500 lbs.
Sail area	735 sq. ft.

But the ability to sail fast was definitely not at the top of Johnson's priorities.

"If you're going to buy a four-door sedan," he said, "performance might be fifth on the list. First you may want reliability, comfort, and perhaps other things. We've been the same way with our (other) boats. And people are beginning to realize that cruising catamarans are not rocket ships. This boat will sail faster than our Island Packet 40, and is certainly equal to or better than any monohull in its size range. That's sufficient."

Instead of speed, among Johnson's top priorities were moderate heeling (seven degrees maximum), and enough reserve buoyancy to carry 3,000 or 4,000 pounds of crew and stores on a long cruise. He also wanted a boat that wouldn't tend to bury its bows, as do many cats with fine entries. Other high priorities were roomy, comfortable accommodations, a spacious, solid bridgedeck area extending further forward and aft than on most cruising cats; and easy, uncomplicated handling both at sea and when docking.

To get these features, Johnson went with a hard-chined, arc-bottomed cross section on the hulls and a relatively big footprint for high initial buoyancy. Such an underbody works well given the priorities, but robs performance a bit compared to lighter cats with skinnier hulls and circular bottom cross-sections for lower wetted surface. However, the speed penalty may not be unacceptable for some sailors: Instead of motoring at 8-1/2 knots, you might motor at 7-1/2. And in conditions where you might sail another similarly sized cat at, say, 10-11 knots, you might do 7-8 in the Packet Cat. Also, the Packet Cat carries a relatively modest 15-foot beam, not much more than a powerboat with the same accommodations, whereas lighter, faster cats would need to be beamier to attain the same righting moment for equivalent sail area.

Buoyancy forward is aided by a central nacelle, or DeltaPod® as Johnson calls it, hanging from under the bridgedeck. It's not a new concept; Prout has been using something similar for years. But the Prout pod is a passive design, intended to stay out of the water until the seas get rough, whereas the Packet Cat pod is active, partially submerged at all times. Besides helping to keep the bows from burying, Johnson claims the submerged pod partially cancels the wave train coming off the outer hulls, creating a very flat wave pattern. At the expense of increased wetted surface area, this nacelle also permits standing headroom on the bridge and better cockpit visibility because of the lower cabin top, a bugaboo of many designs. As are so many aspects of sailboat design, it's a matter of trade-offs.

Among the other consequences of the designer's priorities are: oversized berths, color-coded running rigging, roller furling, and no centerboards. Instead of a board or boards, a long shallow keel under each hull helps control side slip while enabling the boat to sail in shallow water (draft 2' 6"), and to sit straight up on the bottom when the tide goes out. This has been the approach of most multihull builders (the Gemini 3200 is an exception), though clearly centerboards or daggerboards provide increased lift and improved windward performance.

Performance and Handling

Depending on who you talk to, you might find people saying this is a 9-knot, or on a very good day 10-knot, boat in smooth water. But in a test sail on a reach with 16 to 18 knots of wind and a 1- to 2-foot chop, we recorded a maximum of 7.7 knots on the speedo.

The 30" Edson wheel is connected to twin rudders via sheathed push-pull cables, and the wheel-to-rudder linkage has an unusually low ratio (1-1/4 turns stop to stop). Nevertheless, in all conditions the boat was easy to steer. In fact, in the breezy test sail, we noticed a neutral to slight lee helm.

To try to correct the lee helm to the slight weather helm which is generally considered ideal, and at the same time gain a bit more speed, we asked our crew (from Island Packet) for more vang tension. We were then told that the rigid vang is a turnbuckle arrangement with a locking pin, and is adjusted to a critical angle to work well with the standard boom-furling Sailtainer™ unit, supplied by Isomat. Once the vang position is set. it's left alone, and you must try to tighten the leech of the main by using mainsheet alone. We cranked in the main until it began to stall, but the lee helm stayed with us and there was no increase in speed. Changing to an easily adjustable vang would be a worthwhile improvement, though at this point it's apparently incompatible with the Sailtainer.

When the wind temporarily slackened to 11-13 knots, boat speed fell off to around 4-5 knots close-hauled. The Packet Cat tacks in about 100 degrees, and we didn't need to backwind the jib to do it. Heel never exceeded five degrees or so-little enough so a beverage can wouldn't start to slide across the cockpit console table. Dead downwind, we made 5 knots in 16 or 17 knots of true breeze.

One of the designer's top priorities was ease of handling, and the boat does indeed handle well for a beamy 35-footer. Control, especially under power, is excellent. We were able to turn on our own axis, helped by the twin screws (not contra-rotating) which provide a huge moment arm, being 10' 6" apart. But despite the wide-set props (which on the test boat were feathering, a $3,900 option), the boat motors quite well with either engine off, with no significant helm compensation needed. Backing into a berth is made easier by the configuration of the cockpit helm console; you can stand facing aft, forward of the console, and steer the craft precisely into a slip with a hand on each of the two throttles.

To help make sail-handling easy, the fully-battened main rolls into a Sailtainer boom; the roller furling jib has a foam luff pad for reefing if needed; the control lines are all color-coded; and winches are big, self-tailing, and well-located. For ease of anchoring, there are twin stainless anchor rollers with matching hawsepipes to a pair of forepeak stowage areas.

Island Packet personnel said that with both engines revved to cruising rpm, the boat burns 1-1/2 gallons per hour (3 quarts per engine), to make 7-1/2 knots. If you shut one engine down, they said, the boat will steam at 6 knots, burning 3 quarts an hour. That gives a two-engine cruising range of something like 250 miles with a 10-percent reserve in the single 55-gallon fuel tank, or longer if you use one engine (there's room to add more tankage if you want.)

Like other catamarans, the Packet Cat's motion is different from a monohull. Some describe it as "jerky," though "quick, lively motion" might be a less pejorative-sounding phrase. The reason has to do with the fact that (A) there are two separate hulls, and when underway, what's happening on one side of the boat isn't necessarily happening on the other side; and (B) the boat is lighter per square foot of waterplane (or "footprint" in today's vernacular) than a monohull. In any case, we quickly got used to this different motion, but, like "the green-blue thing," either one does or one doesn't.

Construction

By typical cat standards, the Packet Cat is moderately heavy, with a solid (no foam core) hull and a special deck composition that Island Packet calls PolyCore®. The hull and deck, each molded in one piece, are joined using an elongated shoe box design, overlapped a good 6 inches and bonded with 3M 5200 urethane sealer all the way around. This creates an enormous area of bonding in the hull-to-deck joint. In addition, stainless bolts with lock nuts are placed every 6 inches along the joint.

Triaxial glass is extensively used in molding, along with ISO/NPG gelcoat on which Island Packet gives a 10-year limited warranty. The PolyCore deck structure uses a matrix of microspheres and resin to add stiffness, strength, and resistance to delamination, and to avoid the risk of rot that's always a worry with a plywood substrate. The lower portion of the central pod, plus chambers under the cockpit sole, are foam filled, first with Styrofoam® blocks to take

up most of the volume, then with a nitrogen-frothed, two-component foam around the blocks. The net result is an unsinkable structure.

Port lights are 1/2-inch acrylic, which should be plenty strong for most conditions. Aluminum 1/4-inch backing plates are used behind all cleats. The entire hull/deck structure is designed to ABS (American Bureau of Shipping) standards.

Twin 27-hp. three-cylinder Yanmars are quiet and effective. Soundproofed engine compartments, accessible via walk-in access from the twin shower stalls and via hinged panels in the cockpit lockers, each have two lights and plenty of space to move around, and to add extras such as gensets, watermakers, and so on. The fuel tank is pre-plumbed for a diesel genset, one of many thoughtful touches. On Deck Comfort at the helm is excellent. The helm seat, with ample (2' x 3' x 2') storage under, is 19 inches over the sole and has a 2-inch soft cushion and a suitable cushioned backrest nicely positioned at the small of one's back. On our test boat, the instruments and controls mounted on a large, sturdy console were generally easy to use treading the engine monitoring instruments being a minor exception). To the right of the helm seat is a 1-1/2-cubic-foot day-cooler compartment, insulated with about 2 inches of expanded urethane foam.

On most cruising cats, the wheel is mounted on the cabin bulkhead, with the seat on a tall post with footrest above the cockpit sole, and crew benches unsociably behind the helm. But, the forward helm position is better protected by the dodger—another trade-off.

The forward deck is spacious and, with the double solid stainless rails all around, imparts a feeling of

---

The Island Packet Cat is essentially a two-couple boat, with two staterooms and two heads.

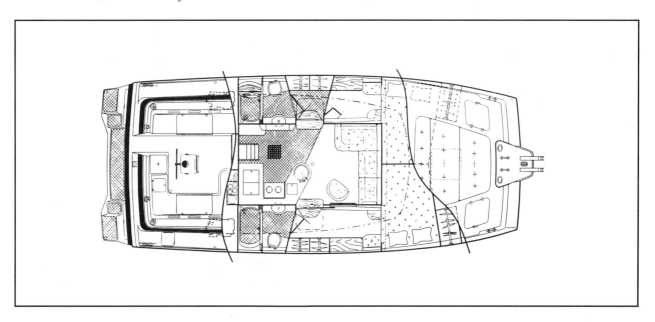

Note the center nacelle or DeltaPod® of the Packet Cat, which is always at least partially submerged.

security. Unlike the trampolines on most cruising cats (to help keep weight out of the ends), the Packet Cat has a full fiberglass foredeck extending almost to the very bows, complete with a cushioned sun lounge area featuring a tilt-up back. (The one-position angle of the back seemed a bit horizontal to us—but probably could be made adjustable with a little redesign). The glass foredeck adds weight, but is in line with the designer's emphasis on comfort and convenience.

So are twin anchor rollers, twin chain lockers, and three large foredeck storage bins. We also liked the design and number and size of cleats, all stainless 10-inch open base type: Four for mooring, two for the anchors, and two midship cleats for spring lines (the last, sadly, not often seen on production boats).

Built into the transom, abaft a gated walk-through to the cockpit, is a small swim platform and hinged stainless ladder. Scuba tanks, swim gear, and extra ground tackle may be stowed in two deep storage compartments with flip-up doors built into the transom.

Interior

The Packet Cat layout is well conceived, with a big saloon between the hulls for lounging, chart work, cooking, and dining, and in each of the two hulls, sleeping quarters, heads, and storage for personal gear. The Packet Cat has about 6' 4" headroom throughout. The decor is pleasantly light and bright: Ash that's been stained a pastel "Hatteras white," sealed, and lacquer finished; and matching tones in mica laminates and upholstery.

We like inventive touches in interior design, and the Packet Cat is full of them. For example:

• A special rocker switch, just inside the companionway, is wired direct to the batteries rather than through a master on-off switch. and illuminates the main companionway steps, the steps going down

into each hull, and the master electrical panel.

• A nesting teak stool beneath the companionway can be pulled out to give better access to the overhead shelves in the galley, and down into the icebox, which is a deep 26-1/2."

• The dining table folds down and into a recess in the bulkhead to starboard, so if you just want a "living room" with no table, you can have it.

• Two drawers under the saloon settee are sized for ChartPaks. Adjacent are two large, deep cedar-lined storage drawers for blankets and such. The designer is obviously from the "place for everything, everything in its place" school.

• A trash-bin is built into the face of the galley, and a dustpan and grate are built into the cabin sole.

The L-shaped dining area seats three with the hinged table unfolded to its 54" x 24" position (folded it's 27" x 24"), and a fourth can be accommodated with a heavy but portable chair upholstered to match the decor. The chair is low for the table, being only 13 inches above the cabin sole, whereas the table is 30-31 inches off the sole.

The table is high in order to match the settee, which is also high (19 inches above the sole), purportedly to provide sitting visibility through the port lights. However, short folks still can't see the horizon, even when sitting ramrod straight, as the windowsills are about 51 inches above the sole.

Still, if you stand, or buy yourself a high stool to sit on, the four windows across the front will provide enough visibility to steer with a remote-controlled autopilot from the shelter of the cabin in bad weather.

The galley has a Hillerange stove (two-burner with oven), a big storage area for pots and pans underneath, and an abundance of cabinets with shelves in the sink area—though some are shallow because they run into the head bulkhead in the starboard hull.

Lockers overhead give more stowage over the galley counter. The top-loading, 13-cubic foot icebox is heavily insulated and pre-wired for an owner-installed refrigeration system. Galley hardware is all first class and works smoothly. The saloon settee converts to a double berth.

The owner's stateroom in the starboard hull, down two steps, features a sliding entrance door, which gives privacy to the owner throughout the entire side, including head, double berth, and connecting passageway.

On the port side, guests sleeping in the forward cabin or saloon need common access to the head, precluding a door to the port passageway.

Otherwise, the layout in each of the two hulls is a mirror image of the other. Each stateroom has a 'thwartships double berth, 6' 6" long by 5' 0" at the head end and 4' 0" at the foot, with a 5-inch mattress.

A problem with this commonly used arrangement is that the inside sleeper must crawl over the outside sleeper to get in or out of the berth.

There's a big (17"x12") ventilation hatch over the wide end of each berth, and an opening port outboard. Each stateroom has adequate drawer and shelf storage (including one shelf with an outlet for a portable TV), a cedar-lined hanging locker measuring 4' 8" from floor to bar, a cushioned seat, and a step to climb onto the berth.

We judged the two heads to be above average in functionality and practicality. Each has 6' 4" headroom (6' 3" in the separate, curtained-off stall shower, which includes a seat and foot tub), a Raritan PH-2 toilet with ceramic bowl, big round sink, and enough room to move around without injuring yourself.

Throughout the interior, ventilation and light is superlative, with a total of 12 opening ports (each 4-1/2" x 12" stainless framed, all screened) and six hatches in the hulls, and five more overhead hatches and a pass-through window between galley and cockpit, plus a very large companionway opening, 26" wide and 36" high at the aft end, and 29" fore and aft, in the salon. The companionway is equipped with an acrylic hatch overhead plus an acrylic combination bifold door/dropboard at the entrance, lockable from both inside and out.

Conclusion

The $217,950 1994 base price tag ($225 ,000 and up sailaway) is a lot of money—more than most people pay for a house.

But, on the other hand, the quality of workmanship and finish is high, the performance is good compared to a similarly-sized monohull or a fuel-guzzling trawler, the accommodations are very livable, and the amenities are excellent. So if you're in the market, can afford it, and can get past the "green-blue thing," we think the Packet Cat is a boat that succeeds in what it tries to do.　• **PS**

Pearson 35

Rugged, versatile and handsome, the Pearson 35 has held her value well over the years.

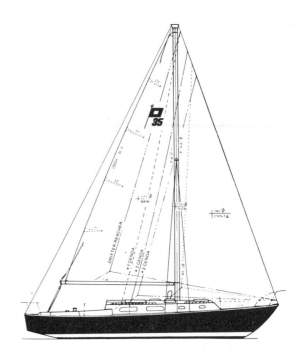

Even to those of us who had begun serious sailing in that era, 25 years ago seems like history. *Finisterre,* a beamy centerboarder by the standards of the time, with a yawl rig, had won a remarkable three straight biennial Bermuda Races at the end of the 1950s. In 1964 another relatively beamy centerboard yawl, a Pearson Invicta, won again. It was the beginnings of an era of shallow wide boats that not only sailed through a gaping loophole in the popular rating rule of their day but also offered interior space unavailable in the typically narrower, deeper boats that preceeded them.

Thus, in the mid-1960s when Pearson Yachts sought to replace in its line the venerable but "old fashioned" Alberg 35, it chose to do so with a centerboard 35-footer. Retaining the traditional long overhangs, modest freeboard, curved sheer and moderate displacement, Pearson's in-house designer Bill Shaw put together the Pearson 35.

The 35 was introduced in 1968 and remained in production for the next 14 years. In all, 514 P35s were built, almost all for East Coast and Great Lakes owners attracted by the 35's shoal draft (3' 9" with centerboard up) and "classic" proportions. Even the popular Pearson 30, usually heralded as the enduring boat from a builder otherwise noted for its frequent introductions of new boats and short production runs, remained in production only 10 years, albeit with almost 1,200 boats built.

Equally remarkable during an era when builders were quick to make regular changes to existing boats in concert with their marketing departments (and afix a "Mk" whatever to to designate changes), the 35 remained essentially unchanged. A yawl rig continued to be an option and the original dinette layout was replaced by a traditional settee layout, but otherwise the most significant changes were the variety

Specifications

LOA	35' 0"
LWL	25' 0"
Beam	10' 0"
Draft	3' 9"/7' 6" (board up/down)
Displacement	13,000 lbs.
Ballast	5,400 lbs.
Sail area	550 sq. ft.

of auxiliary engines used over the years. Thus in talking about the Pearson 35 we can talk about 14 years of production all at once.

A Close Look at the Boat

The success of the Pearson 35 was no accident. Like the Tartan 27, the Alberg 30, and its Pearson predecessors the Alberg 35, Vanguard and Triton, the P35 gave a broad spectrum of sailors the type of boat they were looking for: traditional design, contemporary styling, solid construction, and eminently livable space both in the cockpit and belowdecks. And those same qualities continue to make the Pearson 35 a highly sought after boat on the used boat market almost 25 years later.

Introduced in the midst of the how-many-does-she-sleep era and, with that, the convertible dinette fad, the 35 boasted six berths, only three or four of which promised comfort. It took a number of years but the discomfort of the dinette/double berth combination became evident and the small upper berth became shelf space. Remaining have been the good sized forward V-berths and a reasonable transom (pull-out) berth in the main cabin. In the mid-1970s a pull-out double berth replaced the dinette although it remained better as a single berth with the boat capable of sleeping a total of four without crowding.

Excessive berths notwithstanding, the 35 has a livable interior. However, note that it does not have a navigation table, the galley tends to interfere with the companionway, and the head is small by modern standards. We do not consider any of these shortcomings serious.

Although the interior is more spacious than the average boat of her era (but less so than 35-footers nowadays), perhaps the strongest appeal of the 35 is her cockpit. By any standard old or new it is big (over 9' long), comfortable, and efficient, equally suitable for sailing or dockside entertaining, especially with wheel steering and a sloop rig to leave it uncluttered by tiller or mizzenmast. The lack of a quarterberth results in sail lockers port and starboard as well as a usable lazerette.

Below, the decor is strictly functional with a fiberglass head and hull liner and lots of Formica, a plastic enactment of the typical decor of the 1970s.

The performance of the Pearson 35 is moderately good (average PHRF base rating, about 180). Like many moderately beamy boats with full keel and low aspect sailplan, she quickly picks up a weather helm as she heels. However, the combination of adjustable centerboard and judiciously shortened sail makes that helm only inconvenient, not annoying, especially if the 35 is equipped with wheel steering. She tends to be at her worse in lighter winds, particularly when seas are sloppy, at her best on a close reach in at least moderate winds, then she feels fast, solid and seaworthy.

Owners report no lack of confidence in the 35, either in her strength or performance, in storm conditions. However, the size of the cockpit is a serious drawback in heavy seas offshore.

The original engine in the 35 was the Universal Atomic 4, about the largest (and heaviest) boat for which that engine is suitable, with the prop in an aperture. By 1975 the Farymann diesel became an option, followed by a variety of Westerbeke and Universal diesel engines. Accessibility to the Atomic 4 was marginal; for the diesels it became next to impossible, prompting the most common owner complaint about the boat: retrofitting a diesel to replace the Atomic 4 is difficult.

The 35 would never be mistaken for a motorsailer, given her succession of modestly powered engines. It would be a shame to further saddle her mediocre light air performance with the drag of a three bladed prop to improve performance under power; backing down will always be "an adventure," as one owner deems it, regardless of engine or prop.

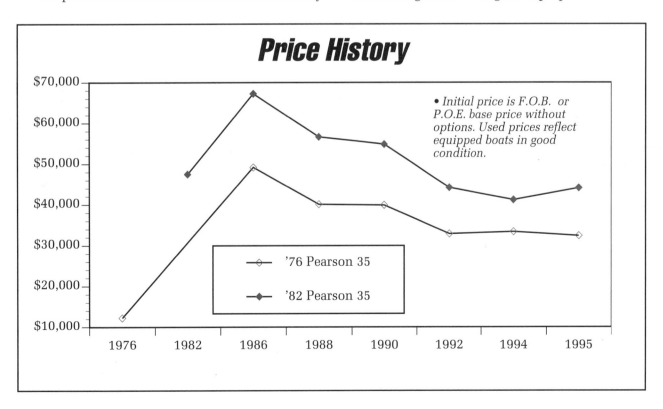

Price History

• Initial price is F.O.B. or P.O.E. base price without options. Used prices reflect equipped boats in good condition.

'76 Pearson 35

'82 Pearson 35

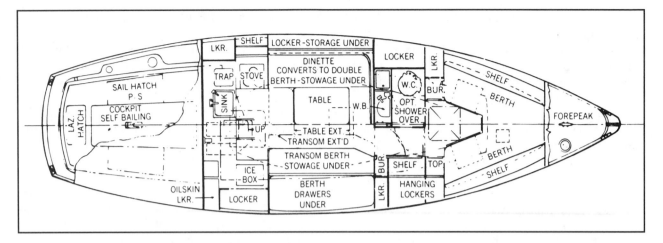

The spars and rig of the 35 are workmanlike. Owners of yawls extol the opportunity to "get anywhere in anything" with jib and jigger. However, with slab reefing we'd opt for the sloop rig. Sail area is not so large that it cannot be worked even with a shorthanded crew, and "modern" conveniences such as roller jib furling and roller travelers make the task even more feasible.

As a further aid, several owners report having fitted their 35s with an inboard staysail, in effect a double head rig, but the short foretriangle base ("J") of the 35 would seem to militate against much effectivess from that rig except in extreme conditions.

What to Look For

With the few changes in the Pearson 35 during her long production run, any basic faults with the boat were soon cured in the earliest models. There seems to have been few even of these. Indeed, the 35 is structurally a rugged vessel. As a result, buyers in the market for a 35 should concentrate on the effects of age on particular boats. Following is a sampling of the problems owners report:

• The aluminum ports, fiberglass hatches, and through deck fittings such as stanchions and chainplates are prone to leaking. So too on occasion does the hull-to-deck joint. These are largely annoying rather than serious and no more so than any boat of the vintage of the 35.

• The centerboard boat definitely has appeal, but with that appeal goes difficulties of maintenance including that of the pennant and pivot. Any survey of a prospective purchase should include a thorough inspection of the board, trunk, pivot and pennant. Incidentally, some owners report having permanently pinned the board up (and wedging them to prevent thunking), but we'd think twice before both compromising windward performance and control of balancing the helm by such a move.

• Gelcoat crazing is a common complaint, although most owners have learned to endure the disfigure-

Originally, the Pearson 35 had six berths. Eventually someone must have listened to reason and altered the layout, adding some welcome storage space instead.

ment while enjoying the rest of the 35's aesthetic qualities. Bottom blistering seems about average for 10+ year old production boats.

• The rig is the typically rugged one that Pearson is noted for, and its problems are apt to be largely corrosion and age.

• Check the condition of the auxiliary engine with the help of a professional. The same goes for the fuel tank. Major repairs or replacement are not easy.

Conclusions

If we were looking for a Pearson 35 we would spend our time checking out those built from the mid-1970s and later but not, if price were an object, one of the last ones built. We would want one with the "standard" (not dinette) accommodation plan, a sloop rig, and a diesel engine, preferably a Westerbeke. Cosmetic abuse would not bother us particularly; the basic quality of the boat lends itself to refinishing with polyurethane outside and even extensive refurbishing inside. A number of owners report upgrading of the interior with woods, fabrics and fittings, reducing or eliminating the formidibly antiseptic fiberglass liner and "teak" faced laminate on the bulkheads.

The degree that the Pearson 35s have retained their value—and seem destined to continue to do so—has to impress any potential buyer faced with the prospect of paying a high price for an older boat. And on this score, make no mistake; a vintage Pearson 35 in good condition has become one of the more expensive used boats of her type and original price on the market. For the kinds of use she is best suited for—coastal cruising for up to four—she is a rugged, versatile, and handsome craft for which there should continue to be a healthy market for many years to come.

• PS

Nicholson 35

A real-live, serious ocean cruiser. The hard part will be finding one on the used market in the U.S.

Today's new boat market has fragmented about as far as it can: cruiser/racers, racer/cruisers, cruiser/cruisers, racer/racers. But not so long ago, there were a few boats built as plain-old cruisers, with decent performance (but no racing aspirations), seaworthy construction (without overkill), and design that allowed you to take an out-of-the-box sailboat on a cruise for a week, or a year.

Maybe you have to go to a real old-time boatbuilder to get that kind of quality. How old-time? Will 200 years of yacht building experience do?

If not the oldest yacht builder around, Camper & Nicholsons has to be in the running. Over the years, Nicholsons built every kind of boat imaginable, including pure racers and boats that came precariously close to being sailing houseboats. Nicholsons have never had the type of exquisite joinerwork you find in Far Eastern boats, nor have the looks of most of their boats fallen into the category of classic. But the boats have always been built with a high level of integrity, and a few of the designs are classic not in looks or detailing, but in overall quality.

Just over 200 Nicholson 35s were built over more than a 10-year period, with production tailing off in the early 1980s. Most boats were sold in England, but a number were built for American owners, and still more found their way to the U.S. during the rampage of the dollar against foreign currencies in the mid 1980s.

The Nicholson 35 is a cruising boat, plain and simple. Its proportions are about as common-sense and moderate as you can get. The boat is clean, almost austere in appearance, with very little exterior wood trim. You'll find a teak caprail, teak grab rails, teak ply cockpit seats, and that's about it.

It is a true medium-displacement boat: heavy by contemporary racer/cruiser standards, but very rea-

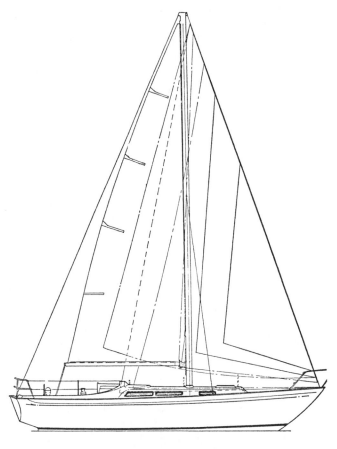

Specifications

LOA	35' 3"
LWL	26' 9"
Beam	10' 5"
Draft	5' 6"
Displacement	15,650 lbs.
Ballast	7,300 lbs.
Sail area	736 sq. ft.

sonable for an offshore cruiser with a waterline almost 27' long.

Sailing Performance

The Nic 35 is no racing boat, but she's no slug, either. Her PHRF (Performance Handicap Racing Fleet) rating of about 156 is some six seconds per mile slower than the Ericson 35-2, but some 20 seconds per mile faster than a "pure" cruiser such as the Tayana 37 or Crealock 37.

A moderate fin keel and skeg-mounted rudder underbody allows reasonable performance in light air, despite a smallish sailplan. The working sail area is just about evenly divided between the foretriangle and mainsail.

The rig is a simple masthead sloop, with double

lower shrouds and single, airfoil spreaders. The mast is a tapered, anodized Proctor spar, which is filled with foam to deaden sound. Halyard winches are mounted on the mast.

While the sailplan never changed, there were many minor revisions to the rig over the years. Early boats have roller-reefing booms, while late boats have slab reefing. Winch specifications and options changed over the years.

Most early boats have halyard winches that are large enough for hoisting sail, but too small to allow you to easily get a person to the masthead. We wouldn't want to hoist a 90-pounder up the mast with the standard Lewmar 8C winches. Larger halyard winches were optional—Lewmar 16 or 25. The 25 is as small a winch as we'd want to use to hoist anyone aloft, and even that would be work for most people.

The mainsheet traveler bisects the cockpit just forward of the wheel, so that you have to step over the traveler and onto the cockpit seats to go forward from the steering position.

While the mainsheet's position just forward of the helmsman is reasonable, the driver cannot easily trim the mainsheet, which secures to a cleat on the front of the teak traveler support. It would be a simple matter to replace this awkward arrangement with a modern traveler, with the sheet ending at a cam cleat on top of the traveler car.

The cockpit seats themselves are short and not very comfortable, with a high, nearly vertical fiberglass cockpit coaming. The deep cockpit does give excellent protection from seas and spray.

One of the best features of the cockpit is a molded-in dodger coaming, much like you find in this country on S&S-designed boats such as the Tartan 37. When fitted with a good dodger, the entire forward half of the cockpit will be bone-dry in almost any conditions.

Despite the fact that the aft side of the deckhouse slopes forward, the companionway is built out slightly, making it vertical. This allows you to remove the top dropboard in light rain, even with the dodger down. The companionway hatch slides have Tufnol runners, allowing the hatch to move easily. This is typical of the good structural detailing in boats from C&N.

Cockpit volume is huge. A bridgedeck protects the companionway, but the high coamings could allow the cockpit to fill almost to the top of the hatch in a major pooping. Later boats have large flapper-protected pipe scuppers through the transom in addition to big cockpit scuppers. We'd suggest retrofitting these to any older boat to be used for offshore voyaging.

Shroud chainplates are just inboard of the low bulwarks. They consist of heavy stainless steel "hair-pins," and are bolted through what would be the beam shelf on a wooden boat. We had some reservations about this construction when we first looked at it more than a decade ago, but after finding no chainplate damage on a similarly-fitted Nicholson 40 that had been rolled over and dismasted, we can't argue with the strength of the installation. Lloyds approves it, and they're notoriously conservative.

Like most boats of the 1970s, Nicholson 35s tend to be under-winched. Standard jib sheet winches are Lewmar 40s or 43s. Larger Lewmars were optional. We'd go for the biggest self-tailing genoa sheet winches that could fit on the coamings, and we'd make it a high priority for shorthanded cruising.

The low bulwarks give an enormous feeling of security under sail. The side decks are wide, and there is a grab rail atop the cabin trunk on each side, although the rail's flattened shape takes a little getting used to. The molded-in fiberglass non-skid is so-so. Teak decks were an option, but not a commonly chosen one.

In general, sailing performance is what you would look for in a serious cruising boat. The hull shape is uncompromised by any rating rule. The ballast/displacement ratio of 42%, with the lead concentrated quite low in the molded keel, results in a reasonably stiff boat by any standard.

Sailing performance can be improved on any boat by replacing a main and genoa more than a few years old. You'll never get racing boat performance out of the Nic 35, but you also won't have to work yourself to death to get acceptable speed, either. That's not a bad trade-off.

Engine

A variety of engines have been used in the Nic 35, all diesels. Early boats have the ubiquitous Perkins or Westerbeke 4-107. Later boats have a smaller Westerbeke L-25 or a marinized Volkswagen Rabbit diesel. Given our druthers, we'd take the Perkins engine. But there's a complication here. Early boats, recognizable by a prop shaft that emerges from the aft end of the keel, utilize a hydraulic drive rather than a conventional transmission. The engine faces aft under the cockpit bridgedeck, with the hydraulic pump mounted on its back end. The hydraulic motor is in the bilge at the aft end of the main cabin.

Hydraulic drives are a mixed blessing. They allow the engine to be mounted anywhere, but most marine mechanics don't know how to work on them. However, heavy equipment mechanics anywhere in the world can solve most hydraulic problems. On the downside, a major problem requiring replacement of the hydraulic motor or pump in a non-industrial area could be a real headache.

Later boats have a more conventional exposed shaft and strut. The engine is mounted further aft, under the cockpit, and the shaft is driven through a V-drive. Access to the engine in either installation is poor. On V-drive boats with a quarterberth, you can get to the front of the engine through the quarterberth. With no quarterberth, it's a crawl through a cockpit locker. The back of the engine is accessed through removable hatches behind the companionway ladder.

Control when backing is better with the V-drive installation, since the prop is much further aft. Likewise, tight maneuvering ahead is better with the same prop configuration, since you get good prop wash over the rudder.

In all boats, the fuel tank is a fiberglass molding. It is not integral to the hull, but is glassed in after the hull is laid up. We have heard no reports of failures of the tank.

Fuel capacity varies from 33 to 40 gallons—adequate for a cruising boat, but a little on the skimpy side for true long-term independence.

Construction

There's nothing to fault in the construction of these boats. Some hulls—but not all—were built under Lloyds survey. A Lloyds Hull Moulding Note—which covers the basic layup of the hull, installation of bulkheads, and the deck molding—is fairly common, as it added nothing to the cost of the boat other than a survey. A full-blown Lloyds 100 A-1 certificate is rarer, since it added substantially to the price of the boat.

Nicholsons was an early user of isophthalic polyester resin, although it was only used for gelcoat. This made Nicholson 35s more blister-resistant when new, but it probably doesn't substantially reduce a boat's tendency to blister if it is left in the water constantly for years. Structural work in these boats is first-class. We've never understood why good-quality European boats in the late 70s and early 80s seemed to have much neater glass work than most production American boats of the same period, but they do.

The lead ballast casting is dropped into a molded keel cavity, then heavily glassed over. The outside of the keel molding of any boat with internal ballasting should be carefully examined for grounding damage.

There is a deep bilge sump under the cabin sole just aft of the fiberglass water tank. This will keep bilge water where it belongs until it can be pumped overboard.

Two 90 amp-hour batteries were standard on early boats. They were increased to 128 amp-hours each on later boats, and the alternator size was increased

Many changes were made to the interior layout over the years; most were improvements. Pictured here is a standard interior from a mid-'70s model. Many of the boats have custom interiors.

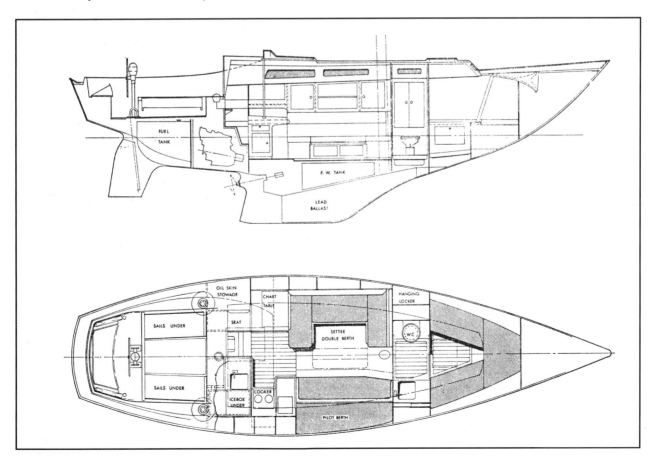

to 60 amps. If you want to go to bigger batteries on an older boat—a must for serious cruising—you'll need to install a bigger alternator if you don't want to run your engine all the time.

Interior

Many small changes were made to the interior design and decor over the years. In addition, the Nicholson 35 was built to order—you didn't buy one off some dealer's lot—so there is a lot of minor interior customizing. This was encouraged by the builder, and the prices for modifications were reasonable. It makes buying a used boat more complicated, however, because the combination of features you're looking for may be hard to find.

The forward cabin on all boats is pretty much the same. There are the usual V-berths, but unlike a lot of boats, they don't come to a point at the bow; there's plenty of foot room. The berths could be converted to a big double, but you won't find that on most boats.

A chain pipe runs vertically between the berths to the chain locker on many boats, rendering moot any modification to a double berth. The chain locker under the berths does keep the weight of chain low and fairly far aft, if you're willing to make the trade-off.

Padded vinyl liners are used on the hull sides, rather than wood ceiling. This looks good when new, but gets tired after a few years. We'd prefer wood. Wood ceilings can be refinished; vinyl can only be cleaned.

The earliest boats have white melamine-finished bulkheads, which lend to the general austerity of older models. Later boats have teak-veneered bulkheads, but the teak used is generally fairly light, so it doesn't dramatically darken the interior.

Ventilation in the forward cabin is poor. A low-profile Tannoy ventilator installed in the aluminum-framed deck hatch was standard, but these don't move nearly as much air as big cowl vents. Original specs called for cowl vents over the forward cabin, but we've never seen them.

Aft of the forward cabin is a full-width head. Camper & Nicholsons used this same basic design on several boats, and it works well. You may not like the idea of walking through the head to get to the forward cabin, but it allows a much larger head than you'll find on the typical boat of this length built in the 1970s.

There are good touches in the head, such as a stainless steel grab rail in front of the sink, and a mirror that angles upward so you don't have to bend over to shave. Using the full width of the boat for the head allows its use as a dressing room without undue contortions.

Early boats do not have pressure water, nor do they have hot water for a shower. These creature comforts came later in the production run, but they can be added to older boats without much trouble.

There is very little wood in the head—just trim around locker doors—which makes it easy to keep clean and dry. A single Tannoy vent provides limited ventilation, but there's plenty of room on deck over the head to add two cowl vents in Dorade boxes. This would help ventilate the entire boat, and would be high on our priority list.

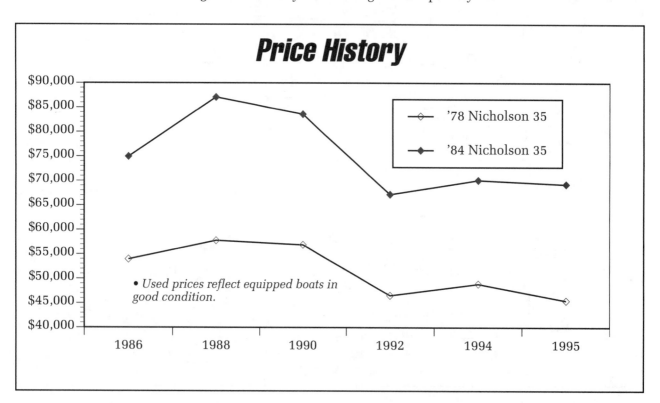

Price History

Legend: ◇ '78 Nicholson 35 ♦ '84 Nicholson 35

• *Used prices reflect equipped boats in good condition.*

You'll find a lot of variations in the main cabin, and which ones are most desirable is really a matter of choice.

All boats have a U-shaped dinette to starboard, with a permanently mounted dropleaf table. On the later boats we've looked at, the table is mounted on a heavy tubular aluminum base, securely bolted to the cabin sole. It is one of the sturdiest tables we've ever seen. The design allows the table to be reached from both the dinette and the starboard settee, giving lots of elbow room for five for dinner, with elbow-to-elbow seating for seven close friends if a lot of passing of food isn't required.

There is storage space under the dinette, with lockers and bookshelves behind the seat back.

Starboard side layout varies. As originally designed, there is a straight extension settee, with a pilot berth outboard. The pilot berth was deleted on many boats, increasing storage space but visually narrowing the cabin. On a serious cruising boat, the extra storage would be a plus, since both the dinette and settee can serve as good sea berths. All berths, incidentally, are fitted with lee cloths—something you don't find as standard on most American boats, even boats sold as serious cruisers.

Ventilation is provided by an aluminum-framed hatch over the middle of the cabin, plus two small water-trap cowl vents at the aft end of the main cabin. For use in the tropics, you really need to add more cowl vents, at the very least.

Minor changes were made in the galley over the years, but they were not earth-shaking. The earliest boats have good locker space, but no cutlery drawer. This was added under the counter on later boats. It would be a simple retrofit.

Nice molded teak counter fiddles on early boats were replaced by functional but tacky aluminum fiddles on later boats. Galley counters are covered with plastic laminate, and some of it is hideous: God-awful speckly-tweedy stuff, sort of in keeping with the interior decor we've experienced in unnamed cheap bed and breakfast joints in the UK.

There's good storage space in the galley, with lockers outboard, a big pantry locker under one counter, a pot locker under the stove well, and another locker under the sink. The sink itself is quite small.

The icebox is outboard of the sink, next to the stove. It's a good-sized box—five cubic feet—and insulation is adequate for northern climates. In the tropics, we don't think it would make the grade.

A gimbaled two-burner Flavel propane stove with oven and broiler is standard equipment. It is painted steel—as are most European galley stoves—and will be a ripe candidate for replacement on older boats. The stove well is narrow, so it may take some searching to find a stove that fits. Force 10 makes a stove that is narrow enough to fit most European stove wells, but you'll probably have to special-order it, as most American boats take a wider model.

The propane supply is a paltry 10 pounds, so you may well end up looking for ways to expand that. A Marine Energy Systems two-tank molded gas locker should fit in the starboard cockpit locker if you don't mind giving up some storage space.

All in all, the galley is very good for a 35' cruising boat; exceptional when you compare it to most American boats of the early 1970s.

Although all boats have a nav station at the port after quarter, the layout varies tremendously.

There are two basic configurations: an aft-facing nav station, which uses the dinette for a seat; and a forward-facing station, using the quarterberth head as a seat.

With the aft-facing station, there is no quarterberth; you get an extra cockpit locker. You also get a real curiosity: a belowdecks watch seat next to the companionway, elevated high enough so you can see out both the companionway and the cabin trunk windows.

This is a real seagoing feature, but will be wasted space on boats that are only used for coastal cruising. Offshore, with the boat running under autopilot or steering vane, the watch seat allows you to sit below, out of the weather, while still keeping a reasonable watch unless you're in crowded shipping lanes.

On some boats, the watch seat was deleted, and replaced with a big hanging locker. This would be a feasible and desirable modification on boats not used for serious cruising.

Both nav station layouts have a big chart table, good bulkhead space for mounting electronics, and space for navigation books and tools. It's a tough call as to which arrangement is better.

The quarterberth would make an excellent sea berth. We'd rather sleep in a quarterberth than a pilot berth, particularly in a warm climate. At the same time, a wave down the companionway can douse you in big-time fashion in the quarterberth. We'd take our chances, opting for the quarterberth and forward-facing nav station.

Headroom is over 6' throughout. The long windows of the main cabin make for a well-lighted interior.

A molded fiberglass water tank holding about 70 gallons fits under the sole in the main cabin, smack on top of the boat's longitudinal center of flotation, where it belongs. This is marginal water capacity for long-distance cruising—we'd like to see at least 100 gallons, even for a couple—but it would be simple enough to install auxiliary tanks under both the dinette and settee. A second tank is a good idea on any boat, in case of a leaky tank or a contaminated water supply.

On early boats, the tank is filled from inside the boat—no deck fill. This avoids any chance of salt water contamination from a leaking filler cap, but it complicates tanking up: you have to drag hoses or jerry cans belowdecks.

The tank vents properly, inside the boat rather than outside. Most American boats have water tank vents on deck, many of them in the side of the hull. To put it bluntly, this is really dumb. If a boat spends a lot of time on one tack with the vent submerged, salt water will siphon back into the tank. Heavy water on deck can even get into vents mounted on the side of the cabin.

With the exception of the aluminum galley fiddles, most of the interior changes over the years are a distinct improvement. Storage is excellent for long-term cruising.

Conclusions

This is a real-live, serious ocean cruiser. It's not pointy at both ends, doesn't have a full-length keel, isn't shippy looking, and doesn't have oodles of nicely-fitted exterior teak to drive you wild with pleasure at the boat show, delirious from endless maintenance when you have to live with it.

The cockpit is uncomfortable, but can be improved with seat cushions and back cushions. It's a shame the cockpit seats aren't long enough to lie down on.

The interior is roomy and comfortable for cruising, lacking only a permanent double berth—a shortcoming that can be remedied, albeit with some work. The interior lacks the space and privacy of current 35-footers best suited for marina living or coastal cruising, but is functional for offshore sailing, particularly for a couple.

We wouldn't hesitate to sail this boat anywhere, with virtually no changes. It demonstrates common-sense design and high-grade construction, even though it's not fancy, and there's not a gimmick to be found: no microwave, no stall shower, no recessed lights, none of the things that some people think they need for comfortable cruising.

The hard part, of course, is finding one. English boating magazines have a lot of Nicholson 35s for sale, but there are not too many on this side of the pond. Actually, that might be an advantage.

Buying a boat overseas is relatively painless, and you save yourself the trouble of sailing across the ocean before you can cruise Europe. Buy a boat in England, cruise there for a couple of summers, laying the boat up over the winters. Then, when you retire or get that long-awaited sabbatical, you can do some "real" cruising. You could do a lot worse. • **PS**

The J/35

She's fast and she's fun—sailing is what this boat is all about. We like the J/35 a lot.

The "J" stands for Johnstone and the "35" stands for 35 feet. Straightforward—a characteristic of both the boat and the company that sells them.

The Johnstones were originally two: Rod Johnstone started things in 1976 when he designed a 24-footer and built it in his garage. He convinced his brother, Bob Johnstone, that the boat could be a success, and Bob became chief salesman, in charge of the business.

The relationship continues to this day, but the family owned company is now run by children of both Johnstones, all serious sailors like their parents. Rod's sons Jeff, Alan, and Phil are president, vice-president, and legal counsel respectively. Bob's son Stuart is chairman of the board and marketing manager, while second son Drake oversees the dealer network and is sales manager of the company.

The original J/24 was sold as a "fast" boat that ignored the existing racing rules. At the time, there was a large group of serious racers who felt that the handicap rules, particularly the International Offshore Rule (IOR) and the Midget Ocean Racing Club (MORC), were encouraging unhealthy extremes in design—not necessarily good, fast sailboats, but rather boats that would sail marginally faster than their low handicap ratings said they should sail, boats that required huge crews to go fast.

At the time, the word on the J/24 was that it spit in the eye of the rules; Rod Johnstone had designed a boat that went fast and was fun to sail, and if it didn't do well in the handicap rating game, then it was the game that was at fault. Except for a couple of aberrations—a 34 and a 41 designed to beat the IOR rule—the J/Boats have remained faithful to that idea. And it is significant that the rating rules have come around to the J/Boats, rather than vice versa. There

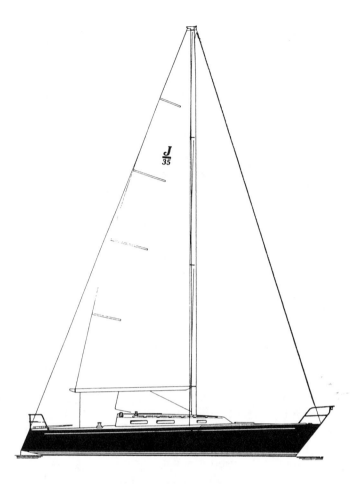

Specifications

LOA	35' 5"
LWL	30' 0"
Beam	11' 8"
Draft	6' 11"
Displacement	10,000 lbs.
Ballast	4,400 lbs.
Sail area	633 sq. ft.

are more J/Boats than any other brand, by far, racing under the current PHRF and IMS handicap rules.

Unlike most sailboat companies, J/Boats decided from the beginning to stay out of the boatbuilding end of the business. Rather than a J/Boat factory, the completed boats come from Tillotson-Pearson, an independent company whose president, Everett Pearson, was one of the pioneers of fiberglass boatbuilding.

The arrangement has been mutually satisfactory over the years, with J/Boats having relatively little invested in manufacturing overhead, concentrating on the design and marketing; and Tillotson-Pearson has another steady and successful customer to complement the other lines of boats that they build—Alden and Garry Hoyt's new Manta 32—along with

Owners' Comments

"This is a wonderful sailing boat with the ability to be very, very fast and yet not difficult to handle. The interior is minimal but okay for weekends."
—1985 model on Long Island Sound

"There is almost no interior storage, even though we bought all the interior options. But at least we can't accumulate too much stuff. This is an easy boat to sail—my wife and I cruise it each year and have little trouble."
—1984 model in Lake Erie

"I've been very pleased with the construction. Took a hit broadside by a Beneteau 44 on a reach with minimal damage."
—1983 model in Florida

"Buy the boat; you'll love it. It is very fast, very powerful and easy to sail—always seems to be in balance and easy to steer. My wife and I cruise ours alone. There is nothing like a J/35 going upwind in a breeze and waves."
—1986 model in New York

"I am 6' 5". Otherwise the boat is perfect."
—1987 model in Massachusetts

"The boat is a high-performance rocket. It rocks and rolls upwind in big seas, and I downgrade it for wet sailing—low freeboard and no coamings. But I have never had any problems with the hull, deck, rudder, rig, rigging, etc. The fixed ports need to be resealed every two years."
—1984 model on Lake Michigan

some high-tech endeavors, such as fabricating giant carbon-fiber propellers for wind generators.

Over the years, Tillotson-Pearson has established a reputation for high-quality production work, often at the leading edge of fiberglass technology, that has helped J/Boats maintain an image of quality near the top-end of the production spectrum.

The J/35 was a successful racer from its introduction in 1983, and with more than 300 built so far, it has had a successful production run for the company. The 35 is still available as a new boat and will continue to be. A new design, the 35C, is unrelated to the 35, a different design, slower, aimed more at cruising than the original 35.

In design, the 35 looks like a typical Rod Johnstone boat, with short overhangs for a long waterline, relatively low and flat sheerline, a low cabin house, and a moderate well-balanced rig. Obviously, Johnstone knows something about the harmony between a boat's underbody and the water, but a large part of the boat's speed is also dependent on the light weight—10,500 pounds on a 30-foot waterline—as well as a good distribution of that weight.

Traditionalists may think the J/35 is a little plain, but its proportions are pleasing, and many people consider it the most attractive grand prix racer around. If you didn't know the boat's record, you probably wouldn't pick it out of a crowd as a speedster, or know that it's one of the most successful racing boats its size of the 1980s.

The boat has primarily been known as a racer, but the company touts it as a shorthanded cruiser as well. The boat's big cockpit, while principally designed for a racing crew, does make the boat good for day sailing, ideal for taking out guests and for dock partying. The boat has frequently been involved in singlehanded racing (both Tony Lush and Francis Stokes raced J/35s across the Atlantic), and we would agree with the company that it is easily handled by a couple, and could make for good cruising for two people or a family with small children.

Though the hull is a bit more beamy and saucer shaped than would be ideal in an offshore boat, it is one of the few modern racers under 40 feet in which we would consider doing an ocean crossing. In storm or hurricane conditions, it has a greater chance of achieving inverse stability than a narrower, heavier boat, but its speed makes it more likely that the prudent sailor will be able to sail away from such extreme conditions.

Construction

As is necessary to make a strong but lightweight boat, the J/35 uses some sophisticated construction techniques. Both the hull and deck are balsa-cored, with the end-grain balsa inside layers of biaxial and unidirectional fiberglass. As with any cloth, there is less stretch and more strength parallel to the glass fibers than across them, and the biaxial and unidirectional cloth used by Tillotson-Pearson lets the builder arrange the cloth throughout the hull so its strength is in line with the forces that occur under sail.

Unlike most boats, the main structural bulkhead which takes the forces of the rig is a molded fiberglass piece, and the floors are made up of glass beams to which both the mast step and the external lead keel are fastened.

The hull and deck are strong and, perhaps more importantly, stiff, so that there is a minimum of flexing when the boat is being pushed. The quality of the construction is evident in the six- and seven-year-old boats that are still able to handle the rig forces of a pumped-up backstay on a hard beat.

We have a lingering concern about the longevity of balsa-cored boats, since we have seen many 10- to 20-year-old boats with deck delaminations and a few with substantial delamination in the hull. Tillotson-Pearson obviously disagrees with us and continues to be committed to balsa cores.

With other builders, a major part of our concern is that balsa cored laminates seem to be more demanding of good engineering and high-quality workmanship than solid fiberglass laminates. Tillotson-Pearson is one of the few companies that we would trust to consistently do a good job in laying up a balsa-cored hull.

An unusual feature of hulls built after 1988 is that the company provides a 10-year warranty against blistering. In molding the boat, they use a vinylester resin on the first layer inside the gelcoat, and—along with a clean shop and careful workmen—they think this is enough to warrant the guarantee. The guarantee is transferable to later owners.

New J/35s can also be purchased with an American Bureau of Shipping (ABS) certificate. ABS is similar to the better known English Lloyd's certification, in that an independent surveyor periodically checks the shop and the boat during construction to make sure it meets minimum standards. While relatively new to cruising sailors, ABS certification is important to racers in the top echelons. International offshore regattas require it. It seems worthwhile because it is about the only way buyers can get an independent evaluation of the boat without overseeing the entire construction process themselves.

The boat comes with a thorough list of standard equipment. The company lists only 18 options for a new boat, and most of these are aesthetic preferences or cruising options, such as a dark-colored hull, two-tone deck, V-berth, swim ladder, and propane locker.

The rig is excellent, with a Hall Spars mast, rod rigging, and complete state-of-the-art running rigging. All winches are adequate, but if we were planning shorthanded cruising in addition to racing, we would consider larger, self-tailing primaries.

Tiller steering is standard on the boat. In its latest brochures, the company doesn't even list wheel steering as an option, but many earlier models had wheels, and some owners may still want it installed. We sailed both a tiller model and a wheel and believe the tiller is far superior, especially for racing. However, wheels seem to be sufficiently in vogue that there are a preponderance of them on the used 35s for sale.

Interior

The J/35 is primarily a racing boat, and its interior is spartan compared to similarly sized cruising boats. But the interior is decent, and well-finished given the plainness of the boat. The company advertises the high-quality of the interior woodwork, but we would describe it as so-so—better than the cheapest production boats on the market but definitely not "yacht" quality.

The arrangement is conventional. Forward you will find either sail bins or an optional V-berth, decently sized, with a head just aft of that, and a hanging locker and bureau opposite. Two comfortable settee berths are aft of the main bulkhead in the saloon, with an optional fold-up table between them.

The galley is minimal, with a two-burner alcohol stove and sink on the port side and an ice-box with chart-table top opposite. There are two big quarter berths underneath the bridgedeck and cockpit.

Ventilation is good, with eight opening ports and two hatches in addition to the companionway, but there is no provision at all for pushing air through the cabin when underway.

Except for the poor headroom and storage space, the J/35's interior is workable for short-term cruising. Still, racing is the boat's forte.

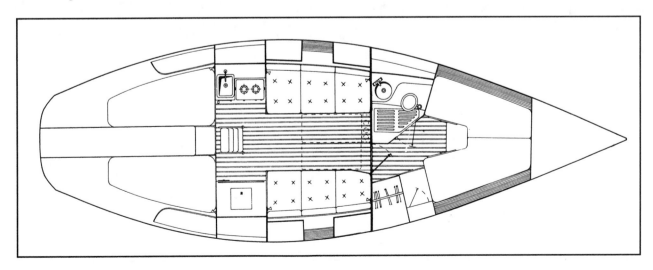

Storage is minimal, adequate for a racing crew or for a couple on a short cruise, but every 35 we looked at had sails and crew gear spread all over the settees and berths.

We would be quite comfortable weekending or cruising on this boat, but it does lack the amenities which most people demand nowadays, like hot-and-cold pressure water, propane stove and oven, and refrigeration. All these things could be added, of course, but they rarely are because they represent weight which is anathema to the high-performance sailor.

For us, the main shortcoming of the interior is the lack of headroom forward, in the head and V-berth, and a tall person will be uncomfortable even in the main cabin.

While this interior may not sound like much to the cruising sailor who looks at other boats with VCR stations and queen-size after berths, it is far superior to the one-off custom racers and almost all other racing boats that are in the same speed class as the J/35. Though the "cruiser" part is minimal, this boat is a true racer-cruiser. Where compromises are made, the racer is clearly favored, but the owner won't feel compelled to check into a motel at the end of a long passage as is the case with most racing machines.

Under Power

The Yanmar 3GM engine has become almost a standard in this size boat. It is a good engine, dependable, relatively quiet, and its 28 horsepower is plenty big for the J/35. A 20-gallon fuel tank gives about 150 miles of range, adequate since this boat will still be sailing in light airs when most others have cranked up the diesel. The boat comes standard with a Martec folding prop, and the boat powers easily to hull speed. The J/35 turns sharply and handles well under power, and it will back up more or less where you want it. Access to the engine is decent, behind the companionway steps underneath the cockpit. Installation of the engine and the other mechanical systems is workmanlike—good but nothing spectacular.

Under Sail

Sailing is what this boat is all about.

We sailed twice on a 35 during their first two years of production, and again last fall, in two heavy-air triangular races.

The boat is obviously quick. With a PHRF rating around 70, it is significantly faster than almost all boats its size. It is 50 seconds-per-mile faster than our own 16-year-old Carter 36 and most other IOR racers between 34 and 37 feet. In the class we raced in last fall, only a Schock 35, and a C&C 37 were comparable in speed. Like most good sailing boats, the J/35 has an "effortless" quality about its motion through the water. To us, it seems that most boats make quite a fuss as you push them up toward hull speed, especially on a beat. Often, you can "hear" how fast you're going by the amount of noise the boat makes. But a J/35 moves easily up to speed, and you have to look at the knotmeter to know whether you're moving five knots or seven.

It's a well-balanced boat, with excellent feel (if you have a tiller model) on all points of sail.

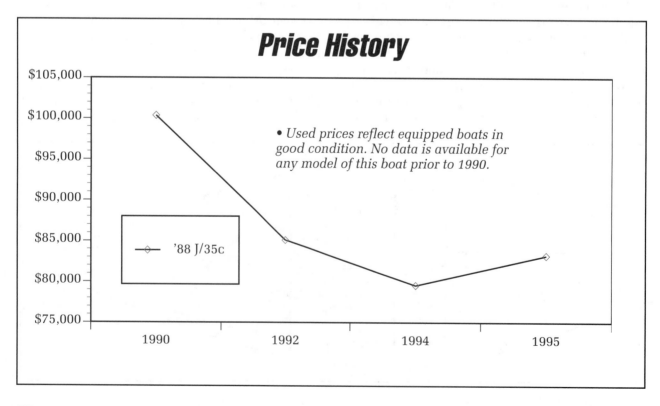

Price History

- Used prices reflect equipped boats in good condition. No data is available for any model of this boat prior to 1990.

'88 J/35c

The boat can be wet working to weather in waves, especially given the lack of cockpit coamings, but otherwise it has few faults in sailing. Unlike many high-performance boats, it's also quite forgiving, so an inexperienced helmsman and crew can achieve good speed and at least finish a race or a passage ahead of other boats, even if losing on handicap.

Conclusions

The J/35 is a pricey boat. A new basic boat will run over $100,000 ready to race, and if you add premium electronics and get into the high-tech sail game, you can up the ante considerably.

However, unlike most boats these days, the J/35 will likely hold its value quite well. The boat will continue to appeal to the die-hard racer and thus maintain its value better than most other boats.

It is obviously not a boat for everybody. If you're looking for a weekend cottage or a floating condominium, go elsewhere. But if you are in the group of sailors who want a boat between 30 and 40 feet, whose time afloat is spent more than 50 percent in racing, you might want to consider the J/35. And if we were rolling in dough, we'd have to have one to park out in front of our condo, just for the fun of sailing it.

For the used boat shopper, the main consideration after price will be the quality of equipment, especially sails. Unlike some boats, it is quite probable that a J/35 has been raced, and usually raced hard, so in many instances a total refit of the basic boat may be in order.

Given that the latest models have several advantages—an ABS certificate and a 10-year anti-blister warranty—most used boat shoppers will probably want to also go the extra distance to get a new boat.

We like the J/35.

It gets down to basics—if sailing is what sailing is all about, you won't find a much better boat anywhere. • **PS**

Bristol 35.5C

Ted Hood knows all there is to know about centerboard cruisers; he applied it well to this boat.

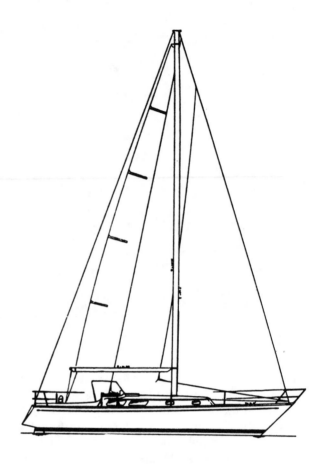

Around Bristol, Rhode Island—made famous by Nathanael G. Herreshoff—they tell this story: In the beginning, Bristol Yachts made rather ordinary boats. Along the way to success, Bristol's boss, Clint Pearson, collected some of the most skilled workmen in the business. Somewhere in the 1970s, in order to support about 130 craftsmen, Bristol upgraded sharply and took aim at the big boat, high buck market. It made good sense.

And that's when the centerboard sloop called the Bristol 35.5C was born. She debuted in 1977 and disappeared with the rest of the line a few years ago.

The inestimable Ted Hood designed her. He probably knows more than anyone alive about centerboard cruising boats. He's done a lot of them.

"This one just turned out great," he said. "She's about as small as you can get and still have really big boat appearance and performance. The interior just worked out very well." Hood owned one himself.

"She goes right along, doesn't she?" he said.

The Bristol 35.5C, which also came in a full-keel version (without the "C"), is an extraordinarily orthodox boat. There simply are no extremes in design, construction or performance, unless it is in her ability to flaunt her stern downwind and burn a lot of boats when beating in light to moderate air.

She's what is called medium displacement. Look at her dimensions. Nothing jumps out, except perhaps for slightly less beam than is seen in 35-footers of that era and certainly far less than is seen in more recent designs.

The Interior

Despite the 10' 10" beam, the interior reflects Ted Hood's attention to comfortable detail. There simply are no tight spots, no clumsy corners and no head or hip knockers.

Specifications

LOA	35' 6"
LWL	27' 6"
Beam	10' 10"
Draft	3' 9"/9'6" (board up/down)
Displacement	15,000 lbs.
Ballast	7,000 lbs.
Sail area	589 sq. ft.

You can walk into the head, turn around and even take a shower standing erect, if you're no more than 6' 2" in height.

The forward berths are more than adequate. Especially comfortable for one (but tight for two) are the pull-out extension berths in the main cabin. The big quarter berth is for that nose tackle in your racing crew. Luckily, only a few boats were built with pilot berths, because not having them means that the storage space is that much greater. With pilot berths, the boat theoretically sleeps no less than nine, but you'd feel like a 49er on a crowded clipper ship headed for the California Gold Rush.

The galley is a joy, with more counter space than many larger boats. Unobstructed, durable flat surfaces are always at a premium when preparing meals

Owners' Comments

"Three Bermuda races, three prizes, once second overall. Good sea boat. Broke a centerboard after four years while racing upwind in very heavy going. Builder has treated me well. I'd choose the same type of boat if I were starting over again."
—1978 model in Westwood, MA

"Could use more interior lights in better places. Next to impossible to change oil filter without major spillage into bilge. She's fast and rugged."
—1982 model in Shelton, CT

"Only good V-berth I've ever seen. Completely satisfied, except that you can't even see much less get to shaft stuffing box. Engine access worries me, too."
—1980 model in Norfolk, VA

"Good looking, fast and interior is very livable."
—1979 model in McAllen, TX

"Everywhere you can put a foot is solid as a rock. Passing sailors comment on her good looks."
—1981 model in Long Island City, NY

or washing dishes. The truly huge ice chest obviously has superior insulation. Even with the engine running the ice lasts well.

The spacious cabin interior is enhanced by a well-engineered fold-down table, which, unlike many, can be rigged in five seconds.

If one were to be picky, the lack of a wet locker aft in a boat of this size might be noted.

Engine access is, at best, mediocre. It's in a narrow compartment, with access in the front only by removing some drawers and the heavy step panel and on the port side through a panel in the quarterberth.

All joinery, laminates and solid wood, reflect the individual skills of Bristol's work force. The main and forward cabins are wood-sheathed. The sole is teak with a handsome ash inlay, all hand-layed, screwed, glued and bunged.

Many Bristol 35.5s were customized to some degree. Interior wood, for instance, could be mahogany, cherry or teak, with the latter two carrying a considerable premium. Double sinks in the galley were another fairly expensive option.

However, most equipment is standard. Bristol used topflight components, like Racor filters, Brunzeel bulkheads, Nicro vents, Schaefer hardware, Almag 35 ports, Bomar hatches, Edson steering and Lewmar winches.

The boat's deck is a first-rate work platform and, for comfort, the cockpit is the equal of any 35-footer. However, because the seats run the full length of the cockpit, one must climb up and over to reach the steering station behind the big wheel. It's annoying. You can't even slide aft.

Construction

The Bristol 35.5s are solid fiberglass. The hull is built in halves and joined down the middle, which makes possible Bristol's fine hull-to-deck joint. The hull is flanged inward and the deck is bolted on top of the flange with a teak toerail also through-bolted. It makes for both a watertight joint and a very rigid structural beam at the rail.

Centerboards frequently are a source of major headaches. However, the Bristol 35.5C's board, which does not protrude into the cabin sole, must be well designed and executed.

The board is controlled by a low-geared horizontal winch on the coachroof. A stainless steel wire runs forward to a stainless vertical pipe at the corner of the chart table, down and across to the centerline under the floorboards. It makes three turns. The cable is entirely enclosed. If it were to cause trouble, it would be difficult to fix. However, only two of the *Practical Sailor* readers who own Bristol 35.5Cs report problems. Only a few boats were built before Bristol made modifications to the centerboard.

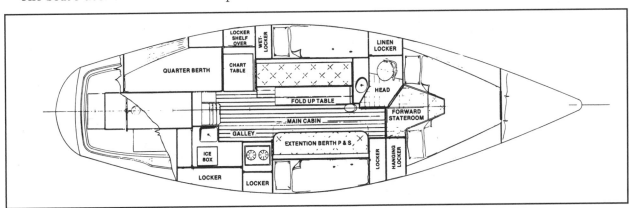

Sailing Characteristics

Make no mistake: The Bristol 35.5C is tender, as are most centerboarders. In return you get a very lively boat that is quick in any air, like many more modern fin keelers except that with her moderate keel and centerboard, the Bristol 35.5 doesn't require slavish attention to the helm.

The centerboard version has an IOR rating of 25.38, which means she should move out on a C & C 35, an Olson 38, a Hughes 38, a Pearson 35, a Tartan 37, a Morgan 38 and a J/34. That's pretty good company for a design of this vintage.

The IMS numbers show the centerboard version to be faster than the keel version. The heavier centerboarder (with 500 pounds more ballast) gives the keel model 6.8 seconds a mile in light air and 9 seconds a mile in 20 knots.

Despite being a centerboarder, the Bristol 35.5C, because of her ballast, has a very respectable calculated static stability of 115°.

The boat's phenomenal light-air performance is delineated in the Performance Package supplied by the United States Yacht Racing Union. In a true wind of 6 knots, close-hauled (44.5 degrees), the Bristol 35.5C, with a 120% jib, should do 3.9 knots. The velocity made good will be 2.8 knots. She'd be heeled only 5°. Beam reaching in the same conditions, the boat should do 5.4 knots.

In 20 knots true, the boat would do 6.1 knots, but would be heeling 31°. Broad reaching in 20 knots, she'd turn up slightly more than eight knots.

We've spent many happy hours sailing out of Newport, Rhode Island, aboard a 35.5C owned by Dwight Webb, who never has been known to overuse the engine. He's a sailorman. Beautifully maintained (with all exterior teak varnished) and with excellent sails, including Hood furling on the headstay and a Doyle Stackpack on the main, Webb's boat always moves well in any air.

In the past, Webb has owned quite a few boats: a Meridian, Triton, Morgan 30, Pearson 33, Pearson 35, Bristol 39, C & C 33, Sea Sprite 34, C & C 34 and a C & C 38.

He's passed on 10 years with the Bristol 35.5C, which he deems simply, "Best boat I've ever owned."

Conclusion

If a Bristol 35.5C takes your fancy, try for one with either a Westerbeke diesel or the equally satisfactory three-cylinder, 24-hp diesel made for a time by Universal. Avoid the Yanmar 2QM 20H, a two-cylinder diesel that struggles unsuccessfully to get up to hull speed.

Beware of a 1978 model without the modified centerboard.

Also, don't pay extra for a boat with a half dozen headsails. The Bristol 35.5C achieves her polar diagram optimums with a single 120% or 130% jib, which ideally will be on furling gear. Jibs bigger than that simply overpower the boat.

You'll pay heavily for a newer one, and because so few were built, the older used ones also are somewhat dear. 1981 is about where the ideal prices seem to occur. Those built later than 1981 seem to carry premium prices. **• PS**

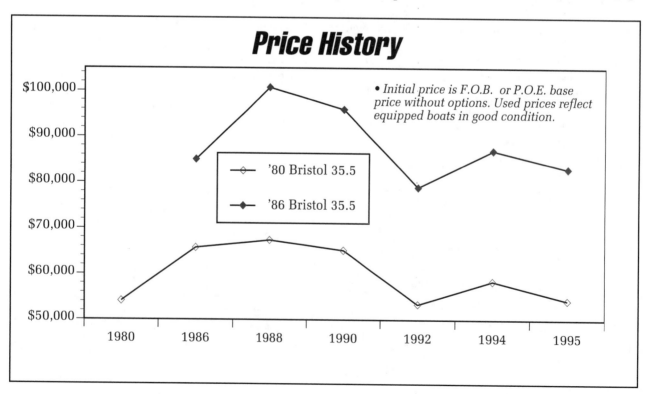

Price History

• Initial price is F.O.B. or P.O.E. base price without options. Used prices reflect equipped boats in good condition.

— ○ — '80 Bristol 35.5
— ◆ — '86 Bristol 35.5

Hans Christian 34/36

In many ways this blue-water cruiser represents the best and worst of Taiwan boatbuilding—heavy but maintenance-intensive construction.

The story of the Hans Christian 34 and 36, and their successors, is a microcosm of the history of the Taiwan/U.S. boatbuilding industry. That is to say, a mixture of good designs, fine hand craftsmanship, knockoff gear, occasional shoddy finish and detail work, double-dealing and broken promises. Sometimes out of the mix comes a well-built, good-sailing blue water cruiser like the Hans Christian 34.

The Designer(s) and Builder(s)

Hans Christian Yachts got its start 24 years ago when a former Long Beach, California high school teacher named John Edwards approached naval architect Robert Perry about a plan to build quality yachts economically on the island of Taiwan. It wasn't an original thought; the Formosa Boat Building Co. in Taipei and Cheoy Lee in Hong Kong had been at it since the 1950s. Edwards and Perry had collaborated on an earlier Taiwan-built boat, the CT 54. For Edwards, Perry came up with plans for the hull, keel and rig for what would become the HC 34.

Before the first 34 was built, Perry says he was informed that Hans Christian had "blown up" his design to a 36-footer but that, no, he wouldn't be getting any royalties. Thus ended, for a time, Perry's role with the design, although the company continued to credit (or exploit) his name in connection with the 36.

Under Edwards' Taiwan arrangement, he "owned" the designs and
controlled the distributorship. An outfit called

Specifications, 34/36

LOA	33' 11"/35' 7"
LWL	29' 0"/30'6
Beam	10' 11"/11' 4"
Draft	5' 6"/5' 11"
Displacement	18,300/22,000 lbs.
Ballast	7,000/NA lbs.
Sail area	676/711 sq. ft.

Union oversaw construction, and the yard basically owned the tooling. House designer for subsequent designs such as the 33 and the 41, was listed as Harwood S. Ives of Cruising Design in Winterport, Maine (Perry says he's tried unsuccessfully to track down "Woody" Ives, has found no one who knows him and tends to doubt his existence. Hans Christian's new president, Jerry Finefrock, who took over this year, says he understands that Ives is English, but that he hasn't been able to locate him either.)

Finefrock, a lawyer who concedes his knowledge of the firm's earlier history is somewhat incomplete, says that through some sort of "Chinese chicanery" someone took the HC 36 molds and began building the Union 36. He said a lawsuit, filed by Edwards after Union lightened the scantlings and reverted to

High bulwarks add to the height of the perceived freeboard and may be a factor in this boat's tendency to "sail" at anchor. on the other hand, they provide tremendous security while working on deck.

the Hans Christian name, ended the chicanery. Perry, who meanwhile had retaliated by designing the Tayana 37, disagrees with that version. He suspects that Edwards somehow alienated the yard, which owned the molds, much as he had with the earlier project, the CT 54.

Later, the Union people asked Perry to lend his name to the 36 in return for royalties. He agreed to a compromise in which the yard could claim the boat was "based on a hull by Bob Perry," which was true to the extent it was a knockoff of his 34. When the company continued to claim it as his design, he disassociated himself and the royalties stopped.

In the middle of all this, a Union employee asked Perry at a meeting in Taipei to redesign the 36's keel, paid for the job with a personal check, then took the design and began building his own boat at the Mao Ta yard. The 36, ultimately more successful than the 34 in sales, popped up as the Mariner Polaris 36 and

EO 36. None did as well as the Tayana 37, however, of which 570 eventually were made.

Hans Christian went on to create a number of successful models ("John Edwards has a good eye for a boat," Perry concedes), eventually parting ways with the Hansa yard, which had taken on the line land presumably dropping "German-built" from its advertising claims, claims that made a lot of people believe the boats were built in a little Bavarian village high in the Taiwan Alps). The boats then were built at several other Taiwan yards before relocating, in 1989, to Thailand. Edwards then faded from the scene ("He's out of the business," Finefrock said) and the new ownership took over early in 1993 from Edwards' former partner, Geoffrey White. Hans Christian now consists of two distributorships, one headed by Finefrock in Annapolis, another in Europe, and a new plant in Bangsaray, Thailand. Finefrock said the factory has air-conditioned lay-up facilities, a new quality control program directed by Michael Kaufman of Annapolis, and is certified to build to ABS standards.

Gone from production, the president said, are the 33 and 38; the 33T (traditional) is suspended, the 38T has been idle since 1990, and the 38 MK II is dead and buried. The 43T, out of production since 1989, will be reactivated, while the 43 Christina, part of Hans Christian's updated Euro line, will continue. The 40 Christina is gone, but a new version of the 48T will be made. Plans are in the works for a 60-footer. In all, there are some 1,100 Hans Christians sailing the oceans of the world, including the 34 and 36.

Don't ask Hans Christian for the plans or any data, however; all was lost when the company relocated from California to Annapolis.

You can, however, call Perry (Robert Perry Yacht Designers, 6400 Seaview Ave. N.W., Seattle, WA 98107; 206/789-7212), who feels "a connection" to Hans Christian owners, even if he didn't design all their boats. His consultation fee of $250 entitles persons to "ongoing access and consultation, drawings and any technical backup you need."

The Boat

As designed by Perry, with a little help from Edwards/Ives, the Hans Christian 34/36 is a heavy, double-ended, cutter-rigged cruising yacht designed specifically for ocean sailing. Like others of its kind, it's often described as a traditional North Sea double-ender, although the tradition exists mostly in the imaginations of builders and owners rather than with any vessels that actually existed. "They are exaggerated caricatures of old boats," says Perry. Nevertheless. the 34/36 has pleasing lines that draw admiring glances. And it was boats like this that helped Taiwan expand its boatbuilding industry during the 1960s and 70s.

The boat is typical Taiwan in other ways—solid construction (it displaces 18,300 pounds), its real teak decks and all-wood interior. The craftsmanship is excellent and affordable only because native carpenters were paid a tenth of what their U.S. counterparts earned. All this weight, of course, tends to make it a poor light-air sailer.

The 34/36 has a low chin bow, a short canoe stern, a long flat run aft and a fairly straight deadrise in the mid-section over a V-bottom, similar to Perry's U.S.-built Valiant 40. Perry said he began rounding his hulls for boats like the Tayana 37 and FD 35 before realizing he'd gotten it right the first time. "That's a hull shape I went back to as time went on."

The hull is solid (and thick) hand-laid fiberglass. The deck is 5/8" teak planks over a sandwich of 3/8" glass, 3/4" plywood, and another 3/8" glass layer. The cabin top is cored with 1/2" plywood. Although the deck bungs are bound to loosen with time (this is a boat that requires lots of maintenance) we saw no evidence of deck delamination in the 1978 model we inspected. The hull-deck joint is glassed over on the inside and appears to be through-bolted as well. Solid bulwarks allow the lifeline stanchions to be mounted vertically for better strength than those through-bolted to the deck. Interestingly, the nuts are embedded in the glass, a practice used elsewhere on the boat. (Hans Christian, incidentally, in the future will drop the thick glass and wood-cored hulls in favor of lighter Divinycell foam-cored hulls.)

The solid bronze traveler is definitely heavy-duty, although its position well forward on the boom makes sheeting difficult (photos of other 34s show boom-end sheeting). The bronze, like the wooden blocks, is part of the traditional aesthetic. Despite the overbuilt nature of the boat, little flaws here and there can create problems. On the 34 we sailed out of

Newport in the summer of 1993, the *Rosalie,*, a worker had failed to drill a weep hole in the port stanchion of the boom gallows. The result was a persistent leak over the galley that took the owner many hours to track down and remedy. And there's occasional mismatching of metals-in one case we saw stainless steel screws inserted into a bronze fitting.

Another complaint was a squared-off leading edge on the 7,000-pound full keel, described by the owner as looking like a cheese wedge. Perry says that probably was his fault as a relative newcomer, who neglected to give precise enough instruction to the yard that built the keel. The best solution, he said, is to reshape the leading edge with foam and fiberglass.

Accommodations

This is a good-sized boat with commodious, if less than perfect, storage and space below. The galley, to port at the foot of the companionway stairs, is small, with a two-burner stove, ice chest for cold storage and limited counter space.

Rosalie's owner, Frank Girardi, cut a door into the compartment under the sink to convert otherwise dead space to storage. To starboard aft is a quarter berth that the owner says is his favorite sleeping berth. There's also a generous chart table, positioned and sized for the dedicated navigator.

In the saloon is a settee berth to starboard and to port a U-shaped dinette; there's plenty of stowage behind and under seats. Six opening bronze ports, oval in size, and a large rod-reinforced skylight

The interior of the HC 34 is straightforward, with plenty of headroom and ventilation. The all-wood construction makes it warm and comfortable, though you might want to reupholster the original Naugahyde cushion covers, which tend to get sticky in humid weather.

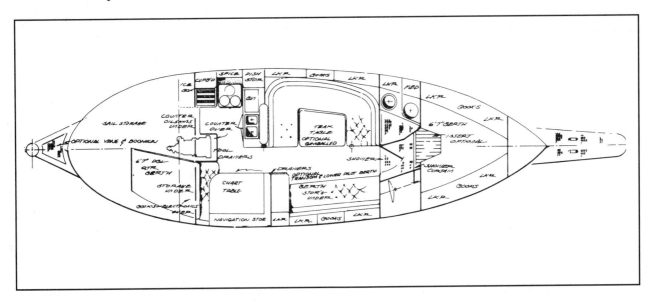

introduce lots of light to the main living area. A second, smaller hatch and several more ports forward provide natural light for the head, and the V-berths.

This is a deep boat with a big bilge, good access to the systems including the engine, and lots of tankage; the original boat came with two stainless steel water tanks under the main salon and a smaller one forward. A previous owner removed the saloon tanks and replaced them with a single fiberglass unit that holds 150 gallons—sufficient for almost any trip. Girardi installed filters between tank and head and galley for better-tasting water.

Other alterations made (and worth checking on any boat) included replacing an (illegal) T-joint in a propane line behind the dinette, leading to a LPG water heater, and replacing a gate valve in the head with a Wilcox-Crittenden seacock. The owner also cut another door under the head sink for better access to seacocks. A check of all the seacocks, which may or may not be cheap knockoffs, is a good idea.

Performance

At 18,000-plus pounds and with a 5' 6" full keel (with cheese wedge up front), this is not your ideal light-air cruiser, despite its three sails (main, Yankee and staysail) and total sail area of 676 square feet. In fact, it requires a good 15 knots to get up and go at anywhere near its hull speed. We were doing 5.6 knots close-hauled, relatively-speaking, in 13-15 knots and small Narragansett Bay waves. The owner

has reached a top speed of 11 knots (while surfing in a following sea) and recorded a high of 9 knots on the return of this year's Bermuda One-Two race. For the record, the only PHRF data for the 34 and 36 we could find, one boat each, was 204 and 186 respectively.

Despite Hans Christian's one-time claim that the 34/36 "has a genuine appetite to go to weather in a drifter or a blow." this boat is best on a reach. The highest you're likely to get to point is 45 degrees; we tacked through an even 90 degrees on our outing. A bigger jib should help the boat's overall performance, according to comments *Practical Sailor* has received. In fact, Perry recommends sailing with a genoa and without the staysail to maximize light-air performance. Sailed as a sloop, he says the 34's performance compares favorably to other boars of this genre.

While hardly the boat for a drifter, it's definitely a good boat to be on during a blow. Owners report that it rises exceptionally well to the steepest of waves. High-sided with big bulwarks, it may not be the aerodynamic ideal, but it is dry and safe. The cockpit, surrounded by teak staving, is comfortable in size and configuration, but small enough to be safe at sea and with adequate drainage. The bulwarks make going forward feel quite safe.

Although OSTAR and BOC veteran Francis Stokes calls a cutter sail plan the best for ocean sailing, it can be difficult to learn to trim. Perry agrees that the "clutter rig" is the most difficult for the beginner to master, noting that an over-trimmed staysail acts like

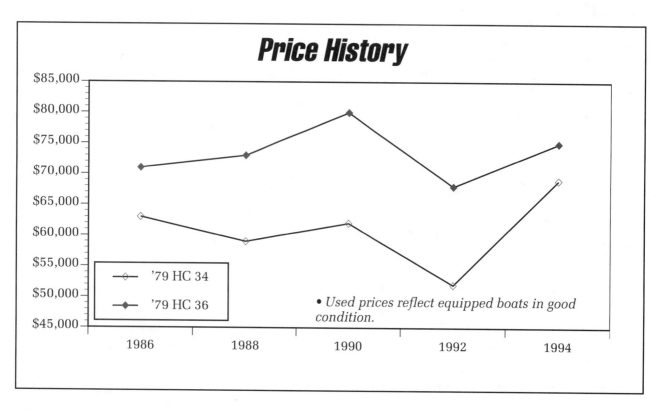

Price History

Legend:
- —◇— '79 HC 34
- —◆— '79 HC 36

• *Used prices reflect equipped boats in good condition.*

a "parking brake." We experienced some backwinding of the mainsail by the staysail tin part because its foot was too long for the club and had quite a hook in it) and felt occasional weather helm. Part of the problem may have been the extreme forward location of the mainsheet traveler, which made trimming difficult; a dodger also interfered with cranking the winch a full turn.

The boat itself balances well; the owner reports that his Monitor wind vane works well in most conditions. On the wind, he was able to simply lock the wheel and sit back and relax while the boat held its course.

Heeling was not excessive at 15-17 degrees in 15-knot winds. Reefing should not be necessary until well into 20 knots of wind; easing the mainsheet will buy some extra time without suffering undue consequences.

Hans Christians came powered with a variety of engines. Two 34s we know of, one with an Isuzu 40, the other with a 3-cylinder, 35-hp. Volvo, got about the same results in speed—about 6 or so knots at 1,800 rpm. *Rosalie's* performance under power improved (for a time) to about 8 knots with a three-bladed propeller, but fell off during the season, possibly because of bottom fouling. The owner had switched from his two-blade because it "thumped" when passing behind the deadwood; fairing the aperture would help this condition.

Conclusion

While not a good boat for the weekend coastal cruiser, or for anyone who does much sailing in light-to-moderate air, this is an excellent choice for the serious blue-water sailor. This is a boat that will take you offshore to Bermuda or just about anywhere and will stand up to a gale. The 34/36 won't get you there fast, but it will get you there safely.

The teak decks and wood interior are attractive, but carry with them the burden of constant upkeep. This is a good-looking boat, particularly to those who like the "traditional" canoe stern and all the trimmings. And you can probably pick one up in the $50,000-$55,000 range.

• **PS**

Columbia 36

A bargain-basement racer/ cruiser from a grand-daddy of American production boatbuilders.

It's hard to believe, especially for those of us who learned to sail in the 1960s, that fiberglass sail boats built back then are now a part of history. The "fiberglass revolution" that seems like just yesterday, is now 30 years in the past. A lot has happened in the world of boatbuilding since then, but many of those old boats are still sailing.

The Design

The Columbia 36 was in production between 1967 and 1972. One reader estimates that more than 600 were built, making it a very successful model.

The boat was designed by William Crealock, the California naval architect who today is more readily associated with the Pacific Seacraft line of bluewater cruisers bearing his name. The Columbia 36, with its transom stern, aluminum frame windows, and step-down cabin, bears little resemblance to the Crealock 34 and 37, whose canoe sterns and bronze portlights give it a tough, traditional, go-anywhere look.

The Columbia 36 was a pretty slick looking boat in its day, and though its lines have worn reasonably well with time, we're reluctant to call it a "classic." The sheer is essentially flat, with modest spring, the sidedecks wide and the cabin nicely proportioned. The rig is on the small side for this size boat.

Underwater, the divided underbody shows a swept-back fin keel that looks like an inverted shark's dorsal fin, and a skeg leading to the spade rudder. Interestingly, the propeller shaft (not shown in the drawings) is situated at the aft end of this skeg, which places it above and aft of the rudder and nearer the surface than one might expect.

The long cockpit rates highly with owners. One reader said it doesn't feel crowded even with a crew of eight.

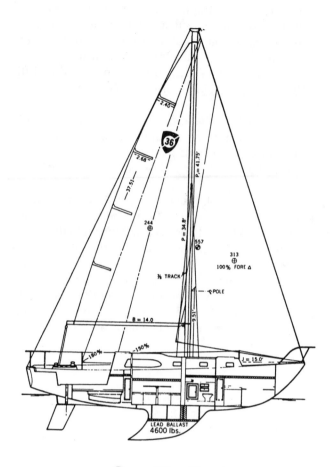

Specifications

LOA	35' 9"
LWL	28' 3"
Beam	10' 6"
Draft	5' 5"
Displacement	12,000 lbs.
Ballast	5,000 lbs.
Sail area	557 sq. ft.

The displacement/length ratio is 261, which is a nice number for good all around performance—too high for a hot rod, but just right for comfortable family sailing.

A subtle point about Columbias is the tooling. A wooden boatbuilder in Maine once told us that one of his objections to fiberglass boats was the absence of crisp, sharp lines and edges. Study a glass boat, especially an old one like the Columbia 36, and you'll see what he means. Every edge is generously radiused. Of course, some of this is necessary to pull a form from the mold, but not to the extent that Columbia rounded everything. In our opinion, many of the old Columbia's lose a few points in looks for this reason. An exception would be the Columbia 50, where wooden toerails (instead of the usual rounded, molded fiberglass toerails) go a long way toward alleviating the impression of an amorphous, egg-shaped structure.

Construction

Like nearly all production builders in the 1960s, Columbia used standard hull laminates of polyester gelcoat, chopped strand mat and 24-ounce woven roving. Columbia was a pioneer in developing what it called the "unitized interior," or fiberglass pan, in which the engine beds, stringers and furniture foundations are all molded. This pan is then "tabbed" to the hull with wet fiberglass and is presumed to provide the necessary stiffening.

Finish work goes quickly after such a pan is in place. Teak trim, cut and milled in the woodshop, is simply screwed into place. The cabinet doors, juxtaposed against the gleaming white pan, and ubiquitous pinrails are as telltale of the late 60s and early 70s as shag carpeting.

The hull-to-deck joint is unusual in that it incorporates a double-channel length of aluminum into which the hull and deck flanges are fitted top and bottom. It probably made good engineering sense, but given the complaints about leaking, and the fact that this method, to our knowledge, has not been used by other builders, suggest it had its problems. Because aluminum has little or no springback, we imagine that bumping a piling could permanently "dent" this channel, causing leaks that would be very difficult to repair properly.

The deck was cored, and to finish the interior a molded headliner was glassed in. The old Columbia brochures are rather funny to read, showing as they do plant workers dressed in lab coats, installing winches, cleats and windows as if building a boat was no more difficult than assembling pieces from a kit. In fact, Columbia fomented this idea, marketing its boats in kit form and calling them Sailcrafter Kits.

The basic structure of the early Columbias was reasonably sound, and sold with a two-year warranty. That many of those boats are still around says something positive about general construction quality.

On the other hand, the boats were pretty much bare bones. No frills. But then, they were more affordable than a comparable boat today. We don't mind the opportunity to do our own customizing, but the interior pan limits what you can do.

Most readers responding to our Owner's Questionnaire rate the construction quality of the Columbia 36 as above average. No major problems were reported, though we do have some complaints of deck delamination. In all fairness, separation of the fiberglass skins from the coring is common in many older boats and should not be judged as a weakness peculiar to Columbia. But you should have your surveyor check the deck for soundness before buying.

Miscellaneous complaints include inadequate ventilation, need for a sea hood ("The companionway hatch is a joke"); various leaks at windows and hull-deck joint; and mainsheet and wheel poorly located. The brochure says the keels are lead, but at least one reader said his was iron.

Performance

The Columbia 36 was intended to be something of a hot boat when it was introduced. In fact, it was offered with a trim tab on the trailing edge of the keel for better control off the wind. A brochure credits the inspiration to the Twelve-Meter *Intrepid*'s "lopsided defense of the America's Cup."

We don't know how successfully the boat was raced, but do know that its PHRF rating is about 162, making it just a hair faster than a Catalina 30 (168) and a Cal 34 (168). None of our readers indicate that they race. One said, "Built for comfort, not speed." Typical reader ratings for speed are "average" upwind and "above average" off the wind. Several note the importance of sail trim (true of any boat!); annoying weather helm (excessive weather helm is unforgivable, but we suspect there's always a few whiners in this department who must not understand that a boat without any weather helm is a bear to steer); and one reader noted that the spar doesn't bend much to optimize sail shape (bendy rigs weren't in vogue at that time).

The standard sloop rig doesn't carry a lot of sail. One reader said he had a "tall boy" mast, which presumably was available as an option, as was—surprisingly—a yawl rig.

Overall, readers have positive remarks about seaworthiness, stability and balance. "The boat is a very good sailer," wrote one reader, adding that his boat "...has taken all Lake Michigan has to offer and never broken."

Most Columbia 36s were equipped with Atomic 4 gasoline engines. Several readers complain that the 30-hp. doesn't move the boat fast enough—about five knots. One reader had an Albin 20-hp. diesel. Another said engine access was very poor: "No room even to check oil."

Fuel tankage is 29 gallons; water is 44 gallons.

Interior

The layout of the Columbia 36 is standard, with a V-berth forward, U-shaped dinette amidships, and quarter berths aft. The sideboard galley puts the cook in the way of traffic, and the sink may have difficulty draining on port tack.

The most unusual feature of the plan is placement of the chart table opposite the head. This certainly isn't convenient to the cockpit for navigator-helmsman communications, but it does allow two quarter berths instead of just one. Readers note that the boat sleeps an honest six people, and tall ones at that. Headroom is listed at 6' 3".

Fiberglass interior pans tend to make for a rather sterilized appearance—the proverbial inside look of a refrigerator or Clorox bottle. We're not fond of them for several reasons: Pans restrict access to parts of the hull, tend to make the interior noisier and damper, and make it difficult to customize. But, that's the way it is with most production boats.

Conclusion

The Columiba 36 was a popular boat in the late 60s and early 70s, and still has its fans today. The basic structure is good. The interior is plain. We suspect that prospective buyers will find a wide range of customizing by previous owners. The quality of this workmanship will have a lot to do with your decision to buy or look elsewhere.

The *BUC Used Boat Guide* lists average prices for Columbia 36s ranging from about $25,000 to $33,000, depending on year and condition. Our original research showed those prices to be reasonably accurate. In today's market, you should be able to pick up a Columbia 36 in decent shape at a great price. One reader wrote, "The boat can be bought at bargain rates as it is the most underrated boat on the market."

Prices for all boats tend to be higher on the West Coast than the East Coast. Freshwater boats from Canada and the Great Lakes are most expensive (BUC Research says 25-30 percent more), and those in Florida and nearby states are the least expensive (about 10 percent less).

We think the boat represents an outstanding value for the person who wants the most boat for the least money. On the other hand, it suffers from the usual economies and slap-together techniques of large production builders. And the design is beginning to look a bit dated. We doubt that you'll make any money on the boat. **• PS**

The only unusual element of the Columbia 36's interior layout is the placement of the chart table forward, opposite the head, rather than in its more common location near the companionway. Since radios and instruments are usually mounted near the nav station, we prefer it aft.

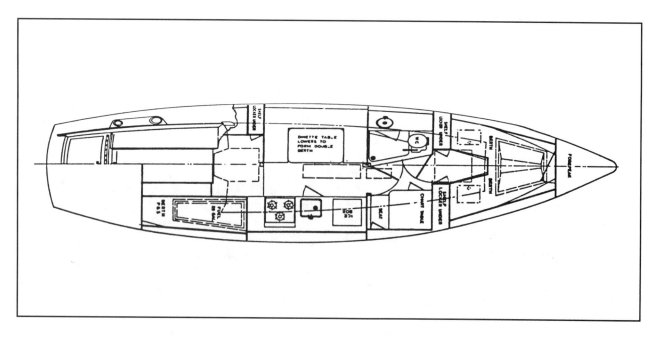

Allied Princess 36

An able cruiser with a springy sheer that, despite some shortcomings, can take you (almost) anywhere.

The Allied Boat Company built its first boat about 1962. It was the Seawind ketch, de–signed by Thomas Gillmer, a professor of naval architecture at the United States Naval Academy.

Later the Seawind would become the first fiberglass boat to circumnavigate the globe; she was Apogee, sailed by Alan Eddy of Boston.

As the Catskill, New York company grew, the 30' 6" Seawind was replaced by the 31' 7" Seawind II, And the product line was expanded to include the Greenwich 24. Luders 33, Seabreeze 35 sloop/yawl, Allied 39 and XL2, among others. The Princess 36 was introduced in 1972 along with the center-cockpit Mistress 39, both designed by Arthur Edmunds. Production ceased in 1982. We don't know how many were built, but see quite a few in the listings of Soundings. Also, many small changes were made during the course of production, and we won't attempt to report all of those that we know.

Allied was plagued with financial difficulties throughout much of its life, changing ownership several times, and finally succumbing in 1982. With the exception of one Britton Chance racer, all of Allied's boats were cruisers that, according to our 1982 review of the Seawind II, suffered from "bland expanses of fiberglass, and mediocre woodwork." On the plus side, they were solidly built.

Like its big sister, the Princess has a shoal draft, full keel, drawing just 4' 6". Clearly, this boat is not going to point as high as a good fin keel design, but for cruising, especially in the shallow waters of the Chesapeake, Florida and the Bahamas, it'll be ideal. Plus, with the rudder hung off the trailing edge of the keel, the boat shouldn't suffer too much damage in

Specifications

LOA	36' 0"
LWL	27' 6"
Beam	11' 0"
Draft	4' 6"
Displacement	14,400 lbs.
Ballast	5,000 lbs.
Sail area (sloop/kth)	595/604 sq. ft.

the event of a grounding.

Compared to some more contemporary designs of similar size and intent, the Princess has a middle-of-the-road beam of 11' 0". The Pearson 365, for instance, measures 11' 5-1/2".

The waterline is close to the 28-foot minimum that author and circumnavigator George Day considers desirable for passagemaking; heeled, it should lengthen nicely as the ends submerse.

When you first see this boat, either in the water or on paper, the two things that immediately strike you are the sheer and bow. Edmunds put the low point of the sheer at the right place, about two-thirds of the distance aft from the bow. But the bow seems awfully high. In fact, when you walk forward along the sidedecks, you have the definite sensation of walk-

Owners' Comments

"This is a very seaworthy vessel that is easily single-handed. It is not a fast boat. I would be happier with a cutter for many reasons other than sailing ability. Have made a total of four round trips to Bermuda, one to Antigua. Cockpit is very large: not too good for offshore."

1973 model in North Kingstown, Rhode island

"Not so good in light air. But in 10-15 knots, with 150-percent genoa, it moves well. Well-designed for heavy weather. Originally a little tender. Ballast added. Full-keel design (which has certain advantages) completely spoils maneuverability and reverse directional control [under power]. It is very rugged."

1978 model in Old Saybrook, Connecticut

"Moderately heavy displacement with very little teak (thank God) above of below. Never had to use the dodger in fair weather underway (includes ocean sailing up to 35 knots)."

1976 model in Short Hills, New Jersey

"Out-sailed a CSY 37 and Irwin 37, but can't keep up with a Pearson 35, Luders 36, Cape Dory 30 or 33. Can be balanced under a variety of sail combinations and tracks beautifully. In severe conditions—short, steep seas—hobbyhorses and Westerbeke 4-91 can't push it very well."

1973 model in Wilmington, Delaware

"Allied never did have good cabinetry or joinery work inside. Formica looks cheap."

1978 model in Fort Myers, Florida

---

ing uphill. Too much, we think, though the look certainly sets the Princess apart from boats with flatter sheers (again, the Pearson 365 comes to mind). Perhaps because of the high bow, Edmunds drew a sort of mini-clipper curve that in the drawing can be seen as an almost S-shape. We like clipper bows on wooden boats, but seldom on fiberglass boats, especially without trailboards, the absence of which makes the boat look like a skinhead without even a ring in its nose to add interest. The high freeboard forward doesn't help windward sailing ability, and may increase the tendency to sail at anchor. On the plus side, the foredeck is likely to stay a bit drier in a seaway. In fact, owners report the boat is unusually dry.

The coachroof or cabin top has a good deal of camber, which also is distinctive.

The cockpit is large at 10' long and 6' wide. There is a bridge deck to minimize the size of the companionway (protected by a storm hood) and make it that much harder for water to get below. An added benefit of bridgedecks, often overlooked, is the amount of interior space opened up for the galley, electrical system, headroom en route to the quarter berths, etc.

An unusual feature of the Princess is its Edson worm gear (or chain-driven pull-pull, or rack and pinion, depending on model) steering, seldom seen on production fiberglass boats.

The forward-facing wheel takes some getting used to, but it affords three convenient seating positions, to port, starboard and aft. And it doesn't take up as much cockpit space as a pedestal steerer. There is the mizzenmast to reckon with, but it's at the forward end of the cockpit, where it makes a convenient handhold for crew coming up from below. The seats are long enough for a tall person to sleep on, an important consideration for cruising.

Though there is considerable volume to this cockpit (you don't worry about how much water one will hold until you've been pooped), the bridge deck and aft seating/steerer housing go a ways toward keeping it safe.

All this said, the Princess has an exceptionally comfortable cockpit that is easy to move about, albeit at some expense of safety.

Construction

Allied always enjoyed a reputation for building strong hulls and decks. No hull cores were employed, though balsa was used in the Princess' deck, as is customary, and to our minds preferable to plywood.

One wouldn't expect any exotic fibers in a boat built in the mid-1970s, and there aren't any in the Princess, just 24-ounce woven roving and mat, plus a final layer of cloth, all laid up by hand. Hull thickness increases at the turn of the bilge and more at the keel. The internal ballast (meaning the keel cavity is part of the hull mold) is lead, glassed over with two layers of mat and woven roving so that if the keel is punctured during grounding, no water will presumably enter the cabin.

An early brochure says voids between the lead and hull are filled, but it doesn't say with what material. (We discovered, to our chagrin, that the voids in our 1967 Pearson Vanguard were partially filled with sheets of balsa core, which absorbed water like a sponge.)

Bulkheads are bonded or tabbed to the hull, which is the proper way to build a fiberglass boat. Many boats, because of inner liners or pans, do not have the bulkheads bonded on all sides to the hull and deck. (Because of the Princess's one-piece overhead liner, we couldn't tell whether the bulkheads were tabbed to the deck.) This creates a strong basic structure, but tabbing (strips of fiberglass mat) does occasionally break away from the bulkhead due to continual working of the hull or because the builder didn't first remove the veneer from the plywood bulkhead to achieve a stronger bond. Check it. If the fiberglass tabbing is exposed, repairs to it aren't all that difficult.

The hull and deck (which includes the toe rail molding) are caulked by an unspecified "bonding" material, then through-bolted on 5" centers and glassed over. The flanges are on the outside, and so to protect them from collision with, say, pilings, the joint is covered with an aluminum extrusion.

We're not all that fond of outward-turning flanges, and protecting them is, indeed, important. We think the aluminum does a good job of that, but if it was ever damaged, replacing it could be a major problem.

The rudder stock is 1-1/2" bronze riding on a 32-lb. bronze heel casting.

One of the things we like best about the Princess is its wooden interior—no fiberglass cabin sole, bunk foundations, etc. Teak, naturally, is the wood used for the cabin sole and trim. The bulkheads are covered with a simulated wood veneer that some owners may want to paint to relieve any phobias about cave dwelling. Just remember that for paint to bond to Formica and other laminates, the surface must be well sanded; it isn't easy and the paint may still peel when nicked. It's a one-way street, because you can't strip the paint and go back to sanded laminate. Other alternatives are to use a tie-coat as a primer (our experience is that they can be difficult to apply smoothly), or to glue on a new thin veneer of real wood.

For ventilation, there are two Dorade vents and an opening hatch forward; opening portlights were optional. Retrofitting a small deck hatch over the saloon table would do a lot to improve air flow in the main cabin.

The interior of the Princess has good sea berths and galley. Variations on the head and quarter berth were made over the years.

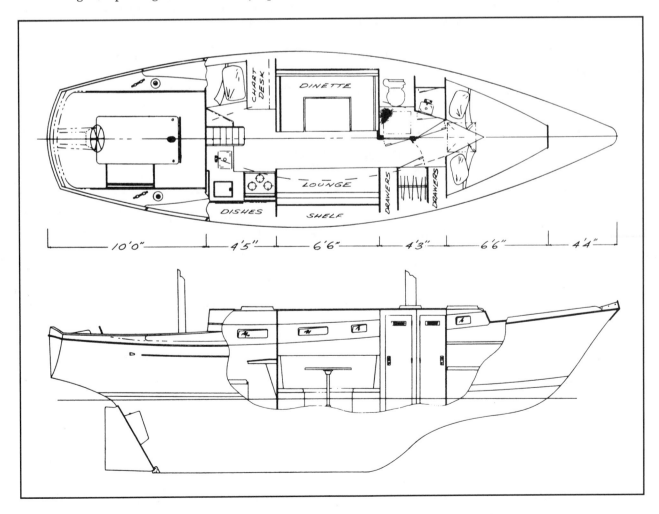

Interior Plan

The almost style-less line drawing of the interior shows a fairly standard layout, with just a few wrinkles. Each V-berth forward measures 6' 7" x 2' 8". There is a sink separated by a half-bulkhead from the toilet; a shower and sump were optional. A 1972 brochure shows the sink behind the forward door to the head, while a 1973 brochure shows it outside the head entirely. This move did add space to the forward cabin, but we wonder how the person sleeping would like it when some guest washes his hands after a nocturnal urination?

Elsewhere, there is a U-shaped dinette measuring 6' 6" x 2' 0" (later models had settees with drop-leaf table), with stowage compartments behind the backrest; hanging locker and bureau drawers; L-shaped galley; and combination port quarterberth/navigation table. Like the other berths, it is of adequate length at 6' 6". On a few boats we've seen, this area has been enclosed with bulkheads to make a very small aft quarter cabin. Fortunately, a large cutout in the forward bulkhead allows for some ventilation to this otherwise tight area.

Other details worth noting: Headroom is a generous 6' 4". Freshwater capacity is variously reported at 80 and 90 gallons in a stainless steel tank under the main cabin sole. Fuel is reported as 40 gallons, first in a black iron tank, later in one of Corten steel, which is preferable. The first boats were equipped with a single 60-amp battery, which is almost laughable today. This was quickly increased to 90 amps, but today's owner surely will want at least two series 27 105-amp batteries, much more if he has 12-volt refrigeration or an autopilot.

Performance

Owners responding to our Boat Owner's Questionnaire report that the Princess has just average to below average speed sailing upwind. This is not surprising considering its long, shallow keel and ketch rig. Off-the-wind performance is rated average.

But the seaworthiness ratings give credit to the design, coming in at above average to excellent. Says one owner, "I've owned nine boats, and this is the best of all."

In terms of stability, a number of owners say she is initially tender but settles in nicely, seldom putting the rail under. Walter Schultz, builder of Shannon sailboats, used to deliver Allieds down the Hudson River to Long Island, and says the Princess is the second most tender boat he's ever sailed (the first is the Seawind II).

The Princess tracks well, and the rig can be balanced nicely if the right combination of sails is set. Owners with steering vanes say they do a good job on this boat, no doubt due to the lateral surface area of the keel and balanced rig (remember that when sailing upwind, the mizzen may cause weather helm and so is often struck).

"Have left helm for half-hour with 20-30 knots on beam in 6-8-foot seas!" croons one owner of a 1976 model.

This is in part possible because of the worm gear

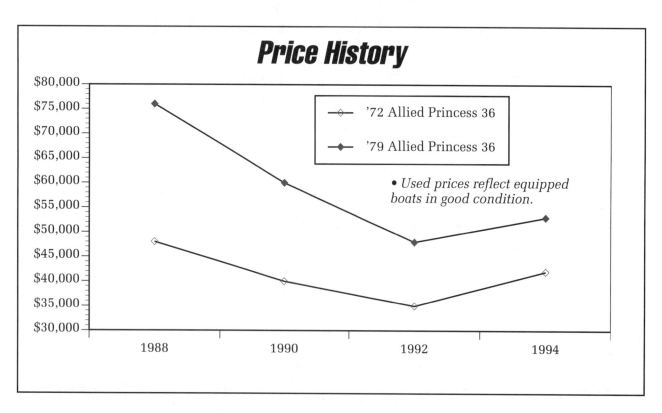

Price History

Legend:
—◇— '72 Allied Princess 36
—◆— '79 Allied Princess 36

• *Used prices reflect equipped boats in good condition.*

steering, which is non-reversing (and so gives no feedback to the helmsman). Worm gear steering is practically bomb-proof and easy to steer upwind. Off the wind, however, we have found the three turns lock to lock too many to comfortably handle quartering seas.

The Princess is powered by a 25-hp. Westerbeke 4-91 diesel with 2:1 reduction gear, a good engine but, if original, probably growing tired. It turns a 17" by 11" three-blade propeller, which gives it good thrust but lots of drag under sail. There are the usual complaints of handling in reverse.

"Terrible," says one owner, adding, as did several others, that the high bow adds to docking problems in a cross wind. A number of owners complained that the engine is too small for the boat, citing difficulties powering into head seas. If repowering, consider an engine of about 40 hp.

Despite the fact that it's slow and somewhat tender initially, we think the Princess 36 represents an outstanding value for the dreamer on a short purse string.

Conclusion

Despite a few drawbacks (unusually springy sheer, draft too shoal for a 36-footer, large cockpit, and tenderness) we like this boat, and think it is an exceptional value for the budget-minded cruiser. Though one owner said he doesn't recommend it for blue-water passagemaking ("too tender"), we have heard from others who have traveled far and wide on the Princess, including one circumnavigation.

It is not a fast boat, but comfortable, as a cruising boat should be. One would think that the diesel and big prop would give it the power to handle the head seas so often encountered in coastal cruising, but a number of owners say it doesn't (this may be partly due to the high bow and hull shape). The shallow draft, a potential liability when sailing offshore, makes it ideal for cruising the Intracoastal Waterway, the Chesapeake Bay, Florida Bay and the Bahamas.

The interior has three good sea berths, which is all you can ask for in most any boat. A strap will hold the cook securely to the galley, and the chart table, though modest, will suffice for navigation purposes. At anchor, the large V-berth with overhead hatch will be the bunk of choice due to superior ventilation.

The introductory price of the Princess was $25,995, ketch or sloop (we've never seen a sloop). Today, the BUC Research *Used Boat Price Guide* reports that 1972 model as being worth between $37,600 and $41,800. Later models (built by Wright/Allied after a change in ownership) may be worth, BUC reports, as much as $59,300 to $65,900. We've tracked 1970's Princess 36 prices pretty closely and believe you can buy one in decent shape somewhere in the mid-40s, a bit more for later models in great condition.

We doubt we'd pay a $10,000 premium for a 1980's model unless (a) we had a lot of easy cash to spend, and (b) the boat had been repowered with a newer diesel, and equipped with other still-functional goodies we wanted, such as an autopilot, radar, electronic instruments, etc.

The beauty of the Princess, as we see it, is a robustly character ketch at an affordable price. Compared to the Pearson 365, it's better built (we still don't like the fiberglass inner liner and screwed together hull-deck joint of the P365, though there is much else to appreciate, e.g., the bathtub!) and less expensive.   • **PS**

Morris 36 Justine

This semi-custom gem is exceedingly rare on the used market, but worth looking for.

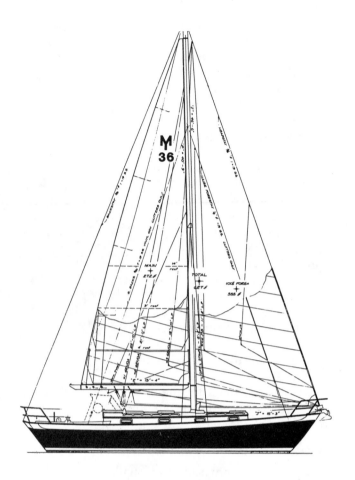

A few decades ago, when you wanted a new boat, you chose a designer, commissioned a design, selected a builder, and nursed your dream through to completion. Not many people could afford boats in those days, and not too many people today could afford to have a boat built in this fashion. Now, you're more likely to go to a boat show, look at a lot of boats, and pick one off a dealer's "lot," just like buying a new car. Until you get into large, very expensive boats, most of the options you can get are add-ons like bigger winches, perhaps a different rig, and more electronics.

You want a bigger nav station? Find another boat. A bigger icebox? Ditto. A non-teak interior? Just keep looking.

Few things are more frustrating than finding a boat that has 90% of the characteristics you're looking for, and 10% that you really can't stand. You can grit your teeth and grin and bear it, or you can keep looking.

Most of today's sailboats are marvels of production line efficiency, but with production lines comes standardization, and with standardization comes a numbing sameness that can remove a lot of the pleasure of owning a boat.

Morris Yachts can hardly be accused of running a production line operation. In his 20 years in the boatbuilding business, Tom Morris has built only about 100 boats. Catalina probably turns out more boats than that every month.

But Morris's boats fall into that intriguing category called the "semi-custom yacht," boats based on a standard hull and interior that can be modified to the desires of individual owners.

This isn't a cheap way to build a boat. Imagine going into the Chevrolet plant—or to Mercedes-Benz, for that matter— and asking to have the dash-

Specifications

LOA	36' 3"
LWL	29' 6"
Beam	11' 7"
Draft	4' 4"/5' 6" (std/Scheel)
Displacement	15,602 lbs.
Ballast	6,500 lbs.
Sail area	627 sq. ft.

board rearranged, or the interior layout changed to suit you.

For most people, the semi-custom boat doesn't make sense. If you're satisfied with what you can find in a production boat, you should by all means buy it. If you're looking for the most amount of boat for the least amount of money, the semi-custom boat isn't for you. If you're an experienced boat owner, have definite ideas about what you want, and are willing to pay significantly more to get it, the semi-custom boat may be the answer.

The Morris 36 Justine is built by Tom Morris and his crew of 16 in Southwest Harbor, Maine. Southwest Harbor is a tiny village that supports an astonishing number of boatbuilders, including the prestigious Hinckley company. Fortunately, this means that there is a reasonable pool of skilled labor in the area, between native Mainers and boatbuilders from further south who have migrated north for the more bucolic downeast lifestyle.

Morris's reputation was built on smaller boats: Frances (26'), Linda (28'), Leigh (30'), and Annie (30'). All are Chuck Paine designs, and all share the Paine characteristics of moderately long keels, nearly symmetrical waterlines, moderate displacement, and lovely, lively sheer. Justine was the first Morris boats with "modern" underbodies, having longish fin keels and skeg-mounted rudders. The patented Scheel shoal draft keel is an option chosen by about 3/4 of Morris 36 owners.

Construction

Despite their traditional appearance, Morris yachts utilize materials as up-to-date as any builder, including biaxial fabrics, isophthalic gelcoat, and vinylester resin in the mat layers immediately beneath the gelcoat. The primary laminating resin is a more typical orthopthalic resin.

Morris is convinced that the answer to hull blistering lies not just in the choice of materials, but in the care with which the hulls are laid up. At most production builders, the glass shop is at the low end of the totem pole. No one likes working in the intense styrene atmosphere of a molding room, and many builders use their less-skilled labor there.

This, according to Morris, is a serious mistake. He believes that the more care that is taken in the molding process, the less likely problems are to develop with the laminate. He is fanatical about the removal of air and excess resin from the laminate. Excess resin adds weight while reducing structural properties, and Morris believes that air in the laminate is a breeding ground for blisters.

A core sample we examined, removed for installation of a through hull fitting, had been burn-tested. It showed a 56/44 resin/glass ratio—nearly perfect.

The hull of a Morris 36 takes two to three men about a week to lay up. The hull stays in the mold at least an additional week while interior structural components such as bulkheads, floor timbers, and supports for hull ceiling are installed.

Leaving the boat in the mold at this stage prevents any distortion of the hull, making sure that the interior furniture modules and deck fit without complication.

For an extra $1,750, Morris will core the hull with Airex foam. If you're going to live aboard the boat in a cold climate, the extra insulation of the Airex hull would both make the boat warmer and reduce condensation. From a pure hull performance and strength point of view, it is unnecessary.

There are no interior molded fiberglass body pans in Morris boats. The interiors are built up of plywood, which is glassed to the hull. This method of construction allows substantial latitude in interior design.

Between the major and minor bulkheads, each area of furniture is self-contained, and can be changed to suit the owner's desires. In Justine #14, for example, the standard arrangement of nav station and quarterberth on the port side aft was replaced with lockers, drawers, a huge refrigerator-deepfreeze, and a big standup chart table, while the layout of the forward section of the main cabin remained unchanged.

The hull-to-deck joint is made with an inward-turning flange at the sheer, which is actually raised well above the deck level to form a bulwark. The edge of the deck molding turns upward, then outward, overlapping the hull flange, creating the inner surface of the bulwark.

Hull and deck are bolted together, the joint bedded in 3M 5200 polyurethane.

The keel is an external lead casting, bolted to the hull. Just aft of the ballast there is a deep, molded fiberglass bilge sump, which should do a good job of keeping water out of the bilges and lockers low in the hull.

Glasswork and gelcoat are done to very high standards, although the two-tone deck gelcoat on the new boat we sailed had some variations in color which gave a slightly splotchy appearance.

A year-old boat we examined had several minor gelcoat cracks in various locations on deck. These were not stress-related: they had probably been in the deck since it was removed from the mold, but showed up over time as dirt worked into the tiny cracks. We do not consider them significant. All glass surfaces exposed inside the hull are finished with grey gelcoat.

Chainplates and through hull fittings are electrically tied to a copper strap grounding system, which is glassed over to prevent oxidation and the resultant reduction in conductivity. The strapping is then tied to a keelbolt.

While there are substantial backing plates on deck hardware such as stanchions, there are no backing plates under the foredeck cleats—potentially some of the most heavily-loaded hardware on the boat. Hoses on hull fittings below the waterline are not double-clamped. In some cases this is because Spartan seacocks—which do not require double clamps—are used, but in other areas it simply appears to be an oversight.

Handling Under Power

The hull of the Morris 36 is easily driven. The engine is the three-cylinder Volvo 2003, rated at 28 hp at 3,000 rpm. At a more normal cruising rpm of 2,000 this will give a speed of about 5 1/2 knots.

The boat handles well under power. There is little vibration or noise, although only the forward portion of the engine box is insulated for sound reduction. The boat we sailed was equipped with a feathering Max-Prop, which is probably the single best investment that any cruising sailor could make to improve performance under both sail and power. Max-Props aren't cheap, but they're worth every penny if you're concerned about performance and have an extra $1,000 or so to spend.

Access to the front of the engine for service of filters and belts is good, although it does require removing the companionway ladder and engine box. Access for checking the oil is more difficult— you have to remove the lid to the engine box, which is a tight fit with the ladder in place. This could be easily solved with a small access hatch on the side of the engine box. Oil checks should be a routine part of engine operation.

There is no oil drip pan under the engine. Having rarely succeeded in changing or adding oil without spilling some, and having never seen an engine that didn't eventually leak a little lubrication and fuel oil, we think a drip pan is a must, despite Justine's deep bilge sump.

Handling Under Sail

Chuck Paine likes fast boats. Although the standard rig is a sloop with a fairly conservative single-spreader rig by Metalmast, there is an optional taller, lighter double-spreader rig with the chainplates set well inboard.

No one has yet ordered this rig, but both Paine and Morris would like to talk an owner into the hotter rig, flush through-hulls, and other little goodies that would make the boat faster. The double-spreader rig adds $950 to the base price of the boat. With the standard deep keel, a Justine set up this way should be a formidable IMS racer for an event such as the Marion-Bermuda Race.

Thus far, however, all the owners are cruisers.

Most have opted for the shoal draft Scheel keel rather than the more conventional long fin, which adds 1' of draft.

The Scheel keel is by all reports very slightly less efficient upwind, but about the same speed on other points of sail. The Scheel keel adds $1,200 to the price of the boat. Unless shoal draft is critical for you, we'd stick with the normal keel.

With a half-load displacement of only 15,600 pounds on a 29' 6" waterline, the Morris 36 has a lot of speed potential, particularly when you consider her 42% ballast/displacement ratio. She is no slouch. The boat we sailed was equipped with a rig 2' taller than standard, a Doyle fully-battened main, and a roller-furling Doyle Quicksilver genoa. Despite a slight hook in the leech of the genoa, the boat pointed and accelerated as well as any fast cruiser of her size, and a lot better than most of them.

On Deck

The deck layout of the Morris 36 is simple and clean. Shrouds are set a few inches inboard of the bulwarks—just far enough to be in the way when going forward along the deck, so that it's easier to go forward over the deckhouse.

The helmsman's seat is a little low for looking over the cabin house, but the cockpit coamings are wide enough to sit on in reasonable comfort in order to see the jib telltales.

Sail handling hardware is excellent, with Harken traveler and mainsheet blocks. The other deck hardware comes from a variety of sources: stainless steel genoa track from Hinckley, Lewmar winches, Bomar hatches, and other suppliers for bits and pieces.

The combination of bulwarks and lifelines that are 27" tall give a great feeling of security on deck. Yet the bulwarks are not high enough to be visually

Though there is a "standard" interior, many owners choose to take advantage of Morris' customized layouts.

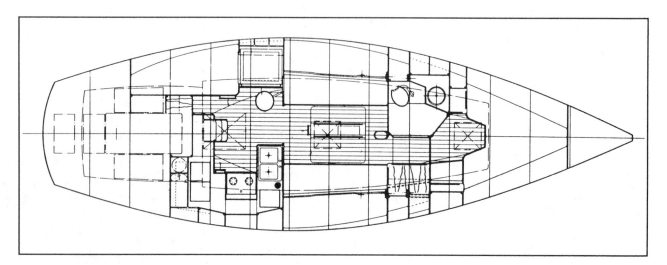

obtrusive—you don't even notice they're there, you just feel more secure.

The stemhead fitting includes a substantial roller for a CQR anchor. A chafe pad should be fitted on the deck at the inboard end of the anchor shank, or a hole will quickly be worn in the deck from the anchor shackle. There is no anchor well on deck, and the forepeak locker for anchor rode storage is so far forward in the hull that we would not suggest storing large amounts of chain there.

We can't imagine a much more secure cockpit for offshore sailing. There are four large cockpit drains, although the actual low point in the cockpit sole requires a quirky little fifth drain to get the last bit of water out with the boat sitting at anchor. The upper parts of the cockpit coamings are angled comfortably outward.

With the optional cutter rig, two staysail sheet winches are fitted to the aft end of the coachroof. With the dodger in place, you can't swing the starboard winch handle in a full circle without fetching up on the dodger frame, an inconvenience. The mainsail sheet winch is also mounted on the coachroof, but there are no obstacles in the way of its operation.

Access to the rudder head for installing the emergency steering requires opening a bronze deckplate and inserting the welded stainless steel tiller. With the tiller in position, you will have a good-sized opening in the cockpit sole, which can allow water below in heavy weather. Some sort of boot over the opening would be a plus. Large cockpit lockers port and starboard will hold all the extra sails, anchors, and other assorted junk you care to load in them. Merriman pedestal wheel steering with Ritchie compass are standard.

Belowdecks

If you're looking for acres of varnished teak and complex joinerwork, the interior of the Morris 36 won't be your cup of tea. If you appreciate honest, solid workmanship to a high grade, and interior finish that is traditional in the best sense of the word, you're going to like this boat.

There are two standard, no-extra-cost interior finishes: oiled teak, or white Formica trimmed in oiled teak. We don't like oiled teak interiors—they're drab. An oiled teak interior is not in any sense traditional. Builders like them because they're cheap to finish. Teak plywood costs just a little more than regular marine plywood. One worker can completely oil the interior joinerwork of a boat the size of the Morris 36 in a couple of days. Varnishing or painting, on the other hand, would take weeks.

If you find that hard to believe, consider the fact that you can get all that interior teak varnished if you want, but it is an option that costs $6,250. At the Morris standard labor rate of $26 per hour, that means that they spend 240 hours—six man-weeks—varnishing the interior.

The interior of white Formica with oiled teak trim is a practical combination that is airy, light, and attractive. It is so superior to the drab varnished or oiled teak interiors of most boats as to defy comparison, although it will appear stark to those with little grounding in traditional yacht interiors. If it were our

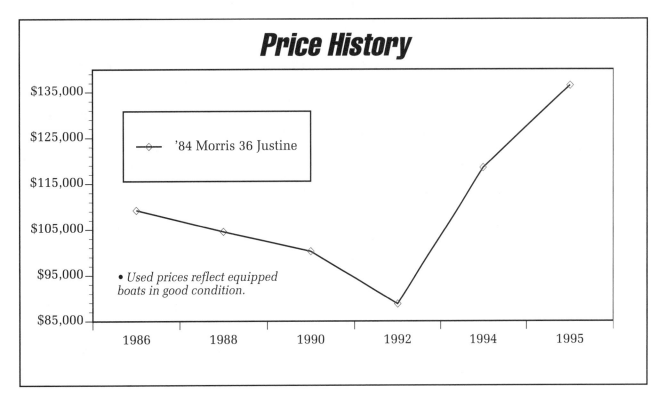

Price History

—◇— '84 Morris 36 Justine

• *Used prices reflect equipped boats in good condition.*

boat, we would get the Formica interior with teak trim, but we would not have the teak trim oiled. We would either have Morris varnish it, or do it ourselves at our leisure. Varnishing just the trim should cut the extra finishing cost by about half, and give you a truly elegant interior. You cannot put varnish over an oil finish, so you have to make a conscious decision about what you're going to have before you start.

Given the cost of domestic labor, there's no way that a US builder can turn out a boat with the exquisite, labor-intensive interior details of the best Taiwan-built boats, such as the Little Harbors, and still deliver a boat at a price much less than that of the space shuttle. You won't find every locker of the Morris 36 lined with varnished wood ceiling, and you can see the hull structure in places that even a lot of cheaper Oriental builders cover up with wood sheathing.

At the same time, Morris refuses to line the overheads, hull, and inside of lockers with the ubiquitous foam-backed vinyl that you find glued into almost every American-built boat from Hunter to Hinckley. For insulation, Morris will line lockers with cork if you want—a practical, if not particularly elegant solution. As another option, you can get the hull above the waterline lined with non-structural foam to reduce condensation and noise.

There's nothing wrong with opening a locker and being able to see what holds a boat together, even if fiberglass construction details lack the hard-edged beauty of traditional wood structural components. But for those not used to seeing fiberglass surfaces, parts of the Morris 36 will have an unfinished appearance.

The forward cabin has V-berths port and starboard, with an insert to form a double. The forward cabin is pushed far into the bow, and the boat's fine entry angle results in a berth which narrows sharply at the foot. Because the berths are quite long, we doubt if the narrowness will be a problem unless the berths are occupied by two giants. Headroom in the forward cabin is an honest 6'.

Aft of the forward cabin, there is a large hanging locker to port, with the head to starboard. The passage between the main and forward cabins is quite narrow, as is the door to the head. There is adequate locker space and elbow room in the head, and a six-footer can stand up without bending. The only interior fiberglass molding in the boat is the head floor pan, which makes sense on a boat with a shower. However, this white, non-skid molding will be tough to keep clean. There is a small teak grate over the shower sump, but the drain is not actually at the lowest point in the head sole, so that you may end up with a small puddle in the aft corner of the head after showering. This is a problem on a lot of boats, and

could be remedied in this case by changing the pan molding so that it angled upwards slightly just aft of the drain grate.

One of the big advantages of a semi-custom boat without a molded hull liner is the ability to alter the interior arrangements without breaking the bank. While the standard main cabin arrangement has settees and pilot berths both port and starboard, there are several other accommodation plans offered as reasonably-priced options. Hull #14, which had just been completed when we visited Morris, has a U-shaped dinette to starboard, and storage lockers in place of the pilot berth to port. This is fine on a boat that will not be sailed offshore, but it means that the only sea berth in the boat is the quarterberth. A more practical arrangement for occasional offshore work would be to retain either the port or starboard pilot berth. With a pilot berth to starboard and the standard port quarterberth, there would be at least one comfortable offshore berth on each side of the boat—a necessity for two-person passagemaking, when an adequate place to sleep can spell the difference between being rested and getting fatigued.

Headroom in the main cabin varies from 6' 3" on centerline at the forward end to 6' 5" on centerline just forward of the companionway.

Aft of the settees, partial bulkheads on both sides of the boat separate the galley and nav station from the main part of the cabin. In the standard arrangement, there is a good wet locker just to port of the companionway ladder, and a large quarterberth outboard of the locker. Forward of the quarterberth is the nav station, which faces athwartships rather than the more common fore and aft. The chart table is big enough to accept almost any chart folded in half, and has adequate space for electronics, navigation paraphernalia, and books. The navigator's bench is a bit narrow for maximum comfort, and we would miss having a backrest when trying to navigate with the boat heeled a lot on port tack.

The electrical panels are fitted behind the companionway ladder, sheltered under the bridgedeck. While this is a good location, it is somewhat vulnerable to spray, and the panels should be protected behind an opening clear acrylic splash shield.

To starboard is a well laid out galley, which includes a three-burner Force 10 propane stove with oven. This is one of the best galley stoves made, and is typical of the quality components which go into the Morris 36. It is also one of the reasons the boat costs so much. Propane is stored in a cockpit locker holding three six-pound aluminum bottles.

The icebox and lid are well insulated, and the box itself has 4" of foam insulation. Sea Frost engine-driven refrigeration is an option costing $2,350. If you're going cruising in warm climates, a good refrigeration system is a must.

On one boat we examined, the owner wanted a larger refrigerator and freezer than would fit in the allocated space, so the nav station was replaced with a huge refrigerator/freezer, retaining the top for chart work. While this wouldn't be everyone's cup of tea, it shows the design flexibility that is the primary advantage of the semi-custom boat.

Deep double sinks manufactured by Polar are pretty much the norm on larger boats, but here, Morris uses a double sink, one large and deep, one small and shallower than usually seen. We like the idea of unequal size sinks—there always seems to be one pot on board that won't fit into the relatively small Polar sinks. At the same time, we'd like the sinks to be at least 9" deep. We wish some sink manufacturer would put out deep double sinks of these proportions, but we haven't seen them yet.

Hot and cold pressure water are standard.

Designer Paine has also drawn a tri-cabin interior for those who want an aft stateroom, although none of the first 14 owners selected this extra-cost option.

Conclusions

The Morris 36 is an expensive boat. It is also a well-built, very attractive boat. The builder is flexible enough to alter the interior in almost any way you want, as long as the main structural bulkheads stay in the same place.

This all comes at a price, of course.

There's no written warranty on the boat. Morris shrugs, and says if something is wrong, he'll fix it. We believe him.

If you take full advantage of Morris's ability to customize your boat, the final price will be a lot higher than the base price. Hull #14, for example, has a custom interior plus such niceties as radar, central heat, and Alpha Marine autopilot. If you want to go all out, you can increase the price of the boat by 40% without batting an eye.

Besides price, the only disadvantage of a semi-custom boat is that you may in creating the boat of your dreams be building a boat that's a nightmare for anyone else, a boat that no one else is willing to buy when the inevitable time comes to sell. Thus far, that hasn't been a problem with the Morris 36. Only one of the boats has come on the resale market, and it was sold before the broker even received the listing. The buyer had only been interested in one other boat: a new Morris 36.

Obviously, the primary advantage of a semi-custom boat is to create a boat you'll keep for years. Many Morris 36 owners do just that. **• PS**

Freedom 36

Though expensive, the Freedom 36 is a boat that sails well and is very easy to handle.

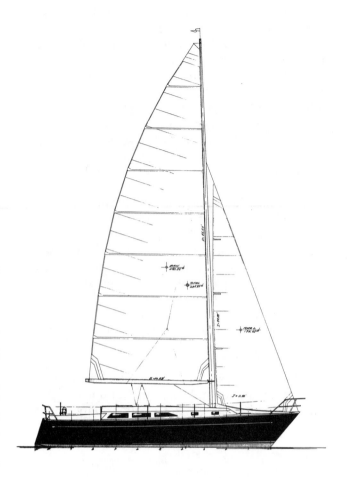

Freedom Yachts were the invention of Garry Hoyt back in the early 1970s. An advertising executive and champion one-design sailor, Hoyt reached a stage in his life when he wanted a cruising boat, but he found the existing fleet ordinary and unsatisfactory. So—the story goes—he set about designing himself a boat. The result was the Freedom 40, an unusual-looking cruiser with a long waterline, conventional hull, and a peculiar wishbone cat-ketch rig.

Hoyt marketed the Freedom 40 with the diligence and success you'd expect of an accomplished advertiser—claiming speed, quality, and simplicity of handling for his innovative-looking boats. In time he designed (often with the aid of professional naval architects like Halsey Herreshoff) and sold a whole line of Freedoms—a 21, 25, 28, 32, 33, and 44, as well as the original 40.

At the time, Hoyt's company was unusual—because Freedom Yachts was a "boatbuilder" that didn't build the boats. Instead, Hoyt went to Everett Pearson, pioneer in the fiberglass boatbuilding industry and one of the founders of Pearson Yachts.

Tillotson-Pearson took on the Freedom line, establishing a reputation for Freedom yachts as top-end, high-quality production boats. Ultimately, Hoyt sold the company to Tillotson-Pearson.

One of the first moves of the new owners was to revamp the Freedom line. The company commissioned new designs from California-based naval architect Gary Mull, well known for his race boats and his wholesome racer/cruiser designs like the Ranger 29 and Ranger 33 in the early 1970s. The Freedom 36 was the first of the Mull designs, and it was followed by a 30, a 28, and a 42. The 36 went out of production in 1989.

The Mull-designed Freedoms share a profile that

Specifications - Sloop

LOA	36' 5"
LWL	30' 7"
Beam	12' 6"
Draft	4' 6"/ 6' 0" (shoal/deep keel)
Displacement	14,370 lbs.
Ballast	6,500 lbs.
Sail area	685 sq. ft.

is rather different from the older Freedoms—with fewer curves and more sharp turns, most noticeable in the square, boxy cabinhouse that is remarkably reminiscent of a Ranger 26. The boats are generally plain and simple looking, with virtually no exterior wood trim.

The most noticeable characteristic of the line continues to be the unstayed carbon fiber mast that had become a hallmark of all the Freedom boats. Most traditional sailors would describe the new designs as big catboats, with the enormous-diameter mast set well forward, but they do carry a vestigial jib and are technically sloops. All the new Freedoms are rigged with the aim of simple handling that has always been associated with the line.

The Mull boats have also maintained the general

Some Freedom 36s were built with the unusual Freedom cat ketch rig.

concept of enormous beam and long waterline with almost no overhangs, and the boats have more interior volume for their length than almost anything else on the market. The major difference from the older boats is that the hull underbodies are thoroughly modern in the Mull designs, with flat bottoms, fin keels, and spade rudders.

Hoyt originally tried to market the Freedoms directly to customers, but the company has since developed a widespread network of dealers which generally have a good reputation for servicing the boats they sell. The company has also developed a good reputation for responding to warranty problems and other customer complaints.

For example, the Freedom 36 that we sailed for this evaluation had originally been sold to an owner on the west coast, and had developed some gelcoat problems on the deck. The company eventually replaced the boat with a new one—an incredibly rare occurrence among boatbuilders—had redone the deck completely, and then re-sold the boat to the current owner at a reduced cost.

Similarly, while we were evaluating the 36, the owner received a package from the company with a kit to modify the lightning protection system in the

boat. The new boats were being set up differently, and the builder thought the change was advisable for all boats. They provided retrofit kits—at no charge.

On its latest boats, the company is also offering a 10-year warranty on the hull—even against gelcoat blisters—and a lifetime warranty on the spar to the first owner.

While there has never been a boat line with no problems, buyers of Freedoms should have better expectations than most of successful dealings with the company.

Hull and Deck

Both the hull and deck of the Freedom 36 are fiberglass with a Contourkore balsa core throughout. There are potential problems with water absorption in both hull and deck of balsa cored laminates, with little way for the owner to guard against it except by depending on the integrity of the manufacturer. Tillotson-Pearson is one of the few companies that we would count on to produce a good, long-lasting hull in boat after boat. Basic construction is solid.

The fiberglass itself is a laminate of E-glass mat and stitched unidirectional fiberglass, with vinylester barrier resins in the exterior layer of the hull below the waterline. The outside layer is an isophthalic gelcoat. Both the vinylester and the isophtalic resins are believed to provide the best protection against water absorption and blistering. This is a high-cost fabrication, but Freedom obviously has faith in it.

One of the big advantages of balsa coring is the thermal and acoustic insulation it provides. Condensation problems inside the hull are greatly reduced, and the hull has a solid, quiet feel to it going through waves.

The drawback of balsa coring is that one must exercise more care than normal when installing through-hull and through-deck fittings, for example being careful not to compress the whole laminate and allow for penetration of water. Cracks or other damage to the hull must be attended to promptly.

The hull and deck are laid up separately and joined with an inward-turning flange on the hull on which the deck molding sets. An adhesive caulk, 3M-5200, is laid in the seam, and the joint is through-bolted with 1/4" stainless bolts through an external aluminum toerail.

We examined a number of hulls and found them generally fair, with no obvious problems. Exterior gelcoat work is generally good.

Two keels are available—either a deep fin or a shoal draft fin. The 36 we sailed had the deep fin, which is an external lead casting, bolted to the hull. The shoal keel is encapsulated in a keel cavity and fiberglassed to the hull. If you can stand the draft, the deeper keel will be preferable in terms of performance as well as construction.

Overall, the construction of the Freedom 36 is high-quality, with everything being done pretty much the way industry standards say they should be done. The single exception we found was not in the 36 but in a Freedom 28 we examined. The 28 had a chintzy plastic through hull fitting for a sink drain, with no seacock—an odd oversight in an otherwise well-built boat.

Rig

The unstayed carbon fiber masts were quite radical when Freedom first used them, but they are well-established and proven by now. They are laid up somewhat like fiberglass, with carbon fibers wound around a form and impregnated with resin. For equivalent strength, they are much lighter and stiffer than an aluminum mast.

Under sail, it's a bit shocking at first to see the mast bend in puffs, especially since it's so tall (55' 6" above the waterline). But once you're accustomed to that peculiarity, there should be little to worry about in terms of strength or longevity. We were unable to find any statistics or insurance figures on carbon fiber mast failures compared to aluminum mast failures, but we suspect the odds of a dismasting or other significant failure are no more likely—perhaps even less likely—with the carbon fiber than with aluminum. We are aware of at least one mast that was damaged in a lightning strike.

The Freedom 36 was available with both a sloop rig and Freedom's trademark cat ketch rig.

Handling Under Power

A three-cylinder 27 hp Yanmar diesel is standard. The engine is adequate, though certainly not over-sized.

Engine installation is well done, in a small compartment lined with a lead/foam sound deadener. Access to the engine is possible from the front by removing the companionway steps, and from the port cockpit locker by removing a panel. It's hard to get at the Yanmar's dipstick on the engine's starboard side. There is a small screw-out port for access from the aft cabin, but the port is about a foot ahead of the dipstick.

The boat comes with a solid two-bladed prop which most owners will want to trash immediately, replacing it with a folding or feathering prop. The

With her broad beam, the Freedom 36 has lots of room belowdecks. The layout is fairly conventional, but quite comfortable.

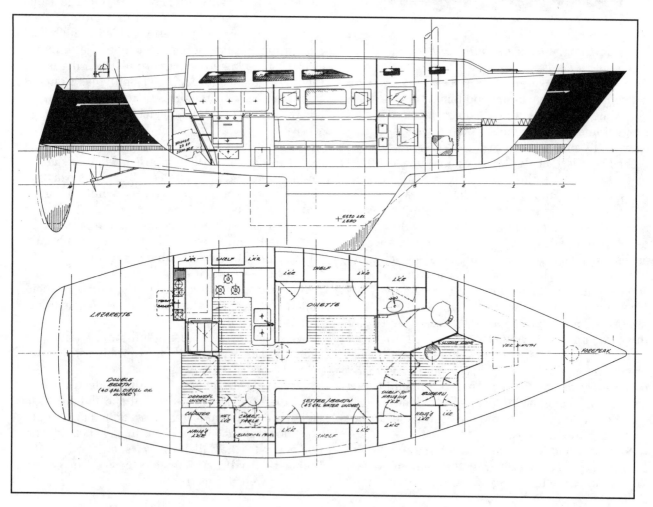

boat we sailed had a three-bladed feathering prop, which not only lets the boat live up to its sailing potential, but also seems to improve backing power. A folding prop would be much cheaper, though motoring performance would not be as good as with the three-bladed feathering prop.

It surprises us that companies which tout the sailing performance of their boats continue to fit them out with solid propellers. There's almost nothing you can do that will degrade sailing performance more than carry an exposed, solid prop, especially when the wind turns light.

With the three-bladed feathering prop, the Freedom 36 performs well. The boat backs out of a slip, goes where you want it to go in reverse, and powers easily to hull speed without overloading the engine. The engine is mounted slightly off-center so the shaft is at an angle to the centerline of the boat, and some people will tell you that this helps the boat track in a straight line under power. The 36 did track straight, but then most boats with centerline installations track straight, too.

With the deep fin to pivot on and the spade rudder located way aft, the boat turns sharply. The large mast and the high topsides provide plenty of windage, but generally the Freedom 36 should be nimble enough to make handling in close quarters no problem.

Handling Under Sail

"Easy" is the key word in the company's promotion of their sailboats. We found the mainsail a bit of a nuisance to hoist and lower, with the full-length battens fouling the lazy jacks, but other than that the boat is truly easy to sail.

All the gear is of good quality. Halyards are led aft to the cockpit, through stoppers to self-tailing winches. The jib can actually be hoisted by hand, but the main requires the winch to raise it the last 10' or so. Other controls (outhaul, reef lines, boom vang, cunningham) also lead to sheet stoppers in the cockpit. A neat feature is the "panel" for hanging the coiled lines, just behind the winches at the front of the cockpit.

The mainsheet is a four-part tackle at mid-boom, running to a Harken traveler ahead of the companionway. Frequently, the mechanical advantage of a mid-boom sheeting arrangement is so low that mainsail trimming is hard, but we found we could handle the mainsheet by hand easily in winds up to about 12 knots. Thereafter, we used the winch. All winches are adequately sized, though self-tailers are an option that almost everyone will want.

The non-overlapping jib uses a sprit that fits in a sleeve on the sail. The jib is self-tacking, with a single sheet that is easily controlled by hand. It is amazing how much speed the dinky little jib adds to the boat. Though the company's literature talks about sailing under main alone, for performance you need the jib. Though we haven't sailed a Nonsuch 36 and a Freedom 36 side by side, we suspect the Freedom will be noticeably faster, largely because of the jib.

The pulpit-mounted spinnaker pole and the other spinnaker handling gear (all optional) are remarkable in making the spinnaker easy to hoist, jibe, and lower. Of course, the spinnaker is tiny for a boat of

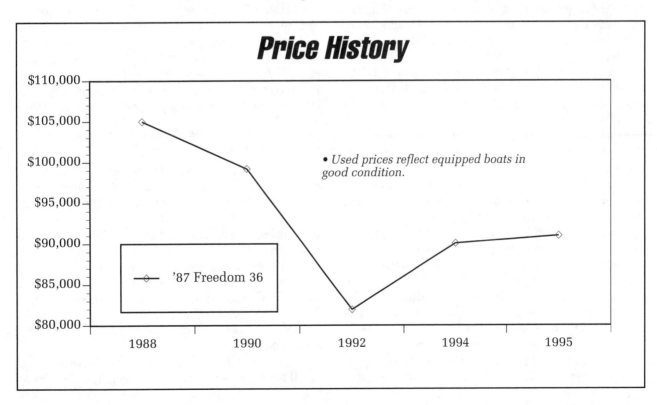

Price History

• *Used prices reflect equipped boats in good condition.*

'87 Freedom 36

this size—closer to what you'd get on a J-24 than on a conventional 36' sloop. Using the pole—which is pinned at the center so that it pivots on top of the pulpit—takes some getting used to, but once you figure things out it's a lot easier than jibing a J-24.

We raced the 36 in two PHRF triangle races to try her performance against more conventional boats. In most respects, we found the boat admirable.

Full crew for the racing was two people, and in terms of performance per amount of energy expended, the boat was a clear winner. It is amazing how getting rid of a big jib lowers the activity required on a sailboat.

We did find that the fully-battened main on the bendy mast required new skills, particularly going to windward. The sail has a very wide "slot" in terms of trim, and does not seem to stall out. We messed with the mainsail almost constantly, first trimming it as we would a conventional main, then dropping or raising the traveler, adjusting sheet tension, cunningham, and so on.

The conventional wisdom concerning the rig is that it will not go to weather: you should foot off for maximum performance. But we found that we could point with most of the fleet, and the boat had a B&G Hornet system which kept telling us that our VMG was highest when we were pinching.

Reaching is the boat's strong suit—as you would want in a good cruiser—and the boat is a surprising combination of effortlessness and power. Handling, including sail trim, is a piece of cake, even with the spinnaker up.

Running, the boat is a little sluggish, even with the spinnaker. We didn't test the boat fully, but we suspect that jibing downwind on broad reaches may be faster than running dead down, at least in lighter air.

Whatever the point of sail, the sailor used to conventional rigs will have to do quite a bit of experimenting and relearning to get the most out of the Freedom 36.

In terms of absolute speed, the boat was a bit disappointing to us. We expected a little more than we got out of her long waterline.

Her PHRF rating is 150, comparable to the speed of racer/cruisers of 10 years ago like the C&C 33 and 34, or the Pearson 10M. Our impression is that the boat will sail much faster than those boats on a reach, but quite a bit slower on a beat or a run. Her strongest performance will be in stronger winds rather than light air.

There is not a lot that you can do about the fundamentals of yacht design, but we sort of expected that the boat would outsail a 15-year-old Mull design like the Ranger 33. In fact, it won't. Of course, any passage on the Freedom will be much easier than on the Ranger, much less demanding, and much less tiring. But it won't be faster, unless you can always make arrangements for a reach.

Nonetheless, after our experience on the boat, we strongly recommend the Freedom 36 as a sailing machine, with the ease of sailing far outweighing any drawbacks. She is a pleasure under sail.

On Deck

You sail the Freedom 36 almost entirely from the cockpit, and it is big and roomy, with plenty of space to do the minimal chores of sail handling.

The benches are wide and comfortable, long enough to use as outdoor berths. It's not a T-shaped cockpit—one of the few straight cockpits we've seen recently, and we decided we sort of like that. There's ample room for lounging about, and with a dodger and bimini it would be an excellent cruising cockpit. There's a propane tank locker, and a cavernous portside locker that will be hard to use well unless you can figure out a way to subdivide it.

Wheel steering is standard. The boat we sailed had an optional oversized wheel that simplified steering from the side decks, but made passage around the wheel difficult.

From the cockpit forward to the mast, the Freedom is wide open. It would be an ideal working platform, though of course there's little working of the boat to be done except from the cockpit. The nonskid of the decks and cabin top seemed generally mediocre.

From the mast forward, the rig gets in the way of things. With the turret-mounted spinnaker pole, the spinnaker in its storage sock, and the wishbone in the jib, the foredeck is crowded. Anchor handling and docking are complicated by having to step over and around the gear, and we suppose many cruisers will think about not having the spinnaker equipment at all. To us, this congestion on the foredeck seems the one major shortcoming of the Freedom rig. Otherwise, the Freedom has a spacious, comfortable deck.

Belowdecks

As you might expect with the long waterline, short overhangs and wide beam, the area belowdecks is huge. We thought the size, especially the beam, might even be a problem under way, but found that that the boat is stiff enough that you should rarely be tossed about.

The interior arrangement is fairly ordinary. A big forward cabin has a good V-berth which can be made into a comfortable double by using an insert in the V. There's a bureau and hanging locker to starboard and a door to the head to port. Headroom is 6' 1" near the entry door.

There is good stowage under the V-berth and in a small forepeak—in fact, this boat generally has more storage than is common in more conventional modern designs.

The head is roomy, mostly a fiberglass molding, and has a second door to the main cabin. Opposite the head is another bureau and storage space.

The main cabin is large, with an L-shaped settee around a table which folds up against the forward bulkhead. The table can be folded out so that the starboard settee becomes the outboard seat for an enormous dining table. There is good storage space behind both settees and beneath the port settee. Headroom is a true 6' 4".

The galley is U-shaped, with deep sinks, a good dry-storage locker, a gimbaled stove with oven, an adequate icebox, and lots of storage space. A garbage trap in the aft bulkhead lets you drop stuff into a wastebasket stored in the cockpit locker. Now if someone would just come up with some similar way to store your returnable cans and bottles.

Opposite the galley is a navigation table with a swing-out seat. Above the table is the electrical panel, and mounting space for most of the electronics.

The aft cabin, mostly under the starboard cockpit seat, is also good-sized, with a bureau, hanging locker, and decent headroom just inside the door.

Finish below is generally good—lots of teak veneer with a nice contrast in the ash battens used as hull ceiling. The cabin overhead is vinyl panels—OK, but a nuisance if you need to mess with the deck hardware fastenings.

Ventilation is adequate, but would be minimal for offshore passages. You might want to look for the optional dorades to improve air movement below.

Conclusions

In general, we came away from the Freedom 36 with renewed respect for the work of Tillotson-Pearson. For us there's no question of the quality of construction or general workmanship.

Though high-quality, the Freedoms are plain. If you're into hand craftsmanship or the sort of excessive teakwork that you find in the best Oriental imports, you probably won't like the Freedoms, though their belowdecks joinery and finish is very good.

In general, we also like the roominess and livability of the boat. In a 36-footer, it's hard to imagine more space, or think of a way the space could be better used.

In sailing, the strong point of the boat is ease of handling, and after our trials on the water, we have no reservations about the unusual rig—it works, and it works pretty well. In a 36' cruiser, we might hope for a little more absolute speed, but the Freedom is no slouch. She will make smart passages, and make them easily.

The sloop rig is somewhat out of the ordinary, with its fully-battened mainsail and vestigial jib.

The major drawback, of course, is price, since the Freedom is on the high end of the price spectrum. With sails and a few "necessary" options like the spinnaker package, self-tailing winches, electronics, and refrigeration, the price of a new boat could easily have topped $110,000.

And if you fully outfitted the boat, including things like customized interior fabrics, you could have quickly gotten the bottom line up to $125,000 or so—a lot of money, even for one of the biggest 36-footers around.

For the price you got a good boat, with assurance of quality construction and a company that will stand behind its products. For many who've owned cheap boats, those characteristics will be worth paying for.

Probably the most distinctive thing you'll be getting in the Freedom 36 is the ease of handling. We can't imagine how you could get a 36-footer that sails well and make it any easier to handle. A lot of the joy of sailing is making the wind work for you, and the Freedom 36 gives you more return for your labor than any other boat we've sailed.   • **PS**

PDQ 36

In this size range, we cannot think of any production cruising cat that as successfully combines good construction, pleasing lines and decent sailing performance.

The PDQ 36 was designed by Alan Slater and is built in Whitby, Ontario, Canada, utilizing, we are told, some of the workers from the now-defunct Whitby Boat Works, builders of the Alberg 30 and 37, and the Whitby 42. Since the first boat was launched in 1990, about 40 or 50 have been built.

Though promotional literature makes much of the PDQ's high-speed performance, it is definitely a cruising catamaran. In such designs the accommodations usually are built on the bridge top; this is necessary to provide the spacious saloon with 360-degree view that makes buyers so gaga. The amas or hulls, which tend to be narrow and without portlights, contain the sleeping cabins, head and sometimes the galley. The bridge structure quickly distinguishes the cruising catamaran from the racer because it adds windage, weight and often necessitates lowering the bridge (to provide headroom in the cabin above it) closer to the water than is often considered desirable. But if performance is sacrificed, it is only when compared to other lighter, more streamlined multihulls. We'll talk more of this later.

First let's examine the choices Slater made with regard to the major design considerations.

Like most production cruising multihulls today, the PDQ 36 has U-shaped hulls. A hull waterline length-to-beam ratio of 8:1 is considered about the minimum for decent performance, with 12:1 being more efficient and 16:1 being super high-perfor-

Specifications

LOA	36' 5"
LWL	34' 4"
Beam	18' 3"
Draft	2' 10"
Displacement	8,000 lbs.
Sail area	542 sq. ft.

mance, but not suitable for cruising. The PDQ 36 comes in at 12:1—right on.

Traditionally, the common practice was to give the catamaran an overall beam equal to about half the waterline length. The 18' 3" beam of the PDQ, measured against the 34' 4" waterline, gives it a .53 BOA/LWL ratio, just over standard. By comparison, the Lagoon 37 we previously reviewed has a 20' beam and a 33' 4" waterline for a .60 ratio. On the one hand, increased beam improves stability, permits carrying more sail area, and reduces the possibility of hull waves converging and causing interference. On the other hand, narrower cats are easier to park in marinas.

Many cats of conventional beam have full bridgedecks, meaning the deck is solid between the

The PDQ 36, thanks to the addition of scoop transoms and new window styling, is much better looking than its original configuration as a 34.

two hulls, as opposed to those with trampolines or netting across the bows (called partial bridgedecks; Hobie cats and others with no solid deck whatsoever between the hulls are called open wings).

The PDQ is therefore a partial bridgedeck design, despite its standard beam/length ratio, and this helps to save some weight.

Underwing clearance is 2', which we consider minimal, though preferable to the Prout and Packet Cat nacelle that easily immerses (the nacelle does soften the ride and add headroom above, but also increases wetted surface, hence drag). We would expect the flat underwing of the PDQ to pound somewhat in heavy seas.

Speaking of weight, the displacement/length ratio is just as informative for multihulls as it is for monohulls. The PDQ 36, which is available in three progressively heavier versions—Sports/Cruiser, Classic and LRC—comes in at 79, 88 and 96 respectively. In his book *The Cruising Multihull*, designer and author Chris White says that fast cats have D/L ratios of between 50 and 70, and slow cruisers about 100 to 120. So, the PDQ comes in probably right where it should be, on the performance side of cruising.

Like most production cats, the PDQ also has fixed keels, which are the simplest, least expensive and most foolproof way to enhance windward performance. They also don't require complicated kick-up rudders. The PDQ's keels are comparatively short, as

they should be for good maneuverability. Unfortunately, they don't provide the resistance to leeway or necessary lift for superior windward performance; you need centerboards or daggerboards for that. But with the exception of the Gemini cat, nearly all cruising cats sold in this country have fixed keels. While we understand the reasons (expense), it would be nice to have a choice.

The rig is a moderately high aspect ratio sloop intended to carry overlapping headsails. The Sports/Cruiser has a 3/4 rig on a rotating wing spar; to date none have been sold, so it appears most buyers desire the cruising convenience of the masthead rig installed in the Classic and LRC versions. (The latter stands for long-range cruiser, and features twin 18-hp. Yanmar diesel saildrives as opposed to the twin two-stroke Yamaha outboards of the Sports/Cruiser and the twin four-stroke 9.5-hp. Yamaha outboards of the Classic.)

The PDQ 36 started life as a 34-footer, with rather chopped off transoms. Before long, the hulls were extended with a far more pleasing shape incorporating molded-in stairs for easy boarding from the water or a dinghy.

All things considered, we think the PDQ represents sensible design choices. Yes, we'd like to see a bit more underwing clearance, but to achieve that, plus have adequate headroom inside, the overall profile of the boat would have to be raised to ungainly heights (bridgedeck cats already stand quite tall with enough windage as it is). We'd also like to have the option of daggerboards or centerboards, but they would add cost and complicate the interior. When we asked PDQ's John Farrow about boards, he did say the company has engineered them but so far there have been no takers. It would hike your cost, but might be worth exploring if you want to get the most out of this boat.

Construction

The PDQ 36 is built of solid fiberglass below the waterline and cored with Klegecell above the waterline and in the deck. Where deck fittings are attached, the core is omitted in favor of solid glass, which is the proper procedure. The boats are built entirely of AME 4000 modified epoxy resin. With the optional Interprotect epoxy barrier coating, the hull is guaranteed against blistering for five years; everything else is covered for one year (the Yamaha outboards carry their own two-year warranty).

In each boat there are more than more than 110 molded components tall vacuum bagged), which after bonding to the hulls and bridge, require only trimming out, making it fairly production efficient. Wood is ash, the overhead is vinyl (the panels are removable), and the cabin sole is teak and holly. A gray carpeting is used on cabin walls.

On deck, it's another matter, with no wood whatsoever. Handrails, for example, are stainless steel. This represents quite a reversal from 10-20 years ago, when everyone wanted loads of teak; today wood is regarded as too maintenance intensive; owners would rather be sailing than sanding and varnishing.

The hull and deck are sealed with 3M 5200 and through-bolted with 1/4" stainless steel machine screws.

The mast is made by Isomat with 3/8" shrouds and forestay, and twin 5/16" backstays. Due to the wide staying base, there are no spreaders. The boat we sailed was outfitted with Harken jib furling, Lewmar winches, and Spinlock XL rope clutches, all good quality.

The deck hatches are made by Lewmar. Total ventilation openings are 16. Several years ago the saloon windows (made of smoked acrylic) were redesigned, increasing visibility and for more attractive styling.

The companionway doors are also smoked acrylic, and if you are venturing offshore you should plan to either protect it or beef it up as its large area makes it vulnerable.

Tankage is 44 gallons (more on the LRC) in a narrow stainless tank under the cockpit floor. Water capacity is 50 gallons.

The forward double berths measure 58" x 77". Headroom in the hulls is 6' 7". When you enter the saloon, headroom is 6' 0", less where you sit.

Steering is push/pull cable, as on outboard boats. It is easy to route and apparently is strong enough, though pull/pull seems safer.

Quality of construction and fittings appears to be very good. We came away from our inspection with positive feelings about the boat.

Deck and Interior

Deck and interior space is what really sells cruising catamarans, and the PDQ is no exception. We like the tramp forward for lightness and lying on, but walking on them takes some getting used to. The aluminum extrusion connecting the two bows nicely handles the forestay and ground tackle systems.

The side decks are a bit narrow, and you will find yourself often going over the cabintop instead— watch out for jibes. Lifelines are 24". The cockpit is spacious of course, and the helm, as is customary, is a bulkhead-mounted wheel with padded skipper's seat. The optional dodger and Bimini combination is huge, accounting for its $3,500 price.

About our only gripe on deck is the inability to fit a boom vang due to clearance problems.

Below, the accommodation plan speaks for itself. The two double-berth cabins forward are commodious; a reviewer from another magazine noted that some extra sound insulation could be used on the separating bulkhead. There is a generous nav station and the galley has plenty of counter space.

The aft port stateroom can be configured several ways, as an office, day room or sleeping cabin.

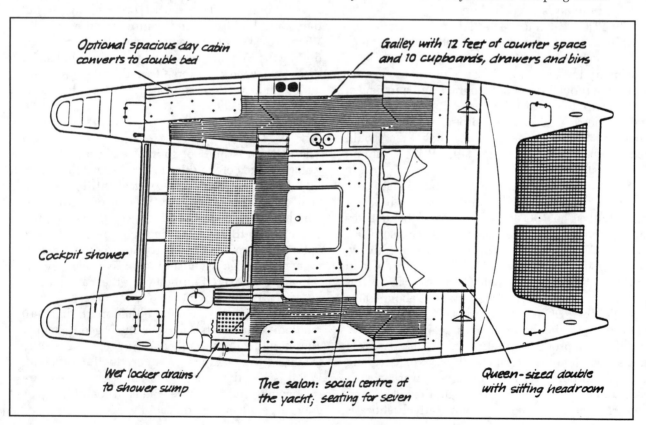

Optional spacious day cabin converts to double bed

Galley with 12 feet of counter space and 10 cupboards, drawers and bins

Cockpit shower

Wet locker drains to shower sump

The salon: social centre of the yacht; seating for seven

Queen-sized double with sitting headroom

Performance

The sailing speed of the PDQ 36, like all multihulls, depends a great deal on how heavily it is loaded. Clearly the 7,200-pound Sport/Cruiser will outperform the 8,700-pound LRC. And the family who can limit stores to 500 pounds will sail faster than those adding 1,500 pounds. Which means that if you can resist the temptation to add a genset, air conditioning, windlass, excess tools and entertainment, you'll not only make faster passages, but ride higher and pound less.

That said, we think the PDQ is basically a 7-10-knot boat, with speeds in the teens possible in higher winds with a gutsy skipper. PDQ literature states that sailing speeds will be "25-50% higher than a monohull of equivalent length." This fits in well with our experience; where you might have made 6 knots in your Islander 36, you'll now go 7-1/2 to 9 knots.

The boat points reasonably well, given the absence of deep daggerboards, tacking most comfortably through about 100 degrees (multihulls generally are not able to strut their stuff until the sheets are eased for reaching).

Conclusion

If you are looking for a production cruising catamaran in this size range, what are your choices? Let's see: There is the Packet Cat 35, Jeanneau Lagoon 3 7, Tobago 35 by Fountaine Pajot, and several from Prout—the Event 34 and Snowgoose 37. Because looks count for a lot, especially among cruising cats where it's easy to be ugly, we immediately discount the Prouts for what we perceive as clunky styling as well as an odd rig with tiny mainsail (granted, these are personal feelings).

The Tobago 35 looks sporty and it is priced a bit below the PDQ 36. But we have some doubts about construction as well as the large-roach mainsail that does not allow a backstay. The Packet Cat 35 seems well built, but it's just too heavy for us; perhaps when we retire we could live with it. That leaves the Lagoon 37 and the PDQ 36.

We like them both. The Lagoon 37, though with the same approximate waterline, displaces nearly 12.000 pounds and carries 839 square feet of sail versus 8,000 pounds and 532 square feet for the PDQ Classic. It sells for about $35,000 more, so we're not really comparing equal boats.

While the Gemini 3200 probably represents the best value in small cruising cats (about $85,000; it's one of the few cats that's been around long enough to find used—you can pick up a 10-year-old Gemini in the $50s), the PDQ is certainly a viable next step up. Quite a bit more money at $165,000, to be sure, but sound construction, good looks, and performance that should satisfy monohull converts. **• PS**

Tayana 37 Cutter

This product of the Far East would make a good choice for the retired couple who want to travel.

With several hundred boats sailing the seas of the world, the Tayana 37 has been one of the most successful products of the Taiwan-built boat invasion of the US that began in the early 1970s. Her shapely Baltic stern, scribed plank seams molded into the glass hull, and lavish use of teak above and below decks have come to epitomize the image that immediately comes to mind when Oriental boats are mentioned.

Not all thoughts of Far Eastern boats are pleasant, however. To some, Taiwan-built boats mean poor workmanship, overly heavy hulls, unbedded hardware of dubious heritage, wooden spars that delaminate, and builder-modified boats light years removed from the plans provided by the designer. Add to that a serious language barrier and the inevitable logistical problems of dealing with a boatyard halfway round the world, and you have a situation ready-made to generate potential nightmares for the boat buyer. To the credit of the builder, the designer, the primary importer, and a powerful owners' association, the Tayana 37 weathered an astounding sixteen years of production—a lifetime in the world of boatbuilding—while making steady improvements and maintaining a steady output of over 50 boats per year.

Washington-based designer Bob Perry had just hung out his own shingle when the Tayana 37 was designed in the early 70s. The Sherman tank Westsail 32 had just come lumbering onto the scene, bringing with it a resurgence of interest in the double ended hull form, and more people than ever before were beginning to have the dream of chucking it all and sailing away to a tropical paradise.

Bob Perry has become an enormously successful designer of cruising boats, from traditional full keel designs such as the Tayana 37, to modern fin keel

Specifications

LOA	36' 8"
LWL	31' 10"
Beam	11' 6"
Draft	5' 8"
Displacement	24,000 lbs.
Ballast	7,340 lbs.
Sail area	864 sq. ft.

cruisers such as the Nordic 40, Golden Wave 42, and the Valiant 40. A remarkable number of his designs have been built in the Orient, in both Hong Kong and Taiwan.

Perry conceived the Tayana 37 as a cruising boat of traditional appearance above the water, with moderately heavy displacement, a long waterline, and a reasonably efficient cutter rig of modern proportions. (A ketch rig is also available). Below the water, the forefoot of the long keel has been cut away, and a Constellation-type rudder utilized rather than a more traditional barn door. Perry sought to cash in on the popularity of the double ended hull while keeping displacement moderate and performance reasonable, avoiding the plight of boats such as the Westsail 32—the inability to go to windward, and sluggish performance in anything short of a moderate gale. The stern design of the Tayana 37 borrows heavily from the well known Aage Neilsen designed ketch Holger Danske, winner of the 1980 Bermuda Race. It is one of the more handsome Baltic-type sterns on any production sailboat.

The Tayana 37 began life as the CT 37. In 1979 the boat became known as the Tayana 37, named for Ta Yang Yacht Building Company. While some snobbishness exists among some owners who own the CT version, Perry insists that this is illusory. According to the designer, the CT 37 and the Tayana 37 are the same boat, built by the same men in the same yard. In much the same way that the early Swans imported by Palmer Johnson were known by the name of the importer—the names Nautor and Swan were unknown here in the late 1960s—early Tayanas were known as CTs because the name CT had already become known in this country.

Perry, who has worked with many yards in the Far East, considers Ta Yang one of the best. The yard has been very responsive to input from both dealers and owners. Over the years the Tayana 37 has been in production, this has resulted in steady improvement in the quality of the boat.

The vast majority of Tayanas now imported into this country are brought in by Southern Offshore Yachts, which has offices in eastern Canada, Rhode Island, Maryland, and both coasts of Florida. By working closely with the builder and maintaining good contact with the owners' association, Southern Offshore has had significant input into improving the quality of the boats.

Owners report that Southern Offshore has been very responsive to handling warranty problems. The same cannot be said for all Tayana dealers. One west coast Tayana 37 owner responding to our owner survey reported that "basically, the dealer treated us like second-rate citizens." A similar comment was voiced by a midwestern owner.

Construction

The hull of the Tayana 37 is a fairly heavy solid glass layup. Some roving printthrough is evident in the topsides. The hull-to-deck joint has in the past occasionally been a problem with the boat. There is no doubt it is strong, but there have been numerous reports of leaking.

Part of the problem with the hull-to-deck joint is the fact that the hull and deck moldings form a hollow bulwark extending well above the main deck level. This bulwark is pierced by hawsepipes and several large scuppers at deck level. Careful bedding of all fittings that penetrate the bulwarks is essential to avoid leaks. On new boats, the entire hollow bulwark is glassed over from inside the hull, greatly reducing the possibility of leaks. This results in an incredibly labor intensive joint, but labor intensive is the name of the game in Taiwanese boatbuilding.

None of the numerous through hull fittings is recessed flush with the exterior of the hull. The argument is frequently made that this is unnecessary on cruising boats. Nothing could be further from the truth. The cruising boat is frequently undercanvassed for her displacement and wetted surface. Add to this the low speed drag associated with projections from the hull, and you have a boat that spends a lot of time motoring in light air, when she should be sailing. While the Tayana 37 is far from undercanvassed, she could benefit from a little more bottom fairing as much as the next boat. An option to recessing the through hull fittings would be to fair them in with large microballoon blisters—not as effective as recessing, but perhaps easier to do after the fact.

The rudder stock is a substantial stainless steel rod, with the rudder held on by welded arms riveted through the rudder blade. The heel fitting is a bronze casting. This is fastened to the hull with stainless steel bolts. Inevitably, there will be galvanic action between the bronze and the stainless, with the fastenings coming out on the short end. There is provision for protection of the rudder straps with zincs.

All hardware, including cleats and stanchions, is through-bolted and backed with stainless steel pads. Most hardware is fairly accessible from belowdecks.

The ballast keel is an iron casting dropped into the hollow fiberglass keel shell. The casting is glassed over on the inside of the boat. We prefer an external lead keel for its shock absorbing qualities in case of grounding.

The glasswork of the Tayana 37 is of good quality. There are no rough edges, the fillet bonding is neat, and there is no glass or resin slopped about. Tayana warrants the hull against defects for ten years.

Until recently, the standard steering system was a Taiwanese worm gear system copied from the Edson worm gear. Recurrent problems with this system, notably extremely sloppy and mushy steering, have resulted in significant changes. The standard system is now a pedestal system Taiwanese-built but remarkably similar to the Edson pedestal steerer.

Seacocks are used on all through hull fittings. The seacocks appear to be copies of US-made Groco valves. Hoses to seacocks are all double clamped.

Handling Under Power

Three different engines have been used in the Tayana 37: the Yanmar 3QM30, the Perkins 4-108, and the Volvo MD17C. The standard engine is now the Yanmar. This makes good economic sense, as Japan is rather closer to Taiwan than either England or Sweden. Both the Volvo and Perkins are still available as options. We see no reason to choose either engine over the Yanmar.

While the engine box removes completely to provide good access for service, there is no provision for easy access to the oil dipstick. This means that this vital task is likely to be ignored. A simple door in the side of the engine box would solve the problem.

The placement of the fuel tank has caused substantial discussion on the part of owners. The standard 90 gallon black iron tank is located under the V-berth in the forward cabin. When full, this tank holds almost 650 pounds of fuel. This is about the same weight as 375 feet of 3/8" chain—a substantial amount to carry around in the bow of a 37-footer. A Tayana 37 with the bow tank full and a heavy load of ground tackle will show noticeable bow down trim. The design was originally drawn with the fuel tanks under the settees, but the builder put the tank forward to create additional storage in the main cabin.

This is a good example of one of the basic recurring problems with Far East built boats. Frequently the builders have good glass men and good inside joiners, but their inexperience in sailing results in inconsistencies which compromise their boats.

Fortunately, thanks to the pressure from owners, the builder offers optional tankage amidships, where it belongs. By all means select this tankage option so that the fore and aft trim of the boat will remain unchanged as fuel is consumed.

Although any of the engines is adequate power for the boat, don't expect the Tayana 37 to win any drag races. With her substantial wetted surface and fairly heavy displacement, performance under power is sedate rather than spritely. Owners report handling under power fair to good, although one reported that his boat "backs up like a drunken elephant."

Handling Under Sail

The Tayana 37 comes as a ketch or cutter, with wood spars or aluminum, with mast stepped on deck or on the keel. Few builders offer you so many options.

The standard rig is a masthead cutter with wooden spars, the mast stepped on deck and supported by a substantial compression column. The designer strongly recommends the aluminum cutter rig, and we heartily concur. The wooden mast is poorly proportioned, with a massive section and extremely thick side walls. One new mast we looked at had a large knot on the forward side of the mast just at spreader level. Despite the huge mast section, we feel the knot could weaken the mast significantly.

In contrast to the large section of the mast, the boom is an extremely small spruce box section. With mid-boom sheeting, this spar will probably be about as stiff as a rubber band, complicating mainsail shape. The clew outhaul slide is far too flimsy for a boat of this size, and owners report that the outhaul slide frequently distorts or explodes. Once again, these problems are not atypical in Taiwan boats, where you frequently find excellent craftsmanship but a poor understanding of engineering or the forces involved in ocean sailing.

In contrast, the aluminum rigs, which may come from a variety of sources including France, New Zealand, and the US, are well proportioned and suited to the task.

We see no reason to select the ketch rig. Both performance and balance with the cutter rig will be better. The cutter's mainsail is 342 square feet. Any couple healthy enough to go world cruising should be able to cope with a sail of this size.

The cutter rig is tall and well proportioned. Perry has drawn an unusually high aspect rig for a cruising boat, and the result is a boat with good performance on all points of sail. With the aluminum rig, the optional Nicro Fico ball bearing mainsheet traveler, and a well cut suit of sails, the Tayana 37 will be surprisingly fast. Her working sail area of 864 square feet is generous.

This "standard" interior arrangement is unlikely to reflect any given Tayana 37. The builder offers custom interiors at no extra charge, and nearly all owners have taken advantage of the opportunity.

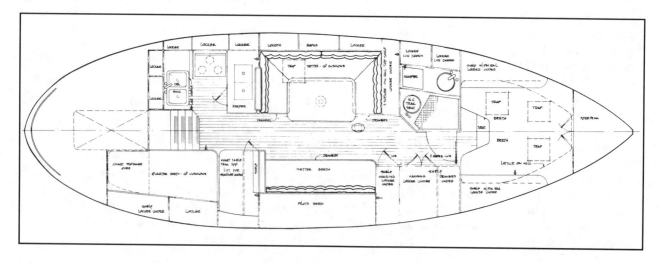

Despite a ballast/displacement ratio of 33 percent, the Tayana 37 is not a stiff boat. This is due in part to the tall, heavy rig and the substantial amount of other weight above the boat's vertical center of gravity. Much of the boat's heavy joinerwork and glass work is well above the waterline, raising the center of gravity and reducing initial stability. Perry believes the initial tenderness to be an asset, reducing the snappiness of the boat's roll and making her a more comfortable sea boat. We agree.

Many owners report that the boat carries substantial weather helm. The sail plan is drawn with significant rake to the mast. This creates just enough shift in the center of effort of the sail plan to create a lot of weather helm. Bringing the mast back toward the vertical by tightening the headstay and forestay while loosening the backstay should cure much of the problem, according to reports from other owners. It may be necessary to shorten the headstay to do this.

The weather helm and initial tenderness may also be due in part to the poor cut of the standard sails provided with the boat. For years, the standard sails have been made by Lam of Hong Kong. The sails have the reputation of being stretchy and having very poor shape. Mainsail draft with this fabric is almost uncontrollable, with the sail becoming baggy and the draft moving aft as the wind increases. This will create weather helm and increase the angle of heel.

Deck Layout

With her bulwarks, high double lifelines, and substantial bow and stern pulpits, the Tayana 37 gives the sailor a good sense of security on those cold, windy nights when he's called out for sail changes. A teak platform grating atop the bowsprit coupled with the strong pulpit relieves that appendage of its widowmaker reputation.

The bowsprit platform incorporates double anchor rollers which will house CQR anchors. Unfortunately, there is no good lead from the rollers to any place to secure the anchor rode. Line or chain led to the heavy bowsprit bitts would chafe on the platform, An anchor windlass mounted to port or starboard of the bowsprit would provide a good lead, and is an available option.

There are hawsepipes through the bulwarks port and starboard well aft of the stem. These will be fine for dock lines, but are too far aft to serve as good leads for anchoring. There is room at deck level outboard of the bowsprit to install a set of heavy chocks for anchoring, although anchor rode led to this point will chafe on the bobstay as the boat swings to her anchor.

This is a classic problem of the boat with bowsprit. The anchor rode must really lead well out the bowsprit to avoid the bobstay, yet the long lead complicates securing the inboard end of the rode.

The long staysail boom makes it difficult to cross from one side of the boat to the other forward. The standard staysail traveler is merely a stainless steel rod on which a block can slide on its shackle. Under load, this can bind when tacking, so that it may be necessary to go forward and kick the block over after every tack. By all means look for the optional Nicro Fico travelers with their roller bearing cars. Complaints about the standard travelers are rife. Stan-

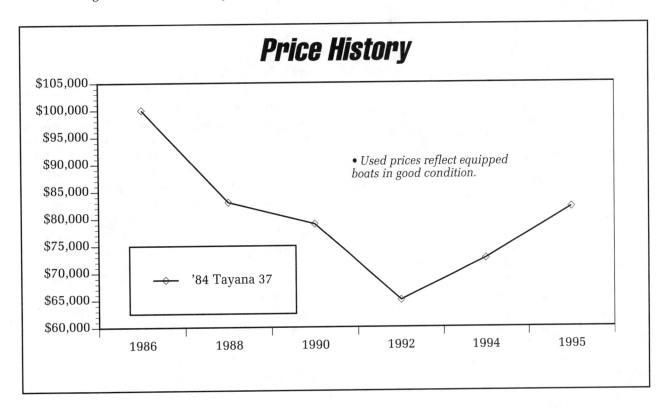

Price History

• *Used prices reflect equipped boats in good condition.*

◇ '84 Tayana 37

dard winches on the boat are Barlow. We suggest that you try to find self-tailing winches for all sheets.

Although the side decks are relatively narrow due to the wide cabin trunk, there is reasonable access fore and aft. A full length hand rail on either side of the cabin trunk provides a good handhold.

The cockpit of the Tayana 37 is small, as befits an oceangoing sailboat. There are cockpit scuppers at each of the four corners of the cockpit well, with seacocks on the through hull outlets.

With the now-standard pedestal steering, the cockpit seems to have shrunk. Only three can be seated in real comfort, although this is no real problem for the cruising couple. It is not a cockpit for heavy entertaining in port. The elimination of the coaming around the stern of the boat has made the cockpit seats long enough for sleeping on deck, but at the expense of exposing the helmsman to a wet seat in a following sea. The coaming can optionally be continued around the rear of the cockpit. Cockpit locker configuration varies with the interior options chosen, but the lockers are large enough to provide reasonable storage, although you should resist the temptation to load them heavily so far aft.

Belowdecks

The interior of the Tayana 37 probably sells more boats than any other feature of the boat. There is not really a standard interior. Every boat that comes through is custom built, and almost every owner takes advantage of the opportunity to create an interior suited to his or her own needs.

The cost of producing these interiors is not prohibitive. Interior joinerwork is labor intensive, but labor in the Orient is still far cheaper than it is here.

Like other Taiwanese boats, the interior of the Tayana 37 is all teak. This results in an interior that can be oppressively dark to some people, exquisitely cool to others. To keep it looking good, someone is going to have to do a lot of oiling or varnishing.

The interior joinerwork is some of the best we have seen on any boat, whether it is built in the US, Taiwan, or Finland. Joints were just about flawless, paneled doors beautifully joined, drawers dovetailed from solid stock. There were no fillers making up for poorly fitted joints, no trim fitted with grinders, no slop anywhere. The men who put the interior in the new boat we examined were real craftsmen. Older boats we have looked at did not boast quite this caliber of workmanship, but their joinerwork was certainly of good quality.

With such an array of interior options it is difficult to really evaluate the boat's interior. Naturally, if you're considering a used Tayana, you're stuck with whatever the original buyer had installed. However, if you're thinking of ordering a new boat, the choices are wide open.

This may be a mixed blessing to the buyer. For the couple who have owned other boats, have kept copious notes about what they want and don't want in their next boat, and who are experienced, well read, and knowledgeable, the ability to plan their own interior offers an opportunity that is probably unequaled in a boat in this price range.

If you have only vague ideas of what you want in the interior of a cruising boat, one of the real advantages of owning the Tayana 37 may be lost. Do you want a pilot berth or storage? Drawers or bins? Propane or kerosene for cooking? Quarterberth or wet locker? Fold up or drop leaf table? To the inexperienced, the choices may be bewildering. To those who know what they want, the opportunity is a gold mine.

In all fairness, there is a "standard" interior. It is prosaic but good, with V-berth forward, followed by head and lockers just aft. The main cabin has a U-shaped settee to port, straight settee and pilot berth to starboard. Aft is a good U-shaped galley to port, nav station and quarterberth to starboard. For not much more money, you can have pretty much what you want, from a "standard" array of interior options to a fully custom interior. You're missing a good bet if you don't spend some time creating your own dream interior.

Conclusions

The Tayana 37 is both typical and atypical of Taiwanese boats, She is typical in the problems that existed due to the builder's inexperience with seagoing yachts, typical with communication and language problems.

She is atypical in that many of these problems have been solved over many years of production, in that a good owners' association has resulted in real improvements in the boat. Anyone considering a Tayana 37 should join the owners' association and read all the back newsletters before buying the boat.

Because of the myriad options, we don't really suggest a new Tayana 37 as a first boat. Between pilot house and trunk cabin versions, ketch and cutter, and the incredible array of interior options, the first time boatowner would have a great deal of difficulty coming up with just the right boat.

The total cost of a well-equipped Tayana 37 with most of the desirable options compares very favorably with other boats of her size, type, and displacement.

The Tayana 37 would make an excellent retirement cruiser for the experienced sailing couple. Properly handled and equipped, she could take you anywhere with confidence and reasonable dispatch. If you want to design your own interior and are willing to wait for your boat to be built, she just may be the right boat for you. • **PS**

Jeanneau Lagoon 37

Built by TPI forthe giant French builder Jeanneau, this cat is fast, roomy and pricey.

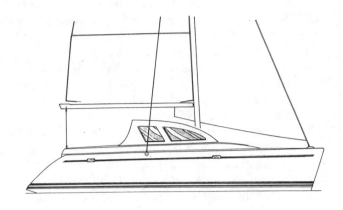

Jeanneau's Lagoon 37 catamaran, launched last December, is the second cruising catamaran produced as part of a joint venture between the French firm and TPI of Warren, Rhode Island. (As a side note, TPI is the new name of Tillotson-Pearson Industries, following Tillotson's sale of his share to John Walton, owner of Corsair Marine. Walton, who builds the F-24 and F-27 trailerable trimarans, is a member of the family that owns WalMart department stores). The venture was intended to give Jeanneau a foothold in the American market without building its own plant, as arch rival Beneteau did several years back. The first fruit of the collaboration was the Lagoon 42, introduced two years ago and named "Boat of the Year" at the next Annapolis Boat Show. However, the 42 proved too big and too expensive to interest individual buyers, and those built to date have either been acquired by charter fleets or shipped back to France for sale. Not so with the 37. Of the 16 sold in the first two months, more than half are going to individuals.

The Boat

As designed by Marc Van Peteghem and Vincent Lauriot-Prevost, best known for their Route du Rhum-style racing multihulls, the Lagoon 37 is a refined, down-sized version of the 42. This is a fairly light but stable cat aimed at the cruising sailor rather than the adventurer.

In appearance, the 37 like its bigger cousin, is sleeker and sportier than many of the lumbering cruising "cats" that have come onto the market in recent years. At 36' 9" length overall, the boat carries a generous beam of 20 feet. Because the height from the waterline to the top of the coach roof is only 8' 9", the squat look is avoided. The scoop-shaped cabintop adds to the dynamic look. In short, the 37 looks like

Specifications

LOA	36' 9"
LWL	34' 1"
Beam	20' 0"
Draft	4' 0"
Displacement	11,833 lbs.
Sail area	835 sq. ft.

a boat instead of a boat-shaped condominium.

The deck-stepped mast from Sparcraft is white-painted aluminum supported by a forestay, two cap shrouds and tri-diamond innerstays to hold it in column. The backstay was eliminated to permit use of a big-roach main of 473 square feet. The overlapping jib (120 percent) is tacked manually, unlike on the 42. Shore Sails has been making most of the sails for the Lagoon, which are optional. Engine power comes from twin Perkins 20-hp. freshwater-cooled diesels.

Construction

Hull construction is typical TPI, consisting of hand-laid fiberglass over a balsa core, the core ranging from 3/4 inches to as much as 1-inch thick in the mast area. The skin coat is vinylester resin for protection against osmotic blistering, and the Lagoon, like most TPI products (J Boats, Alerion Express, Sundeer, etc.), comes with a 10-year blister guarantee. The twin keels, which have 4 feet of draft, measure about 8 feet fore and aft (with a rake on the leading edge) and are molded in as part of the hull. Also molded in are the stern boarding steps.

The hull-deck joint, as is becoming the norm on other TPI boats, is connected by urethane glue, with additional stainless steel bolts fastened at the stanchions and cleats. We heard of one instance in which the hull-deck joint on one of the 42s opened under enough heavy pounding to create "a pretty good leak" in one of the amas. When we asked TPI's Phil Mosher about it, he said there was no glue in that area and that it was quickly fixed. Mosher further believes that his patented glue joint is superior to caulked and through-bolted joints, and simpler for the builder than fiberglassing over the joint.

Hardware, as expected on a Tillotson-Pearson, is of high quality: Harken traveler, five Lewmar self-tailing winches (30s for the jib lines, 40 for the main), Schaefer fair leads, Spinlock clutches. Hatches and ports are Lewmar; there are 12 opening hatches for ventilation, six opening ports. The large smoked windows that light the saloon are made at the Warren plant of 1/2-inch acrylic.

Performance

We sailed hull #1 on a brisk December day shortly after its launching. On the docks, the wind was just a whisper—not enough to consider taking the average monohull cruiser out for a spin. Once on the open waters of Narragansett Bay, however, the cat seemed to create, as mulithull enthusiasts like to say, its own wind. There were no speed indicators to refer to, but the 37 seemed to be doing 6 or 7 knots, fast enough to catch a tug and its tow (okay, it was slowing for a turn).

According to Chris Bjerregaard, a TPI engineer, the boat should do 8-9 knots in 15 knots of wind, 10 or 11 when the water is flat. Our water was flat and the cat skimmed along as though on a pond, gliding easily over the mild wake kicked up by the tug. Ted Genard of Hellier Yacht Sales of New London, Connecticut, had been out two weeks earlier in snow squalls and winds gusting to more than 25 knots, and reported a smooth ride at 10 knots with less than five degrees of heel.

The 37's steering mechanism incorporates two tillers connected to a crossbar that passes inside the bridgedeck and is hooked by cables to the wheel. All cables run at 90-degree angles for purely linear motion. The system is designed to minimize friction, and the helm in fact is light, almost like power steering. On calm waters, the boat tacked neatly, recovering easily.

No matter what the multihull people say, few cats can sail as close to the wind as a hotshot monohull, although the speed they gain by cracking off a few degrees will often as not negate the difference. The problem usually is in the shallow stub keels, common to many production cats. The 4-foot draft of the keels on the 37 give a measure of lift but not as much as a deeper centerboard would provide. Bjerregaard put it this way: "The 37 will sail upwind with any monohull of 4-foot draft, but there aren't any (of that size)." Deepen the draft, and you'll get better windward performance, he said.

For comparison, the PDQ 36 cat draws just 2' 10", and the 37-foot Antigua by Fountaine Pajot draws 3' 6". Few production catamaran builders use centerboards, presumably due to higher costs and the usual maintenance difficulties. An exception is the Gemini 3200, which, in our experience, profits greatly from its centerboards.

The shallow underbody and comparatively light displacement of the Lagoon 37, or any cat, also make it difficult to slow in heavy air, or heave to. Multihull sailors often deploy parachute anchors tied to a bridle off the bows. One of two Lagoon 42s caught in heavy winds en route to the Caribbean last winter, reportedly tried an alternative measure, trailing its bimini as a drogue to reduce speed (see sidebar).

We can't testify to the 37's heavy-air capabilities, but we can make some educated guesses. It was hull #1 that was abandoned by its delivery crew less than two weeks after our test sail. Although the cockpit is high and dry under light to moderate conditions, one (French) delivery skipper we talked to said cat sailors get used to sailing underwater when the seas rise up and the bows dig in.

We also talked to a passenger on one of the 42s that got caught in 30-plus knots of wind and 8-foot seas during an offshore passage. Beating under a single reef, the boat began hobbyhorsing as the seas grew to more than 5 feet, the leeward bow plunging into the waves and the windward lifting out on occasion. Although he never felt the boat was out of control, the motion was uncomfortable and all on board were seasick. The ride was wet as well, with periodic waves washing the deck. At one point, he said, "there were fish in the cockpit." The bows also tended to labor underwater, possibly because of a tight weave on the forward 6' x 10' trampoline. Bjerregaard said that shouldn't be a problem, but in any event the builder has switched to a looser, 1-1/2-inch weave.

There's nothing like a rough passage to point out shortcomings that escape notice on a calm day. The 37 offers wide sidedecks and comes equipped with double lifelines, but there is a lack of handholds—no problem on light-air days but a worry when you must go forward under adverse conditions.

Minor points: The main halyard, which is led internally and has 2:1 purchase, according to the manufacturer, still took much hauling even with the #40 winch. Presumably, this will become somewhat easier as the sail slides wear.

Jib sheets also tended to hang up during tacking on the earliest 37s, primarily because the winches were angled forward on pads. On new models, the winches have been squared away to the mast.

Under engine power, the 37, like all non-displacement boats, moved smoothly with none of the laboring familiar to monohulls. Cynics might say you need the engines just to tack one of these cats, but that was not the case on our sail. Of course, the drawback of two hulls is the need for two engines—double the trouble. The Lagoon has 52 gallons of fuel capacity.

Accommodations

One of the attractions of a true cruising catamaran is the incredible amount of interior space you get for the length. The 37 has a large, open saloon whose ports offer a 360-degree view as well as lots of light. A semi-circular bench behind a good-sized convertible table looks aft to the cockpit through a folding smoked-acrylic door. The bench, which seats eight according to promotional material, is cushioned with a backrest and can be converted to an extra bunk. The saloon interior is finished with light-colored laminates with teak trim.

The standard interior offers three double sleeping cabins, two with queen-size berths at the forward end of each hull or ama, and a double-size berth aft. The separate hulls, which offer a sense of privacy

rarely found on monohulls this size, are three steps down from the saloon and offer 6' 3" headroom wherever a person is likely to stand. Cabins are well lit from a variety of portlights, including low-level ports in the bows. Ventilation via the ports and opening hatches seems adequate. There's plenty of stowage space, including hanging lockers in each cabin.

The starboard passageway contains a pilot berth/storage area across from a fold-down nav table and station, including electrical panels. The standard setup on the 37 has four 12-volt batteries and includes two electric bilge pumps in addition to two manual pumps operated from on deck. The prototype boat we looked at was equipped with an optional walk-through head between the nav area and the forward cabin.

To port, you step down into a sizable galley area that offers lots of counter space and stowage, double sink, freezer/refrigerator, which can be either electri-

---

Smaller catamarans are rather cramped inside, but given the size of the Lagoon 37 there's space to spare, much more than in a monohull of similar size. The separate hulls lend a high degree of privacy, as well.

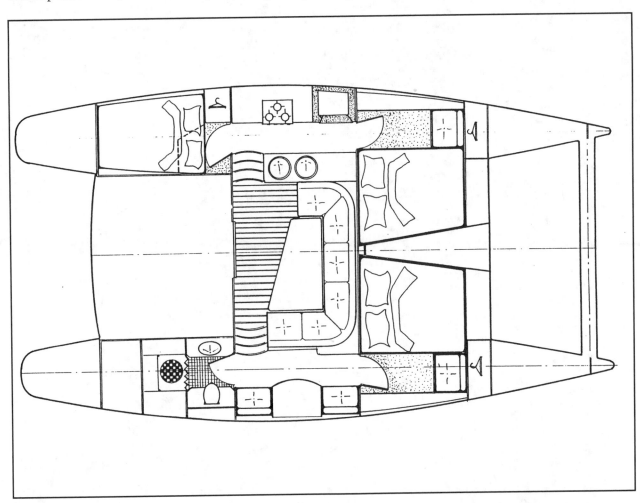

cal or mechanical, and a three-burner Force 10 stove. Aft to starboard is a roomy main head with shower stall. This compartment, like the portside sleeping cabin, provides access to the engines. The color scheme throughout is white or near-white, offset by green bands around the ports and green cushions (and countertops in the galley). A padded headliner is standard; where we saw the bare hull it was well-finished.

The cockpit, intended to serve as an extension of the saloon in temperate weather, is commodious and features two tables that fold to make one larger table. The two-person helm has a padded bench. There's a big anchor locker and seven storage lockers, accessible from the deck. The transom also sports a folding swim ladder. Overall, given the size of the platform and the cockpit, there's plenty of room for five or six people without any need for shifting or scrambling to get out of each other's way.

Conclusions

With the Lagoon 37, Jeanneau has brought its catamaran line within useful range for the individual owner. This is a good-looking boat with seemingly excellent performance capability in light to moderate wind speeds. For those who like to cruise with company or do a lot of entertaining, underway or at the dock, the Lagoon provides plenty of space to socialize or make yourself scarce. Lots of initial stability and lack of heeling under most conditions also make it an attractive option for those who prefer to stay comfortable and dry, rather than experience the traditional sailing experience complete with salt spray in the face.

At a 1993 price of $199,500 plus sails, the 37 isn't cheap (The Fountaine Pajot Antigua 37, for example, has been selling for about $177,000; the PDQ 36 is in the same ballpark.) Still, we'd recommend that those seeking similar accommodations on a monohull, and who do most of their cruising in milder weather and waters, at least check it out. For those who intend to spend a lot of time sailing to windward in coastal or offshore waters, where the winds and waves tend to kick up, a monohull probably remains the better choice. Obviously there's a market out there for the 37; with just four in the water by early 1993, Jeanneau North America and TPI had received orders for 12 more.   • **PS**

Crealock 37

A conservative boat that is sold as a "go-anywhere" yacht—and it is, in both design and construction.

The Crealock 37 is the largest boat built by Pacific Seacraft, a California company that has carved a comfortable and ever-growing niche in the boat market by specializing in smaller, high-quality cruising boats. Pacific Seacraft boats could be termed "modern traditional," with pronounced sheerlines, traditional bronze hardware, moderate displacement, and conservative modern underbodies.

This boat was first built by Cruising Consultants, a short-lived California company that built 16 Crealock 37s in 1978 and 1979. In 1980, Pacific Seacraft acquired the tooling.

There's no way around it. To someone who appreciates a traditional-looking boat, the Crealock 37 is about as pretty as they get. The canoe stern isn't for everyone, but Bill Crealock draws it perfectly, in a way that both Will Fife, Jr, and L. Francis Herreshoff would have appreciated.

Because freeboard is fairly low, the cabin trunk must be quite tall to give good headroom below. Its height is somewhat disguised by low bulwarks and teak eyebrow trim dropped down below the actual top of the cabin trunk.

The Crealock 37 was conceived and marketed as a go-anywhere boat, and in both design and construction it fits the bill. That's not to say it's perfect—no boat is.

Hull and Deck

This is a conservative boat, devoid of construction razzmatazz. The hull is an uncored, solid laminate. For those living in colder climates and wanting more insulation, the boat can be built with either foam or balsa core, but these are added to the normal hull layup, resulting in a somewhat heavier boat with slightly reduced interior volume.

Specifications

LOA	36' 11"
LWL	27' 9"
Beam	10' 10"
Draft	4' 5"/5' 6" (Scheel/std)
Displacement	16,000 lbs.
Ballast	6,200 lbs.
Sail area	619 sq. ft.

Longitudinal and transverse stiffness are provided by a full-length molded liner which contains recesses for bulkheads, floors, major furniture components, engine beds, and water tanks. A liner like this can be a mixed blessing. If properly designed and installed, it adds considerable rigidity to the hull structure, and greatly speeds assembly of the boat's interior. Poorly designed or improperly installed, liners can inadequately support the thin outer skin of the boat.

In the Crealock 37, numerous openings in the liner allow it to be securely glassed to the hull, using resin and fiberglass fabric. This is the way it should be done.

Hull liners are not without disadvantages. They constrain the interior layout to that defined by the liner, and they can make later installation of additions to the wiring and plumbing systems difficult.

One unusual feature of the Crealock 37's construction is that the water tanks are an integral part of the hull liner. The sides, ends, and bottom of the tanks are molded. The tops of the tanks are Formica-faced plywood. This is a reasonable way to do the job. We would not recommend using the inside of the hull itself as part of the tank, since this could aggravate a hull's tendency to blister.

The main structural bulkhead at the forward end of the main cabin is both glassed and bolted in place. Since the bulkhead and compression post must absorb the load of the deck-stepped mast, this belt-and-braces attachment is a good idea. Below the hull liner, mast compression is transferred to the hull via a glass-filled PVC pipe. This is a reasonable installation, and we have never seen signs of excess compression loading on a Crealock 37's deck.

Chainplates are stainless steel straps bolted through the topsides. This is a simple, strong, leak-proof installation. But aesthetically, it breaks up the clean flow of the sheerline, and we have seen chainplates like this bleed brown oxidation down the topsides after lengthy ocean passages. Functionally it means the shroud base is a bit wider than necessary, slightly constraining upwind performance.

Hardware and its installation are first-rate. Most of the deck hardware is bronze, and it is both well designed and well finished. Since Pacific Seacraft recently changed porthole suppliers, the familiar trademark oval ports have been replaced with more rectangular models. We think the oval ones look better, but according to the builder, the new ones seal better and have an improved spigot design.

Hull and deck are joined together at the bulwarks. At the top of the bulwarks, there is an inward-turning hull flange. On the deck, the edge of the molding turns upward to form the inner bulwark face, then outward at the top to overlap the hull flange. The joint is bedded in polyurethane sealant and through-bolted. The top of the bulwark is covered with a teak cap. You can't fault this type of joint.

All through hull openings are equipped with either ball valves or tapered-plug seacocks, with the fittings bolted through the hull. This is the right way to do it, but it makes it difficult to use flush skin fittings.

Fiberglass work is excellent. Even on dark-colored hulls, there is no roving print-through, and there are no visible hard spots in the topsides. We have found minor gelcoat cracks around the mainsheet traveler supports, but these may well result from pulling the deck from the mold, rather than from stress on the traveler itself.

Decks are cored with plywood, rather than the more commonly used end-grain balsa. A balsa cored deck is both stiffer and lighter than a plywood cored deck, but you have to put plywood or glass inserts in the balsa deck under heavily-loaded hardware.

The keel is an external lead casting, bolted to the hull with stainless steel bolts. A conventional low-aspect fin keel is standard, but many owners choose the shoal draft Scheel keel.

Rig

The mast is built by LeFiell. It is untapered, and is normally supplied with external halyards. Internal halyards are optional, and while unnecessary on a cruising boat, they do reduce windage and neaten things up around the mast.

Halyard winches are Lewmar 16 self-tailers. At least one of the winches should be upgraded in size so that the smallest member of the crew can hoist the largest member to the masthead if necessary.

The mast and boom are painted. Painted spars look great when they're new, but they tend to get a little bedraggled after a few years of cruising. Anodized spars aren't as pretty, but they usually hold up better over time.

The rig is simple and straightforward, rugged and functional. It's not what you'd put on a racing boat, but it won't fall down in heavy weather, either.

Engine and Mechanical Systems

Over the years, Pacific Seacraft has used both Universal and Yanmar diesels in the Crealock 37. The engine currently used is a four cylinder, 100 cubic inch Yanmar 4JHE, normally aspirated. This is about the ideal size engine for the boat, and it's a very good installation.

A hinged panel lets you lift up the top of the engine box for quick access. You must remove the companionway ladder to get at the front of the engine, which you'd need to do to change the water pump impeller or alternator belt. A removable panel in the quarterberth gives access to the left side of the engine, as well as to the stuffing box. The engine compartment itself is properly sound insulated.

Two 120 amp-hour batteries are standard. The 55-amp alternator supplied is just barely adequate for the standard batteries. If you want more electrical storage capacity, you'll also need to upgrade the alternator.

Wiring and plumbing are neat and workmanlike. Surprisingly, however, some components of the electrical and plumbing systems that should be standard on a boat of this quality, like lightning grounding, hot and cold pressure water, and an electric bilge pump, are options.

Handling Under Sail

You can have the Crealock 37 rigged as a sloop, cutter, or yawl. A divided rig offers no advantages on a boat this size. A double headsail rig is highly desirable, particularly if you use a headsail roller reefing system, since it allows you to hank on a heavy weather staysail without having to remove the genoa from the furling headstay.

The optional cutter rig adds to the price of the boat, but it's worth it.

Another popular option is the singlehander's package, which shifts halyards, reefing lines, jib downhaul, and halyard winches from the mast to the top of the cabin trunk at the front of the cockpit. Unfortunately, this puts the halyard winches directly in the way of a cockpit dodger, preventing you from swinging the winch handle in a complete circle.

Genoa sheet winches are mounted on the molded cockpit coamings. Winches are adequately sized.

The lead from the genoa track through the turning blocks to the winches needs to be altered slightly to reduce friction. An angled shim under the turning blocks would do the job. We'd also go up one size on the turning blocks. Turning blocks are very heavily loaded—roughly twice the sheet load—and are frequently undersized.

Since the boat is fairly narrow by modern standards, the outboard chainplates are only a slight compromise in windward performance. The typical cruiser/racer of this length is almost a foot wider, meaning that sheeting angles on the Crealock 37 are roughly the same as they would be on the cruiser/racer whose chainplates were 6" inboard.

The Crealock 37's rig is very well proportioned. The mainsail's aspect ratio of about 2.7:1 is about ideal, and the main itself is only 272 square feet—no sweat for one person to handle. With a divided foretriangle and headsail roller furling, sailing this boat is a piece of cake.

Compared to a cruiser/racer, the Crealock's waterline is short by contemporary standards. This pushes her displacement/length ratio to 334, decidedly toward the heavy end of the spectrum. But with a sail area/displacement (SA/D) ratio of about 15.6:1, the boat offers pretty good performance in anything other than drifting conditions.

The displacement/length ratio is a tricky number to use. It is meaningless for evaluating performance without considering the SA/D ratio at the same time. For a 37' boat, the Crealock 37's displacement is moderate. For a serious 37' cruising boat her displacement is actually fairly light.

All in all, the Crealock 37 will perform perfectly satisfactorily under sail, particularly on long passages.

Handling Under Power

The Yanmar engine is plenty of power for a boat of this displacement and type.

The boat was designed with a strut-mounted exposed prop. However, this was modifed to provide a prop aperture in the skeg supporting the rudder. The aperture is nicely faired, and the position of the prop immediately in front of the rudder gives good flow over the rudder for steering.

A two-bladed prop is standard, and you can reduce drag under sail by painting a mark on the shaft to help in aligning the blades with the deadwood for long passages. Alternatively, fit the boat with a two-bladed or three-bladed feathering prop. At the risk of sounding like a broken record, we can only reiterate that nothing will improve the typical sailboat's handling in reverse more quickly than adding a feathering prop.

A 40-gallon aluminum fuel tank is located in the bilge under the main cabin sole. It is completely removable without disassembling joinerwork. Although it's unlikely you'll ever have to take it out, this installation is a big plus. You can expect about a 250 mile range under power, which is reasonable for a boat this size. Somewhat greater fuel capacity

The standard layout is a good one for comfortable long-term cruising. That's fortunate, since the molded hull liner makes altering it difficult.

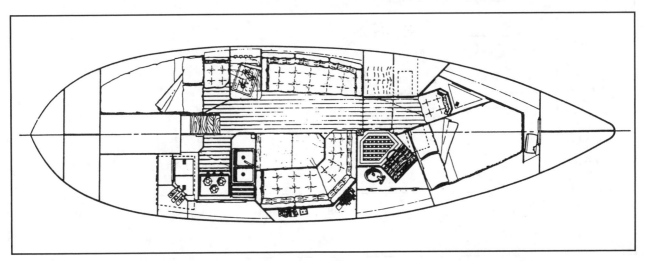

would be desirable for a serious cruiser, but the boat doesn't really have the displacement to carry a lot more fuel and water.

On Decks

The deck is quite well laid out for cruising, but where the heck do you put the dinghy? There's not quite enough room between the mast and the mainsheet traveler for a decent-sized rigid dinghy.

There are dual anchor rollers at the bow, but they don't project far enough forward to get a CQR or Bruce anchor safely away from the topsides. One Crealock 37 we looked at has a custom drop-nose extension on the rollers, an excellent idea that should be incorporated by the builder.

The foredeck is a clear, unobstructed work area. There are four foredeck cleats: two 10" cleats mounted on the inside of the bulwarks next to the hawseholes, and two 12" cleats near the centerline for anchor rodes. Thanks, Pacific Seacraft, for an arrangement that acknowledges the reality of anchoring.

A raised fiberglass boss in the deck forward of the anchor cleats will accommodate an optional anchor windlass. Raising the windlass slightly above deck level greatly reduces the amount of water that gets below through the chainpipe. You'll definitely want a windlass on this boat if you do any serious cruising.

Since the stanchions are bolted to the inside of the bulwarks rather than to the decks, decks are remarkably clear of clutter. Stanchions are 30" high, a good height for a cruising boat. On the downside, the face of the bulwarks can be deflected by leaning against the stanchions.

Despite the wide cabin trunk, the side decks are plenty wide enough for unobstructed passage, and there are teak grabrails along each side of the cabin trunk.

The cockpit is deep and comfortable, with coamings angled slightly outboard. Cockpit seats are just long enough to lie down on.

There are three cockpit lockers: a deep one on the starboard side that can serve as a sail locker, and two smaller lockers under the helmsman's seat. A lazarette on deck aft of the cockpit serves as a propane storage locker. It is properly sealed and scuppered, but it also functions as storage for the stern anchor rode. The lazarette is also big enough that it is tempting to use it for other storage as well.

According to ABYC (American Boat and Yacht Council) standard A-1.11.b(4), lockers used for LPG tank storage "shall not be used for storage of any other equipment." Even storing the anchor rode in the lazarette would violate that section of the standards.

One excellent feature of Pacific Seacraft boats is the removable cockpit sole, which is bolted down on heavy gaskets. On this boat, the entire sole was originally removable, but with the now-standard steering pedestal in place (the boat was designed for tiller steering) you had to remove the entire steering gear and pedestal before the cockpit sole could be taken out. The deck molding has been retooled so that only the forward half of the sole is removable— a substantially more practical arrangement.

A narrow bridgedeck protects the companionway. The sliding companionway hatch itself is an

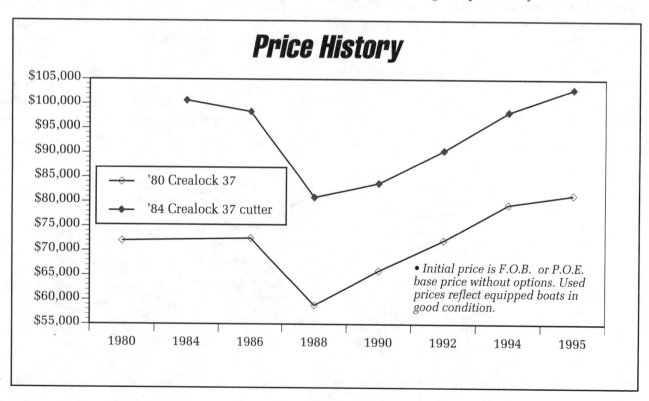

• Initial price is F.O.B. or P.O.E. base price without options. Used prices reflect equipped boats in good condition.

excellent design, one of the most carefully thought-out and watertight we have seen.

Surprisingly, there is no molded breakwater for a cockpit dodger. The dodger must be fitted around the mainsheet traveler supports and handrails. This makes it almost impossible to get a watertight seal around the bottom of the dodger—a serious drawback on a cruising boat. In general, however, the deck layout is clean, simple, and functional.

Belowdecks

Everyone has a different idea of what the interior of a serious cruising boat should be. The trend today is toward multiple cabins, queen-sized berths, and heads with stall showers. Instead, the Crealock 37 uses a very basic layout devoid of gimmicks and visual tricks, but one that is nearly ideal for a cruising couple.

The Crealock 37 has enough headroom even for tall folks. In the main cabin, there is an honest 6' 4" throughout. In the head and forward cabin, headroom is over 6'.

Despite an interior that is heavy on teak, the boat doesn't look dark inside. The feeling of lightness is helped by multiple ports and hatches, an off-white padded vinyl headliner, and the exposed white fiberglass settee and galley dresser risers that are part of the molded hull liner.

Although an oil finish on the interior teak bulkheads and trim is standard, we highly recommend that you ask the builder not to oil the teak at all. Instead, varnish it. If you really want the interior to look good, use gloss varnish on the teak trim and fiddles, satin varnish on the bulkheads and any other flat areas of teak veneer.

The forward cabin has a nice-sized double berth—50" wide and about 7' long—along the starboard side. The space below it is largely taken up by the forward water tank and the holding tank, although there are several drawers under the head of the berth. A comfortable seat fills what would otherwise be dead space between the berth and the hanging lockers to port. There are cubby lockers above the seat along the port side of the hull.

Using the space under the double berth for tankage is a reasonable solution, but not one free of drawbacks. When the water tank is full, you're adding about 300 pounds at the forward end of the waterline. If you also carry a lot of chain in the anchor rode locker forward, this is enough weight to noticeably alter the boat's trim and increase pitching moment, especially since the entry is fairly fine.

Ventilation in the forward cabin is good, with three opening ports and a double-opening Bomar hatch. The cowl vent over the passageway between the forward cabin and main cabin will help ventilation in bad weather.

The head compartment is on the starboard side, immediately aft of the forward cabin. Ventilation is provided by an opening port and a cowl vent.

A slatted teak seat folds down over the toilet if you want to sit down while showering, which is a good idea if you're doing it while underway. Since the entire lower half of the head compartment is a fiberglass molding, cleanup is quite simple. The shower sump pumps directly overboard with its own pump—a good solution to the problem.

Main cabin seating consists of an L-shaped dinette to starboard, and a straight settee along the port side. A drop-leaf table folds up against the forward face of the galley dresser, and can be folded out in two sections to use for dining. Since you can't reach the table from the settee, you're really limited to four for dinner at the table.

We find the folding table a little awkward. It isn't really sturdy enough to brace against at sea, so you'll tend to leave it folded up. The halfway open position will be useful in port, although that doesn't give you a table that two people can sit at comfortably.

A folding table is used for two reasons. First, the cabin sole in front of the dinette is removable so you can get at the fuel tank. Second, someone somewhere along the line decided that with a drop-in insert, the dinette would make a nice big double berth. Unfortunately, there's no good place to stow the big piece of plywood you need to create that double berth, and you need another double berth on a 37' cruising boat about like you need a hole in the head.

Using the dinette as a single berth is a little awkward, since the corner of the L is a gradual curve rather than a right angle, limiting foot room.

There is good storage space under both the port settee and the dinette, and there are various lockers and shelves outboard of the settees. Surprisingly, the locker doors do not have positive catches. Instead, they rely on friction latches—a mistake on a cruising boat, as you'll discover the first time the lockers empty onto the cabin sole.

The nav station is aft of the port settee, and it has its own seat rather than using the head of the quarterberth. The chart table itself is a reasonable size, but the piano hinge that joins the opening lid to the fixed portion of the table top is not recessed flush, limiting the space you can actually use for plotting. In addition, the fixed part of the table is flat, making it a good place to put your coffee cup, but the rest of the table is angled. If the whole table were in one plane, it would make for a more usable work surface.

A well-designed electrical panel is mounted on the bulkhead next to the navigator. The forward section of this bulkhead is meant to be used for flush-mounting electronics, but the space behind the bulkhead is really too shallow for a lot of equipment, and the location places the instruments at an awkward angle for the navigator. Pacific Seacraft will build an instrument-mounting rack over the forward end of the chart table, and we recommend it.

Cruising boats really need a big, easy-to-use nav station, with plenty of shelf space for electronic goodies, sextant, and navigation books. A couple of drawers to hold small nav tools would also be useful.

Aft of the nav station is a large quarterberth. The boat's accommodation plan shows this as a double, but it's really too small for that, being 42" wide at the head, tapering to about 2' wide at the foot.

Batteries are mounted under the head of the quarterberth, and the second water tank occupies most of the rest of the space below it.

The U-shaped galley is opposite the nav station. With one exception, it is a very workable galley. The exception is that the bottom of the deep double sinks is right at the load waterline, so water sloshes back through the drains, particularly when the boat is on port tack. Since the galley counter is only 34" high—36" is standard household height—a simple alteration would solve that problem.

The icebox is large and well insulated, with 4" of pour-in-place foam. The icebox lid, while insulated, needs to be gasketed to reduce heat transfer.

There is reasonable storage throughout the galley for food and utensils, although a cutlery drawer would be helpful. As a $440 option, you can get a good-sized locker suspended over the sinks. We'd go for it on a boat used for extended cruising.

Access to the bilge is somewhat limited, except for the large hatches over the fuel tank. Opening the small hatch over the aft end of the bilge sump requires removing the companionway ladder, a nuisance.

Light and ventilation in the main cabin are excellent, with four large and two small opening ports, plus a second large Bomar deck hatch. We'd add a second pair of Dorade boxes over the main cabin to improve heavy weather ventilation.

The interior of this boat is very livable for long-term offshore cruising. The three berths in the main cabin are all pretty much parallel to the centerline of the boat, an important consideration for sleeping under sail.

Our quibbles with the interior are small, and none of the faults we find is in any way fatal. The molded hull liner makes for an inflexible layout, but the standard one is good enough that this won't be a problem for most people.

Conclusions

For an off-the-shelf serious cruiser for two people or a small family, you couldn't do much better than this boat. The hull shape and design are pretty ideal, and the looks are classic without being dated or cute.

The Crealock 37 has held its value extremely well in a time when most boats are depreciating rapidly in a glutted market. This is largely due to the reputation of the boat and the builder, and due to the relatively small number of boats produced by the builder.

Pacific Seacraft's ads have stressed the ruggedness and seaworthiness of the boat. One ad shows a Crealock 37 lying on her side on a reef, basically undamaged. Another ad promotes the Circumnavigator package, ready to go anywhere and complete down to the steering vane.

It's pretty clear what the targeted market is: people who want to go places in small boats, who want good boats to carry them there, and have the money to spend. In today's market, that's a pretty good type of boat to build.   • **PS**

Irwin 37

A lot of boat for the money, as long as minor points like sailing performance aren't important to you.

An evaluation of the Irwin 37 threatens to expose all our prejudices about boatbuilders and cruising boats. In general we like sturdily built, finely finished, well performing boats that reflect traditional standards (if not design) and lasting value.

Irwin Yachts built boats of mediocre quality and finish and marketed them to buyers looking for as much boat as possible for the price. In every sense of the word, Irwin boats, of which the Irwin 37 is archetypal, are production boats. They were mass produced, carefully priced, simply advertised, and widely sold to a broad spectrum of customers.

More than 600 Irwin 37s were sold between the time the boat went into production in 1971 and its demise in 1982.

The last version was designated the Mark V, representing the popular strategy of numbering the steps in the evolution of a design even though the changes may be minor.

From the outset the Irwin 37 was a roomy, appealing cruising boat that was once described as the Chevrolet Belair of the boat market. Her greatest appeal was to the sailor/owner who is not into tradition, sailing performance, elegance, construction details, or investment.

Irwin Yachts was considered to have the most notoriously slipshod quality control among the larger boat builders. No other boats have as poor a reputation for warranty claims, delays in commissioning, missing or incorrect parts, and mislocated hardware as Irwin. Similarly an examination of virtually any Irwin-built boat reveals details that reflect cost savings but are problems; some, in our opinion, serious (gate valves on all through hull fittings) and some trivial (through hull fittings not installed flush with the hull).

Specifications

LOA	37' 0"
LWL	30' 0"
Beam	11' 6"
Draft	4' 0"/5' 6" (shoal/full keel)
Displacement	20,000 lbs.
Ballast	7,800 lbs.
Sail area	625 sq. ft.

Construction

There are no basic industry standards for fiberglass construction; the primary criterion for adequate hull laminate strength seems largely a matter of in-use durability. Some builders, in the absence of such standards, overbuild their products (CSY, for example). Irwin Yachts, on the other hand, have hulls and decks molded to specifications that are, by industry comparison, light. By our standards the Irwin fiberglass layup is minimal; that is one reason the boats have a low price. Yet basic laminate is not where cost savings are most apparent.

More conspicuous are cosmetic flaws. In two of the later 37s we looked at, there were obvious deep hollows in the bottom. These are evidently the result of pulling a still "green" hull from the mold and setting it in a four-point building cradle. The supports dished the laminate, probably permanently.

For years Irwin Yachts suffered from printthrough whereby the pattern of the underlying roving in the laminate was visible in the topside gelcoat. This later was considerably reduced with the use of Cormat between the roving and the gelcoat; in the later 37s we examined, printthrough was negligible. This printthrough remains an unsightly feature of older 37s, especially in the dark paint of the sheerstrake.

In our examination of the 37s we also noted sloppy underwater fairing around the rudder gudgeon and where the "Adapt-A-Draft" keel is attached. These types of flaws, coupled as they are with such details as protruding through hull fittings and squared off trailing edges, produces needless drag for a boat whose performance under sail is already suspect.

The earliest Irwin 37s did not have bowsprits. The result was a hazy gracelessness that was accentuated by obvious unevenness in the sheerline, unrelieved topside expanse, and Clorox-bottle styling, not to mention dimples and gelcoat blemishes. To improve performance with more sail area Irwin added a molded fiberglass bowsprit. Serendipitously the extension did wonders for the aesthetics. Less fortuitously the glass sprit also became a source of warranty claims when, if tightening the rigging caused it to flex, the gelcoat crazed.

The final version of the bowsprit is of welded aluminum. In a mid-production boat we examined, the bobstay is a threaded stainless steel rod with jaw terminals at each end. The newer boats have the rod welded between two plates on each end, a less costly fitting. As the lower end will be continually awash and thus vulnerable to corrosion, we think the welded construction is a mistake. Similarly we are concerned about the stainless steel rudder gudgeon, which has shown evidence of stress corrosion.

The Irwin 37 has a history of warranty claims against defective gelcoat—too thin (or missing), too thick, discolored, crazed, or covering voids. Where this happened in the diamond pattern non-skid deck surfaces that Irwin produced into the early '80s, inconspicuous repair was well nigh impossible.

The problem drove Irwin dealers and new owners to distraction and fueled much of the scuttlebutt about Irwin's poor handling of warranty claims. In the last boats Irwin put on a random non-skid pattern, easier to repair. Irwin also went to a better quality gelcoat.

Another common question about Irwin Yachts has been its hull-to-deck joint. Contrary to common industry practice, the joint in the Irwin 37 consists of overlapping flanges joined with a polyester slurry and fastened on about 6" centers with stainless steel self-tapping screws. Most builders now use a semi-rigid adhesive and bolts, a technique we favor. We believe this more positive attachment is called for on boats going to sea.

The chainplates of the 37 are stainless steel webs laminated into the topsides during the hull layup. This technique was developed by Irwin and is imitated by a number of builders whose chainplates are at the outer edge of the deck. It seems to be a satisfactory installation and indeed preferable to early Irwin 37s which had the chainplates through-bolted to the topsides.

Handling Under Power

Virtually everyone from whom we elicited information on the Irwin 37 either dismissed as unimportant or derided her performance under sail. She seems a classic example of the all-too-common cruising boat that does everything better than handle as a sailboat. A number of owners we talked to do not seem bothered by this shortcoming. We, again with our prejudice, would be.

The Irwin 37 comes standard with a sloop rig; the roller furling genoa was an almost unanimously specified option. A cutter rig (with a club jib) and a ketch rig were two other options. In any configuration she is a boat that seems ideally suited for a couple to sail. The sail area is modest with the ketch carrying about 60 square feet more sail than the sloop, just about enough to compensate for the windage of the mizzen mast. Personally we think the cutter rig is the best answer of the three, the staysail providing a handy headsail in hefty conditions and doing away with the clutter, expense and windage of the mizzen.

Plainly the standard shoal draft keel without a centerboard is inadequate for sailing to windward. If a buyer wants shoal draft, he should consider the centerboard version. The board does thunk in its trunk when down, a harmless if annoying distraction. Fully raised it remains quiet; what a relief in the middle of the night at anchor.

For optimum performance we recommend the deep keel. Still, do not hope too earnestly for scintillating windward work; for such joy you should consider a host of boats other than the Irwin 37.

Owners have indicated to us their willingness to accept indifferent performance under sail. However, we have heard complaints about the amount of attention the helm needs and some difficulty in steering the boat both under sail and under power ("Steering is stiff and my wife (98 lbs) has difficulty at times."). We suspect some of this chore is the result of an unbalanced semi-spade rudder being driven by a relatively small diameter steering wheel through an aft-cabin layout that requires considerable routing of the steering linkage.

Handling Under Power

The Irwin 37 has a 40 hp Perkins 4-108 diesel engine driving a three-bladed propeller with 2:1 reduction through the after edge of the keel. That is a combination that bespeaks of performance under auxiliary power. In fact, with the standard shoal keel and that combination for power, the Irwin 37 might reasonably be labeled a motorsailer if that term had not fallen into such disfavor in recent years.

The combination also suggests that the Irwin 37 should appeal to the powerboat owner looking to sail as a way to reduce his fuel consumption without sacrificing the room and amenities of the moderate sized powerboat. Certainly we think it is a worthwhile alternative to the ad hoc conversions of sailboat hulls and rigs to sailing powerboats with their high deckhouses, awkward sail handling systems, and sundry other hermaphroditic compromises.

Interior

If performance is not a priority in the design of the Irwin 37, livability is. The Irwin 37 is a coastal cruiser for two couples or a family of four. She has the most practical aft cabin layout we have seen on a stock boat under 40 feet. The layout has remained essentially unchanged since the 37 was introduced and features a spacious aft cabin, a step-down galley, a more-than-adequate walk-through passageway, and a forward cabin that should not make its occupants feel like they are in steerage.

Fundamental to the Irwin Yachts design and marketing philosophy is that the interior should instantly appeal to women. The decor is Production Boat Contemporary: tufted velour cushions, plenty of teak, and "color coordinated" carpeting. We are not impressed with the so-so craftsmanship and unsanded finish of the joinerwork nor with the antiseptic molded hull liner, but these are details that do not immediately affect the illusion of quality, comfort, and spaciousness.

Thus the interior of the 37 minimizes seagoing machismo: there are no handrails, sea berths, navigation sanctum, or sailbag stowage. Below, with the possible exception of the gimballed stove, one can easily forget that under certain circumstances a sailboat may not always be upright or free from motion.

It would be hard to imagine being aboard an Irwin 37 at sea. There is no berth one could sleep in comfortably. The settee berth to port is too narrow and the settee to starboard is too short. One owner remarked that even when the settee berth is to leeward, a nap-taker is rolled out of it during a gentle afternoon sail.

But what the 37 may lack at sea she more than makes up for at bedtime at anchor. Both the athwartships after berth and the forward V-berth are queen-sized with 4" mattresses. The two cabins are separated by 30 feet of boat and closed doors. Each has a private head.

There are good hanging lockers, lots of drawers, a few scuttles and assorted nooks and crannies. Yet someone forgot to build in places to store dry, warm food. For cold food there are, now get this, one front opening Norcold refrigerator (standard) and two, yes two, large top-opening iceboxes. In fact, both iceboxes are so sizable that their bottoms are difficult to reach. One of them (under the rudimentary chart table) might be better used for dry food storage except that getting at its contents would be at best inconvenient. The alternative is to use the galley icebox as a dry well and rely on the Norcold despite our longtime prejudice against using front opening boxes which depend on electrical power away from a dock. Perhaps this refrigerator is the best giveaway as to what type of cruising the 37 is best suited for.

Two other points about the interior deserve comment, one favorably and one not so. Engine access

We may not like the way she sails or her construction quality, but the interior layout is very good. Still, there are some problems when it comes to storage.

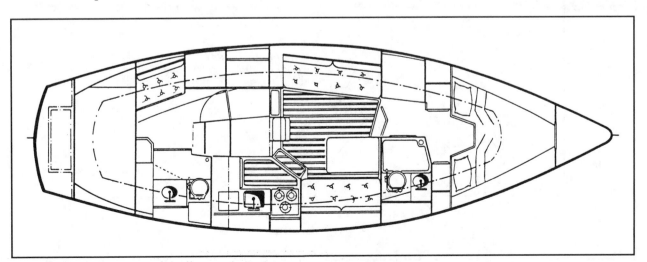

and sound insulation are among the best we have seen in a production boat, helped by removable panels on the sides of the walk-through. To check the dipstick and heat exchanger water there is no need to move the companionway ladder. In short, if the engine of the 37 seizes from lack of oil or overheats for lack of water, the owner has only himself to blame.

On the other side, the bulkhead-mounted fold-up, drop-leaf cabin table will not survive the first fall against it when a powerboat leaves a wake. It might not even withstand the weight of a rib roast. The first thing we would do after buying an Irwin 37 that still had the stock table is find ourselves a rugged, attractive fixed cabin table. (The next thing we would do is to make the seats comfortable.)

Deck Layout

The Irwin 37 is a handy boat to sail. The sidedecks are wide, the rail rises to a low bulwark forward to give a sense of security and the cockpit coaming has an opening to starboard but is low enough to climb out of anywhere. The bowsprit is designed to carry a 30 lb plow anchor housed in a roller chock. Hawseholes (of polished aluminum, replacing the line-chafing fiberglass on older boats) are mounted in the bulwark for docklines. Oddly enough neither the hawseholes nor the roller chock give a fair lead to the pair of deck cleats.

The stanchions are mounted through the deck into blocks drilled to fit, a system that we think gives a rugged support. In early 37s the stanchions went into fiberglass tubes glassed under the deck; in later

boats they go into wood blocks (saving cost and complexity). In contrast to this sturdy structure, the bow and stern pulpits are screwed on the teak rail cap. We hardly recommend that attachment.

The cockpit is small, accommodating at the most four adults at a time. Yet the seats are long enough to stretch out on and access below is easy. We are not bothered by the absence of a bridgedeck or companionway sill for safety because the cockpit is high and amidships, hence dry. Besides, Irwin's advertising notwithstanding, we doubt if many owners would consider offshore passages, given all the limitations the 37 would have at sea.

We like the number, design, and placement of the "smoked glass" opening hatches/skylights. Like many designs that have tropical cruising and chartering as part of their destiny, the Irwin 37 has a well ventilated interior.

On deck stowage is limited to one gigantic locker, the lazarette. The trouble is that for storing fenders, docklines, sheets, snorkeling gear, etc. as well as an odd sail or two, it would leave everything hard to get at. You cannot reach the bottom from the deck and without some owner-installed shelves, hooks, and bins the contents would be in chaos.

Conclusions

Having exposed our prejudices we hasten to add that the more than 600 Irwin 37s sold conclusively prove that many sailors do not share those prejudices.

When new in the early '80s, the Irwin 37 was about $15,000 less expensive than, say, the Tartan 37 or the Pearson 365. A Hunter 37, by contrast, could

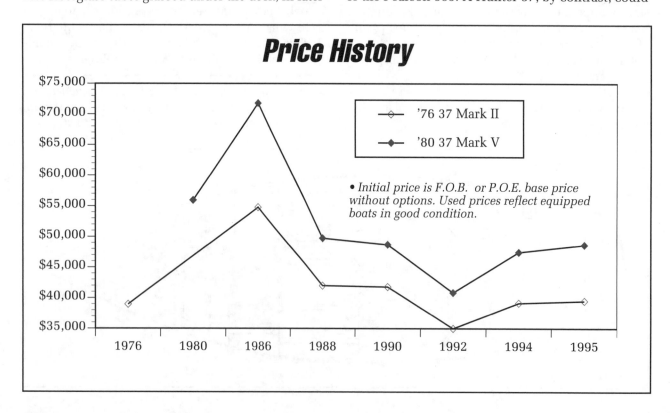

Price History

Legend:
- ◇ '76 37 Mark II
- ◆ '80 37 Mark V

• Initial price is F.O.B. or P.O.E. base price without options. Used prices reflect equipped boats in good condition.

be sailed away for about $10,000 less than the Irwin 37.

Ironically, considering the persistent badmouthing of the Irwin 37 around the waterfront, older models have retained their value reasonably well. The reason seems simple: the Irwin 37 offers many buyers what they are looking for in a boat.

And for the dollars the Irwin 37 is a lot of boat. Many owners report looking seriously at smaller boats and settling on the 37 when they (and their wives) see the spacious 37 for the same price as the smaller boat. For that price they get what they see as a summer home afloat. Deep water cruising may be a distant dream but the immediate desire is a comfortable and impressive boat for weekending and two weeks in the Bahamas, the Eastern Shore, or out of Long Island Sound.

For any boat that retains its stock features, we'd plan systematic and regular upgrading. Expect to replace the standard through-hull gate valves with seacocks or ball valves. Divide the humongous lazarette. Run the halyards aft to the cockpit when they need replacing. Build some pitch into the seats of the settees. Rebuild the "navigation station" into handy food storage. Mount a larger diameter steering wheel so you will no longer have to steer standing up or perched on the edge of your seat.

Finally, take a sail on a boat meant to sail effectively to windward, just so you'll see what you are missing.   • **PS**

CSY 37

A strongly built cutter designed with a particular purpose in mind—bareboat chartering.

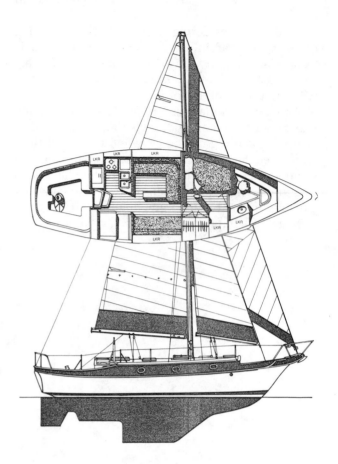

The CSY 37, designed by Peter Schmitt, is the mid-sized boat In the CSY line. Primarily designed for the Caribbean bareboat charter trade, 87 of the raised-deck cutters were built.

Schmitt has combined some features most often found in "traditional" boats—the oval stem, raised deck, and semi-clipper bow—with a relatively modern underbody featuring a fairly long fin keel and a skeg-mounted rudder. On paper, the boat looks pretty good. In person, she is rather tubby and high-sided.

The CSY 37 most closely resembles the Ericson Cruising 36. The styling of both these boats can best be termed "ersatz traditional."

With the short standard rig and shoal keel, she is no performance cruiser. With her huge cockpit she is not really a sea boat. Rather, she is a boat designed for a specific purpose, bareboat chartering, a purpose which she serves admirably. To expand her appeal to the general sailing public would be difficult, as CSY discovered. The company went under in 1981.

Most CSY 37s went into charter service, usually on lease-back arrangements. The boats have to be strong and reliable, for a week out of service for repairs means lost revenue to the charter operator. That the boats can stand up to this constant use and abuse is a credit to both designer and builder. Few other boats could, as CSY's charter experience has shown.

Construction

There are really only two words to describe the construction of the CSY 37: massive overkill. This is a mixed blessing. It means you have a strong, heavy hull. It often also means that you end up with a boat that is undercanvassed in light air. Very often it means a boat that has a fairly low ballast-to-displacement ratio.

Specifications

LOA	37' 3"
LWL	29' 2"
Beam	12' 0"
Draft	4' 8" (shoal), 6' 2" (deep)
Displacement	19,689 lbs.
Ballast	8,000 lbs.
Sail area	610 sq. ft.

Forty percent of the CSY 37's advertised displacement is in the ballast keel. With a 29' waterline, the displacement of about 20,000 lbs is about average by traditional standards, heavy by modern standards.

The hull is an extraordinarily heavy solid glass layup as is the deck. No core materials are used anywhere. Without coring such as balsa or Airex, a glass hull can sweat in a cold climate and can be excessively warm in a hot, humid climate.

The hull-to-deck joint is simple and effective. The hull and deck flanges, which overlap to form a molded rail, are bedded in 3M 5200 and through-bolted with stainless steel machine screws on 4" centers. 3M 5200 is about the most effective and tenacious adhesive sealant on the market.

Keel construction is unusual. The cast lead keel is

glassed into the hollow keel molding, any voids being filled with fiberglass slurry. This is then glassed over to form a double bottom and to keep the ballast in place. This ballast arrangement is identical in both the shoal and deep draft versions. The deep draft boat, however, has a 16" deep keel extension filled with about 600 lbs of cast concrete. If a shoal draft boat is desired, this extension can simply be cut off. The shoal draft boat with less lateral plane will, of course, make more leeway.

The hull is molded in two pieces, then joined in the middle with heavy overlapping layers of mat and roving. This allows some flexibility in hull design allowing such features as a molded-in rubbing strake and a stern with substantial tumblehome.

Installation of hardware is excellent. This is one of the few boats we have ever seen with through-bolted bronze seacocks. Backing plates are used on deck hardware such as cleats and winches.

The rudder stock is a solid 2" round bronze bar. The cast bronze rudder heel fitting would look more at home on a 60' boat than on a 37-footer.

The bow fitting is a massive stainless steel weldment, incorporating an anchor roller, a welded chock, and the headstay chainplate. The edges of the bow chock are not rounded, and could easily chafe an unprotected anchor rode. This bow fitting could double as an effective battering ram. We suspect that the dock boys in the West Indies are pretty wary every time an inexperienced charterer brings one of the CSY charter boats into the slip.

The chainplates are heavy stainless steel flat bars with load-distributing welded webs through-bolted to the hull. The hull layup is further reinforced in the

There are six large opening hatches on deck, making ventilation excellent. There's also plenty of room for lounging about, crucial to the charter trade. There's even enough space to carry along a dinghy.

way of the chainplates, an almost extraneous precaution, given the extreme heaviness of the regular hull layup.

Interior bulkheads are heavy waterproof plywood, attached to the hull with solid and neatly made fillets. Airex pads along the outboard edges of the bulkheads distribute the bulkhead stresses on the inside of the hull, preventing hard spots.

Cabin sole supports are clear fir. The teak-faced cabin sole is screwed to these bearers, with only limited access openings to the bilge. *The Practical Sailor* would prefer that most of the cabin sole be removable, providing access to the bilge spaces in an emergency. CSY appeared to be counting on the massiveness of the hull construction to prevent holing. This conceit could backfire. Remember the *Titanic*?

Hatches are molded fiberglass with translucent panels. They have good gasketing and good holddowns, but a short person will have trouble reaching overhead to open the hatches due to the tremendous headroom.

Exterior finish is of good stock boat quality. Joinerwork is clean with the exception of an awkward transition from the railcap on top of the raised deck to the sheer-level railcap in the foredeck well.

The molded fiberglass trailboards are shielded below the bow by a somewhat awkward molded glass panel. This became standard after a number of

CSY boats blew off their trailboards in heavy seas. We would have preferred it if they had just left the trailboards off entirely.

Handling Under Sail

The CSY 37 was available in two keel configurations, and with two rigs. The four possible combinations offer very different performance characteristics.

Most boats were delivered with the standard short rig. In areas of normally heavy air, such as the West Indies in winter, the normal rig is adequate. In light air with the short rig, the boat is a slug. The engine will come in handy under these circumstances.

Performance is greatly enhanced by the tall rig, which is about 8' taller than the standard rig and incoroplates two sets of spreaders.

With the chainplates set at the outboard edge of the hull, the sheeting base is excessively wide. Sheeting a genoa in tight enough to go to windward effectively is difficult.

To avoid the necessity for running backstays, the intermediate and after lower shrouds are attached to the deck several feet aft of the mast and the upper shrouds. Unfortunately, when broad reaching, the

Anchor handling is made easy by the bow roller arrangement. This boat was fitted with the optional stainless-steel anchor chain. We recommend using galvanized chain instead.

boom and main fetch up on these shrouds far too soon. This is ironic in a boat whose best point of sail is off the wind.

Our test boat had the tall rig and the shoal-draft keel. This is not the combination we would choose to own. Performance with the tall rig is greatly enhanced. However, the higher sail plan does make the boat more tender, and with the cut-down keel combines to produce a boat that makes excessive leeway when heeled more than about 20 degrees. We would prefer to combine the tall rig with the deep keel.

Our test boat was overpowered with full main, staysail and large jib topsail by gusts of a little over 15 knots over the deck, sailing hard on the wind. She also made substantial leeway. With a reef in, the helm eased, the boat stood up, and leeway was less.

Off the wind, the CSY 37 comes into her own. She is stable as a church and visions of long tradewind passages instantly come to mind. Under those conditions she would shine if you had plenty of chafe protection on those aft-leading shrouds.

Halyard winches are mounted on the keel-stepped painted aluminum mast. The boom does not overhang the cockpit, and has a well-made boom gallows which provides a good handhold on deck as well as being an excellent place to store the boom when at rest, or when sailing under the storm jib alone in heavy weather.

Handling Under Power

With such high topsides, the Perkins 4-108 is the smallest engine we would want in the boat. As it is, handling at slow speeds in a crosswind can be tricky. A great deal of practice is required to handle such a high-sided boat under power in a breeze.

The turning radius of the CSY 37 is substantially larger than with a shorter-keeled boat. With her heavy displacement, acceleration is not exactly neck-snapping. She should have enough power to get her out of tight spots, however.

Handling in reverse is tricky. The boat does not go where you aim it until you learn to use a combination of rudder and bursts of throttle.

Engine access through the large cockpit hatch is good, but the heavy hatch should have a more positive means of holding it in the upright position. If it fell on your head, you'd remember it, if you were lucky enough to then remember anything.

To those who have been spoiled by the handling under power of some modern boats, the CSY 37 may be a disappointment. It handles like a boat, rather than a compact car, requiring some patience and planning ahead.

Deck Layout

With her raised deck amidships, the CSY 37 has an amazing amount of deck space, giving the on-deck impression of a small ship. There is plenty of space on deck to carry a rigid dinghy. Designer Peter Schmitt's own CSY 37 carried a beautiful little dory with a varnished transom as a tender; she fit quite neatly on the starboard side and served as a catchall for fenders and lines.

Deck space is important in boats used extensively in the charter trade. Lounging on deck is the primary charter boat activity. In this category, the CSY 37 gets five stars.

Anchor handling is fairly easy with the stub bowsprit. There is, however, only a single bow cleat. This is a pet peeve of *The Practical Sailor,* for it greatly complicates anchoring with two anchors, a common practice for cruising boats. The optional "anchoring package" included a good length of stainless steel chain, which is miserable stuff to handle by hand. Use galvanized instead.

We do not recommend the electric anchor windlass. If you plan on using a windlass, get a boat with the manual unit.

Heavy travelers for both the main and the staysail are located on the main deck. Thwartships control lines should really be used with these to get optimum performance from the sails—essential on a boat which must be tweaked to get a reasonable level of performance on the wind.

The cockpit of the CSY 37 is huge—too big for an offshore boat but good for the charter trade. The large cockpit lockers are well divided and are partitioned from the engine space under the cockpit.

The starboard cockpit locker contains the best battery box installation we have seen on a stock boat.

The port locker contains the optional 110-VAC refrigeration compressor. Unfortunately, its wiring is exposed to the weather when the locker lid is opened. The sound-insulated engine room hatch occupies much of the cockpit sole.

There are four large cockpit scuppers, which are imperative to have with the huge cockpit. The companionway sill should be higher if the boat is to be used offshore. A fiberglass seahood, protecting the forward end of the companionway slide, is standard equipment.

Interior

Two interior arrangements are available, a two-stateroom, two-head plan, and a single-stateroom, single-head plan. The two-stateroom plan is used primarily in the charter trade. It is really too much interior to try to cram in a 29' waterline and designer Schmitt was not particularly proud of it.

The single-stateroom layout is also unconventional, It gives over the forward 40% of the interior space to a large cabin with built-in double berth and a huge head compartment in the forepeak. The problem with this arrangement is that should you have guests aboard, they must troop through the owner's cabin in order to use the head—a major inconvenience.

The space given over to the head in the single-stateroom model is almost exactly the same space occupied by the forward cabin in the two-stateroom model. With a single-stateroom layout, interior space might have been better utilized with a "conventional" layout of sleeping quarters forward with the

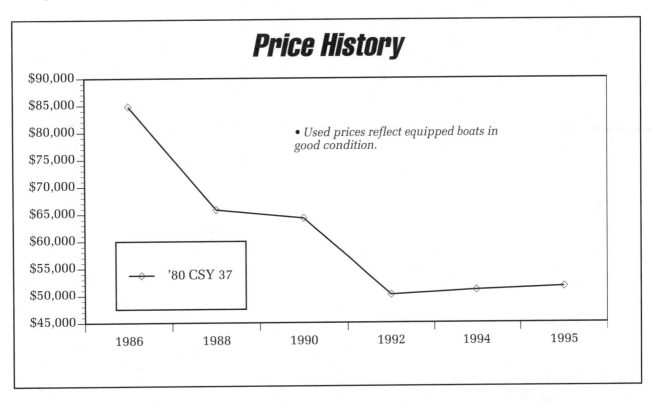

Price History

• Used prices reflect equipped boats in good condition.

◇ '80 CSY 37

head and hanging lockers dividing the forward cabin from the main cabin. Unfortunately, the "conventional" layout was not an option.

The interior volume of the CSY 37 is huge, thanks to the raised deck. There are many well-thought-out interior details, too many, unfortunately, to catalog here. The ice box, for example, is divided into two compartments with separate opening traps. The ice-box has a minimum of 4" of urethane foam insulation, probably more than any other stock boat on the market.

There are, however, lapses in this good design. Galley counter tops in our test boat were covered with a slatelike laminate, difficult to clean and too bumpy for a good work surface. Head counters and some shelves were covered with marble-grained plastic, looking more like a slice out of a multi-colored bowling ball than real marble.

The mixture of excellent design details, strange lapses in taste, and execution which ranges from fair to excellent is difficult to evaluate reasonably. It was pleasing to see, that after years of using teak-grained mica-covered bulkheads, CSY switched to real oak-faced bulkheads in newer production boats.

Ventilation of the interior can only be described as excellent. There are six opening hatches or skylights in addition to the companionway. Some dorade boxes, however, might be welcome in steamy climates with frequent rain. One could spend a great deal of time analyzing the interior details, primarily because a lot of thought has gone into them. Both of the interior layouts are unusual, and each will have adherents and detractors.

Conclusions

CSY was an unusual company, and the CSY 37 is certainly an unconventional boat. The boat is strongly built—overly built, in fact, The 1980 base price of $91,670 seems high until you consider that this is a 20,000-lb boat, and very well equipped. Hot and cold pressure water, Edson pedestal steering, and gimballed propane stove were all standard, for example.

CSY boats were probably the strongest production boats ever marketed. They may be ungainly, and not the hottest performers under sail, but they are tough. That's an important consideration if you're trying to get the most for your money.　• **PS**

Tartan 37

Good manners and attention to detail set this well-bred Sparkman & Stephens design apart.

The Tartan 37 is a moderately high performance, shoal-draft keel-centerboarder that went out of production in 1989, to be replaced by the Tartan 372.

Over the years, Tartan specialized in the production of well-finished boats geared toward the upper income cruising sailor. Most of these boats were Sparkman and Stephens designs, and many were keel-centerboarders. Tartans were also geared toward "civilized" racing, with boats such as the Tartan 41 and Tartan 46. With their Sparkman and Stephens designs and high quality joinerwork, Tartans provided a somewhat lower priced alternative to lines of boats such as the very expensive Nautor Swans.

Several hundred Tartan 37s were built. Most of these were the keel-centerboard version. An optional deep-keel version was also available. A racing version of the 37, called the Tartan 38, was built in limited numbers.

The Tartan 37 is attractively modern in appearance. She has a gentle sheer and a straight raked stern profile, with moderate overhangs at both bow and stern. Underwater, the boat has a fairly long, low aspect ratio fin keel, and a high aspect ratio rudder faired into the hull with a substantial skeg. Freeboard is moderate. The boat is balanced and pleasant in appearance. She is not a character boat, but is attractive, fairly racy, and functional—a typical modern Sparkman and Stephens design.

Construction

The Tartan 37 is a well-built boat. Tartan made use of both unidirectional roving and balsa coring in stress areas. This yields a stiff, fairly light hull that is less likely to oilcan than the relatively thin solid layup used in many production boats.

Specifications

LOA	37' 3"
LWL	28' 6"
Beam	11' 9"
Draft	4' 2" (cb), 6' 7" (deep keel)
Displacement	15,500 lbs.
Ballast	7,500/7,200 (std/deep keel)
Sail area	625 sq. ft.

Some roving printthrough is evident. There are also some visible hard spots on the outside of the hull. These may be the result of the heat of secondary bonding of bulkheads and partitions. Gelcoat quality is very good.

The rudder is faired into the skeg with fiberglass flaps to minimize turbulence. All through-hull fittings are recessed flush to the hull skin. For a cruising boat, remarkable attention was given to reducing skin friction and improving water flow.

Tartan's hull-to-deck joint is simple and strong. The wide internal hull flange is bedded with butyl and polysulfide, the deck dropped on, and the two bolted together via the stainless steel bolts which hold on the teak toerail. This toerail is not always properly bedded. We were able to easily insert a

thick knife blade under the toerail in several areas near the bow, where the rail is subject to the most twist. Water will lie in this joint if it is at all open, making it impossible to keep varnish on the toerail.

Most deck hardware, such as cleats, is backed with thick aluminum plates. Pulpits are through-bolted but lack backing plates. The hull-to-deck joint is through-bolted across the transom—one of few boats so built. Running lights are mounted in the topsides, about a foot below the sheerline. The wiring for these lights is located in the forepeak locker, where it could be damaged by anchors or rodes stored there. We generally dislike running lights mounted in the hull. They look neat, but they are nearly invisible at sea, often leak, and frequently stain the topsides with long tears of oxidation after periods at sea.

Interior glasswork is some of the best we have seen. Fillet bonding is absolutely neat and clean. There are no raw fiberglass edges visible anywhere in the hull.

One of the reasons that the Tartan 37 cost so much is that there was a lot of expensive engineering and construction in the boat. The starboard main chainplate assembly, for example, is a complex construction of stainless steel weldments and tie rods that probably added hundreds of dollars to the cost of the boat.

To keep the interior of the boat neat, the centerboard pennant comes up on deck through the center of the mast. This necessitates a complex mast step with transverse floors and a massive hat beam under the mast step to absorb compression. Add another few hundred dollars of engineering and construction.

If price was not a concern, perhaps this is little ground for complaint. However, the more complex a piece of construction is, the more subject it may be to failure, and the more expensive to repair or replace.

Tartan uses bronze ball valves on through hull fittings below the waterline. Exhaust line, cockpit scuppers, and bilge pump outlets are above the waterline, and have no shutoffs. The cockpit scuppers, which would be submerged while the boat is underway, should have provision for shutoff.

Handling Under Sail

Owners report that the Tartan 37 is a well-mannered boat under sail. The boat will not perform at the Grand Prix level, but she is no sluggard, either.

A large percentage of the boats were purchased for family cruising. On these boats, headsail roller furling systems are usually installed. Almost inevitably, there will be some sacrifice in windward performance with roller-furling headsails.

The optional inboard genoa track should be considered essential to those concerned with optimum windward performance. Coupled with the standard outboard track, this allows versatility in sheeting angles.

Headsail sheets and winches are within reach of the helmsman. This feature is vital for short-handed cruising, and can help make the difference between a boat that is easy for two people to handle, and one that is a pain. However, no real provision was made for the installation of secondary headsail winches, should you wish to carry staysails. Small winches could be mounted on the cockpit coamings forward, but they could well interfere with the installation of a dodger.

With good sails, performance of the Tartan 37 is not disappointing on any point of sail. Tartan brochures showed the 37 happily romping along on abeam reach in a 15 knot breeze. We suspect that under those conditions her owner is likely to be as happy as any sailor afloat.

Handling Under Power

The standard 41 horsepower Westerbeke 50 diesel is more than adequate power for the Tartan 37. The tendency in many production boats today is toward smaller, lighter, lower-powered diesels—the opposite of the past American boatbuilding practice, which, like our automobiles, tended toward excessive horsepower.

For a cruising boat, the mechanical power represented by a 40 horsepower engine in a 15,000 lb boat makes sense. The cruising boat needs the ability to punch into a head sea when necessary. Frankly, we prefer a boat to be slightly overpowered, rather than underpowered. We'll take the greater weight and the higher fuel consumption without complaint.

The engine box of the Tartan 37 is only partially sound insulated.

Access to the front end of the engine is good, by removing the companionway ladder. Access to the oil dipstick is another matter. To reach the oil dipstick, one must climb into the starboard cockpit locker. This necessitates removing much of what could be stored in that locker every time the oil is checked. If one is conscientious enough to check the oil every time the engine is run, a lot of loading and unloading will be required. In practice, it means that the oil level is unlikely to be checked regularly. Most sailboat owners rather shockingly neglect their engines. Making the oil dipstick inaccessible can only exacerbate that tendency toward neglect.

Deck Layout

With wide decks, inboard chainplates, and a relatively narrow cabin trunk, fore and aft movement on the deck of the Tartan 37 is relatively easy. It would be easier if the lifeline stanchions had been positioned further outboard, rather than about 3" inboard of the toerail.

There are proper bow chocks, and two well mounted cleats forward. However, a line led through the chocks to the cleats bears against the bow pulpit. Shifting the cleats further inboard would provide a better lead.

Surprisingly, there is no foredeck anchor well. This means that an anchor must be stowed in chocks on deck, if one is to be readily available. Then, you must face the problem of anchor rode storage. Molded foredeck anchor wells are becoming almost universal in modern boats. While the weight of anchor and rode—about 65 lbs in a boat this size—might be objectionable stowed all the way forward, the convenience of such a system generally outweighs the increase in pitching moment that might result. Removing the ground tackle from the deck also reduces clutter and toe stubbers, and simplifies foredeck work.

There are strong, well-mounted teak grabrails on top of the cabin trunk, although the reasoning for using two short rails on each side rather than a single long rail escapes us. The molded breakwater/cockpit coaming is a common Sparkman and Stephens feature, and greatly facilitates the mounting of a dodger—almost standard equipment on a cruising boat.

The T-shaped cockpit of the Tartan 37 is very comfortable for five while sailing. It has several unusual features. Rather than the usual unyielding fiberglass, there are teak duckboards on all cockpit seats. This means that you won't sit in a puddle when it rains, or when heavy spray comes aboard. These duckboards are comfortable, but they are held in

The forward cabin is very comfortable, with its own door to the head and plenty of room. In the main cabin, the fold-down table is a poor feature—hard to set up, and flimsy to boot.

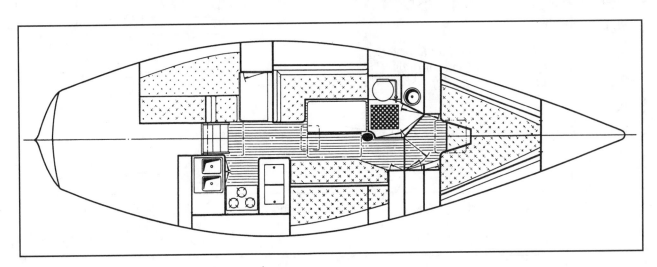

place only by wooden cleats, with the exception of the starboard seat. A more secure arrangement should have been provided for offshore sailing.

There is a teak-grated cockpit sump under the helmsman's feet. This shifts the cockpit drains inboard from the edge of the cockpit. The result is that a puddle can collect in the leeward corner of the cockpit when the boat is well-heeled in a blow, with heavy spray coming aboard.

Access to the steering gear is via the lazarette hatch. There is good provision for an emergency tiller, but the lazarette hatch must be held open in some way to use the emergency steering. There is a drop-in shelf in the lazarette which allows using the locker with less risk of damage to the steering system, but we would be reluctant to store anything small there that might possibly jam in the steering gear.

With a low cabin trunk, visibility from the helm is excellent. We suspect that many helmsmen would prefer a contoured seat to the flat bench provided, however. The relatively wide flat top of the cockpit coaming provides reasonably comfortable seating for the helmsman who prefers to sit well to leeward or well to windward.

The main companionway is narrow and almost parallel-sided—features we like—but the sill is much lower than we prefer for offshore sailing. The low sill facilitates passage of the crew below. Unfortunately, it also greatly facilitates passage of water below should the cockpit fill. Coupled with the thin plywood dropboards, we feel this is a potential weakness in watertight integrity, compromising the boat

as an offshore cruiser. For offshore racing, for example, the Special Regulations require that the companionway be permanently closed up to the main deck level or the height of the lowest cockpit coaming.

Belowdecks

Due to an abundance of teak and teak plywood, the interior of the Tartan 37 is dark and cavelike. This is much the same criticism we have made of other well-finished boats. Mind you, it's a rather elegant cave, with excellent joinerwork throughout. Somehow, boat designers and builders have convinced most of the consuming public that teak is the only wood to use belowdecks. The fact is that there are many wonderful woods—ash and butternut, for example—that yield interiors that are lighter in both weight and color than teak.

The forward cabin of the Tartan 37 is truly comfortable for a boat of this size, with drawers, hanging lockers, separate access to the head, and enough room to dress in relative comfort. The completely louvered door separating the forward cabin from the main cabin looks nice, and does assist in ventilating the forward cabin. It limits privacy, however, and one good blow from a crew member caught off balance in a seaway would probably reduce it to a pile of teak toothpicks.

The head is quite comfortable, and it is possible to brace adequately for use offshore. The shower drains into a separate sump—not into the bilge.

Layout of the main cabin is conventional, with settee and pilot berth to starboard, dinette to port. Including a pilot berth on the starboard side necessi-

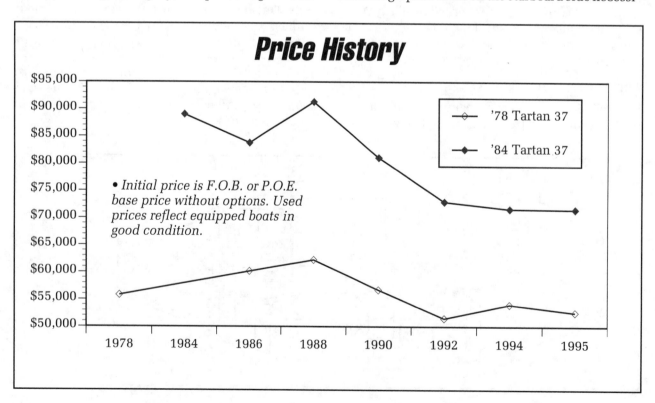

Price History

• Initial price is F.O.B. or P.O.E. base price without options. Used prices reflect equipped boats in good condition.

Legend: ◇ '78 Tartan 37   ◆ '84 Tartan 37

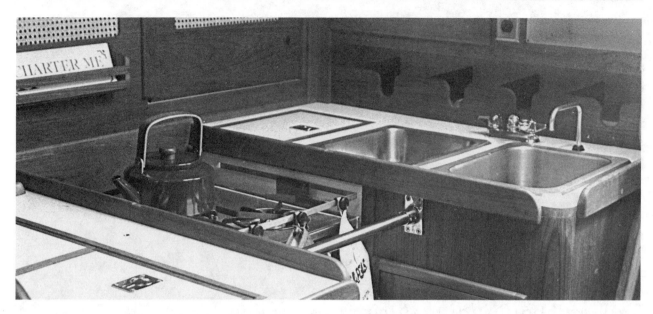

tates the complex chainplate arrangement mentioned earlier, for the berth prevents a simpler and cheaper bulkhead-mounted chainplate.

In what is a rather remarkable lapse in good design for such a boat, there is a bulkhead-mounted, fold-down cabin table. Pins in the bottom of the two legs must be inserted in corresponding holes in the cabin sole—no mean feat at anchor, and a ridiculous expectation offshore. The new Tartan 37 we examined already had a pockmarked cabin sole from setting up the cabin table for potential buyers. Metal plates recessed in the cabin sole would at least minimize the potential for damage here. Once set up, the table is disappointingly flimsy.

While there is excellent storage space in the galley, one must reach across the stove to reach much of it—and it's a long reach for a short person. The stove is securely mounted and has a grab bar across its well to protect the cook, but this grab bar also inhibits the stove's gimballing function.

There is no on-deck provision for storage of propane bottles, should you wish propane rather than the standard alcohol stove. There is room for CNG bottles in the starboard cockpit locker, but CNG has never really impressed us because of its bulkiness compared to propane.

The icebox appears to be well insulated. Why Tartan, like many other builders, fails to insulate and carefully fit the tops of their iceboxes totally escapes us. We have found this shortcoming on every variety of boat, from the cheapest to the most expensive, and it represents a rather strange disregard of the basic laws of thermodynamics.

The Tartan 37 has a large, well-designed navigation station. The quarterberth converts to a double berth.

Ventilation is excellent, with eight opening ports and three hatches. There are also four ventilators for the accommodations areas—two exhaust type and two low plastic cowls in dorade boxes. We think four taller cowls in the dorades would be more effective, or better still, the five tall cowls shown in the original plans for the boat. The vertical aft deckhouse bulkhead also allows a drop board to be left out when it rains, further improving ventilation.

Despite our complaints about the darkness of the interior, joinerwork is of excellent stock boat quality throughout.

The degree of enclosure of the interior of the hull can complicate access to deck hardware, and certainly does not facilitate survey of the vessel. In traditional wooden yacht construction, structural members are often left exposed for their intrinsic beauty, as well as for ventilation and preservation. In fiberglass boats, it is rather difficult to find intrinsic beauty in the structural material. Perhaps we are better off with it all hidden—as long as we know what holds the boat together. We certainly have confidence in what holds the Tartan together, even if we do pay a premium for that confidence.

Conclusions

The Tartan 37 is a well-built, well-mannered fast cruising sailboat. Like many S&S designs, there is a lot of complex engineering in the boat, which helped to boost the price. The boat also shows a generally high degree of finish, and a fair amount of attention to detail—perhaps more than most consumers are willing to pay for.

The Tartan 37 is a gray flannel Buick of a boat, the perfect banker's, lawyer's or stockbroker's boat. She's neither ostentatious nor plain. She is neither cheaply designed, nor cheaply built. One pays a lot for good breeding. Whether it is too much to pay is something only you, and the loan officer at your bank, can decide.   • **PS**

Island Trader 37/38

In many ways, this overweight ketch exemplifies the worst of Taiwan boatbuilding during the 1970s.

During the late 1970s, when Taiwan-built boats began to appear on the U.S. market in increasing numbers, few boats better illustrated the Far East yacht than the Island Trader 37 or 38. (Same boat, different name depending on which brochure, in which year, you read.) Imported to the U.S. by Marine International of Bay Head, New Jersey, between about 1977 and 1988, the Island Trader line apparently embodied the general misconception of what a real ocean-going boat should look like: Clipper bow, taffrails, pinrails, wooden spars, and enough spring in the sheer to mimic the curl of a breaking wave. And don't forget the interior teak carvings of five-clawed Chinese dragons (symbol of good luck), poppy flowers and Dr. Fu Manchu. You can't exactly trace these designs to some turn-of-the-century Scandinavian lifeboat design; in fact, the designers seemed to have invented their own history, a history without a past.

The Design

Good subject. Who did design this boat? You won't find any names on the brochures or in old sailboat magazine directories. William Garden gets at least occasional credit for the infamous Island Trader 41, built by a handful of yards and variously called the Yankee Clipper 41, Formosa 41, CT 41 and Sea Wolf 41. Did some American broker/distributor pen the lines, or, more likely, did some Taiwan builder flash the molds sitting behind his cousin's chicken coop?

Maybe even he doesn't even know who designed the boat, or if he did, he darn sure doesn't want to pay royalties. Taiwan, in the early days of fiberglass boatbuilding, had the unsavory reputation of freely

Specifications

LOA	37' 4"
LWL	30' 4"
Beam	12' 0"
Draft	4' 6"
Displacement	26,400 lbs.
Ballast	7,000 lbs.
Sail area	567 sq. ft.

modifying plans to avoid unnecessary expenditures. In this culture, everything's fair in love, war and business.

In profile, the Island Trader 37 looks like she caught a wave on the chin. The sheer seems exaggerated, rising too high in the bow and stern.

The low-aspect rig is short, carrying just 567 square feet of sail on a 30' 4" waterline. Displacement is reported anywhere from 18,600 lbs. to 26,400 Lbs. Holy cow! Did we say *twenty-six thousand, four hundred pounds?* This gives the 37 an incredible displacement/length ratio of 422, and an abominable sail area/displacement ratio of 10.7!

Lastly, check out the keel. This is the literal and pure conception of "full keel." (Maybe the Island

Owners' Comments

"Super sea boat. With full keel and proper sail trim, she sails herself."

1980 model in Bristol, Connecticut

"Terrible and unsafe steering mechanics that had to be changed immediately, at considerable cost."

1979 model in West Hampton Beach, New York

"Lost mast because of defective stainless steel turnbuckles. Had three steering breakdowns. Ice-box is poor. Replace galley and head fixtures."

1976 model in PelhamManor, New York

"Be prepared to spend about $10,000-$15,000 over and above to set up boat properly. Insist on sea cocks vs. gate valves. Isolate batteries and alternator Replace lifeline stanchion screws with stainless steel. Cockpit hatches should be re-built. Steering sheaves should be replaced. Temperature cut-off switch on hot water heater. Boat comes equipped with a ridiculous manifold riser which cracks and permits water into the engine. Leading edge of rudder needs to be faired. Prop turbulence on rudder is excessive. Not well rigged for genoa sheets. Porthole gaskets are poor. Sail tracks are poor. Samson posts have sharp edges. Scupper construction poor and too small."

1983 model in New York, New York

Trader does have a 19th century heritage after all!) At the least, we'd like to see the forefoot cut away to reduce wetted area.

Construction

Typical of this era, the Island Trader 37 hull is solid fiberglass, and has lots of it. One owner of a 1982 model, responding to our questionnaire, said he was "bounced around by a small whale without damage." Other owners, too, praise the heavy construction, alluding only to mysterious defects: "Chinese glass work needs some help." Or, "Chinese 'stain-

less' is interesting."

But it's the teak that invariably draws interest. And, of course, there's lots of it. Though more than capable of first-class work, the Taiwan yards don't always deliver a first-class product. The owner of a 1979 model said, "The finish work (teak), while plentiful, is only fair." Others, however, noted that some care had been taken in matching grains, and that the joinerwork was for the most part good.

The owner of a 1983/84 boat wrote us a lengthy note saying, "Some models built in the 1970s had plywood cabins that rotted, giving bad name to

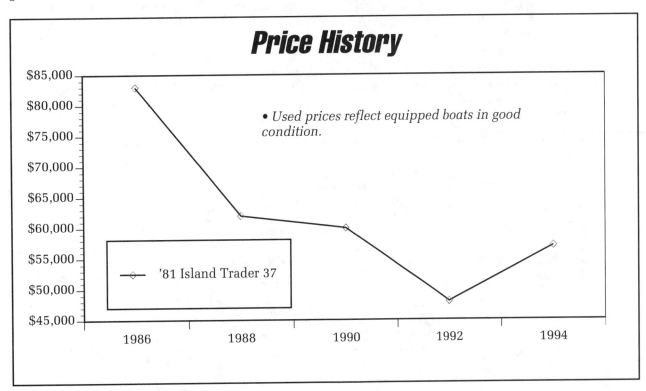

Price History

• *Used prices reflect equipped boats in good condition.*

—◇— '81 Island Trader 37

company. Boat had a few minor oversights that were easily corrected. Protruding chainplates on outside of hull and a wide (3-1/2") caprail of unvarnished teak were subject to abrasion. Therefore, I faired out the teak caprail to extend outboard of the chainplates, then installed 3/4" x 3/8" half-round brass rub rails on the full length of the caprails."

The inappropriate use or handling of plywood is another dubious trademark of early Taiwan boats. We've often seen cockpit seats made of plywood with teak on top and sprayed gelcoat underneath to make them look like fiberglass; they don't last too many years before moisture delaminates the plywood, busts through the gelcoat and reveals the horrendous soggy mess. We're not sure how the seats of the Island Traders were made, but we'd check them closely, too, especially since one reader said his needed reconstruction.

Respondents to our questionnaires report a number of other endemic problems: gate valves instead of sea cocks, poor quality turnbuckles, poor quality sheaves for the cable steering system, poorly designed exhaust system that can lead to engine damage, inadequate support for the rudder stock, and wiring problems, such as connecting the engine starter directly to one battery.

Based on an inspection of Taiwan boatyards about nine years ago, we think there are two principal causes of such misguided efforts: inadequate supervision by American marketers, and inadequate knowledge on the part of the Taiwan workers.

While the best yards, such as Ta-Shing, now rate well against American and European builders, there still are a lot of backyard builders who do things the old-fashioned way, which for the most part means outdoors using the cheapest, most easily available materials. During our visit, we seldom saw workers using power tools. Often a group of workers travels from one shed to the next doing carpentry, metal or electrical work for various yards. One day it's Hans Christian, the next it's Island Trader. And to expect that such people understand, let alone have ever heard of, the American Boat & Yacht Council standards for, say, color coding wiring or sea cock installation, is unrealistic.

The bottom line, we feel, is that with good management and supervision, Taiwan can produce quality boats. But judging from the litany of problems associated with Island Traders, we think owners of these boats are likely to get more problems than they've bargained for.

Performance

Earlier we noted that the displacement/length ratio of the Island Trader 37 is 422 and a sail area/displacement ratio of 10.7, easily putting it in the "heavy" or "motorsailer" category. With its short, divided rig, we would not expect sparkling performance. Owner reports bear out this assumption.

Owners consistently rate the 37 as slow upwind and only average off the wind; we think they're probably being generous at that. "Better in heavy weather," one owner put it nicely. "Be aware that the boat is very slow," said another more directly.

On the other hand, the tradeoff is comfort, no doubt due, at least in part, to an easy motion. "Solid and dry. Very stiff and stable platform," said one owner. The boat also balances well, according to most owners. "We went to windward for four hours without helm adjustment," wrote the owner of a 1982 model. Given the ketch rig and long keel, the 37 should be hard to knock off a course.

Though the 37 no doubt possesses some attributes of a good cruiser, the extraordinarily heavy displacement and small sail area are severe strikes against it. A good cruising boat is also a good sailer, at least a decent one. The Island Trader 37, by most counts, does not perform well under sail.

Owners praise the roomy interior, generous stowage and teak. Unfortunately, that's about where the good things stop.

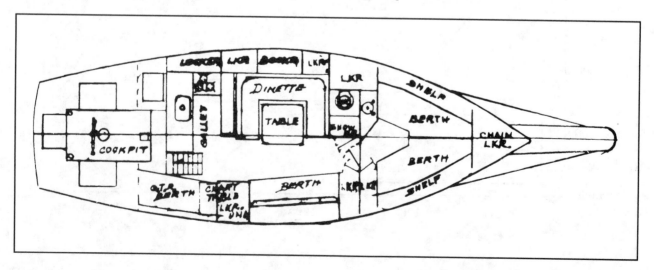

Early brochures do not specify a brand of diesel engine, but owners of late 1970s' models report no serious problems with the Volvo MD3B. Later models had the Yanmar 3QM30H, indicating slightly higher levels of satisfaction with reliability and accessibility. These first-generation "Q" series Yanmars, however, had a reputation for being noisy; when Yanmar re-engineered the line later in the 1980s, considerable improvements were made. Owners report good maneuverability under power with the Standard 3-blade prop, though one owner said, "Too much prop wash on big rudder; tough to hold on course." We also have several complaints about being underpowered.

Interior

With a 12' beam, the Island Trader 37 has plenty of accommodations and stowage for its length. As can be seen in the drawing, there is a V-berth forward, head with shower, convertible dinette and extension berth in the saloon, and an aft galley to port and quarter berth to starboard. The Taiwanese love to build doors and louvers and knick-knacks, and the 37 has plenty of these to showcase. Every fashion has its time, however, and the dragons and poppies are beginning to disappear. All-teak interiors tend to be darker, heavier and require more maintenance than bright, modern, high-pressure laminates.

Ventilation is good, with seven portlights and two skylights. "This boat has room and comfort, and she is warm to the eye," wrote one owner, adding that the "icebox is too big; tough to get to stuff and doesn't drain well. "

"Her spaciousness is one of her major attractions," wrote another owner who sails on Long Island Sound.

Headroom is an astonishing 6' 8" maximum, 6' 4" minimum, according to one owner (which may explain why another owner said he has trouble seeing over the cabintop).

Overall, it seems that many people bought the 37 because of its large, teak interior with oodles of stowage.

Conclusion

Judging from the hull numbers of readers' boats, close to 200 Island Trader 37s were built over about a 10-year period. Company literature describes them as a Best Buy. In 1981, the base price for what was then called the 38 was $69,900. Today, according to the BUC *Used Boat Price Guide*, that boat is worth between $55,000 and $60,000. Based on the few ads we've seen in sailing magazines, this seems about right.

In the same price range, however, you can buy a 36-foot Allied Princess ketch, perhaps an older Pearson 365 ketch or, if you really want the Far East look, a Japanese built Mariner 36 or 40, all of which are much better performing boats with far fewer problems. For our money, we would not touch the Island Trader 37/38. **• PS**

Endeavour 37

She's comfortable and heavily built, but her performance leaves a lot to be desired.

Tampa Bay, in some respects, is the new Taiwan of American boatbuilding. Lost in the miles of nondescript tin warehouses, surrounded by chain link fences, where hundreds of virtually anonymous businesses come and go like the rain, it is easy to become disillusioned: My yacht was built *here*?

Relic molds lie about the dirty industrial zones like whitewashed bones. Riggers become salesmen. Salesmen become builders. Builders *never* become businessmen, which is about the only difference between Taiwan and Tampa. An eager, low-paid workforce (read Cuban), favorable business climate (low taxes), and sunny weather (considered 50% of an employee's compensation here) combine to make the environs of Florida's largest west coast city a logical place to rent a shed, buy some used tooling, hire a couple of glass men and a carpenter (there's a sort of floating labor pool in the Tampa area), and hang your shingle—I.M. Starstruck Yacht Co.

In the 1970s, Southern California—Costa Mesa more than any other city—was a major boatbuilding center. It was much the same as South Florida is today, until Orange County got tough on environmental emissions, and for the sake of a few parts per million of styrene fumes, essentially drove the boatbuilders out. Two early giants, Columbia Yachts and Jensen Marine (Cal boats) fled. Islander stuck it out until succumbing to bankruptcy just a few years ago.

Endeavour Yacht Corporation traces its lineage to those good ol' days in Costa Mesa. Co-founder Rob Valdez began his career at Columbia, managed, incidentally, by brother Dick Valdez, who later founded Lancer Yachts. Rob followed Vince Lazzara to Florida to work for Gulfstar. The other co-founder, John Brooks, had worked for Charley Morgan and then

Specifications

LOA	37' 5"
LWL	30' 0"
Beam	11' 7"
Draft	4' 6"
Displacement	21,000 lbs.
Ballast	8,000 lbs.
Sail area	580/640 (sloop/ketch)

Gulfstar and Irwin. "It's so incestuous," he once said, "it's pathetic."

In any case, Rob Valdez and John Brooks founded Endeavour in 1974 using the molds from Ted Irwin's 32-footer to launch the business. The company built about 600 32s in all. Spurred by this success, Valdez and Brooks began looking around for a larger sistership to expand the line. Just how they "developed" the 37 is a tale best left untold until the principals pass away or become too senile to read the yachting periodicals. Brooks calls the 37 a "house design," and that is generous. The total number of Endeavour 37s built is 476—a lot for a boat that size.

In 1986 Brooks sold the company to Coastal Financial Corporation of Denver, Colorado. Despite upgrading the pedigree of its model line with designs

Owners' Comments

"For what the boat is, it is a good value. Lots of room for the length. Well built, solid feel. Would like a better pointing boat, and larger, fewer berths. Otherwise very happy."

—1985 model in Manitowoc, WI

"Boat is a little slow, but otherwise sails well. We took out the electric refrigerator and put in an icebox—great move. Also eliminated the pilot berth for more storage."

—1981 model in Braintree, MA

"I live aboard and love the "A" plan layout. I like not having a V-berth. Very good, seakindly boat, put together very well. I spent four years looking for a Plan "A." Added an electric windlass, Cruisair heat pump, roller main and jib, 4KW generator and am very happy."

—1981 model in Norfolk, VA

"There's lots of weather helm in strong (20-knot) winds. Seems to be a design flaw. Nice use of teak inside and out. Very spacious belowdeck. Spacious cockpit, well suited for entertaining and coastal cruising. Not laid out for offshore, but I don't do that."

—1979 model in Lompoc, CA

"Not a pretty boat due to high freeboard and higher still cockpit coaming. Well built and luxurious if you care nothing for performance. Use your engine when going to windward. Can be bought cheaply."

—1981 model in Huntington, NY

by Johan Valentijn, Endeavour's position was plagued by declining sales and competition with its own products on the used boat market.

Brooks said, "When boats started to blister, I said, 'God's on our side! Maybe they'll disappear and go away. Everything else becomes obsolete—your car, your clothes. We're the only ones building a product that won't go away!' "

The Endeavour 37 represents a decent value for the cruising family more interested in comfort and safety than breathtaking performance. Let's take a closer look.

Sailing Performance

Most Endeavour 37s are sloop rigged, though the company did offer the ketch as an option—an extra $1,800 in 1977. The sloop is somewhat underpowered, so the ketch would appear to give the boat some much needed sail area. With either rig, it is not a fast boat, nor was it intended to be.

A bowsprit was added at one point to increase the foretriangle area and to facilitate handling ground tackle, though some photographs show the forestay still located at the stem despite the presence of an anchor platform, which was an earlier option. Also, a tall mast option was offered. Many readers complain of heavy weather helm in higher wind velocities, and moving the center of effort forward by means of enlarging the foretriangle would be one solution.

PHRF ratings range from a high of 198 for the standard rig in the Gulf of Mexico area, to 177 for a tall rig with bowsprit racing in Florida. PHRF ratings, of course, are adjusted according to local fleet performance, so variances between regions are to be expected. Most 37' club racers rate 10 to 40 seconds per mile faster, and a high-performance boat such as the Elite 37 or J/37 will clean its clock by 80 seconds per mile and more. Make no mistake, the Endeavour is a cruising boat.

Some of the boat's other troubles are presumably attributable to hull design, something most of us can do little about. The boat points no better, despite a fairly fine entry. One reader says he tacks through 115°, a number competitive only with schooners. Another notes excessive leeway.

Such performance may be expected from a boat with a long, shoal-draft keel, though it is cut away at the forefoot and terminates well forward of the spade rudder. Many owners report satisfactory balance as long as they pay attention to trim, reefing, and sail combinations. And it deserves mentioning that the Endeavour 37 has been happily employed as a charter boat by several companies, including Bahamas Yachting Services, which moves its fleet between the Bahamas and the Virgin Islands each season. It has and can make safe ocean passages.

Engine

The standard engine was the freshwater-cooled, 50-hp Perkins 4-108 with 2.5 to 1 reduction gear, a real workhorse that is something of a stick against which all others are measured. It rated tops among mechanics in *Practical Sailor*'s 1989 diesel engine survey. The company began phasing it out that year in favor of a new line. The Perkins 4-108 is a good engine for this boat, adequately sized for the waterline and displacement.

Access to the engine compartment is reasonable; the companionway steps are removable and there are sound insulating materials glued to the inside of the box.

Fuel capacity is about 65 gallons in a baffled tank.

A two-blade, bronze propeller was standard, though many respondents in our owner's survey stated they had switched to a three-blade to improve control backing down. This, of course, is a problem with many boats. A three-blade, automatically feathering prop would improve performance under power and minimize drag under sail. It seems a shame to further destroy the performance of this boat by turning a three-blade, fixed prop, just for control in reverse; at that point one must ask himself just how much time he intends to spend going backwards.

Construction

The Endeavour 37 is a good example of low-tech construction—nothing fancy—no exotic fibers, core materials or unusual tooling. The hull is a single-skin, solid fiberglass laminate. No owners reported structural problems with oilcanning panels or moving bulkheads. Numerous owners, however, complained of gelcoat crazing, a condition also cited of the Endeavour 32. Gelcoat repair kits seldom match old and faded gelcoat colors, so owners are faced with an expensive re-gelcoat job or painting with an epoxy or polyurethane paint system. Since most older fiberglass boats inevitably suffer gelcoat crazing in areas of stress or impact (a dropped winch handle will do it), we'd be more concerned with the condition of gelcoat below the waterline. The results of *Practical Sailor*'s 1989 Boat Owner's Questionnaire showed 8 of 19 Endeavours had blistered; 42% is high.

The interior is built up of plywood with teak trim. Workmanship is generally good. In fact, one owner who said his hobby is woodworking, said, "The trim joints are excellent." In general, owners liked the boat because it feels solid, "built like a tank."

Problem areas included gate valves on through-hulls, which some owners have correctly replaced with sea cocks; side-loading refrigerators on some boats that were replaced with top-loading ice boxes; pumping of the Isomat spar; inaccessible electrical wiring; V-berths too short for people over 6'; listing due to water and holding tank placement; and plastic Vetus hatches crazing and dripping. Ventilation seems to be a concern of many owners, though with 10 opening portlights and three hatches, there's not

The "A" interior plan (top) is popular with those who live aboard their boats; the "B" plan (bottom) was designed more with the charter trade in mind. Both arrangements have pros and cons.

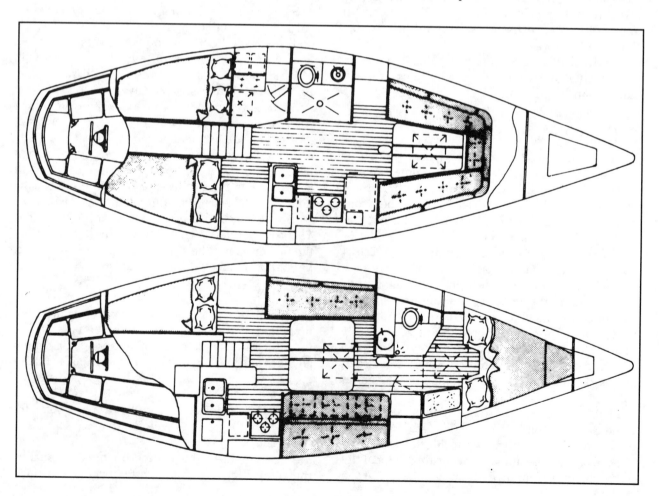

much more to be done except add cabin fans and rig wind scoops.

An Endeavour trademark is the teak parquet cabin sole, which makes you feel like you're dribbling down center court at the Boston Garden. Some like it, some don't, but at least it's different.

The keel is part of the hull mold, with internal lead ballast dropped in and glassed over. There are no keel bolts to worry about, but in the event of a grounding one should look to see if the skin has been punctured and water entered the cavity. The laminate must be thoroughly dried before repairs are made, and this can mean a fairly long waiting period. The shape of the keel is what is sometimes called a "cruising fin," shallow and long with a straight run. The boat should take the bottom well, whether it is an accidental grounding or intentional careening for bottom work on some distant island.

Interior

Two arrangement plans were offered—"A" and "B." The first is a bit unusual in that the forward V-berths are dispensed with in favor of an enormous U-shaped dinette; owners of this plan like it. In its lowered position, the table converts to a huge, sumptuous double berth.

And there is a handy shelf forward for books, television and knick-knacks. The hull sides are decorated with thin teak slats that are widely spaced and fastened flat against the liner. This plan has a large forepeak, divided into two compartments, one for chain and the after one for sails, accessible from the deck.

The galley is a sideboard affair located to starboard and the head is opposite to port, just about midships. Hot and cold pressure water and a shower are standard equipment. The sink is porcelain and there is a full-length mirror. Plumbing has copper tubing and there is an automatic shower sump pump. Aft in Plan "A" are two large double quarter berths.

Plan "B" is the more conventional, with V-berths forward (no sail stowage in the forepeak), the toilet compartment just abaft the head of the bunk, settees in the saloon with an offset dropleaf table, pilot berth outboard above the starboard settee, aft galley and a port quarter cabin.

There is a privacy door to this stateroom (not shown in the layout illustration), which is no doubt what the public demands; however, some owners complain that it is stuffy and cramped. That, of course, is what you get with a small, enclosed cabin aft in the boat; despite overhead hatches, vents, and portlight opening into the cockpit footwell, ventilation is bound to suffer.

There seem to be pros and cons to both plans. "A" is certainly more open, which will suit a couple with few overnight guests. Ventilation is better as air coming in through the forward deck hatch freely circulates in the main cabin; the main bulkhead in "B," as in most boats with this type of layout, obstructs air flow, and nowhere is this problem more acute than in the tropics, where every breath of ocean breeze feels like the difference between life and death.

Both plans offer sleeping accommodations for at least six, including decent sea berths. Plan "B" has a

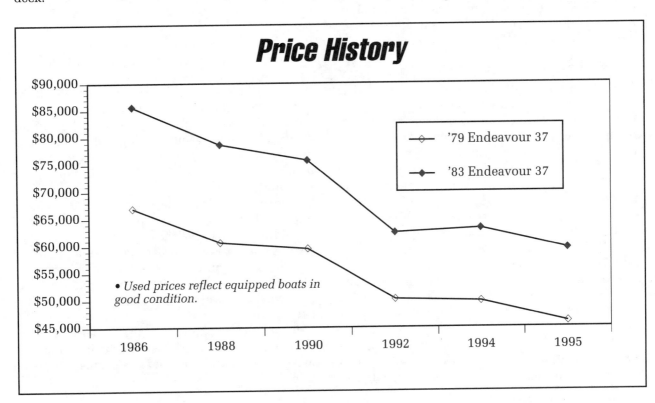

Price History

'79 Endeavour 37
'83 Endeavour 37

• Used prices reflect equipped boats in good condition.

pilot berth that ups the count to seven, but most owners of this layout had converted it to stowage space.

The deep, double sinks in both "A" and "B" are reasonably close to the centerline of the boat, and should drain on either tack.

In the late 70s, a three-burner alcohol stove and oven was standard. On the boat we chartered for a week in the Bahama Islands, the stove was LPG and there was a nifty tank locker in the cockpit coaming, well hidden yet easily accessed. The garbage container and insulated beverage container in the cockpit are nice features.

Both plans also have chart tables, which of course is appreciated. The longer you study the arrangement plans, the more you realize just how much has been fitted into the available space. If any corners have been cut to make this happen it's probably the length of some berths, which a few owners criticized (presumably the endomorphs and Ichabod Cranes among us).

A high percentage of the owners surveyed are live-aboards and almost without exception they consider the boat ideal for their purposes. And it's not difficult to see why. During our week of chartering, there was plenty of space for two couples to move about without knocking elbows at every turn.

The aft cabin is, however, cramped, and getting into the high berth would be easier with a step; one is leery of jumping in, especially given the low overheads of boats. Also, one has to get his bottom on the berth first, then swivel around to get the feet aimed in the right direction. If your mate is already in bed, this can be a maneuver almost impossible to perform politely! The V-berths are preferred for ventilation and ease of getting in and out.

On Deck

The Endeavour 37 is easily appreciated on deck. The side decks are wide and uncluttered. The foredeck, though narrow at the bow, is adequate for sail handling, and the high cockpit coaming makes for a good backrest and a sense of protection. The toerail rises forward so that there is a sort of mini-bulwark for security when changing sails or handling ground tackle.

In profile, the coaming seems too high, especially on top of the high freeboard; one owner said he'd have liked to see an Endeavour 37 without this great, wraparound coaming.

From the helm it's a different story. The varnished cap board on the coaming defines the attractive curve, and does impart a feeling of safety and well being.

Coamings such as this, which extend over the sea hood (a good safety feature), make installation of a waterproof dodger much easier, though the dodger will be large and extend athwartship nearly the full beam of the boat at that station.

The large size of the cockpit is worth noting. In fact, it probably borders on being too large for off-shore sailing. A pooping may temporarily affect handling, but given the considerable volume of the hull, the presence of a good bridgedeck, and assuming that weather boards are in place, water shouldn't get below or unduly sink the stern. Still, it is a boat we'd like to see with large diameter scuppers for safety's sake. One owner said he thought it was possible to run two large scupper hoses aft through the transom, which is a sensible idea. Another said the cockpit was too wide and that it was difficult to brace his feet when heeled.

Conclusion

The Endeavour 37 is a Florida boat. Windward sailing performance was purposely sacrificed for shoal draft, which is a requirement of cruising the Florida Keys and Bahama Islands. The cockpit is large and the deck area spacious.

Either you like the Endeavour 37's distinctive cockpit coaming or you don't; we found the cabintop area just abaft the coaming useful for stowing suntan lotion, hats and the usual cockpit clutter; in calm conditions, it even makes a fairly decent, elevated seat when you want to pontificate to the rest of the crew.

Sailing performance is marginal, especially upwind. The rig, however, is very simple and will seldom get the beginner in trouble, which explains the boat's appeal to charter companies. A light, nylon multi-purpose sail will be essential to light air performance, but it is probable that many owners turn on the engine when the wind drops below about 10 knots, and when going to windward to get that extra few degrees.

Our most serious concerns with the boat are, unfortunately, those that are uncorrectable. You can replace the gate valves with sea cocks, rewire the electrical system, even install flexible water and holding tanks to correct minor listing tendencies, but there's nothing practical that can be done about poor hull design.

One reader suggested fitting a hollow keel shoe to improve the boat's windward performance...hollow, he said, because the boat is heavy enough as it is. The boat also appears not to balance well, and though this tendency can be mitigated to some extent by mast rake and sail trim, it may well extend to the shape of the ends of the hull's waterline plane when heeled.

In all fairness, however, the Endeavour 37 is heavily built, reasonably well finished, comfortable to cruise and live aboard, and it sells for an attractive price.

• **PS**

C & C Landfall 38

We've yet to find the perfect cruiser, but much of what we'd want can be found right here.

The C&C Landfall 38 was the midsize boat in the Canadian company's three-boat Landfall range, which also included a 35- and a 43-footer. This series was produced as a distinct line until 1987, when the Landfall name was dropped.

Unlike other C&Cs, whose interior and deck layouts are designed for racing as well as cruising, the Landfalls are geared toward cruising, with more comfort, a slightly higher degree of finish detail, and deck layout concessions to the cruising couple.

These are performance cruisers, however. Despite more wetted surface, more displacement, and a slightly smaller rig than the original C&C 38, the Landfall 38 is a fast boat, designed for cruisers who want to get there quickly, as well as in style.

The Landfall 38 is a direct descendant of the old C&C 38, the older hull design having been modified with slightly fuller sections forward, a slightly raked transom rather than an IOR reversed transom, a longer, shoaler keel, and a longer deckhouse for increased interior volume.

Nevertheless, the hull is more that of a sleek racer rather than a fat cruiser. For the additional performance that makes the boat a true performance cruiser, you trade off a hull volume that is slightly smaller than you would expect in a pure cruiser of the same waterline length. This is most notable in the ends of the boat, where the V-berth forward narrows sharply, and the hull rises so quickly aft that C&C's normal gas bottle stowage at the end of the cockpit is eliminated.

C&C was a pioneer in composite fiberglass construction. Balsa coring became synonymous with the company name over the years.

Construction

Construction of the Landfall 38 is typical of the C&C line. Hulls are a one-piece, balsa cored molding. The

Specifications

LOA	37' 7"
LWL	30' 2"
Beam	12' 0"
Draft	4' 11"
Displacement	16,700 lbs.
Ballast	6,500 lbs.
Sail area	648.5 sq. ft. (100% jib)

deck and the top of the cabin trunk are also balsa cored. Hull and deck are through-bolted with stainless steel bolts on 6" centers. The hull-to-deck bolts also serve as fasteners for the teak toerail, which replaces the familiar and businesslike slotted aluminum toerail used on other boats in the C&C line.

C&C used butyl tape as a compound in the hull-to-deck joint. Although this is a good, resilient bedding compound, it has no real structural properties. We would rather see an adhesive rubber compound such as 3M 5200 used in the joint to provide a chemical backup to the strong mechanical fastening.

The keel is an external lead casting, bolted to an integral keel sump. The keel is a fairly low aspect ratio fin, keeping the draft of the Landfall 38 to 5'. The keel is flat on the bottom, and the boat will stand on its keel, something that can't be said for a lot of fin keel boats.

All deck hardware is through-bolted, and is equipped with either backup plates or oversize washers. The relatively narrow hull-to-deck flange, however, means that some of the backup plates do not lie flat on the underside of the deck, as they bridge the narrow flange. This can result in uneven local stresses which can lead to gelcoat cracks in the vicinity of hardware such as lifeline stanchion bases.

The Landfall 38 uses bronze seacocks on all underwater through hull fittings. These are properly bolted to the hull, and their hoses are double clamped. The skin fittings are neither recessed flush to the hull nor faired in, however. This would be a fairly easy task for the owner.

In contrast to many boats, the mast step does not sit in the depths of the bilge where it can slowly turn to mush, taking the bottom of the mast with it. Rather, the mast step spans two deep floor timbers in the bilge sump, keeping the heel of the mast out of the water and providing stiffness in an area which is frequently too weak in fin keel boats.

Although most construction details are excellent, there are some shortcomings surprising on a boat of this quality. The engine compartment has no sound-proofing, despite the fact that the engine sits a few feet from the owner's berth.

C&C construction is light but strong. The Landfall 38 is heavier than the old C&C 38 because of extra ballast, more interior joinerwork and molding, and a longer deck.

Handling Under Sail

Although the Landfall 38 is a cruising boat, her performance approaches or exceeds that of many production racer-cruisers. Her hull is basically an undistorted IOR shape, and the rig is a slightly shorter version of the old C&C 38 rig.

The Landfall is a full 2,000 lbs heavier than the original C&C 38. Nevertheless, there is relatively little difference in the performance of the two boats.

In typical C&C fashion, the rig is aerodynamically clean, with airfoil spreaders and Navtec rod rigging. Shroud chainplates—also Navtec—are set inboard for good upwind performance.

The large rig and big headsails of the Landfall may be intimidating to some cruising couples. The 100% foretriangle area of 385 square feet is pretty intimidating, since it means that the 150% genoa has an area of almost 580 square feet.

Because of the large foretriangle, the boat is a natural candidate for a good roller furling headsail system if it is to be cruised by a couple.

Main halyard, reefing, and cunningham lines are all led aft to the cockpit. Headsail halyards, however, lead to winches atop the cabin trunk just aft of the mast. This prevents the helmsman from assisting with headsails when the boat is sailed by a couple. This may or may not be a problem, depending on how agile the foredeck crew is. Since you can get two headsail halyards and two headsail halyard winches, a better solution might be to relocate one of the headsail winches aft, leaving the other near the mast. Then, headsail hoisting and dropping can be tailored to the particular crew's needs.

Surprisingly, self-tailing winches were not standard on the boat, except for the mainsheet winch. On an expensive boat which has hot and cold water as standard items, we'd certainly expect to see self-tailing genoa sheet winches, particularly if the boat is to be used for shorthanded sailing. Self-tailers make sail handling so much easier when cruising that they are just about the first thing we'd add to any cruising boat. And they'd be the biggest self-tailers we could fit on the winch islands.

The Landfall 38 is stiff and well-balanced under sail. Owners report that she is as fast or faster than similar boats of the same size. The Landfall 38's PHRF rating, for example, is 120, squarely between the 114 of the Cal 39 and the 126 of the Tartan 37—two boats to which the Landfall 38 will inevitably be compared in size, type, and price.

To our way of thinking, performance cruising is what it's all about. It's all well and good to have a heavy, underrigged boat if you're cruising around the world. Most people's cruising, however, is limited to a few weeks a year, with moderate distances between ports, and schedules that have to be met. A boat that will get you there fast, safely, and in comfort is a highly desirable type of boat for this kind of cruising. From a performance viewpoint, the Landfall 38 meets those requirements.

Handling Under Power

C&C was one of the first boatbuilding firms to introduce Yanmar diesels into the US market, and they stuck with Yanmar through thick and thin. Yanmar engines have been a paragon of reliability, but they have had the reputation for vibration and noise. Vibration has at times been so bad that engine mounts have broken and shafts have refused to stay in their couplings. It is always difficult to say in an engine installation whether the engine, the design of the installation, or the person doing the installation is at fault when there are problems. One Landfall 38 owner has had three prop shafts in his boat. Now, after careful matching of the shaft flanges and careful alignment of the engine, he reports satisfaction with the installation. C&C picked up a hefty bill on that one, but they did it without hesitation.

Careful engine and shaft alignment is a key to good engine performance, particularly in a modern boat with a short shaft and a flex-mounted diesel engine.

The 30 hp Yanmar 3HM, which replaced the 3QM in the Landfall 38, is perfectly adequate power for the boat, easily achieving hull speed. The boat handles well under power in either forward or reverse.

Engine access for service is a mixed bag. The engine is tucked well aft, under the cockpit, and drives the prop through a V-drive. The oil is checked by removing a panel in the quarterberth in the owner's cabin. The companionway ladder and a bureau next to it remove fairly easily for access to the back of the engine, although it will probably be necessary to empty the drawers before the bureau can be lifted out. The oil filter is reached by climbing down into the starboard cockpit locker. Once again, emptying the locker may be necessary.

Since there is no engine drip pan, you must exercise great care when changing oil and oil filters to keep the bilge clean. The engine is wedged so tightly under the cockpit sole that a funnel is required—with a long hose—to add either oil or engine coolant. A partial plywood bulkhead that hangs over the engine complicates this, and could easily be cut away to give slightly better access.

Battery access is poor. A mirror is required to check electrolyte levels, and filling the batteries just about requires removing them from the battery boxes.

The standard prop is a solid two bladed wheel. To reduce the considerable drag of this installation, we'd change to either a folding two bladed prop such as a Martec, or a feathering prop such as the Maxprop.

Deck Layout

Although the deck layout of the Landfall 38 is similar to that of other boats in the C&C line—performance oriented—some changes have been made to make the boat more suited to cruising. The stern rail incorporates a fold down swimming ladder, and the bow pulpit is the walk-through type, suited to tying up bow-to at the dock. The bow pulpit also incorporates international style running lights, rather than the running lights mounted in the topsides that were a C&C trademark for years. Thank God for progress.

Unfortunately, the wiring for the running lights is relatively unprotected inside the anchor locker, and the electrical connections there are simple butt splices with no weathersealing.

The anchor locker has strong hinges, but lacks a positive latch. There is also no means of securing the bitter end of the anchor rode. Prudent owners will install an eyebolt or through-bolted padeye.

A new stainless steel stemhead fitting incorporates bow rollers for both chain and rope. There is no provision for a keeper pin in the bow roller, however, and the cheeks of the fitting do not extend high enough to guarantee that the rode will not jump out of the roller when the boat pitches at anchor.

With the shrouds set well inboard, fore and aft access is excellent. There are handrails along the cabintop, and a stainless steel guardrail over the forward dorade boxes to keep headsail sheets from fouling.

C & C managed to cram three cabins into the Landfall 38 with fair success, and was even able to include an enclosed head with separate shower stall. The nav station and owner's cabin aft of the head need some protection from the weather, however: if the companionway is left open under sail, spray could get below and ruin everything from charts to instruments to bedding.

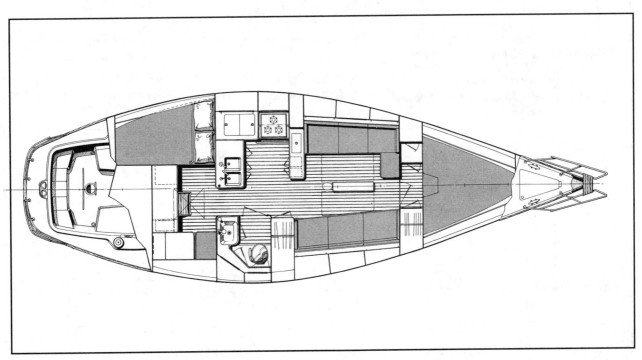

A few Landfall 38s were built with teak decks. This $10,000 option really makes the boat elegant, and is practical underfoot.

Although this is a cruising boat, there is no molded coaming for the attachment of a cockpit dodger, except a small lip around the companionway hatch. Admittedly, leading all sail controls aft along the cabin top complicates the installation of a dodger, but it can be done. Of course, the dodger can be installed even without a breakwater, but it won't be as effective in keeping water out of the cockpit.

The cockpit is a fairly typical T-shaped C&C design. A large-diameter Edson wheel makes it possible for the helmsman to sit to weather or to leeward, but requires making the cockpit seats too short to lie on. On some C&C models, molded seats in the aft corners of the cockpit serve both to support the helmsman's seat and as storage for propane bottles. On the Landfall 38, the cockpit has been pushed so far aft—because of the longer deckhouse—that the hull is too shallow under the aft end of the cockpit for the traditional gas lockers. A separate molded bottle locker that fits under the helmsman's seat is installed when a gas stove is used. Unfortunately, this eliminates the normal life raft storage position. Owners who want both propane and a life raft are going to have to figure out another place to stow the life raft.

A shallow locker under the port cockpit seat is handy for small items, and there is a deep locker under the starboard seat. Changing oil filters requires climbing down into this locker, as does adjusting the stuffing box.

The forward end of the cockpit is protected by a good bridgedeck. Although the companionway is slightly off center, it is not enough to be concerned about in heavy weather. The companionway has other problems, however. Since the bulkhead slopes forward, the drop board must be left in place when it rains. Also, since the bottom of the companionway is below the top of the cockpit coamings, ORC requirements demand that it be left in place when racing offshore. Although this isn't a racing boat, the ORC requirements make good guidelines for offshore cruising practices. Because the drop board is a single teak-faced plywood board, in either situation the companionway must be all the way closed—or left all the way open.

The companionway sill has no lip, so that water can enter the cabin under the drop board. This is a simple fix for owner or factory. The prudent owner will also install a barrel bolt to secure the drop board in place when sailing offshore.

Belowdecks

C&C's interior designs are among the best in the business, and the interior of the Landfall 38 is no exception. The preponderance of teak is a little overwhelming, but it is varnished, rather than oiled, making it slightly lighter than you might expect.

It takes quite a bit of ingenuity to cram a three-cabin interior and huge head with separate shower stall into a 38' boat. In the Landfall 38, this has been accomplished with a reasonable amount of success.

The forward cabin has the usual V-berth, drawers, several lockers, and a cedar-lined hanging locker. This hanging locker is the only really usable hanging

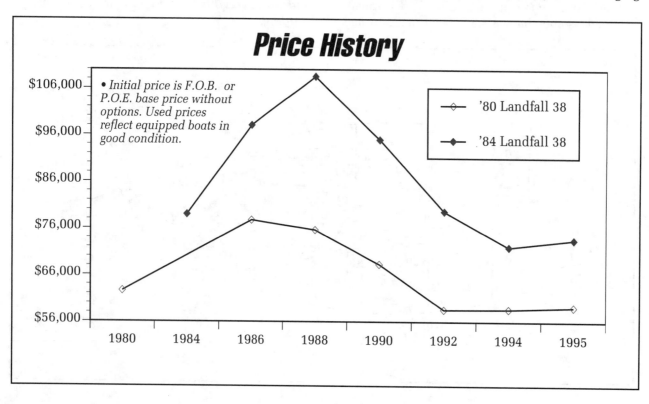

Price History

- *Initial price is F.O.B. or P.O.E. base price without options. Used prices reflect equipped boats in good condition.*

'80 Landfall 38
'84 Landfall 38

space on the entire boat, despite the existence of a rudimentary hanging locker in the aft cabin.

A large hatch over the forward cabin can be used as an escape hatch; a single step is mounted on the bulkhead to make it possible to climb out the hatch. There is solid 6' headroom in the forward cabin, and enough standing room for comfortable dressing. The V-berth, however, is too pointed at the foot for reasonable comfort for two tall people. There are reading lights over each side of the berth, and a light in the hanging locker—a welcome feature.

The main saloon begins aft of the forward cabin, with no intervening head compartment.

Lighting and ventilation of the Landfall 38 is about the best we've seen in a production boat. Both fluorescent and incandescent fixtures are located throughout the main cabin. Remember that you should not use fluorescent lights when you are operating the Loran, as the RF noise of fluorescent lights may interfere with signal acquisition.

The main cabin, galley, and head are ventilated by four large cowl vents in dorade boxes, plus small opening hatches in head and galley. C&C gets an A+ for ventilation in this boat.

Water tanks are located under the main cabin settees, where they belong. Unfortunately, these tanks vent to the outside of the hull, risking contamination of the water supply. This is a common fault in American production boats, and one with no real justification. We'd rather risk spilling a little water in the inside of the boat by overfilling the tanks than risk salt water in our fresh water supply from water siphoning into the tanks in heavy weather through vents mounted in the topsides.

The Landfall 38 uses molded polyethylene water tanks. Occasionally, these tanks are "overcooked" during manufacture, imparting an unpleasant taste to the water that cannot be removed. We've seen it on more than one boat, including C&Cs.

Fresh water plumbing is butyl tubing rather than the more commonly seen clear PVC. Butyl is far less likely to impart any taste to your water, and is highly desirable. It is easily recognized by its battleship gray color and relative rigidity. A manifold under the sink allows switching between the three water tanks, which have a total capacity of 99 gallons. In addition, the 30 gallon holding tank could easily be replumbed as a fresh water tank, giving a very respectable water capacity properly distributed throughout the boat.

In typical C&C fashion, the galley is well laid out and well executed, with deep centerline sinks, kickspace under the counters, and a large icebox. The icebox lid is insulated (hurray!) but ungasketed (boo!), and the icebox melt water is pumped overboard (hurray!) rather than draining into the bilge.

Counter space is excellent. In an attempt to get more, a fold-down counter is fitted over the stove.

Unfortunately, it must be folded up when the stove is in use, making the locker behind the stove inaccessible. Since the boat already has good counter space, we'd eliminate the folding nuisance.

The standard stove is a large gimballed alcohol affair. Don't even consider it. Get either the optional propane installation, or the optional CNG stove. Alcohol has no business as a cooking fuel on any boat to be used as a serious cruising boat.

The stove recess is protected by a stainless steel grabrail which gives the cook a handhold and prevents him from being thrown against the stove in a seaway. A counter with built-in bottle storage separates the galley from the main cabin.

Generally, the galley is usable at sea or at anchor, with excellent storage, usable spaces, and functional appliances. Hot and cold pressure water is standard, and a backup fresh water foot pump is provided at the galley sink.

The main cabin table is strongly mounted to both cabin sole and mast, and easily—and honestly—serves six at dinnertime. Port and starboard settees can be used for sleeping, although the backrests at the head and foot of each settee will have to be removed and stored somewhere for anyone over about 5'8" tall.

Storage is provided outboard of each settee. The handy owner will install shelves in these lockers to better utilize the space.

Opposite the galley is a huge head complete with separate shower stall. The sink and counter are a single fiberglass molding with a large sink and a high protective lip, making this part of the head infinitely more usable than the usual tiny oval sink.

Although at first glance there appears to be a great deal of storage in the head, much of the locker space is occupied by plumbing. The only locker really suited for linens is located in the shower stall, and is equipped with a latch which must be reached through a finger hole in the locker door. Water will inevitably find its way into this locker. The locker could easily be fitted with another type of catch, and ventilation holes could be bored through to the head compartment to help prevent mildew. The separate shower stall will make those unused to boat living far more comfortable, although some might prefer the additional storage space the boat had before the separate stall appeared.

Oddly, the water closet is tucked so far under the side deck that it's impossible to sit upright on it. While you may argue that few people sit upright on the toilet, there will be plenty of cracked crania before you get used to the required position.

Another oddity is that the head door is louvered. Admittedly, there is little privacy in the head on any boat. Since the Landfall's head is already well-vented by a cowl vent and an opening hatch, we'd eliminate the louvered head door to restore at least a bit of privacy.

The aft cabin makes a good owner's stateroom, with large double quarterberth to port and chart table to starboard. Unfortunately, the chart table makes a better dressing table than chart table. There is no provision for the installation of instruments such as radio or Loran in the nav area. A shallow hanging locker occupies the space outboard of the chart table where these instruments would normally be mounted. It's a poor hanging locker, since the garments face thwartships rather than fore and aft. The only thing you can see is the last item you put in. It is unusable as a wet locker, since you'd have to drag your foul weather gear over the chart table.

For serious cruising, we'd eliminate this hanging locker, using the space to mount radios, Loran, repeaters, and provide a bookcase for our navigation books. This has the serendipitous byproduct of allowing the shallow chart table to be made deeper, which it sorely needs.

What about hanging space? Well, here goes. Make the linen locker in the shower a hanging locker by eliminating or reducing the size of the holding tank under it. Or (we can see marketing people putting guns to their heads), eliminate the separate shower stall and create more storage. So much for redesign.

In the way of modifications, however, the nice double quarterberth is going to get soaking wet the first time a big one comes over the weather rail and water pours through the companionway when the boat is on starboard tack. In the same situation on port tack, the chart table will get soaked. A set of plexiglass screens on either side of the companionway should solve that one, and should be considered if the boat is to be used offshore. For shorthanded cruising, that quarterberth is the ideal place for the off watch, provided it can be kept dry. The necessity for keeping the sacrosanct nav station and its fragile electronics—and equally fragile navigator—out of the weather should be obvious.

The basic interior layout of the Landfall 38 is excellent for the cruising couple that likes a private cabin aft, and will sometimes entertain others for extended periods of time. As with most boats, a certain amount of fine tuning of interior spaces will be necessary to get the most out of them. The boat has a fair number of complex systems: hot and cold water, electric pumps, multiple tanks. In fact, the 16 circuits provided for in the electrical panel are almost all used up before you get to things like navigation and performance electronics. Fortunately, there is space for an additional electrical panel. You're probably going to need it.

Conclusions

With an average used price for a 1984 model at around $70,000, the Landfall 38 is not a cheap way to go cruising. The price is typical of luxury performance cruisers in its class.

General design and construction are excellent. The hull is a proven design, the rig is efficient and strong. There are a number of design details that should be improved for serious cruising, notably the companionway, cockpit protection, life raft storage, and provision for shorthanded handling under sail.

A serious cruising boat must function as well bashing to windward for days on end as it does at the dock. Above all, it must keep its crew dry and comfortable. We have yet to find the perfect cruising boat, but many of the things we'd look for are found in the Landfall 38. We wish they were all there, but the fact that they aren't is what keeps designers and builders in business. • **PS**

Morgan 38 and 382

Charlie Morgan's hurrah becomes Ted Brewer's success story becomes today's pseudo-classic.

We receive many requests from readers to review certain boats. Almost without exception, the requests come from owners of the boat suggested. Few boats have been the object of more requests than the venerable Morgan 38. At first blush, it is difficult to determine which Morgan 38 we ought to address, as two distinct designs were built since the first one appeared 22 years ago. After some thought, we decided to trace the history of both as best we could, including also the Morgan 382, 383 and 384.

History

The Morgan 38 was designed in 1969 by Charlie Morgan. He had founded Morgan Yacht Company in St. Petersburg, Florida, in 1965. The Morgan 34 was his first production model. A hometown boy, he had made a name for himself in the 1960 and 1961 Southern Ocean Racing Conference (SORC), winning with a boat of his own design called *Paper Tiger*. While not a formally trained naval architect, Morgan demonstrated his skill with a variety of designs. Many of these were keel/centerboard models, owing to the shoalness of Florida waters. Seventy-nine were built before production halted in 1971.

In 1977, the Morgan 382 was introduced, designed by Ted Brewer, Jack Corey and the Morgan Design Team. According to Brewer, the boat was loosely based on the Nelson/Marek-designed Morgan 36 IOR One Ton. The most obvious difference between the 38 and 382 was the elimination of the centerboard and the addition of a cruising fin keel (NACA 64 012 foil) with skeg-mounted rudder. They are two completely different designs from two different eras in yacht design.

In 1980, the 382 was given a taller rig and called the 383. About 1983 the boat underwent other subtle

Specifications - 38

LOA	37' 8"
LWL	28' 0"
Beam	11' 0"
Draft	3' 9"/8' 4" (board up/down)
Displacement	16,000 lbs.
Ballast	7,500 lbs.
Sail area	640/681 (sloop/yawl)

changes, now called the Morgan 384. The rudder was enlarged and the interior modified. In its three versions, the Brewer model registered about 500 sales.

The company changed ownership several times during this period. It went public in 1968, was later bought by Beatrice Foods and then Thor Industries. Presently it is owned by Catalina Yachts, who built just 24 38s (three were kits) before discontinuing production in 1986.

Design

The first Morgan 38 was a development of the highly successful 34, which Morgan called a "beamy, keel-centerboard, CCA (Cruising Club of America)-style of yacht. We had a good thing going and didn't want to deviate; we found little interest in those days in

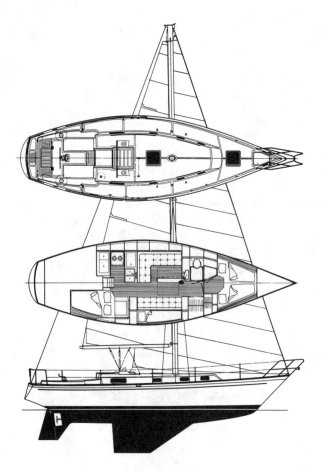

Specifications - 382

LOA	38' 4"
LWL	30' 6"
Beam	12' 0"
Draft	5' 0"/6' 0" (std/deep keel)
Displacement	18,000 lbs.
Ballast	6,800 lbs.
Sail area	668 sq. ft.

keel boats. Centerboards have their own sorts of problems, but there's an awful lot of thin water in the world, and safe refuge and quiet anchorages are mostly in shoal water."

The boat has a long, shoal keel drawing just 3' 9" with the board up. The rudder is attached and there is an aperture for the propeller. "Beamy," in 1969, meant 11 feet. The waterline was fairly short at 28 feet, but the overhangs give the hull a very balanced and pleasing profile. The stern is pure Charlie Morgan—a finely proportioned shape that is neither too big nor too small. In profile, the angle between the stern (which interestingly is a continuation of the line of the backstay) and the counter is nearly 90 degrees. It's a trademark look.

Sloop and yawl rigs were offered, which was typical of CCA designs. The rig has a lower aspect ratio (the proportion of the hoist to the foot of the mainsail) than later designs, including the Brewer-designed 382. Yet this is a very wholesome rig for cruising. Owners responding to our questionnaire said the boat balances very well.

Owners of the 382 and subsequent permutations seemed less pleased. They didn't rate balance as highly, noting most frequently the difficulty in tracking (keeping the boat on a straight course) when sailing off the wind (not uncommon with beamy fin keel designs; it's a trade-off with speed, pointing ability and maneuverability). Others said that they raked their masts forward to improve balance. One thought the problem was caused because the rudder was slightly undersized. Still, these owners liked the way their boats sail.

The rig, of course, isn't the only difference between the Morgan and Brewer designs. The latter has a foot wider beam—12 feet—and a longer waterline. Two keels were offered, the standard five-foot draft and an optional deep keel of six feet. Displacement jumped a thousand pounds to 17,000 despite a reduction in ballast from 7,500 pounds to 6,600 pounds. Centerboard boats, naturally, require more ballast because it isn't placed as low as it is in a deep fin keel boat.

The look of the 382 is much more contemporary. The rake of the bow is straighter, as is the counter, which is shorter than the original 38 as well. Freeboard is higher and the windows in the main cabin are squared off for a crisper appearance.

Construction

The hulls of the early 38s were built of solid fiberglass and the decks of sandwich construction. Some 382 hulls were cored, others not. A variety of core materials were used, mostly Airex foam. The lamination schedule was your basic mat and woven roving, with Coremat added as a veil cloth to prevent print-through.

Both designs have internal lead ballast, sealed on top with fiberglass.

The early 382s did not have the aft bulkhead in the head fiberglassed to the hull, which resulted in the mast pushing the keel down. All boats "work" under load, and bulkheads bonded to the hull are essential to a stiff structure. Anyone who has a boat in which major load-bearing bulkheads are not attached to the hull should do so before going offshore. To its credit, the company launched a major recall program.

The owners of all Morgan 38s, as a group, note the strength of the boat. One said he hit a rock at 6 1/2 knots and suffered only minor damage. Very few problems were mentioned. The owner of a 1981 model, however, said he "drilled through hull at

Owners' Comments

"One of the best combinations of design, workmanship, strength, sailing characteristics available. I live aboard. I know of no other sailboat new or used that offers the knowledgable sailor as much for the money."

—1972 model in Florida

"To my knowledge, the only problem areas have been centerboard cables and the mast foot where it sets on the keel. They don't build hulls and decks that thick anymore."

—1970 model with two Transatlantic crossings

"It is among the finest of the vessels our family has owned. I am a construction engineer and can appreciate the quality."

—1983 model in Connecticut

"She is a great boat to cross the Gulf Stream. A little too much draft for cruising in the Abacos—but you can't have both. She is holding up well in the charter business."

—1980 model in Florida

"The accessibility to the engine leaves a lot to be desired."

—1970 model in Florida

waterline and was surprised at thinness of glass on either side of the Airex: 1/8" inside, 1/16" outside." With the stiffness that sandwich construction provides, not as much glass is required; still, protection from collision and abrasion would recommend greater thickness outside. Brewer, incidentally, discounted the report.

Interestingly, Hetron-brand fire-retardant resin was used for a time, prior to 1984; if you recall, this was blamed for the many cases of reported blistering on the early Valiant 40s. About half of the 382 owners responding to our surveys reported some blistering, none serious.

The attached rudder of the early 38 is stronger than the skeg-mounted rudder of later models. But we do prefer the skeg configuration to a spade rudder, at least for cruising. A problem with skegs, however, is the difficulty in attaching them strongly to the hull. One owner said his was damaged in a collision with a humpback whale, but that is hardly normal usage!

Several owners of later models commented that the mast was a "utility pole," recommending a custom tapered spar for those inclined to bear the expense.

Other problems reported in our survey were only minor and were corrected by the company. In fact, owners were nearly unanimous in their praise for Morgan Yachts' customer service.

Interior

The layout of the Morgan 38 is quite conventional and workable. In both incarnations there are V-berths forward, private head with shower (separate enclosure in the 382), dinette in main cabin with settee, galley aft in the port quarter area and nav station with quarter berth opposite to starboard.

Specifications for the first 38s included "attractive wood-grained mica bulkhead paneling, with oiled American walnut trim." This was a popular treatment in the 1960s, and practical, but often done to excess. By the 1980s, fake teak didn't play so well. Owners wanted real wood, and that's what they got in the 382.

Owners of early 38s complained of poor ventilation ("I added six opening ports, and would like an additional center cabin hatch," wrote one), short V-berths ("Could be 4" longer, but I'm 6' 2."), and more closet space (from a live-aboard).

Owners of later models mentioned the need for a larger forward hatch to get sails through, a hatch over the galley, larger cockpit scuppers, and Dorade vents. (Teak Dorade boxes were added on the 384.) They complained of not enough footroom in the V-berths and poor location of the main traveler in the cockpit. (The traveler was moved to the cabinhouse top on the 384.)

Despite these minuses, most owners cite the volume of the interior and many stowage compartments as major reasons for their satisfaction with the boat.

Performance Under Sail

As implied in our comments on balance in the "Design" section of this review, the centerboard 38 sailed beautifully. She is dry and seakindly, stable and relatively fast for her generation. Its PHRF rating ranges from 145 to about 150. The yawl rig is probably not as fast as the sloop, but for the cruising couple, the mizzen sail gives the skipper another means of balancing the boat, as well as a means to fly more sail when reaching if he's prepared to fuss with a staysail.

The 382 rates between 128 and 150, about 137 on average. The Morgan 383 and 384, which are grouped together, rate a mite lower at 135, on average.

It is not surprising that Brewer's redesign is faster, even though it's 1,000-2,000 pounds heavier. This is due to it's deeper fin and higher aspect rig with the ability to carry larger headsails. There is also less wetted surface.

Performance Under Power

The centerboard 38 was powered by the seemingly ageless Atomic Four gasoline engine, though a Perkins 4-107 or Westerbeke 4-107 was available at extra cost ($1,940 in 1969). The early 38s cruise at about 6 1/2 knots.

A first-generation Yanmar—the 3QM30—was used on some 382s, and as owners of those engines know, they tend to be noisy and vibrate a great deal. Yanmar engines improved a great deal after the manufacturer redesigned and retooled the entire line. But the most common powerplant was the magnificent 50-horsepower Perkins 4-108. If we were looking for a Morgan 38 to purchase, we'd certainly lean toward one with this engine.

Both designs handle reasonably well under power, as well as most sailboats do, meaning that backing down with a two-blade prop is a necessarily cautious procedure.

A number of owners recommend changing to a three-blade prop, but that will affect sailing performance. One should examine his sailing style closely before making the move.

Conclusion

The Morgan 38, in any incarnation, is a handsome boat that sails well and is built strong enough for most people's purposes. Some may pause before taking a centerboard boat far offshore, but it has certainly been done—recall, if you will, Carleton Mitchell's hugely successful racer *Finnisterre*.

Both centerboard and fin keel versions seem to us to have advantages and disadvantages that are essentially tradeoffs.

On the one hand, we like an attached rudder for cruising, as it provides the best protection from collision with logs and other hard objects. On the other, we recognize the importance of placing ballast low, as in the fin keel version, and we appreciate Brewer for giving a nice slope to its leading edge so that damage from hitting logs will be minimized. Brewer said that a 382 that passes survey is capable of cruising just about anywhere. "They've crossed oceans," he said.

To our eye, we admit to being fond of the CCA designs with low freeboard and graceful sheer lines. The yawl is a versatile rig that is especially attractive, though it does require more in the way of tuning and maintenance.

An early Morgan 38, in good condition, should sell in the high 20s. Expect to pay a thousand or so more for the yawl. For sellers, considering that in 1969 the base price of the boat was $22,995, that's not a bad return on investment.

Fifteen years later the price had jumped to $84,995 (1984 model). Those boats today are advertised in the mid to high 60s, and occasionally the low 70s. (What anyone is actually getting for these days is another matter entirely).

Considering the changes in the economy, that's still not bad performance. What it means most to the prospective buyer is that the Morgan 38 and 382 are popular, much admired boats that should, we expect, hold their value as well as or better than most others.

• PS

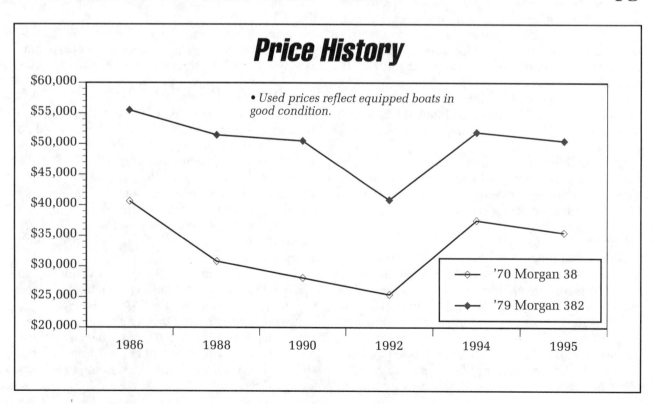

Price History

• *Used prices reflect equipped boats in good condition.*

Legend: ◇ '70 Morgan 38   ◆ '79 Morgan 382

Sabre 38

This stylish sloop with an all-wood interior is a premium fin-keel, spade-rudder club racer.

Sabre Yachts of South Casco, Maine, was founded by Roger Hewson in 1970. Its first boat was the Sabre 28, whose quick acceptance by the public was a portent of good things to come for the fledgling company. In the following years, Sabre built boats up to 42 feet in length. Hewson's formula was to design and build to a curious blend of contemporary hull shapes and traditional interior styling. At one point in time, during the mid-1980s, Sabre was probably the largest builder of production fiberglass boats with built-up wooden interiors. Others, such as Pearson, C & C, O'Day, Hunter, Catalina, et. al., used molded fiberglass pans for furniture foundations. Many custom builders use all-wood, but at about 125 boats per year during its heyday, Sabre built the most. In 21 years, the company built about 1,800 boats.

Unfortunately, Sabre recently joined the growing list of defunct American builders. The company ceased production in January after its major creditor withdrew its line of credit, forcing Sabre to close its doors. A number of boats were claimed by the bank.

The Design

The Sabre 38, like all Sabres, was designed by Roger Hewson and his in-house team. It was introduced in 1982, with an aft-cabin (still with an aft cockpit) version available the next.

In 1986 the boat was redesigned, informally referred to as the Mark II. While this report focuses primarily on the early design, we will touch on some of the changes found in the 1986 redo.

Any builder wishing to produce lots of boats must offer its customers a design that does many things well. It cannot be a flat-out racer, or a lumbering cruiser.

This generally translates to moderate displace-

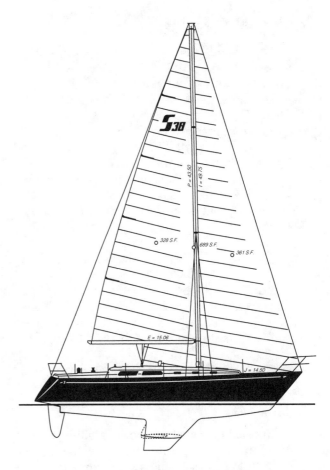

Specifications - Mk I

LOA	37' 10"
LWL	31' 2"
Beam	11' 6"
Draft	6' 6"
Displacement	15,200 lbs.
Ballast	6,400 lbs.
Sail area	688 sq. ft.

ment, long waterline, fin keel and spade rudder. And so it is with the Sabre 38.

The Sabre 38 has a waterline length of 31' 2" and the choice of a deep, fixed keel or keel/centerboard configuration. A partial shallow skeg provides some support for the rudder to swing on. Sabre called the skeg a Tracker™, saying it improves directional stability.

The coachroof has a fairly low profile with 12 windows and portlights. The 38 has a curious little step-down in the coachroof, which disappeared in the Mark II. Steps were not uncommon in older designs, but today, cleaner lines are favored.

Beam of the early 38 was a relatively modest 11' 6", widened to 12' 4" in the Mark II. Neither is so extreme as to produce unusual handling characteristics.

Owners' Comments

"Best ventilated boat I have seen. Self-bleeding feature of the Westerbeke 33 is a real boon! Refrigerator is too close to the engine for good efficiency. Standard head not up to overall quality of boat. We had a Wilcox Imperial substituted. Varnished interior we now have is far superior to the oiled teak. With offset shaft, boat needs a folding prop for top performance under sail."

—1983 model in Connecticut

"The 150-percent genoa needs to be furled early. If you're not racing, use 135-percent genoa instead."

—1982 model in New York

"Trim affected by amount of water in port and starboard tanks. Even though this is rigged as a racing boat, it is easy for two people to sail and even use the spinnaker in up to 12 to 16 knots of wind."

—1983 model in Michigan

"A true delight to sail in strong winds and seas, or light winds. I would prefer an annodized spar as Awlgrip chips easily. Would prefer a varnished interior. Earliest production models have a much poorer icebox design and do not have a molded fiberglass head compartment. When buying, be sure to have weight balanced due to installation of extra equipment (my boat has starboard list)."

—1989 model on Chesapeake Bay

"I recommend the boat highly. Design, construction and attention to small detail are outstanding. Design and tall rig produce good boat speed in the lighter airs. I wish the boat was not quite so tender, but that's the price for speed and high pointing ability."

—1984 model in Florida

"The crew at Sabre cared about their owners, whether their boats were purchased new or used."

—1982 model in Maine

The hull is fairly shallow, with firm bilges, as is typical of this type. The displacement/length (D/L) ratio is 224. For the sake of comparison, the performance-oriented J/40 has a D/L ratio of 199 and the Hunter Legend 40 226. The Cabo Rico 38 cruiser, with much slacker bilges, has a D/L ratio of 375 and the Caliber 38 293. So you can see that the Sabre 38 is intended to sail fairly fast.

One consequence of moderate to light D/L ratios is the necessity of locating the water tanks under settees rather than on centerline, deep in the keel. This robs precious stowage space and makes trim calculations important.

In fact, several owners said their boats had pronounced lists, especially if they didn't carefully monitor tank levels. This is regrettable and somewhat difficult to understand in a boat of this size, quality and price.

The bow, viewed in profile, is a straight line with an aggressive rake. The reverse stern on the early 38 is conservative; on the Mark II it was given additional rake and convexity for a more modern look.

Beauty lies in the eye of the beholder, but we will say we prefer the lines of the Mark II, largely due to the improved stern shape, the absence of the step in the coachroof, and the ever-so-slight slope to the forward end of it.

Construction

Before about the mid-1980s, all Sabres were built of solid fiberglass, with balsa-coring only in the deck. All of the later designs incorporate balsa coring in all or parts of the hull.

Hence, the early 38 was built without a core and the Mark II has a balsa core. We have in the past had some misgivings about the use of balsa coring below the waterline, not because water entering through a crack might migrate across the grain (it doesn't), but because moisture does enter most laminates and may wet the endgrains, potentially contributing, along with fatigue, to delamination.

Fiberglass skins in sandwich construction (on either side of the core) are by design much thinner than a single-skin hull, and while the sandwich is very stiff, the outer skin won't endure abrasion (say, grinding on a beach or rock) as long. Also, balsa-cored boats, especially for the long-distance cruiser, are more difficult to repair.

We think the newer balsa-cored boats are quite good. We'd consider one for coastal cruising, and think balsa or foam core is mandatory for a competitive race boat. For serious cruising, however, we'd stick with a single-skin, solid glass hull.

In a survey of readers' boats several years ago, we reported that Sabre had a below-average incidence of blistering—about 19 percent.

Still, a few readers completing our Boat Owner's Questionnaire stated their boats had blistered, none seriously. Not surprisingly, Hewson elected in the Mark II edition to use Blisterguard gelcoat and immediately inside it a layer of chopped strand glass fibers and vinylester resin.

Vinylester resins, as we reported in our June 15, 1991 report on barrier coatings, are superior in preventing the ingress of moisture through the laminate. The reason for using chopped strand fiber is that it may be sprayed from a gun, eliminating the sizing used to hold the random fibers together in chopped strand mat (CSM); the sizing is highly suspected in the formation of some forms of blistering.

Sabre called the system DuraLam™, though it is, to the best of our knowledge, the same method originally developed by Tillotson-Pearson and used in a variety of yachts, including J/Boat, Freedom, and Alden boats.

Interior construction is where, to our minds, Sabre has really distinguished itself. The all-wood interiors are strong and warm feeling. Bulkheads, stringers and furniture are bonded directly to the hull, with more contact points than many fiberglass pans.

Wood is a better accoustic and thermal insulator than glass, so the interior is warmer and quieter. And, chances are, an all-wood interior provides better access to all parts of the hull, not to mention greater ease of modification should you desire to make changes at some future time.

Oiled teak is the wood of choice at Sabre. Too bad other woods weren't offered. At the least, we'd prefer a nice varnish job to brighten up the interior. Sabre's interiors have always seemed a bit dull to us.

On deck, there are numerous instances of special attention, from the teak coaming caps to the companionway hatch sea hood to the double lifelines and twin gates.

Readers rate the construction of their Sabres from above average to excellent. None cited any complaints. "Interior joinery is as fine as I have seen on any boat," wrote one owner.

Performance

Owners seem pleased with the performance of the early 38, rating its speed upwind and downwind as above average. It has an average PHRF rating of about 114. The Mark II rates about three seconds per mile faster.

This isn't as fast as the J/40, which rates about 75, the Baltic 38 at about 96, or the C & C 37 at about 105. But then the Sabre's all-wood interior suggests that owners are after more than ultra-light weight and all-out speed. For what it is, the Sabre 38 performs and handles well.

Seaworthiness is another category in which the 38 is well regarded. One owner said he'd sailed his to the Virgin Islands three times. Another said his performed well in "30-knot winds and 10-foot seas off the Jersey coast."

On the down side, most owners cited tenderness as troublesome. We don't know what percentage of the owners responding had centerboard models, but suspect the lack of initial stability is true, to some degree, of both centerboard and deep keel models. This is probably a function of the large, double-spreader rig and modest beam.

Perhaps it explains why the Mark II version was given 10 additional inches of beam; that, of course, would help increase form stability.

Remember, however, that in order for a boat to perform well, it must be able to carry a lot of sail area. And when the wind pipes up, reducing sail is necessary and expected.

A heavier boat with less sail area naturally will be able to carry full sail longer, but then it won't be nearly as fast in lighter airs.

None of the owners who cited tenderness said it would stop them from buying the same boat again. We don't think it should either.

One owner recommended using the 135-percent genoa, instead of a 150, when not racing. That sounds like good advice.

The main sheet traveler is located on the cabin top, out of the way of crew in the cockpit. Mid-boom sheeting, however, requires greater purchase to trim the sail.

A Westerbeke 33 diesel engine was standard in most Sabre 38s. This is a good engine, which owners rate as above average to excellent in terms of reliability and performance.

One owner said the boat "backs straight due to offset prop shaft and strut." Accessibility was rated as pretty good, with no more than the usual difficulties reaching some components.

Several owners said reaching the oil filter is not easy. The fuel capacity of the early 38 is 30 gallons in a single aluminum tank; this was increased to 45 gallons in the Mark II.

Interior

The original layout incorporates the usual V-berths forward. Just aft is the head with separate shower stall and opposite are two hanging lockers.

The saloon has opposing settees with a drop-leaf table on centerline. The galley is aft to port and, with the addition of a safety belt, would be secure in a seaway. To starboard is a navigation table with quarter berth.

The aft-cockpit version is a bit unusual for a boat of this length, but shows several clever features. The galley is about amidship, but instead of locating the sink outboard where it would not drain well, it is placed in an island on centerline.

The head is to starboard of this island, but lacks the separate shower stall of the standard plan. The aft cabin has a double berth to starboard and a single

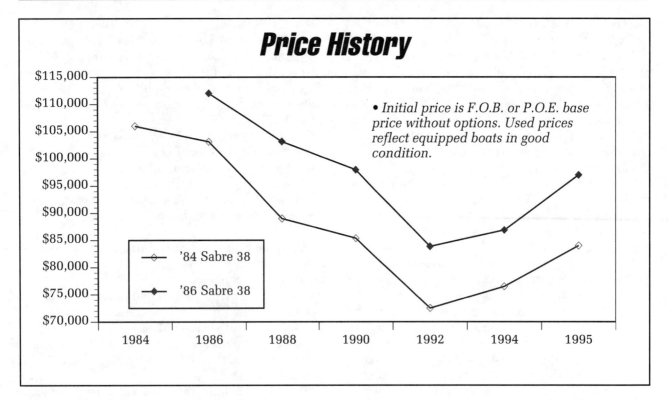

Price History

- *Initial price is F.O.B. or P.O.E. base price without options. Used prices reflect equipped boats in good condition.*

Legend:
- ◇—— '84 Sabre 38
- ◆—— '86 Sabre 38

with nav table to port. Berth lengths in both versions are 6' 6" and have five-inch foam cushions. Headroom is 6' 3".

The interior of the Mark II is somewhat more open. The V-berths do not require an insert cushion to make up a double, and there is a changing seat plus wash basin in the forward cabin.

The galley has plenty of space, and just aft of it, in the port quarter, is a double berth under the cockpit. To starboard is the large head, and a separate nav station.

All three plans provide decent sea berths in the settees and quarter berths. Interestingly, no dinette model was offered; while sometimes considered less seaworthy, offsetting the dinette to one side or the other permits meals without obstructing access fore and aft from the forward cabins, as is the case with centerline drop-leaf tables.

Fresh water capacity of the early 38 was 94 gallons and the holding tank held 24 gallons; in the Mark II these numbers were increased to 106 and 30 respectively.

Conclusion

The Sabre 38 is a well constructed boat with few deficiencies. It is a cut above the plethora of typical fin keel-spade rudder production boats. We like especially the all-wood interior. The only complaints we've read are its initial tenderness (in the early models) and sensitivity to trim.

If you are a serious racer or have dreams of long-distance cruising, you can do better with, say, a J/37 or Crealock 37. With a design such as the Sabre 38, versatility is the operative word. The design and construction of the Sabre 38 will suit the average American sailor just fine.

Hewson earned a reputation for good customer service, and his annual owner rendezvous helped spark a certain esprit de corps. It'll be a shame if he can't find the resources to resume business. • **PS**

Irwin Citation 38

The main reason to choose the Citation 38 is sailing performance: she has the feel of a well-designed boat.

The "Irwin" in Irwin Yachts is Ted Irwin, a boat designer and builder who has been around nearly as long as production fiberglass boats have.

Over the years, Ted Irwin has designed, and Irwin Yachts has built, a variety of sailing boats—from flat-out cruising condos to full-bore racing machines. Starting with the combination racer/cruisers that were then fashionable, Irwin began producing in the 1970s not only cruiser/racers like the Irwin 28, 30, and 37 one-ton, but also roomy center cockpit cruisers like the 37, 38 and 43.

The company has been consistent in the niche they occupy in the sailboat market. Their line has been known as middle of the spectrum, better in quality than the cheapest boats on the market, yet with low enough prices to make the economy shopper think twice before jumping for the cheaper alternatives.

In style, the Citations continue the moderate tradition of Irwin designs. The Citation models are all similar, fairly high-sided with very short overhangs and a low cabin top. The distinctive profile is usually accentuated by a dark sheer stripe that makes a sharp downturn to follow the reverse transom.

In all modern boats with flat bottoms, it's hard getting good headroom without making the boat look ugly. The choice is to keep the sheer line low and attractive and use a high cabin house, or use high sheer and a low cabin top. The Citations use the second method and depend on the sheer stripe to keep the high freeboard from looking ugly. The sculpted cabin top keeps the entire profile low, with a high coaming flowing from the back edge of the cabin to the back of the cockpit.

A distinctive characteristic of the Citations is a complex swim ladder at the aft end of the cockpit.

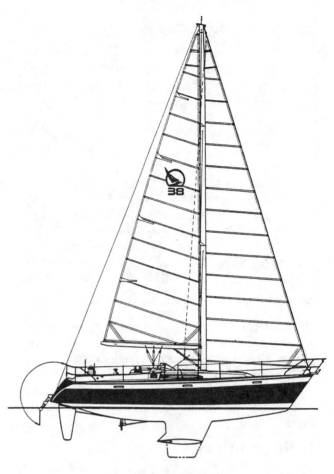

Specifications

LOA	38' 0"
LWL	30' 8"
Beam	12' 6"
Draft	4' 11"/6' 11" (wing/fin)
Displacement	15,000 lbs.
Ballast	5,800 lbs.
Sail area	675 sq. ft.

The ladder is molded into a section of the transom which opens up and swings down for boarding. With the rear end of the cockpit open, it is an effective ladder, but owners report that it is somewhat awkward and difficult to prepare for use. The owner of the boat we sailed described the deployment of the ladder as a "nuisance."

As the largest of the Citations, the 38 is probably the best looking, handling the high-sidedness better than her smaller sisters. The boat has three windows set in the sheer stripe on each side, so they are not very noticeable. Like the other Citations it is distinctly modern-looking—not pretty, but not ugly either.

The company touts the 38 and the two smaller Citations as developments of Irwin's custom racer,

Owners' Comments

"The boat is built to a price for livability and coastal cruising. She's fine for that—extremely roomy, and therefore ugly. Finishing details are fair, sometimes sloppy and cheap. (Of course, I wanted cheap.)

"The boat sails better than I expected. For her size, she's one of the best designs for the Caribbean, where I sail.

"The manufacturer has been extremely uncooperative in shipping replacement parts. It took seven months to get parts after a grounding and sinking. However, for chartering in the Caribbean and northeast US, I'd trade up to another Irwin—I'm crazy."

—1983 model in the Caribbean

"With the shoal keel, the boat is tender but well balanced—you can lock the helm and go for a walk. I bought it because the price was right and I got a good deal. I've been treated reasonably enough—but very slowly—by the dealer and builder.

"Warranty claims included refrigeration, head, gelcoat, and stanchions. The deck lifted at the halyard turning blocks at the base of the mast. I changed these to cheek blocks mounted on the mast. The trim on the drawers is coming off—very cheaply finished.

"Upwind performance is average. Downwind speed is excellent."

—1983 model in RI

Razzle Dazzle, which performed very well on the Southern Ocean Racing Circuit. But they seem to us at best distant cousins of that flashy racer.

Though Irwin has never gone for super-lightweight boats, the production Citations are so much heavier that the comparison seems to be primarily a marketing ploy.

Hull and Deck

In general, Irwin uses conventional modern techniques in building the fiberglass hull and deck. The hull is a one-piece hand-laminated molding, using 24-ounce roving and biaxial fiberglass. Forward of the mast, the hull molding has a foam core—a design feature to provide stiffness and save weight. In today's market, such cored construction is economically feasible if you want a stiff hull and can charge a price above the bottom of the market.

The hull is further stiffened and strengthened by the interior fiberglass grid which incorporates fiberglass stringers to support the keel, mast, and major components of the cabin interior.

The deck is also a one-piece molding, with foam core in the cabin top and walkways, plywood core underneath the winches and hardware. Hull and deck are bolted together through an aluminum toerail.

Standard keel on the 38 is a lead wing design drawing 4' 11". A conventional lead fin is available as an option, and the boat we sailed had the conventional fin. Both keels are external, bolted through the hull and the interior grid.

The shoal draft of the wing, saving 2' compared to the fin, is an obvious advantage. We generally remain skeptical of the value of the wing keel, having seen some very poorly performing ones which were about as effective going to windward as a flopperstopper. But Irwin apparently has enough faith in

their design to make it standard. If we were never going to race the boat, we'd consider trying a wing, but otherwise we'd probably opt for the fin and pay the draft penalty.

The rudder is a conventional modern high-aspect spade driven by a 36" wheel on a pedestal.

Exterior finish of the boat is generally good. The gelcoat does not have a high-gloss finish, but rather more of a matte appearance. This should be easier to maintain, making nicks and scratches less noticeable. The hull molding is fair, with no evident hard spots or ridges, and the deck molding is well done. The non-skid pattern is adequate, but minimal; it should be easy on bare feet.

There is hardly any exterior wood to care for—four teak grab rails and two plywood companionway hatch boards. The hatch boards on our test boat were poorly finished. A meticulous owner will want to finish them properly, or perhaps replace them with some higher-quality plywood, teak or plastic.

Rig

The rig is made in-house by Irwin and would generally be considered overbuilt by modern standards. The mast has two sets of spreaders and is stepped on the keel. The backstay is split to accommodate the fold-out boarding ladder in the transom, and the boat we sailed had single lower shrouds with a babystay forward. Halyards and other running rigging are internal.

Although the top quarter of the mast is tapered, the extrusion is so heavy that we had trouble bending it with the backstay adjuster. The adjustable babystay was also arranged in such a way that there was minimal pull forward, but we re-rigged it and were finally able to get enough mast bend to flatten the mainsail in heavy winds. It is not clear to us why

Irwin uses an adjustable babystay rather than forward lower shrouds, especially when the mast is so stiff. Cruisers would more likely prefer the more conventional rig with double lowers, which would be somewhat stronger.

The boom and fittings are good quality, with jiffy-reefing lines and topping lift led internally from the outboard end to exit at the mast.

Halyards and all other running rigging are Dacron. Standing rigging is conventional stainless steel wire with swaged fittings, plenty heavy, but lighter than you might expect with the super-heavy mast. Shroud chainplates are set well inboard, with stainless tierods belowdecks leading to anchor points on the hull grid.

Handling Under Sail

We raced four triangle races on the Citation 38 to judge her sailing ability. In general, she proved to have good sailing characteristics, well behaved with no obvious flaws or other problems.

Irwin advertises her PHRF (Performance Handicap Racing Fleet) rating as 130 with the wing keel, 120 with the fin keel—roughly about the same speed as a C&C 35 or many of the 1970s one-ton racer/cruisers like the Irwin 37 and Morgan 36. However, the local handicap of the boat we sailed is 108, a rating she could sail to only in light air off the wind.

In light winds the boat sails exceptionally well. In heavy winds, she certainly sails well enough to satisfy any serious sailor other than the dedicated racer, but she will not sail up to her rating relative to other modern lighter boats. She is generally fast enough to make good, satisfying passages for the cruising sailor. But we would generally not recommend her to the serious racer since the boat sails to her rating only in one condition, and it will be a struggle to win with the boat in heavy winds. For the very occasional racer who cruises most of the time, she should be satisfactory.

Specifically, the boat is exceptionally close-winded in light air, and ran very well in all winds. Reaching, she is sometimes a handful in a breeze, but overall she is a good sailer, typical of the best modern production boat designs.

We were surprised at the apparent thoughtlessness in many details of the rigging. While the hardware and fittings such as blocks, winches and shackles were all top quality, the way things were set up made for all sorts of problems.

For instance, the backstay adjuster was arranged with what looked like a clever idea. The split backstay was equipped with a typical double-ended block and tackle arrangement. To cleat the line, a tunnel was cut through the coaming so the line could be led to a cam cleat inside the cockpit. Unfortunately, given the anchor points for the tackle, the line bound on itself and on the block, creating so much friction that the tackle was almost impossible to use—we resorted to one person hanging on the line while a second took the slack through the cam cleat.

Similarly, the mainsheet traveler is well forward—a good place to keep it out of the way of people, but a poor place for getting good leverage on the boom. Unfortunately, the traveler hardware was set up so that it was impossible for a single person to move the traveler car in heavy air. Two people were required: one to pull up the boom by hand and the other to pull in the traveler control lines. Before the third race we replaced the whole traveler with a multi-part Harken system that made it possible, if not easy, to control the traveler.

There are a number of other details in the rigging—such as the fact that none of the exits from the mast or boom are labeled in any way—that indicate corners cut in rigging the boat. Fortunately, all the problems are fairly easily corrected by an owner, but it is surprising to see a boat with good sailing poten-

The interior is cavernous, but is well-divided. For long-distance cruising, the Citation 38 could use some extra storage space.

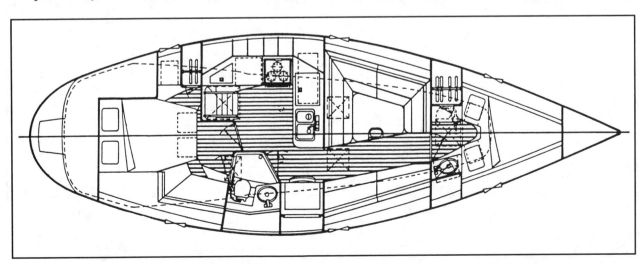

tial handicapped by this rather sloppy attention to detail.

Handling Under Power

The boat is equipped with a 27 hp 3-cylinder Yanmar, which is adequate for the boat's size and weight, although it is certainly not an excess of power. The boat backs well, turns sharply, and is easily driven to hull speed by the engine. The cruiser addicted to powering at a knot over hull speed may want to talk to Irwin about a larger engine, though one is not currently offered as an option. Irwin installs the same engine in the Citation 35, which seems like a better match. The tank on the 38 holds 30 gallons of diesel fuel—ample for good cruising range.

The engine is located in the center of the boat above the keel, underneath part of the settee and the galley cabinet. With an aft-cabin boat, this seems a sensible arrangement to us, giving good access to the engine while keeping the weight centered in the boat.

Like many builders, Irwin continues the practice of shipping the boat with a solid two-bladed prop, a crude way of keeping the price down. Anyone who is likely to order this type of well-performing sailboat will want to get a folding prop immediately. Most similar practices—such as offering the boat without lifelines as standard—have disappeared from the marketplace, but this peculiarity continues with almost all manufacturers.

On Decks

The low cabin house of the 38 makes the decks very usable, both for working the boat under sail and for lounging around. Furthest forward is an anchor roller beside the forestay, just ahead of an ordinary anchor locker to fit a Danforth-type anchor. The foredeck is wide and roomy enough to handle foresails. A big forward hatch in the low cabin top is usable for passing sails up and down.

The walkways are wide, with inboard shrouds, and the cockpit coaming is an easy step. Halyards and other control lines are led aft to the back of the cabin house where two Barient 17s are located. Small Dorade-type air inlets are molded into the cabin top just ahead of the traveler. The companionway hatch is off-center to port.

The cockpit is T-shaped, with comfortable benches and backrests. Barient 24 primaries are just adequate for the boat, but most owners will probably go for self-tailers all around.

There is a shallow cockpit locker on the port side, but the starboard locker is cavernous. We have yet to see a really good way of organizing these huge cockpit lockers, or of handling the oversize locker lid made up of the bench seat and part of the backrest. The helmsman's seat is peculiar in that it is removable as part of the process of folding out the transom ladder. Engine controls are on the steering pedestal.

Double lifelines, pulpit, and stern rail are standard.

Belowdecks

With a 12' 6" beam and a 30' 8" waterline, the interior of the Citation 38 is enormous, but it is broken up enough not to seem like a cavern. Forward is an

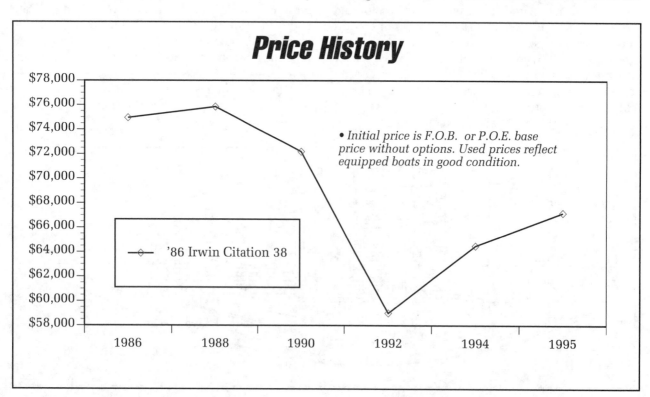

Price History

• Initial price is F.O.B. or P.O.E. base price without options. Used prices reflect equipped boats in good condition.

◇ '86 Irwin Citation 38

ordinary V-berth that should be good for sleeping or sail storage. There's a small bureau and hanging locker opposite, just aft of the berth.

In the main cabin, a U-shaped dinette is opposite a settee which can be used for a berth. The galley is roomy, open, and quite workable.

On the starboard side opposite the galley is a good navigator's station with a swing-out chair and electrical panel above it. Just aft of the nav table is the head, with entrances from both the galley and the aft cabin.

The aft cabin is quite roomy, made possible mostly by the offset companionway hatch and forward engine location. The berth is huge and comfortable, and this cabin will undoubtedly be one of the selling points of the boat.

In general, interior equipment is of good quality, with propane stove, 90-gallon water tank, hot water heater, a dozen opening ports, and good lighting.

Like most modern boats, the interior seems set up for weekending, with very little real storage space. A long-distance cruise will require converting some of the space for basic storage.

The only other shortcoming of the interior is that it looks like a standard, run-of-the-mill production boat, with lots of veneer and plastic, finished a little crudely in spots. But, for a relatively low-priced boat, it's better to compromise here than in the hull construction or mechanical systems.

Conclusions

Overall, the Citation 38 is a good boat that seems a little ordinary, generally representative of mid-line production boats. Though such a statement may sound like faint praise, it really isn't.

The boat is not as well finished as competitive boats like the Pearson 37, but it is generally better done than lower-priced boats such as the Hunter, and the price is appropriately in between.

Why would anyone choose this Irwin rather than one of her competitors? There are, of course, the personal considerations of appearance and aesthetics. Many people will consider the Citation 38 better looking than some of her boxier competitors.

To us, the main reason for choosing this boat would be the sailing performance. She has the feel of a well-designed boat, unlike so many other contemporary models which get their performance merely by combining big sail areas, long waterlines, and light weight. This boat sails very well.

The other consideration, of course, will be price. You can buy cheaper boats and you can easily buy more expensive boats. To us, Irwin has kept the price down in the most sensible way—not by compromising basic construction or eliminating layers of fiberglass, but by going to conventional components and easy construction in the interior.

For the avid racer, the Citation 38 is too much of a cruiser—something like the J/35 would be a better racing boat. And for the pure cruiser more interested in room than in sailing performance, a boat like the center cockpit Irwin 38 might be more suitable.

For a serious cruising sailor who likes a boat that sails well but still wants the size necessary for cruising in comfort, the Citation 38 would be a reasonable choice. **• PS**

O'Day 39 and 40

She started life as a Jeanneau, but wound up as an American boat. She is a good alternative to imports.

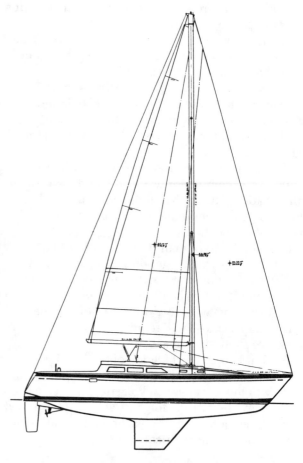

The O'Day 40 began life in Europe as a 39-footer, from the drawing board of the French IOR designer Phillipe Briand, and was first built by Jeanneau as the "Sun Fizz." O'Day reached an agreement with their sister company to build the boat in America and began selling her as the O'Day 39 in 1981.

After about 120 boats were built, O'Day had Hunt & Associates do a redesign, leaving the basic hull the same, but lengthening the cabin house, rearranging the interior, moving the mast aft a bit, and adding a platform extension with boarding ladder to the transom. The new version was christened the O'Day 40, and by the end of its first year—in the summer of 1986—50 boats had been built, to make the 39/40 a successful product for the company during a period when most other American builders were not doing too well. The 40 continued as part of the line until O'Day shut down in 1989.

The 39/40 is very typical of modern racer-cruisers in design. She is moderate in displacement by current racing standards, but has a cutaway underbody with fin keel and spade rudder. The widest beam is carried far enough aft to allow for a good sized after cabin and roomy galley, and the shallow bilges are compensated for by rather high topsides, to provide lots of living space below. At a distance of 200 yards, she would be nearly indistinguishable from a dozen Jeanneau and Beneteau models, if she had blacked-out windows and different hull stripes.

Construction

The hull construction is a departure from O'Day's traditional solid fiberglass laminate, since it is balsa cored.

The balsa core makes for a strong and stiff hull and has the advantage of reducing the amount of fiber-

Specifications

LOA	38' 7"/39' 7"
LWL	33' 6"
Beam	12' 8"
Draft	4' 1"/6' 4" (shoal/draft)
Displacement	18,000 lbs.
Ballast	6,600 lbs.
Sail area	701 sq. ft.

glass and resin required for a given strength; consequently it reduces weight and cost. The balsa also provides insulation against heat and sound, and helps to eliminate condensation inside the cabin.

The disadvantage of the balsa cored hull is simply that much greater skill and quality control are required in the laminating process to ensure the potential strength inherent in the fiberglass-balsa-fiberglass sandwich.

There are skeptics with questions about the longevity of the balsa-glass laminate as well as potential problems with water absorption. But the technology has been used in production sailboats for the last 15 years, and a great many hull moldings have been made—particularly by C&C and J-Boats—with little evidence that there has been any more laminate failure or osmotic blistering than with conventional layups.

We extensively examined the hull of one 39 and did a quick examination of a 40, and the glass work looked good. Unfortunately, with balsa coring, there is no way to see the quality of the laminate. Potential owners must depend on the reputation and track record of the builder.

The exteriors of both hulls we examined were fair with no evident hardspots. Gelcoat work seemed to be average production line quality, though the 39 had a bad color flaw in the bootstripe and some peculiar "crinkles" on the transom. Overall, the glass work on the O'Day 40 appeared to be somewhat better than on the O'Day 25, 27, 28, and 32 models that we have examined in the past.

The keels are external lead, bolted to a keel stub on the hull (some early keels were iron). Two versions are available—deep or shoal. The deep keel is a better shape and much to be preferred, unless the extra 17" of draft is a critical consideration. The one keel we examined was poorly faired—anyone thinking of racing the boat in PHRF will have to spend quite a bit of time with fairing compound and a grinder.

The deck layup is a standard balsa core laminate, with plywood inserts under cleats and winches. Non-skid is a molded pattern which is marginally adequate when wet. The 39 we examined had a number of small voids in the cockpit gelcoat, but there was little evidence of stress cracking anywhere outside the cockpit—a sign of decent workmanship.

In the hull-to-deck joint, O'Day adopted the European practice. There's a standard inward-turning flange on the hull, on which the deck molding rests, with polyurethane compound serving as a sealer. Stainless bolts are then inserted through the hull flange, the deck, and an exterior aluminum toerail. A thick layer of fiberglass is laid over the interior of the joint, bonding the hull to the deck. It's a good strong joint, the only concerns being the difficulty of tracing any leaks that develop and the problems of repair resulting from collisions with docks, pilings, or other boats.

Inside, a fiberglass pan forms the foundation for interior cabinetry and is bonded to the hull for additional stiffening. The chainplates are also anchored to this fiberglass pan, with Navtec Rod between the pan and the deck. Early on, O'Day 39 brochures claimed that this construction resulted in "quite possibly the strongest production sailboat of its size built in the United States"—a case of the advertising department conquering both common sense and reason.

Bulkheads are conventional teak-faced plywood, and the overhead is covered with a fiberglass hull liner. For ceiling, cabinetry is used is some spots, carpeting in some spots, and wood strips on a plastic fabric in some spots.

There's nothing very distinctive about the mechanical systems, but the boat comes pretty completely equipped, with shore power, propane stove, pressurized water system and water heater, twin batteries, and 110 gallons of water tankage.

Undoubtedly the best part of the mechanicals is the engine compartment—enormous in the 39 and big and roomy in the 40, to provide plenty of room for add-ons, such as engine-driven refrigeration or multiple alternators. Access is good on the 39—the companionway steps hinge upward—and excellent on the 40, where additional access is provided through the aft cabin.

All the interior woodwork is standard issue production line pre-fab—decent looking from a distance but with a number of sloppy joints, rough interiors, cheap hinges and latches, and loose drawer and door fits when examined close up.

Handling Under Power

The 39 was fitted with a Universal 44 diesel, and the 40 has a Westerbeke 46, both fresh water cooled. The four cylinder engines run smoothly, with minimal vibration. The noise from the engine compartment is muffled by insulation, but if we cruised the boat much, we would want to add a better lead/foam sandwich to quiet things down a bit more.

Both engines provide more than enough power to drive the boat at hull speed in strong head winds and seas; in fact, the horsepower/weight ratio is closer to that of a motorsailer than a typical racer-cruiser. With a 42 gallon aluminum fuel tank, powering range will be well over 200 miles.

We chartered the 39 for a week in the Virgin Islands and found in about 10 hours of powering that the boat handled well with the two-bladed solid prop, backing where it was told to and powering forward in a good straight line. There should be no problem fitting a folding or feathering prop, which would improve sailing performance while retaining ample powering ability.

One bad design detail is that the engine's key and instrument panel is at the front end of the cockpit, well out of reach of the helmsman.

Handling Under Sail

During our week in the Virgin Islands, the boat proved to be a good sailer. The shallow draft keel keeps it from pointing well, but it sailed fast on every point off the wind. With the deep draft keel, she should be a good all around performer. The sail area is divided a bit unevenly—a smaller high-aspect mainsail and a larger jib, on a double spreader mast.

The small main and large foretriangle undoubtedly reflect the designer's racing background and mean that, for high performance off the wind, a spinnaker will be required. However, the mast is tall enough and the sail area great enough that satisfactory performance can be obtained in most conditions with the standard roller furling 150% jib and a main with two reefs. A Hood Stoway mast and mainsail are options, but the main is small enough and easily enough handled that the added expense is probably not a reasonable investment.

The spade rudder far aft makes for quick response to the helm, and the boat demonstrated no serious bad habits in a wide variety of conditions, though it does pound a bit going to windward in a chop. Some might find it a bit tender, and an early reef in the main is necessary to keep the boat upright and sailing well. But, overall it is definitely on the performance end of the cruising boat spectrum, rapid enough to make owners at least think of entering a Wednesday night race. With a PHRF rating of around 114 for the deep draft version, it is the same speed as all out racing boats in that size range were 10 years ago.

Standard equipment on the latest 40 includes a Hood LD furler, but only one pair of Barlow 27 self-tailing winches. The winches are absolutely minimal for easy handling of a 150% genoa; to make for more reasonable jib trimming we would probably want to upgrade to Barlow 32s or their equivalent. The cockpit coaming has built-in recesses for an extra set of winches—only necessary for the racer.

The short boom is sheeted to a traveler ahead of the companionway. With the mainsheet so far forward, hand trimming of the main is impossible, but the standard equipment self-tailing winch is adequate. The traveler has only mechanical stops, so adjustment under load is impossible. With the traveler—as well as most other sail controls—anyone wanting to race the boat will have to add a number of fine-tuning devices to make racing trim feasible.

On Deck

As you might expect on a 40' boat, there is plenty of deck space all around. The side decks are wide enough that the inboard shrouds can be smack in the middle of them and still allow sufficient walk around room. The design of the hull means that the foredeck is relatively pinched, but still there's enough room for sail and anchor handling.

The 39 had a stainless "pulpit" around the mast as standard equipment—a good feature for heavy weather work—but the pulpit was made an option on the 40.

The stanchions—set in aluminum toerail sockets—the bow pulpit, and the stern pulpit are substantial enough, and there are double lifelines all around. The stern pulpit opens up to a transom-mounted ladder on the 39 and to a foot-wide swim platform and off-center ladder on the 40.

The cockpit is long and roomy but has a couple of irritating flaws. The main one is that the wheel is just wide enough that you have to squeeze between it and the cockpit seats. Unfortunately, the hasp for the cockpit lockers is exactly opposite the wheel, and anyone using the boat extensively will have permanent bruises on the shins at hasp level.

The lazarette hatches are outboard of the wheel. The lids are made up of not only the seat but also part of the coaming. This makes for a cavernous opening, but the lid is big and heavy enough to also be an effective guillotine.

The lazarette compartment itself is huge, but in practice too deep for the bottom to be usable. An owner will want to divide up the compartment in some way—with partitions or netting—to provide reasonable access to frequently used gear.

In the 39, a large storage compartment under the cockpit sole offered space for a life raft or other gear, but the compartment was eliminated to provide more aft cabin room in the 40. Propane tanks fit under the helmsman's seat.

The O'Day 40's interior was changed around from that in the 39, the most notable difference being the switch from two small aft cabins to one large one. Overall, the 40's interior is better.

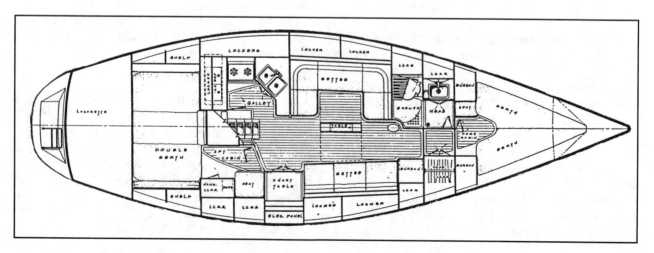

Belowdecks

The principal difference between the 39 and 40 interiors is that the 39 had two aft cabins—one port, one starboard. While this is ideal for charter work, both aft cabins are a squeeze for double occupancy.

On the 40, the port side aft cabin was eliminated, the starboard aft cabin was expanded with a huge athwartship double berth, and the galley was enlarged to occupy what was left of the former port cabin. The 40's arrangements are clearly preferable for an owner or family using the boat.

The galley is good sized and convenient, the only shortcoming being the minimal dry storage areas. The chart table opposite is adequate, with a cute little swing-out seat that looks to be unusable in heavy weather. On the 39, a second icebox frequently replaced the chart table for charter. Unlike many earlier O'Days, the iceboxes are well insulated.

The main salon is comfortable and will seat a crowd, the head is adequate for family use (the 39 had a second toilet and washbasin in the aft cabin), and the forecabin is big enough for an adult couple to use on a two week cruise. Throughout, the dead spaces are used pretty well to provide storage bins and bureaus, as well as two smallish hanging lockers. The bilges are very shallow, so there's no storage there, and any water taken on will make a real mess.

There are hatches and opening ports all over the place and, in fair weather and calm sailing, ventilation is excellent. With hatches and ports closed, however, there are only two dorades on the 40 and there was nothing on the 39. Opening ports into the cockpit footwell alleviate the problem a bit, but additional dorades or other waterproof vents would be mandatory for wet weather cruising.

The opening ports in the topsides are likely to be a concern for some buyers. Sailing, we found it hard to put the ports under water, and when we did leaking was minimal. If we ever went offshore in the boat, we would install storm shutters.

Other than the potential ventilation problems, the interior is well thought out, and the balsa cored hull provides good insulation.

Conclusions

In general, the O'Day 39/40 is a wholesome boat that fits a definite niche in the American cruising boat market. It would be inappropriate to think of her as finished like a high quality yacht—she is definitely mid-line production quality—or to consider her as an offshore or world cruiser.

Rather, she is a contemporary coastal cruiser, the sort of boat to be used mostly for weekends, occasional casual races, and a two or three week cruise each season. For those purposes, we can only conclude that her design and production have been well executed. She will be no one's ideal boat but a moderate and satisfactory compromise for many.

More notably, she is about the only American-made boat her size which is a reasonable alternative to the host of foreign imports that have invaded the American market. There are American-mades in her price and size range—like the Hunter 40 or Morgan 38—but we think she is somewhat better made and an overall better value than those.   • **PS**

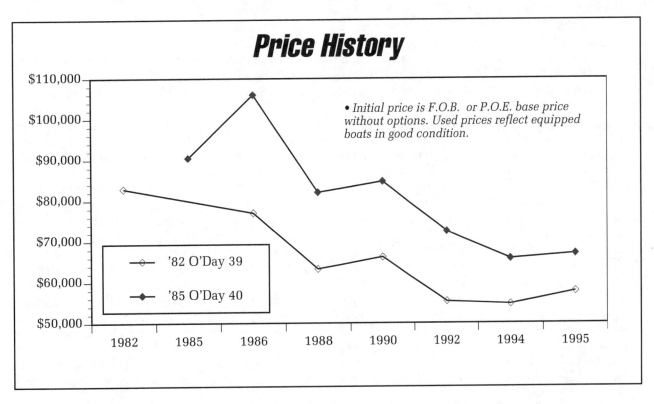

Cal 40

Though now an old and dated design, the Cal 40 was a hot boat when new, and she carries that legacy.

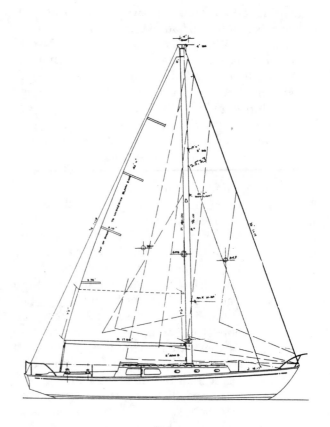

Thunderbird, a Cal 40 owned by IBM president T. Vincent Learson, took first in fleet over 167 boats in the 1966 Bermuda Race. Because this was the first computer-scored Bermuda Race, Learson got a lot of gaff about the IBM computer that had declared him the winner—and about beating out his boss. Thomas J. Watson, IBM's chairman of the board, sailed his 58' cutter, *Palawan*, second across the line, but ended with second in class, 24th in fleet, on corrected time.

In fact, the computer scoring system was not especially kind to Learson. Both he and Watson would have fared considerably better under the old system that calculated scores from the NAYRU time allowance tables. *Thunderbird*'s victory was a legitimate win, another in a stunning series by Cal 40s that was establishing the boat as a revolutionary design. The first Cal 40 was built for George Griffith in 1963. That winter, hull #2, *Conquistador*, took overall honors in the 1964 Southern Ocean Racing Circuit (SORC). The Transpac races of 1965, '66, and '67 all went to Cal 40s. Ted Turner's Cal 40, *Vamp X*, took first place in the 1966 SORC. In the '66 Bermuda Race, five of *Thunderbird*'s sisterships finished with her in the top 20 in fleet, taking five of the first 15, four of the first nine places. And so on. In their first few years on the water, Cal 40s chalked up an astonishing record.

The 40 was the fifth in a line of Cal designs that C. William Lapworth did for Jensen Marine of Costa Mesa, California. Lapworth had already designed a series of moderately successful racing boats, the L classes, including an L-24, L-36, L-40 and L-50, when he teamed up with Jack Jensen. The Cal designs were built on concepts he had tried in his L-class boats. The first Cal was the 24, Jensen's first boat, launched in 1959. The Lapworth-Jensen team

Specifications

LOA	39' 4"
LWL	30' 4"
Beam	11' 0"
Draft	5' 7"
Displacement	15,500 lbs.
Ballast	6,000 lbs.
Sail area	700 sq. ft.

then produced a 20, 30, and 28 before getting to the Cal 40, which proved to be a successful distillation of Lapworth's thinking up to that time.

Aspects of the boat that departed from the conventional wisdom were her light displacement, long waterline, flat bilges to encourage surfing, fin keel and spade rudder. The masthead rig is stayed by shrouds secured to chainplates set inboard of the toerail, a then unusual innovation that allows a reduced sheeting angle. The success of the design helped legitimize fiberglass as a hull material, establish Jensen Marine as a significant builder of fiberglass boats, and propel Lapworth to the forefront of yacht design.

Three decades have passed since Lapworth drew the Cal 40. In that time, using computers to score

Owners' Comments

"At her best in dirty weather. Has been driven mercilessly; nothing ever seems to fail. Old Westerbeke lost by poor exhaust design. New Perkins and new exhaust expected to outlive me."
—1963 model in Gig Harbor, WA

"Wet, pounds in gales, some waves—green—go over the boat. Good sea boat. Can balance with no one on helm for hours in 15 to 30 knots of wind. Excess sail makes little difference—rail at surface. Classic, large comfortable cockpit, good drainage. Minimum wood, white unpainted gelcoat looks good, plain by today's standards."
—1968 model in Kailua, HI

"Very well built compared to today's stock boats. A used Cal 40, in good condition, should be an excellent buy."
—1964 model in Long Island Sound, NY

"This is a most satisfying boat. She is stable, safe and seakindly. Faster than all but the race machines. Doesn't point as well as high aspect rigs. This only reflects the stage of development when boat was built. Few boats of her size will pass her off the wind. I plan on keeping her forever."
—1969 model in Radnor, PA

"The cockpit is outstanding; the interior is small and not roomy. She sails like a dream and is twice as much boat as I could have afforded new. With another new sail or two, I am convinced she will be a successful club racer again. There is nothing which can touch her performance designed prior to 1974."
—1969 model in Corpus Christi, TX

"Design of mast truck pulleys allows halyards to jump sheaves. Not a roomy cruising or liveaboard boat."
—1965 model in Mitchellville, MD

races has become commonplace—boat measurers and designers would be paralyzed without them. The CCA Rule, the NAYRU tables and the Portsmouth Yardstick have been replaced by IMS, IOR, and PHRF, with the effects of their parameters expressed in the shape, size and weight of new boats. New building materials and techniques have changed the meaning of terms such as "light displacement," "long waterline," "fin keel," and "fast sailboat." Today the Cal 40 is a dated design, having been surpassed in her revolutionary features by her descendents. She remains among the esteemed elite of racing yachts, but she is not especially light, long on the waterline, or fast compared to current designs.

The Cal's builder was transformed by time, as well. Jensen Marine was bought by Bangor Punta Marine, and the Cal production line was moved to Florida about the time that the Cal 40 went out of production in 1972. For the next decade, the company's name and address shifted between combinations of Cal, Bangor Punta and Jensen in California, New Jersey and finally Massachusetts, where it joined O'Day under Bangor Punta's umbrella in the early 1980s. After 1984 the company was called Lear Siegler Marine, Starcraft Sailboat Products, and finally emerged as Cal, a Division of the O'Day Corporation, in Fall River, Mass. Cal and O'Day ceased production in April, 1989.

Construction

The construction of the Cal 40 is typical of Jensen Marine boats of the 1960s. The hull is solid hand laid fiberglass with wooden bulkheads and interior structures. Strips of fiberglass cloth and resin secure the wooden structures to the hull, but this tabbing is rather lightweight and has been reinforced in some Cal 40s where it has failed. If it has not been reinforced, it probably needs it.

Because saving weight was a priority in building the Cal 40, the reinforcement provided by the bulkheads and furniture is critical to hull stiffness. Failure of the bonding can be a significant structural concern.

The hull-to-deck joint is an inward-turning hull flange, upon which the deck molding is bonded, then through-bolted and capped with a through-bolted teak toerail. This is a strong type of joint, but there is some complaint of minor leaking along it in a few boats. The leaks are most likely one result of the relatively light construction of the hull skin, which has a tendency to "oilcan" in heavy weather, creating stresses at the joint.

The deck, also a solid fiberglass layup, has reinforcement designed into it during layup, so no interior metal backing plates are provided under winches, cleats, and other hardware. *PS* generally recommends backing plates behind high-stress hardware as a matter of course. We found little indication of trouble with leaking or working of most of the fittings, but one owner said that his lifeline stanchion bases had to be reinforced. This would be an area to inspect carefully.

Colors and non-skid surfaces are molded in, but due to the age of any Cal 40, the finish will look tired unless it has been renewed. A good Awlgrip job will do it wonders, and is probably warranted for this boat unless it is in general disrepair.

The deck and cockpit of the Cal 40 we inspected have numerous cracks in the gelcoat in corners and other stress areas. Check these areas closely—they are unsightly, but in most cases are not a structural concern.

Ballast is an internal lead casting dropped into the keel before the insides were assembled. If there is evidence that the boat has suffered a hard grounding, invesitgate the ballast cavity to see that it was properly repaired. It should not have a hollow sound when rapped, and there should be no cracks, weeping, or other evidence of moisture inside. Due to the construction sequence, major repairs could be awkward.

Wiring was also installed prior to the interior, which makes it quite inaccessible in some areas. What may be of more concern is that it is low enough in the boat to get wet if the last watch forgot to pump the bilges and the boat heels over to her work. That's what happened to one owner, who lost all the electricity on the boat when approaching Nova Scotia's Bras d'Or Lakes after an all night sail. Fortunately, dawn arrived in time to avert a navigation problem. They anchored in the harbor and found that the electrical system worked fine, once it got dry again. Before the next season rolled around, the boat's entire electrical system had been replaced in elevated, accessible locations. The implication is that you should look carefully at the wiring in a Cal 40 before you make any decisions. If it has been replaced, try to learn who did the work and how well qualified he/she was for the job. If it has not, you may have to work the cost of rewiring into your acquisition expenses. We would suspect the worst until proven otherwise.

You might expect wheel steering on a boat this size, but the stock Cal 40 came with a big tiller. The boat is well enough balanced to be controlled with a tiller, and many helmsmen prefer it to a wheel, which masks feedback from the rudder and makes sensitive steering more difficult.

The cockpit is roomy, but properly designed for offshore work with relatively low volume, a bridgedeck and small companionway. The tiller sweeps the cockpit midsection, allowing the helmsman to sit fairly far forward, a help to visibility.

Winch islands are located aft of the helmsman, where there is room for the crew, but it also makes the sheets accessible to the helmsman for short-handed sailing. The teak cockpit coaming has cutouts giving access to handy storage bins.

The aluminum mast is stepped through the deck to a fitting that meets it at the level of the cabin sole. The shroud chainplates are secured to a transverse bulkhead at the mast station, and then tied into an aluminum weldment in the bilges. This weldment also supports the mast step. While chainplates have been an area of concern in some designs, because they can work under the large loads they carry, our indications from Cal 40 owners are that the chainplate/shroud/mast step attachments have served well.

Sailing Performance

The Cal 40 is in her element in heavy air, especially off the wind. Her long waterline and flat bilges help her get up and go on reaches and runs, surfing in heavy air. On the wind, the flat hull forward pounds in waves and chop, which slows the boat somewhat and is irritating. Owners agree that she sails best with the rail in the water. She is not dry on the wind, so a dodger is a welcome feature.

The masthead sailplan allows relatively easy reduction of headsails to suit heavier conditions, and Cal 40 owners extol the survivability of their boats. "Simple rig, nothing breaks, strong, easy to use," is a typical comment.

Despite her stellar racing record, the Cal 40 is only ordinary in performance by today's standards. She carries a PHRF rating between 108 and 120 seconds

A traditional '60s-style layout with eight berths is found in the Cal 40. Eight people is really too many on this boat, and the spare berths are likely to be used as storage space.

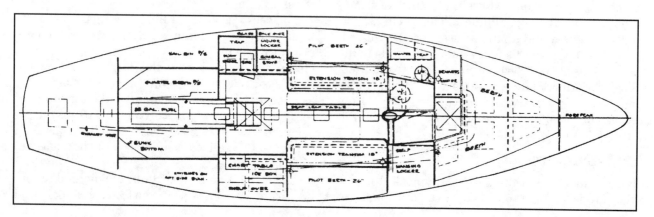

per mile, depending on the region. That's about the same as a C&C 38 or an Ericson 36, both IOR designs of the late 70s. Compared to a mid-1970s design such as the Swan 38, the Cal 40 is a bit slower on the wind and in light air, a bit faster off the wind and in heavier going, about equal in speed overall. It's not surprising that these boats perform alike if you look at the length of their waterlines and their displacements.

In comparing the Cal 40 to boats of her own vintage one sees what all the fuss was about. The Columbia 40, for example, is a 1965 Charles Morgan design, an "all-out racer" with a 27' waterline, displacement of 20,200 pounds, and a PHRF rating of about 170. Or look at the Hinckley 41: 29' on the water, 18,500 pounds, PHRF about 160.

The Cal 40's waterline is almost 31', but she displaces one or two tons less than the Columbia or the Hinckley, and rates nearly one minute per mile faster under PHRF. In that context, she is indeed a fast, light displacement boat with a long waterline. Just look at her "fin keel" and you can see the progression. Compared to a full keel with attached rudder, it is small. Compared to a modern fin keel, it hardly seems small enough to qualify for the name. If Cal 40s win races today, it's because they are well sailed, not because the boat is the fast machine on the race course.

Interior

In the 60s, "accommodations" tended to imply the number of berths in a sailboat, and the more the better. It also included the notion of a basic galley with sink, stove, icebox, and a table of sorts, plus a head with toilet and sink. Space age electronics had not arrived in the galley or the nav station, nor had space arrived in the concept of the main saloon.

Inside, as elsewhere, the Cal 40 is well designed and functional, but she speaks of her own era. The layout is very traditional, with a V-berth forward, separated from the main cabin by a head and hanging locker. Pilot berths and extension settees port and starboard provide sleeping for four. The dropleaf table seats four, six if you squeeze. Next aft is the galley to port and a nav station to starboard, consisting of a chart table over the voluminous icebox. The galley has a usable sink next to the well for a gimbaled stove with oven.

Flanking the companionway steps are the entrances to the quarterberths, known affectionately as "torpedo tubes," which gives you an impression of their dimensions. They extend from the main cabin through to the lazarette, which allows good circulation of air. In fact, on a return trip from Bermuda, one seasick sailor found great solace between tricks at the helm by climbing into one of the cocoon-like torpedo tubes, where he was washed with a fresh breeze from the dorade vent on the lazarette cover. The fact that the quarterberths flank the engine compartment doesn't matter as long as you are under sail, but it's a different story when under power.

So you have sleeping accommodations for eight, which is too many people on a 40-footer, except perhaps when racing. The extension transom berths, however, do not lend themselves to use under way. The interior, not spacious by modern standards, fills up fast with extra bodies aboard. Owners tend to

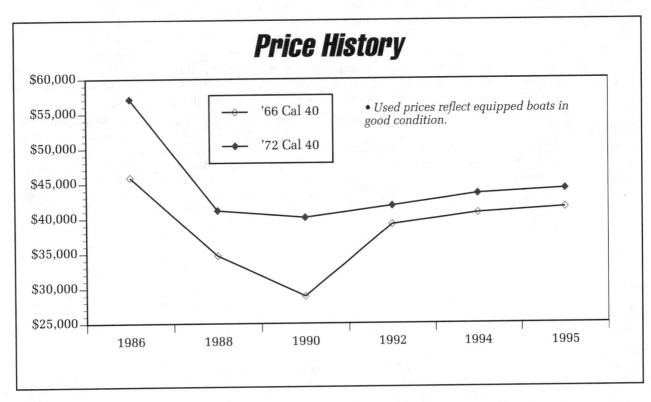

convert some of the berths to storage space. The pilot berths are especially tempting for that use, but since they are also the most comfortable berths on the boat, the quarterberths are often sacrificed for storage.

One of the best features about the Cal 40's interior is the dining table. Set slightly to port, it is supported by a sturdy sole-to-overhead stainless steel post at each end with a 4' 4" gimbaled mahogany tray between them above the table. The posts make excellent handholds, and the gimbaled tray can serve for everything from salt and pepper holder to bookshelf to diaper-changing table. The table has a drop leaf to port and to starboard, so it can be set up for use from the port settee without blocking fore-and-aft passage through the boat.

Engine

A variety of powerplants will be found in Cal 40s. Some early hulls were equipped with Atomic 4 gasoline engines. Later hulls got Graymarine 4-112 gasoline or Perkins 4-107 diesels. It's likely that the original engine will need to be replaced if it has not already been done. Even the newest Cal 40s are rather old, and the early models have passed the quarter-century mark.

Boats in our files have Volvo MD2B, the Perkins, Pathfinder 50, Westerbeke 4-108, and Pisces 40 from Isuzu listed as replacements for the original engine.

The engine is located under the cockpit, between the torpedo tubes, which allow access to both sides, but are not especially convenient, particularly if the area has been turned into storage space. Better is the companionway ladder, which removes to expose the front of the engine. That can be an inconvenience, too, if the engine needs some attention while under way.

Used for the minimum requirements of a racing yacht, primarily getting in and out of port, you can probably make do with any of the engines. If the boat is to be used for cruising, with greater demands to be made on the engine, the Atomic 4 would likely be inadequate.

Generally the boat will do about six or seven knots under power, depending on the power plant and propeller. We suspect that many Cal 40s will have folding propellers, good for racing but not the best for

powering, especially in reverse. The spade rudder set well aft confers good maneuverability under most conditons.

Conclusions

The Cal 40, a hot racing boat when new, carries that legacy with her into maturity. Generally, the boats have been raced hard, some cruised hard as well. Owners have tended to be the type to add gear and modifications to keep the boat comfortable and competitive. The boats are likely to have a large inventory of much-used sails.

Because of her age and dated design, a Cal 40 may be available for much less money than a newer boat offering comparable quality and performance. Prices will vary according to the condition of the boat and gear, but will likely fall in the range of $40,000 to $50,000. If the boat has lots of add-ons in the galley and nav station, modern racing hardware, renewed standing rigging, new finish on the topsides, and the bottom is in good condition, it might fetch something higher. One performance extra to look for is a special (non-factory) fairing job on the keel and rudder that was available when the boats were young.

On the other hand, it should not be a surprise if there are areas that require attention, and you should calculate the cost of the work into the price you are willing to pay. Twenty or 25 years of hard sailing will take its toll. Significant expense could be incurred if the boat needs new wiring, an Awlgrip job on the topsides, extensive reinforcement of the interior furniture tabbing, a new engine, or new rigging. If racing is in your plans, new sails might be scheduled in as well.

This would be a good boat for a handy do-it-yourselfer. Over the years, most of the boat's problems have been solved more than once by other Cal 40 owners, many willing to share their wisdom. You would probably have a choice of solutions, and indications of which worked best.

Although there is not currently an active owners association, there persists a loose fellowship among present and former owners. If you buy a Cal 40, you will acquire a modest boat, with good pedigree and performance, and—should you desire them—a few new friends, as well.   **• PS**

Passport 40

Built in Taiwan under American supervision, this handsome sloop can be compared to the Valiant 40.

When Seattle yacht designer Robert Perry designed the Valiant 40 in 1973/4, he broke new ground in the usually conservative world of yacht design. With a fin keel, skeg-mounted rudder and displacement/length ratio of 264, critics said it was unsuitable for serious offshore work. The idea of going trans-oceanic with a divided underbody challenged a lot of old beliefs about what constitutes a safe passagemaker.

Time has certainly proven the critics wrong and Perry right. The Valiant 40 has made numerous circumnavigations, including Dan Byrne's credible showing in the first (1983) BOC Challenge. Ten to 15 years ago, it was considered a fast boat for such an undertaking. Today, alack, it's too slow for competitive long-distance ocean racing. But the fact that all of the circumnavigations of which we are aware were made safely, and with little complaint by the skippers, is strong testimony to the soundness of the design.

The Passport 40, introduced in 1981, represents Perry's evolving ideas about "performance cruising," a phrase originating from his work. "Performance," he once told us, "is a moving target."

The Design

The Passport 40 design was commissioned by several parties, including the Taiwan builder and former furniture maker Wendel Renken, who was to supervise construction and handle distribution in the U.S. According to Perry, he was first given an interior drawing, "an extrapolation of the Islander Freeport 36" with the head in the bow and a Pullman double berth aft of it. "It was," he added, "a classic case of a hull wrapped around an interior." Some readers may be astonished, but this is frequently how the yacht business works.

Specifications

LOA	39' 5"
LWL	33' 5"
Beam	12' 8"
Draft	5' 3"/5' 9" (shoal/std)
Displacement	22,771 lbs.
Ballast	8,500 lbs.
Sail area	771 sq. ft.

In order to place the head so far forward, the cabin trunk had to be extended farther forward than what might be considered normal. Perry said that if he deserves any credit for having done a good job, it was in making a pleasant looking boat with such an extended trunk.

There are numerous differences between the Valiant 40 and Passport 40. Gone is the so-called canoe stern (which Perry calls the "Moses Theory of the stern parting the waves") and the nearly flat coachroof. The Passport 40 has a rather large, conventional transom, which allows beam to be carried well aft and to increase cockpit space. And the coachroof has considerable camber, which, of course, is quite a bit stronger than a flat one.

Perry calls the two boats "totally different." "The

Owners' Comments

"Bob Perry draws beautiful lines. The woodwork is first class all the way. Everything is geared for comfort and livability."

—1985 model in Seattle, WA

"No failures or hints of failures after six years. Interior perfect for two couples. The large galley is important. The cockpit is a bit cramped. Nanni (Mercedes) parts and maintenance support are iffy. Stern ladder is awkward to use. Newer models have been improved."

—1983 model in San Francisco, CA

"The rubrail should be above the wale stripe to be effective. Do not expect the boat to perform well in light air (less than six knots). I'm very impressed with the quality of the rig and its strength. The interior is the best I've seen on any 40-footer. Gelcoat work is not the best but I've been told the yard has been working to improve the problem. I would buy another just like it."

—1983 model in Grand Rapids, MI

"Tracks very well. It's a heavy, spacious boat easily handled by two people. Evokes favorable comments wherever we go. Stable and stiff. Women are very comfortable with this boat."

—1982 model in Brigantine, NJ

"Gelcoat probably not as fine as the other aspects of the boat. Deck drains not at most dependent point. Small amounts of standing water."

—1982 model in Oakland, CA

"My Passport has the Pathfinder diesel and I am very happy with it. It consumes about three-quarters of a gallon per hour.

"Upwind performance is hindered by the roller furling, but I would never give it up. The boat tracks well, stays upright and goes fast.

"I equipped the Passport for comfortable cruising with forced-air heating, microwave oven, roller furling, radar, autopilot, electric windlass, etc."

—1982 model in Seahurst, WA

Passport 40 is a wide-stern boat with assymetrical waterlines, a wedge shape, and flat bottom. The Valiant 40 has symmetrical waterlines and higher deadrise."

Both boats do, however, have large fin keels, often called "cruising fins" due to their comparatively long run and shallow draft. The leading edges are raked for several reasons: to get some ballast further forward, absorb the force of collisions with logs and other objects, and to facilitate removing the ballast casting from its mold. Combined with the skeg-mounted rudder, which is more forgiving than a spade and gives additional lateral plane aft to help tracking, this is a nice underbody configuration for cruising. About all it gives up to the full keel boat is an exposed propeller.

The essential specifications differ somewhat, though not greatly. The Passport 40 is six inches shorter overall, with a waterline seven inches shorter. Beam is four inches wider, and draft is three inches shallower. Displacement and sail area are roughly the same, though Perry says all of the Passport 40s weigh more than listed—"24,000 pounds at least."

In appearance, the sheerlines are also quite similar, as are the bows. Both are very handsome boats and will continue to look good for many years to come. If he had to design the Passport 40 again, Perry said he wouldn't make the stern quite so wide and give it more deadrise for more bilge.

Construction

Passport boats were constructed in Taiwan, first at the King Dragon yard and later at Hi Yang. Renken lived in nearby Taipei with his Chinese wife. His close supervision in the construction of the Passport line, ranging from 37 to 51 feet (the latter designed by Stan Huntingford), represented a changing trend in Far East boatbuilding.

Anyone who has owned one of Taiwan's famous "leaky teakies" knows that Chinese craftsmen are highly capable in some areas, and woefully inept in others. Most of the problems were caused not by lack of skill, but lack of modern boatbuilding knowledge. And, to some extent, by poor facilities and archaic tools. Wiring often wasn't color coded, cockpit seats were plywood thinly covered with layers of fiberglass, and custom metal fittings were cast from inferior alloys.

What Renken and others did in the early 1980s was to move on site and teach the glass men and carpenters how to build to higher standards. The work produced by Passport Yachts International, Ta Shing (builders of the Mason and Tashiba lines), and Ted Hood's Little Harbor yard, are vastly superior to the early clunkers built by Formosa and others. You remember those old pirate ships—the Marine Traders, Sea Wolfs and Yankee Clippers—with the Chinese dragons carved on the doors, and dozens of tiny drawers inside drawers, don't you? In fact, today Taiwan is capable of building boats about as well as any country in the world, *if* they are properly supervised. During our visit to Taiwan in 1987, it appeared to us that nearly all of the good yards had Western supervisors or agents watchdogging construction. The exception was Ta Shing, which builds and markets its own boats.

The hull of the Passport 40 is solid fiberglass (one owner responding to our Boat Owner's Questionnaire said Airex foam core was optional, but Perry said he's never heard of one), hand laminated with 24-ounce woven roving and 1.5-ounce mat. Polyester resin. Very traditional. Wooden transverse stringers are glassed inside the hull to increase stiffness. Hull thicknesses vary, naturally, but one report stated it was about 9/16-inch thick near the keel. According to Perry, the deck is cored with mahogany plywood. The hull/deck joint is through-bolted every eight inches, sealed with polysulfide and the seam filled with resin and filler. Ballast is an iron casting fit into the one-piece hull/keel cavity.

The interior of a Taiwan-built boat is what really grabs people. The Passport 40's doors, frames and trim are solid Burmese teak, amply varnished. Same goes for the chart table and dinette. The cabin sole is teak and holly. Even the cockpit seats have inlaid teak. And the deck is laid 5/8-inch teak bedded in Thiokol. Okay, that's a lot of teak, but Renken used some restraint compared to the earlier Taiwan-built boats. The interior looks great, but you still gotta like teak!

According to one brochure, the diesel auxiliary offered was either a Perkins 4-108 or Nanni diesel (Mercedes Benz). However, owners report also owning Pathfinders (Volkswagen), Isuzu and Yanmar diesel. We'd prefer a boat with the Perkins for reliability and parts availability. The engine is located under the dinette settee, which may seem odd to some, but is in fact a good place for it. Weight is kept close to the center of the boat, it is convenient for maintenance and repair, and there is no need for a V-drive, which would be necessary had Perry put the engine aft under the companionway steps. The only concern with its placement in the saloon would be noise, but generous sound insulation—lead-lined foam—does a good job of muffling even a large diesel.

Fuel tanks (two) were "fiberglassed black iron," according to the brochure. The two water tanks,

---

Top: The standard layout places the head forward, which required Perry to extend the cabin trunk farther forward than he would have liked. Bottom: The optional interior plan has a double berth forward and a large head, with tub, in the conventional location. Both plans should work well for the live-aboard couple.

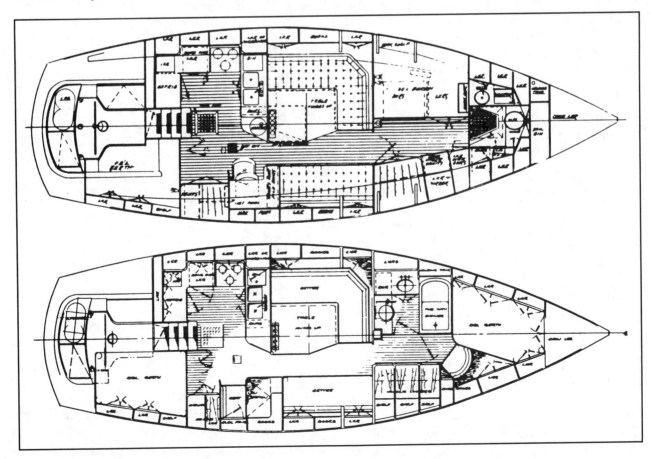

holding about 125 gallons, were either fiberglass or stainless steel. The latter were apparently optional for a time, then later made standard.

A key difference between boats built in Taiwan under people like Renken and the previous generation was the installation of familiar Western hardware and equipment. Stateside distributors realized that to sell successfully to the American public, items such as winches and pumps had to be familiar brands, easily repaired and serviced. The Passport 40, for example, is equipped with products by Lewmar, Barient, Schaefer, Marinetics and Raritan.

There are 10 bronze opening portlights with screens for superior ventilation. The four hatches are by Atkins-Hoyle and are top quality. Like many builders, Passport Yachts apparently often changed suppliers. Some readers report owning Kenyon masts, others Isomat. Owners had the choice of a deck- or keel-stepped mast. All say they are satisfied.

Overall, owners rate construction of their Passport 40s as above average to excellent. "No leaks, no gear failures," wrote one owner. The only complaints involved less than perfect gelcoat. Considering that these boats, like most boats built in the countryside of Taiwan, were built in open-air sheds, it is not surprising. Just 18 percent of owners reported any blistering, none major.

This is a heavily built boat that we consider suitable for serious cruising. We wouldn't expect to find bulkheads working or large, unsupported structural panels that oilcan. The abundance of teak, especially on the decks, will require additional maintenance and probably some repair as the boat ages.

This is not a criticism of the Passport, just a fact of life for owners of boats with laid teak decks.

Performance

Just what is a "performance cruiser"? It certainly isn't a race boat. Nor is it a lumbering, full-keel, heavy-displacement, traditional cruiser. To our mind, a performance cruiser is heavy enough to handle rough, offshore conditions, yet has an easily driven hull form, a nice foil shape to the fin and sufficient sail area to keep moving in lighter air. That would sum up the performance of the Passport 40 with reasonable accuracy.

As is usually the case, owners' ratings of their boats' performance are all over the mark. Some Passport 40 owners rank their boats' upwind performance no better than average, others say it's excellent. Much depends on past experience and the variety of boats sailed for comparative purposes.

"It's amazing how well this heavy boat moves in light air," one owner commented. Another said, "Needs 10 to 15 knots of wind to move it well."

Perry acknowledges that the rig is short and that light air is not its strong suit. "The happiest owners seem to be in San Francisco. This is a full mainsail boat," he said, adding that while a lot of people think they want a high sail area-to-displacement ratio, many owners are more comfortable with a more conservative rig that doesn't need shortening in moderate wind speeds.

The majority of owners rate the boat's offwind performance better than upwind, but not all. One owner, who rated upwind performance as excellent

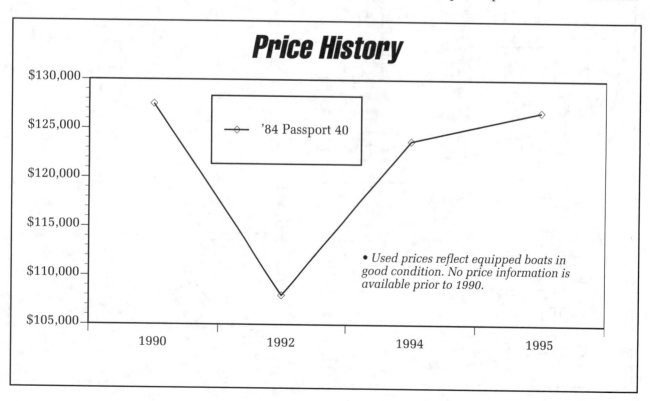

Price History

- '84 Passport 40

• Used prices reflect equipped boats in good condition. No price information is available prior to 1990.

and offwind as above average, said, "Points high, a joy to sail upwind."

Seaworthiness, stability, and balance also rate well. "Very dry. No need for dodger," said a San Francisco, California, owner. "Even in 25 knots of wind, the rail does not go under," said another.

Several owners praised the boat's maneuverability, with a few noting that the helm requires constant attention. Well, you can't really have both maneuverability and no-hands steering. The key is good balance, and the Passport appears to have it. "One of the easiest handling boats I've sailed in 20 years," said an Oakland, California owner.

For some perspective on the boat's speed, a check of PHRF handicaps shows the Passport 40 rated anywhere from 114 to 138 seconds per mile. For the sake of comparison, the Valiant 40 and the durable Freya 39 with tall mast also rate about 138. The Crealock 37, which is similar in its designed purpose, though a bit smaller, rates between 168 and 180. A middle-of-the-road Pearson 40 rates about 108 as does the Ericson 39. The more race-happy C&C 40 rates about 90. So it seems safe to say that among offshore cruisers, the Passport 40 has a good turn of speed, not much slower than mainstream fin-keel, spade-rudder sloops of similar length. And, of course, it cannot compete with the hard-core racer.

Perry said that despite its flatter bottom, a Passport 40 can be beaten by a well-sailed Valiant 40. If the boat was built with hull coring and brought down to its designed displacement, he said, it would perform better. It also suffers, he said, from dragging its wide transom when heeled hard over.

In any case, we think the Passport 40 is a very pleasing combination of design tradeoffs that enable her to make safe, reasonably fast passages. And, she can climb away from a lee shore with confidence. That's important.

Interior

Two basic interior layouts were available, though the builder encouraged customization. Consequently, in a used Passport 40 you might find all sorts of adjustments that may or may not suit your taste.

As mentioned, the original layout locates the head virtually in the forepeak, with the forward stateroom just aft of it. The head of the offset double berth is at the main bulkhead, right where the toilet would be in the second plan. The advantage of this layout is locating the seldom-used head away from the principal living area. In the bow it will be well ventilated, but riding the throne in a big sea could be a wild experience! Moving the berth aft increases its utility as a sea berth. The disadvantage is that ventilation of the berth won't be quite as good for sleeping on hot, tropical nights.

The saloon features either an L- or U-shaped dinette to port and a settee to starboard. The galley is aft to port and quite large, too large according to one owner. At eight feet, there's enough room for two people to work together. The stove fuel of choice is propane, which we think is the only way to go. To starboard is an enclosed stateroom with double quarter berth, seat and chart table. Enclosing such a cabin looks appealing at the boat show, and is nearly a prerequisite of the charter trade, where, we are led to believe, every outing is like some scene from the movie "Four Seasons." In reality, such cabins are stuffy and uncomfortable. In fact, in the tropics, even open quarter berths may become untenable, despite overhead hatches (always too small, by necessity) and electric fans.

If we were planning a one-couple cruise, we'd seriously consider removing part of the bulkhead and the door. Communication between the navigation station and the helm would be improved. If, however, we were weekend summer cruisers who liked to cruise with other couples, we'd just install the biggest fan we could afford to run on available battery power.

As implied above, the second basic plan locates the head just forward of the main bulkhead and gives the owner the choice of a V-berth forward or an offset double berth with changing seat. We've tried both types of berths and admit there is no perfect solution. A couple that likes sleeping together must, on a V-berth, install the insert board and cushion. Cushion beading and cracks between cushions may be a bother, but can be at least partially solved by laying down a padded comforter under the bottom sheet. The problem then is climbing into the berth head first from the head compartment. The offset double allows room to stand in the cabin next to the berth. The seat is handy, and entry into the berth is easier. The only drawback is that the person sleeping outboard must climb over the other person to get in and out. We can't remember which was worse: doing the climbing over, or being the one getting trampled.

The joinerwork is, by most standards, very nicely done. Lots of varnished teak. Lots of stowage bins. Many thoughtful details. We like an all-wood interior for its warmth and sound-deadening qualities.

Conclusion

Readers continually ask us to recommend seaworthy cruising boats. The Passport 40 is one. We like Perry's concept of the performance cruiser. If you're planning to venture to remote sections of the world—say, Patagonia or Sri Lanka—we'd probably opt for a full keel design as added protection against the possibility of severe groundings, collision with deadheads, or beaching, but for the Caribbean or the South Pacific, the Passport 40 would be an intelligent choice.

• PS

C&C 40

Originally built to race under the IOR, this boat remains competitive as a club racer.

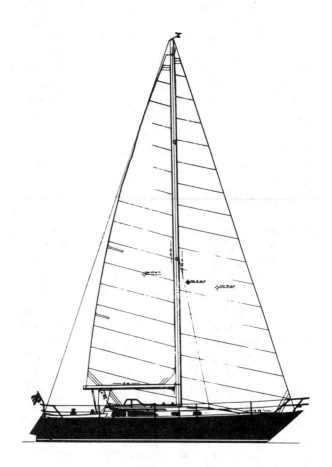

While C&C did not invent the racer/cruiser, the Canadian-based company has remained dedicated for two decades to the concept of the dual-purpose boat.

With the notable exception of a few pure cruisers—the relatively low-performance Landfall 35, 42, 43, and 48—a racer-based cruiser (the Landfall 38), and a real oddball (the Mega 30), most C&Cs have paid at least lip service to contemporary trends in racing boats.

In some cases, C&C's boats have been closely designed to the racing rules. The C&C 38 was a somewhat modified old IOR (International Offshore Rule) one-tonner, the later C&C 41 was a development of several C&C custom IOR boats, and the C&C 37+ was designed to be competitive under the current IMS (International Measurement System) handicapping rule.

The C&C 40 entered production as a 1978 model, and was phased out in 1983, replaced by the higher-performance C&C 41—a bigger, much faster, slightly lighter, more powerful boat, which still managed to be cheaper than the last C&C 40s built.

Sailing Performance

The 40 was an IOR design, but she was not heavily optimized to the rule. In the late 1970s, custom IOR designs featured not only somewhat tortured hull shapes to fool the rule into thinking they were slower than they were, but in many cases had grapefruit-sized "bumps" at critical measurement points. By comparison, the hull of the C&C 40 is undistorted, fair, and conservative.

This lack of distortion was reflected in the boat's IOR rating. A reasonably optimized custom 40' IOR design of the late 1970's rated about 10' lower than her overall length. The C&C 40, at 39.58' long, typi-

Specifications

LOA	39' 7"
LWL	31' 6"
Beam	12' 8"
Draft	7' 0" (std keel)
Displacement	17,100 lbs.
Ballast	7,910 lbs.
Sail area	740 sq. ft.

cally rated from 29.5 to 30.5, depending on the keel and rig configuration of the boat.

With a rating as high or slightly higher than that of custom boats, which most likely were lighter and had better weight distribution, the C&C 40 was reasonably competitive under the IOR in her first year, marginally competitive by the second, and a good club-level racer by 1980. Top-flight IOR boats then had a serious competitive life of two years or less, which was a major factor leading to the near-demise of the rule.

Fortunately for the C&C 40, the MHS (Measurement Handicap System, later renamed the IMS) began to grow in popularity after 1980, giving the boat a new lease on competitive life, at least at second-echelon levels of competition. The boat is no

IMS rule-beater; she's handicapped fairly by IMS, which means she'll do neither better nor worse racing under the rule than the crew sailing her.

This boat has good all-around performance upwind and downwind, in both light and heavy air. Despite a wide maximum beam, the boat's ends are fairly well balanced, and the rudder is deep enough to stay in the water in all but a flat-out broach.

You'll find a number of different keel and rig combinations. As designed, the boat has a high-aspect-ratio fin keel drawing 7', with an "I" (height of foretriangle) dimension of 53'. This configuration is reasonable for all-around performance, but is a little lacking in power for lighter air. A rig 2' taller was introduced, and to increase sail-carrying ability, this is usually coupled with a 4" deep, 300-pound lead shoe bolted to the bottom of the keel. Stability of the two versions is virtually identical: the addition to righting moment from the shoe is almost exactly offset by the heeling moment of the taller rig.

The tall rig, deep keel version is on the average about three seconds per mile faster than the standard rig, standard keel model.

With a draft of 7' or more, this is not a boat for gunkholing, nor is it a good cruiser for areas of shallow water. A keel/centerboard variation was also built, drawing about 4' 9" with the board up, 8' 6" with the board down. To maintain the same stability as her deeper-draft sisters, the centerboard boat carries an additional 885 pounds of ballast, making her noticeably slower in light air. The IMS velocity prediction program shows the standard rig, centerboard model to be about four seconds per mile slower than the standard keel, standard rig version in eight knots of breeze. In 16 knots of wind, all three configurations are virtually identical in speed.

In areas traditionally known for heavy air, a keel shoe coupled to the standard rig has proven to be a powerful and competitive combination.

Like many IOR boats from the mid and late 1970s, the C&C 40 has a very high-aspect-ratio mainsail: about 3.5:1 with the standard rig, almost 3.65:1 with the tall rig. The result is a mainsail of just over 300 sq. ft., but a 100% foretriangle of about 440 sq. ft. This means lots of headsail changes, since reefing the mainsail has relatively little impact on total sail area.

With a racing crew of eight, headsail changes are no big deal. For a cruising couple, wrestling down a #1 genoa of over 650 sq. ft. would be no fun. For shorthanded cruising, a modern headsail reefing system is an absolute must for this boat. We'd also forget the 150% genoa for cruising, using a 130% genoa—about the size of a racing #2—which could be effectively reefed to about 100%.

It's not realistic to expect more reduction from a single sail. In winds of 10 knots or more, the loss in speed from the smaller genoa is virtually meaning-less when cruising: it's still faster than 90% of the 40-footers out there.

C&C rigs are generally well designed, with masts of reasonably high-performance characteristics. The 40 has a keel-stepped, double-spreader rig with single lower shrouds, Navtec rod rigging, and a forward babystay. This allows good mast control for racing. Tensioning the babystay pulls the middle of the mast forward, flattening the mainsail in heavy air. With all the shrouds in a single plane, the mast can assume a fair bend from top to bottom.

Most of these boats are equipped with a hydraulic backstay, with the babystay adjusted by a traveler on a track mounted atop the cabin. Boats that have been set up for racing may also have hydraulics for the babystay and vang. Without hydraulic mast controls, it's virtually impossible to take advantage of the spar's sail-shaping capabilities.

The mast is made from a reasonable section for a racer/cruiser. It is bendy enough for sail control when racing, but not nearly as fragile as you would find on a flat-out IOR racer of the same rig size.

If you intend to use the boat only for cruising, and you install a headsail reefing system, it would be almost imperative to add an inner forestay, particularly if you're headed offshore. The existing staysail track in the middle of the foredeck is not really strong enough for the attachment of a true heavy-weather staysail or storm jib.

In addition, we'd add running backstays to counteract the pull of the inner forestay, but you'd only have to set these up in heavy weather when sailing with a staysail or storm jib on the forestay.

The deck layout is definitely designed for racing. Halyard and spinnaker gear winches are mounted atop the deckhouse, aft of the mast. This works fine on a racing boat, keeping the center of gravity low, making it possible for one person to jump the headsail or spinnaker halyard while another tails, out of the way, further aft.

For shorthanded cruising, however, mast-mounted winches are superior. When reefing the mainsail with mast-mounted winches, one person can ease off the halyard, hook in the reefing tack, crank down the clew, and grind up the main halyard, all without moving. With deck-mounted winches, it's back and forth between the mast and the deck if one person has to do the whole job.

Construction

Like most C&Cs, the 40 was built with a balsa-cored hull. The result is a hull that is extremely stiff for its weight, but balsa coring is not without its potential for problems. In the event of delamination or rupture of the hull skin, the balsa coring can absorb moisture. Moisture penetration of the outer laminate could ultimately reach the balsa coring. It is imperative that a balsa-cored hull be carefully examined by a knowledgeable surveyor before purchasing a used boat.

As with most boats, the deck of the C&C 40 is also balsa cored. The deck, too, should be carefully sounded to check for delamination. In our opinion, deck delamination is potentially a very serious problem in almost any boat—not just this one—and the cost and difficulty of repair is frequently grossly underestimated.

C&C uses a basic inward-turning flange for the hull-to-deck joint, with a through-bolted aluminum toerail providing the mechanical fastening. Unlike many builders, C&C uses butyl tape in this joint. Butyl tape has no structural or adhesive properties; it just keeps the water out.

Uniform tensioning of the bolts in the joint is important with this type of bedding compound. Leaks in the joint can frequently be solved by careful re-torquing the bolts, but don't tighten them so much that all the compound's squeezed out.

As is typical of C&Cs, owners give the boat high marks for quality of construction, and in general, their enthusiasm is justifed. The boat does, however, have a potential weak point. Like most late IOR boats, the hull is virtually flat on the bottom, with the shallow bilges having little depth for strong transverse support. The keel has a relatively short root chord, so the keel stresses are very concentrated. In a hard grounding, the trailing edge of the keel can be levered up into the hull, resulting in devastating damage.

We examined one C&C 40 that ran into a rock at about seven knots during a race. The aft edge of the keel punched through the bottom of the boat, and the owner just managed to power the boat 20 miles to a boatyard, which hauled her instantly to keep the boat from sinking.

That boat required massive bottom rebuilding—the boat was actually replaced and the damaged hull repaired and re-sold. Over the years, we have looked at several C&C 40s with similar, though less dramatic, bottom damage as the result of grounding while racing. Remember that with this boat, you need more than 7' of water under you.

Beginning with 1981 models, both the deck and rudder installations were more heavily reinforced.

Most boats were retrofitted with these upgrades, and you should check with previous owners to see that they were done.

Engine

Several different engines were used in the C&C 40. Early models usually have a Yanmar 3QM-30. Later boats typically were fitted with a Westerbeke 30, although some boats were equipped with the more powerful VW-based Pathfinder engine.

All the engines are capable of driving the boat to hull speed in calm water.

The engine is mounted under the bridgedeck, just below the companionway. You must remove the companionway ladder and the front of the engine box to get access to the front of the engine. You can get at the port side through the quarterberth.

The boat handles extremely well under power, thanks to a big rudder well aft, very little wetted surface, and a prop mounted just forward of the rudder. Most boats are equipped with Martec folding props for racing—not the best installation for handling in reverse—but since the prop is so far aft, the boat handles very predictably when moving astern. For cruising, we'd rather see a feathering prop, which is an expensive but worthwhile retrofit.

Interior

C&C never skimped on the interiors of its racer/cruisers, and the 40 is no exception. The interior is built up of teak-faced ply, rather than incorporating a fiberglass liner with molded furniture bases.

The oiled teak ply makes for a darkish interior, which could be lightened considerably by varnishing both the ply and its solid teak edging. A nice combination is to use satin finish varnish on the ply, glossy varnish on the solid teak trim. This is time-consuming, of course, but it can noticeably brighten a drab interior.

The C&C 40's original layout (left) had a conventional racing boat interior with a large galley, a head in the forward section and two pilot berths. The last few boats built had a revamped interior (right). The pilot berths were eliminated, the galley and nav station were flopped, and the head moved aft, all to create a private aft cabin.

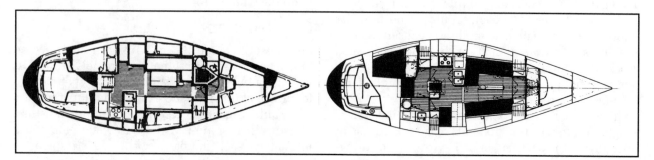

The cabin sole is teak and holly-faced ply, and the teak veneer is so thin that it chips easily, particularly at the edges when you pry up the floor boards.

There are plenty of berths for racing, and too many for cruising. The V-berths forward can be made into a double with an insert, and the quarterberth is wide enough to form a very tight double or a very big single.

Interior layout is fairly prosaic: V-berths forward, settees and pilot berths both port and starboard in the main cabin, quarterberth aft. Some early boats were built with a split quarterberth, with a narrow inboard berth and a narrower pilot berth outboard, tucked under the side deck. This is a particularly useless arrangement for cruising, and we wouldn't be too happy getting stuck in either of those berths when racing, either.

The head compartment is good-sized, and is accessible from either the main cabin or the forward cabin. We're not sure you really need two doors mere inches apart to get into the head, but perhaps the additional privacy for head access from the forward cabin is important to some people. We'd rather have the separation that a solid bulkhead between head and forward cabin would provide.

Main cabin storage is sacrificed to get in the two pilot berths. If you're planning long-distance racing with a big crew—or weekending with lots of friends—the pilot berths are nice. But the lower third of the pilot berths is recessed behind a longitudinal bulkhead which serves as the shroud anchorage. There will be no air circulation around your lower body in this berth.

Space over your feet is further reduced in the pilot berths by a locker tucked into the upper part of this longitudinal bulkhead. The result is a pair of berths that would be okay in cooler climates, miserable in the tropics.

Ventilation below is generally inadequate for anything but cooler climates. While there are good-sized aluminum-framed hatches over both the forward and main cabins, plus a small hatch over the head, the only provision for ventilation in bad weather is a pair of cowl vents in dorade boxes at the aft end of the main cabin.

C&C racer/cruisers have good galleys. The galley—aft on the starboard side—is the classic U-shape, with double sinks and a large bin in the forward counter; a large, well-insulated icebox under the aft counter; and the stove in the middle, at the base of the U.

The builder was a pioneer in the use of propane aboard boats, and that's what you'll find as a cooking fuel in virtually all C&C 40s. It's a good installation, with gas bottles located in small lockers on either side of the helmsman's seat at the aft end of the cockpit.

This is a very usable galley, with good storage outboard, a fair amount of counter space, and a practical layout.

The nav station opposite the galley has its own seat (you don't sit on the quarterberth) and a big chart table.

The bookshelf outboard is usually sacrificed for navigation and communication electronics, leaving you no place for your navigation texts. In fact, that

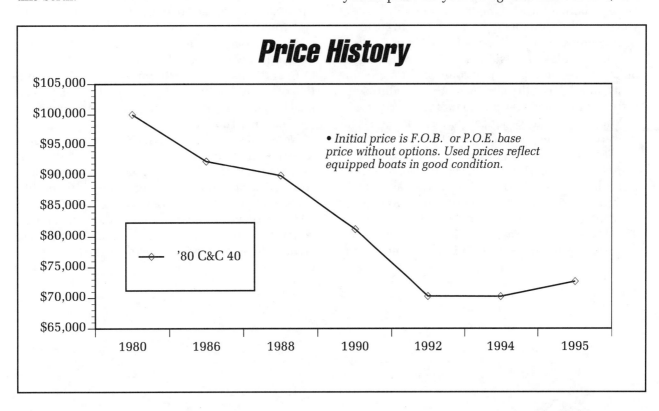

Price History

• Initial price is F.O.B. or P.O.E. base price without options. Used prices reflect equipped boats in good condition.

'80 C&C 40

single 2' shelf is the total amount of book shelving in the entire boat!

If you're thinking of cruising, you may want to sacrifice one or both of the main cabin pilot berths, replacing them with storage lockers and shelves. Otherwise, there's little readily accessible storage space in the boat.

In these days of tri-cabin layouts in 30-footers, it's unusual to find the basic two-cabin layout in a 40' boat. In fact, virtually every 40' cruising boat built since the early 1980s has a three-cabin interior.

With the racing competitiveness of the C&C 40 decreasing, and its desirability as a cruising boat limited by lack of a good owners' cabin with a double berth, a major re-thinking of the boat was required if it was to continue in production. This resulted in the short-lived aft cabin version of the C&C 40. In the last year of production, the deck was re-tooled, and the interior redesigned to create a tri-cabin boat with a stateroom aft.

The new interior was a mixed success. The pilot berths were eliminated, replaced by much-needed storage. The galley lost some space—it became L-shaped, giving up one leg of the old U—and was shifted slightly forward and to the port side. The nav station was flopped to starboard .

Aft, to starboard, is the head. On the port side aft is the owners' cabin, with a double quarterberth, hanging locker, and a seat. A doorway through the starboard bulkhead gives access from the owners' cabin to the head, and there's another doorway to the head from the main cabin.

In order to accommodate this new arrangement aft, the companionway was shifted forward, so that you must climb on top of the deckhouse to get to the companionway, which is a sliding hatch in the deck.

This deck layout is similar to that used on some older Swans, and it's a poor solution for a cruising boat, since it basically eliminates the possibility of a full-width dodger over the front of the cockpit.

You can install a dodger, but it will be so far forward as to offer minimal protection to the cockpit, and it makes climbing down the companionway a gymnastic effort with the dodger in place.

With the aft cabin C&C 40, you still have a high-performance boat, and you still—unless you opt for the centerboard—have a boat that draws at least 7'. The deep-draft, high-aspect-ratio fin keel and small mainsail are not the best combination for most cruising.

On the plus side, the aft cabin boat has significantly more privacy, eliminates unneeded berths, and has much more storage space.

Ventilation and light below are also much better in the aft cabin boat, although the big hatch over the main cabin is lost to the main companionway. In addition to the large hatch over the forward cabin, there are two small hatches over the main cabin, plus small hatches over both the aft cabin and the head. There are also additional fixed ports in the deckhouse, adding light to the main cabin.

Relatively few aft cabin boats were built. It was an expensive layout to construct, and the 40 was already getting pricey due to the built-up interior, which is much more labor-intensive than an interior based on a liner with molded furniture.

Conclusions

Despite her heavy interior, the C&C 40 was a reasonably competitive racing boat when introduced in the late 1970s. On the plus side, the interior was comfortable enough for cruising when the racing was over—as long as deep draft and a big rig don't intimidate you.

Some 200 C&C 40s were built, and many of them did a lot of racing. It's not unusual to find a 40 with very complete electronics, a full hydraulic rig control package, and a big inventory of racing sails.

Since the design's days as a serious racing boat are pretty much over—although you can certainly compete at the local level—many owners interested in racing have unloaded C&C 40s at near fire-sale prices.

In general, the C&C 40 is a well-built boat, in the same class as other boats from the company. The construction is not particularly high-tech, however, and some boats may have suffered under the strains of very heavy racing.

In particular, we'd recommend careful examination of the hull bottom in the way of the keel, and the attachment of structural components in the way of the mast and rudder.

Newer designs from C&C have taken advantage of higher-tech materials such as molded interior and hull support modules, and in general are probably stronger per pound of structural weight than older boats such as the C&C 40. Nevertheless, a C&C 40 which surveys cleanly can be an excellent value for club racing, and—with some re-working of the deck layout—for shorthanded cruising in areas where the deep draft is not a problem.   • **PS**

Valiant 40

A semi-custom yacht from Texas that's a true high-performance blue-water cruiser.

The Valiant 40 has a long history. In 1972 Nathan Rothman decided to start a boatbuilding business and approached old friend Bob Perry to design the ultimate cruising yacht. At that time Rothman and Perry were young, poor, relatively inexperienced, and full of ideals. Perry accepted the offer without even asking to be paid right away.

The decision to make the Valiant a double-ender was a marketing one based on the skyrocketing success of the Westsail 32. The Westsail had just been featured on the cover of *Time* magazine; double-enders were "in." Rothman sent Perry a photo of Aage Nielsen's *Holger Danske* and said, "Let's have a stern like that."

"So I took that fanny," said Perry, "and with all my experience on race boats, I designed a high-performance cruising boat." Rothman contracted with Uniflite to build the boats in Bellingham, WA, and the first Valiant was launched in 1973.

In the late '70s Rothman sold Valiant to Sam Dick Industries, who continued to build the boats under contract with Uniflite. Uniflite eventually bought the company from Sam Dick Industries. Finally, in 1984, Rich Worstell, one of Valiant's most successful dealers, bought Valiant Yachts, and began building the boats on Lake Texhoma.

Everyone knows that everything is bigger and better in Texas. Rich Worstell would not disagree with that—at least not if you were discussing the Valiant. Rich is a Valiant zealot.

Since 1984, he has built a relative handful of Valiant 40s. He also manufactures the Valiant 32, 37, Pilothouse 40, and 47. Every boat is semi-custom and each Valiant buyer comes to the factory at least three times—once to decide exactly which options he wants, once to oversee the building, and once to

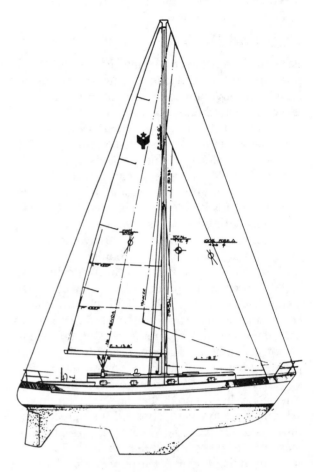

Specifications

LOA	39' 11"
LWL	34' 0"
Beam	12' 4"
Draft	5' 2"/6' 0" (shoal/std)
Displacement	22,500 lbs.
Ballast	7,700 lbs.
Sail area	753 sq. ft.

commission the boat. "We like every customer to shake his boat down at our lake facility so any minor problems can be fixed right here at the factory," says Worstell.

Over the years Valiant has gained a considerable reputation. Veteran singlehander Francis Stokes sailed his Valiant 40 *Mooneshine* to victory (first American monohull) in the 1980 Ostar; in 1983 Mark Schrader sailed a Valiant 40 safely around the world singlehanded, and again, in 1986-87, Schrader's Valiant 47 *Lone Star* completed the BOC.

"But the Valiant is not a boat for everyone," says Perry. "If I were going to hang out in St. Tropez or Portofino, I'd need a different boat—no question— I'd need pointy deck shoes—and a pointy boat. But there's a comfort that comes with being in a slightly less than all-perfect, smarmy environment—and the Valiant seems to suit that."

Hull and Deck

Early in Valiant's boatbuilding history, Uniflite Corporation experienced extensive hull blistering problems both above and below the waterline due to their use of a fire-retardant polyester resin.

To combat the problem, Worstell began using a 100% isophthalic resin used in conjunction with an isophthalic gelcoat. Although tests performed by Comtex Development Corporation in Bridgewater, MA, prove that vinylester blisters less readily than isophthalic resin, Worstell claims he has had no problems with blistering since 1984.

Valiant is convinced that the answer to hull blistering lies not just in the choice of materials, but in the care with which boats are built. Resin is catalyzed a gallon at a time, and hulls are laid up by hand. Valiants also come with 21 mils of epoxy, about eight coats, applied to the bottom of the hull. Topsides are coated with Imron polyurethane paint. While Imron is not as durable as Awlgrip or Sterling, Valiant prefers it because it's easy to repair.

The Valiant hull is an uncored, solid laminate. The deck is balsa-cored fiberglass with molded non-skid surface. Anywhere "stressed" through-bolts enter the deck or cabin house, Valiant puts in high-density foam or hot-coats the end-grain balsa to prevent water from seeping in. All heavily-loaded deck hardware, including grabrails, is installed with backing plates or heavy-duty washers.

Chainplates are stainless steel straps that extend through the deck. Valiant V-cuts their chainplate slots so that extra 3M 5200 sealant can be forced in to form a pressure gasket against the chainplate. Two chainplates through-bolt to 1 1/2" to 2" knees glassed to the inside of the hull. One of the chain plates through-bolts to the main bulkhead. All are very accessible.

The hull-to-deck joint on the Valiant is hard to fault. At the top of the bulwark there is an inward-turning flange. On deck, the edge of the molding turns upward to form the inner bulwark face, then outward at the top to overlap the hull flange. The joint is bedded in 5200 and through-bolted. The bulwark is then capped with a teak or aluminum toerail. We'd be tempted to opt for the aluminum one since it eliminates the upkeep of teak and is more protective against chafe.

The rubbing strake is made of high-density foam glassed to the hull with a sacrificial teak strip on the outside. There is also a stainless rub rail option.

The keel is an external lead casting, bolted to the hull with stainless steel bolts and backing plates. A conventional 6' fin keel is standard, but some owners choose the shoal draft model. Valiant will build the keel anywhere from 5' 2" to 6' in depth, but it can only be cut down in 2" increments.

Rather than molding the skeg as an integral part of the hull, a steel weldment is encased in a two-piece fiberglass shell filled with high-density foam and mish-mash. The skeg is then epoxied to the bottom of the hull and bolted in place with stainless steel bolts, nuts, lock washers, 5200, and a backing plate. Valiant glasses over the skeg again once it is in place to cover the seam. This type of skeg construction is very strong, and should provide adequate protection if you hit a submerged object or run aground.

The skeg heel is through-bolted to the bottom of the skeg. The rudderpost, made of 1 3/4" diameter stainless steel bar, rides on three bearings—one in the gudgeon, one where the rudder post goes through the hull, and a final bearing at the top in the rudder support bracket. Like the skeg, the rudder is filled with high-density foam and mish-mash, and molded in one piece with the rudderpost.

Valiant fabricates over 50% of the components for its boats in-house, including the mast step timber, which is the same for the Valiant 37, 40, 47, and Pilothouse 40. To form the mast step, 1/2" aluminum plate is TIG-welded to form a massive H-beam. The H-beam is then through-bolted to the floor timbers, and the mast sits in an oval-shaped aluminum weldment that is bolted to the custom mast step. This arrangement provides a strong platform, and eliminates corrosion problems that occur if a mast is stepped in the bilge. A tie rod extends from the mast step to the deck to keep the deck from overflexing or "panting."

Wooden bulkheads, which end at the cabin sole, are glassed to the hull with three layers of fiberglass mat and cloth. Valiant also glasses in a series of 12 transverse floor timbers, made of 2 1/2" to 3" high-density Divinycell closed-cell foam, to stiffen the hull.

Many production boats use continuous bulkheads or a molded floor pan for the same purpose. Installing floor timbers, rather than a molded fiberglass body pan, not only provides strength, it also gives Valiant the freedom to customize its interior.

The deep bilge is gelcoated, and all furniture is structurally bonded to the hull. Valiant believes that glassing furniture to hull and bulkheads replaces the need for longitudinal stringers. We question whether this is the best way to reinforce a hull in a semi-custom boat where furniture components are rearranged constantly.

Valiant uses bronze ball-valve seacocks screwed directly onto the threaded tail of the through-hull fitting. We consider this type of seacock potentially unsafe because it can put too much stress on the fitting. Instead, we recommend a flange-type seacock with mechanical fastenings and a doubling plate.

Two water tanks located under the settees port and starboard hold 140 gallons of water. Tanks are built of high-density polyethylene. Each tank has a large inspection plate, and vents to the bilge.

Valiant bonds their boats to protect them from electrolysis. Seacocks, prop shaft, and all underwater hardware are tied to a 6"x6" zinc that is recessed into the hull. Opinion is divided on the efficacy of bonding underwater metal. We've seen bonding solve a boat's galvanic corrosion problems. We've also seen boats suffering from electrolysis solve their problem by eliminating the bonding system. To insure lightning protection Valiant grounds the chainplates and mast base to the keelbolts. A single sideband counterpoise, consisting of copper strapping tied to the keelbolts, is also available as an option.

Engine and Mechanical Systems

The Valiant has a large, well-designed engine room. There's plenty of space to sit down to check the batteries or work on the engine or generator. However, the engine room sole, which follows the curve of the hull, is slippery. We advise coating the sole with non-skid.

Over the years Valiant has used Westerbeke, Perkins and Volvo engines in the 40. Currently, Valiant installs a three-cylinder Volvo 2003 Turbo, rated at 42hp at 3000 rpm with a V-drive transmission and a 3:1 reduction gear.

The front of the engine is accessible from the engine room for servicing filters and belts or changing the oil. The aft ends of the engine and transmission are accessible from the owner's stateroom or head, depending on which interior layout you choose. The engine compartment is properly sound insulated.

Volvo's flexible mounts are bolted to pieces of 4"x4" aluminum angle through-bolted to two high-density foam beds glassed to the hull. The engine has a Volvo water-lift type exhaust system. The exhaust sytem hose is looped high to prevent salt water from back-siphoning into the engine. In general, installation is very good.

However, many mechanics believe that a turbocharged engine is too complicated for a small sailboat, and can present a lot of extra headaches for the cruising sailor. We'd prefer to see the Valiant fitted with a normally aspirated four-cylinder engine of about 100 cubic inches.

The electrical system includes 110-volt AC and 12-volt DC service, and is controlled by a well-designed custom distribution panel mounted next to the navigator. Wiring is to ABYC specification. Wires are color-coded, and neatly run through a PVC pipe to the engine room. There's a handy pennant line supplied for running extra wires. Two 105-amp-hour deep-cycle batteries come standard on the 40, and you can order two extra 105-amp-hour batteries wired in parallel with the original two batteries. (You can also buy four Prevailer gel-cell batteries which Valiant properly installs in wooden battery boxes.) However, we consider wiring batteries in parallel poor practice. As an alternative, we'd recommend you buy two 180-200 amp-hour deep-cycle batteries, or two extra-large Prevailers, and upgrade the size of the alternator.

For those who want all the amenities of home, Valiant neatly installs an auxiliary generator (Northern Lights 5kw) behind a sound-proofed door in the aft end of the engine room. We think installing a generator in a 22,500 lb., 40' sailboat is overkill.

The plumbing system includes hot and cold pressure water. As an option you can also order a Whale foot pump in the galley or head that can be used for fresh or salt water. We consider manual foot pumps mandatory equipment for long-distance cruising. We'd also be tempted to purchase the handy Jabsco deck washdown pump.

There are two standard layouts, but the builder will do anything a buyer wants, within reason (and budget). As a result, a given interior may be very different from the standard one shown here.

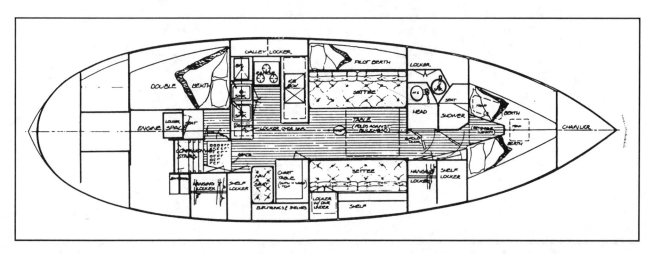

The standard electric bilge pump is a Par 36600 (eight gallons per minute capacity). This pump is inadequate for emergency bilge pumping. We'd recommend adding a second electric pump, even though there is a manual Whale Gusher mounted on the forward end of the cockpit well.

Handling Under Power

The Valiant 40 hull is easily driven; the Volvo 2003 Turbo at a normal cruising rpm of 2400 gives you a speed of 6 knots through the water in flat seas. The boat handles particularly well under power in tight quarters or when docking stern-to.

A two-bladed fixed propeller is standard equipment. You can order a two- or three-bladed feathering Max-Prop, which will improve your performance both under power and sail.

If you order the gen-set option, fuel is stored in two aluminum saddle tanks with a total capacity of 110 gallons. Without a generator, fuel is carried in one 90-gallon aluminum fuel tank. There's a handy fuel gauge mounted at the nav station which eliminates guessing how much diesel you have left.

Handling Under Sail

With a fine entry, a long waterline, a reasonably efficient underbody, and moderate wetted surface, the Valiant sails as well as any fast cruiser of her size.

The Valiant's broad flared bow makes her least efficient in a steep chop to weather. As soon as you bear off, however, the big flared bow becomes all sailing length, and the boat becomes very powerful, especially on a reach or broad reach in heavy air. She also performs respectably downwind. She's not as fast as a more modern, lighter racer/cruiser, but she's no slouch, either.

The Valiant is cutter-rigged with the mast stepped fairly well aft. This makes for a small, manageable mainsail (306 sq. ft.), and a foretriangle that is substantially larger than it would be on a typical sloop-rigged 40-footer. Still, the boat is unusually well-balanced and easy to handle. You can sail it either as a sloop or cutter (there's a quick release option on the inner forestay), but if you're shorthanded you'll probably prefer the double headsail rig.

Perry broke tradition when he designed a fin keel and skeg rudder for the Valiant. (At that time full keels were considered de rigueur for serious offshore cruising.) Since 1973 Perry has updated the keel twice.

"The initial keel was expensive and difficult to build, so Uniflite asked me to design a stiffer, less expensive one," Perry told us. His second keel design lowered the VCG (vertical center of gravity), deepened the bilge, and generally improved the boat's performance. It was also much easier to build.

The last change was again an effort to make the building effort more efficient, and provide a variety of keels. "With new foil developments we thought we could make it better yet," said Perry, "so I called up Dave Vacanti, who specializes in keels, and we came up with another foil—the same foil shape that was used on *Mongoose* in the Transpac."

The latest keel packs more weight into a shorter chord length and changes the leading edge angle. With increased stability, the newer deep-keeled Val-

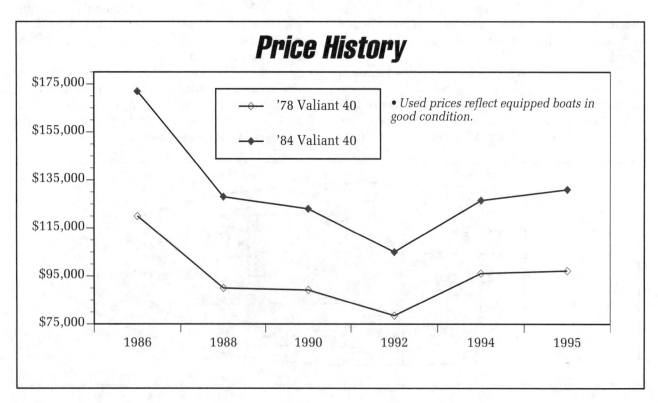

Price History

- ◇ '78 Valiant 40
- ◆ '84 Valiant 40

• *Used prices reflect equipped boats in good condition.*

iants can carry more sail and are faster than older boats. The shoal draft models are a compromise. They don't point as high as the 6' keel, but they do permit the cruising sailor to venture into shallower waters. Still, unless shoal draft is critical for you, we'd stick with the normal keel.

On Deck

The Valiant comes with continuous Navtec rod rigging; the inner forestay and intermediates, however, are wire. Instead of using running backstays to counteract the load of the inner forestay, the standard Valiant rig incorporates fixed intermediate shrouds which lead just behind the aft lower shrouds. The intermediates give minimal fore and aft support to the mast, and could cause unnecessary chafe on the mainsail downwind. We'd opt for running backstays.

A Navtec hydraulic backstay adjuster is optional, but you might want it if you go for roller furling on the headstay. The tapered mast is custom-welded by Spar Tech Inc. in Seattle, and then painted with Imron.

Sail handling hardware is excellent, with Schaefer genoa and staysail tracks. Winches are Lewmar and adequately sized. The halyard winches can be mounted on the mast or on the top of the cabin trunk at the front of the cockpit. Unfortunately, the staysail winches are located directly in the way of the cockpit dodger, preventing you from swinging the winch handle in a complete circle.

Wheel steering is Edson with radial drive. The drive wheel is easily accessible from the cockpit locker. The emergency tiller arm is offset 90° so you don't have to remove the wheel to install the tiller, but there's no comfortable place to sit when using it.

Because the cockpit lockers are huge, the hatches should be gasketed and fitted with latches that can apply pressure to the seal.

Surprisingly, there is no molded breakwater for a cockpit dodger. This makes it almost impossible to get a watertight seal around the bottom of the dodger.

Hatches are Lewmar except for the main hatch, which is custom-made of fiberglass and Lexan. Two dorades and a mushroom vent provide extra ventilation below. While these help beat the heat in the tropics, we are prejudiced against cutting unnecessary holes in the deck.

Belowdecks

One of the biggest advantages of a semi-custom boat without a molded hull liner is the ability to alter interior arrangements to meet an owner's needs. Presently, the Valiant 40 has two standard layouts, but Worstell is willing to make any changes a buyer wants provided they don't interfere with the seaworthiness or integrity of the boat.

The original standard belowdecks arrangement has V-berths forward with an insert to form a double. There's a divided chain locker in the bow, and a 3" PVC pipe can be led to a locker under the forward berth for anchor chain storage. Although we agree with keeping weight out of the bow, we'd worry about the anchor chain jamming in the PVC pipe. Closed cell foam, 1/2" thick, is used throughout the boat above the waterline for insulation.

Aft of the forward berths to starboard are two cedar-lined hanging lockers plus additional storage. The head is to port. The head door has a complicated, levered door handle that, on the boat we inspected, did not catch properly; we prefer very simple closing devices on all doors to avoid this type of problem.

There is ample locker space in the head for towels and sundries. The oval-shaped stainless steel sink is moderately deep, but we'd opt for a manual foot pump as well as the standard hot and cold pressure water. On the boat we inspected the shower and head occupied one space. As an option, you can order a molded fiberglass shower stall with built-in seat and removable teak grates. There's no separate shower sump; shower water is pumped directly overboard. In the main cabin there are settees port and starboard with a choice of shelves or a pilot berth above the settees. You can even opt for a special television shelf. The port berth has a pull-out option that makes a narrow double (6' 8" x 3' 2"). There is a white Formica drop-leaf dinette table which measures 3' 5" x 4' 3" when fully extended. To port, aft of the saloon, is a well-laid-out U-shaped galley. A four-burner Regal propane stove with oven and broiler is standard, but a Force 10 can be installed as an option. We'd buy the Force 10. Propane is stored in a vented lazarette locker holding two 11-lb. tanks. We'd prefer two 20-lb. tanks for long distance cruising, but the propane locker would have to be redesigned.

There are four cedar-lined lock-in type drawers for cutlery, and oodles of storage above the sinks and stove for food stores, spices, and dinnerware. However, we'd like to see the large port side sliding locker divided into smaller cubicles to keep things orderly offshore.

There are adequate double sinks (9" deep) located across from the icebox. Foam insulation in the ice box measures only 2" on the lid, and 3" on the sides. This might keep things cold in northern latitudes, but it won't be effective in the tropics.

A good-sized nav station, facing fore and aft, sits to starboard opposite the galley. The chart table is large enough for any chart folded in half, and has adequate space for electronics, navigation instruments, sextant and books. There is also storage for charts under the nav table, as well as extra storage under the nav seat.

Just starboard of the companionway ladder are three vented storage lockers. One is a wet locker with a canvas door that unzips for ventilation. To port of the companionway is a double stateroom—again with plenty of stowage under bunks and in lockers.

As an alternate arrangement, Valiant has recently designed an interior which we think a couple cruising without children may prefer. As you come down the companionway steps there's a quarterberth to starboard, and a head to port. The layout in the main cabin is the same as the original interior layout. However, forward of the saloon on the port side is a good-sized double berth with hanging lockers and storage opposite. The forepeak then becomes a well-appointed storeroom for sails.

This layout is preferable offshore. First, the head is easily accessible from the cockpit—and aft where the motion is less violent. Second, the off-watch can sleep snugly in the quarterberth, but still be in earshot of the person on deck, or within arm's length of the nav station or galley. The double berth forward can be used for sleeping in harbor.

Headroom everywhere is 6' 2". Lighting is good throughout the boat, especially in the nav station and engine room.

The Valiant comes with two standard interior finishes: oiled teak, or white Formica trimmed in oiled teak. Some people love oiled teak. We don't. If we chose the teak interior, we'd pay the extra money to have it varnished.

An interior of white Formica with teak trim is a practical combination that provides light and a feeling of space, but it may appear stark to those familiar with wood interior spaces. We'd at least opt for the white Formica with teak trim (varnished) in the head and galley.

The cabin sole is not a cheap veneer—it's 1/2" teak with poplar strips mounted on 3/4" ply. Again, we'd choose to have it varnished rather than just sealed, but some people find a varnished cabin sole too slippery.

Conclusions

The Valiant 40 is a true high-performance blue-water cruiser. It's also a well-built boat. You'll be hard pressed to find another builder who is more dedicated to his product than Rich Worstell. Basically, he takes pride in building the Valiant, and, if you buy one, he wants you to be proud of it, too.

For this reason he's willing to pretty much build the boat to an owner's specifications—within reason.

This all comes at a price, of course.

There are a few things we don't like about the Valiant. Most of them, (except for the seacocks) have nothing to do with seaworthiness. They're purely aesthetic. For example, the cabin trunk is too boxy for some people's tastes, and we'd like to see the boat built with oval instead of rectangular ports. The joinerwork is good, but no better than you'll find on other boats in this price range.

Basically, the Valiant is just not as flashy as more expensive semi-custom boats like the Alden 44. But the Valiant is an honest boat. It's strong, it's seakindly, and as Perry so aptly said, it's "been everywhere, and done just about everything." **• PS**

Bristol 39 and 40

The looks of these twins are strictly traditional, but so is the interior room—modern 33-footers have more.

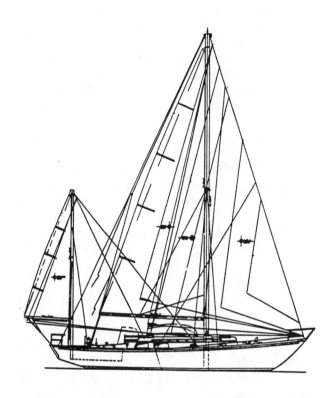

The Bristol 39 and Bristol 40 are basically the same boat, even though the specifications state that the Bristol 40 is nearly a foot longer than the Bristol 39. According to the builder, the hull sections aft were made slightly fuller on the Bristol 40, and the stemhead fitting was altered. After very careful scaling of plans, we can say with reasonable confidence that from one end of the hull to the other, excluding the bow pulpit and the anchor roller, the Bristol 39 and Bristol 40 are about 39' 8" long. Whether you call it a 39-footer or a 40-footer is up to you.

But this is not a 40' boat in the modern sense. Yes, if you take a tape measure to the boat, you'll read almost 40'. But if you go below, you'll swear you stepped onto a 33' boat—at least if you're used to looking at the 33-footers built today.

With a waterline length of 27' 6" and a beam of 10' 9", The Bristol 40's proportions are about as typical as you can get of cruising/racing sailboats built between about 1930, when the CCA (Cruising Club of America) rule was conceived, and 1970, when it was replaced by the International Offshore Rule (IOR). For those 40 years, about 30% of the average boat's length was in overhangs. Today, you find the waterline length and beam of the Bristol 40 on boats less than 35' long.

About 150 Bristol 40s were built. This does not include the relatively small number of boats in the Bristol 39 series.

The 39 was one of the first models built by Bristol Yachts, entering production in 1966. Beginning with 1972 models, the boat was rechristened the Bristol 40. The last Bristol 40 was built in 1986.

If you like traditional yachts, you'll find the Bristol 40 appealing. The boat has the long overhangs, lovely sheerline, low freeboard, narrow cabin trunk,

Specifications - 40

LOA	39' 8"
LWL	27' 6"
Beam	10' 9"
Draft	4' 0"/7' 10" (board up/down)
Displacement	17, 580 lbs.
Ballast	6,500 lbs.
Sail area	707 sq. ft. (yawl)

undistorted hull shape, and narrow beam we associate with the beautiful yachts of the past. If you didn't know she was a Ted Hood design, you might mistake her for a boat by Olin Stephens, John Alden, or Phil Rhodes.

The trade-off for these traditional good looks is a boat with a small interior compared to today's 40-footers.

Sailing Performance

"Fast" is a very relative term when you're talking about sailboats. The Bristol 40 is not fast relative to more modern 40-footers, but her performance is similar to that of other boats of her length built under the CCA rule, when boats were heavier and shorter on the waterline than they are today. The boat is close in speed, for example, to the Hinckley Bermuda 40 yawls with the original low aspect ratio rig. It is about 30 seconds per mile slower, however, than the Cal 40—a boat of the same length on deck, but with a longer waterline, less wetted surface and slightly less displacement.

In both keel and centerboard versions, the Bristol 40 is a fairly tippy boat, as you would expect from her narrow beam, shoal draft, and modest amount of ballast. Like "fast," however, "tippy" is a relative term.

Most narrow boats have relatively low initial stability, even if their ultimate stability is good. For example, the McCurdy and Rhodes 62-footer *Arcadia*, built in 1972, is about 2' narrower than a new IOR 60-footer would be, and has a righting moment about 15% lower than that of the new boat, even though *Arcadia* is significantly heavier.

Yet *Arcadia*'s range of positive stability is about 143°, while the typical "modern" racer/cruiser loses positive stability at 120° or less.

Unfortunately, being narrow and tippy doesn't guarantee a good range of ultimate stability. The keel version of the Bristol 40 loses positive righting moment at about 120°—the absolute minimum we would consider for a serious offshore cruiser. The centerboard version's range of stability is less—about 110° for the only boat rated under the International Measurement System (IMS).

It is not unusual for centerboarders to have very low positive stability. The Hinckley Bermuda 40—the classic keel-centerboarder—typically loses stability at an even lower angle than the centerboard Bristol 40, yet few people would consider the boat unsuitable for passagemaking.

Owners report that the Bristol 40 is very sensitive to the amount of sail carried. We'd suggest a modern headsail reefing/furling system for shorthanded cruising to reduce the number of headsail changes required.

Like most CCA boats, the Bristol 40 is a good reaching boat, lacking the rounding-up tendency of many modern boats with full sterns. The trade-off is that the boat tends to squat when running downwind, digging a hole that's hard to climb out of. A Bristol 40 with a full keel won the 1983 Marion-Bermuda Race, an event that consisted largely of four days of close reaching in light to moderate breezes.

Because the boat is narrow, there is no need to move the genoa track inboard of the toerail. The only real disadvantage of toerail-mounted genoa track is that you may have to relead the sheet to clear stanchions when changing headsails or reducing sail area with a headsail furler, unless there are turning blocks at the aft end of the genoa track. The two most common mainsheet arrangements on the boat are a short traveler spanning the cockpit immediately in front of the steering wheel, or a longer traveler over the coachroof in front of the companionway. The short traveler in the cockpit doesn't really offer much mainsail control, but it is a convenient location for the sheet.

The rig is a basic masthead sloop or yawl, using an untapered, keel-stepped anodized mast with single spreaders and double lower shrouds: basically foolproof. The lower shroud chainplates do not line up exactly with the pull of the shrouds, which will tend to fatigue the chainplates over time, as well as increasing the likelihood of leaks due to an unfair pulling angle.

Since this is a boat that was in production for the better part of 20 years, it's difficult to generalize about the sailing gear you'll find. On the Bristol 40s we've looked at, the stock winches tend to be one or two sizes smaller than we'd put on the boat today. You're unlikely to find self-tailers on older models.

A lot of Bristol 40s were built as yawls. While the yawl rig is pretty and looks very traditional, the mizzen is generally only useful to help balance the helm, as a convenient place to mount a radar antenna, and to serve as a support for a mizzen staysail on the rare occasion that it pays to carry one. The mizzen makes the boat more tippy and increases windage—disadvantages for upwind sailing.

Engine

Before 1970, Bristol 39s came with either Atomic 4 or Graymarine gas engines. Later model 39s and Bristol 40s were powered either by the Atomic 4 or by a variety of diesels, including the Westerbeke 4-91, Westerbeke 4-107 and 4-108, Perkins 4-108, or Volvo MD2B and MD3B engines. That should be enough variety to satisfy everyone.

The Westerbeke and Perkins 4-108s are essentially the same engine, and in our opinion would be the best engine for the boat, although they're more power than it needs. Diesel engine installations in the Bristol 40 are not without problems. There is little room between the shaft coupling and the stuffing box—so little, in fact, that several owners surveyed reported that it is almost impossible to reach the stuffing box for adjustment or repacking.

In all models, the fuel tank is located under the cockpit sole, above the engine. Fuel capacity is about 30 gallons. Early diesel-powered models have black iron fuel tanks, and at least one owner surveyed reported having to replace a rusted-out tank after a few years. Later models have aluminum fuel tanks, which are less likely to corrode. Range under power with the Perkins 4-108 and 30 gallons of fuel will be about 180 miles.

The gasoline engines used in early models swing a small prop. Unfortunately, when the switch was made to bigger diesels—the Perkins 4-108 displaces

108 cubic inches, the Atomic 4 only 65 cubic inches—the propeller aperture was not enlarged, limiting prop size. We measured the height to be 16 1/2", which means you can really only swing about a 15" prop and still maintain adequate tip clearance. The result is that you end up turning an oversquare prop (more pitch than diameter), which is not the most efficient way to utilize the engine in a sailboat.

Our prop choice would be a three-bladed feathering Maxprop for the best combination of performance under both sail and power. The Maxprop would also slightly improve handling in reverse, which is rated as poor by most owners. A tiny fixed prop tucked in an aperture in the deadwood and rudder is a bad combination for handling in reverse. Powering ahead, the boat handles just fine.

There is no sound insulation in the engine compartment. Access to the front of the engine is fair, requiring removal of the front of the engine box which doubles as the companionway ladder.

Construction

Bristol Yachts has gone through a lot of changes over the years. The prime mover behind Bristol was Clint Pearson, one of the pioneering Pearson brothers—the other, Everett, now runs Tillotson-Pearson.

The boats built by Bristol today are a far cry from those of 15 years ago. Current Bristols are targeted toward the middle to upper end of the production and semi-custom markets, with very good finish detail and systems. Originally, Bristols were aimed at the mass market, and were finished and equipped accordingly.

Since the Bristol 40 was built over a period of 20 years, there were a number of minor changes during the production run, but the last boats are essentially the same as the first ones.

The Bristol 40 is not a particularly lightly built boat, but she is certainly not heavy for her overall length, even by modern standards. The boat is substantially lighter than most long-keel CCA 40-footers. The Hinckley Bermuda 40, for example, displaces about 20,000 pounds in normal trim. The Cal 40, considered a real lightweight in 1966, weighs about 16,000 pounds in IMS measurement trim; the average Bristol 40, right at 17,000 pounds in the same configuration.

By way of comparison, the Little Harbor 38 that won the 1986 Newport-Bermuda Race tips the scales at a hefty 25,000 pounds, and the newer Bristol 38.8 has a designed displacement of just over 19,000 pounds.

None of the Bristol 40 owners we surveyed report any major structural flaws. They do, however, complain of annoyances such as leaking ports, deck

Though there's somewhat less room below than in a more modern 40-footer, the interior is reasonably well laid out. This is one of several different interiors that were offered.

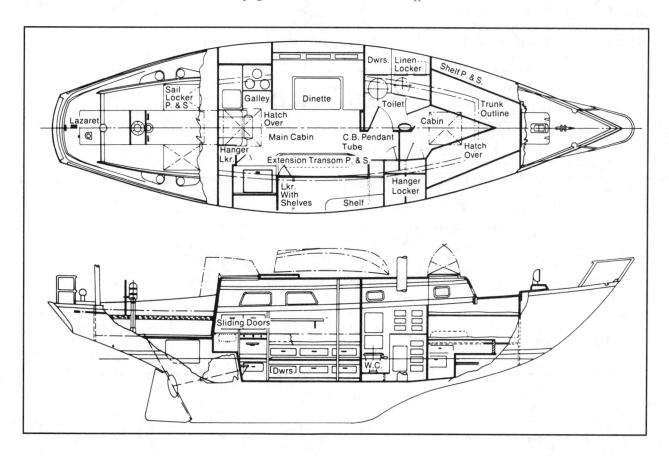

hardware, and hull/deck joints. These are generally assembly and quality control problems, and most can be solved by the owner, albeit with a fair amount of labor. A leaking hull/deck joint may be more of a problem, but this type of leak should show up during a careful examination of the boat. Discoloration and water streaks inside lockers and on bulkheads, rust and drips on through-fastenings, and mysterious puddles of water may indicate leaks in the joint.

From a cruiser's point of view, a nice feature of the Bristol 40 is its water capacity: 130 gallons in two fiberglass water tanks.

Any sailboat hull older that about eight years is getting on toward being a candidate for painting. While the gelcoat in the Bristol 40s we examined still looks reasonable, most of the colored hulls—pastels were popular in the 70s—are badly faded. The colored gelcoat used was not colorfast.

We also noted numerous gelcoat flaws on decks: cracks around stanchion bases, some voids at sharp corner transitions. During the survey, the surveyor should carefully sound the entire deck for voids. If you're going to go to the trouble and expense of painting, you might as well catch all the problems at the same time.

Deck non-skid is a molded-in basket weave pattern, and we have found it to be less effective than more aggressive non-skid designs.

The cockpit is huge, with seats almost 7' long. The well is narrow enough that you can brace your feet against the opposite seat—a good feature on any boat, but especially important on a tippy boat. The big cockpit is a mixed blessing. It gives plenty of space for daysailing or in-port parties, but it is also vulnerable to filling in extremely heavy offshore conditions.

In our opinion, the cockpit scuppers are too small. Each of the two scuppers is about the size of a bathtub drain. Since there is no bridgedeck—just a raised companionway sill—it is particularly important that the cockpit drain quickly. This is a pretty reasonable retrofit job. For offshore sailing, the bottom dropboard should be caulked and permanently secured in place.

There is a reasonable amount of exterior teak trim on the boat, including toerails, cabin eyebrow trim, handrails, and cockpit coamings. A Bristol 40 with a freshly-Awlgripped hull and varnished teak trim would look handsome, indeed.

On the port and starboard quarters, there are large chocks for dock lines. While these look substantial, they are only screwed to the toerails, and can easily tear out. Chocks can be very heavily loaded during panic dockings, and should always be through-bolted, as should all deck hardware.

Through hull fittings are not recessed flush, but can easily be faired in to reduce drag in very light air. The Constellation-style rudder is set slightly above the aft edge of the keel, so that the boat will ground out on the keel rather than the rudder.

Instead of a bolt-on external keel, the Bristol 40 has a molded keel cavity filled with 6,500 pounds of lead. One owner we surveyed had added 1,500 pounds of lead pigs in the bilge to improve stability.

Interior

Bristol has always made extensive use of built-up

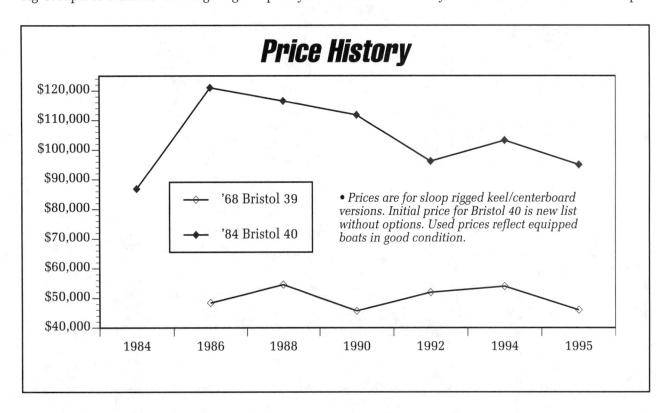

Price History

- ◇ '68 Bristol 39
- ◆ '84 Bristol 40

• *Prices are for sloop rigged keel/centerboard versions. Initial price for Bristol 40 is new list without options. Used prices reflect equipped boats in good condition.*

interiors of plywood and solid wood, rather than fiberglass molded components trimmed out in solid wood. The company has also made extensive use of mahogany rather than teak in interior construction.

If you're used to the dull brown of teak, the brighter reddish-brown of the mahogany interior of the Bristol may or may not appeal to you. Mahogany must be varnished: it is not suited to an oil finish in a marine environment. If you let the varnish wear off, the wood will turn grey, particularly after exposure to water.

At the same time, mahogany is lighter and brighter than teak, and can make an all-wood interior slightly less gloomy. If all else fails, you can always paint out the mahogany bulkheads and leave the mahogany trim varnished. Teak plywood is much harder to paint out, since its waxy surface doesn't hold paint very well.

The built-up interior allowed a number of interior options in the Bristol 39 and 40. As originally drawn, the boat had a wide-open offshore racing interior, with a sail locker forward, the head in the area normally reserved for a forward sleeping cabin, and symmetrical pilot berths, settees, and quarterberths in the main cabin. While it provides six sea berths, this interior has little appeal for a cruising family. Most boats were built with one of several more conventional interior layouts.

One advantage of long-ended boats is that the V-berths don't have to be jammed into the bow. Instead, you get berths that are wide enough at the foot for normal-sized people. The forward cabin of the Bristol 40 is quite roomy, with two berths and various lockers and drawers. An insert turns the V-berths into a reasonable double berth.

The head compartment is aft of the forward cabin, on the port side. It is a big, roomy head, with rather remarkable storage, including 10 small drawers and three lockers. All boats came with hot and cold pressure water, and have a hand-held shower attached to the head sink fixture.

Opposite the head are the usual hanging lockers.

Several different main cabin layouts were offered, with an arrangement to please just about every fairly conventional taste. On the port side, you'll find either a settee berth with storage outboard, a U-shaped dinette, or a narrow pull-out settee with a pilot berth outboard. On the starboard side, you'll usually find a settee with a folding pipe berth above, although some boats were built with a conventional pilot berth outboard of the starboard settee.

On boats without a dinette, the main cabin table folds up against the port forward bulkhead—a reasonable solution in a narrow boat.

Main cabin storage space is quite good, with a number of drawers and lockers. The actual storage arrangement varies with each interior layout.

Ventilation in the main cabin, as well as in the entire boat, is so-so. There is an opening port in the head, and a cowl vent overhead. There is another cowl vent on the other side of the cabin trunk opposite the head, providing some air to the forward cabin and main cabin in foul weather. Over the forward cabin is a large fiberglass hatch.

A fiberglass hatch over the main cabin was optional. The main cabin ports do not open. Ventilation would be greatly improved by adding Dorade boxes just in front of the dodger breakwater at the aft end of the main cabin. If you also put a reversible aluminum-framed hatch directly over the middle of the main cabin, and added a small dodger to it for heavy weather protection, you'd go from lousy ventilation to good airflow in one fell swoop.

We're not keen on the fiberglass hatches used in production boats in the 1970s. They distort easily, and never seem to seal completely.

Headroom is about 6' 4" on centerline aft, decreasing to about 6' in the forward cabin.

In all interior layouts other than the original ocean racing one, the galley is at the aft end of the main cabin. There are two aft galley arrangements. One is spacious but not particularly efficient, the other is tight. On boats equipped with a quarterberth and nav station on the port side, the galley is jammed into the starboard aft corner, and is small for a 40-footer. On boats without a nav station, stove and sink are on the port side, with a large icebox opposite to starboard. The top of the icebox is then used as a navigation table. Neither galley layout is as good as the U-shaped galley used on more modern boats such as the Bristol 38.8.

You'll have to make a choice on the galley layout. A nav station is very desirable if the boat is used for more than daysailing. Yet the starboard galley you get on boats with nav stations is quite small, and doesn't have much storage for foodstuffs or utensils.

Even on boats with the port nav station, the electrical panel is located on the starboard side, above the galley and next to the companionway, in a fiberglass box that's a molded part of the cabin liner. We'd want to give better protection to the panel by building a frame with an opening clear acrylic cover.

Despite the narrowness of the Bristol 40 compared to newer boats, the interior is reasonably laid out and not cramped. Headroom is good, and you can easily make improvements in ventilation. The interior doesn't seem as spacious as a lot of boats due to the fairly narrow, tall cabin trunk. Newer designs have more freeboard, allowing a lower cabin trunk and increasing the feel of interior space.

Conclusions

Like the better-known Bermuda 40, the Bristol 40 is an exceptionally pretty boat, and those good looks are one factor that kept the boat in production for such a long time. But the Bermuda 40 has been carefully refined, and its reputation nurtured by a group of nearly-fanatical owners who are willing to pay rather remarkably high prices for a design that is now 30 years old.

The Bristol 40, on the other hand, lacks that reputation and following. A few Bristol 40s were built for die-hards even after the boat was superseded in 1983 by the faster, roomier, stiffer Bristol 38.8—a design that is a distinctly more modern Hood cruiser/racer.

Because of her large cockpit, small cockpit drains, slightly vulnerable companionway, and fairly low initial stability, this boat wouldn't be a good choice for extended offshore cruising, although Bristol 40s have certainly done their share of it. For cruising in the Chesapeake, Bahamas, or Gulf of Mexico, the keel-centerboard version would be a reasonable choice, and even the deep keel model draws substantially less than most 40-footers.

A late-model, sloop-rigged boat with Perkins or Westerbeke diesel would be our first choice. Since relatively few changes were made in the boat during the years of production, however, you might also find a good older boat on which a lot of attention has been lavished.

If you like traditional looks, and you cruise in shoal coastal waters without extremely heavy winds a lot of the time, the Bristol 40 should appeal to you. You're a natural candidate for the boat if the looks of the Bermuda 40 catch your eye, but you don't have the pocketbook to indulge yourself in Hinckley quality. **• PS**

Hinckley Bermuda 40

With the longest production run of any boat built in the U.S., the 40 is as seaworthy as she is beautiful.

The Henry R. Hinckley & Co. The name is known to every American sailor. Or should be. It connotes different things to different people, mostly depending on their politics: Down East craftsmanship, big bucks, Yankee work ethic, East Coast blue-blooded snobbery. For those familiar with the company's work, it more likely means mirror-like varnish, custom stainless steel castings, the trademark dust bin in the cabin sole and "frameless" portlights. Still, critics are quick to complain that other builders produce boats that are just as good for less money. More often than not, these sentiments are just sour grapes from people who can't afford a Hinckley or even a different brand of comparable quality. While we acknowledge that there probably are a few builders around the world which build boats to the same exacting level, Hinckley is nonetheless unique in North American boatbuilding.

History

Henry R. Hinckley started the company that bears his name on graduation from Cornell University. His first boat, launched in 1934, was a 26-foot lobster-type powerboat. Soon moving to sail, he designed and built the Sou'wester 34 and 30-foot Sou'wester Jr. During World War II he built mine yawls, coastal pickets and tugs. While his "production" wooden boats weren't regarded as anything exceptional, his yard did do some first-class work, building the 73-foot *Windigo* (nee *Ventura*) and *Nirvana*.

After the war, Hinckley began experimenting with fiberglass as a potential boatbuilding material, though, true to his conservative Maine heritage, he didn't rush into it. The Hinckley Bermuda 40, introduced in 1959 and still in production today, was a watershed for the company.

Specifications - Mk III

LOA .... 40' 9"
LWL .... 28' 10"
Beam .... 11' 9"
Draft .... 4' 3"/8' 9" (board up/down)
Displacement .... 20,000 lbs.
Ballast .... 6,500 lbs.
Sail area .... 776 sq. ft.

According to company notes on the B 40, "The firm had built a wooden 38-foot yawl in 1959 and had called her a Sou'wester Sr. It was Henry's plan to sail the boat hard the coming summer and if she proved her worth, he would use her as a plug from which to build the mold for the first fiberglass Hinckleys. But this was never to occur."

At the 1959 New York Boat Show, Hinckley was approached by a consortium of eight men, who had commissioned Bill Tripp to modify the Block Island 40 for them. The group's front man, Gilbert Cigal, persuaded Hinckley to build the boats. The decision to abandon the Sou'wester Sr. was difficult, but from a business point of view, it made more sense to invest in tooling for boats already sold.

The first B 40 was delivered to consortium mem-

Owners' Comments

"One is hard-pressed to find a critical Hinckley owner. Their boats are solidly built and cabins are beautifully finished. Pride of ownership, and purchase price, lead to well-maintained used offerings, generally."

—1977 model in Pennsylvania

"If buying a new B 40, count on spending an additional 33 to 50 percent on options. The best route might be a used B 40. I've sailed many of these and even 15-year-olds hold up very well. Hinckley has an excellent restoration program for all their boats. It's difficult to imagine another yard providing as much interest and expertise."

—1988 model in New York

"Barn door rudder. Tough to maneuver in close quarters and situations with heavy crosswinds. The Bermuda 40 is one of the classic yawls in CCA design. An absolute pride and pleasure to own and to sail."

—1969 model in Michigan

"Given the traditional layout in this hull, it is not too generous by today's standards, but it does work, especially with four or fewer people. Big lack to us is a really comfortable place to sit below (transoms are not quite the right shape). We also made a mistake in giving up the wet locker for a larger refrigerator. She is a comfortable cruiser, no speed demon, but also easy to sail with limited crew."

—1978 model in Washington, DC

---

ber Morton Engel in time for that year's Bermuda Race. Though not completely finished, she finished in the top third of the field. In 1964 she won the Northern Ocean Racing Trophy and the next year the Marblehead to Halifax Race.

Many other B 40s achieved notable accomplishments both racing and cruising. One of the more publicized circumnavigations was done by Sy and Vickie Carkhuff, who wrote about their adventures in numerous magazine articles. It is therefore no surprise that the combination of Hinckley quality and Tripp seaworthiness produced a boat that boasts the longest-running production span of any fiberglass boat—32 years.

Hinckley's Rigdon Reese said the company does not sell a lot of B 40s nowadays, in part because their 42 and 43-footers represent many of the major advancements that have been made in yacht design over the past three decades. These are primarily in the areas of increased interior volume and better sailing performance. "But," Reese says, "every now and then someone appears at the door who feels he *must* own a B 40. If we can't sell him a brokered boat (Hinckley sells the vast majority of used—or should we say 'pre-owned'—Hinckleys) or talk him into a newer design, then we'll build him a B 40." The last one launched was during the summer of 1991—hull #203.

The Design

Unlike the Block Island 40, the Bermuda 40 is a centerboarder, and a major reason for its continuing appeal. If shoal draft is a requirement, as it often is in some areas of the U.S., one is forced to consider a centerboard design or, when available, a wing keel. Though not terribly beamy by today's standards, the

B 40's 11' 9" beam is substantial. If you can't get stability through ballast located deep (remember, the design parameter was for a shoal draft boat; and, fin keel boats weren't considered suitable in 1960 for offshore work), you must get it from what is called "form stability," that is, the shape and dimensions of the hull. Similarly, the interior would not be considered very spacious by today's standards, but in 1960 it had the room of a wooden 50-footer.

Typical of the CCA (Cruising Club of America) rule, the B 40 has generous overhangs, which contribute greatly to her exceptional looks. The sheer had a nice spring to it, rising just a bit at the stern and considerably more so at the bow. The low point is about two-thirds of the distance aft, helping give the profile its classic lines. Tripp was fond of the concave counter and nearly vertical transom.

The keel draws 4' 1" with a gently cutaway forefoot (no "chin") and straight clean run on the bottom. The rudder, attached to a vertical rudderstock, is hung off the trailing edge of the keel. This is a boat that, should she run aground, won't suffer a lot of damage, and should give the owner a fighting chance to float her, without crippling the rudder, utilizing his own on-board resources.

The down side of this design approach is less than stellar upwind performance. She does not tack as quickly as a boat with a more modern underbody (such as the McCurdy & Rhodes-designed Hinckley 42), and has a tendency to lose speed through the tack until she has a chance to pick up a head of steam. Then again, the B 40 has a heavier displacement than many modern boats of similar length. The Tripp 40 (designed by Bill Tripp's son), an all-out racer, displaces 12,750 pounds. The shoal keel J/40 displaces 18,650. Full-blown cruisers such as the Tashiba 40

(29,000 pounds) and the Lord Nelson 41 (30,500 pounds) are considerably heavier. So the B 40 is actually of moderate displacement, representing a nice comfortable figure for offshore sailing without forsaking light air performance.

Three different versions have been offered over the years—the Bermuda 40 Custom, the Mark II, and the Mark III. The yawl was the rig of choice until the Mark III, which also is available as a sloop. The Mark II was given an airfoil centerboard and a slightly taller mainmast (49' 3" bridge clearance) than the Custom (47' 0"). This increased sail area from 725 sq. ft. to 741 sq. ft.

The Mark III was changed further. According to the company's notes, "In response to the 'new' IOR rule, Peter Cooper of Sound Spar conspired with Bill Tripp and Henry once again to raise the aspect of both mizzen and main. This time the main mast was raised a full four feet three inches and moved aft almost two feet. This enlarged the foretriangle to the point where larger primary sheet winches were needed. The additional sail area raised the center of effort, and it was necessary to add a thousand pounds to the boat's keel. This added weight made her sit lower on her marks and added a foot to her waterline." Obviously, the company was trying to pump up performance to keep up with consumer expectations.

As one would expect, there have been many other refinements made to the original design, though most are minute compared to the changes in rig and ballast.

Construction

The B 40 is built of solid fiberglass—always has been and still is. A "hybrid knit fabric of Kevlar/E-glass" fibers is used in current boats. The deck was originally solid glass. Later it was balsa-cored, and now it is cored with 3/4-inch PVC foam, and vacuum-bagged for good bonding of the skins. The hull-deck joint is unusual in that the fairly standard deck-to-hull flange system is incredibly strong. The flange is 1/2-inch thick and about six inches wide, increasing around the chainplates. There also is a lip on the flange than gives the deck a snug fit. In his book, *The World's Best Sailboats*, Ferenc Mate describes at some length the process of fitting the deck to the hull. The deck is lifted with a chain hoist and lowered onto the hull to determine where the bulkheads should be trimmed. He quotes Bob Hinckley as saying, "We raise it, lower it, raise it, lower it, up and down like whore's drawers until all the tops of the bulkheads fit perfectly." The two mating surfaces are ground and filled until the two match like a piece of joinerwork. Wet fiberglass mat is laid on the flange and then the two pieces are bolted together. The entire process "takes two days for a small crew."

As implied above, the interior is built before the deck is fastened. It is almost a cliche, but true, that Hinckley builds a wooden boat inside a fiberglass hull. No fiberglass is visible. You can probably have any specie of wood you want, including cherry, white ash or the traditional Maine white paint and varnished mahogany trim. Whichever you choose, rest assure it will be gorgeous.

Lead ballast is mounted externally, fastened with one-inch stainless steel bolts. The cast bronze centerboard is not operated by a wire pennant but by a worm gear.

All deck hardware is through-bolted; holes are not oversized for dropping bolts through but tapped so that each machine screw threads not only into the backing plate and lock nut, but also through the deck itself.

Hinckley prides itself on manufacturing as many components as it can, including the stainless steel stem casting, custom tapered mast, steering pedestal, even the stanchions. One could go on and on describing how the through-hulls are countersunk flush with the hull, the number of coats of phenolic tung oil varnish applied to all natural wood surfaces,

The Bermuda 40's wide side decks force a tradeoff below—lessened living space. Overall, there is less space than would be found in a more modern design. Detail and finish work are excellent.

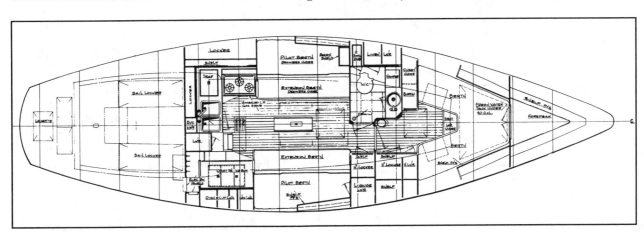

and how sheet copper is used to bond all sea cocks to the boat's lightning and bonding system.

The engines, of course, are not made by Hinckley, but each is test run for several hours and the standard 55-amp alternator replaced with a 105-amp model to charge the house batteries. A 53-amp alternator charges the engine start battery. The Westerbeke 4-107 diesel was standard for many years, though today you can also have the Yanmar 4JH2E. Hinckley makes its own shaft log and muffler. Fuel capacity is 48 gallons in a single Monel tank. Three stainless steel water tanks hold 110 gallons.

The cockpit seat lockers are gasketed and can be locked from below via a latch in the galley. Lockable, watertight seat lockers should be, but seldom are, a requirement of offshore sailing.

Interestingly, Hinckley recommends Marelon ball-valve sea cocks, through-bolted with Monel fasteners (of course, you can have whatever you want). Of equal interest is the one opening portlight. All others are fixed safety glass, which is preferable to Plexiglas or Lexan in terms of scratch resistance and resistance to ultraviolet rays. The frames are mounted inside, so that they are not visible from the outside. One owner said he wished ventilation was better.

Not surprisingly, owners responding to our questionnaire rate construction as excellent—without exception. One reader called his B 40 "bullet proof, over-engineered."

Performance

As mentioned under the "Design" section, the B 40 is an adequate performer. She is not particularly fast

upwind, due in part to the fat, shallow keel, but does much better off the wind, according to owners. They rate stability as about average, often citing the relatively low 28 percent ballast-to-displacement ratio. One reader said, "It heels early to about 15 degrees, then stiffens." Another said, "It's hard to keep the rail in after initial 15- to 20-degree heel (with centerboard down)."

On a more positive note, the mizzen sail and centerboard allow the boat to be balanced much better than most designs. One owner said, "On most courses we can almost eliminate weather helm with appropriate sail trim." Another said balance was "especially good from beam reach to a very broad reach." These points of sail, for most other boats, cause the most difficulty in handling.

Owners rated seaworthiness as excellent. One said he'd taken one knockdown and suffered no damage.

Under power there are the usual complaints about losing steering control in reverse, but this is to be expected of a full-keel design with the propeller in an aperature. One reader said, "We sometimes use the centerboard for docking." The 37-hp. Westerbeke auxiliary, while rated as an excellent engine, has barely sufficient power to punch through headseas. (We have no comparative information on the Yanmar.) Access to the engine, incidentally, was rated as fair. One reader wrote, "All service is from the front end. The sides are accessible through cockpit lockers. You can get right down and sit on the reverse gear if you wish." Another noted that the shaft and log are "buried," and difficult to work on.

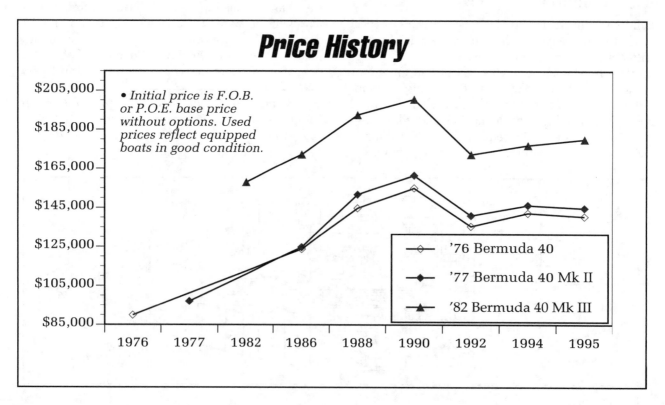

Price History

• Initial price is F.O.B. or P.O.E. base price without options. Used prices reflect equipped boats in good condition.

◇ '76 Bermuda 40
◆ '77 Bermuda 40 Mk II
▲ '82 Bermuda 40 Mk III

Interior

Details of interior layout vary from boat to boat since each B 40 is built to order. The basic plan, however, remains essentially the same.

There are V-berths forward which may be converted to a sumptuous double with the addition of the insert board and cushion. The head has a sink and shower as standard equipment, and opposite are a number of cedar-lined lockers for clothes. Stowage space is generous.

The standard saloon layout has berths for four: two extension settees, and pilot berths port and starboard. These tend to push the furniture in toward the centerline, making the cabin seem less spacious than more contemporary designs. (This also is partly a function of the B 40s very wide sidedecks—a blessing on deck and a trade-off below.)

While a narrow cabin provides better handholds and is therefore safer at sea, the drop leaf dining table restricts access fore and aft when the starboard leaf is up. That can be annoying. The optional U-shaped dinette eliminates the problem.

The galley is aft and is adequate, though compact. There isn't much counter space other than the lid tops of the icebox and stowage bin. Worse, the navigation station is above the icebox on the starboard side. The optional layout features a navigator's seat; in the standard layout one must stand. We'd prefer to see a separate nav area with additional room for electronics.

For extended cruising, the B 40 is best suited to a couple, with occasional guest crew. For a family with children, the kids would have to sleep in the pilot berths, which is okay but means that their junk will rain down on the settees.

Most owners commented on the lack of interior space, but accept it as part of the package, knowing full well that if they'd required more, they could have bought a different boat.

The finish detail of the B 40, indeed, any Hinckley, is legendary, and there isn't space here to describe the many intelligent features that help set this boat apart from the rest of the field. You'll have to see for yourself, as the interior design and workmanship represent a good part of the total cost.

Conclusion

Hinckley takes enormous pride in its work, and offers to its customers a wide range of services. In effect, you become part of the Hinckley family. Most Hinckleys are serviced by the builder, and most used Hinckleys are sold through Hinckley's own brokerage arm. They also run a charter service, which is a good way to test sail a Hinckley for longer than an afternoon.

Because of the substantial investment owners made in purchasing a Hinckley, and because of the continuing support offered by the company, most used Hinckleys are in excellent condition. And the B 40, because of its 32-year production run, may be found with a wide range of options, and can be purchased at a wide range of prices. Resale value is excellent. For example, the base price of a 1975 B 40 was about $90,000. BUC Research today lists the value of that boat at about $120,000 to $130,000. Assuming the original owner spent, in addition to the base price, another $25,000 equipping his boat, he could still expect to break even 17 years later! If you purchase a good used Hinckley at a fair price, you could conceivably expect to make a small profit on resale, and while that was not uncommon during the 1970s, it is almost unheard of in the late 1980s and early 1990s. BUC lists an average low retail of about $80,000 for a 1960 model and an average high retail of about $350,000 for a 1990 model.

Every B 40 is a bit different than the last, so it would be advisable to check several before making a decision. Looking at used B 40s would also be helpful in selecting features for a new model.

The base price of a 1992 Bermuda 40 yawl is $354,740.

Obviously, Hinckleys aren't for everyone. They are expensive and only you can decide whether the many little quality details are worth the cost. As one owner said, "The B 40 is to be bought on the day that the full significance of 'you only have one life to live' becomes clear." **• PS**

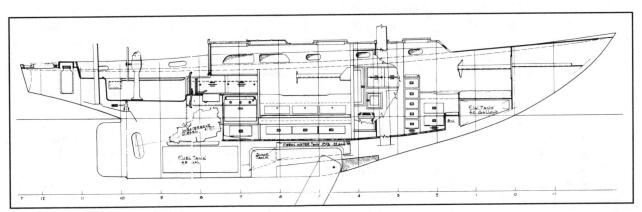

Block Island 40

Bill Tripp's fabled yawl is still being built, almost to the original plans. It has few vices.

Eric Woods, wearing shorts and sneakers, and a baseball cap with the bill backwards, looks a lot like Johnny Carson as he finishes setting the mizzen staysail and jumps back to the cockpit. He has the same impish grin, the sort of grin a 10-year-old boy has after dropping a frog down a girl's dress.

It's no accident. He's just launched hull #10 of Migrator Yachts' version of the Block Island 40 yawl, we're steaming along at better than seven knots, and he's happy. *Really* happy! And why not? After a lifetime in the boatbuilding business, and a long-time love affair with the BI 40, he's finally his own boss; his two sons Rob and Eric, who work with him, are sailing a sistership abeam of us; sales are picking up; and, hey, this is a perfect day!

History

Richard Henderson, in his book *Choice Yacht Designs*, credits the inspiration of the Block Island 40 to the Sparkman & Stephens-designed *Finnisterre*, a centerboard yawl that won the Bermuda Race three consecutive times. That boat led to the production model Nevins 40, and later to several similar boats by other designers. The Block Island 40 and Hinckley Bermuda 40, both drawn by William H. Tripp, Jr., are the best known.

Tripp's first effort along these lines was the Vitesse class, which he designed in 1957. It was constructed in the Netherlands, and imported to the U.S. for Van Breems International. Not long after that the American Boat Building Corporation of Warwick, Rhode Island, purchased the molds, changed the name, and built 22 boats before in turn selling the molds to Metalmast Marine, Inc. of Putnam, Connecticut. Metalmast, which built 14 of them, at one point commissioned Tripp to modify the underbody by

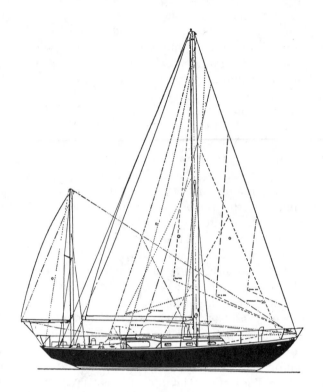

Specifications

LOA	40' 8"
LWL	29' 2"
Beam	11' 10"
Draft (board up/down)	4' 2"/8' 10"
Displacement	20,000 lbs.
Ballast	7,800 lbs.
Sail area	738 sq. ft.

separating the keel and rudder. They also gave the rig a higher-aspect ratio mainsail.

Numerous accomplished yachtsmen have owned or do own Block Island 40s, among them John Nicholas Brown and *Volta*, Niebold Smith and *Reindeer*, Benjamin DuPont and *Rhubarb*, Van Allen Clark and *Swamp Yankee*. The BI 40 dates to a time when you could own a true dual-purpose boat, equally adept at racing and cruising. Today, unfortunately, it's a rare boat that so qualifies.

In time the molds grew weary and were retired. Until that is, Eric Woods decided to leave his job at C.E. Ryder Corp. (builder of Sea Sprites and Southern Crosses). He and his wife Joan had been interested in having a BI 40 built for their own cruising pleasure. Metalmast declined to build the boat, but

The standard rig on new Block Island 40s is a yawl, though ordering a sloop rig can be done. To date, however, all the new boats have been delivered with yawl rigs.

said they'd sell him the molds so he could do it himself. Accidentally and providentially, Woods found himself in 1985 completely retooling the molds and forming his own company for the dubious purpose of building a 1957-vintage yawl. "The more I sail this boat," he told us, "the more I'm convinced this a better boat for cruising than most of the newer models on the market."

Woods' Migrator Yachts hasn't exactly taken the world by storm, but he's survived some of the toughest years in the sailing industry.

The Design

The BI 40 enjoyed a successful racing career (largely under the CCA rule), which may surprise younger readers whose experience begins with the IOR, IMS or PHRF. The long overhangs quickly immerse when heeled, adding to sailing length, which, of course, relates directly to speed. Freeboard is relatively low, and the keel is long, with a nice flat run. The rudder is attached and the propeller is located in an aperture.

The standard rig is a yawl, though a sloop is possible. Woods, however, says he's delivered only yawls, and isn't sure he'd want to build a sloop, believing as he does in the advantages of a two-stick rig. Because centerboard boats tend to have some initial tenderness in moderate to higher wind velocities, the ability to drop the mainsail and jog along nicely under jib and mizzen is very attractive. This option keeps the center of effort low.

At 11' 10", the BI 40 was quite beamy by 1950 standards, and still provides a nice wide platform by today's standards. A trademark of both the BI 40 and Hinckley B40 are the wide side decks, which enable one to walk forward without ducking or sidestepping the shrouds. This also moves the settees inboard, providing generous stowage outboard as well as minimizing distances between handholds—important features for cruising and rough weather safety.

Woods has made several changes, which aren't immediately obvious, but nevertheless important. He gave his version a more hydrodynamic centerboard (solid fiberglass weighted with lead) for improved windward performance (Woods likes to adjust it to about a 45-degree angle). Off the wind, the board is completely retracted.

Aware that interior volume of the original design was limited, and that so many boats are purchased based on livability, he also lengthened the cabin trunk fore and aft. This has allowed him to install a true U-shaped galley and sit-down chart table, features not found on earlier BI 40s or B40s.

A minor improvement was cleaning up the aperture for a smoother flow of water over the propeller. Ever mindful of performance, Woods is a strong advocate of a three-bladed feathering Max Prop for less drag and better performance backing down.

By nearly any standard, this is a handsome yacht, indeed, what many folks would call a "proper yacht." It's sure to draw praise in any harbor.

Construction

Woods has assiduously followed developments in fiberglass boatbuilding technology. While there is nothing particularly high-tech about the layup, he's doing what he's supposed to for this sort of boat: combination 1-1/2-ounce mat, 18-ounce biaxial, and 24-ounce directional fiberglass set in polyester resin with an isopththalic gelcoat. The first two laminations are vinylester, which as we have reported has proven superior in preventing blistering. Airex core, 5/8-inch thick, is standard. The deck is balsa-cored.

Hull #10 was given a Ferro Copper Clad treatment on the bottom. It's 14 mils thick, adds 126 pounds to the hull, and costs $3,500. Woods, as well as some other builders such as Tom Morris, believe that Copper Clad is very cost effective, even if it doesn't last as many years as the Ferro Corp. claims (15 years-plus). It also looks great.

The interior is all-wood and though perhaps not finished to the same degree of perfection as a Hinckley, it is very nicely done. Bulkheads are tabbed to the hull. Ceilings are ash. Joinery is teak-faced plywood or solid teak. Mahogany is used where concealed. Locker doors are louvered. The headliner is foam-backed vinyl, and is removable. Eleven opening portlights, two hatches and two Dorades provide excellent ventilation. The only fiberglass pan is in the head, where moisture and shower water make this the correct choice.

The hull/deck joint is bonded with 3M 5200 and through-bolted every six inches.

The standard auxiliary is the Yanmar 4JHE 44-hp. diesel with 2.17:1 reduction gear.

Performance

In its heyday, the BI 40 had a good racing record. In the 1960 Bermuda Race six of the first 11 places were won by BI 40s, and in 1978, the BI 40 *Alaris* won her class. Its PHRF rating varies between rig (sloop or yawl) and fleet from a low of 156 to a high of 186. The average seems to be 165. It's difficult to make comparisons, but more contemporary boats with similar ratings include the Hunter 33, Irwin 34 Citation and Island Packet 38. But what's the point? The BI 40 is not a round-the-buoys racer. She's a cruising boat displacing 20,000 pounds.

Upwind is never the forte of a centerboard design,

though the BI 40 delivers decently. In 20- to 25-knot winds with just jib and mizzen, we were able to make good speed with the apparent wind at 30 degrees. The ability to proceed safely and comfortably without the mainsail is an advantage that must be experienced to be appreciated—no excessive heel, no sudden heeling in gusts, no mainsail noise.

On our return to Marion, Massachusetts, with the wind just aft of the beam and the Buzzards Bay chop pushing us, we set the mainsail and mizzen staysail. It was a delightful romp, with speeds of eight knots. The helm was nicely balanced. It was, as the saying goes, one of those days that God will not subtract from our allotted time.

Interior

The drawing shows the essentials of the BI 40 interior. Not so obvious is the large forepeak, separated from the forward cabin by a watertight bulkhead. Access is by means of a hatch in the foredeck. Inside is plenty of room for sails and ground tackle.

Some customization is possible. For example, Woods has built boats with nav stations oriented either fore and aft or athwartship.

When the molds were retooled, Woods extended the cabin trunk a little to make room for a U-shaped galley and sit-down nav station. Note the large forepeak locker.

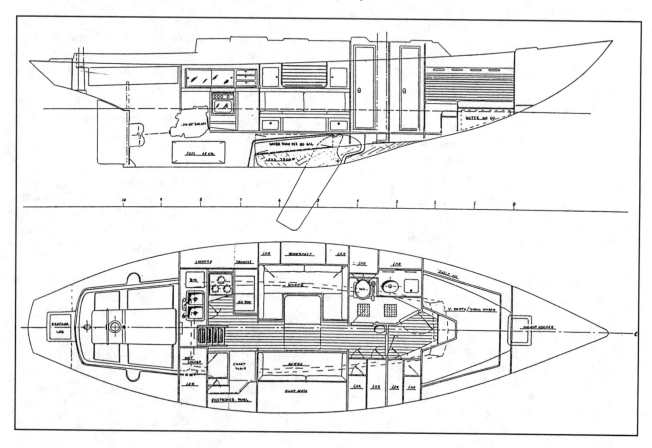

Note also the generous number of stowage areas, including the four hanging lockers opposite the head, bins behind the port-side settee, and the wet locker right where it should be—next to the companionway.

One owner opted for a quarter berth aft of the nav station, but Woods warns about the amount of stowage space lost.

Headroom is 6' 1-1/2" in the main cabin, slightly less forward. Berth lengths range from 6' 4-1/2" to 6' 7". Foam cushions are 6 inches thick.

It is no secret that many boats are purchased on the basis of the interior. Without being chauvinistic, it is often the wife, nearly oblivious to the deck and rig, who either blesses or condemns her husband's choice based on her impression of the interior. This may mean many things, such as overall spaciousness, large galley, adequate stowage. The BI 40 shows well on all counts, though not by some contemporary standards, where the settees are moved outboard to the hull, freeboard is raised as high as possible (often necessitated by bolt-on keels and shallow bilges), and extra berths are shoved in where possible, sometimes even under the cockpit. After viewing, say, a Hunter 40, in which the accommodations have been pushed into the extreme ends of the hull, the BI 40 interior may appear cramped. Such comparisons infuriate Woods, and rightly so. The BI 40 is an honest cruising boat for a couple or small family. Its long overhangs are very traditional. It has adequate tankage (120 gallons water, 45 gallons diesel) and stowage to really go somewhere, a fact that cannot be appreciated until you've gone. The low freeboard helps performance. The wide sidedecks promote safety. All of the berths in the main cabin make comfortable sea berths (you can't sleep in chairs, fashionable in some modern boats). In short, this is an excellent interior arrangement for real cruising.

Conclusion

Over the eight years that Woods has been building BI 40s, he's made numerous small refinements, such as adding a ball-bearing Lewmar traveler to the stern pulpit for trimming the mizzen more efficiently. Breast cleats amidship. A new outhaul and reefing arrangement. Gradually increasing the height of the toerail as it approaches the bow. And he'll work with customers to incorporate their ideas insofar as the basic structure and concept allows.

We can find little to fault in Woods' version of the BI 40. It won't be the right boat for everybody—none is. If you're planning on living aboard at a dock, you can get more space for your buck. If you must have 8-inch teak bulwarks, look at the Lord Nelson or Hans Christian. If you must have more speed, especially upwind, look for a divided underbody.

If it isn't apparent already, we'll admit it here: This is our kind of boat. Moderate displacement. Long keel and attached rudder. Prop in an aperture. Low freeboard. Clean decks. Easy to handle. Strong construction. Good looks. Altogether, a wholesome thoroughbred. But then, ours is a cruising mentality.

The 1992 price was $198,000, fully commissioned including sails. The BUC Research *Used Boat Price Guide* lists those BI 40s built by American Boatbuilding as selling between $31,500 and $48,500. A 1976 or 1977 Metalmast BI 40, the last years that company built the boat, sells between $63,000 and $72,000. Because not that many were built, and because most owners seem to hang onto their BI 40s until death do them part, they are seldom seen on the used market. If you really want one, you'll probably have to have Migrator Yachts build one for you. We should all be so lucky.   • **PS**

Tartan 41

This boat offers a good introduction to real-live ocean racing—but watch out for tired equipment.

For a design whose production run totaled only 86 boats over four years, the Tartan 41 has had a rather remarkable impact on the ocean racing world. The newest Tartan 41 is more than 15 years old, yet in long distance races run under the International Measurement System (IMS), the Tartan 41 still shows up regularly near the top of the heap.

In the 1989 Marion/Bermuda Race, for example, two of the top seven boats were Tartan 41s. That's typical of the boat's performance in that race since it began.

The Tartan 41 was an early International Offshore Rule (IOR) design, a boat from back when production racer/cruisers could still do well even in big-time competition. Sparkman & Stephens was still a dominant racing design firm in those days, as they had been for 40 years. The IOR was in its infancy, and unlike recent years of racing under that rule, there were as many series-produced boats as custom boats in big regattas.

1972 was the first year of production of the Tartan 41. The previous year, the company had introduced the 46, a big IOR racer/cruiser that was not particularly successful as a racing boat.

The 41 was conceived as a flat-out racing boat. Late CCA (Cruising Club of America) boats such as the Tartan 34 had been rendered fairly obsolete by the international rating rule. Charlie Britton at Tartan felt he could move a lot of his more competitively-minded customers into a larger racing boat designed to the new rule.

In 1969, just before the advent of the IOR, Palmer Johnson began importing a line of boats from a small builder in Finland by the name of Nautor Ky. One of these PJ boats, an S&S 43-footer, had the general appearance Britton was looking for: flush deck with

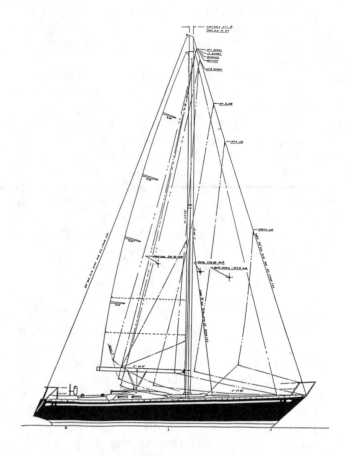

Specifications

LOA	40' 8"
LWL	32' 5"
Beam	12' 3"
Draft	6' 4"/7' 2" (std/deep keel)
Displacement	17,850 lbs.
Ballast	9,200 lbs.
Sail area	725 sq. ft.

small deckhouse, good freeboard, and moderate ends. Britton asked S&S for a similar boat, but one that fit more precisely into the new rating rule. The result was the Tartan 41.

When Palmer Johnson began importing their boats from up near the Arctic Circle, they were marketed under the PJ name, since few in this country had ever heard of Nautor Ky. They were graceful boats, well finished and well thought out in typical S&S fashion. The name "Swan" seemed to suit them well. The rest, of course, is history.

1975 was the last model year for the Tartan 41, but the hull design resurfaced from 1980 to 1984 in the form of the Tartan 42. The 42 was a cruiser, with shoal keel, a heavier interior, and a new deck which provided considerably more light and air below than was found in the flush deck Tartan 41. The 42's pinched early IOR stern looked odd in 1980, by which time the rear end of the typical racer/cruiser was about twice as wide as that of the Tartan 41/42.

The slightly reversed transom and flush deck of the 41 make for a much better looking boat than the rather ho-hum deckhouse and more traditional transom of the 42. They're very different boats, but the 42 gave the venerable old design a new lease on life, albeit in a well-disguised form.

Sailing Performance

The Tartan 41 is not as fast as a more modern 41' IOR production racer/cruiser such as the C&C 41. The two designs have similar wetted surface and sail area, but the C&C 41 is faster on every point of sail in every wind condition that you'd want to experience.

Advances in hull and appendage design aside, one big difference is displacement. The designers' specifications called for the Tartan 41 to come in at 17,850 pounds on a waterline length of 32' 5". In fact, the typical Tartan 41 displaces very close to 21,000 pounds before consumables are added. The C&C 41 is about 2,500 pounds lighter.

That doesn't mean that the Tartan 41 is slow in either absolute or relative terms. Her PHRF (Performance Handicap Racing Fleet) rating of 96 to 102 makes her some 15 seconds per mile faster than the Cal 40. Back in 1972, the Tartan 41 was one mean machine.

This is not the world's easiest to handle boat. Just a few years earlier, Sparkman & Stephens had begun separating the rudder from the back of the keel, moving the rudder all the way to the aft end of the waterline.

The increased lever arm of the aft-mounted rudder meant that rudder area could be reduced, cutting down on wetted surface. Likewise, keels were getting smaller, deeper, and more efficient.

But this was a time of experimentation, and not all of the experiments were completely successful. The original rudder and keel of the Tartan 41 were very small. On a close reach, the boat was not extremely stiff, and the rudder was sometimes hard-pressed to generate enough turning moment to bring the boat back on course in puffy conditions. Naval architect Scott Graham, who raced against Tartan 41s on the Great Lakes, remarked that they should have been equipped with turn signals: you weren't sure whether the boat was going to round up or round down in the puffs.

Several solutions to this handling quirk were developed. For several early boats, S&S designed a simple lead shoe weighing several hundred pounds, which bolted directly to the bottom of the keel. This increased draft by about 6" and righting moment by about 8%.

In 1974, S&S designed a new keel for the boat. The new keel fit directly onto the old bolt pattern on the hull, but was about 7" deeper and 700 pounds heavier than the orginal keel, raising the total ballast package to 9,900 pounds. The new keel was offered as an option in 1974 and 1975, and many of the last 20 boats were built with the deeper, heavier keel. In addition, a number of earlier boats were retrofitted by Tartan with the new keel.

It takes a trained eye to determine which keel is on any Tartan 41 you're looking at, since the differences are fairly subtle unless you have both versions standing side-by-side. You can't go by draft or hearsay alone, since almost all of these boats have changed hands several times, and the current owner may not know his or her own boat's history very well. A call to the factory should tell you which keel is on which boat.

The rig, on the other hand, was never altered. The boat has a big, bullet-proof mast, with single spreaders and single lower in-line shrouds. This is no toy rig: lower shrouds are 7/16", other shrouds and stays are 3/8" wire—the same size you'd find on a lot of 50-footers today. The Tartan 41 was meant to be raced, and raced hard.

Many boats have upgraded components of the rig. A more modern boom with internal reefing lines would be a plus. Hydraulic rig controls on vang, backstay, and baby stay have also been fitted to some boats, although they are certainly not essential. It takes a lot of force to bend this telephone pole of a mast, although the single lower shrouds make it somewhat possible.

Sailhandling equipment was state-of-the-art for 1972, but some of it is a little long in the tooth by now. The original Barient 32 primaries are big enough, but the lack of self-tailers is tough for shorthanded cruising or racing. Likewise, the Barient reel main halyard winch should be approached with caution. Safe use of a reel halyard winch on a boat this big requires concentration and a strong arm on the winch handle, particularly when reefing.

For cruising, you'd want to fit a modern headsail reefing system, big self-tailers, and an up-to-date boom—some $10,000 worth of upgrades, but definitely worth it. For your money you'd get a fast, powerful boat that could be handled by two reasonably normal people.

According to IMS calculations, the typical Tartan 41 has a 124° limit of positive stability. This is well above the 120° minimum limit that we consider reasonable for serious offshore cruising and racing.

Despite the tall sail plan and heavy rig, the boat is fairly stiff by contemporary standards, particularly with the modified keel. She is not quite as close-winded as a more modern racing boat. In 12 knots of breeze with flat water, the Tartan 41 tacks through

84°, according to the IMS velocity prediction program. In the same conditions, a C&C 41 tacks through 80°. The C&C 41's computer-predicted VMG (velocity made good to windward) in those conditions is 5.019 knots, while the Tartan 41's is 4.693. Lighter displacement does have its virtues. Interestingly enough, the two boats show about the same velocity prediction differential on all points of sail, in all wind conditions.

Engine

The original engine is probably the Tartan 41's single worst feature. It's not that the engines themselves were bad; they were just too small for a boat of this displacement. Since this was a racing boat, the purpose of the engine was to get the boat to the starting line, and home after the finish. That's about all it was good for.

When first introduced, the boat was fitted with a two-cylinder, 20 horsepower Westerbeke (Bukh) diesel. In mid-production, this was changed to a similarly-sized Farymann. By now, many of these engines have been replaced with bigger, more modern engines. At over 20,000 pounds, this boat needs close to 100 cubic inches of engine displacement for good performance under power.

Fortunately, the engine sits directly under the companionway ladder, and is not jammed under a galley counter. It may be necessary to build new beds and a new engine box to install some larger engines, but there's room to do the job. If you're looking at a boat with an original engine, factor in the cost of a replacement—including the installation—within the next few years.

Unfortunately, the aluminum fuel tank is sized for these small engines. The 26-gallon fuel capacity is marginal for cruising with a bigger, more fuel-hungry engine. It would be a fairly straightforward job to add more tankage, but it does cost money.

Construction

The Tartan 41 is a rugged boat. Fiberglass construction was not terribly sophisticated in 1972, and that's one reason the boat is about 3000 pounds heavier than designed.

Over the production run, a lot of effort went into reducing weight. All of the boats are balsa cored, but the amount of coring varies from boat to boat as changes in the hull layup were made to save weight. According to Charlie Britton, later boats have more extensive coring and a correspondingly lighter fiberglass layup.

The drive to save weight peaked in the seven or so stretched versions of the boat, known as the Tartan 44. The hulls of the 44 were about 20% lighter than those of the first 41s, and some weight was also carved out of the deck. Britton reports that the longer waterline and lighter displacement of the 44 resulted in a boat that was faster both reaching and downwind.

There were actually three hull configurations of the Tartan 41. The hull tooling was for a 43-footer with a conventional transom. An insert in the mold produced the familiar reversed transom of the 41, and an extension on the back of the hull resulted in the 44. The overwhelming majority of the boats were built as the Tartan 41.

Despite the constant weight-saving battle, this is not an underbuilt boat. Owners report no structural problems, even though many Tartan 41s have done thousands of miles of ocean racing. The boat is a racing Sherman tank, if that's not a contradiction in terms.

Cosmetically, however, many of these boats have paid a price for their hard life. Ocean racing is not kind to decks, topsides, or interiors, nor are 15 years of exposure to the elements. Some of the boats look tired.

Several boats we have examined have gone through spectacular cosmetic upgradings, including polyurethane-painted topsides, and decks painted with

Despite a flush deck, there's a remarkable amount of headroom below. Overall, the interior is well suited to the Tartan 41's calling, i.e. ocean racing. Many 41s have owner modifications to improve livability.

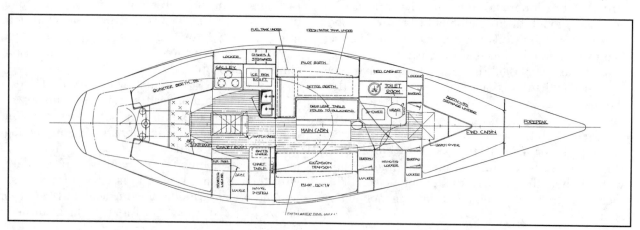

contrasting nonskid areas. The effect is pretty impressive. The boat is particularly good-looking painted dark blue, so that the apparent height of the topsides is camouflaged. A dark hull, however, shows every flaw in the topsides, and would be considerably hotter belowdecks in the tropics.

The Tartan 41 is frequently referred to as a "poor man's Swan," and for good reason. The hull and deck bear a strong family resemblance to Nautor's boats of the mid-1970s, and the Tartans are ruggedly built to similar specifications. But the vast expanses of elegant on-deck and belowdecks joinerwork for which Swans are known are totally absent on the Tartan 41. The boat is pure business.

Typical of S&S designs, structural and hardware specifications for the boat are very complete, down to the round-head screw draft marks on the hull centerline. S&S deck layouts in this period were the most functional you could find, with leads properly positioned, winches and hardware adequately sized, although winches are small by current standards.

The boats were designed and built for ocean racing. You don't have to guess whether a turning block is big enough, whether the deck is adequately reinforced for the hardware—provided it's in the original position—or whether the steering quadrant is going to stay attached to the boat. It ain't elegant or high tech, but it's sturdy.

Interior

Belowdecks, the Tartan 41 continues the fairly Plain Jane theme. There are no fancy touches, no leaded glass liquor cabinets.

On some boats, permanent forward berths were deleted, replaced by sail bins with folding pipe berths over. We'd almost rather have the boat with this configuration. You could tear out the forward cabin and install a big double berth with no compunction whatever.

Headroom in the forward cabin is about 6' 2". An aluminum-framed hatch overhead can provide ventilation in port, and there's a small built-in ventilator in the deck molding, but that's it for fresh air. A big cowl vent in a dorade box is a must addition to the foredeck, despite what it does to that big, clean working area.

The head compartment is just aft to port. It has a pressurized, cold-water shower. Needless to say, many boats have added a water heater. There's a big hanging locker opposite the head.

The main cabin is "offshore racing yacht plan A:" pilot berths both sides, straight settee berth to starboard, L-shaped settee to port. Most boats have water tanks located under the settees.

A drop-leaf table folds up against the port bulkhead: a reasonable arrangement for racing, but a poor substitute for a permanent table on a serious cruising boat. Building a real, live, sturdy main cabin table would be an excellent winter project for a new owner.

You'll find a variety of water tank installations. The original capacity of 60 gallons has in many cases been augmented, particularly in boats used for either cruising or racing in salt water. We've seen fiberglass tanks, polyethylene tanks, and bladder tanks in Tartan 41s. Since many of these are owner retrofits,

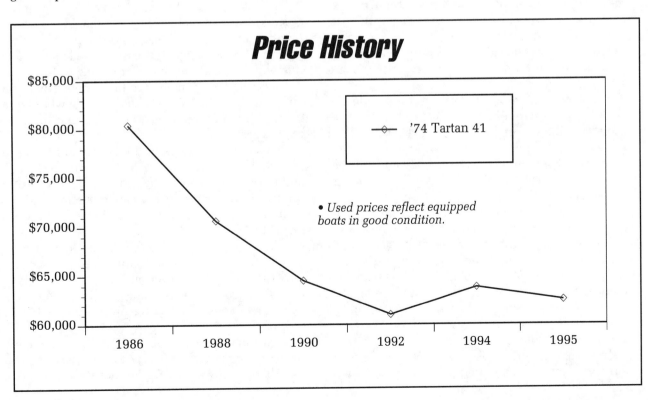

Price History

—◇— '74 Tartan 41

• *Used prices reflect equipped boats in good condition.*

examine them carefully for proper installation, including correct venting inside the hull.

The main bulkheads in most boats are teak-faced ply, with furniture risers of plywood faced with plastic laminate and trimmed in teak. In most cases, ivory-colored laminate was used, and it frequently just looks dirty and yellow after 15 years.

The appearance of the interior can be dramatically improved by varnishing the oiled teak trim with high-gloss varnish, and by installing new upholstery.

Despite the flush deck, there's a lot of headroom below. The bubble-type deckhouse extends over more than half the main cabin, giving 6' 7" of headroom, with about 6' 4" in the galley and nav station.

As with many flush-deck boats, both light and ventilation below are pretty mediocre. In fact, you'd want to augment them substantially before taking a Tartan 41 to a warm climate. If it hasn't already been done, a small opening hatch can be fitted at the forward end of the deckhouse, just aft of the mast. With careful work, big dorade boxes could also be fitted into the front of the deckhouse.

Galley and nav station are a small step up from the main cabin. Locker space in the galley is reasonable, but counter space is limited to the top of the icebox.

A gimbaled pressurized alcohol stove was standard equipment. By now, many of these antiquities have been retired, and justifiably so. Some boats we have looked at have installed CNG stoves, with the fuel bottles stored belowdecks. CNG is lighter than air, and will rise if there is a leak in the system. However, CNG should be treated with the same respect as propane, with the bottles kept above decks in a properly-vented enclosure. A lighter-than-air gas is no substitute for caution.

Opposite the galley is the nav station, with a good-sized table and reasonable mounting space for instruments.

Aft of the galley and nav station, tucked under the cockpit, is an area euphemistically labeled "aft stateroom" on the original drawings. It isn't exactly a stateroom, to put it politely. There are two quarterberths, with a narrow area of cabin sole between. On most boats, this area is used for sail storage when racing.

You could, were you so inclined, rebuild the port quarterberth to form a double, but that would mean reducing or eliminating the access from the galley to the quarterberth area, reducing air flow and nurturing a feeling of claustrophobia. You'd be better off converting the forward cabin to a double, saving the Tartan 41's "aft stateroom" for stowage, open-minded overnight guests, and use at sea when passagemaking in temperate climates.

In general, the interior of the Tartan 41 is well-suited for the boat's original purpose: racing. With

the exception of the rather coffin-like quarterberth area, there's a lot of volume and headroom in the hull—enough to make you want to start redesigning for a cruising interior.

That, of course, is what the Tartan 42 was all about. On a very similar accommodation plan, the 42 gives you light, ventilation, and a good aft cabin. You lose, however, the flush-deck good looks that are a great part of the Tartan 41's appeal.

Conclusions

For a design that is almost 20 years old, the Tartan 41 still looks strikingly modern and functional, despite her marked tumblehome and pinched stern. The growth of IMS racing has given the boat a new lease on her racing life. With new sails, a smooth bottom, and some upgrading of deck equipment, the Tartan 41 will still be competitive in any IMS event longer than a standard Olympic course.

The boat's moderately heavy displacement and deep sections result in an extremely seakindly motion—a real plus for either racing or cruising.

We would look for a boat with the optional deep keel, particularly if we were interested in racing. The original rig is fine for either racing or cruising, although it's time to consider replacing the standing rigging—including turnbuckles—if it's original. Since the rigging is so big, replacing it is a fairly expensive job: 3/8" wire isn't cheap, and neither are big rigging terminals and turnbuckles.

This is a minimum-cost, entry-level, ocean-going racer. The new-boat price in 1975 was about $65,000.

Watch out, however, for old engines and old sails. A Tartan 41 is likely to come with a huge inventory of sails, many of which are most suitable to use as painting drop cloths. Racing sails more than three years old are probably pretty tired. Tired racing sails do not necessarily make good cruising sails.

Since the foretriangle is so big, a new genoa is a fairly costly item. A fully-battened main would be a good addition for cruising, as would a new headsail reefing system.

Boats that have been used for years of racing are likely to have old luff groove devices on the headstay, and these do get bent, dinged and generally beaten up by the spinnaker pole whacking them—and the afterguy will occasionally get loose, even on the best-sailed boat.

Likewise, an original Bukh or Farymann diesel may also be tired. An old folding prop—most 41s have them—may need to be bushed to get rid of blade slop. Better yet, if you're going cruising, budget in a new three-bladed feathering prop along with the new engine.

At any one time, a number of Tartan 41s are likely to be on the market, so it pays to shop around. You buy this boat by its condition, not its age. It's one thing to get the boat at a bargain price, but if a paint job, a new engine, and new sails are on the list, you're going to spend a good chunk of change before you've got what you want.

If you want a bargain-basement, rugged ocean racer, the engine and cosmetics may be unimportant, but you're likely to want new sails, and you'll almost certainly want to refair the bottom—years of bottom paint make a poor racing finish.

If you want a sturdy, fast long-distance cruiser, tote up the dollars to see what it will cost to bring the creature comfort factor to an acceptable level.

Since there was variation in construction techniques, and since you may find a variety of factory and non-factory keel or rudder molds—at least one boat was built as a centerboarder, and another was converted to a deep, free-standing spade rudder rather than the original small, skeg-mounted rudder—the provenance of the individual boat is important. Many of the boats have changed hands and names several time, so it may take some sleuthing.

Over the years, Tartan has produced a number of boats that deserve reputations as classics: the 27, 30, 34, and 37 come to mind. But the 41 has introduced scads of sailors to real live ocean racing, and will probably continue to do so for another generation, long after many of today's hot boats have disappeared into the ranks of the also-rans.   • **PS**

Shannon 39

One man's vision of the perfect ocean cruiser, this new design incorporates dozens of hidden lessons learned from a lifetime of boatbuilding.

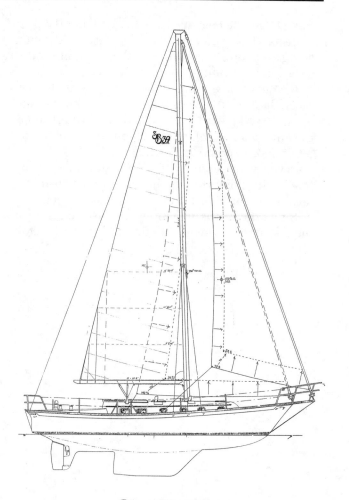

Specifications

LOA	41' 7"
LWL	38' 7"
Beam	12' 0"
Draft	5' 6"
Displacement	18,700 lbs.
Ballast	6,900 lbs.
Sail area	749 sq. ft.

You're buying a boat. Dozens of decisions to make. A careful checklist against which to measure new boats...and an even more bewildering variety of used boats. You're looking for a match-up with your preferences, prejudices and pocketbook...and for the waters you'll sail. So many boats from which to choose, almost all of them involving compromises.

And then...there's a Shannon. Absolutely no compromises—if your pocketbook is not involved.

Read the chapter about Shannons in Ferenc Maté's book, *The World's Best Sailboats.*

Writing about Hinckleys, Swans, Little Harbors, Aldens, "Rassys", Morris yachts, "Nicks" and Cherubinis, the respected Canadian author says of the Shannons, "...monstrously strong hulls...." "...lockwashers everywhere...," "...most sophisticated gelcoats, resins and fibers in the industry...," "...massive hull-deck flange...," "...completely thought out and superbuilt...," "...everything double-caulked...," "...amazing attention to detail."

The Company

The Shannon Boat Company of Bristol, Rhode Island, was started in 1975, by Walter Schulz, a designer/builder, and David Walters, a super salesman. They had some financial backing from the late F. William Stechmann, III.

They shared a single focal point: Build the world's best ocean-cruising sailboat—at any cost.

They named it for the river in Ireland, Schulz's ancestral home.

Their Shannon 38, a jewel that reflected Schulz's admiration for the Allied Princess and the Block Island 40, was an instant success. Then followed the Shannon 28, which, pound-for-pound or by the foot, was perhaps the most expensive semi-production sailboat ever built. Other models followed.

Walters was a dedicated racer who wanted to build boats to compete with European boats like the light, fast Swan 46. Schulz, properly leery about competing with Europe's government-subsidized marine industry, wanted to stick to cruising boats. Walters, who later built Cambrias, sold out to Schulz in 1982.

Schulz continued by himself.

Shannon got a big boost when in September of 1981, a widely-known yachting writer named

The Shannon 39 with a moderate displacement/length ratio and generous sail plan, is a spirited performer on a reach.

Moulton H. "Monk" Farnham, at age 72, made a five-week, single-handed crossing of the Atlantic in *Seven Bells*, his Shannon 28, and wrote extensively about it. It helped to position Shannon sailboats squarely in the premium ocean cruiser class.

Awash in success, Schulz admits he made a crippling mistake in 1986 by bringing out a 32' power boat he was not equipped to produce when the orders poured in.

Blithely riding the yellow brick road of success, Shannon got caught in the horrendous downdraft that withered the marine industry...and in 1988 was forced into Chapter 11. It was a humbling experience for the so-proud Schulz.

Everyone thought it was the end of a boatbuilder who, in every last detail, zealously insisted on simply the best. There followed an incredible three years of entanglement with banks, an interim owner and shifting locations. It takes Schulz. a onetime New York street kid, an hour to trace out the financial maze.

"Maybe I should write a book about how to survive in the business worldd," he said, but immediately recanted: "No, no. I'm a boatbuilder."

Shannon's plight attracted the business acumen of a host of wealthy Shannon owners. They taught Schulz to track man-hours, improve purchasing, keep records and bird-dog the budget. One result: The company has what it claims is the most sophisticated computer systems of any boatbuilder.

Through it all, Schulz continued to build boats and keep intact the company's extraordinary band of dedicated craftsmen. Outstanding among those 20-odd "core" employees are Dave "Bucky" Frazier, a gelcoat expert; Tom Quinlan, a finish carpenter; and Mike Drywa, an electrical magician with a Welch name.

By 1991, soundly reorganized with five Shannon owners as partners, Shannon emerged, in the words of Schulz, "...with the dream still very much alive...and no debt."

Is a Shannon a dream boat? Shannon owners think so.

Used Shannons command premium prices. When asked about used Shannon prices, Bill Ramos, Schulz's longtime right-hand man, said a 1977 Shannon 38 ketch sold in the summer of 1994 for $91,500, exactly what it cost new.

As of late 1994, there were 99 Shannon 38s, 60 Shannon 28s, 36 Shannon 43s. 22 Shannon 51s, 17 Shannon 37s and the new Shannon 39, the subject of this review. Along the way, there have been cutters and ketch rigs (about half of the buyers choose ketches), full keel and centerboard versions, a few pilothouse models and, most importantly, a relentless pursuit of boatbuilding technology.

Construction

The Shannon 39's hull, which takes seven days to lay up, is a highly engineered unit built in a six-piece, bolted-together mold that permits a massive hull flange and facilitates different transom and keel configurations. Starting on the first day with an NPG isopthalic gelcoat and 1.5-ounce mat set in vinylester resin, the second day gets another 1.5-ounce mat and a 2.6-mm layer of Coremat (thick compacted fibers) and a layer of biaxial S glass.

Subsequent days get three more layers of S glass and half-inch Airex. (Schulz is considering using in place of the Airex a next-generation PVC foam called Corecell, which has even better heat resistance and stiffness.) More S glass is applied, along with blankets of S glass and roving-mat in stress areas. The flange is reinforced with Fabmat. The centerline and stern corners are heavily reinforced with Kevlar hybrids.

The hull cures in the mold for a week (far beyond the 72 hours generally recommended], after which the mold is dismantled to release the hull.

At the sheer, the lay-up is about 3/4" thick; at the bottom it's nearly 2". It's very stiff construction, but not good enough for Schulz.

Longitudinal stringers with biaxial laminates are added. Bulkheads are stitched (with drilled holes through which short fiberglass cords are laced for imbedding in the hull-bulkhead joint) and glassed in place against Klegecell foam ribs. The stringers and ribs leave space between the hull and the interior for sound insulation and air circulation.

The hull-deck joint is caulked and bolted on 5" centers with locking aircraft nuts, alternately through the deck, teak toe rail and genoa tracks.

What results is a rigid monocoque, cored hull (20 percent lighter and 36 percent stronger than solid fiberglass) framed by four powerful longitudinal lines, two at the rails, the others along the reinforced bottom.

The 6.900-pound lead ballast, encapsulated and sealed in fiberglass laminates, goes inside the boat, where Schulz firmly believes it belongs (he cites a 20-year life expectancy of keel bolts and a host of associated problems). The engine bed is a pair of 4" x 16" laminated oak timbers both sealed and bonded to the hull. Schulz says the wood engine beams absorb engine vibration and noise much better than a fiberglass structure. The engine compartment, well-insulated with lead-lined foam from Soundown to minimize noise, provides excellent access.

Hung on a stainless post on a detached skeg (with a stainless steel shoe), which protects the propeller (on an Aquamet 22 shaft in a stainless tube with removable Cutlass bearing), the rudder is solid fiberglass over a huge reinforcing steel plate. According to Schulz, no Shannon ever has lost a rudder.

Schulz, in his design approach, never has worried about weight. "Build the boat exactly right, plan to put aboard what you need to work the boat and be comfortable and then calculate the needed sail area," he said.

Interior

Shannon owners don't buy Shannons to take a crowd sailing. They like comfort and storage space. Although most interiors have at least a bit of customizing (all Shannons are semi-custom), the standard layout of the new Shannon 39 has two single and two double berths, with one of the latter in the form of a pull-out settee in the saloon.

A big head compartment, with a good shower stall, is to starboard, nicely placed at the foot of the companion ladder. lust forward of the head is the nav station, with a swivel chair that does not protrude into the walkway.

The large, angled portside galley, aft of the settee with a drop-leaf table, has exceptional counter space for food preparation, a top and front-opening refrigerator and a lot of locker space for food and cooking implements.

The interior is hand-fitted with solid mahogany framing...not the customary 3/4" stock, but with 2 x 3s both screwed and epoxied in place.

Drawers and cedar-lined lockers are built of Baltic Plywood, again a very expensive way to go.

The layout of the Shannon 39 is fairly conventional, though the head is located aft where there is less motion and it's more convenient to the companionway.

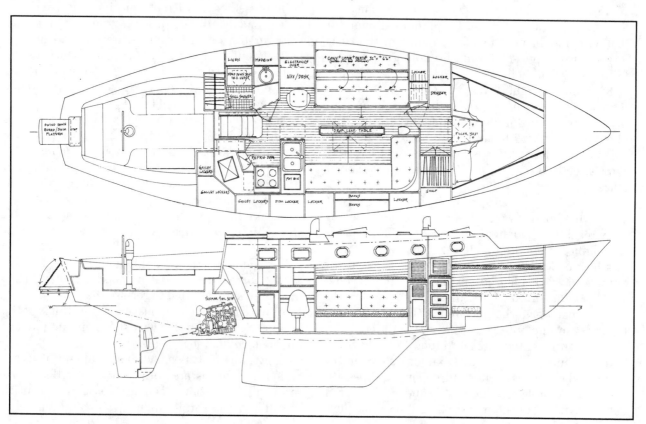

Shannon's Kinship With a 1967 Ford Truck

Walter Schulz doesn't like teak decks. "Too heavy, too hot, too many holes and too hard to maintain."

Shannons built before 1975 had a variety of non-skid deck treatments. Schulz struggled with various commercial mold patterns and a British product called Treadmaster.

None of them pleased him. No fault of the products. It's just that Walter Schulz is not easy to please.

One day, while loading a 1967 Ford stake truck, he noticed that the steel-plate truck bed had a very pleasing pattern. He closely examined it and decided that although the diamond design was very nice, the top surfaces of the diamonds were too smooth.

He returned to his office, to smoke a pipe, think and doodle. Finally, with his mind made up, he cleaned up the truck bed and marked off a 4 x 8 foot section. Over the next two weeks, working 12 hours a day with a hand-held, sharp-point die grinder, he stippled every one of the several thousand diamonds.

"What the hell is Walt doing now?" everybody asked.

Finally satisfied, he took off a fiberglass mold, backed by a 4 x 8 sheet of plywood.

He got his reward when he and Shannon employees tested it and found that it made the best

Unsatisfied with conventional non-skids, Schulz made a mold from the steel bed of a 1967 Ford truck.

non-skid deck short of teak. In addition, the easy-to-clean pattern, although unique, can be repaired if it gets dinged or gouged.

Every Shannon built since then has distinctive 8-foot, non-skid sections, necessarily separated by smooth waterways, taken from that original mold personally hand-tooled by an extremely dedicated man known for his near-maniacal attention to detail.

(Unknown even to some Shannon owners, there is aboard every Shannon a drawer, not always the same one, that if withdrawn and turned over, displays under a coat of varnish the names of every Shannon employee who worked on the boat.)

As with any Shannon, the choice of interior finish wood is up to the buyer. Early Shannons were all wood inside, but Shannon recently has been using white Formica with teak trim to brighten up the interiors. (The second Shannon 39 has a cherry wood interior.)

The solid teak plank sole, splined with holly, is 5/8" thick.

Well-ventilated, the deck has three overhead hatches, 10 opening portlights and four 4" Dorades, all with screens.

All the reinforcing and heavy interior framing lead Maté to comment that a Shannon "meets the specifications of an icebreaker."

On Deck

The Shannon 39 is an easy boat to work.

"We take our gang sailing—day sails, deliveries and off to the boat shows," Schulz said. "They come to appreciate what works and what's comfortable."

Shannon also maintains very close contact with its owners, who are quick to suggest improvements. (Of about 300 Shannon sailboats sold, the company has "lost" only 20 boats; the Spring 1994 Shannon Owners' Newsletter offered a prize for information on wayward owners.)

For instance, because most Shannon owners indicate that they sail shorthanded, and trimming the headsails and main can be a problem, on the new 39-footer, the mainsheet winch is on a raised pad to starboard on the stern deck. The helmsman need only turn slightly to trim the main. (If the owner is left-handed, Shannon will put the winch to port.)

On this particular boat, the main and secondary winches are located far aft on the port and starboard coamings, placed there for easy access to the helmsman (but a bit clumsy for the crew).

Sail controls, even the main traveler, all are managed from the cockpit.

The crew remains in the cockpit, other than to ready the main for hoisting and to gather and furl it when finished. Even the single-line main reefing can be accomplished from the cockpit.

A well for a hard-canister life raft is under the teak grate in the cockpit.

Because most Shannon buyers opt for a dodger, which on most boats makes going below a bend-over trick, the new Shannon's bridgedeck has a new, cut-out step that makes it easy. A well-designed boarding ladder and platform. set into the stern, is an expensive option.

A recessed engine panel to the left of the helmsman is easy to monitor.

Performance

The new Shannon's double headsail cutter rig, with both headsails on Harken furling gear, is not for the beginning sailor (the typical Shannon buyer has owned an average of three previous boats). It takes some sailing "savvy" to get the most out of a cutter or ketch.

Carrying 749 square feet of sail on a displacement of 18,700 pounds (6,900 of it in ballast) and a 32' 10" waterline, the new 39-footer cutter has a 17.02 sail area/displacement ratio and a displacement/length ratio of 243. Those are very sound, moderate numbers, with the D/L indicating that Shannon has done a fine job of building a very strong, rigid boat of modest weight.

Practical Sailor took her out on a moderately stiff day. The wind varied from 12 to nearly 30 knots. Under power, with a three-bladed prop (an owner option), the new Shannon backed down in a straight line and smartly gathered forward way. She did require a bit of helm effort to resist turning due to prop wash.

Under sail, with one reef in the main and the 120-percent genoa (the headsail on the inner forestay), she turned up a nice 6.5 knots to windward. However, in the really stiff gusts , she was overpowered, rail down, and showed a marked tendency to be hard-mouthed, meaning that it required vigor at the helm to keep her from rounding up. When the big genoa was furled and the high-cut Yankee on the forward headstay was deployed, the boat settled in comfortably, with no diminution of speed.

Cracking off, the Shannon 39 comes into her own. She's easily managed under any combination of sail (we even tried a dead run with the reefed main and the genoa and Yankee run out wing-and-wing). All three sails pulled like Clydesdales.

(Shannon, for each of its models, furnishes a chart showing combinations of Yankee, genoa, main, and staysail, and mizzen—in the case of ketches—for wind speeds of five to 40 knots, including when to reef the headsails and the main.)

As with any double headsail cutter or ketch, the Shannon 39, compared with a sloop, pays a small penalty going to windward, especially if racing in very light air. However, she is, like most Shannons, a "reaching machine." Given her conditions and course, she'll show her heels.

(A Shannon 38 won three consecutive Daytona-Bermuda races; a Shannon 37 was first in class and second overall in the 1991 Marion-Bermuda race; and a Shannon 43 last year made an Atlantic crossing—Padanaram, Massachusetts, to Kinsale, Ireland—in 17 days and 22 hours.)

Conclusion

A Shannon is, perhaps more than any production or semi-custom fiberglass boat ever built, a singularly-exact expression of one man's view (backed by the opinions of 300 experienced sailors) of what a fine-handling, seagoing sailboat should be.

The new Shannon 39 is not a round-the-buoys racer. The numbers suggest that, in light air, a J/40 will move out on her. On a passage, you might start out with a Valiant 40, and at the end of the day, find her astern but still in sight.

For quality, she has few structural peers. For finish work, a Swan, Morris or Hinckley might be a shade better. As with other semi-custom, high-quality boats built up with excellent materials and huge blocks of fine craftsmanship, the new Shannon carries a hefty price tag—$273,000 for the basic sail-away boat in 1994 (which Schulz describes as "a sextant and off to Bermuda"). Because a Shannon is handmade, interior modifications, such as lengthening a berth or adding a locker or the choice of finish wood, are no-charge options, as is the choice of engine, prop and basic equipment like blocks and winches.

Electronic instrumentation, a Delta-wing or Scheel keel, air-conditioning, a cabin heating system, a desalinator and other such equipment can take the price up around $300,000.

As Maté observed, a Shannon is a "long-distance cruiser that can sail the seven seas ably and with good speed, built without compromise...to serve her crew well regardless of the weather."

The new 39-footer will do nothing but accentuate that viewpoint.   **• PS**

Whitby 42

Solidly built and easy to maintain, the Whitby 42 is good both at dockside and going places.

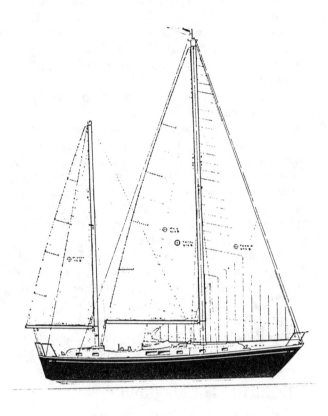

The Whitby 42 was one of the small success stories of the boatbuilding industry. Designed by Ted Brewer in 1971, the Whitby 42 went into production in 1972. A few hundred boats were built.

While most boats were built by Whitby in Canada, hulls numbered between 200 and 300 were built under license by Fort Myers Yacht and Shipbuilding in Florida.

When the Whitby 42 was introduced in 1972, cost of the boat, including such features as diesel auxiliary generator, hot and cold pressure water, and refrigeration, was $42,000, including US duty. In the same year the Morgan Out Island 41 had a base price of $33,000, and the Coronado 41 was $30,000.

In 1983, the Coronado 41 was a memory, an Out Island 41 cost about $130,000, and the Whitby 42 would have cost you just shy of $103,000 with the US duty paid. Today, an early-'80s Whitby 42 commands about $3,000 *more* than an Out Island 41 of the same vintage. In other words, the Whitby 42 has good staying power, and, if anything, has improved on its value position in the market.

When we first saw the Whitby 42 in 1973, it seemed an ungainly whale of a boat, with high topsides, white decks, white everything. Over the years, through the subtle use of color—dark sheer strake, two-tone decks—the appearance of the boat was quietly altered. While the Whitby 42 will never have the sleek grace of an ocean racer, she has a sturdy grace of her own, the product of endless refinement and subtle improvement over the many years of her production history.

The Whitby 42 is a fully-powered auxiliary, rather than a motorsailer. Although she won't go to windward like a light fin-keeler, the boat is fully capable of performing well as a sailing vessel.

Specifications

LOA	42' 0"
LWL	32' 8"
Beam	13' 0"
Draft	5' 0"
Displacement	23,500 lbs.
Ballast	8,500 lbs.
Sail area	875 sq. ft.

Many owners have put tens of thousands of sea miles on their boats. A fair number of owners are retired couples who purchased the boat as a cruising home. Since the boat has the elbow room, accommodations, storage, and comforts that you would associate with a retirement home, it has proved a remarkable success in that capacity.

The Whitby 42 does not particularly look like an oceangoing boat, with her center cockpit, high topsides, wide beam, and shoal draft. Nevertheless, an astounding percentage of the boats are used for serious passagemaking.

Construction

Construction of the Whitby 42 is sturdy, but without the dramatic overkill frequently seen in cruising boats. The hull is balsa-cored from just below the sheer to just below the waterline.

Hull and deck are joined with an internal flange, which is glassed together and mechanically joined with stainless steel rivets. In the way of the genoa track and some deck fittings, hull and deck are also bolted together. The builder would use bolts throughout to join hull and deck, for a slight additional charge.

On newer boats, all through-hull fittings are equipped with through-bolted bronze seacocks. Older boats may have gate valves on underwater fittings.

Deck and deckhouse are also balsa-cored. Solid glass is used in the way of deck hardware. In some older boats, owners report that the area under the mizzenmast was not solid glass, resulting in compression of the deck in the vicinity of the mast. Owners of older boats also report that the under deck support for the mizzen was marginal. Later models appear to have these problems solved.

For those used to looking at the massive construction of some cruising boats, notably those built in the Far East, some of the construction details of the Whitby 42 may look a little light. The success of these boats as cruisers indicates that proper proportioning in design and construction are more important than massive scantlings.

Handling Under Power

With a fuel capacity of 210 gallons, the Whitby 42 has a range under power of about 1,500 miles. The Lehman Ford 4-254 diesel produces about 67 hp, enough to drive the moderate displacement hull in almost any conditions.

Fuel tanks are located amidships. This means that the trim and balance of the boat will not change significantly as fuel is consumed.

Although a three-bladed prop in aperture is standard, light air performance would be significantly improved by replacing the prop with a feathering prop such as the Maxprop or the Luke feathering prop. Using this prop there would be little or no sacrifice in performance under power, but there could easily be an increase in speed of a half knot or more under sail in winds under 10 knots. If you're off cruising in the South Pacific, just carry along the standard prop as a spare.

Amazingly, none of the Whitby 42 owners we talked to had added a feathering prop. It would be one of our first major changes if we owned the boat.

Because of her windage and fairly long keel, the boat does not exactly handle like a sports car under power. One owner says that his boat "turns like the Queen Mary," so give yourself plenty of room and take your time when docking.

Like most center cockpit boats, the Whitby 42's engine is located under the cockpit. The result is a

huge engine room with stooping headroom. The entire cockpit sole is the engine room hatch cover, and it can be unbolted in an hour or so to allow removal of the engine without tearing the interior of the boat apart. For a cruising boat that puts a lot of hours on the engine. this is a real plus.

The engine room has enough space for a small auxiliary generator. A generator was standard when the boat was first built, but later became an option. If you intend to do extensive cruising in the boat, a generator of about 3.5 kw would be worth installing. Unfortunately. the weight of the generator, which is mounted on the port side, may give the boat a slight port list.

Access to the stuffing box is good, through hatches in the cabin sole in the aft cabin. General access to the engine is excellent.

Handling Under Sail

Owners characterize the Whitby 42 as slightly faster than other boats of the same size and type. When equipped with a mizzen staysail and a spinnaker—a very reasonable combination for offwind sailing offshore in this boat—the boat is quite fast. One West Coast owner has raced his boat with remarkable success, but that is certainly not the boat's forte.

In the past, there have been problems with the mizzenmast. Since the main boom ends fairly close to the mizzen, the mizzen forestays do not have a very good angle for forward support. Until relatively recently, it was also absolutely necessary to use the mizzen running backstays when carrying a mizzen staysail. Earlier boats also reported problems with the under deck support system for the mizzen.

All of the mizzen problems are exacerbated if the boat is equipped with a radar antenna mounted on the mizzen mast—the natural location for it on a ketch.

Fortunately, most of these problems have been resolved on later boats. The mizzen spreaders are swept back enough to provide good after support without the use of running backstays, although we would probably still rig them in heavy weather or sloppy seas. Forward support of the mizzen was improved by the addition of a triatic stay between the main and mizzen mastheads.

The use of a triatic probably constitutes a second-best solution, as loss of one mast could well result in the loss of the other, since the masts are tied together. However, there is no simple way to improve the staying of the mizzen.

On later models, the mainsail is equipped with slab reefing, a great improvement over the roller reefing found on older models of the Whitby 42. A separate track on the mainmast for a storm trysail is something we'd go for if the boat is to be used offshore.

Another highly desirable rig option was the doublehead rig, which came in a package with a platform bowsprit and a removable inner forestay. Owners report that the extra sail area forward improves the balance of the boat as well as giving her some extra power.

Despite the great beam of the boat, her midships hull section is almost round. This means that the boat picks up very little form stability as it heels. Coupled with a ballast/displacement ratio of about 35%, this yields a boat that is not particularly stiff under sail, according to owners.

Although the boat comes with hydraulic steering, it is also possible to use an Edson pull-pull system. Since this is a less powerful steering system than the hydraulic steerer, you should go with the maximum size steering wheel that will fit in the cockpit—about a 40" diameter wheel. In addition to providing the extra leverage for the pull-pull system, a larger wheel lets you sit further outboard, an absolute necessity on a center cockpit boat when using a large genoa.

We prefer the pull-pull steerer because it gives the helmsman feedback about the balance of the boat. In the long run, the steering feedback will make you a better sailor. When the boat steers hard, it is out of balance, and is not being sailed to maximum efficiency.

With a high aspect rig and a generous sailplan for her moderate displacement, there is no excuse for the Whitby 42 to be a dog under sail. If you have the boat heavily loaded, you'll just have to add more sail to maintain performance. Fairing in the through hull fittings and adding a feathering prop will also help performance, particularly in light air.

Finally, by all means spring for the bowsprit and the extra sail area it gives you. According to one owner, designer Ted Brewer said the addition of the bowsprit is the single greatest improvement in the boat over the years.

Deck Layout

The deck layout of the Whitby 42 is about as simple as the deck on a boat can be. There are sturdy Skene chocks and large cleats forward, and chocks plus big cleats aft. With the platform bowsprit, anchors can be made self-stowing.

The foredeck has plenty of space for an anchor windlass, an absolute must if the boat is used for extended cruising. The forepeak locker could be used to hold anchor chain, but we'd be reluctant to add another 500 lbs of ground tackle in the front of the boat, since there's already a large water tank under the forward berths.

Despite a wide cabin trunk, access forward along the deck is good. To go from the cockpit aft, however, it is necessary to go over the top of the aft cabin, as the mizzen standing rigging takes up much of the side decks aft. Stanchions, bow, and stern rails are tall and sturdy.

There are two lockers on the afterdeck, one useful for lines and fenders, the other containing the propane bottles. Although the lids of both lockers are equipped with gaskets, surprisingly flimsy turnbutton latches are used to secure the lids. For offshore passagemaking, we'd replace these with sturdier latches.

There is also a large locker on the port side of the cockpit. This locker, too, lacks a good set of hatch

One of the more livable interiors is to be found in the Whitby 42. Engine access from the passage to the owner's cabin is excellent. The two chairs shown here are often replaced by a settee.

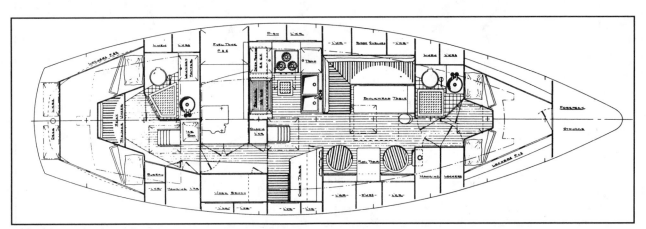

dogs, and since it opens into the engine room, we'd give high priority to making it secure, despite its location well above the water.

The cockpit is huge. However, it is not particularly vulnerable, since it is fairly high. We've seen few cockpits which would be better in port. There's even a big icebox next to the helmsman, making it unnecessary to truck down below for a cold one.

A sturdy molded breakwater protects the front of the cockpit. We'd add a dodger for offshore use. The original drawings of the boat also show a permanent windshield, which would be a good feature on a boat used primarily in northern latitudes.

One Whitby 42 we've seen has a permanent shelter over the front end of the cockpit, which both improved the looks of the boat—the shelter was designed by someone with a good eye—and gave remarkable protection to the front of the cockpit, allowing the companionway hatch to be left open in all but the worst weather offshore.

For offshore use, the louvered companionway drop boards should be replaced with solid boards, since a remarkable amount of water can get below in heavy weather. This is particularly important in the companionway to the aft cabin, which faces forward.

The companionway to the aft cabin makes it impossible to fit a mainsheet traveler. Therefore, a good boom vang is a must.

Belowdecks

Down below, the Whitby 42 really shines. The boat has one of the more livable interiors we've seen.

The owner's cabin aft has two large berths. If they are to be used as sea berths, they must be fitted with lee cloths. Since the berths are not parallel to the centerline of the boat, they do not make particularly good sea berths. The person sleeping in the leeward berth will find his head lower than his feet, while the occupant of the weather berth will be in the opposite situation.

Although there are a fair number of storage bins and a good hanging locker, the aft cabin has few drawers. Although drawers are not a particularly efficient way to use space, they are extremely convenient, particularly for those who have lived their lives in houses.

The aft head is huge. A few handrails would make it more comfortable offshore.

A passageway with stooping headroom joins the aft cabin to the rest of the boat. Getting full headroom in this passage would unnecessarily complicate the cockpit layout.

A workbench which can be converted to a berth is on the starboard side of the passage. The space below the bench is filled by a fuel tank, some storage space, and a big chart storage locker.

Outboard of the workbench is the electrical panel. Despite the stooping headroom, this is just about the ideal location for the electrical panel, since it is completely protected from spray.

On the port side of the passage, just aft of the companionway, there is a large locker for foul weather gear. Little touches like the chart storage area and the wet gear locker make the difference between a floating condominium which is miserable at sea and a true cruising boat.

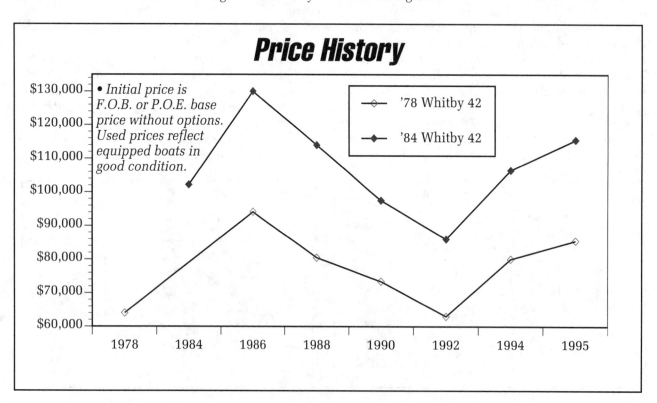

Price History

• *Initial price is F.O.B. or P.O.E. base price without options. Used prices reflect equipped boats in good condition.*

Legend: '78 Whitby 42 / '84 Whitby 42

The main cabin is roomy, light, and well-ventilated, The galley to port has a large refrigerator and deep freeze—Grunert holding-plate refrigeration, driven by an engine-mounted compressor—a three burner propane stove, and, on newer boats, deep double sinks.

The only weak point in the galley is the mounting of the stove. On starboard tack, it fetches up against the back of the stove well when the boat heels much over 15 degrees. On port tack, the stove blocks access to the drawers under the sink counter.

There is a ventilation hatch over the galley, a real boon for the cook in hot weather. Except for the stove limitation, the galley gets an A+.

To starboard is the navigation table, with adequate room for the mounting of instruments and a good chart table. The chart table slopes toward the navigator, making it easier to work on from a seated position, but it is equipped with a folding support which allows the table to be leveled for use in port, making a handy desk.

Originally, there was no settee on the starboard side of the boat. Rather, the boat had two swivel chairs, a familiar touch to those used to life ashore. However, if the boat is to be used offshore, it should be ordered with the optional starboard settee, since the main cabin settees are the only good sea berths on the boat.

There is plenty of storage space outboard of the settees on both sides, including a rather excellent liquor locker with a folding cocktail table.

The main cabin table folds up against the port forward bulkhead. On a boat of this size, a fixed cabin table makes more sense. If we owned a Whitby 42, we'd build a narrow dropleaf table with deep fiddles, incorporating a pipe to the cabin overhead for a handhold when sailing offshore.

While this would intrude into the main cabin space, it would reduce the chance of a bad fall in rough conditions, would free up the bulkhead for other uses, and would create a storage space on the cabin sole where bulky objects like spare sails could be stowed offshore.

The forward cabin and head are almost as roomy as the aft cabin. In port, the occupants of the forward cabin are not second class citizens. Except for light

air sailing downwind, the forward cabin will probably not be used for sleeping offshore.

All in all, the interior of the Whitby 42 is an excellent compromise between the needs of the long term live-aboard and the long distance cruiser.

Conclusions

In these days of astronomical prices, the Whitby 42 represents a good value for living aboard or cruising. While finish detail is not particularly fancy, the boat is solidly built, and should be easy to maintain.

The boat came with a rather remarkable list of standard equipment, with such items as hot and cold water, refrigeration, huge tankage, two showers, dual voltage electrical systems, and ground tackle.

The options were practical and born of experience. Many of them are highly desirable, such as the double headsail rig option with bowsprit, contrasting deck, dark sheer indent, autopilot, and windlass.

Fully equipped for cruising — and we mean fully equipped—a new boat in the early '80s cost about $120,000. That boat used in 1992 could bring about $75,000 or thereabouts, depending on condition.

You can expect reasonable sailing performance from the Whitby 42. Obviously, her best point of sail will be reaching in moderate to heavy air.

Most owners are very enthusiastic about their boats. For most of them, this is not a first boat. Although most consider the boat a good boat dockside, they also consider it a boat in which to go places. We agree.   **• PS**

Slocum 43

A semi-custom yacht that excells in comfort and livability. Be sure to check out the options, though.

There is no doubt about the Slocum 43's mission in life. This boat is made for blue water cruising. Named for Joshua Slocum, the most famous blue water sailor of all, she has been designed, built and equipped by and for people who spend a considerable amount of time living aboard and sailing offshore. Long and lean she is not. The effort here has gone into making functional and comfortable spaces in a sturdy passagemaker.

The Slocum 43 is a semi-custom double-ender designed by Stan Huntingford of Vancouver, BC, who designed traditional displacement cruising boats for three decades before retiring in 1987. The Slocum 43 is descended from the Passport 42—or perhaps we should say "ascended," because the Slocum is a bit larger than the Passport: 9" longer, 1" wider, and 3,000 pounds heavier. A comparison of the two boats would soon be reduced to a search for the places where they differ. Most of the differences will be in the details of the deck and interior, as both boats are custom designs to one degree or another.

Slocum Yachts also builds a 37' cutter, similar in character to the 43, but even more traditional. She displaces only 1,000 pounds less than the 43, and carries a full keel and attached rudder, in contrast to the 43's long fin keel and skeg rudder. The 37 is also a development by Huntingford of one of his earlier designs, the Rafiki 37.

The Slocum 43 was originally built by Cruising Yachts International, of Houston and Taiwan. Jan Stadman, President of CYI, split Slocum Yachts away from CYI in order to pursue another boatbuilding project. Slocum Yachts was purchased in 1988 by Walter Brown, who is continuing to operate the business out of New York much as Stadman did.

The Slocums are built at Hai-O Yacht Building

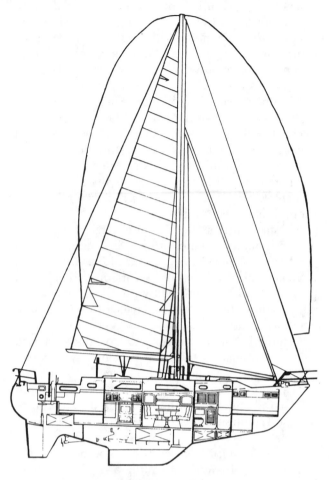

Specifications

LOA	42' 6"
LWL	35' 10"
Beam	12' 11"
Draft	5' 6"/6' 4" (shoal/std)
Displacement	28,104 lbs.
Ballast	9,000 lbs.
Sail area	808 sq. ft.

Corp, Taiwan, and imported into the US for final commissioning. Stadman has been building boats in Taiwan for almost 20 years, and claims to have solved the infamous Taiwan quality control problems by maintaining an on-site British supervisor, who is charged with making the boats come out of the yard according to specifications. In addition, Stadman's hands-on style of management takes him several times a year to Taiwan to implement his design modifications (he has designed most of the interior of the boats himself). As the Slocums' builder, he personally works the boat shows, and maintains a relationship with Slocum owners, garnering feedback on which innovations work and which don't, trading ideas for modifications, and incorporating the owners unofficially into his sales structure by connecting them with prospective buyers eager to admire their yachts.

Slocum owners are a small but devoted cadre of sailors. They are lavish in praising their boat, praise laced with references to Stadman's personal participation in their boat owning experience. Inevitably, the new owner of Slocum Yachts will have a different style of relating to the boats and owners. Brown has adopted much of Stadman's format, and is now making the trips to Taiwan himself. Additionally, Stadman himself continues to work with Brown.

Construction

The Slocum 43 has been designed and built with enormous attention to detail. It boasts many thoughtful and carefully designed features of the sort that can be done when labor costs are at the low end of the scale. Jan Stadman has obviously spent time at sea, and he has incorporated his experience into the Slocum 43. It is surprising, then, to come across the occasional oversights and omissions, a few of which are fairly significant and contradictory.

For example, the hull of the Slocum 43 is a fiberglass sandwich cored with 20 mm of Airex R62-80, a stable and lightweight material that both stiffens and insulates the hull. Full-length box stringers provide further stiffening. The bulkheads are 3/4" marine plywood, set in place with an Airex shock absorbing strip between the edge of the bulkhead and the hull, and taped with fiberglass strips extending 8" from the joints. The deck is also cored, but with balsa instead of Airex.

This is a reasonably sophisticated, modern approach to hull construction, evidencing concern for saving weight, so the cabin sole comes as something of a surprise. It is made of 1/2" plywood faced with 1/2" solid teak and holly—strong, but heavy. The weight of the floorboards soon becomes a matter of personal experience. The entire cabin sole and support system can be removed for full access to the engine, tanks, and bilges. The accessibility is wonderful. Moving all those floorboards around is not.

Another contradiction is in the cockpit. The size, design and layout of the cockpit is generally good and appropriate for a blue water cruising boat. However, the cockpit lockers have three serious problems. First, the massive molded fiberglass lids are heavy and are not equipped to stay up in an open position. Some kind of retainer should be rigged to prevent them from accidentally closing. There's not likely to be a second chance for any fingers in the way of a good slamming from those lids. It might even be worth replacing the lids with something more sensible.

Second, the lockers are cavernous—big enough to enter to repair the steering gear, wiring or plumbing therein. That sounds like a big advantage—it *is* a big

advantage when you need to get to those things. The flip side is that anything stowed in those cavernous lockers also has access to the steering gear, the plumbing, and the wiring, and could foul or jam them in rough conditions. The lockers should be subdivided with removable shelving to keep items within reach and away from the works below. Shelving to protect the steering mechanism was added to later hulls (we examined #43).

Third, the lockers are not sealed off from the bilges. That's a common situation, but with lockers this size it becomes more of a concern. If water came aboard when a locker was open, a lot of it could get below very fast. (Maybe when you opened it in those rough conditions to clear the steering gear?) Not likely, perhaps, but it's the sort of unlikely event that can spell the difference between making it or not in survival conditions.

In general, though, the Slocum 43 has the strength and characteristics appropriate to passagemaking. She is quite stable, despite the seemingly low ballast/displacement ratio. The internal iron keel weighs 9,000 pounds, on a displacement of 28,000 pounds. Our rough calculation of her capsize screen value puts her at 1.69, the low end of the scale, comparable to the Bermuda 40, Luders 33, and Fast Passage 39. Her stability can be accounted for in part by the location of the engine in the bilge, below the waterline. Further, the boat is relatively beamy over much of her length. The water tanks are also below the waterline, and will add to stability when they are full.

The hull-to-deck joint is an inward-turning hull flange, overlapped by the bulwark flange at the perimeter of the deck molding. The joint is sealed with 3M 5200 adhesive and through bolted with 3/8" carriage bolts on 5" centers. The assembly is topped with an L-shaped teak caprail. This is a strong joint, and all but the bow is fairly well protected from potential impact by the tumblehome of the hull. A large teak rubbing strake in the area of maximum beam offers some protection to the midsections of the hull.

Below the rubbing strake, the white hull has been scored to simulate planking, which tends to hide irregularities that might show up in smooth gelcoat. Above the strake, a blue stripe fills the area to the caprail. The boat we examined showed some printthrough in the blue gelcoat, which is not scored, but in other areas the gelcoat finish appeared good.

The rubbing strake and sheer stripe reduce the appearance of height of the topsides, making the Slocum 43 seem, from some angles, sleeker than she really is. She is actually rather egg-shaped, and large for her length, a fact that can be appreciated for the roominess it confers below.

Fifteen through hull fittings on the boat exit at or

below the waterline, and are fitted with Taiwan-made bronze seacocks and, as needed, with vented loops to prevent back-siphoning. Although the hull is solid fiberglass laminate in the way of the seacocks, there is no backing plate behind the seacocks—the flange rests directly on the inside of the hull—and there are no additional screws or bolts to secure them. Some of the hoses attached to seacocks at the waterline were not double-clamped. We would prefer to see double hose clamps on all through hull fittings, plus mechanical fastenings, and backing plates to distribute the load. Two nice touches: the seacocks are labeled as to function, and emergency wood plugs are taped to the hull near many of them. There are, however, a lot of openings through the hull, more than we like to see.

The plumbing system includes hot and cold pressure water systems to the head, galley, and cockpit shower, plus manual cold fresh water and salt water systems to the head and galley. Two Rule 2000 electric bilge pumps are backed up by a Henderson manual pump mounted in the cockpit. Most of the domestic plumbing lines are copper tubing. Bilge pumps and drains have 1 1/2" or 2" hoses.

The electrical system includes 110-volt AC and 12-volt DC service, controlled by an American-made Newmar electrical panel. The 12-volt system is supplied by two 120 amp-hour batteries located in a convenient locker in the owner's stateroom at the base of the companionway.

We were unable to see the chainplate attachments because the hull is lined with teak strips glued to plywood sheets, which are in turn screwed to vertical furring strips attached to the hull. According to Stadman, the stainless steel chainplates extend from the deck to near the waterline, and are interconnected below by a welded stainless steel cross-member. They are through-bolted to the hull in the area of the rubbing strake, so the bolts are not visible from outside. Inside, the chainplates are further secured with fiberglass, and, in the area of chainplate

attachments, the hull is a solid fiberglass laminate. While this arrangement seems plenty strong, it would be difficult to repair.

The deck reinforcement in the way of hardware is unusual. A stainless steel plate is sandwiched inside the deck molding, in place of the balsa core. Because it is pre-drilled and tapped, deck hardware can be attached without struggling to attach nuts from below while turning bolts from above. Structurally, this system appears to distribute the loads on the hardware only to the upper skin of the deck sandwich. We would be more comfortable with through-bolted attachments, backed up with an interior plate, that would utilize the entire thickness of the deck.

Handling Under Power

A 50 hp Perkins 4-108 diesel, set on flexible mounts near the midpoint of the boat, provides adequate power for the Slocum 43. This engine was rated in our 1989 mechanics' survey as one of the best.

The three-bladed bronze propeller is strut-mounted just forward of the rudder skeg, a good position for balanced maneuvering under power.

Accessibility to the engine is excellent. The engine compartment is provided with a light (great) and soundproofing (could be better). Locating the engine in the bilge is a compromise. It puts 500 pounds where it serves as centrally-located ballast, enhancing stability and reducing pitching moment. It eliminates a large engine box in the cabin, or cramming the engine inaccessibly under the cockpit. The location also allows a nearly horizontal propeller shaft, which is more efficient than an angled shaft. The drawback is the engine's vulnerability to flooding if the boat takes on a lot of water. The Slocum 43 has a large sump which should help avoid

The interior is the best feature of the Slocum 43. Storage, lighting, ventilation and workmanship are all excellent. We could find almost nothing to criticize about it.

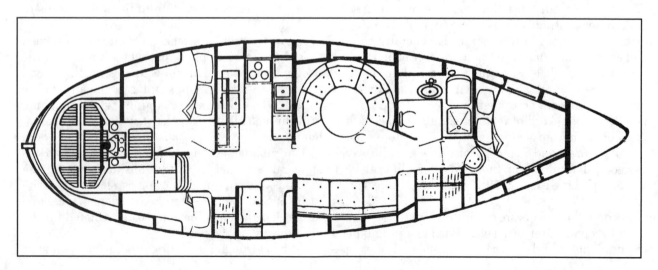

problems, but the owner should be aware of the potential for trouble.

Engine controls are conveniently mounted on the steering pedestal, with the instrument panel recessed into the starboard cockpit coaming and protected with a clear plastic cover. This location might be too vulnerable to spray in some boats, but this cockpit seems to be fairly dry.

Fuel tanks are under the cockpit, with filling ports located at the base of the steering pedestal, a good location because of proximity to the tanks and easy clean-up in case of a fuel spill. The two black iron tanks hold 150 gallons. This capacity gives a powering range of about 700 miles.

We think black iron fuel tanks are a bad idea in sailboats. The Slocum's tanks are painted on the outside with an anti-corrosion coating, but fuel tanks rust from the inside out. Diesel fuel frequently has water in it, and the water settles to the bottom of the tank. The water displaces fuel which would normally coat the sides of the tank. Without a protective coating of diesel fuel, iron tanks can rust out quickly, particularly along welded seams. The additional cost of a fuel tank of high-grade aluminum is minimal compared to the cost of disassembling joinerwork to repair or replace black iron tanks, but iron tanks are still quite common on Taiwanese boats.

Handling Under Sail

The Slocum 43, while not a high performance boat, nevertheless performs adequately for cruising. On the sparkling autumn day that we sailed her, we had optimum conditions: winds of 14 to 16 knots with relatively flat seas. Although the rig was not tuned, the boat was reasonably fast, surpassing our expectations.

Her weakest performance will come when the wind drops below 8 or 10 knots and when working to windward. She will not sail as close to the wind as a narrower boat with finer entry. The genoa sheets to a car on the caprail, which keeps the decks uncluttered, but the rails on a beamy boat present a sheeting platform too wide for good upwind performance. Many new sailboat designs have a wide beam, but the shrouds have been engineered to inboard chainplates, and genoa tracks run inboard instead of along the rail, achieving a closer sheeting angle for the genoa and improving a boat's ability to go to windward.

In general, running rigging is led to the cockpit, so that the boat can be sailed without leaving the cockpit once the sails are up. An exception is the mainsheet traveler, a Nicro 610 X-track and car that require going forward to make adjustments, which proved difficult. The X-track is designed to not bind up when the mainsheet pulls at an oblique angle. In our tests of mainsheet travelers, *PS* concluded that this feature did not offer better performance than other types of travelers tested. In any case, the Slocum's mainsheet lead is perpendicular to the traveler, and so does not demand this special feature. At the very least, we would rig a better athwartships adjustment, perhaps leading the adjustment line to the cockpit. Better, get the Harken traveler system offered as an option.

Standard sail inventory is made by Cheong Lee,

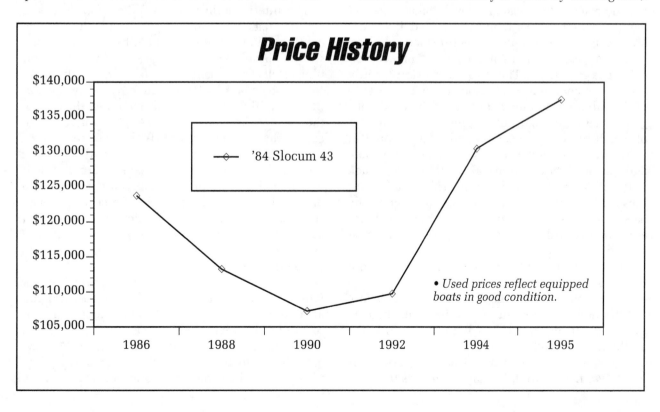

Price History

● *Used prices reflect equipped boats in good condition.*

Taiwan: mainsail rigged with two slab reefs, 150% genoa, #2 working jib, and staysail. The keel-stepped mast, boom, and staysail club are Isomat; internal halyards lead to mast-mounted winches. The double-spreader cutter rig is supported by stainless 1x19 wire and swaged terminals.

On our test boat, all sheet winches were self-tailing Barients, and adequate in size: 32ST as primaries, 22ST on the main, 17ST on the staysail. The halyard winches were generally of adequate size, although none was large enough to winch a person to the masthead, so it might be advisable to upgrade the mainsail halyard winch from a Barient 18 to a 22 or larger. Winch bases are insulated to prevent metal-to-metal contact and resulting corrosion on the mast.

On Deck

The cockpit and decks of the Slocum 43 offer a sense of security and comfort, due to the high freeboard, bulwarks, high lifelines (30" above the deck), heavy stanchions and stanchion bases, beefy pulpit and pushpit, and plenty of handholds and grabrails the length of the boat. Secure footing is provided by the teak underfoot everywhere: in the cockpit, on deck, and on the coachroof.

The T-shaped cockpit is not enormous, but is roomy enough, with comfortable seating on all four sides. The most popular lounging spot is the custom pushpit bench, a crescent-shaped innovation situated above the stern that confers superiority on the occupant.

A massive stainless and laminated wood boom gallows serves multiple functions. Besides holding the boom above head-banging level, it makes a good handhold and, along with the molded fiberglass breakwater, forms a support structure for the dodger.

If we have a complaint, it is that there might be too much of a good thing. There would probably be little lost if the stanchions were made of 1" in place of the 1 1/4" tubing used on our test boat. The teak looks great and is functional, but it represents a fair amount of weight in a high location, and a fair amount of work, whether oiled or varnished. The cockpit sole and side decks have raised teak planking set in black polysulfide, screwed and bunged. The thought of all those screws piercing the fiberglass through to the balsa core is a bit worrisome, but if the screw holes are properly sealed and the bungs stay in place it should not be a problem.

The teak on the coachroof is thinner—inlaid into the deck mold during construction, routed with a dovetail groove which fills with resin during layup. A little non-skid instead of teak in some strategic places might improve things without affecting the aesthetics too much.

The sidedecks are clear and passage forward is easy. Two mast pulpits of 1 3/4" stainless tubing—massive, again—offer good handholds, a place to secure gear and lines, and provide protection for the optional deck boxes.

The foredeck is somewhat obstructed by the staysail boom, but there is ample room to move and work around it. An electropolished stainless steel bow fitting accommodates two anchors. A double rope/chain locker in the bow of the boat can accommodate the anchor rode, but it is not a sensible place to carry the weight of a long anchor chain. There is a hatch on the foredeck which can be useful for sail changes underway.

Despite the fact that much of the deck equipment is overscale, the two 8" bow cleats are grossly undersized for a big, heavy boat. For passage through the Panama Canal, for example, regulations call for docking lines at least 7/8" in diameter. Try bending those around an 8" cleat, and you'll see what we mean.

We recommend the optional Nilsson V-3000 electric anchor windlass, rather than a manual windlass, on this size boat. However, take care that the foot switch is installed out of the way, to avoid losing a finger by accidentally starting up the windlass when you are not prepared.

Belowdecks

Below is where the Slocum 43 is most impressive. The interior is attractive and well thought out in details important to living in confined spaces on a moving platform for extended periods of time. Systems are accessible for maintenance and repair. In spite of extensive use of teak, there is a sense of light and space, and ventilation is good.

The interior joinerwork is quite good, from the circular teak table in the port side settee to the contoured nav station with slant-top opening table, stowage beside and under the seat and table, and hinged electrical panel. The teak and holly cabin sole has recessed dust/drip pans covered by grates at the base of the companionway steps and the base of the mast. A hanging wet locker at the base of the companionway drains directly to the bilge.

In the galley, the double icebox is fitted with a foot pump that delivers ice melt directly overboard, so it won't smell up the bilge. A built-in dish rack also drains overboard. The gimbaled Force 10 propane stove is recessed behind a safety bar. Overhead cupboards have a movable peg system which allows you to custom fit spaces inside to the size and shape of your dishes.

Throughout the interior, ample lighting is provided—brass reading lamps over the berths, broad area illumination by 16 overhead fixtures, and indirect fluorescent lamps above bookshelves.

Stowage is plentiful and well organized: 25 drawers with solid teak front panels slanted to allow ventilation when the drawers are closed; shelves, bins, cabinets and lockers in staterooms and work areas; and good use of potential "dead" spaces around settees and berths.

Two places on the Slocum 43 which would be especially significant to livaboards and passagemakers are the owner's stateroom and the head. The head is a double-compartment, one-piece molding with built-in shower. In the full headroom shower are handholds, alcoves and a seat—better than some shoreside showers. The head compartment is roomy enough for maneuvering, and offers stowage above and below the wash basin as well as in a bulkhead cabinet.

The owner's stateroom has room for two standing adults, a queen size berth, bookshelves, hanging locker, four drawers and three cabinets. Located at the foot of the companionway, it is convenient to most parts of the boat, yet offers good privacy and comfort. Some might object to having the fuel tank and battery access through this cabin, but we are not among them.

The nav station is comfortable, with good working space for chartwork, flat stowage for charts and tools, and ample room for installing electronics. The boat we sailed had an autopilot, Satnav, loran, depthsounder, performance indicators for boat speed, wind speed and direction; log, timer, VHF radio and a stereo receiver/tape player. The pilot berth is aft of the nav station, separated from it by the wet locker. An odd oversight is the lack of a red light for night work at the nav station, although three red floor lights are provided at strategic locations for maneuvering safely from one end of the boat to the other.

Conclusions

The Slocum 43 resides toward the lower end of the price scale for her type of boat, but certainly not in the very lowest position.

The Slocum 43, like all boats, is a mix of compromises. She excells in comfort and livability below. Her shortcomings lie in some of the technical details of construction and equipment, although the boat is generally adequate in those areas as well. A new-boat buyer with a lot of cruising experience could, and should, specify appropriate options to meet those shortcomings. Because the boat has evolved over the years, the earlier models will be different from later hulls, and a prospective buyer might do well to investigate the changes before deciding what to specify for his own boat. Of course, the buyer of a used Slocum 43 will have to live with whatever decisions the first owner made.
• **PS**

Mason 43/44

Owners say this powerful, Taiwan-built world cruiser carries Hinckley quality at half the price.

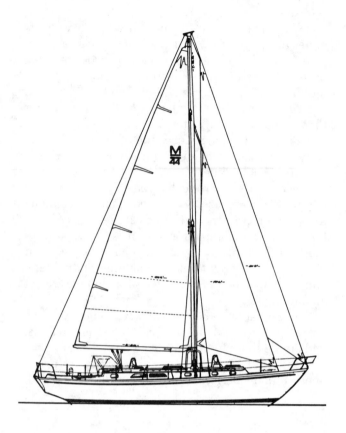

The Mason 43 was introduced in 1978 by Pacific Asian Enterprises (PAE), a California-based "developer" of Taiwan-built yachts. The Mason 44, which uses the same hull but a different deck mold, appeared in 1985, and is still in production today. In all, 180 43s and 44s have been sold. Due to a program of continual refinement, it is probable that no two are exactly the same.

The Masons have earned a reputation for offering quality approaching that of Hinckley, Swan, Alden and Little Harbor at a lower price, largely due to lower labor rates in Taiwan.

The Boat and the Builder

The Mason 43 was designed by Al Mason. During his career Mason worked with Carl Alberg, John Alden, Philip Rhodes and Sparkman & Stephens, as well as independently. His bent is generally traditional, with pleasing proportions and gentle sheer lines.

According to PAE's Joe Meglen, the 43 is an "evolution of a successful CCA ocean racer named *Sitzmark,*" which in turn evolved from the Nevins Yawl, *Finisterre,* and farther back, the New York 32.

The 44 was redesigned by PAE's in-house design team. Changes included modifying the rudder, lowering the cabin 2-1/2 inches, increasing fuel tankage, eliminating the single quarter berth, bringing the companionway aft, and making the mainsheet traveler run the full width of the cabin trunk.

PAE was formed by three yacht brokers (including Meglen) who first formed their own brokerage, Lemest Yacht Sales, and later decided to develop their own boats. Besides the Mason line, they've also done the Nordhavn 46 and 62 trawlers and are presently working on a Jim Taylor-designed 52-foot IMS boat.

Ta Shing Yacht Building Co. of Tainan, Taiwan, builds the molds and the boats for PAE. During a tour

Specifications

LOA	43' 11"
LWL	31' 3"
Beam	12' 4"
Draft (shoal/deep)	5' 6"/6' 3"
Displacement	27,400 lbs.
Ballast (43)	8,400 lbs.
Sail area (cutter)	899 sq. ft.

of Taiwan boatbuilders in 1986, we felt that Ta Shing was doing the best work of any Taiwanese-owned and operated yard in the country (the other superior yard at that time was Ted Hood's Little Harbor facility). Ta Shing also builds or has built the Norseman 447, Skye 54, the Babas, Flying Dutchmans and Pandas, and its own Tashiba and Taswell lines, which it markets directly.

The design of the Mason 43, with its long trunk cabin, generous overhangs and full keel, makes no pretenses of modernity. Apt adjectives include traditional, classic, handsome. and, according to the ads, "timeless." With its heavy displacement (d/l ratio = 400) and cutter or ketch rig, cruising is clearly its intention.

Owners' Comments

"She is a seakindly yacht and a joy to sail. According to our B&G we have had her as close as 30 degrees off the wind, although she (and we, too) are happier a little more off the wind."

1991 model in California

"I am absolutely captivated by the boat and am not objective at all in my feelings toward her. The general construction is of the highest standard. Like an Irish hunter, she is a workhorse and a lady—maybe not quite as fast around six furlongs as a racehorse, but for the long pull, through timber, brush and over walls, she is really something."

1986 model in Maryland

"Almost all Masons I have seen list to starboard. This, I think, is because the starboard fuel tank is 100 gallons and the port fuel tank is 70 gallons. In consuming water and fuel, it is important to balance the use of one's tanks.

"I have certain options that I feel are essential: foam insulation, a must for Maine; a freshwater deck pump for washing down the boat; the saltwater deck pump for cleaning the rode and anchor; screens for all ports and hatches; the drain and teak grate at the base of the companionway; bronze edge and channel for companionway drop boards; aft cabin berth four inches longer (I am 6' 1"), which makes the port cockpit locker smaller; fuel skimmer at bottom of fuel tank.

"Boats should be as beautiful and as functional as they are fun. The Mason 44 is all three."

1968 model in Massachusetts

Construction

The Mason boats are heavily built with solid fiberglass hulls, balsa-cored decks, and eight longitudinal foam/ fiberglass stringers for added stiffness. Bulkheads are 3/4-inch mahogany plywood bonded to the hull with foam in between to prevent hard spots (the right way to do it). The hull/deck joint of the 43 was originally through-bolted, caulked with Thiokol and reinforced with stainless steel flat stock. Meglen told us they later felt the stainless steel wasn't doing anything structural and dropped it, in part to save its 600-pound weight. Current boats are through-bolted on 8-inch centers, alternating with self-tapping screws also on 8-inch centers; the entire joint is laminated over with three layers of mat and woven roving. This, plus some other changes, enabled PAE to add 1,000 pounds to the ballast of the 44, without adding to overall displacement.

Fiberglass work is generally very good. One owner responding to our call for reader input said his boat arrived with a slight print through, but that the dealer, Bass Harbor Marine in Maine, painted the hull with Awlgrip at no charge to correct the problem.

A boat yard owner who has worked on a number of Masons said. "Areas the average owner will never see are finished with smooth, clean surfaces. The total absence of fiberglass 'meathooks' in such spots is much appreciated by yard workers."

A number of owners reported minor blistering, none serious.

Teak decks were standard on the 43, but not the 44. Teak is a wonderful non-skid surface, and nothing quite matches its looks. But there are usually attendant problems, especially leaks. One 44 owner said, "I do not have a teak deck, and am not sorry."

The amount of bright work on these boats is considerable. After all, fancy joinerwork is the essential feature Taiwan builders have to offer, and many American buyers lap it up. But savvy owners know it requires a lot of upkeep. The owner of a 1989 model said, "Bright work maintenance has become a nuisance in my life. I could do without the toe rail and have them aluminum. Also, I would eliminate the bright work 'eyelids' around the deck house, as in the Cambria 44, as well as the cockpit coaming and the Dorade boxes."

Speaking of Dorade boxes, the owner of a 1985 Mason 43 said his are mounted on plywood blocks screwed to the deck, which after four years began to delaminate and rot. The inappropriate use of plywood is, or at least was, a common problem on Taiwan-built boats.

Much Taiwan metalwork, such as custom welded stainless steel fittings, has also been suspect. Several owners of earlier Masons mentioned it.

The mast is a Forespar aluminum extrusion, painted with polyurethane. As the cost of anodizing increases (due to the difficulties and expenses of toxic waste disposal), we'll see more and more painted masts. They look great when new, but extra care should he taken to prevent scratches that penetrate to bare metal.

Turnbuckles are by Navtec, which we have rated highly in past evaluations. Blocks are by Schaefer. Running intermediate backstays are provided on the cutter and double headsail ketch rig for added support in heavy air.

Interior

Both the 43 and 44 are aft cockpit, tri-cabin designs. As can he seen in the plan, there is a V-berth or offset double berth forward, U-shaped dinette, galley and nav station amidship, and a private stateroom aft, partially extending under the cockpit.

The companionway is offset to starboard and on the 43 it is positioned several feet forward of the cabin bulkhead. This unusual feature means added distance from the cockpit to the safety of the cabin, a movement that some owners feel is less than ideal when sailing on port tack in a blow (the mainsheet also tends to inhibit access). An additional problem was the difficulty in constructing a full dodger. Of course, a partial dodger over the companionway is possible, but this does little to protect the crew in the cockpit.

In response to these complaints, the companionway of the 44 was moved aft, and the cockpit seating lowered to provide higher backrests; this latter change eliminated the single quarter berth.

As noted above, Taiwan builders are noted for their joinerwork, sometimes performed to ridiculous excess in the form of Chinese dragons, poppy flowers, and as designer Bob Perry is fond of observing, the building of "drawers inside of drawers." Happily the Masons show considerable restraint; their interiors are in fact exquisite.

Owners report very few problems, only a handful of gripes concerning the interior. These include leaky teak hatches (several highly recommend the optional Lewmar hatches), absence of a good sail locker on the 43 (despite voluminous stowage areas). marginal ice box insulation, settee too narrow for maximum comfort, no positive latches for securing cabin sole panels in event of knockdown, and difficulty in accessing tanks for cleaning.

The engine (usually a Perkins 4-108 in the 43, a 55-hp. Yanmar diesel in the 44) is located below the cabin sole. Owners of both engines report high levels of satisfaction with performance, though some feel the Perkins is "one size too small." Sound insulation is excellent ("I can hardly hear it running."). While this location places its weight low and presents no problems building furniture around it, several owners did note that a surprise flooding of the bilge immerses it. An automatic float switch for the bilge pump is now standard: one owner recommends the added measure of an alarm. Another noted that the engine "...is difficult to access, especially at the forward end where there are belts for the alternator and refrigerator compressor." Because of its enormous sump, Meglen says it's not a worry. And the location allows a horizontal propeller shaft for greater efficiency under power.

Fuel tanks are painted steel and water tanks stainless. The owner of a 1988 Mason 44 said, "Her fresh water capacity of 205 gallons is more than enough. The manifold for the five tanks is a work of art." Fuel capacity of the 44 is 160 gallons (a bit less in the 43), giving meaningful ranges under power of 400 miles minimum in worst-case head seas.

Performance

Underway, the Mason 43/44 is a big boat with the displacement to power through choppy seas. Naturally. it does not have a racer's speed or close-windedness (partially due to a fat keel), but owners are generally pleased with their boats' performance. They consistently rate off-the-wind speed superior to upwind speed, and balance as above average.

The one area which nearly every respondent commented on is stability. Due to its comparatively narrow beam, low ballast-to-displacement ratio, and large sail area, the boat heels quickly to 15-20 degrees, to lengthen the waterline, then digs in. This appears more true of the 43 than the 44, which was given additional ballast.

Various layours were offered, including one or two heads, and in the forward cabin, choice of V-berth or offset double. The single quarter berth in the aft cabin was eliminated in the 44.

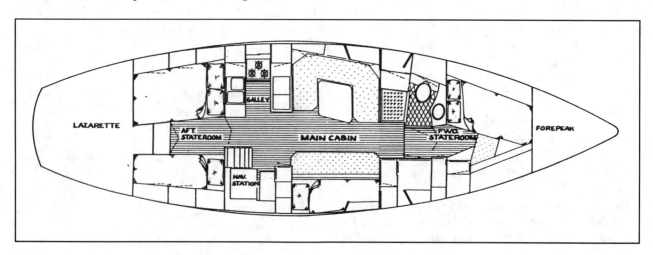

The owner of a 1984 model echoed the sentiments of many when he wrote, "My earliest experiences sailing the boat were frustrating as I found we had to reef beating in 15-16 knots of wind. I thought I'd bought a very tender boat. It took me a while to realize that the enormous mainsail, such a boon to light air breezes, made me crazy when the wind increased. When the first reef is in, the rail comes up and the boat goes like a shot. Once I understood the trade-off between light-air performance and the first reef, I grew to appreciate the design decision leading to the larger main."

In heavy weather, both models are exceptionally seakindly. The owner of a 1985 model recounted spending the night 60 miles offshore in the remnants of a hurricane, with 35-knot sustained winds and much higher gusts. Wave heights averaged 15 feet. "We made progress upwind at 4-5 knots under double-reefed main and staysail, until I was too tired to stay on watch. I hove to for eight hours. The motion was comfortable enough to sleep and not once did I feel unsafe. The boat needed zero attention, staying perfectly balanced."

For powering, owners recommend a feathering prop such as the Max Prop, which one owner said improved handling, and gave him an extra half knot of speed under sail. Several owners noted sluggish response to the helm at slow speeds.

Conclusion

Mason 43 owners have mixed feelings about the changes made in the 44. Some appreciate the 44's additional ballast and conventional companionway, which allows easier fitting of a full dodger. Others feel that the 44 is somewhat less attractive, with a "less sophisticated interior finish."

Mason 44 owners retaliate, saying that their cockpits are "much better" than the 43s, which suffer from a lack of ergonomics, especially backrests that are too low.

Almost all owners emphasized that their complaints are for the most part niggling, and that on the whole they adore their boats. "The Mason 44 is probably the prettiest vessel I have ever seen," wrote one owner. "She has sweet lines, capped by a perfect sheer. Her finish is outstanding and her belowdecks woodwork rivals Hinckley and Little Harbor." Not one regretted his purchase, and many see their Mason as the last boat they'll ever own. With few exceptions, owners feel PAE is a conscientious company that addresses its customers' problems with care and expedition.

The Mason 43/44 is a heavily built cruising boat with complex systems. Most problems are associated with accessories, not with the basic structure and rig. She is seakindly, balances well, and is good in light air, though the large mainsail needs to be reefed early when the wind pipes up.

Prices vary considerably according to age, condition and equipment. Earlier models probably represent better values, as rising labor rates in Taiwan have increased the cost of producing the later models.

It's a good production boat for long-distance cruising. But the large amount of bright work demands constant maintenance. • **PS**

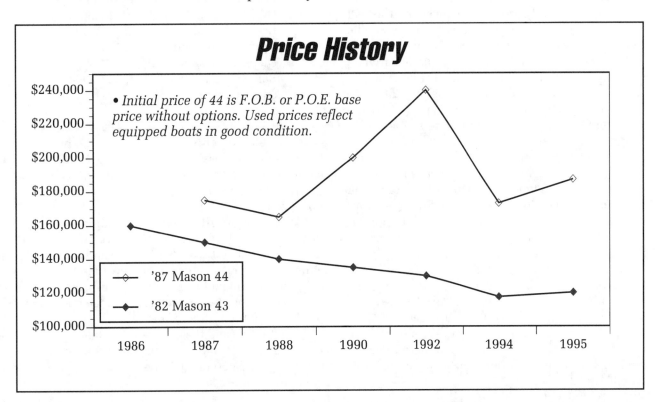

Price History

• *Initial price of 44 is F.O.B. or P.O.E. base price without options. Used prices reflect equipped boats in good condition.*

◇ '87 Mason 44
◆ '82 Mason 43

Brewer 12.8
Brewer 44

The venerable Whitby 42 has evolved into these two blue-water cruisers, both good, solid values.

The Brewer 12.8 and the Brewer 44 are developments of the Whitby 42, a cruising boat from the board of Ted Brewer. Brewer is one of the great modern cruising boat designers. His boats are well-mannered, attractive and practical.

According to the designer, the Brewer 12.8 and Brewer 44 use the same basic hull and deck as the Whitby 42, a boat that was designed in 1971. Hull changes to the Whitby 42 were made by cutting out the long keel and attached rudder, replacing them with a more modern short keel and skeg-mounted rudder. This eliminated a lot of wetted surface, improving the light-air performance.

To improve windward performance, a high aspect ratio centerboard extends through the bottom of the 12.8's shallow keel. Since the board is not ballasted, it does not affect stability, but can be used when reaching to shift the center of lateral resistance.

The Brewer 44 is the same boat as the 12.8, with the stern extended slightly, increasing the size of the aft stateroom. This has the fortunate side effect of making the boat slightly narrower aft and reducing the size of the transom.

Both the Brewer 12.8 and the Brewer 44 are semi-custom boats: you don't go down and buy one from a dealer, you have one built. Eliminating a dealer network does away with commissions of approximately 20%—a significant saving to the customer on a boat this size.

Since the Brewer 44 is slightly larger—more boat for the buck—has a better aft cabin, and doesn't cost a lot more to build, it has replaced the Brewer 12.8 as the "standard" model. You can still get a 12.8 on special order if you want a 42' boat. We'd opt for the bigger boat because it's better looking and has a much better aft cabin. Otherwise, the boats are virtually identical.

Specifications

LOA	42' (12.8), 44' (44)
LWL	33' 9" (12.8), 35' 6" (44)
Beam	13' 6"
Draft	4' 6" (shoal & cb), 5' 2" (deep)
Displ.	23,850 (12.8), 27,500 (44)
Ballast	9,000 (12.8), 12,000 (44)
Sail area	867 sq. ft. (cutter)

Absolutely the only advantage the 12.8 has over the 44 is that it is easier to lower a dinghy stowed in davits down the vertical transom of the 12.8. On the reverse transom of the 44, the dinghy tends to hang up as you drop it.

It's easy to get a little confused reading the specifications for the three boats. The beam of the 12.8 and the 44 is listed as 13' 6", while the Whitby 42 is 13' wide. According to the designer, the difference probably comes from including the molded-in guardrails of the Brewer 12.8 and Brewer 44, since no change was made to the hull width.

Both the 12.8 and the 44 have 4' 6" standard draft, yet the 44 has from 2,000 to 3,000 pounds more ballast, from 2,650 to 3,650 pounds more displacement (depending on which ad you read), and a

Owners' Comments

"Exterior cosmetic finish is great. Interior joinerwork—drawers, doors, etc—is only average. For the first time, my wife is ecstatic with the livability of a boat.

"The centerboard version handles well in all winds. She is easily singlehanded even without an autopilot—or a wife—for long passages."

—1984 model 12.8 in New York

"With a 150% genoa, you need turning blocks to lead properly to the sheet winches. The builder is very willing to customize at a reasonable price.

"Delivery time was quoted as four months, but was actually five. Be prepared to spend a month in Fort Myers after the boat goes in the water.

"Excellent electrical and refrigeration systems, but I should have bought a generator. I recommend the cutter rig with a quick-release forestay. I tie it back when using the 150% genoa, then use the staysail when the wind reaches 20 knots.

"There are so many good things about the boat, and so many little problems. So what's new?"

—1985 model 12.8 in Maryland

"The boat sails well, but can't go to windward like my old IOR boat. The base price is low, but by the time you put on the extras, it adds up. It's still much cheaper than a Bristol or an Alden. For the first time, my wife really enjoys spending time on a boat, although she thought we were too old for another boat."

—1987 model 44 in Rhode Island

waterline from 1' 3" to 1' 9" longer. According to the builder, the 44 started out with 11,000 pounds of ballast, but that has gradually increased to almost 12,000 pounds.

Since there is no actual change in the keel depth or position in the two boats, it is reasonable to assume that the increasingly heavier 44 actually draws more than the advertised 4' 6". The extra displacement of the 44 probably translates into a base draft of about 4' 9". In practice, both the 12.8 and the 44 will draw even more in cruising trim, since owners of these boats frequently load them up with heavy items such as generators and bigger-than-standard batteries.

The 12.8 and the Brewer 44 are built by Fort Myers Yacht and Shipbuilding. The yard has built 40 12.8s, and 24 of the 44' version have been sold. The yard also built 33 Whitby 42s under license from the Canadian builder.

The 12.8 and the 44 were conceived as good-performing, long distance livaboard cruisers. The members of the original syndicate which commissioned the Brewer 12.8 were experienced racing and cruising yachtsmen who wanted the livability and layout of the Whitby 42, coupled with a higher-performance hull and rig configuration.

Hull and Deck

There is nothing fancy about the construction of the Brewer 12.8. The hull is a conventional layup of mat and roving, with balsa core from just below the waterline up to just below the sheer.

The hull-to-deck joint is formed by a glass hull bulwark with an inward-turning flange. The outward-turning bulwark flange of the deck molding overlaps this, and the hull and deck are bolted and bedded together. This is a good, solid joint. It is capped with teak.

A fiberglass rubbing strake is molded into the hull just below the sheer. It's a toss-up between a molded fiberglass rubbing strake and a bolted-on wooden one. Certainly maintenance will be easier with the fiberglass strake, but a wooden strake might absorb a little more impact without damage to the hull, and would probably be easier to repair or replace. In any case, a rubbing strake is a good idea on a boat that may well be laid alongside primitive docks in far-off places to load fuel or water.

Some of the construction details strike us as a little light for a serious cruising boat of this displacement. The shroud chainplates, for example, are 1/4" stainless steel. If this were our own boat, and we were planning serious offshore cruising, we'd want those chainplates to be 3/8" material.

Likewise, rig specifications call for 9/32" wire for shrouds and backstay, plus a 5/16" headstay. We'd rather see at least 5/16" shrouds, plus a 3/8" headstay. The specified wire sizes are adequate, but we prefer a little more margin in an offshore cruiser. The lighter wire saves some weight and windage aloft, and a little money.

Some of the construction details are very good. Lifeline stanchions are 29" tall, spaced closely together, and properly backed with aluminum plates. Some finishing details on the early 12.8 we sailed, on the other hand, were less satisfactory. For example, rather than using solid teak molding in the door frames, the Brewer 12.8 had glued-on veneer edging. Likewise, aft of the settee backs there are access hatches to storage areas. These access hatches are merely cutouts in the plywood, and the edges were not even sanded smooth before painting.

The Brewer 44 we looked at was a totally different animal in finish detail. Doorways have solid teak edge moldings; detailing is much better throughout. Where the early 12.8 rates only "average production boat" in the detailing category, the 44 detailing is "very good production boat" in quality. When we looked at the 12.8, we figured it needed another 200 hours of detailing to match its potential. The 44 is just about there.

Rig

The standard rig of both the 12.8 and the 44 is a well-proportioned, modern, high aspect ratio cutter. The mainsail area of 368 square feet is about the maximum size conventional mainsail that a retired couple would want to handle. If the boat is going to be a long-term retirement home, we'd consider going to a roller-reefing mainsail such as the Hood Stoway or Metalmast Reefaway. This type of decision should be made when the boat is built, since a retrofit is an expensive proposition involving replacement of the spar.

The mast is by Isomat, with Lewmar halyard winches mounted on the spar. The rig is stepped through to the keel.

Engine and Mechanical Systems

Standard engine for the Brewer 44 is a 62 hp Perkins 4-154. A larger 85 hp Perkins is optional. Either engine is more than adequate power for the boat. We prefer the smaller engine for its better fuel economy, but if you want a real motorsailer, the bigger engine is a reasonable choice. The Brewer 12.8 used the 62 hp Lehman Ford engine.

With the standard 135 gallons of fuel and the smaller engine, range under power is about 700 miles. This is just about what you'd want in a big cruising boat that sails well.

Plumbing and wiring systems are good, but the standard batteries are too small for the boat. Although the standard equipment list is reasonably thorough, a lot of equipment you'd want for serious cruising is optional. The basics such as hot and cold pressure water, propane for cooking, fuel tank selection system and fuel filters are standard, and well-executed.

Handling Under Power

The Brewer 12.8 with the Lehman diesel motors comfortably at 6 knots at about 1700 rpm. This is a very economical cruising speed. Both of the Perkins engines are capable of pushing the boat faster, but when you're cruising, fuel economy is more important than how quickly you get there.

The boats have a lot of windage. A major criticism of the Whitby 42 was that it was difficult to handle at low speeds when docking, particularly in a crosswind. Both the 12.8 and the 44, with their more cutaway underbodies, maneuver substantially better. This is still a big boat, and it will not spin on a dime like a smaller boat.

One change that would dramatically improve both speed under sail and handling under power would be to install a feathering prop such as the Maxprop instead of the standard solid prop. The 44 we looked at had a three-bladed Maxprop, and the owner wouldn't have it any other way. A feathering prop gives full thrust in reverse—unlike either fixed or folding props—yet offers little more resistance under sail than a folding prop.

Midships cockpits with engine rooms below can be noisier both ondecks and belowdecks. These boats have fairly good sound insulation in the engine room; you know the engine is running, but it's not obtrusive.

Handling under Sail

The Brewer 12.8 sails as well as you'd want for a cruising boat. The boat is extremely well balanced. In about 12 knots of true wind—16 knots or so over the deck—we could trim the sails for upwind sailing, then walk away from the helm without even setting the wheel brake. In smooth water, the boat tracks and holds course well.

In puffier conditions, the boat tends to round up sharply when close reaching with the board fully extended. This is not much of a surprise, since most beamy boats do this.

With a large-diameter steering wheel and mechanical pull-pull steering, response and feel are excellent.

The boom on the 12.8 we sailed was very high off the deck. We ended up climbing onto one of the halyard winches to hook up the main halyard. This is a disadvantage, particularly if the crew is older and less agile.

Furling the main is also complicated by the high boom. You can reach the boom for furling at the mast and atop the aft cabin, but it's difficult to do it over the center cockpit. Likewise, with the big dodger up, you can't get to the boom over the main companionway. The boom is probably placed this high to clear a Bimini top, but it sure makes it a chore to set and furl the mainsail.

In contrast, the boom of the new 44 we examined was just enough lower to make hooking up the halyard and furling the mainsail a straightforward proposition.

Most of the standard winches for the boat are marginal in size, particularly if the boat is to be used for retirement sailing. Standard genoa sheet winches, for example, are Lewmar 52 self-tailers. These are approximately equivalent to the Barient self-tailing electric 28s that were on our test boat. Larger Lewmar primaries are optional, and should be chosen. We'd pass up the optional electric primaries at over $6,000, unless it's the only way you can trim the sails.

The main halyard on the boat we sailed—one of the original eight Brewer 12.8s—had a poor lead: from a block at the base of the mast, through a deck-mounted cheek block, through the dodger coaming, to a stopper and winch atop the cabin just forward of the cockpit. The turning block at the base of the mast was too high, allowing the halyard to chafe at several points, particularly on the cheek block. In fact, we could barely crank up the main using the Lewmar 30 halyard winch. This is easily corrected, but it was annoying to see the same poor lead on the brand new 44 we examined. In fact, the owner of the 44 had ordered a larger than standard main halyard winch to overcome the friction in the system.

Our test boat was rigged as a cutter. Staysail sheet winches are self-tailing Lewmar 30s mounted on the forward end of molded winch islands just outboard of the cockpit coamings. With a large cockpit dodger in place, it is difficult to impossible to use these winches: they're actually hidden outside the dodger, and the dodger side curtains have to be unclipped to trim the staysail.

The primary headsail sheet winches are also awkward to use. The winch handle swings through the lifelines. This is a function of the wide, midships cockpit; sailhandling has been compromised to create cockpit room.

There are properly through-bolted aluminum genoa tracks mounted atop the bulwarks. On our test 12.8, there was also a shorter inboard genoa track, which could be used to advantage going to windward, since the main shroud chainplates are set inboard of the rail. In practice, few of these boats will be equipped with a deck-sweeping genoa, so the inboard track is probably superfluous.

The 12.8 we sailed had large Schaefer turning blocks aft for improving genoa sheet leads to winches. However, these blocks were mounted almost flat on their welded winch islands. Since the winch is higher than the turning block, the lead from the block to the winch is not fair, which can cause chafe on the sheet and increased friction in the system. The blocks should be angled upward slightly to correct this, which could be done with shims or with a slight redesign of the mounting weldments.

On the Brewer 44, aft turning blocks are not standard. With a very high-cut genoa whose lead was very far aft, you could end up with an awkward sheet angle at the winch unless turning blocks are installed. This is a disadvantage of sail handling from a cockpit in the middle of the boat.

A full-width mainsheet traveler is mounted atop the aft cabin. Our 12.8 used a Schaefer traveler, while the 44 has a Lewmar unit. Controls for the Lewmar traveler cars are at the back end of the aft cabin. You have to climb out of the cockpit to adjust them. The original Schaefer traveler has car adjusters just aft of the helmsman, with stoppers and a Lewmar 30 winch. We're at a loss to explain why a good setup was traded for a bad one.

The mainsail is trimmed by a Lewmar 30 self-

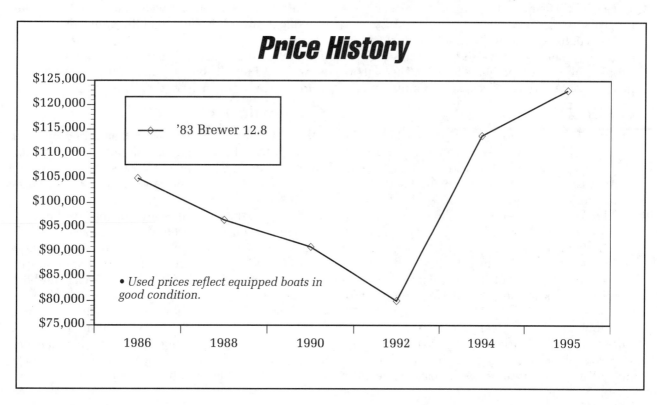

Used prices reflect equipped boats in good condition.

tailer mounted atop the aft cabin, reasonably accessible to either helmsman or crew. This winch is powerful enough for a mainsail this size.

A double-headsail ketch rig with bowsprit is an option that will set you back about $7,000 by the time you buy the mast, sail and fancy bowsprit. Frankly, if you want a ketch rig because it's easier to handle on a boat this size, you'd be better off spending that seven grand on a Stoway cutter rig, huge self-tailing sheet winches all around, and roller furling on both the genoa and staysail. It would probably be easier to handle than the ketch, and you'd keep the better performance of the single-masted rig.

Despite relatively shoal draft, the Brewer 12.8 is reasonably stiff. With full main and 150% genoa, the boat heels about 20° with 18 knots of breeze over the deck. With the optional deeper keel she would be a little stiffer, but the keel/centerboard combination is probably slightly faster on most points of sail, if a little tippier in heavy air.

We think the extra ballast in the Brewer 44 will make her an even better performer than the Brewer 12.8 in winds of over about 15 knots. Although the extra displacement and wetted surface will slow the boat slightly in very light winds, the standard rig is big enough to keep the boat moving in winds as light as most people care to sail in. When it's too light, you can always turn on the engine. Most cruisers simply aren't interested in squeezing out every ounce of performance in light air.

There are actually three different underwater configurations for the Brewer 44: a shoal fin keel; the same shoal keel with a high aspect ratio centerboard; and a slightly deeper—but still relatively shallow—fin keel.

The centerboard has become optional—it was originally standard on the 12.8—because a lot of people simply never bothered to use it. The boat sails fine without it; it just goes sideways a little more.

On Decks

Sailhandling limitations aside, the cockpit is just about ideal for a cruising sailboat. You can comfortably seat eight in the cockpit for idle hours at anchor.

An Edson wheel steerer dominates the cockpit. It has custom boxes with electrical switches for anchor windlass, autopilot—you can practically run the boat from here. We're a little concerned about the proximity of all this wiring to the steering compass, however. When having the compass swung, be sure to operate every piece of electrical equipment on the steering console to make sure that nothing affects the compass.

A high molded-in breakwater makes installing a full-width dodger fairly easy. A good cockpit dodger is essential on a center cockpit boat. Without a dodger, a center cockpit is a wet place to live sailing or motoring to windward in a blow. Both of the dodgers we looked at, however, blocked access to the staysail sheet winches.

Side decks are very narrow due to the wide cabin trunk. This is a definite compromise. The shroud chainplates come down right in the middle of the side decks, yet there isn't room to walk outboard of the shrouds. Instead, you must step up and over the cabin.

Although it's a $1,500 option, most owners will choose the stainless steel stub bowsprit with twin anchor rollers. The 12.8 we sailed had a CQR plow in the starboard roller, and a Danforth stowed sideways in the port roller. It was not the best arrangement. The 44 we examined had plows in both rollers, and they fit, although it is a tight squeeze.

A lot of these boats are equipped with custom davits for carrying a dinghy off the stern. They're a good idea, since there's little deck space for stowing a dinghy aboard.

At the same time, carrying a dinghy in davits offshore can be a risky proposition, particularly in a following sea. The skipper of one 12.8 had the dinghy fill with water during a rough passage—someone forgot to take the plug out—and was afraid the entire arrangement of davits and dinghy was going to be lost. For passagemaking, we'd probably bring the inflatable aboard and break it down for stowage, as awkward as that may seem.

Fuel fills are located in the waterways at just about the low point in the sheer. Water fills are in the waterways forward. As we found, you have to be careful if you're taking on fuel and water at the same time. We overfilled the water tank, sending water straight toward the open fuel fill. Quick hands—not ours—got the cap back on the fuel fill before water could pour into the tank. It wouldn't be a bad idea to raise the fuel fill about an inch off the deck on a pad to reduce the chances of this happening.

Belowdecks

Some of the compromises in sail handling and deck layout have been made for the sake of the interior. The wide deckhouse that makes for narrow side decks creates a huge interior volume, and the space is used very well.

Because the forward cabin is pushed well into the eyes of the boat, the forepeak anchor locker is small. You can lead the anchor chain aft to the locker under the berths in the forward cabin, which has the advantage of moving a lot of weight further back in the boat, where it has less effect on pitching moment.

The forward cabin has V-berths, with an insert to form a double. The berths are quite narrow at the foot, and are only comfortably long for someone under 6' tall. Outboard of the berths there are storage lockers, and there are drawers below.

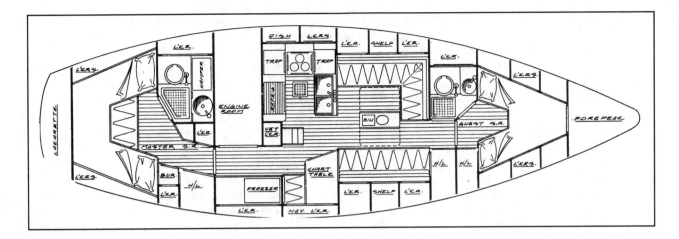

Ventilation in the forward cabin at anchor is provided by a large Lewmar hatch and Beckson opening ports. Offshore ventilation consists of a cowl vent in a Dorade box.

You can enter the forward head from either the main cabin or the forward cabin, since there are two doors. Unfortunately, the door to the forward cabin wipes out the space that would otherwise be used as the head dresser. Instead, you get a little sink with not much space for laying out the essentials of your toilette.

The forward door also means that the head sink is pushed fairly far outboard. With the boat heeled over on starboard tack, seawater backs up through it. One boat we looked at had a big wooden plug to stick in the drain, while the other owner had added a shutoff valve to the drain line just below the sink.

Ironically, the small head dresser is quite low, and could easily have been raised up another 4" or so. This wouldn't eliminate the problem, but the boat could heel over a little more before you'd have to do something about it.

Both the forward and aft heads use inexpensive, bottom-of-the-line waterclosets. Our experience is that cheap heads work fine for daysailing and coastal cruising, but are a curse for the serious livaboard cruiser. We'd rather see a Wilcox-Crittenden Imperial or Skipper on a serious cruising boat.

A solar-powered vent overhead provides exhaust ventilation, but we think in addition that every head should have an opening overhead hatch. A cowl vent in a Dorade box would also be a good idea. It's impossible to have too much ventilation in a head.

The main cabin has a straight settee to starboard, an L-shaped settee to port. You can also have a pair of armchairs on the starboard side instead of the settee, but we see no advantage to this. The L-shaped settee has a drop-in section to convert it to a double, so that you can have three double berths on the boat, if you're masochistic enough to want to cruise with three couples. The good thing is that the boat does contain three separate living spaces, with direct access from each of the spaces both to the deck and to a head compartment. That's a tricky thing to do, and Ted Brewer has pulled it off as well as you can.

Aluminum water tanks holding 200 gallons are located in the bilge under the main cabin.

There is good locker space outboard of the settees in place of the more commonly-seen pilot berths that usually become useless catch-alls. One locker is designed as a large booze locker. When you think about the imbibing habits of a lot of sailors, this makes a lot more sense than stuffing one bottle here, another over there.

Ventilation in the main cabin is good for in port, less good for offshore. There are four opening ports in the main cabin. The standard ports are plastic, which we think is not an acceptable material for an offshore cruiser of this type. Stainless steel opening ports are an option costing $1,890. This buys you very good cast-frame opening ports, which we think should really be standard on a boat of this caliber.

There are also two aluminum-framed hatches over the main cabin. The hatches currently used are single-opening Lewmar hatches with extruded frames. The older 12.8 we sailed had double-opening Atkins & Hoyle cast hatches. A double-opening hatch allows you to open the hatch forward in port for maximum air flow, aft when sailing to keep water from getting below. We wish they had stuck with the more expensive cast hatches.

Two cowl vents in Dorade boxes are provided for sailing ventilation. Like the cowl vents on a lot of boats, the downtake pipes into the cabin of the Brewer boats are improperly proportioned: they should never be smaller than the nominal pipe diameter of the vent itself.

The galley has undergone a lot of minor changes since the first boats in the Brewer 12.8 series were built. The early boat we examined had sinks that were too small, water fixtures that were too low relative to the sinks, drawers that were difficult to operate, and fiddles without corner cleanouts. The 44 we examined had changed all of these things.

One thing has not changed. Between the sinks and the stove, there is a large dry well for storage. This is about the size and shape of a large grocery shopping cart. You wouldn't want to have to dig to the bottom of a grocery cart for the cereal and crackers every time you wanted to use them, but that's pretty much what you have to do with this well. It should at least be divided with sliding shelves to make it easier to use.

At the aft end of the galley, there is a large refrigerator and freezer mounted athwartships. It is well insulated, and has a well-gasketed top.

There's another big opening hatch over the galley, and it is properly placed behind the dodger breakwater, where it can serve as an exhaust vent in any conditions—as long as the dodger is up.

Standard stove is a three-burner propane stove with oven—just what you'd want.

A big chart table is opposite the galley. While it has good storage for navigation books, there is no coherent arrangement for the mounting of the array of electronics that you find on the typical modern cruising boat. Since these boats are built on a semi-custom basis, you could probably have the nav station modified to suit your particular electronics. These boats were designed before the contemporary electronics explosion, and some details have not been upgraded to reflect the state of the art.

Aft of the nav station, there is a passageway with stooping headroom to the aft cabin. On the starboard side of the passage, there is a huge workbench with chart storage and tool storage below. This is a great way to use this space, rather than trying to throw in another berth.

On the older boat we looked at, this same space was filled with a huge freezer and battery storage—an advantage of semi-custom flexibility. The big electrical panel is located over the workbench: out of the way, yet reasonably accessible.

Opposite the work area, under the cockpit, is a real engine room. There's room for the main engine, an optional generator, fuel filtration system, hot water storage tank, and batteries. Although you have to climb over the engine to check the batteries, everything is reasonably accessible. A real engine room is a rarity in a boat this size, and is only practical with the center cockpit configuration.

The aft cabin of the 12.8 has two quarterberths which can be joined by a drop-in section to create a large thwartships double. The extra 2' in the stern of the 44 makes it possible to have a big permanent fore and aft double berth. If you want, you can still get the two berth configuration.

A separate companionway at the forward end of the aft cabin gives access to the cockpit without going through the passageway. This companionway has a slatted dropboard, and since it faces forward, it is vulnerable to spray. For offshore sailing, it should be secured with a tight-fitting canvas cover. In port, it will provide good ventilation at the expense of some privacy. There is also another aluminum-framed hatch over this cabin. It suffers from the same limitations as the hatches over the main cabin.

You can get a sit-down shower stall in the aft head, or have a more conventional arrangement using the entire head as the shower compartment. A sit-down shower may be easier to clean, but you give up a lot of head dresser space to get it.

There is excellent locker space throughout the boat, including three hanging lockers and a foul weather gear locker. Instead of packing in extra berths, the designer and builder have chosen to limit the number of berths and maximize storage. It was a wise choice.

With the exception of the under-cockpit passage, headroom is well over 6' throughout.

Conclusions

Since the Brewer 44 is a lineal descendant of the Whitby 42 and Brewer 12.8, a lot of the shortcomings of those boats have been ironed out over the years. Finishing details have gradually improved, and have generally kept pace with the boatbuilding industry trend toward better detailing.

At first glance, the "sailaway" price of just under $160,000 seems like a misprint. That price includes main and genoa, Hood roller furling on the headsail, propane, refrigeration, basic electronics and pumps. There's also a long options list.

The kicker is that a lot of the things on the options list should be standard on a high-quality cruising boat. For example, the bigger primary sheet winches that we think are required cost an extra $1,800. A teak and holly cabin sole is another thousand; two-tone decks (rather than plain white) add $670. Lightning grounding costs $720, an anchor platform $1,500.

Although the boat was designed as a cutter, staysail rigging, winches, and the sail itself add $2,600.

Standard batteries total only 225 amp hours capacity. For batteries the right size, add $400. For metal ports rather than plastic, shell out almost $1,900. Even the centerboard in a boat that was designed as a keel/centerboarder adds $2,600 to the sailaway price.

With the options that we think are really essentials, the "sailaway" price jumps by about $15,000.

What do you get for $175,000? You get a well-designed, good-sailing, well-built ocean cruising home, a retirement cottage for every romantic port in the world. The boats are not as well detailed or equipped as higher-priced boats such as Aldens, Hinckleys, and Little Harbors. But they're good, solid values, and they'll take you to the same places as more expensive boats. In this day and age, that's not a bad recommendation. **• PS**

PJ/Swan 44

A timeless Sparkman and Stephens design that can boast of construction that's as good as it gets.

The Swan 44, originally imported as the Palmer Johnson (PJ) 44, was designed by Sparkman and Stephens as a production offshore IOR racer, a slightly smaller sister of the Swan 48 which won the 1972 Newport-Bermuda Race. Between 1972 and late 1975, 76 44s were built, and many were imported into the U.S.

While custom IOR boats frequently made off with the big trophies even in the early days of racing under the rule, a well-designed production racer such as the Swan 44 was still competitive, particularly for long-distance racing. Few of these boats are seriously campaigned today on a regular basis, but the Swan 44 is still a competitive boat under the International Measurement System (IMS).

Although the term "classic" is grossly overused, this boat is the real McCoy. The handsome S&S profile still looks good two decades after it was drawn, and it will look just as good in another 20 years. A deep, heavy hull gives full headroom under a nearly flush deck, and the low, teak-decked bubble deckhouse disappears unobtrusively into the foredeck with no fuss.

Construction

The Swan 44's construction is rugged, but unsophisticated by today's standard's. The hull itself is a solid uncored laminate of roving and chopped strand mat, with far more mat than is typical in newer boats.

Mat provides reasonable impact resistance but little stiffness. Hull stiffness is added by three full-length longitudinal stringers. In addition, the furniture is securely bonded to the hull.

Most dark-colored Swan 44 hulls we have examined show significant surface irregularities in the way of stringers, tranverse ceiling supports, bulkheads, and bonded furniture. This is strictly a cos-

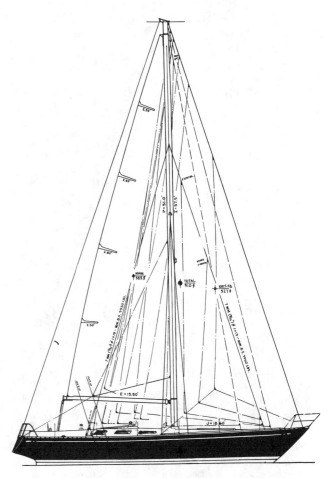

Specifications

LOA	44' 1"
LWL	33' 11"
Beam	12' 7"
Draft	7' 5"
Displacement	28,000 lbs.
Ballast	12,600 lbs.
Sail area	920 sq. ft.

metic concern, but it is a very real one if you wish to paint a light-colored boat a dark color. According to one boatyard owner we talked to, who has considerable experience in repainting older Swans, the typical 44 needs about $1,500 in additional labor and materials for refairing when a dark hull color is chosen over a light color.

Decks are a fiberglass/balsa sandwich, and a teak overlay is standard. Teak decks on a Swan of this vintage are a decidedly mixed blessing. Pride of ownership—and this goes with the territory if you're going to own a Swan—demands that the teak decks be kept looking good. For most owners, this means cleaning the decks at least annually with powerful chemicals.

The chemicals—either acid or a two-step base/

acid combination—are murder on teak decks and their seam compounds. After more than 15 years of religious cleaning, the decks of the typical Swan 44 are pretty tired.

The first signs of trouble are popped bungs, or rusty discolorations around them. Water migrates around the fastenings into the deck core, soaking the balsa and eventually even causing separation of the fiberglass top skin from the core. There usually is little or no leaking belowdecks to tell you of a problem, and by then most of the damage would be done in any case.

If you're buying a Swan 44, an extremely careful survey of the decks is as essential as the hull survey. Replacement of the teak deck covering is an expensive proposition, and could add $30,000 to the price of the boat.

Swan teak decks are not particularly more trouble-prone than teak decks on other boats. The same caveat applies to any teak-decked boat more than about 10 years old. Ironically, the efforts of owners to keep their Swans looking new can cause big problems if enthusiasm is not tempered with a large dose of common sense.

The Sparkman and Stephens-drawn lines of the Swan 44 are a modern classic, especially the flush deck and low-profile deckhouse.

Hull blistering of mid-1970s Swans is about average in frequency. We would be wary of any boat that had spent much of its life in tropical waters, since there is a fairly direct relationship between hull blistering and immersion time.

The hull and deck are bolted together through an anodized aluminum toerail. Inside the boat, the entire hull/deck joint is glassed over—including the fastenings to deck hardware. While this may prevent leakage into the interior, it is a headache when it's time to replace or re-bed deck hardware, and it's time to think about rebedding deck hardware on any boat this age.

Interior

Since the Swan 44 was designed as a racing boat, the interior is not what you would find in a 44-foot cruiser/racer today. The forepeak is given over to sail storage, with two fold-down pipe berths over built-in sail bins. It would be fairly easy to convert this area to a real sleeping cabin. The sail bins are teak-faced ply that could be modified to conventional berths, and there are port and starboard lockers for clothing.

A large sliding hatch over the forepeak provides fair weather ventilation, and serves as a sail hatch. This hatch will leak if solid water comes aboard, so if the forepeak were converted to a stateroom, it would be worth considering replacing the sliding hatch with a modern, watertight aluminum-framed deck hatch. There is no provision for foul-weather ventilation in the forepeak.

The main cabin is positioned immediately aft of the forepeak, rather than being divided from it by the more conventional head and hanging lockers. This pushes the main living area further forward, into a narrower part of the boat. The result is a main cabin that is smaller than you would normally find in a 44-footer.

Pilot berths outboard of the two settee berths make good sea berths, but further restrict the main cabin. At sea, the two extension transom berths, which are parallel to the centerline of the boat, will also be used for sleeping if you cruise or race with a big crew.

Twin 45-gallon stainless steel water tanks are mounted under the settees port and starboard, keeping the weight of consumables in the right location at the expense of under-seat storage.

A large dropleaf table seats four for dining in comfort, six in a pinch. If it's six for dinner, the two persons seated at the aft end of both settees are somewhat cut off from conversation by the mast, which is stepped through the middle of the table to the keel.

The combination of a varnished teak interior and a flush deck make the main cabin somewhat dark, although a fair amount of light is provided by an overhead Goiot hatch and a small deadlight. There are four cowl vents in Dorades over the area for good ventilation.

On at least one boat, the main cabin has been radically altered by removing the port settee and pilot berth, replacing them with a U-shaped dinette.

This would dramatically improve the livability of the main cabin, and is the arrangement most commonly seen on a modern boat of this size and type.

Headroom is 6' 3" on centerline aft, 6' 2" at the forward end of the main cabin.

The galley, navigation area, and head occupy the beamiest section of the boat. The nav station features a large chart table, a comfortable seat, adequate shelf space for books and electronics, and a big bulkhead for mounting instrument repeaters. There's little you could do to improve on it, although for today's offshore cruising and racing you'd tear out the bookshelves to make way for the plethora of electronic goodies most boats carry.

Opposite the nav station is the galley. While it is smaller than you'd find on a boat of this type today, it was huge for 1972, and is more than adequate, with a big, well-insulated icebox, three-burner propane stove, and a fair amount of storage space. Two seven-inch-deep centerline sinks drain directly overboard.

This section of the boat is light and airy, with good light from the two long fixed ports in the low deckhouse, plus the large sliding companionway hatch.

To starboard, immediately aft of the nav station, is the head compartment, with six-foot headroom. It is accessible either from the main living area or from the aft cabin. The lower section of the head compartment is a fiberglass molding, making it easy to clean, while the upper section is the same teak joinerwork that is found in the rest of the boat.

A Baby Blake watercloset was standard issue. This quaint, expensive piece of British marine plumbing is sworn either by or at, depending on your experience with the beast. We can say that replacement parts cost more than a new modern marine toilet.

For offshore sailing, this head location is perfect.

Though the Swan 44 has plenty of good sea berths, she was designed for racing. Adding a double for family cruising would be difficult.

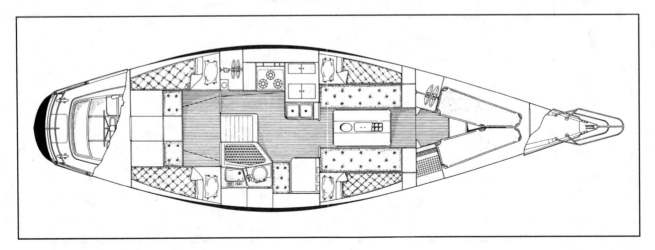

You can come below cold and wet, strip off your foul weather gear, and rinse down without tracking salt water into the living areas of the boat.

The aft cabin was designed more as a sleeping compartment for senior watchkeepers while racing offshore than for long-term living aboard. Twin quarterberths, each 6' 11" long, make good sea berths. For family cruising, many people would prefer a double berth in the aft cabin, but converting this one is a bit of a problem.

The natural location for a double would be the starboard side, but the door to the head makes this impractical without major modifications. Building a larger berth would require sacrificing one hanging locker, a seat, and access from the aft cabin to the head. For long-term cruising for a couple, we'd do it, although a high level of craftsmanship would be required to keep this from looking like an after-thought.

Batteries are located in a fiberglass box on centerline under an unusual locker below the cockpit. A small door at the aft end of this locker, which can best be described as a dog kennel, and is usually used as a catchall, gives access to the steering gear.

There's enough room under the cockpit to mount a belowdecks autopilot, battery charger, and voltage inverter, all of which would be desirable for serious cruising. Since there are no opening hatches in the cockpit giving access to this space, it should remain dry.

Two small hatches overhead, plus a large opening port into the cockpit, provide good light and air to the aft cabin.

In general, interior craftsmanship is excellent, in the Swan tradition. Although the interior tends to be fairly dark and woody, Nautor teak is fairly light in color, which helps avoid the cave-like spaces you often find in a flush-deck boat.

Under Power

All Swan 44s were originally equipped with Perkins 4-108 engines, rated at about 37 horsepower in the normal operating range. The engine is coupled to a Borg-Warner hydraulic reverse-reduction gear, rather than the lightweight mechanical gearbox used today.

This engine is just adequate power for a boat that displaces over 29,000 pounds loaded for sailing. You can expect to cruise at about six knots with good fuel economy—just under one gallon per hour.

Access to the engine for service is reasonable, requiring pivoting up the companionway ladder (it latches to the overhead) and removing the engine box. In the aft cabin, the lower part of the bulkhead removes for servicing the transmission and the back of the engine. You get at the stuffing box by lifting the cabin sole in the aft cabin.

The engine is a tight fit in its well-insulated box. Installing a slightly larger engine when the time comes for replacement might entail rebuilding the box—a minor project.

With the companionway ladder secured to the overhead (it's a head knocker) and the engine box removed, you have sit-down access to the entire engine; there's no excuse for poor maintenance.

A 40-gallon stainless steel fuel tank, giving about a 250-mile range under power, is located below the

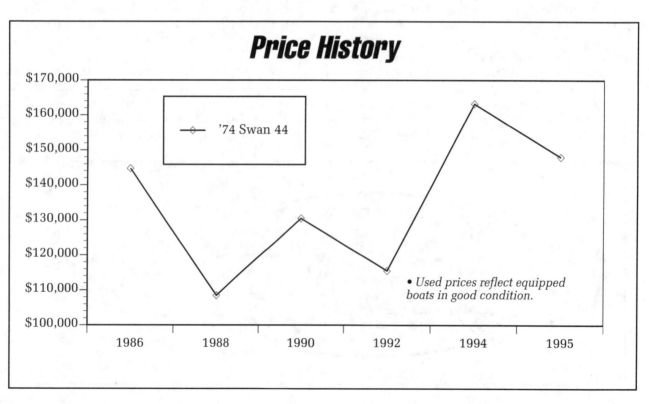

Price History

'74 Swan 44

• Used prices reflect equipped boats in good condition.

cabin sole just forward of the companionway. This is below the vertical center of gravity, smack dab in the middle of the boat. The location could hardly be better to minimize the effect of fuel consumption on the boat's trim.

Under Sail

Sailing performance is excellent. The boat is reasonably fast both upwind and downwind. The PHRF rating of about 84 is some 30 seconds per mile faster than cruiser/racers such as the F&C 44, Alden 44, or Little Harbor 44, although it is slower than a flat-out modern IMS racer/cruiser. The boat is quite competitive under IMS in anything but very light air, where its heavy displacement is a disadvantage.

Over the years, Swan 44s have won more than their share of races. In the 1990 Swan Atlantic Regatta, the unmodified Swan 44 *Temptress* won her class, beating several newer Frers-designed Swan 46s on both elapsed and corrected time, despite being the oldest boat in the fleet.

With a righting moment of about 1,950 foot pounds, this is a very stiff boat, despite a heavy tree trunk of a mast. The original design called for a keel weighing 10,700 pounds, but boats after hull #64 have additional ballast. Typically, Swan 44s have a range of positive stability of 130°. We recommend a range of 120° or higher for ocean racing or cruising.

Both short rig (mast height about 55 feet above deck) and tall rig (mast height about 57.5 feet) were built. For racing or in areas of lighter winds, the taller rig is more desirable, but this is hardly a make or break choice when buying a used boat.

The boat has a big foretriangle, with a 100-percent area of about 540 square feet for the tall rig. This results in a 150-percent genoa of 800 square feet—a large piece of cloth for a small crew to handle. For shorthanded cruising, we'd recommend a genoa of about 135 percent, set on a roller furler. In winds of 10 knots or more, this smaller sail will give comparable performance, and will obviously be much easier to deal with. For racing, the 150-percent genoa is essential for good light-air performance.

The mainsail on the tall rig is about 380 square feet—a comfortable size for a couple to handle, particularly if the boom is modernized.

By today's standards, the rig is old-fashioned. A conservative modern cruiser this size would have a double spreader rig with a mast section of about 6" x 9.5", weighing some six pounds per foot. A contemporary 44-foot IMS racer would have a triple-spreader rig weighing considerably less.

The Swan 44, on the other hand, has a single spreader rig, with a section that is 7" x 10". The big mast section is the result of having a single set of very short spreaders, which allow a tight headsail sheeting angle.

You would have to work very hard to make this mast fall down. Running backstays are standard on the tall rig, but are usually used only when sailing with a storm staysail in very heavy weather.

There is a removable inner forestay, tensioned by a recessed Highfield lever. For offshore cruising, we'd rig it and leave it. Many racers remove the inner forestay entirely. When released, the forestay stows against the mast, wrapping around a fairlead at the base of the mast, held in place by a small tackle on deck. While it's out of the way, you can still trip over the wire when working at the mast.

The deck layout was close to state of the art for racing in its day, but it is not well suited to short-handed cruising.

Originally, the mainsail was hoisted by a self-stowing reel halyard winch. We lived with one of these for years in a state of cautious mutual tolerance without injury, but we've also had one blow up in our face. This type of winch also has a tendency to break your arm if you're not careful when the brake is released, and more than one person has been brained by a free-wheeling handle which got out of control. All in all, the reel halyard winch should be treated with the same respect you'd give an armed hand grenade. In fact, we'd treat it the same way: throw it as far as we can, then duck.

There are twin mast-mounted headsail halyard winches, and deck-mounted spinnaker halyard winches. This is a satisfactory arrangement, although on a modern cruiser you'll probably want self-tailers with low-stretch non-wire halyards.

Cross-linked Barient 35 primaries are mounted at the forward corners of the low deckhouse. For racing, this keeps the headsail grinders out of the cockpit with their weight amidships, but it is a poor location for primary winches on a cruising boat.

You're more likely to use the cockpit-mounted Barient 32 secondaries for genoa sheets when cruising. They are just big enough for a 130-percent genoa, a little too small for a bigger sail or a smaller grinder.

The cockpit, too, is awkward for cruising. The mainsheet traveler spans the cockpit forward of the wheel, and the main is trimmed to a forward-facing winch mounted just below the traveler. This arrangement works as long as there are two people in the cockpit, but it's not so hot for shorthanded sailing.

The cockpit itself is deep and fairly comfortable. There are no cockpit lockers, but the liferaft and propane bottles store under the lift-up helmsman's seat. A lazarette hatch on the afterdeck gives access to under-cockpit stowage for lines and fenders.

A good cockpit dodger is a must for comfortable cruising, but the Swan 44's midships companionway complicates the issue. The companionway is a sliding hatch with no dropboards in the deck forward of the aft cabin. A molded breakwater allows installation of a big dodger, but it is awkward to crawl under the dodger to get below, and the dodger itself is so far forward that it offers protection only for the very front of the cockpit. The helmsman is left at the mercy of the elements.

The major alterations on deck required for cruising would be the replacement of the sail-trimming winches with modern self-tailers, preferably going to bigger secondaries if you can fit them.

We'd also replace the mainsheet traveler and update the boom (early boats may still have roller-reefing booms).

Steering control is less than perfect. As originally designed, the boat has a small, shallow rudder mounted aft of a big skeg. The rudder was quickly found to be too small, and it went through a series of conservative changes. First, the rudder chord was lengthened by four inches. Next, the rudder was deepened by six inches while retaining the original skeg, resulting in a quirky rudder profile and slightly improved handling. In November 1973, the rudder and skeg were redesigned, adding some eight inches of depth to the original rudder.

The new and old skeg/rudder combinations are very similar in appearance. It is easiest to determine which one you are looking at by getting drawings from Nautor and actually measuring the rudder. Of the factory-built rudders, the last design is by far the best, but it is unclear how many boats were built with this configuration.

A large percentage of Swan 44s—usually those that have extensive racing histories—have had rudder, skeg, or afterbody modifications. These range from slight rudder modifications similar to the factory changes, to major alterations to the stern shape, "padding out" of the quarters to effectively increase the boat's sailing length, and any number of skeg/rudder alterations to the thinking of different appendage designers.

For the buyer of a Swan 44, the major concern is more how well the changes were made, rather than just their effect on performance. As a rule, changes have little positive effect on the value of the boat, and if poorly done, can have significant negative impact.

If you're interested in IMS racing, an unmodified early hull would be a good choice, giving you a blank canvas for underwater alteration.

For the more-than-casual racer, naval architect Jim Taylor recommends complete removal of the skeg and rudder, replacing these appendages with a deeper modern elliptical spade rudder having an area equal to about the total of the original skeg and rudder combined.

The Swan 44 *Diane* was modified in this manner, and performance was dramatically improved on all points of sail, according to Taylor.

Because the IMS is fairly weak in handicapping the efficiency of appendages, the improved performance came at very little rating expense.

Even fairly extensive modifications such as these are not too difficult due to the massive construction of the boat. You simply don't have to worry too much about imposing loads the hull is unable to handle.

With the original rudder, maneuvering in close quarters—such as rounding marks when racing—requires careful planning ahead. In addition, you must carry an undesirable amount of rudder angle in heavier air, particularly when reaching. For cruising, these are fairly minor inconveniences. For racing against modern competition, they are significant drawbacks.

Conclusions

There are few production boats of this vintage that can be considered turnkey operations for offshore sailing. The Swan 44 is one of them. Nautor construction is as good as it gets for a production boat, and the S&S design is truly timeless.

Swan 44s vary dramatically in condition and price. Boats that have been raced hard may be cosmetically beat, and worn teak decks can be more than a cosmetic concern. Condition rather than age is far more important in determining the value of any Swan 44, although later boats would be more desirable due to slight improvements in the design.

We have looked at some boats that are unmodifed in layout and equipment, and others that have undergone spectacular upgrading.

Upgrading, of course, is expensive at typical boatyard labor rates of $40 per hour and more, but you'll probably get back more at resale time on this boat than on almost any other.

There's no denying the appeal of Swans in general, and the 44 in particular. Although as a cruiser/racer it is neither fish nor fowl, the boat is a better compromise than most. With an unmodified deck layout and sail handling equipment, the boat is more than a handful for a couple to sail, and while the basic interior layout is good, there are too many berths in the wrong places for extended shorthanded cruising.

Although this boat may not be anyone's ideal cruiser, it is a boat that you can take offshore with complete peace of mind. You don't have to worry whether the hull is strong enough, the furniture will stay attached, the rudder will stay on, or the rig will stay up. The offshore pedigree is there, and the quality is, too.

In today's depressed market for both new and used sailboats, no boat can be considered a good investment in any real sense. But when you look at the cost of a new boat of this caliber, the Swan 44 starts to look like a real blue chip. **• PS**

Morris 44

A rare combination of modern technology and traditional aesthetics, the Morris 44 competes with Hinckley, Alden and Little Harbor.

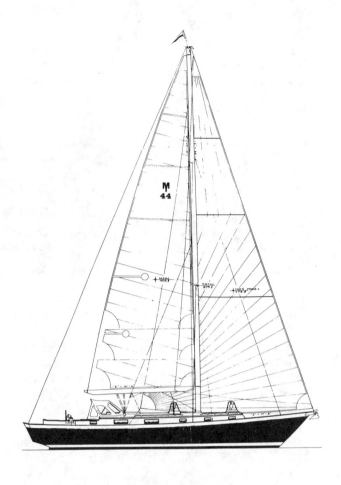

Specifications

LOA	44' 6"
LWL	35' 6"
Beam	13' 0"
Draft	5' 6"
Displacement	23,500 lbs.
Ballast	8,360 lbs.
Sail area	879 sq. ft.

Twenty-three years ago, Tom Morris of South west Harbor, Maine, commissioned Chuck Paine to design his first boat, the 26-foot, flush-decked Frances. Last summer the first Morris 44 left the building that sits at the water's edge at the west end of the harbor. These and the five Paine-designed boats in between illustrate the dynamics of a successful builder-designer relationship. Like most great yards, Morris has chosen to primarily work with one designer, where they can learn each other's likes and dislikes, argue, improve, and develop their ideas together. It requires respect, and Tom and Chuck have that. But Chuck is not a house designer; Morris doesn't build enough boats to justify a full-time person, and a good share of Paine's work is in custom boats.

The Company and the Design

Tom Morris built his reputation with small boats, ranging from the Annie (26'). Leigh (30') and Annie (30'). Somewhere he gave up the tradition of naming his boats after women, calling them simply the Morris 28 or Morris 36 and so on.

Tom is a tall, soft-spoken man with a kind smile, but don't be fooled—he's a keen businessman. Any-one who is still in business after 22 years and nearly 150 boats, has to be. He watches costs. he watches his 22-man crew like an eagle, and he especially watches out for his customer, participating in an intensive commissioning process to make sure everything is right. Everything. After all, these boats are not stamped out *en masse*. They are custom built for each owner.

More properly, we should call them semi-custom. Like Hinckley, Little Harbor and Alden, each boat begins with a standard hull and deck mold, to save design and tooling costs, but from there to the bank, it's up to the buyer, builder and designer to come up with a plan that works for everyone. One or more usual layouts may be offered, but are certainly subject to modification. Fitting out, of course, can have a big impact on the final product. Does the owner want air-conditioning, central heating, electric winches, a huge freezer? Air ducts are best planned prior to construction. If 600 amp-hours of battery capacity are needed, where will the batteries be housed? (On hull #1 of the 44, two batteries were placed in front of the engine, which Morris now says was a mistake because they make bilge inspections

The Morris 44 has traditional good looks with a contemporary underbody; under sail, we could find no particular vices—in fact, she handled beautifully.

difficult.) And if the freezer doesn't fit in the icebox, where does it go? The list goes on—choice of woods (teak, mahogany, cherry, ash?), electronics, even the number of doors to the head. This is what Tom Morris does.

He never really saw himself building a boat this big. His niche was small, quality boats with enduring value. But after the success of the 36, it was probably inevitable. Loyal customers who want to move up will look elsewhere if necessary. Dave and Phyllis Wright were the first to take bait on a 40-footer. Originally planned as a 42 in 1987, it grew as time passed.

In his newsletter, Morris described the design criteria: "In this sailboat we want the capacity to accommodate owners and their guests in two spacious cabins. For comfort and versatility in the choice of cruising grounds there must be the capacity to fit a generator, and a complete complement of cruising equipment and gear; yet she must be easily handled by one or two. And she must be beautiful."

The underbody shows a moderately sized cruising fin with a bulb keel, a skeg-mounted rudder fairly far aft for control, and the propeller shaft exiting through a small stern tube fin to avoid the necessity of a strut and long, exposed shaft. This is a good example of a contemporary performance-oriented cruising boat. It does not have the deep draft of a racer, nor the large wetted surface of a full keel cruiser, just a nicely proportioned compromise.

Paine, who lately has been doing a lot of BOC-type racers, said of the 44 that he was "trying to achieve a very centrist boat, a classic in the best and worst sense, wholesome and forgiving. Not faddish, with very balanced proportions." By "worst" we assume

he means there is nothing particularly unusual about the hull shape, which he described as having "a little more U-shape" than the Morris 36, and being a "little flatter in the stern." The 36 has a displacement/length ratio of 271 compared to the 44's D/L ratio of 255. Other differences include a big rudder and bulbed keel.

Construction

Morris has never liked cored hulls, and though he has offered Airex PVC foam cores on some models he has never built one. He believes solid fiberglass hulls last longer, possess superior abrasion resistance in the event of grounding (because there's simply more glass), are easier to repair, and ultimately hold their value better.

The Morris 44 is built with "longitudinal and transverse stiffeners encapsulated in the final inside laminate supported by the interior monocoque structure bonded to the hull and deck." He calls it "Rib-Core" construction, using 6" balsa for the stringers and luan plywood boards for the bottom transverse floors under the engine and mast. Coupled with biaxial and triaxial fabrics, he says he can reduce the weight of a conventional solid fiberglass hull by 25 percent. A cored hull, he calculates, would save an additional .9 lbs. per square foot of hull laminate, but then he's not building a racer. Additional weight savings are achieved with cored bulkheads (only those that are non-structural), and with hull #1 of the 44, a carbon fiber mast (which, incidentally, gives the boat an incredibly high range of positive stability). Unless lightness is paramount, we like solid hulls, too, and think Morris has taken a very sound approach.

Unlike some builders, who refuse to reveal their lamination schedules, Morris readily offers such information, which in itself gives us a degree of confidence in the integrity of the structure. The general hull laminate consists of 20 mils of NPG gelcoat (28 mils below the waterline), two skins of 3-oz., mat, and 10 lams of 1808 VX and CM 3205 BTI, both unidirectional fabrics with fibers running at right angles in equal number. The woven roving we used to see on most boats has been largely replaced with rovings that are no longer woven; these new fabrics create fewer resin pockets, help achieve a better resin/glass ratio (which Morris works hard at), and virtually eliminate the problem of print-through (where, in the right light, you can see the pattern of the fiberglass through the gelcoat).

The balsa ribs and stringers are reinforced with additional laminates of 3408 triaxial fiberglass, with a third of the fibers running in the direction of the load, as are the keel stub area, skeg, centerline (the hull is molded in halves) and other critical stress points. The deck is cored with 1" end-grain balsa. Bulkheads are tabbed to the hull and deck, which we think is critical for real offshore work. (Many boats with fiberglass headliners can't have the bulkheads glassed to the deck, which allows them to "work" in a seaway, and creak when walking overhead on deck.)

The hull to deck joint is bedded in 3M 5200, through-bolted on 8" centers, and further strengthened by screwing the teak cap rail on alternating 8" centers.

Vinylester resin is used throughout. A growing number of builders are using it for the first lam or two because of its superior resistance to blistering. Morris uses it for all lay-ups because of its superior adhesive qualities (better than polyester, almost as good as epoxy). It adds about $1,000 to the cost of a 44, but worth it, he believes. The end result, we think, is an incredibly strong, stiff hull that barring any unusual events such as collisions should be problem-free for years.

Freshwater tanks (110 gallons capacity) are stainless steel and the 5-gallon diesel fuel tank is aluminum.

Interior

As mentioned earlier, every Morris is a little different, finished to the owner's specifications. The first 44 has the traditional Maine interior with white Formica surfaces trimmed with varnished mahogany. Countertops are Corian, a marble-like plastic.

The list of interior options on Morris' worksheet are revealing: routered drawer pulls, louvered locker doors, mirror with mahogany frame, mahogany soap box holder, galley sink cutting board, rounded corners on bunk tops/fiddles, adjustable bookshelves, etc. The man-hours required to build this sort of cabinet-quality interior, all of which is varnished, is staggering. One quickly realizes why production builders, who are always trying to reduce costs, are forced to preassemble precut wood parts in the shop, drop them into the bare hull and move on to the next job.

The arrangement plan selected by the Wrights

The owners of hull #1 opted for a centerline double berth forward and a private aft stateroom for cruising with friends.

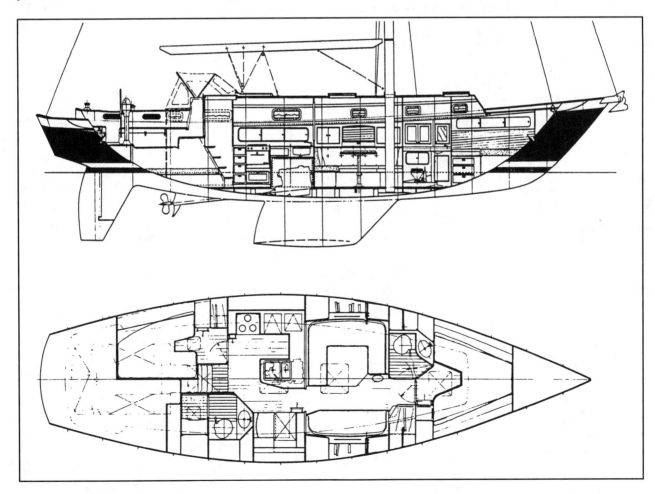

shows a centerline double berth forward, with easy access from both sides. The forward stateroom also has a hanging locker and vanity with sink. Just aft is the U-shaped dinette and opposing settee with bookshelves behind each. The large galley is just aft of the dinette and across the aisle is the navigation station. The head, with separate shower stall, is located in the starboard quarter and a second stateroom in the port quarter area.

Performance

At 22,500 lbs, displacement, the displacement/length ratio of the Morris 44 is a moderate 255. It shows that considerable emphasis was put on performance (without sacrificing too much stowage space, essential for cruising), as does the generous 17.1 sail area/displacement ratio.

So we were not surprised how well the boat moved during our test sail on Narragansett Bay, The boat balanced beautifully, accelerating nicely out of tacks. The helm was light and it seemed to us that the boat responded like a much smaller boat.

Unfortunately we didn't have enough time on the boat to experience it in a variety of wind and sea conditions, but we have no doubt that the 44 will be a pleasure to sail-shorthanded or with crew. We particularly liked the helmsman's seat with rounded corners; there were a variety of positions that felt comfortable, which is important when you spend a lot of time steering.

The auxiliary is a Yanmar 46, which seems right for this boat. It's located under the galley sink, just off centerline, but near the middle of the boat. With good sound insulation, it made just a whisper of noise.

Conclusion

The Morris 44 is a fine way to enter the semi-custom big boat market. We've always admired Chuck Paine's designs for their clean, timeless look. It's hard to find an original way to describe a boat that blends the best of old and new, but if any boat deserves the appellation "modern classic," it's the Morris 44. It's also difficult to find much to nit-pick; Tom Morris and Chuck Paine have succeeded in matching Hinckley, Swan and Alden not only in looks, but quality and performance as well.

1994 base price of hull #2 was $383,000, and while this includes a lot of standard equipment, such as self-tailing winches, roller furling, dodger and ground tackle, clearly you'll be way over $400,000 by the time it's properly fitted out (a varnished interior is a $16,400 option). But, hey, at this level, who's counting? Dave and Phyllis Wright got the boat they wanted at a price they could afford and everybody's happy. **• PS**

Cal 46, 2-46, 3-46

Bill Lapworth's unusual design, with motor sailer accommodations, was ahead of its time.

The early Cal boats were built by Jensen Marine in the old '70s Mecca of fiberglass boatbuilders that was Costa Mesa, California. Columbia and Islander were there, too. For a decade they dominated the burgeoning market for relatively inexpensive, "maintenance-free" boats.

Jack Jensen and designer Bill Lapworth were at the forefront of this revolution, beginning their long association in 1958 with the introduction in 1959 of the Cal 24. The famous Cal 40 sprang from the family tree in 1963, winning the SORC the next. Despite such notoriety as a racer, the Cal 40 and many others in the line were described as good, all-around family boats with modern divided underbodies, relatively light weight, and hence they had an emphasis on performance.

The Cal 46 was introduced in 1967. One reader said he thinks about 10 were built. For several years it was called the Cal Cruising 46. The Cal 2-46, with a redesigned deck, cockpit and interior layout, succeeded it from 1973 until 1976. The Cal 3-46, virtually the same as the 2-46 except for some minor interior changes, was built in 1977 and 1978.

A 1972 profile of Lapworth in *Yachting* magazine said, "A prototype of the Cal Cruising 46, Hale Field's *Fram,* embodying able sailing characteristics with motorsailer cruising comfort, made a circumnavigation of North America (with the help of a train ride from Michigan to the Pacific Northwest)."

David and Beverly Feiges, owners of a Cal 3-46, wrote to us at length about the boat, and in citing the devotion of Cal 46 owners, noted that many have circumnavigated. They added that both Lapworth and Jensen chose the boat as their personal retirement yachts for extended blue-water cruising.

The early Cal boats were built at a time when a handful of big California builders dominated the

Specifications

LOA	45' 6"
LWL	37' 6"
Beam	12' 6"
Draft	5' 0"
Displacement	30,000 lbs.
Ballast	8,000 lbs.
Sail area	784/864 (sloop/ketch)

business. Cal, Columbia (including Coronado), and Islander offered boats from 20 to more than 50 feet. The largest Cal was the 48, modeled more after the highly successful 40. Like some large builders today, such as Beneteau and Hunter, Cal produced two distinct lines—one for racing and short-term cruising, and another for more hard-core cruising. In 1972, Columbia countered the Cal 46 with its Columbia 45 motor sailer, but by most counts it wasn't as successful, nor as pretty.

Today, the Cal 46 stands as a boat that in many ways was ahead of its time, combining as it did a daringly different layout with 270-degree visibility from the deckhouse, a spade rudder and long cruising keel. That they are still revered and sought after comes as no surprise.

Owners' Comments

"We find easygoing days that others think are terrible. Only off the wind in big seas can you work a little. The deckhouse is a bit too high. I have yet to see a boat under 51 feet that can compare to her interior."

—1976 3-46 model in the Caribbean

"Balances well on all points of sail and sea/wind conditions. An outstanding example of a Jensen-built boat."

—1967 Cal 46 model in California

"We have made many minor modifications, including sliding windows, teak sole, roller furling, auxiliary generator, etc."

—1975 Cal 2-46 model in California

"Spade rudder and hull design are excellent. With installation of full roller furling sails, the vessel handles less efficiently, but easily by just me and my wife. We're in our 60s. Most handling at sea can be done from the raised center cockpit, which is dry and comfortable."

—1975 2-46 model in California

The Design

Lapworth certainly knew how to draw a fast hull. Even prior to the fiberglass revolution, he was convinced that light displacement was the way to go. His *Nalu II* won the Transpac in 1959 and his various L-class boats also did well around that time. The Cal 40, as mentioned, won the 1964 SORC.

When it came to designing the ultimate cruising boat, Lapworth wasn't about to settle for a slug. The Cal 46 has a displacement/length ratio of 250, which is considered moderate even today. When in 1973 Robert Perry designed the Valiant 40 with a D/L ratio of 260, many critics said it was too light for offshore work. After numerous, safe circumnavigations, the critics were proven wrong. Of course the Cal 46 is a big boat and when carrying a full load of fuel, water and provisions for cruising, its actual D/L ratio will be higher.

The boat has moderate overhangs by today's standards, though in the 1960s it probably didn't seem so. The spoon bow and carefully proportioned transom balance well. And there is some nice sheer to elevate the bow and keep it drier in bad weather. The deckhouse of the original 46 had large windows and the smallish cockpit was immediately aft of the mast. The coachroof stepped down about midship to the long, windowless cabin trunk, giving it a somewhat awkward appearance.

In the 2-46, the cockpit was pushed aft, the deckhouse windows decreased in size, and windows added to the cabin trunk for a much more handsome and balanced profile.

A sloop rig was the only option until 1973, when a ketch rig was made available. We don't know how many of each were sold, but to our eye, the ketch seems more appropriate to the boat. For cruising, the extra stick enables the crew to sail with "jib and jigger" in high winds, and to fly a mizzen staysail in very light air. Neither rig has a lot of sail area, however. The short rig was mandated by the rela-

tively shoal draft and high center of gravity. It was assumed, correctly, that most owners would find the beefy 85-hp. Perkins diesel the perfect antidote to doldrums and drifters.

One of the more unusual features of the Cal 46 is its large spade rudder. Lapworth wanted to retain some performance features and apparently a keel-hung rudder was anathema to his creed. The keel is quite long, though cut away significantly in the forefoot. It terminates just behind the cabin trunk, leaving space between it and the spade rudder for the propeller, which in the original 46 exits the deadwood horizontally for top efficiency. The Cal 2-46 relocates the engine closer to midships. Both drive the boat at its hull speed of about 8.5 knots with a cruising range of 1,200 miles.

The spade rudder gives the boat better control in tight maneuvering situations than a keel-hung rudder, especially since the keel is so long. The drawback is the potential to snag lines on both the rudder and propeller. Addressing the question, the Feiges' wrote: "It does have a spade rudder, which many people would call a fault in a cruising boat, but considering the advantages, and considering the damaged rudders of all kinds we have seen in boat yards, we'll take our chances with our big beautiful spade."

Draft is shoal at five feet. Clearly this boat isn't going to climb away from a lee shore like an eight-foot draft fin keel racer, but as cruising is its priority, this was a trade-off Lapworth was willing to make. Even the shallow waters of the Florida Keys and Bahama banks won't pose a problem for the Cal 46. And if you need to get to windward in a hurry? Crank up the iron jenny!

Nevertheless, spade rudders do require extra caution, especially in areas where fish nets and lobster pots are prevalent. Indeed, floating lines and logs are a menace worldwide, and the smart skipper will have some plan in mind for the eventuality of cutting free lines or other obstructions.

Construction

The Cal 46, like most early Cal boats, was hand-laid of solid fiberglass using cloth and woven roving. An early brochure states that the hull was engineered for "maximum impact strength," using "compressive strength materials on the outside" and "tensile strength materials on the inside."

The lead ballast was precast in a mold, then lowered into the fiberglass keel cavity and glassed over. The wood bulkheads and structural furniture were fiberglassed to the hull. According to the company's literature, this occurred before removing the hull from the mold, which is highly desirable. Removing the hull before it is fully supported, as some builders do, encourages the possibility of the hull deforming and making the fitting of the deck sloppy. The joint was "bonded together to form a double-thick seam" and "concealed by a decorative rubber or teak rail on the outside, and rendered invisible on the inside by filling, taping, sanding, and painting." The sealant used was 3M 5200 and the joint was through-bolted with 1/4-inch machine screws.

The deck, according to Feiges, was cored with plywood, which structurally is a good material for this application. It is, however, much heavier than end-grain balsa and much more susceptible to far-reaching rot from water leaking through deck fasten-

ers. Interestingly, we have no reports of problems with the plywood. But, if we owned a boat with plywood-cored decks, we'd be certain that all through-deck fasteners were periodically recaulked.

Interior joinerwork is Burmese teak. Overhead panels were covered with vinyl. The sole of some models was plywood supported by 2 x 2s and aluminum angles, with teak and holly over. On other boats, it appears, the soles were fiberglass with carpeting.

The large windows on all models (though their size were progressively reduced after the original 46), are a cause for concern. Most owners mentioned it in completing our Owner's Questionnaire. Not only did they seem weak, but leaked as well. Most owners said they had replaced them with stronger materials or permanently covered them. At the least, some provision for attaching storm shutters should be made.

One owner said the black iron fuel tanks rotted out at 15 years. A 2-46 brochure says the two fuel tanks (totaling 135 gallons) are "10 gauge steel." Water tanks, at least in later models, are stainless steel.

Overall, owners rate the construction of the Cal 46 as excellent. While the smaller Cals may have been

The original Cal 46 had large windows in the deckhouse and just two fixed ports in the cove stripe for the saloon. The head was aft of the saloon, which pushed the engine aft, requiring a V-drive.

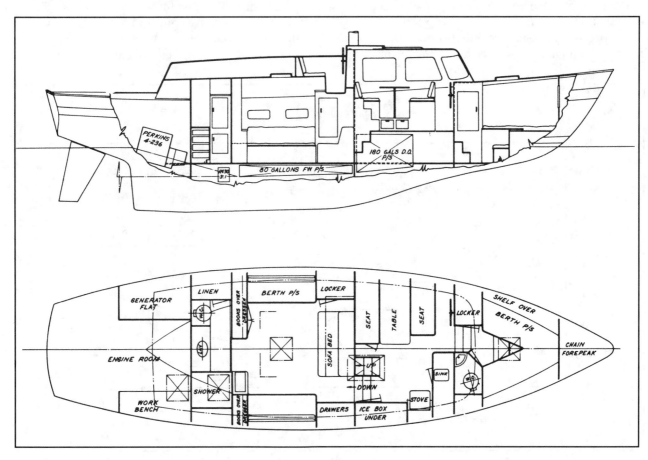

regarded as budget boats, we have repeatedly observed that the larger boats in a company's line are frequently built to higher standards. This appears to be the case with the Cal 46. At the same time, remember that this was a production boat with precut interior components, so don't expect custom quality joinerwork and finish work.

Accommodations

The original Cal 46 featured V-berths forward with its own head compartment, a raised deckhouse with dinette and galley, and a large "living room" aft with settees and a sofa bed. Aft of it is a large head with shower and access to the engine room, which had room for a workbench and generator set. In this configuration, the engine was coupled to a V-drive. Owners of all 46s are unanimous in their praise for the large engine room and its standing headroom. As one owner wrote, when her husband is fixing something on the workbench, "he, and the mess, is not in my hair."

In the 2-46, with its longer deckhouse, two layouts were offered: one with an L-shaped dinette and one with an athwartship dinette with chart table forward of it. Both have sideboard galleys to starboard. The forward and aft cabins were identical, the latter with a double berth and head to port and a settee and hanging locker to starboard. The great appeal of the raised deckhouse is the ability to see through the windows while seated—no need to stand up every time you hear a noise!

An owner of a 3-46 wrote that it doesn't have as roomy an aft cabin, but does have a larger hanging locker and a separate shower stall. It also has a vanity, which she notes contains "a very capacious vegetable bin."

Headroom in the 3-46 is a bit less, and the windows are a bit smaller.

The galley was moved into the passageway aft, making it smaller but more secure. She wrote, "We can hand food directly up into the cockpit through our port located above the sink. The saloon, without the galley, looks huge. There is plenty of storage space, and the largest chart table I've ever seen. At sea, we run a heavy line from the companionway grabrail to the mast to the grabrail on the forward bulkhead, which has always allowed us to move around down below securely." This is an interesting point, as many people don't consider the liability of a large cabin at sea. If one must move from one point to another without benefit of a handhold, there is the danger of being thrown and injured. The safety line is a simple solution, though it won't be as secure a handhold as a solid wood or metal rail through-bolted to a bulkhead.

The center-cockpit layout of the 46 was unusual in the late 1960s and early 1970s. By providing a stateroom at each end of the boat, two couples can cruise in privacy, leaving the dinette "up" all of the time. In a pinch, it could sleep extra crew.

An attraction of the 46 is that neither Lapworth nor Jensen tried to squeeze too much into the hull, leaving plenty of room for stowage and working, which is exactly what a couple or family needs when venturing far from home.

On deck, the cockpit is quite elevated and dry.

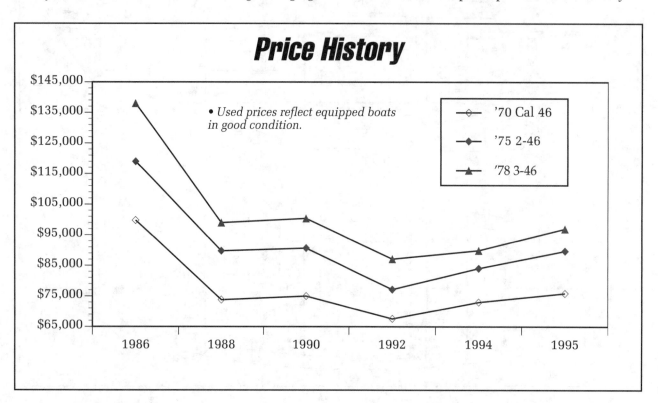

Price History

• *Used prices reflect equipped boats in good condition.*

Legend: ◇ '70 Cal 46　　◆ '75 2-46　　▲ '78 3-46

Consequently, the cabin is tall; some may find it less pleasing to the eye than a lower-profile structure. But that would require higher freeboard, which might impair sailing performance. It may be helpful to install steps somewhere to make it easier to climb from the deck to the coachroof.

The side decks are not as wide as one might expect on a 46-footer, but remember that this design has just 12' 6" beam. And, as is usually the case, the designer wanted to maximize space below. Stepping around the shrouds can be a nuisance, but at least you have a handhold.

The cockpit seats are long enough to sleep on and the backrests are tall.

Performance

As one would expect of a boat with a short rig and shallow keel, sailing performance is not grand prix. The hull, however, is easily driven and the long waterline helps achieve good speeds, especially when the wind is up. Several owners said light-air performance was less than stellar, but then one must remember this boat is part motor sailer, with a large diesel for such exigencies.

On the plus side, the rig fits under the East Coast's Intracoastal Waterway fixed bridges. And, for those venturing to the latitudes of balmy tradewinds, which routinely blow at 20 miles per hour and more, a smaller rig is more easily handled, while still providing sufficient power to reach hull speed. Because it is a bit underrigged, one owner said the boat can carry full sails up to 25 knots of wind.

Most owners rate balance as superb. Several say the boat is a bit tender and that early reefing is a requisite of comfortable passage-making.

Performance under power is good. The Perkins 4-236 diesel is an excellent engine. The reduction gear is 3:1. The standard propeller was a 26-inch, three-blade that gives good power and control. Dragging it around under sail, however, is another matter. A good feathering propeller, such as a Max-Prop, would perceptibly increase sailing speeds as well as improve handling in reverse.

The Feigeses said their 3-46 came with two cutless bearings, counter to Lapworth's drawings. One, they said, was impossible to lubricate or replace. So they removed one and installed instead a pillow block bearing to support the long shaft.

Motor sailers, as critics are wont to say, are neither beast nor fowl, representing either the best of both worlds, or the worst. The Cal 46 represents about a 70/30 split between sail and power. For a blue-water cruising boat, that isn't bad. It sails decently on most points, and has the big diesel necessary not only for long periods of motoring, but also to run all of the convenience items important to long-term comfort at sea, such as refrigeration, inverter, desalinator and electric windlass. Equally important, there's space in the engine room to install all of these goodies.

The original Cal 46 came with a Warner V-drive, which adds expense and complications. We'd prefer the direct drive of the 2-46 and 3-46.

Conclusion

The Cal 46 is a big boat that's sized right for long-distance cruising. It appears that most owners have been devoted to their vessels, and a prospective buyer can only hope that they have maintained them with equal diligence and effort.

Presumably, most of the early bugs have been resolved by now. According to owners, those bugs include large, leaky windows, wooden spreaders, black iron fuel tanks and other items of lesser significance.

The problem, if you're interested, is finding one. Though more than 100 were built, they don't often appear on the market. We'd look for a 2-46 or 3-46, preferring their deck and interior to the original 46. We also like the ketch rig better than the sloop on this design. • **PS**

The FD-12

This German-Dutch designed, Taiwan-built boat is a serious world cruiser with a custom interior.

Sometimes we go to great lengths to look at the boats we evaluate. It might involve a flight across the country to a boatbuilder, or it might be as close as the local boatyard and marina. Evaluating a serious cruising boat, however, often takes a little more effort.

In the case of the Holmann-designed FD-12, we first traveled by air to Belize in Central America, and then by outboard-powered dugout canoe over 20 miles of open ocean to a jungle river in Guatemala. We finally found FD-12 sisterships *Winterhawk* and *Moonshadow* peacefully anchored off the banks of Lake Izabal, 30 miles up the Rio Dulce. We spent a week cruising the FD-12 on this tropical fresh water lake.

Here's what we found out.

The Boat and the Builder

The FD-12 resulted from the collaborative efforts of German designer Eva Holmann and Dutchman Willem Eickholt. In the mid-1970s Eickholt, part owner at the time of Flying Dutchman Yachts, decided to build his dreamboat. A lifelong sailor, he knew he wanted an aft-cockpit, flush-decked cutter of moderate displacement and minimum wetted surface with a fin keel, skeg rudder, canoe stern, and clipper bow. "I also wanted her to be fast. Long passages bore me," says Eickholt. "Last but not least, I wanted her to be pretty in a timeless way."

He chose Holmann, known for her fast, unsinkable cruising designs, to help design the boat.

"Generally speaking, Eva and I got along well," Eickholt told us. "The stormy part of our relationship was Eva's refusal to draw an 'ancient, speed-robbing silly canoe stern,' and my equal determination to have the boat the way I wanted her." But when the German-Dutch war ended, their 'war baby' proved

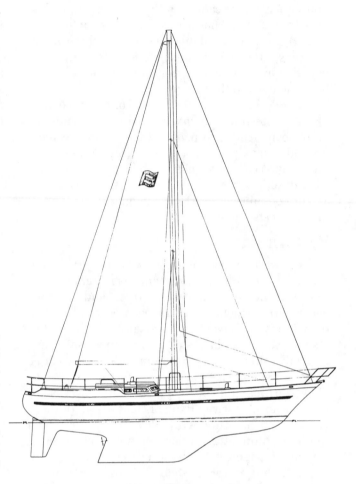

Specifications

LOA	50' 4"
LWL	42' 0"
Beam	14' 3"
Draft	6' 6"/5' 4" (std/Scheel keel)
Displacement	36,000 lbs.
Ballast	14,350 lbs.
Sail area	1,100 sq. ft.

an impressive performer despite, as Eva said, its 'repulsive' stern.

Since the late 1970s, 25 FD-12s have been built at Ta Yang Yacht Building Co. and other yards in Taiwan. In 1980, Eickholt broke away from Flying Dutchman Yachts to form Willem Eickholt and Associates, Inc., and continued to build the FD-12. Each boat is built "on order," and interiors are totally customized.

Construction

The FD-12 hull is a fiberglass sandwich cored with Viny foam, a Japanese product similar chemically to Airex. Viny foam, which is lightweight, and provides both strength and resiliency, also insulates against heat and sound, and helps to eliminate con-

densation within the cabin. A pair of full-length longitudinal stringers and fiberglass and foam floor timbers athwartships provide further stiffening.

Teak plywood bulkheads extend to the base of the hull. A Viny foam wedge insert at the foot of the bulkhead creates a broader bonding angle and distributes transversal stress to prevent bulkhead fractures. The entire bulkhead assembly is fiberglassed to the hull.

The hull-to-deck joint is an inward-turning hull flange, overlapped by the bulwark flange. The joint is through-bolted, filled with Thiokol, coated with fiberglass, and then topped with a teak caprail. This is a strong joint. The owners of the two FD-12s we sailed in Guatemala reported no hull-to-deck joint leaks.

The deck is cored with Philippine fir rather than traditional balsa. Fir is strong, but it's heavy, and puts unnecessary weight high in the boat where you don't want it.

A massive teak rubrail with rectangular-shaped portholes recessed into it offers some protection to the midsections of the hull. However, installing portholes in topsides is always difficult, and both boats in Guatemala had experienced porthole leaks. Leaks in deckhouse ports are simply an annoyance. In a hull they can be dangerous and in extreme cases can lead to loss of the vessel.

The chainplates are stainless steel straps that extend through the deck. Four chainplates (two port and two starboard) bolt to bulkheads, but two chainplates (one port, one starboard) bolt to fiber-

glass knees. The knees are hefty, but several owners of FD-12s report their decks have lifted due to a knee-to-hull bond failure. (On the first dozen or so hulls, Ta Yang Yacht Building Co. gelcoated the hull interior before glassing in the knees. In later hulls, knees were properly bonded to the bare hull.)

To form the mast step, an aluminum H-beam through-bolts to a floor timber, and the mast sits in an oval-shaped aluminum weldment that bolts to the mast step. This arrangement provides a strong platform and eliminates corrosion problems that occur if a mast is stepped in the bilge.

The FD-12's underbody has a cruising fin with a long run and a full skeg. The keel is ballasted with cast lead and molded in one piece with the hull. For careening purposes the hull sits squarely on the fin and skeg to avoid damaging the rudder.

The rudder rides on two bearings, the upper one supporting the steering system. To protect the rudder and the steering mechanism, the skeg is designed to break away in case of a collision. This is also a handy feature for those planning to cruise shallow waters where sooner or later even the best sailors usually run hard aground.

There's approximately 200 cubic feet of polyurethane foam wedged into the bow, stern, keel and other nooks and crannies on the FD-12 to provide positive flotation. Positive flotation is rarely built into a cruising boat because it consumes so much space, but we would definitely consider it if we were building the ultimate cruiser.

Holmann comments: "Most composite boats only

need a bit of help to give them positive flotation, but the amount of flotation must be carefully calculated. If you miss it by one cubic foot, you'll have a very expensive sinker, but it *will* sink."

Size of water and fuel tanks varies depending on interior layout, but all FD-12s carry ample water and fuel for long-distance cruising. One FD-12 we sailed carried 250 gallons of water, the other 150. Fuel is stored in two 125- to 150-gallon black iron fuel tanks. Black iron tanks tend to corrode. Aluminum tanks are a better choice for storing diesel. Water tanks are stainless steel, but the metal is an inferior grade, and the tanks we inspected were rusty.

Performance Under Power

The engine is installed underneath the floorboards at the bottom of the companionway in its own separate bilge. This type of installation keeps the engine weight low where you want it. Spilled engine oil is confined to a small area. The separate bilge also protects the engine from water that might enter the other two bilges.

On the downside, the engine is difficult to access. The front of the engine, located under floorboards inside a galley locker, makes it particularly difficult to change or tighten belts, etc. The rear of the engine is more accessible, but overall it's a poor set-up for a big 50-footer.

The FD-12 is so customized that you're liable to find three different engines on three different boats. In Guatemala, one FD-12 was fitted with an 80-hp Ford Lehman diesel with a two-bladed prop, the other a Lehman-Peugeot 4D61 with a three-bladed prop.

The 64-hp Lehman/Peugeot was noisy, vibrated excessively, and overheated if driven over 2,000 rpm. We'd recommend a larger, more reliable engine. The 80-hp Ford Lehman propelled the FD-12 along nicely, but a similar-sized Perkins might be a better choice for marine use. Still, the FD-12 hull is easily driven and both engines gave us a speed of 6 to 6 1/2 knots through the water in flat seas. Like most sailboats, the FD-12 tends to have a mind of its own in reverse, although one *PS* reader reported that it steered well in reverse with a Max Prop. With a 250- to 300-gallon fuel capacity, you can easily expect a 1,000-mile cruising range under power.

Performance Under Sail

With its relatively fine entry, 42' waterline, and efficient underbody, the FD-12 is a high-performance, blue-water cruiser. It's also a hefty boat (36,000 lbs. displacement), and a comfortable passagemaker under most points of sail. However, like many heavy-displacement double-enders, this boat rolls in heavy air downwind.

The FD-12 is powerful on a reach or broad reach in winds over 15 knots, and performs respectably to weather. It loses speed in light air, but in 15- to 20-knot winds, you can count on averaging at least six knots under sail.

The FD-12 is cutter-rigged with the mast stepped fairly well aft. There's a quick release on the inner forestay to accommodate large headsails, but we doubt you'll use it often. Working sails consist of a Yankee, main and staysail, but in winds under 15 knots a roller furling genoa comes in handy. The boat we sailed also carried a cruising spinnaker which the owners reported using on long passages even when shorthanded.

Double spreaders, hefty 7/16" wire rigging, swage fittings, and Ronstan turnbuckles provide a strong rig. The two forward babystays have a quick release lever so they can be led aft when using a spinnaker pole.

Instead of using running backstays to take the load of the inner forestay, the FD-12 rig incorporates intermediates which lead just behind the aft lower shrouds. The intermediate angle is so acute that the intermediate must be large in diameter and strongly tensioned to provide support. This adds a lot of compressive load to the mast. Intermediates can also

---

There's no such thing as a standard interior in an FD-12. Every one is unique, but all are designed for comfortable, long-distance cruising.

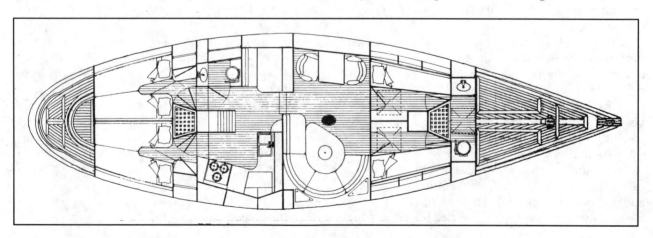

cause unnecessary chafe on the mainsail downwind. Running backstays would be more effective.

The FD-12 is a big 50-footer, but it's well-balanced and easy to handle. Winches on the boats we sailed were self-tailing Barients and Meissners. The Barients were up to par, but the owners complained that the Meissners failed often, and parts were difficult to find and replace.

On Deck

The FD-12's roomy, flush teak deck provides a stable sailing platform. The cockpit is efficient for sailing and safe for passagemaking. It's not too big, has decent cockpit drains, and high coamings that impart a snug, secure feeling, especially offshore.

The steering wheel is hand-laminated teak and spruce. A mainsheet traveler spans the cockpit well just forward of the wheel, and there's an alternative mainsheet arrangement on top of the cabin house. Genoa sheet winches are mounted outboard of the main coamings just forward of the traveler. These winches are well located, but one of the stanchions gets in the way if you are beating to weather and need to ease the sheets to fall off downwind.

Otherwise, the stanchions are strong. They are installed with backing plates and have side braces that bolt to the caprail. To provide a safe way to climb aboard a boat with extremely high freeboard, there are two stainless steel boarding ladders (one port, one starboard) that fold in half over the lifelines.

There were three Bomar hatches forward on one FD-12 we sailed, and one custom teak hatch and Dorade vents on the other. The teak hatch is pretty, but Bomars are easier to maintain, and provide more ventilation.

The aluminum mast is made by Yachtspar of New Zealand and painted with polyurethane. Two stainless steel mast pulpits act as supports when working at the mast, and provide a place to secure gear and lines.

There's a stainless stemhead fitting with double anchor rollers forward. On early hulls this fitting was too flimsy; on later hulls, they strengthened the anchor roller fitting, and also added an extra support strut to the bow pulpit.

The entire forepeak (6' long and 3' to 5' wide) of the FD-12 is designed for storage. You can enter the forepeak cargo hold by opening two huge hatches cut into the deck aft of the anchor chain windlass. These hatches are *extremely* heavy—so heavy they must be tied to the lifelines so you won't lose a finger (or worse) if they slam shut accidentally. They are well-gasketed, but it's disconcerting to see such big holes cut in the foredeck.

The forepeak locker is great for storing sails but it's cavernous and it's sometimes difficult to find things. Also, the anchor chain drops onto a shelf inside this locker, and excess chain can easily get snagged amongst all the rubble.

There are three bronze hawseholes—port and starboard—cut into the bulwarks forward, aft and amidships. They are well-placed but a little under-sized.

Scuppers on the FD-12 do not drain overboard. Instead, hoses are attached to scupper drains and led to through-hull fittings located just above the water-

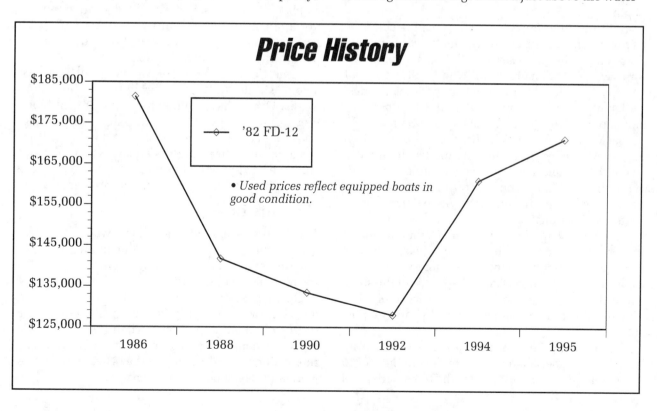

Price History

'82 FD-12

• *Used prices reflect equipped boats in good condition.*

line. This arrangement prevents water from staining the topsides, but we don't like unnecessary through-hull fittings at the waterline.

Owners report that chainplate covers must be rebedded periodically to prevent deck leaks. Stainless weldments on the FD-12 tend to weep rust, and we question the quality of the stainless used throughout the boat. (Taiwan boatbuilders have a reputation for building with inferior stainless. For some reason, the importance of using superior metals is not a concept they readily understand.)

The two FD-12s in Guatemala both had Fleming Major vane gears which were not sensitive enough in light air. A Monitor would be more effective.

Belowdecks

There is no standard arrangement belowdecks. Every FD-12 has been individually customized to meet the buyer's needs. With such a wide possibility of interiors available, we restrict our comments to *Winterhawk* (hull #19), the boat we sailed in Guatemala.

Belowdecks, *Winterhawk* is incredibly spacious—so spacious that with five crewmembers aboard we never felt cramped or hemmed in. Furniture is built of plywood with a grooved teak veneer. The cabin sole is teak and holly. Bulkheads in staterooms and heads are white Formica, and a number of large round mirrors bolted to bulkheads impart a sense of light and space.

Ten bronze opening deckhouse ports, in addition to hatches, provide adequate ventilation, but you might want to install fans or an extra hatch in the aft cabin.

Indeed, *Winterhawk* has all the creature comforts of home. There are two heads, one forward and one across from the galley, each with hot and cold pressure water and manual fresh and saltwater foot pumps. Both heads have showers with teak grates, and sumps which pump overboard. On our cruise, hot showers flowed freely thanks to a Balmar ASC Aqua Master watermaker. (Driven by a Northern Lights 5kw generator, this AC model desalinates about 19 gallons per hour, and completely eliminates the need to take on water from shore, which is especially helpful in countries where the quality of water is questionable.)

A large L-shaped galley on the starboard side of the doghouse has two deep double sinks, plenty of storage, and enough counter space for two people to cook at the same time. The lockers behind the stove are difficult to reach, but there are plenty of additional galley drawers, as well as cubbyholes for pots and pans.

A huge icebox and freezer with AC and DC refrigeration keeps perishables cold, but insulation could be increased all around to make the box smaller and more efficient. We had difficulty adjusting the knobs on the Hillerange propane stove, and given our druthers we'd opt for a Force 10. Two 20-lb propane tanks are appropriately stored under the helmsman's seat in a vented locker.

The nav station, across from the galley, is comfortable with good working space for chartwork, ample stowage for charts and tools, a red flourescent light for night work, and ample room for installing electronics. FD-12s come standard with four 200-amp-hour batteries.

Winterhawk has four Prevailer 8Ds, which the owner praises highly. The electrical system includes 110-volt and 12-volt service. Wiring is supposedly to U.S.C.G. regulations, but the electrical connections for the masthead wiring on *Winterhawk* are in the bilge where they are vulnerable to water damage. Two electric bilge pumps backed up by a manual bilge pump are adequate for emergency bilge pumping.

The saloon has a large U-shaped dinette to starboard and a single settee to port. A Dickinson diesel stove sits amidships for heating the cabin in colder climes. Storage for books throughout the saloon is plentiful, and there are big lockers for canned goods underneath the settees.

Forward, port and starboard, are two almost identical cabins. Each has a single berth with teak leeboards, plenty of drawers and two louvered hanging lockers.

The aft cabin is a large owner's stateroom with a double and single berth and a small night table with mirror. Again, there are plenty of drawers and several hanging lockers. Some might object that there is no head in the aft cabin, but for offshore passagemaking a head in the doghouse by the companionway ladder makes more sense.

Some FD-12s, like *Moonshadow* (hull #2) have layouts similar to *Winterhawk* but with a few more berths. Others have completely different interiors. (For example, hull #7, has the saloon in the doghouse, and the galley in the saloon.) However, all are designed to cruise long distances in comfort, and you'd be hard-pressed to find a 50-footer with more room to accommodate your whims and fancies.

Conclusion

The FD-12 is a moderately fast, well-appointed, comfortable world cruiser. In our minds, positive flotation in a cruising boat is a big plus. We'd like to see more boats built with it.

On the negative side, corroding weldments on deck hardware and rusty fuel and water tanks are a source of potential problems. High freeboard and a canoe stern make for a safe, dry boat, but it would be interesting to see drawings of the FD-12 with an Eva Holmann-designed reverse transom. **• PS**

Santa Cruz 52

Bill Lee's ULDB has been reinvented as a performance cruiser.

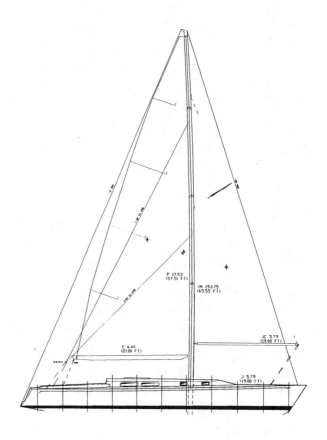

Twenty years after Bill Lee built his first boat in a chicken coop on a hill overlooking the Pacific near Monterey Bay, his designs are still making an imprint on the sailing world. His most recent boat is the Santa Cruz 52, a 53-foot performance cruiser that went into production in 1992. After two years on the water, owners testify that the new boat combines the best of Lee's go-fast methods with ease of handling and creature comforts that rival cruising boats known for their amenities. Although the company has experienced a recent reorganization, the production line is full.

The Man and His Company

Lee, a Cal Poly engineering graduate, was a neophyte boatbuilder when he declared that "fast is fun" (a marketing slogan) and began designing performance boats. His first notable design was the Santa Cruz 27, which incorporated a beamy hull with lightweight construction methods. The boat, in today's vernacular, would be considered a pocket rocket.

By 1977, he'd designed and built Merlin, the first Lee 70, which set a record in the TransPac on her first Pacific crossing, earning him the nickname "The Wizard." Merlin was still setting records four years ago when she won the Victoria-Maui race. Downwind performance was achieved to a great extent by its ultra light displacement, hence the phrase ULDB (loosely defined as having a displacement/length ratio below 100).

Between 1974-1994, five different boats were hatched in the coop, all of which share the same pedigree as Merlin. Bill Lee Yachts produced 140 Santa Cruz 27s, 14 40-footers, 29 50-footers, and 19 70s, the last of which was commissioned in time for the 1993 TransPac. The boats hold their value in the used marketplace so well that 50s still sell for more

Specifications

LOA	53' 0"
LWL	46' 6"
Beam	14' 0"
Draft (deep/shoal)	9' 0"/6' 0"
Displacement	21,000 lbs.
Ballast	9,850 lbs.
Sail area	1,327 sq. ft.

than their original prices.

By 1991, the Wiz concluded that the market for large, grand prix racers was deteriorating, but that there was room for a performance cruising yacht. As a result, he began design work on the 52 with Bob Smith, a veteran architect who'd been providing consulting services since 1988. Before relocating to the West Coast after a stint with Bruce Farr's office in Annapolis, Smith had been responsible for numerous racing and cruising designs, including the Beneteau 52f.

Eighteen months later, the tooling for the Santa Cruz 52 was completed and hull #1 started down the line, bow first. Since encountering a blistering problem with a 27 that had inadvertently moved down the line stern first, the pointy end is always aimed at the coop's swinging doors.

In July 1994, the company declared bankruptcy. Apparently there was a dispute between Lee and the owner of an IMS 72-footer under construction, and Lee found himself faced with the possible seizure of the company by officers of the court. In response, he filed Chapter 7 and the doors of the company were locked, seemingly for the last time.

When the dust settled several months later, John DeLaura emerged as temporary owner of the company. The owner of the Lee 70 Silver Bullet, DeLaura had a SC52 halfway down the production line at the time of the filing, so he bought the company to avoid losing his investment. With the completion of hull #7, he sold the company to Paul Ely, who was also a potential customer. A Silicon Valley venture capitalist, Ely saw long-term potential in the market, so he reorganized the company as Santa Cruz Yachts. Lance Brown, who had been overseeing production of the boats, returned to reassume that role.

Lee, now the ex-officio dean of the ULDB school, operates as an off-site consultant, while Smith continues as resident architect. Sadly, the unfinished 72-footer sits in a pasture while its new owner attempts to sell it to a Hollywood studio as a prop in a demolition scene.

The Design

The SC 52 became a 53-footer as a result of Lee and Smith tinkering with the bow entry and coachroof in an attempt to improve appearance without compromising performance. Consequently, it has finer lines than the 50, to which it is most often compared, though it is 2 feet beamier at 14 feet. Displacement is 21,000 pounds, of which 9,850 pounds is in the keel, giving it a high 47-percent ballast-displacement ratio. The IMS Stability Index (derived from the limit of positive stability measurement) is 121, just above the 120 threshold we have long advocated as a target for safe, offshore sailing.

Smith incorporated some elements of the 70's keel design, intended to increase lift and reduce drag. The keels are manufactured by Mars Metal in Ontario, Canada.

The standard rig is a tapered triple-spreader section that towers 64-feet above the deck, 4 feet taller than the 50. The 52 carries 750 square feet of sail in the main, 577 in the working jib, 1,000 in a 149-percent genoa.

Robert Mann, who sold a Santa Cruz 40 to purchase hull #2, said "She goes to weather with the 70's," and is a vast improvement over the 50. "She's a hunter," he said, referring to a characteristic he defines as "more pointing ability and increased directional stability on any point of sail."

Owners who anticipate sailing in light winds have opted for a 3-foot taller aluminum mast section; a few have paid the dear premium for a carbon fiber spar—about $40,000.

Navtec discontinuous rod rigging is standard equipment, as are running backstays. During our test sails, we noted that runners are used both to improve sail shape and to avoid mast pumping in heavy, choppy seas.

Lee added a cruising touch, a swim platform on the stern for easy access to the cockpit through the wide-open transom.

Construction

While construction methods employed at Santa Cruz Yachts focus on keeping weight to a minimum, Smith's design specifications require that the boat be built to ABS standards (though in and of itself this doesn't doesn't guarantee quality, as ABS requirements occasionally have been found wanting, especially in offshore conditions). Following the reorganization, the same experienced crew that had been doing 30-day hull lay-ups returned to the company.

The outer skin is comprised of combinations of 17- and 18-ounce Nytex and Collins E-glass laid bi-directionally and vacuum-bagged over 3/4" Select Baltek in sections below the waterline, and CK57 balsa above. The same pattern is repeated on the inner skin, which yields a 1-1/8" hull thickness. The inner skin forward of the mast is reinforced with a Kevlar collision mat that extends 12" above the waterline. The cabin top is cored with 1" Baltek, though a carbon fiber deck is optional.

To increase strength at stress points at the mast step, 1" thicknesses of solid glass run across the boat from rail to rail, intersecting bi-directional layers on the floor to distribute loads. Similar strengthening occurs on other load areas induced by the backstay, mainsheet traveler, steering pedestal, ports and hatches, and on the centerline, where the keel bolts are bedded. The hull-deck joint is sealed with AME 4000 vinylester resin putty and stainless fasteners on 4" centers. NPG blister-resistant gelcoats are used.

The elliptical rudder blade is constructed of Aerotek unidirectional carbon fiber bonded to a hollow, fiber-wound carbon rudderpost. The rudders are made by Advanced Composites.

Interior

Once popped from the mold, three pans that define interior spaces are bonded to the hull with two layers of 6" bi-directional glass at each intersection of the hull and pan. The only area of the interior that is inaccessible is beneath the forward shower stall; satisfactory access elsewhere addresses one of our major complaints about many pans and liners.

The master stateroom is a roomy area in the forepeak separated from the saloon by solid wood doors. The stateroom has a double berth, settee, hanging locker and storage areas, plus full head with separate shower stall. The chain locker is forward of a watertight bulkhead in the bow.

The saloon includes a port settee that doubles as a berth, a table with seating for seven, a settee to starboard, two pilot berths, a nav station and galley.

The galley is equipped with a double sink, utensil drawers, 8-cubic-foot ice box insulated with 4" of foam, a Force 10 three-burner LPG stove with oven and broiler. A nice touch is a waste bin that is accessed through the counter top. There's plenty of storage in cabinets behind the stove, which can be modified to accommodate a microwave. A refrigerator/freezer and water maker are optional.

The nav station, located opposite the galley, has plenty of elbow room. Storage in the chart table is supplemented by three built-in drawers. Video displays, GPS, VHF, weatherfax, and ham radio are located on panels at eye level; the panels are easily accessible as they are secured by piano hinges.

One of the boats we inspected had been retrofitted with electronics by a local electrician, which served to highlight the manufacturer's attention to detail. The builder's wiring was neatly installed, including extra wire for drip loops and heat-shrunk numbers for identification purposes. In contrast, the retrofit was ragged.

The companionway doubles as an H-shaped structural bulkhead. A double berth, pipe berth and storage locker are located in the starboard quarter. The insulated engine compartment is located amidships, and a second head is aft of the galley. Large storage areas in the port quarter and aft of the engine are accessed from belowdecks or through the port cockpit lazarette. Though few changes to interiors are possible (another drawback of pans), one owner reduced weight in the ends by eliminating the forepeak accommodations and head, replacing them with pipe berths in the stern.

The interior has less wood below than most cruising boats, but teak battens on the hull, trim on cabinetry, a teak and holly sole and wood veneers on the bulkheads are tasteful accents to a light environment created by white gelcoat surfaces. Tiny red strip lights under the cabinetry illuminate the sole.

Brown told us that the decision to build for the cruising market necessitated a commitment to improve the interior. Two weeks are spent fairing the inside of the hull before the interior is installed so that areas not covered by the pan are neat and smooth, even in storage areas. The wood joinery compares favorably to higher priced yachts. One owner opted for a leather interior, a $7,000 extra.

Deck Layout

The SC52's cockpit is laid out to facilitate easy operation of the boat. Long, angled cockpit coamings offer comfortable backrests, and Lee's trademark drink holders are built into the deck mold. Six winches are located in the cockpit to trim sheets, guys and the running backstays. Halyards, Cunning-

Two interior plans are available. The one shown has a private stateroom aft to starboard and a second head to port. An alternative layout, more for racing, has two pipe berths both port and starboard.

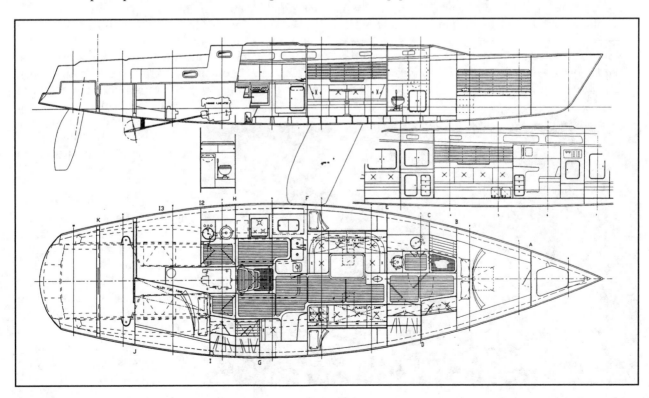

ham, and spinnaker pole controls run aft through sheet stoppers to four winches mounted on the coachroof that can be handled by one person. Winches and most deck hardware are supplied by Harken, though Lewmar winches are available. Mainsheet controls on new boats are in a double-block system on a Harken traveler in the cockpit sole that leads to secondary winches, an improvement over the first boats produced.

With crew and guests forward of a 5' wheel, she is driven effortlessly from a position on the rail, or while standing in the middle of the cockpit, where toerails are built into the sole. The engine control panel, and Navtec controls for the backstay adjuster, flattener and vang are within reach of the helmsman. A propane tank located in a locker to port is covered by a canvas bag that doubles as a sheet holder.

While most sailors will use the starboard lazarette to store fenders, dock lines and cleaning supplies, it is large enough for a six-man life raft. The shore-power cord connects to a plug on the inside of the lazarette.

The bow provides for the below-deck installation of a roller furling drum and a platform below deck for an anchor windlass.

Performance

Based on conversations with two owners and our firsthand experience sailing in two regattas, we'd say the 52 may cut a wide swath through the performance cruising fleet.

Dick Rosic sold a Mason 53 on which he'd logged 40,000 cruising miles, including three TransPacs, before purchasing hull #6 a year ago. Primarily a gunkholer who sails shorthanded in 5-12 knot South-

The Santa Cruz 52 represents the new ownership's attempt to broaded the appeal of its racing line to the performance cruising market.

ern California breezes, he was attracted to the SC52 by its responsiveness and the fact that she's easily handled. He said, "Gear on the boat is smaller. Everything about the Mason is big and heavy, cumbersome. Because there's less load on the 52, she's easier to sail when I'm single-handing. The woodwork is the same quality as the Mason, but requires less maintenance."

Because his plans include extended cruising, he opted for a taller mast, roller furling, an electric winch on the main halyard, and a fully battened mainsail with Harken batcars. His only criticism: A need to increase the capacity of the freshwater accumulator tank.

Mann, by comparison, traded up to a boat that he said "allows me to participate in my own safety." Once the owner of a traditional cruiser he purchased in Europe and sailed across the Atlantic, Mann said he wanted a boat that could be safely and easily handled in a storm by a crew of two.

"We wallowed in the North Atlantic in a heavy displacement boat, and were at the mercy of the storm. With this boat we have better motion in the seas, and we can shorten sails and surf in front of the waves, instead of being overtaken by them," he said.

Mann clearly enjoys ocean sailing, adding that his SC52 "sails downwind at 16 knots in 20 knots of wind." On a recent trip down the California coast, he sailed under a reefed main and jib in 45 knots of wind "and the boat was perfectly balanced, with no rudder stall." Top speed: 20 knots.

He added a three-bladed feathering propeller to the turbo-charged Yanmar 62 horsepower diesel, which delivers 9-10 knots at 2,800 rpm.

We sailed with Marda Phelps aboard hull #5, a replacement for a 42-foot IOR racer, in two Puget Sound regattas in differing weather conditions. Phelps' major concession to racing was a taller mast, so for the most part race preparation is a matter of removing cruising gear and cushions, and replacing the teak and holly sole boards with plywood substitutes so we wouldn't damage the varnish.

Racing in 12-20 knot winds against a fleet of "50-raters," including several SC 50's, we won the regatta easily, despite a handicap that appeared to favor the older boats. The SC52 was easily handled on short buoy races with a crew of 11. It is responsive, goes to weather well, and really stretches its legs on heavy air downwind legs.

The second regatta was sailed in moderate 5-10 knot winds, and we struggled to a second-place finish, suffering under an adjustment to the handicap.

Under IMS handicapping, three of the boats had general purpose handicaps of between 503 and 511; West Coast PHRF handicaps are 12-15, which may penalize those boats with tall masts in light air races. Cruisers of all ilk, however, should be pleased to go to weather at 5-6 knots in 6-8-knot breezes.

Conclusion

Base price of the 52 is $375,000, to which an additional $50,000 will be spent on sails, instruments, and a spinnaker package. For comparison, a J/44 has a base price of about $257,000, and a J/160 (52' 7" LOA) about $425,000.

In our experience, moderately priced boats marketed as "dual-purpose performers" tend to reflect compromises in performance or amenities, but that doesn't seem to be the case with the SC 52.

Unlike boatbuilders that suffer cash shortfalls and become historical reference points, Santa Cruz appears to have a solid future. Hulls #9 and #10 are in production. Compared to similarly-sized cruisers, the 52 is a moderately priced, sturdily constructed, well-appointed yacht that benefits from a 20-year design evolution. Cruisers will travel quickly and in comfort. With proper preparation, racers should find themselves at the top of the fleet in long-distance or buoy races. In either configuration, while the crew is trimming a chute and the boat is hitting 16-18 knots downwind, meals can be prepared in a spacious area while the off watch sleeps in comfort. In this case, there doesn't seem to be a compromise between "fast is fun" and "going in style."　　**• PS**

Deerfoot 61

Steve Dashew's and Ulf Rogeberg's world cruiser is fast, efficient, innovative—and very, very expensive.

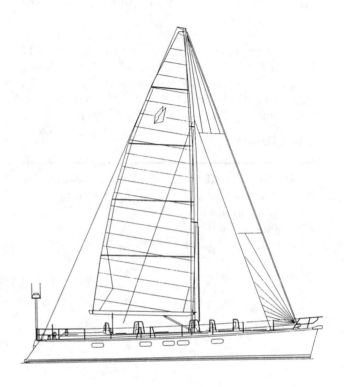

There is no doubt about the Deerfoot 61's purpose in life. This boat is made for long-distance cruising. "We'd sailed thousands of miles on a 50' foot CCA-designed ketch and like most liveaboards we dreamed of the perfect yacht," says Steve Dashew, author of the *Offshore Cruising Encyclopedia*. "We never realized this dream would end in a boatbuilding business."

Dashew built the first Deerfoot, a 68-footer, in New Zealand in 1980. Subsequently, several more Deerfoots, including one for himself, were built in New Zealand and South Africa. "We soon found there was a void in the sailboat market for efficient sailing vessels designed not by the illogical biases of a racing rule, or by concepts thought up by marketing experts," said Dashew.

Since 1980, 16 Deerfoots, ranging in size from 58 to 74 feet have been built. "Four of our fiberglass boats have been built at Scandi Yachts in Finland because they do the best fiberglass work," says naval architect Ulf Rogeberg who worked with the Dashews to create the Deerfoot designs. "The aluminum boats have been built at Walsted's in Denmark."

In 1986, the Dashews, overwhelmed by the size of the Deerfoot project, sold the business to Jim Jackson and Christine Jurzykowski, owners of the 74' aluminum Deerfoot ketch, *Maya*. Jackson, president and executive director of Fossil Rim Wildlife Center, a 2,900-acre wildlife reserve in Glen Rose, Texas, continues to build Deerfoots in the Dashew tradition. Building headquarters have recently moved from New Zealand to Able Marine Inc. in Trenton, Maine.

The Concept

The Deerfoot concept is based on three principles: efficiency, safety, and comfort. "The key is to have a

Specifications

LOA	61' 6"
LWL	57' 6"
Beam	14' 6"
Draft	6' 3"
Displacement	48,200 lbs.
Ballast	16,500 lbs.
Sail area	1,180 sq. ft.

hull which allows you a nice interior while carrying the weight of the boat in the most efficient manner," says Dashew.

Ulf Rogeberg, who previously worked with Paul Elvstrom in Denmark designing 12-meters, explains: "We have tried to create a canoe-shaped hull that is easily driven, a hull with a fine entry angle, narrow waterlines and easy bilges. We have further tried to distribute volume so that the longitudinal center of buoyancy does not move aft when the boat heels. If a boat heels over symmetrically, if its stern doesn't kick up and the bow doesn't bury itself, you'll have better stability, steering control, and performance downwind."

A fine entry angle and a long, narrow hull also reduce drag and provide comfort and efficiency upwind and reaching. With an easily-driven hull, the Deerfoot's rig can be substantially shorter than is needed on a beamy boat with a short waterline. A smaller rig means more stability, less sail changing, less work for a shorthanded crew, and a more comfortable ride.

How does the long, narrow hull affect the interior? While short, fat boats have their beam concentrated amidships, the Deerfoot's relatively narrow beam is carried further forward and aft. This means there's a lot of storage space in the bow and stern. Amidships, the Deerfoot appears spacious because there are few bulkheads, and ceilings are kept void of bookshelves or lockers.

Construction

The Deerfoot's hull, deck and bulkheads are a fiberglass laminate cored with one inch Baltek end-grain balsa. The laminate schedule is unidirectional roving and mat laid up with vinylester resin to resist osmotic blistering. Although balsa is a strong, light core material, a completely water-resistant composite core like Airex seems preferable.

Reinforced with two longitudinal stringers and 13 athwartships stringers made of fiberglass, the hull is strong. There's also extra fiberglass around the mast, and at the turn of the bilge and bow area in case of a collision. The hull-to-deck joint is an inward-turning hull flange overlapped by the bulwark flange. The joint is through-bolted, coated with fiberglass and topped with a teak toerail.

The Deerfoot 61 keel, a NAACA foil fin, is a steel weldment with lead ballast encapsulated at the base. Above the ballast compartment, the keel is divided into three tanks—two for water (140 gallons) and one for fuel (160 gallons). A sump (with bilge pump) divides the water and fuel tanks. Both fuel and water tanks are fitted with Tank Tender pressure gauges for sounding the tanks. The water tanks have an inspection plate on the outside of the keel.

Storing fuel and water in the keel has a number of advantages. First, it gives the Deerfoot 61 a moderately high ballast ratio (about a third of the Deerfoot's weight is in the keel). This lowers the center of gravity and improves stability and windward performance. It also means you have more storage space under seats and bunks. On the down side, there is no way to inspect the tanks from inside the hull, and the water and fuel supply could be jeopardized if your keel is damaged.

Made of aluminum with a six-inch diameter aluminum rudder stock, the Deerfoot's oversized spade rudder improves steering efficiency and windward performance. However, hanging an aluminum rudder behind a steel keel could result in electrolysis. A fiberglass rudder with stainless steel shaft might be a better choice. You also cannot apply copper bottom

paints to aluminum and the proximity of the aluminum rudder and stock to a copper painted bottom could cause corrosion problems.

The mast is stepped on two aluminum plates that are bolted to a fiberglass mount. The steel keel further supports the mast step.

Stainless steel straps form the chainplates, which extend through the deck and bolt to fiberglass knees. In the photos we looked at, the chainplate installation looked strong. However, with the help of two boatbuilders at Able Marine, we unsuccessfully tried to uncover the chainplates by dismantling the interior. Ulf Rogeberg admits getting to the chainplates is "tricky." It might be less so if Deerfoot shortened the valances or bookshelf fiddles running behind the settees.

Seacocks are Marelon. Some people prefer bronze seacocks with bolted flanges (we have had reports of handles breaking off Marelon seacocks), but on a boat with a steel keel and aluminum rudder, Marelon is probably a good idea.

You'll be hard pressed to sink a Deerfoot. The 61 has three watertight bulkheads. One separates the forepeak from the living area, and one separates the living area from the engine room. Each watertight area has its own bilge pump. The bilge pump in the forepeak doubles as a deck wash down pump. There's also a large Edson manual bilge pump mounted in the bilge near the mast.

The 14-foot forepeak, a huge storage area, is a cruising sailor's dream. It has sail bins, anchor bins, and pipes for tying dock lines and sheets. There's also room for fenders and the other paraphenalia that usually collects on deck.

There's a "garage" aft (behind the engine room) for storing propane tanks, outboard motors, and diving tanks. It's also a good place to keep the liferaft where it can be deployed easily if the need arises. The "back porch", a small "sugar scoop" behind the "garage," has a fresh water deck shower, and a stern ladder to make climbing aboard easy. On a boat with such high freeboard, this arrangement could be a real lifesaver if a crewmember were to fall overboard. For everyday use, the fold-up ladder is a bit lethal, however, since the bottom half hinges up but doesn't lock in place. The unwary visitor may reach for a rung and end up in the drink.

Rig

With a 65 foot mast and a working sail area of just 1,150 square feet, the Deerfoot 61 has an efficient, easily-handled cutter rig. Double swept-back spreaders and oversized Navtec 316 stainless steel wire rigging with Norseman terminals provide support for the tapered aluminum spar which has a fair amount of induced bend.

Hydraulics control the permanent double backstays, the boom vang and the inner forestay. The backstays work in tandem to keep the headstay tight for best upwind performance. The hydraulic inner forestay when tightened bends the mast moderately to flatten the mainsail. It can also be removed to facilitate tacking the jib.

Performance Under Sail

The Deerfoot 61, with its narrow, easily-driven canoe shape, fin keel/spade rudder and moderate-sized rig, is a fast passagemaker. Deerfoot claims that one of their 61s averaged 209 miles a day from New Zealand to the Panama Canal. They also claim another averaged 11 knots in 25-knot winds on a broad reach from Marblehead to the Cape Cod Canal. Even if you subtract a few knots (or miles) from these averages, that's still fair sailing.

We sailed the Deerfoot 61 from Newport to the boat show in Annapolis in October, but our story was different. It was a beat to windward the entire way.

In light to moderate winds the boat still averaged seven to eight knots. In 35-knot winds encountered off Delaware Bay, the boat handled well, but pounded in steep, short confused seas.

In most conditions, the 61 is so well balanced that you can steer it with two fingers. There's no weather or lee helm, and you have the feeling you're sailing a racing boat rather than a cruising boat designed for safe, comfortable passagemaking.

In keeping with the philosophy that a cruising boat should be easily handled by two people, the Deerfoot 61's working sails are small. Upwind, the Deerfoot is designed to sail with a jib that just overlaps the shrouds. For light air, there's a reacher that's set on its own stay four feet forward of the headstay and a 1.5 ounce 85% spinnaker for downwind.

Performance Under Power

"Probably 99 percent of maintenance is accessibility," says Steve Dashew. With this in mind, the Deerfoot's large engine room has been designed with attention to detail.

Located aft behind its own watertight bulkhead and entered through either of two cockpit lockers, it houses a four-cylinder 77 hp turbo-charged Yanmar with a 3.2/1 Hurth transmission. There's also an auxiliary two-cylinder, 18 hp Yanmar power plant mounted just starboard of the main engine.

Two 135-amp alternators (one on the larger Yanmar, one on the auxiliary) charge a 600-amp 24-volt Sonnenschein Prevailer Dryfit battery system. A 55-amp alternator (main engine) and a 35-amp alternator (auxiliary engine) charge a second 12-volt system. The 12-volt system is used to start the engines and power some of the navigation equipment. Everything else runs off 24-volt. (The 110-volt AC loads run off an inverter system.)

While 24 volts is good for handling big current draws like an electric windlass or power winches, it's a nuisance when it's necessary to replace equipment in countries where most everything is 12 volt. (For example, 24-volt equipment is quite common in Europe, but usually must be custom ordered in the U.S. or Caribbean.)

The Deerfoot 61 interior shows that a long, narrow hull can be simple and functional, yet spacious and elegant. The 61 is well laid out for long-distance passagemaking or living aboard at anchor.

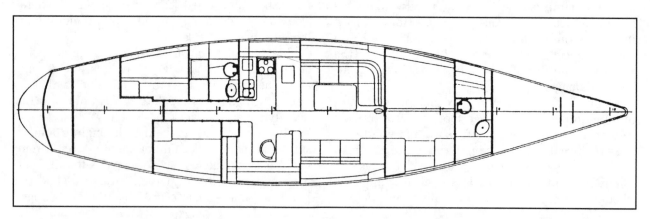

All 24/12 volt DC and AC cabling is laid down in PVC conduits. Wiring is marine grade and tagged with numbers at each end, but the color coding is predominantly red (positive) or black (negative). Color coding the wires to ABYC specifications would be a vast improvement.

Belted onto the engine is a damage control pump (100 gpm) plumbed into the three watertight areas of the boat, and a Sea Recovery watermaker that desalinates 25 gallons of water per hour. The engine room also contains a large hot water heater, two toolboxes, a work bench with sink, and racks for pressure pumps and compressors. There's plenty of work space around the engines, but the watertight bulkhead makes getting to the front of the engine to tighten belts difficult.

At 3,000 RPM the Deerfoot goes eight knots in flat seas. However, the Yanmar runs more efficiently at 2,300 RPM, driving the boat at seven knots in smooth water. Cruising range under power is about 1,100 miles.

Due to hull shape, a 26" three-bladed Max prop, and an extra large rudder, the Deerfoot 61 is extremely handy under power—so handy that it can almost turn (180°) within its own length. The boat handles particularly well in reverse so you're apt to feel smug when docking stern to.

On Deck

The cockpit is in keeping with the Deerfoot philosophy—comfortable for two, a bit cozy for four, but efficient and safe for shorthanded passagemaking. The cockpit drains are huge, four-inch in diameter,

and there are two smaller deck drains all the way aft. The dodger is well made with two opening windows forward for ventilation in warm weather. With forward and side windows closed, it provides a snug, dry place in inclement weather. The trade-off is it hampers visibility for the helmsman.

Two cockpit chairs, one port and one starboard, sit in wells behind the wheel. If you are tall, you can sit comfortably in either with feet planted firmly on the cockpit sole; a shorter person's feet dangle unless you pivot sideways. (In a knockdown the helmsman may go flying since the chairs are not pinned into their sockets.)

The mainsail halyard, main traveler controls and mainsail reefing lines are lead aft to the forward end of the cockpit. However, you must still walk forward to hook the cringle to the reefing hook on the gooseneck. Headsail halyards are located on the main mast along with spinnaker pole controls.

Harken roller furling comes standard on the headstay, although you can opt for jib hanks if you prefer. The cutter stay is left bare for hank-on storm sails.

The Deerfoot 61's long, sleek flush deck provides a stable sailing platform. There are inboard sheeting tracks for the staysail or working jib, and an outboard "T" track bolted to the top of the toe rail from the mast all the way aft for sheeting reachers, spinnakers, and genoas.

Lifeline stanchions, 1 1/4 inch in diameter and 30 inches tall, provide the extra security one needs in an offshore passagemaker. Double lifelines become triple lifelines forward of the mast to help keep crew and

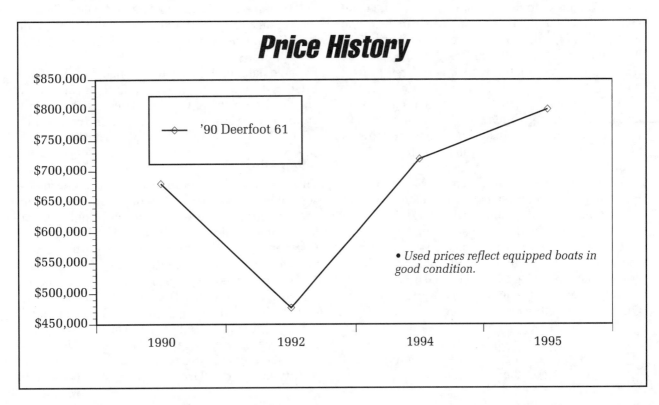

• Used prices reflect equipped boats in good condition.

sails on board. The stainless steel pushpit extends around the cockpit as far as the second stanchion for extra safety aft.

The 61 comes standard with a Lewmar windlass, and the anchor chain self stows neatly into a large anchor chain bin located directly beneath the winch. Because the forestay is located four feet aft of the bow, there's a lot of room to handle the anchor.

Seven Bomar hatches and eight dorades provide ventilation below. Stainless steel guards around the dorades prevent jib sheets from fouling and furnish handholds for crewmembers moving forward or aft.

The Deerfoot we sailed was missing some mooring cleats aft and amidships. Also, cleats and winches, though mounted with through bolts and washers into a thick section of fiberglass, have no backing plates to distribute the load.

Interior

Despite its comparatively narrow beam (14 1/2 feet), the Deerfoot's interior is well designed for living aboard in port or offshore. Emphasis is on having an airy, open saloon. Large hull portholes and light-colored, vinyl-covered bulkheads and ceilings create a feeling of light and space. Plush leather settees and a horizontal teak veneer enhance this feeling and give the boat a Scandinavian flair.

Stepping below from the cockpit, there are two guest cabins—one with bunk beds to port and one with a small double to starboard. When cruising, either cabin provides a good place for children or guests. The port cabin, within earshot of the person on deck, is preferable offshore.

The owner's double stateroom forward is designed for sleeping in harbor. You can hear the anchor chain if it drags, and there's good ventilation. This stateroom has oodles of storage and a spacious head forward with sit-down shower, large mirror, and sink.

Aft is another head with shower, stacked washer and dryer, and large linen closet. The shower compartment has big hooks inside for hanging wet towels and foul weather gear. Both heads, sprayed glossy white, are bright and easy to clean.

The long secure passageway between the companionway ladder and saloon is a good place to don your harness or foul weather gear. It also leads you to the galley to port and nav section starboard.

The nav section/office is C-shaped with plenty of room for charts, instruments and electronics. There are two tables and a rotating chair so you can sit forward or aft. (However, there's no space for knees when swiveling the chair outboard.)

Nav lockers along the hull with roll-top lids furnish a nifty way to store books, cassettes, or extra electronics. There's more room for a computer and other equipment on the desk mounted aft.

Across from the nav section, the galley is a typical U-shape with the stove mounted on the aft bulkhead. Counter tops are Corian which can be lightly sanded if scuffed or scraped. There is handsome stowage for dishes and dry goods in lockers above the stove and along the hull.

Two nine-inch deep stainless steel sinks sit outboard and drain via an electric pump to a thru-hull in the aft head. They would drain more efficiently if they were installed near the centerline and plumbed directly overboard.

Hot and cold pressure water are standard, but surprisingly there are no manual salt water pumps, and only one manual fresh water foot pump underneath the galley sink.

There's an eight-cubic-foot fridge and and a five-cubic-foot freezer across from the stove. The fridge stays cold, but its "side opening" door could be better insulated. There's a microwave and more food lockers along the companionway starboard.

The galley and nav section look out over the saloon. There's a large L-shaped dinette to port and a straight settee to starboard. Fiddles for bookshelves mounted behind the settees are inadequately designed for sailing offshore.

To minimize weight above the waterline, the cabin sole and furniture are constructed of teak plywood on a foam core. A good latch-down system secures the sole. However, on the boat we sailed, the cabin sole was divided into five and seven foot lengths which were much too cumbersome.

Lighting on the Deerfoot 61 is excellent. Overhead lights are round recessed halogens and large rectangular flourescents. The saloon has strip lights behind the valances and in the kickspace along the cabin sole. Small reading lights are mounted above bunks and settees.

Large hatches, which provide plenty of light, are fitted with storm cover tracks so they can be left cracked in inclement weather. They also come with an innovative system of bug and sun screens which conveniently slide in and out of the deck.

Conclusion

The Deerfoot 61 is a luxurious boat. It's also a sensible, liveaboard boat that offers outstanding accommodations, superb craftsmanship, and unparalleled performance. It's obvious that Dashew and Rogeberg put a lifetime of ocean voyaging and boatbuilding experience into the Deerfoot design.

All this comes at a price, of course. New, a coastal cruising version of the Deerfoot 61 runs $680,000, add another $120,000 for the offshore package, which comes with sails, two autopilots, watermaker, refrigerator-freezer, ground tackle, and electronics.

This is a lot to pay for any boat, but you'll get top quality for your dollar.　　**• PS**

Sundeer 64

Steve Dashew's concept of a large, easily handled cruiser for couples becomes a production reality at TPI.

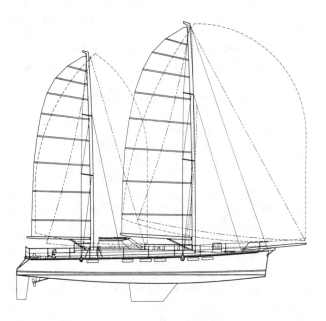

You know his name from the Deerfoot 61 and other models in his line of distinctive bluewater cruising boats. They're easy to pick out of any anchorage: flush decks, plumb bows, comparatively narrow beams and moderately short rigs. His name is Steve Dashew and for nearly two decades he's been rattling the cages of convention, preaching his message that long, skinny boats with small rigs make faster passages and are more comfortable than most of the other cruising boats we're used to seeing.

Steve and his wife Linda have logged better than 175,000 miles cruising over the past 40-plus years. During that time he's formed very definitive opinions about the nature of boats.

His books, the *Bluewater Handbook* and *Offshore Cruising Encyclopedia* are what they suggest, encyclopedic advice on everything from how to keep anchor chain from tangling to sizing mattresses so there's enough space to tuck in comforters. The details accrete to form a philosophy of cruising that is not so thinly veiled: Big boats are better than little boats.

For that reason, much of what he has to say is lost on the average sailor who cannot hope to spend a half million dollars on a boat. Still, examining one of Dashew's designs is a valuable learning experience. (Dashew does most of his own design work, though George Hazen and Peter Schwenn of Annapolis, Maryland, are consulted to check the lines, etc.) Even if you can't afford the Sundeer 64, we urge you to read on.

Design

Beyond its 64' 11" LOA, one of the first things you'll notice about the Sundeer is its long waterline, 64' 0".

Specifications

LOA	64' 11"
LWL	64' 0"
Beam	15' 1"
Draft	6' 7"
Displacement	48,800 lbs.
Ballast	14,200 lbs.
Sail area (cut/kth)	1,626/1,776 sq. ft.

The bow is nearly plumb and the transom is what he calls "immersed." If you write for literature, you'll get 176 pages of very informative discussion on all aspects of the boat, including a half-page in the "Sundeer Series—Addendum" on immersed sterns. Conceding a disadvantage in light air, where an overhanging transom keeps it "from towing part of the quarter wave," at higher speeds the immersed stern, he says, reduces wave drag.

gives more stability to the hull, provides better rudder control, improves powering efficiency and eliminates transom slap at anchor.

Not so noticeable is its comparatively narrow beam of 15' 1". Forget for a moment that that may be the width of your living room at home.

The Baltic 64 has a 17' 4" beam, the Lager 65 and

Oyster 68 beams of 17' 3", and these are nicely proportioned boats. The advantages he cites are less drag; more comfort (due, in part, to a slower roll period); narrower entry of angle (12° compared to a number around 20° for more conventional cruising boats) for "easier wave penetration, and reduced pitching or slamming;" better steering control when heeled; and superior range of positive stability (122°-126° depending on tank levels). Unless you're trying to surf and plane as on a BOC boat, we couldn't agree more. In fact, we think that excessively wide beams are one of the real problem issues for buyers of modern cruising boats.

Part of the "bigger is better" credo is the parallel belief that faster is better. A low displacement/length ratio helps. The Sundeer 64 comes in at an astonishing 77, light for a ULDB! Part of this is construction technique, which we'll talk about in the next section, but mostly it's hull form. The canoe body (hull without keel) is shallow and U-shaped. Water tanks are located at the hull, port and starboard, between the saloon bulkhead and engine compartment, and hold 600 gallons combined. An optional pump system allows the skipper to tweak performance by transferring water in the leeward tank to the windward side. Fuel tanks holding 400 gallons combined are again at the hull, port and starboard alongside the engine compartment. There's no room in the bilge for this much fuel or freshwater, but Dashew has located the recommended (optional) 2.2-volt traction batteries above the keels, concentrating their weight low and amidships. (With 1800 amp-hours capacity, you can spend a week at anchor without running the engine; dual 190-amp alternators do the charging when you leave.) While this location has its merits in terms of weight, it's not without its risks. True, the standard gel cell batteries are sealed, and Hydrocaps are used on lead-acid batteries, but saltwater could cause problems with the connections, which Dashew admits should probably be coated with an appropriate anticorrosive for protection.

The rudder is a large, semi-balanced spade. When asked why he opted against a skeg, he said that at sea control is more important than protection against collisions, and that a spade rudder is the most efficient and easy to handle. The 64's rudder, he said, weighs 325 lbs., four times the weight of a rudder built to American Bureau of Shipping (ABS) standards. The boat, he said, can actually sit on its large fin keel and rudder for maintenance. All things considered, however, for a cruising boat, we still give the edge to the skeg-mounted rudder.

The Rig

The Sundeer 64 is available with cutter or ketch rig, the latter being the most distinctive with its com-paratively short main mast and tall mizzen (58' 6" and 48' 0" off the deck), and large roaches in the sails. The cutter's mast is 61' 5" off the deck. Sails on both rigs are fully battened.

When evaluating this rig, remember that Dashew's concept is based on two-person cruising, which means small headsails, indeed, small rigs altogether so it isn't necessary to reef at the first gust. Viewed from a distance, the ketch rig, which we sailed, looks downright squat, despite its 1,776 square feet. Almost as surprising as the low D/L ratio is the Sundeer 64's sail area/displacement ratio of 19.86 for the ketch, 18.24 for the cutter. These numbers generally are associated with racers tall but the lightest, all-out, go-fast machines). Typical numbers for offshore cruisers are in the 15-16 range. Throw up an asymmetrical spinnaker on the retractable sprit and this boat takes off.

Standard spars are by Forespar, though we suspect some owners will opt for carbon fiber, which saves such a significant amount of weight aloft that one could almost opt for a shoal keel without adding extra ballast.

Both cutter and ketch rigs have inner forestays, swept-back spreaders, and running backstays. The backstay on the ketch has been eliminated, and the angle of the spreaders increased to 25 degrees to improve sideways support. Hydraulics are used for tensioning the inner forestay, vang, and the backstay on the cutter.

There's a lot of rigging on this boat, and it's damn near bombproof. Wire terminals are Norseman or Sta-Lok, which we've reported as being most resistant to corrosion, and the best choice for cruising, especially in the tropics.

Construction

The Sundeer 64, and its smaller sister-ship, the Sundeer 56, are built of fiberglass by TPI. This is the company run by Everett Pearson, which in addition to building J Boats and Lagoon catamarans for Jenneau, is also a leading builder of large windmill blades.

Engineers don't sit still at TPI. Within the past two years we've observed demonstrations at the plant of a new patented method of gluing the hull/deck joint that obviates through-bolts, and the patented Infused Resin Molding (IRM) process. The latter involves placing all fiberglass (a lot of 5605 quadraxial) and balsa coring in the mold, vacuum bagging it more than twice the usual 11 inches of mercury, then injecting the resin, which is supposed to better wet out the fiberglass and penetrate the balsa deeper. Benefits, according to TPI, include the elimination of potential secondary bonding problems between laminations, less air in the laminate (as little as one percent, compared to five percent in conventional laminates), and superior glass-to-resin ratios. Independent laminates expert Bruce Pfund told us that an IRM laminate will have nearly 70 percent glass, compared to about 42-48 percent in conventional woven roving/mat lay-ups.

Dashew calls IRM the "single biggest advance in fiberglass construction in the last forty years." Without it, he says, the 1-1/2" of bow thickness would have to be increased to 3" of woven roving and mat to achieve the same strength.

Additional fiberglass reinforcement is added to the bow and centerline, to protect against collisions. The fiberglass floors are large and extend well across the hull bottom to distribute keel loads. And vinylester resin, instead of polyester, is used exclusively in the lay-up for its superior adhesion and resistance to osmotic blistering.

We've said for years, beginning with a controversial report on balsa about 10 years ago, that we prefer a solid laminate for cruising (no chance of saturating the core, delamination of the core, and greater abrasion resistance), but that problems with balsa-cored construction generally are attributable to carelessness on the part of the builder. A good builder, who knows how to work with balsa, we said, can build a good boat with it. TPI is the acknowledged pioneer and leader in balsa-cored construction, and if we were to trust anyone to build us a boat with balsa, it would be TPI.

Earlier we alluded to a new patented process used by TPI to fasten the hull/deck joints of Lagoon catamarans. This is a urethane glue that TPI's Phil Mosher says eliminates leaks and makes through-bolting unnecessary. The hull/deck joint of the Sundeer, however, is done the conventional way with through-bolts and caulked with 3M 5200 or similar product. Dashew said only that despite some people's perceptions of his boats, he is actually very conservative.

There are watertight bulkheads fore and aft, designed to keep water out of the main part of the boat in the event of a collision. The unusual looking pilothouse is bolted to the deck; the forward Lexan windows are 3/8" thick, 1/4" on the sides. Though well built, there is a conventional companionway with washboards for safety.

The hull structure is guaranteed against blistering and defects for 10 years.

Performance

Our test sail was in mid-November aboard *Artemis*, which had been sold to a Japanese businessman for his son to race in Jimmy Cornell's 1994 Europa Round the World Rally, which departed Gibraltar January 7. Aboard was Kelly Archer, shaking down the boat for the transatlantic passage.

The wind was blowing in the high teens when we left the Barrington, Rhode Island dock, and we broad reached at better than 10 knots. When it was time to jibe, Archer said not to worry about sheeting in as it was better to break something now on Narragansett Bay than in the middle of the Atlantic. So we did a series of flying jibes while Archer watched the rig for any signs of trouble. There were none. During *Artemis'* trip to Gibraltar the crew experienced average wind speeds of 25-35 knots and 18-24-foot seas. The best day's run was 265 miles.

Top speed was 23.4 knots. The only thing that broke, according to Dashew, was a defective casting on the inboard end of the spinnaker pole.

Later we set the asymmetrical chute and pushed boat speed into the teens. Sailing close-hauled back to the dock we jogged along at maybe 6-7 knots,

The interior is set up for a husband and wife team with two smaller staterooms for guests. The use of ceiling-to-sole mirrors on the bulkheads greatly increases the sense of spaciousness.

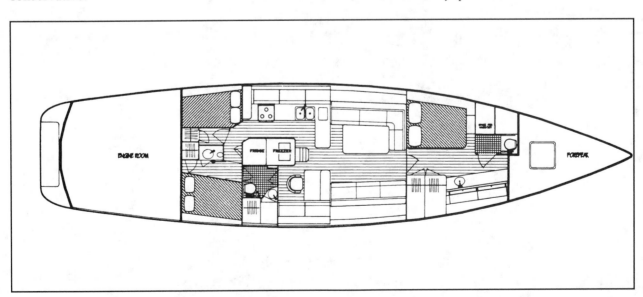

which seemed a bit slow for this big of a boat, and not in line with its reaching performance. Dashew said the boat, because of its shallow keel, doesn't like to be pinched, rather cracked off about four degrees.

On a boat with a 64' waterline, you expect to make nearly double figures, or better, so Archer turned on the 140-hp. Yanmar (88-hp. standard) and handed us the autopilot remote. Protected from the biting cold, we sat inside the pilothouse making minor course corrections as we worked our way up the buoyed channel. The pilothouse, with its 360-degree visibility and long bench/settees, is one of the best features of the Sundeer 64. It's amazing how much more rested you arrive at your destination when protected from the wind and cold; a hard windscreen, we've learned, is much better than acrylic dodger windows because they're easier to see through, causing less eye fatigue and stress.

Interior

Because this is a production boat, you're not going to see the kind of joinerwork found in a custom or semi-custom boat such as the Morris 44. But we found it quite attractive, clean and contemporary, with Formica-faced furniture; vinyl-covered, foam-backed bulkheads, hull sides and headliner; and varnished teak sole. We particularly liked the wood-molded airplane-style stowage compartments used throughout the interior, which seem simpler, more attractive and convenient than hinged or sliding doors.

The standard layout shows an off-set double berth forward and twin double staterooms aft. There isn't a great deal of opportunity to customize, though hi-lo berths in one or both guest staterooms are possible.

The ship's "office" is spacious, as it should be for accommodating all of the electronics, systems monitors, and the paperwork attendant to world cruising.

Conclusion

1994 base price of the cutter-rigged Sundeer 64 was $419,650 (the Sundeer 56 was $287,645), and though this is fairly complete, you'll spend a lot more once you've walked through the options list and fitting-out process. For example, the ketch option is $28,230, the pilothouse $12,828, Maxwell Nilson electric windlass $6,118 (the standard anchor is a 176-lb. Bruce), mini blinds on each window/portlight $2,250, and an American cherry interior $35,735. The average sail-away price of the first six boats was $579,000, which included the above items plus a lot more. Believe it or not, these are attractive prices for a boat this size, which explains why Dashew sold 11 64s and a number of 56s in about a year of advertising. Part of the reason is TPI's extremely efficient operation, part is the relatively simple interior, and part the fact that these boats are sold direct, without dealers. In comparison, a custom 64-footer probably would cost $1-1/2 million.

Whether you find it attractive is an individual matter. Dashew freely admits that he grew up on CCA-type boats with long overhangs and loved their looks. "But what commercial or military boat has overhangs?" he asks. "Once you get over the overhang thing, and see what we're trying to do, it only makes sense."

Frankly, we think the Sundeer 64 has strong, purposeful lines—a classic case of form following function. And that is what this boat is all about, comfortable, high-performance cruising anywhere in the world.   • **PS**

Head-to-Head Comparisons

Four Classy Tenders

A close look at the Trinka, Fatty Knees, Puddleduck and Dyer Dhow. While we like them all, we think the Trinka comes closest to being a "classic," and the Puddleduck rates a Best Buy.

Like all boats, dinghies are the essence of com promise. Too small and they won't carry a load or make way, too big and they become unwieldy to carry and impossible to bring on dock.

"No one's invented the perfect dinghy," one manufacturer's rep told use, "and if they did, it would probably be 17 feet long."

Because the average dinghy is so small and shallow, they get almost all of their stability and performance from hull shape. We tested four top-of-the-line dinghies, which take different approaches to the age-old problem of combining rowing, sailing and towing characteristics in a small package.

Test Conditions

Our dinghy excursions took place over a period of weeks and, unfortunately for the sake of exact comparison, in widely differing conditions, from faint to moderate ocean breezes to light inland air to blustery winds compounded by current. Also, by chance, our original intention to test some smaller models was thwarted, first by the arrival of a Trinka 10, then the availability of the 9-foot Dyer Dhow instead of the popular 7' 11" Dyer Midget. We ended up testing the 9-foot Fatty Knees, not the 8-foot model, and the Puddleduck, which measures 8' 6".

Trinka 10

The Trinka 10 is a smart-looking tender/daysailer that stemmed from designer Bruce Bingham's long experience as a cruiser. Bingham had already designed the Trinka 8 when builder Mark Johannsen

of Miami approached him in 1982 about making a larger version.

"I had a very practical view of what a dinghy ought to be." Bingham said. "What I really wanted was the sailing quality of the old IOD"—the International Optimist Dinghy. So he gave the new boat a somewhat rounded bottom, but made the turn at the bilges high to keep the waterline beam as narrow as possible. The round chine makes the boat somewhat tender initially, but once it's loaded or underway, it develops good stability. This represents the trade-off between round and flat bottoms with hard chines: the round bottom tends to be less stable, but performs better when heeled, and the panels are stiffer.

Bingham also gave the boat a plumb bow, lots of sheer and a fine entry. The 10's relatively narrow

---

The Trinka 10 is as handsome as they come, with its round hull form, high freeboard and plumb bow. It carries a larger sail plan than many dinghies, and as one might expect, at 10 feet it also sails better.

Specifications - Trinka

LOA .... 9' 11-1/2"
Beam .... 4' 0"
Weight .... 125 lbs.
Sail area .... 64 sq. ft.
Capacity .... 4 pers., 640 lbs.
Base Price, 1994
    Row $2,375
    Sail $3,300
Options (sail models)
    Gunwale guard .... Std.
    Oars .... Std.
    Kick-up rudder .... Std.
    Teak .... Std.
Total $3,300

beam, wineglass transom and teak trim enhance its appearance. About 400 of the 10s have been built, edging ahead of the 8 in popularity. Johannsen attributes this to a move away from the old fixation on the 8-foot dinghy, which theoretically could be stowed on deck. "Almost everybody tows these days. Very few people worry about putting their dinghy on deck," he said. A 10-footer is a legitimate daysailer. It opens up a whole new vista."

The Trinka has a rugged fiberglass hull, 1/8" thick at the sheer, 3/16" on the bottom and 1/4" at the stern, forefoot and skeg. There's enough solid teak—in the gunwale, center thwart, and transom reinforcement—to convince the eye you're on a classic yacht tender. A teak breast hook and quarter knees add structural strength.

Thoughtful touches include a sliding cover over the daggerboard trunk (which could use, however, a ridge or ball on the forward edge for wet fingers to grasp), bronze security clamp for the oars, stainless skeg guard, and a hiking stick. The bow and stern seats are watertight, glassed-in chambers, providing the requisite flotation.

Trinka comes with a through-bolted bow eye (with stainless backing plate), close to the waterline; a second, higher bow eye is optional. Bingham disputes the notion that a dinghy's bow should be lifted for towing, which can cause the transom to dig in, inducing drag. He, and Johannsen, prefer the upper eye, adding that having two is cheap insurance, and allows you to shift the load between two painters depending on conditions.

The boat has an optional Elvstrom-type self bailer- a godsend to anyone who's watched a dinghy under tow fill up with water and had to ponder the odious options. The positioning of the little devil, however, invites a bruised or cut toe; the optional floorboards help here.

We sailed the 10 in about 10 knots of wind off Sachuest Beach in Middletown, Rhode Island. The seas were flat and the dinghy sailed about as well as one could expect in terms of speed, stability and leeway. The two-section aluminum mast, carrying 64 square feet of sail, gets the boat moving. Bingham has sailed the 10 with a bendy fiberglass mast, which he says reduces heeling in a puff and generally makes the boat more responsive.

Rowing, with the undersized oars we were provided, was tiring, especially for the outer forearms, a result of what L. Francis Herreshoff called "digging for crabs."

• **Bottom Line:** We found the Trinka 10 to be a well-built, very attractive dinghy that proved a bit more tender than others we tried and, at 125 pounds, on the outer edge of what we'd consider easily handled. Comparing its cost to a Dyer 10 ($3,300 vs. $4,118 with comparable equipment) the Trinka is a good value. Among the 8-footers, the Trinka 8, also appears to be a solid choice. From where stand, we think the Trinkas are the best looking of the lot.

Dyer Dhow

The Dyer Dhow is probably the best known of the mainstream production dinghies. The Dhow dates to WW II when the U.S. Navy asked Bill Dyer to design a plywood lifeboat that could be built quickly and fit

Specifications - Dyer Dhow

LOA .... 9' 0"
Beam .... 4' 6"
Weight .... 104 lbs.
Sail area .... 45 sq. ft.
Capacity .... 3 pers., 650 lbs.
Base Price, 1994
    Row $1,470
    Sail $2,320
Options (sail models)
    Gunwale guard $140
    Oars $118
    Kick-up rudder $40
    Teak $135
Total $2,753

on the deck of a minesweeper or PT boat. Dyer collaborated with Philip Rhodes (with whom he had worked on earlier designs) to produce the 9-footer that has become the signature of the Dyer line.

At that time, Dyer, a former cotton broker, had been in the boatbuilding business for 15 years, beginning with the short-lived Dyer Motorcraft company in 1927, which produced a 19-1/2-foot L, Francis Herreshoff powerboat. Dyer designed several other

sizes until the stock market crash in 1929 put an end to demand. After several years as a boat broker, Dyer and his new firm, The Anchorage, cashed in on the growing sailing dinghy craze, making 10- and 11-1/2-foot Rhodes' designs. The 10-foot lapstrake hull wasn't cheap—$300 in 1930's money—and as interest waned, Dyer asked Rhodes for a new one-design. But the 11-1/2-foot slab-sided boat he came up with didn't catch on immediately and the design reverted to Rhodes (it later became the immensely popular Penguin). Then, during the war, came the request for the 9-footer.

The fiberglass Dyer Dhow built today at The Anchorage in Warren, Rhode Island, is the same as the original plywood model from which it was molded in 1952. More than 6,400 Dhows have been sold over the years, topped only by the Midget, which is approaching the 10,000 mark. It's a snub-nosed, hard-chined, relatively flat-bottomed boat that nevertheless handles well and is still light enough to pick up. The hull is solid glass—two layers of cloth around four layers of mat followed by another two of cloth. Before we could bring the subject up, an Anchorage employee mentioned the tendency of the bottom to flex under load, natural with such a flat panel. "It's flexed for 30 years and hasn't broken," we were told. Still, we have to wonder if flexing of the glass fibers won't eventually take its toll, and it's psychologically disconcerting to feel the floor move.

We sailed the Dhow on a gusty day with the current running three knots in the Warren River. After a few minutes on a reach, and experiencing considerable leeway, we got the boat pointing and, aided by the occasional puff, gained ground to windward. With two aboard, the dinghy tacked and jibed easily. It also tracked well. Our only complaint, a minor one, was the lack of any means to secure the mainsheet; Dyer plans to fix that with the addition of a Harken hexaratchet block. Rowing (short oars again) was fairly easy, even against the current, without the strain we felt on the Trinka 10.

The two-piece Sitka spruce spar and boom not only adds to the looks of the boat, but provide extra flotation—excellent trade-offs for the slight addition of weight. Unlike the Midget, which has a removable daggerboard, the Dhow is fitted with a permanent 28" centerboard. The trunk has a small drain hole for when the dinghy is stored upside down in the winter; a small rubber plug stops it up for towing, although it's not necessary under sail. Rudder (and daggerboard on the Midget) stores under the seats, an advantage of open seating. Kick-up rudders are optional, though we can't imagine why anyone would want a dinghy without one.

• **Bottom Line:** The Dyer Dhow is finished nicely inside, well-constructed, functional, and often imitated by other builders. On the other hand, stiffening

pram, but with more sheer and more of a V-bottom. The result was a boat that kids could safely take out on Narragansett Bay. Baker's students helped draw the plans and he began building them as a sideline at his Warren shop; later, the work was sub-contracted to the Herreshoff family. Eventually, about 400 of the wooden boats were made.

Production of the fiberglass Puddleduck began in 1984 when Jonathan Nomer, a New York native who summered in Rhode Island, took over the business after Baker, really a custom boat builder at heart, had let the dinghy lapse. Nomer, a former charter boat captain, chose building dinghies as an affordable way to get into boatbuilding. Nomer does the fiberglass and woodworking at his shop, New England Skiff Builders, in Perryville, Rhode Island; his wife Nicole makes the 3.9-ounce Dacron sails in a second-floor loft. About 500 of the fiberglass models have been built.

The Puddleduck hull is a single unit of hand-laid fiberglass, beefed up with heavier mat at the stress points. The teak gunwale is fastened with Sikaflex and rivets. Flotation, enough to maintain three inches of freeboard when swamped, Nomer says, comes from built-in air chambers inside the molded-in seats. The stainless steel tow ring (located low on the bow) is reinforced with stainless front and backing

The Dyer Dhow had a centerboard, which is a real convenience when approaching shore. It dates back to WW II; clearly it has withstood the test of time.

the hull with coring or some other method seems like a logical improvement, and it didn't sail as well as the Trinka. In some ways, the design is showing its age. Prices of the 8 and 9 are reasonable compared to the Fatty Knees and Trinka models.

Puddleduck

Puddleducks were developed in the early 1950s when St. George's prep school in Middletown, Rhode Island decided to start a junior sailing program. Robert H. Baker, who taught mechanical drawing and shop at the school, teamed up with Norrie Hoyt to produce a variation on a traditional plywood

Specifications - Other Models

	Dyer Midget	Dyer Dink	Fatty Knees 8	Trinka 8
LOA	8' 3/4"	10' 0"	8' 0"	8' 0"
Beam	4' 1-1/4"	4' 6"	4' 0"	3' 9"
Weight	83 lbs.	135 lbs.	100 lbs.	85 lbs.
Sail area	36 sq. ft.	66 sq. ft.	50 sq. ft.	38 sq. ft.
Capacity	3 pers., 465 lbs.	5 pers., 740 lbs.	4 pers., 750 lbs.	3 pers., 450 lbs.
Base Price, 1994				
Row	$1,435	$2,095	$1,895	$1,675
Sail	$2,280	$3,625	$2,745	$2,300
Options (sail models)				
Gunwale guard	Std.	$150	Std.	Std.
Oars	Std.	$118	$95	Std.
Kick-up rudder	$40	$45	Std.	Std.
Teak	$140	$180	Std.	Std.
Total	$2,460	$4,118	$2,840	$2,300

Specifications - Puddleduck

LOA .... 8' 6"
Beam .... 4' 0"
Weight .... 85 lbs.
Sail area .... 36 sq. ft.
Capacity .... 3 pers., 390 lbs.
Base Price, 1994
    Row .... -
    Sail $1,795
Options (sail models)
    Gunwale guard $105
    Oars $60
    Kick-up rudder .... -
    Teak .... Std.
Total $1,960

plates and a 3" teak block.

The builder continues to refine the product. Cotton-over-foam gunwale protectors will be replaced on new models with plastic shell over expanded polypropylene foam—not as aesthetic, maybe, but more practical. The 12-foot, two-section Sitka spruce spar, gunter-rigged, weighs 12 pounds and can be stored on board.

Prospective customers sometimes are put off by the Puddleduck's pram shape, but shouldn't be. L. Francis Herreshoff liked the one he saw in England so much he produced his own 10-foot version. A properly designed pram—as the Puddleduck appears to be—provides a lot of room for its short length

without giving up too much in terms of performance. The key to a blunt-nosed boat is the amount of rocker, which keeps the transom clear of the water and the bow entry easy; too much and the boat tends to bounce around. Underneath, the V-bottom flattens in the aft sections to facilitate planing when towed. A teak skeg (protected by a stainless steel guard). 6" deep at the stern, keeps the boat on track.

We tried the Puddleduck on an early fall day on the quiet waters of Long Pond in light and intermittent air. Under these conditions, and with its light weight, the pram, not surprisingly, rowed easily. The positioning of the oarlocks (Herreshoff preferred the term "rowlocks") seemed exactly right and only the slight bulge of the daggerboard cap created any hint of discomfort. Anyone 5' 10" or taller can brace his legs against the rear seat for extra pulling power. Instead of the usual three-thwart arrangement, Puddleduck features side seating aft of the amidships thwart. This enables kids to get up from the floor and onto a seat while sailing; it also provides extra flotation.

With two aboard, the boat sailed well enough, despite the relatively small (36 sq. ft.) sail; with just one, it sailed proportionately better. The boat seemed nicely balanced, and the hard chines provided plenty of stability. A cleat on the aft side of the trunk allows you to take a turn with the sheet if you're inclined; two smaller cleats on either side are for tying down the teak cap while towing.

Options include a self-bailer, boat cover, floor grate and a few, such as oars, oarlocks and skeg protector that probably should be standard. Some customization is possible; one customer had handrails on the bottom for grasping in case of capsize, another jacklines! The skiff is rated for a 2-hp. outboard and comes with standard motor pad, offset slightly to counteract the operator's weight.

Puddleduck has a new stripped-down version, developed for the Boy Scouts, that offers the same hull but with virtually no teak trim; it also has a molded-in skeg. At $1,395, this is a less expensive alternative to the $1,795 standard model (including rig).

• **Bottom Line:** We like the side seating but lament the absence of a kick-up rudder. Still, we rate it a Best Buy.

Fatty Knees

The Fatty Knees was designed about 12 years ago by Lyle Hess, designer of the Bristol Channel Cutter, Nor'sea 27 and the Pardey's cruisers. Starting with a 7-footer, which would fit on the deck of his 26' cutter, he gave the little lapstrake-hulled boat a prow bow, 4' beam for stability and a pleasant sheer that minimized its chubby look. The name derives from some

Specifications - Fatty Knees

LOA	9'0"
Beam	4' 3"
Weight	100 lbs.
Sail area	50 sq. ft.
Capacity	4/5 pers., 850 lbs.
Base Price, 1994	
Row	$1,995
Sail	$2,845
Options (sail models)	
Gunwale guard	Std.
Oars	$95
Kick-up rudder	Std.
Teak	Std.
Total	$2,940

banter between Hess' wife and granddaughter, during which each accused the other of having fatty knees.

A cousin, John Hess, built the boat for a time, then turned production over to Joe Nye of Grace Marine in Peabody, Massachusetts, who subbed out the work to several companies.

One was Edey & Duff Ltd. of Mattapoisett on Buzzards Bay, who bought the rights in 1988 and produces the dinghy in 7', 8' and 9' models. All told land assuming John Hess began with hull #1, 388 7-footers have been made, 666 of the 8, and 227 of the 9.

Edey & Duff, begun in 1968 after the two founders admired each other's boat during a cruise, is known for its traditional craft, including a fiberglass version of the S.S. Crocker-designed Stone Horse, and the shoal-draft Dovekie and Shearwater by Phil Bolger. They also build the Doughdish and Columbia tender, two updated interpretations of Nathanael Herreshoff designs. Despite the emphasis on tradi-

tion, the builder employs contemporary techniques and was first in the U.S., for example, to use Airex foam in production molding.

The Fatty Knees has a lapstrake fiberglass hull, which is "terrible" to build, according to sales manager William Haberer, but represents more than an appeal to nostalgia. The lapstrake—10 stringers per side—adds considerable strength and stiffness to the hull. The bare boat, without seats or accouterments, weighs 100 pounds.

The hull is white, the trim and optional floorboards teak. Rowing versions come with mast step, mast partner, daggerboard trunk and gudgeons for easy conversion to sail. The inside rail is teak, the outer rail pressure-treated pine for more durability. The gunwale guard, once 100 percent cotton, now is a longer-lasting Dacron-over-rubber product sold by Johannsen Boat Works.

The seats are fiberglass inserts, glassed and tabbed to the hull.

The forward section is T-shaped, and the stem of the T provides seating for the rower (or sailer); there is enough seat room for the average person, and the arrangement opens up space in the mid-section. Both inserts contain flotation and the forward section has a watertight compartment with an air sock that can be used to store small items.

We tried the 9 on a quiet fall day in Aucoot Cove. A 7-inch-deep skeg (protected by a pine guard) means the boat tracks exceptionally well. There are two rowing stations, the forward one for when the boat is loaded up. We couldn't brace our feet against the rear insert from the regular rowing station, but a block on the floorboards would solve that problem. A teak daggerboard plug, ringed with a rubber gasket, keeps water from welling up while rowing or towing. The mast is a two-part aluminum extrusion from Kenyon; the sail, from Harding Sails in nearby Marion, attaches via a sleeve.

This makes it more difficult to drop during an emergency, but the builders now offer a reefing feature in which you detach the gooseneck and rotate the spar several times, up to the first batten. That's handy, but still better done at the dock.

We expected the Fatty Knees to sail well and it did. "It's first and foremost a tender," Haberer said, "but Lyle Hess wouldn't design a boat that didn't sail." The 9 was lively enough in light air, tacking and jibing smoothly, and making virtually no leeway.

There was a certain amount of water noise underway, possibly due to the lapstrake. We used a 4-1/2' daggerboard, that will be shortened to 4'. A kick-up rudder, once optional, is now standard. We had trouble getting comfortable while sailing, finally sitting on the edge of the T. Although we found sitting on the floor a bit like descending into a deep bathtub, Haberer said sitting on a cushion against the sides works best for most people. A self-bailer isn't available, but you could install your own.

• **Bottom Line:** This is a handsome boat, solidly built, that performs well. It's also labor-intensive to make and expensive at $1,995 for the 9' rowing version, $2,845 with sailing gear. The seating wasn't as comfortable as we'd like. While the lapstrake construction does add to strength, it's also heavier than the others, and we question whether this features warrants its higher price.

Conclusion

All four of these dinghies are well-built. We liked the sailing ability of the Fatty Knees and Trinka best, which isn't surprising given their rounder hull forms and greater sail area. The Dyer and the Puddleduck were excellent rowers, but also sailed well under the conditions encountered. The Trinka's appointments, and traditional styling probably make it the closest to the "classic tender" category, but all of the boats, even the fairly spartan Puddleduck, were pleasing to look at.

Aside from the comments cited, we found few serious flaws in any of the four.

On price alone, we'd rate the Puddleduck a Best Buy. But any purchase decision should carefully weigh appearance, the relative importance of sailing vs. rowing, and price. Among the remaining three, we'd go for the Trinka. **• PS**

Four Trailer-Sailers

The Paceship 23, American 26, Yankee Pacific Dolphin 24, and Aquarius 23 represent different solutions to the problem of easy launching.

In the early 1970s, when the fiberglass sailboat revolution was in full swing, so were the so-called swing keels. Three years after Richard Nixon was elected president, partly on the promise of ending the Vietnam War, U.S. planes still were bombing Cambodia, hippies and peaceniks were marching and both were flashing the V sign. In 1971 Sylvia Plath published "The Bell Jar." Louis Armstrong died, the crews of Apollo 14 and 15 landed on the moon, cigarette advertisements were banned from television, and Joe Frazier outpointed Muhammad Ali to retain his world heavyweight boxing title.

On the domestic level, Americans were taking their leisure time more seriously than ever, taking to the highways in RVs and to the waterways in all sorts of new fiberglass boats. Magazines devoted exclu-sively to sailing began to appear. One of the most popular type of boats was the "trailer-sailer," rela-tively light-displacement sloops with centerboards and swing keels, that could be stored in the backyard or driveway, towed behind the family station wagon and launched in about 45 minutes. Trailer-sailers promised yacht-style accommodations at an afford-able price-in terms of both initial investment and annual upkeep.

Trailer-sailers never really disappeared from the sailing scene, but they haven't been exactly an ex-ploding market force either. Nevertheless, we see indications that trailer-sailers are showing signs of increased interest from boat buyers.

The Ballast Problem

For stability, a sailboat must have an underwater

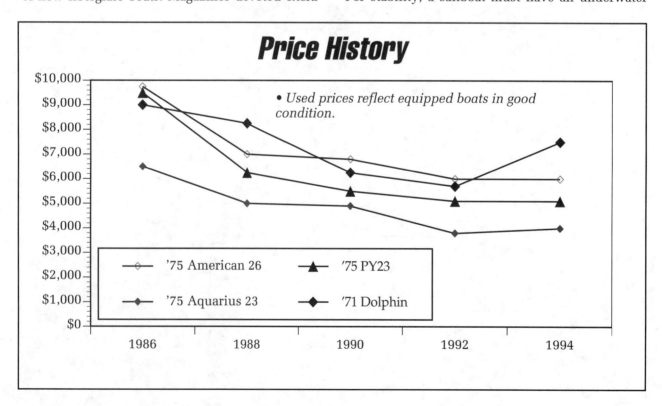

Price History

• *Used prices reflect equipped boats in good condition.*

Legend:
- '75 American 26
- '75 PY23
- '75 Aquarius 23
- '71 Dolphin

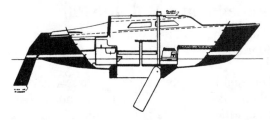

Specifications - Paceship PY 23

LOA .... 22' 7"
LWL .... 19' 4"
Beam .... 8' 0"
Draft .... 1' 9"/4' 9"
Displacement .... 2,300 lbs.
Ballast .... 900 lbs.
Sail area .... 223 sq. ft.
Headroom .... 5' 0"

Catalina 25. The idea is to dump the ballast on haul-out to minimize trailering weight, especially important given the small size of the average car these days. The drawback, as we see it, is that the water ballast works best when it is well outboard, which is the case on race boats with port and starboard ballast tanks. Trailer-sailers with shallow ballast tanks on centerline can't obtain the same righting moments because of the short righting arm. Plus, saltwater is not very dense, just 64 pounds per cubic foot (62.4 lbs. for fresh), compared to lead at about 708 lbs.. While water ballast may be a viable option for lakes and protected-water sailors, we don't think it's the best solution.

Looking back at the Paceship PY 23, American 26, Yankee Dolphin 24, and Aquarius 23, we can examine several other approaches to the same problem.

The PY 23

Paceship Yachts was originally a Canadian builder, located in Mahone Bay, Nova Scotia (it was later bought by AMF of Waterbury, Connecticut, of Sunfish and Force 5 fame). One of its first boats was the popular East Wind 24, introduced in 1963.

The PY 23, designed by John Deknatel of C. Raymond Hunt Associates, was developed in 1974 in response to the trailer-sailer boom. An early brochure describes the PY 23 as "a second generation refinement of the trailerable concept which eliminates the awkwardness in handling and sailing often present in the early trailerables." Indeed, the boat was rated 18.0 for IOR Quarter Ton and 16.9 under the MORC rule. Modern looks were derived largely from the flat sheer and reverse transom.

Instead of the more common swing keel, in which

The Yankee Pacific Dolphin 24 is a classy S&S design, too heavy for everyday trailering, but still capable of being stored in the back yard.

appendage such as a keel or centerboard, and ballast. Both are at odds with the concept of an easily trailerable boat that can be launched at most ramps. A deep fixed keel is untenable. One solution is to design a long, shallow keel, as seen on many Com-Pac boats, and older models such as the O'Day 22. Unfortunately, windward performance suffers because there is little leading edge and foil shape to provide lift.

During the last few years, several builders have experimented with water ballast in the hull and centerboards for lift. Notable designs include the MacGregor 26, Hunter 23.5 and 26, and the new

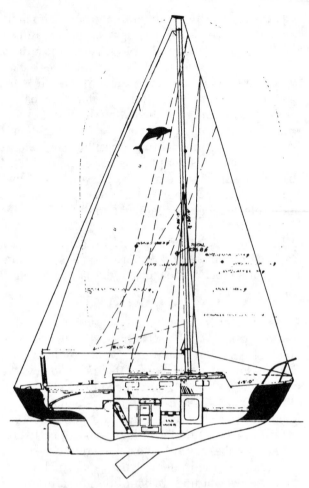

Specifications - Dolphin 24

LOA	24' 2"
LWL	19' 0"
Beam	7' 8"
Draft	2' 10"/5' 2"
Displacement	4,250 lbs.
Ballast	1,750 lbs.
Sail area	297 sq. ft.
Headroom	5' 0"

all of the boat's ballast hangs on a single pivot pin, Deknatel gave the PY 23 a 40-pound centerboard that retracts into a 900-pound "shallow draft lineal keel." This arrangement eliminates a trunk intruding into the cabin space, and places the majority of ballast a bit lower (it draws 1' 9" board up) than in boats such as the Aquarius 23, in which the ballast is simply located under the cabin sole.

The downside is a bit more draft, which means you need to get the trailer that much deeper to float the boat on and off. (We once owned a Catalina 22, which draws 2' 0" keel up, and often had to use a trailer tongue extension—built in—to launch and

haul out.) Based on our experience, any draft under 2 feet should be relatively easy to trailer and launch. Difficulties seem to mount exponentially with every inch of added draft.

Like most trailer-sailers, the PY 23 has an outboard rudder that kicks up for beaching.

Recognizing that trailer-sailers are not built for rugged conditions, and that by necessity they are not big boats, we herewith list some of the more common owner complaints: no backrests in cabin, barnacles in centerboard well, not enough room in head, not an easily trailerable boat, rudder rot, and poor ventilation in forepeak.

On the plus side, owners say the boat is quick, well-built, balances well, has good-quality mast and rigging, a comfortable cockpit, and a livable interior.

In all, we think this is a good example of the trailer-sailer. We like the keel/centerboard arrangement, even though it adds a few precious inches to board-up draft. It sold in 1974 for $8,150 base. Today, it would sell for about $5,100. A superior choice in our book.

Yankee Pacific Dolphin 24

Yankee Yachts of Santa Ana, California, was a major builder during the 1970s, known mostly for its IOR boats.

The Pacific Dolphin 24, designed by Sparkman & Stephens, is a classic-looking boat, not unlike the more familiar S&S-designed Tartan 27. It was built between about 1969 and 1971, when it was replaced by the Seahorse 24, designed by Robert Finch, who helped design the immensely successful Catalina 27.

The reason for its short production run, we surmise, was that the Dolphin has a long keel drawing 2' 10", and though the company initially thought it would appeal to trailer-sailers, its draft, plus 4,250-pound displacement, made it difficult to launch and retrieve. In contrast, the Seahorse drew 1' 8", dis-

The American 26 had nearly hard chines to improve initial stability. The unique feature of this boat is its hollow keel, which creates a sort of trough in the main cabin for 6-foot headroom.

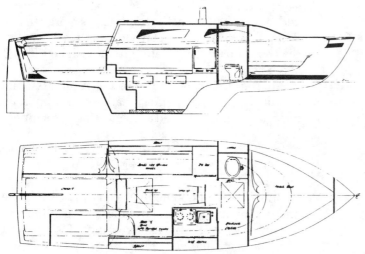

Specifications - American 26

LOA .... 25' 0"
LWL .... 23' 0"
Beam .... 8' 0"
Draft .... 2' 4"
Displacement .... 3,500 lbs.
Ballast .... 900 lbs.
Sail area .... 260 sq. ft.
Headroom .... 6' 0"

placed 2,800 pounds, and has a scabbard-type re-movable rudder.

The Dolphin has 1,750 pounds of ballast, all in the keel. The attached rudder makes this boat a bit more rugged than most trailer-sailers, and its overall quality, including extensive teak joinerwork below, places it in a different category.

Owners report very few problems with the Dolphin other than a comparatively large turning radius, and cramped living quarters; most have only good things to say.

An Oregon owner said, "Using a 3/4-ton pickup with a 390 engine we go uphill at 30 mph and down at 55. It takes us a couple of hours to rig and get underway, but it sure beats paying slip fees." He also cites the Dolphin's speed, saying he keeps pace with a Cal 34, trounces a Balboa 26 and Catalina 27, and has only "lost" to a San Juan 21 going upwind.

A Washington owner says she is very seakindly, with just the right amount of helm, though a bit tender due to narrow beam. Most owners use a 6-hp.

outboard in the well, though one said he opted for a 15-hp. outboard for better performance, and because it can charge the batteries. Construction is reported as heavy.

In 1971 the boat sold new for $5,995. Prices now are around $7,500, which for an original owner would have made it the best investment of these four boats. While we have always liked the Dolphin, we don't view it as suitable for regular trailering.

More likely, you'd keep it at a slip during the sailing season, parking it at home on its trailer after haul-out.

American 26

Costa Mesa, California was the epicenter of 1970s boatbuilding. American Mariner Industries is one company, however, better forgotten. It was in business from about 1974 to 1983.

Its American 26 was a 25 first. A 1974 brochure says, "This 25-footer so completely justified our judgment as to the efficacy of our unique stabilizer keel and hull...that we have moved on to provide the trail-and-sail cruising enthusiast with a choice of two versions—the American 23 and the American 26." This seems to imply that the same hull mold was used.

In any case, what is unique about this line of boats is the wide, partly hollow keel that makes a sort of trough in the cabin sole to provide standing headroom. It is not wide, but does run nearly the length of the main cabin.

Ballast is 900 pounds of lead laid in the bottom of the keel. Draft is 2' 4" for trailerability, but there is no centerboard, and due to the keel's extreme width, you can imagine that windward performance is poor. Unfortunately, we have no owner feedback on this boat to corroborate our assessment.

The boat sold new in 1974 for $8,995 base. The BUC Research *Used Boat Price Guide* says today it's worth about $6,000. Frankly, this design, which severely compromises sailing performance for standing headroom, seems ill-conceived. One can only guess at how many people have cracked their skulls stepping up out of the trough.

Aquarius 23

Coastal Recreation, Inc., also of Costa Mesa, was around from about 1969 to 1983. It acquired the Balboa line of trailer-sailers, and for a time built the LaPaz 25 motorsailer.

The Aquarius 23, and its smaller sister ship the Aquarius 21, were designed by Peter Barrett, a Webb Institute graduate and national champion in Finns and 470s. The Aquarius 23 is not much prettier to

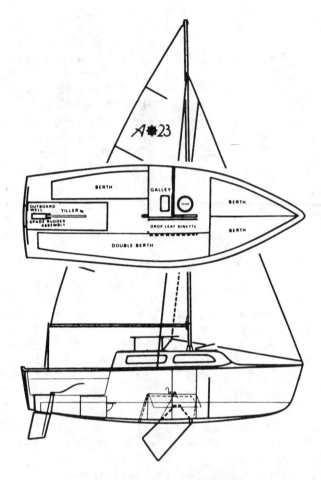

Specifications - Aquarius 23

LOA	22' 8"
LWL	21' 2"
Beam	7' 11"
Draft	1' 1"/4' 7"
Displacement	2,280 lbs.
Ballast	815 lbs.
Sail area	248 sq. ft.
Headroom	4' 11"

look at than the American 26, though it sails surprisingly well. Because highway trailering laws restrict the beam to 8 feet, the Aquarius 23 comes in just under at 7' 11" and relies on it for stability. Most of the 815 pounds of ballast is in the hull. A large centerboard retracts fully into a trunk, which is more or less concealed in the cabin as a foundation for the drop-leaf table. A peculiarity is that persons sitting at the table are all on the starboard side, and the forward person is forward of the main bulkhead, essentially in the head, though there is a fore-and-aft bulkhead making the toilet reasonably private (another important issue for trailer-sailers).

Like the Paceship PY 23 and many other trailer-sailers, the Aquarius 23 has a pop-top to provide additional headroom. We think this is more sensible than the American's keel trough, but we do caution that pop tops can leak and aren't designed for off-shore use.

Another unusual feature of the Aquarius is the absence of a backstay and spreaders. To support the mast, the shrouds are led aft, reflecting, we suppose, Barrett's one-design background. If not suited for wild and woolly sailing conditions, it is at least simple to set up, and that, after all. is the goal of most trailer-sailers.

Friends of ours bought an Aquarius 23 in 1970, and we spent a good deal of time sailing with them, including several overnight crossings of Lake Michigan. The boat handled well, was reasonably quick on a reach, and had more interior room than most 23-footers. Still, we were never very enamored of its looks.

Complaints from owners include lost centerboards and rudder repairs (like the Yankee Seahorse, it is an inside, removable type), poor ventilation, poor windward performance when overloaded, tubby appearance, and lack of a mainsheet traveler. Many owners say they bought the boat for its shoal draft and large interior, but that cheap construction caused numerous problems.

The Aquarius 23, in the early 1970s, sold for $6,195; today it sells for about $4,000. Though our memories of sailing this boat are all rosy, we think there are better boats available.

Conclusion

Our preferred solution to the keel/ballast problem in trailer-sailers is the traditional keel/centerboard as found on the PY 23, Tanzer 22 and O'Day 23, all of which we recommend. The keel/centerboard configuration eliminates the trunk in the cabin, places ballast below the hull, and does not concentrate all of the ballast weight on a pivot pin, as is the case with swing-keel designs.

We do not care for the American 26's hollow keel, believing that if you want standing headroom, either go outside or buy a bigger boat. Nor do we care particularly for narrow shoal keels without centerboards, because windward performance suffers, or boards that leave all the ballast in the hull—whether lead, iron or water—as ultimate stability is compromised.

How one solves the choice between interior space and sailing performance is a personal decision. We, too, appreciate spaciousness down below, but at the same time have always chosen boats that looked and sailed decently, willing to give up a few inches of elbow room for a boat we could feel proud of when rowing away in the dinghy. **• PS**

O'Day 25/ Montego 25

A pair of boats that are quite similar: both represent the transition from daysailer to small cruiser.

The O'Day 25 is really two boats; a fairly fast, stiff, deep keel boat, and a slower, tippier, keel-centerboarder which has made performance compromises in order to create a maximum size trailer sailer.

The Montego 25, on the other hand, despite its shoal and deep draft versions, is too deep, wide, and heavy for ordinary trailering. It is a transition yacht (a small cruiser, often trailerable, that tries to offer the performance and accommodations of a larger boat), by virtue of its size and accommodations.

The O'Day 25 is one of the most successful of all 25 footers. Thousands have been built, and they were cranked out at a steady pace by Bangor Punta's Fall River, Massachusetts plant until the model was discontinued in 1983. The O'Day 25 tries to be the all-purpose 25-footer, with short or tall rig, deep or shallow draft, outboard or inboard power.

In trying to build the 25-footer for everyone, O'Day made a number of compromises:
• The beam is limited to 8' for uncomplicated trailering.
• The shoal draft version lacks the stability to carry the tall rig the boat needs for really good performance.
• The boat is heavy enough to require a size of outboard for auxiliary power that is a big handful.

At the same time, the sheer volume of production of the O'Day 25 means it is a boat whose cost was kept to a minimum, a boat with an established market value and good resale potential almost everywhere, and a thoroughly debugged boat. All of these are important considerations for the buyer of a 25-footer, who may already be looking forward to owning a 27- or 28-footer a few years down the line.

In addition, the keel-centerboard version of the O'Day 25 does provide a maximum-size trailerable

Specifications - O'Day 25

LOA	24' 10"
LWL	21' 0"
Beam	8' 0"
Draft	2' 3" (cb), 4' 6" (keel)
Displacement, lbs.	4,007/3,962
Ballast, lbs.	1,825/1,775
Sail area, sq. ft.	270 (cb), 290 (keel)

cruiser with adequate accommodations for normal vacation-length coastal cruising. This assumes, of course, that you have a vehicle capable of towing 4,000+ lbs., and a heavy trailer—owners suggest a trailer with a capacity of 6,000 lbs. The O'Day 25 adds up to a big package for trailering.

By all indications it's a popular package. Almost 90% of the O'Day 25s sold were the trailerable keel-centerboard version.

Surprisingly, fewer than half the respondents to our owners' survey considered shoal draft or trailerability of primary importance in their decision to buy an O'Day 25. This may be a reflection of a common phenomenon: owners of maximum sized trailerables often find the hassle of trailering, launching, and rigging more than they care to go through for

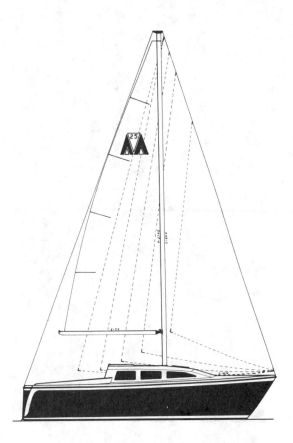

Specifications - Montego 25

LOA .... 25' 3"
LWL .... 20' 6"
Beam .... 9' 1"
Draft .... 3' 6" (std), 4' 6" (deep)
Displacement .... 4,550 lbs.
Ballast .... 1,800 lbs.
Sail area .... 306 sq. ft. (100% jib)

a day or weekend of sailing. After a year or two of this the boat ends up in a slip or on a mooring.

With the Montego 25, the decision has already been made to move from a trailerable to a non-trailerable boat. Despite characteristics such as a shoal draft option and outboard power, the Montego 25 buyer has made the choice to move into a boat whose home for the sailing season is a marina, rather than the driveway at home.

The choice of shoal draft and outboard power for the Montego 25 are determined by the waters sailed and the depth of the buyer's pocket, rather than the need to keep weight and draft to a minimum for trailering.

Construction

The O'Day 25 and Montego 25 are generally similar in construction. Both are solid uncored hull layups

with wood cored deck moldings. The Montego 25 uses plywood coring, the O'Day 25 uses balsa.

Both boats use what we consider to be "small boat" hull-to-deck joints. The O'Day 25 uses a simple coffee can or shoebox joint, fastened with self-tappers and adhesive compound. The Montego 25 uses an outward turning flange which is riveted and glassed over on the inside. Vinyl rubrails cover the hull-to-deck joints on both boats.

This is the maximum size boat suitable for external hull-to-deck joining. External joints are subject to damage in collisions or even in hard docking. Covering the external joint with a rubrail may give the impression that it's okay to use the joint as a bumper. It isn't.

Neither boat uses faired-in through hulls. A handy owner can resolve this lack in a couple of hours using epoxy and microballoons and a little elbow grease. Gelcoat quality of both boats is good.

Although both the Montego 25 and O'Day 25 come in shoal and deep draft versions, their approaches to the problem are quite different. Both the shoal and deep draft versions of the Montego 25 use external cast iron keels, bolted to a shallow keel stub. On the deep draft boat we examined, the keel had been faired to the stub using fiberglass cloth, which had begun to separate from the iron keel in several places after a season of use.

Any dings in an iron keel such as that of the Montego 25 should be ground to bright metal and coated with coal tar epoxy before applying bottom paint. Direct application of copper or tin bottom paint to an iron keel will create severe surface erosion if the boat is used in salt water.

The differing draft versions of the O'Day 25 are very different in character. To make the boat trailerable, the shoal draft O'Day 25 uses a long, shallow keel stub with inside lead ballast. A centerboard gives additional lateral plane for going to windward, but adds little to stability. Over the years, O'Day has gradually added several hundred pounds of inside ballast to the shoal draft 25 in order to improve stability, which has of course increased the weight for trailering.

In the deep draft O'Day 25, a deep glass stub keel replaces the long, shoal keel box of the centerboard boat. A high-aspect ratio fin keel is bolted to this stub keel, giving a substantial draft of 4' 6". The external keel casting is lead, but it took a little work to figure that out. Some at O'Day said the keel was iron, others insisted it was lead. The argument was settled by drilling into the keel casting. It is, we can report with confidence, lead.

It's a good thing that the keel is lead, because it needs a bit of fairing to improve efficiency. The trailing edge is blunt, and the keel casting is poorly faired to the fiberglass stub keel. Lead planes almost as easily as hard wood, so refairing the keel of the deep-draft O'Day 25 is a simple task. Of the dozen or so deep draft O'Day 25s we looked at, about half the owners had taken the time to fair the keels. It should be worth the effort in improved performance.

Some owners report trouble with the rudder of their O'Day 25. In the centerboard version the rudder is five inches deeper than the keel stub. This means that the first part of the boat to contact the bottom when you run aground is the rudder. If you're moving along at a fair clip, a grounding can tear the rudder off the stern of the boat. Construction of both boats is perfectly adequate for usage up to and including coastal cruising. We would not particularly want to take any boat of this size offshore, independent of the quality of construction.

Handling Under Sail

The fin keel, tall rig O'Day 25 and the deep draft Montego 25 have identical PHRF ratings of 219. The rating of the O'Day 25 changes significantly with different rig, keel, and engine combinations.

The outboard powered keel-centerboarder, for example, has a rating of 234—15 seconds per mile slower than the deep keel, tall rig boat. This difference reflects the vastly different character of the two versions of the same boat. The deep keel boat has a more efficient lateral plane and a lower center of gravity, giving much better performance than the keel-centerboard model. Owners report the keel-centerboard boat to be tippy, and the fin keel boat to be stiff.

In addition, the tall rig of the deep keel boat gives slightly greater sail area—enough to make the boat a competitive family racer. Unless very shoal draft and trailerability are essential, the deep keel, tall rig version of the O'Day 25 is the obvious choice. The extra stability, extra sail area, and underbody efficiency add up to a boat that behaves more like a big boat than a small boat.

Both the deep keel and shallow keel versions of the Montego 25 are good performers. If the depth of your sailing waters allows, we would choose the deep keel version for the greater stability and extra lateral plane.

The rigs of the O'Day 25 and the Montego 25 are almost identical Kenyon rigs, but halyards of the Montego 25 lead aft to winches, while O'Day's winches are mast mounted.

These are big boat rigs, with substantial mast sections, airfoil spreaders, and good-sized standing rigging. Booms are set up for jiffy reefing. Mast fittings, tangs, and chainplates are substantially heavier than would be found on boats only marginally smaller.

In other words, these boats have transcended the "toy boat" syndrome so often seen on boats in the 20' to 25' range, and have rigs strong enough for more than fair-weather sailing.

Handling Under Power

The 4,000 lb O'Day 25 and 4,500 lb Montego 25 are at the real outside limit for using outboard power. With high freeboard and no remote controls, starting and throttle operation are a bit of a nuisance, since the outboard must be mounted far down the transom to keep the prop in the water. Remote outboard controls are a must.

Most owners will use a 10 hp outboard on either boat. In a flat calm, it should easily be able to push the boat. However, once there is any wind or sea, the weight and windage of these boats mean that a 10 hp outboard is close to minimum power. Unfortunately, a larger outboard is heavier, more expensive, and stretches the capacity of most outboard brackets. In addition, the propeller of any outboard will have trouble staying in the water as the boat pitches.

The O'Day 25 has a molded-in outboard fuel tank holder in the port side of the cockpit. The Montego 25 has none, so right away you must figure out where you'll keep the gas tank.

There is a growing tendency to put small diesels in boats of this size. Both the Montego and the O'Day offered the Yanmar 1GM as optional auxiliary power. Inboard power adds over 100 lbs to the weight of the O'Day 25 compared to the outboard version.

For a boat that's already pushing the upper limit of easily trailerable weight, every pound hurts. However, inboard power greatly adds to either boat's function as a cruiser. If all your sailing is done on a lake—where strong winds and seas are not likely to be a problem—inboard power is probably an unnecessary expense. On the other hand, if you plan to do a considerable amount of cruising along the seacoast or in the Great Lakes, the convenience, range, and power of an inboard engine begins to make sense.

If we trailer-sailed on Lake Lanier, Georgia, for example, we might choose the centerboard O'Day 25 with outboard power. If we kept our O'Day 25 on a mooring in Newport, Rhode Island, and cruised to Block Island, Nantucket, and the Elizabeth Islands, we'd be more likely to choose the tall rig, deep keel O'Day 25 or the deep keel Montego 25 with inboard.

Deck Layout

Neither boat has a particularly complicated deck layout. Both have an anchor well forward, single lifelines, and a fairly large cockpit.

Because its shrouds are set well inboard, it's far easier to get to the foredeck of the Montego 25. The inboard shrouds should produce narrower sheeting angles and give better upwind performance.

Both boats have cockpit seats long enough to double as fair-weather berths. Both boats also have substantial bridgedecks, fitted with a mainsheet traveler. The mainsheet traveler on the O'Day 25, however, is merely a flat piece of track with a slider. Several O'Day 25 owners said they'd prefer a ball bearing traveler, such as that on the Montego 25. We would, too.

The tiller on both boats takes up a lot of the cockpit. In addition, the tiller fitting of the Montego 25 we examined had a fair amount of play in it. O'Day 25 owners report the same problem. This can frequently be remedied by the owner.

Belowdecks

The trade-off between a trailerable 25 footer and one not constrained in beam by the highway laws is readily apparent when comparing accommodations of the Montego 25 and the O'Day 25. The extra foot of beam of the Montego 25 gives the boat much greater interior volume than the O'Day 25.

O'Day had the fine art of mass production boatbuilding down pat. Nowhere is this better seen than in the interior of the O'Day 25. Much of the interior furniture is incorporated in the body pan. A fiberglass headliner finishes off the overhead. This saves a lot of time in building the boat, and keeps the cost down.

On the other hand, the Montego 25 also uses a molded body pan, but does not use a deck liner. instead, the inside of the cabin trunk is faced with teak veneer, and the overhead is finished with a vinyl liner. The cabin sole of the Montego 25 is teak ply, and the boat uses a solid teak companionway ladder and solid teak companionway drop boards.

By contrast, the O'Day 25 has a fiberglass cabin sole, and uses a molded box step and the top of the galley counter as a companionway ladder. In other words, finish detail of the Montego 25 is better than that of the O'Day 25, and you pay a price for the difference.

Interior accommodations of the two boats are remarkably similar, but the extra beam of the Montego 25 gives greater elbow room. Headroom of the Montego 25 is almost 6' under the main hatch. The O'Day 25 has 5' 6" headroom.

With V-berths forward, two main cabin settees, and a quarterberth, each boat sleeps five, although a slide-out settee in each brings nominal sleeping capacity to six. Do you really want to sleep six on a 25 footer? The zoo that the interior of either boat would be on a rainy morning when everyone was trying to get up and get dressed would probably be enough to turn the most sociable of sailors into a singlehander. Unfortunately, the "How many does she sleep?" syndrome is alive and well in both boats, at the expense of storage space and galley space.

Both boats are big enough to have a separate head compartment. Separate from the main cabin, that is. The head is really part of the forward cabin on both boats, a not unreasonable compromise in a five-berth 25 footer.

Small boat galleys rarely offer much except headaches for the cook, and neither of these boats is an exception. The O'Day 25's icebox is tiny—the auxiliary box in the cockpit is really a daytime beer cooler—and is almost cut in half by the centerboard pennant trunk. While the O'Day 25 has a deep sink,

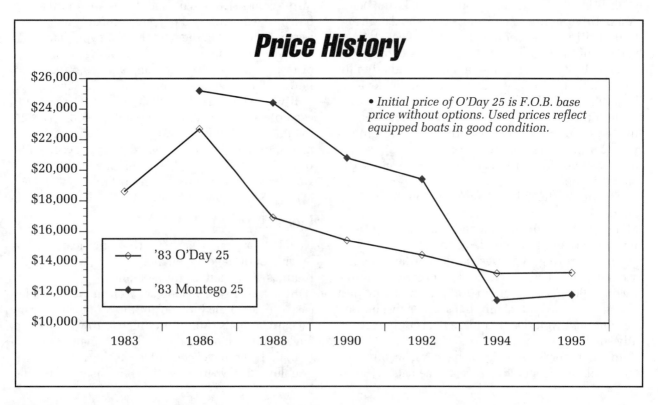

Price History

• Initial price of O'Day 25 is F.O.B. base price without options. Used prices reflect equipped boats in good condition.

◇ '83 O'Day 25
◆ '83 Montego 25

it is almost directly underneath the companionway. Coming below with the boat heeled on port tack you're likely to put your foot in the sink.

The Montego 25 has a larger icebox with an insulated lid. The insulation for the lid is styrofoam, however, and is exposed on the underside of the lid. It is likely to take a lot of abuse.

The Montego 25 has a slide-away two burner alcohol galley stove which stores over the quarterberth. It is slightly easier to use than the same stove on the O'Day 25, which must be removed from a storage compartment and set on the galley counter for use. Since cooking under way is barely practical on a boat of this size, the lack of gimballing for the stoves is not a serious shortcoming.

Both boats have a reasonable amount of storage, as long as you don't want to unpack your seabag. Under-settee storage bins, found on both boats, would be far more useful with drop-in molded plastic trays, which are better for keeping things dry. O'Day offered the plastic trays as an option in the 25.

Conclusions

Both the Montego 25 and the O'Day 25 are good examples of the transition yacht—boats for owners wishing to move up from trailer sailers to small cruisers. Both retain some small boat features — outboard power, shoal draft options—while having many of the basic components of larger boats. These big boat features include deep draft options, sturdy cruising-type rigs, inboard power options, enclosed heads, and permanent galleys.

The shoal draft version of the O'Day 25 is still trailerable, but it is at the outside limit of size and displacement. The compromises in performance to make the O'Day 25 trailerable—short rig, less stability, keel-centerboard configuration—make the trailerable version of the boat more of a "small boat" than a "big boat."

Equipped with an inboard engine and a deep keel, either boat will make a good coastal cruiser for a couple with two small children, Putting more people on the boat for anything but daysailing will be more like camping out than cruising. The deep keel, tall rig O'Day 25 represents just about the minimum investment you can make in an inboard-powered pocket cruiser. For the couple or small family moving up from a trailer-sailer such as the O'Day 22, Catalina 22, or MacGregor 22, either the Montego 25 or the O'Day 25 provides a true transition from the weekender to the true pocket cruiser, at a minimum investment. **• PS**

Catalina 270LE Beneteau 265 Hunter 27

A comparison of three new entry-level cruisers favors the Catalina on price and practicality

People who start in small boats and trade up often view 27 feet as some kind of milestone, and rightly so. At around 27 feet, an inboard engine and the possibility of standing headroom are enticing. Accommodations often become spacious enough for two couples or a family of four to live aboard for a couple of weeks without strain. And hull speed with appropriate sail and engine power typically permits average-weather runs of 35 to 40 miles in an 8-hour day—long enough legs to satisfy the wanderlust of most cruisers.

Three of the newest 27-foot cruising boat designs are from Beneteau, Catalina and Hunter, all major builders. Beneteau bills itself as the largest sailboat company in the world; Catalina lays claim to being the largest in the U.S. Hunter is well-known for its entry-level boats. The new designs of these companies often set the tone for styling by other sailboat makers.

Initially, we'd hoped to be able to test all three boats head-to-head, but Hunter refused due to some criticisms we had of the Hunter 23.5. We did locate a privately owned one later the same year, however, and were able to give it a try; that review can be found later in this chapter. First, though, we'll discuss the Catalina and Beneteau.

Checking out both boats at a mid-1993 show, we noticed that the base list price of the Beneteau First 285 with inboard ($38,050) was less than 10 percent above the base for the Catalina 270LE ($34,775). Their Euro-styled interior layouts were at least superficially similar as well, as were hull and sail plan dimensions. Which boat, we wondered, is the better buy, and for whom?

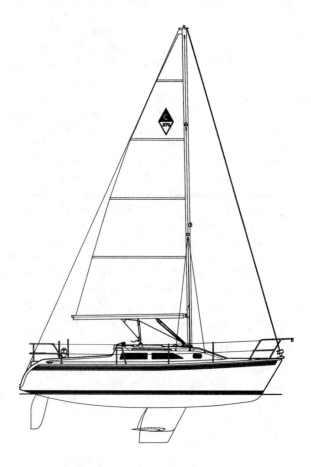

Specifications - Catalina 270LE

LOA	27' 0"
LWL	23' 9"
Beam	9' 3"
Draft (wing/fin)	3' 6"/5' 0"
Displacement	6,400 lbs.
Ballast	2,000 lbs.
Sail area	316 sq. ft.

Design

Both the Beneteau and the Catalina utilize modern wide-body, fin-keel, spade-rudder configurations, relatively long waterlines, and moderate rigs with shrouds moved inboard to permit a narrower sheeting base. The Beneteau has a slightly shorter LOA but longer LWL (length waterline), and a nearly plumb bow. The 285's draft is mid-range (4' 2" vs. the Catalina's choice of 5' 0" deep fin or 3' 6" fin with wings).

Both test boats had inboards. Catalina does not offer an outboard option as it once did with its old 27. Catalina's chief engineer, Gerry Douglas, doesn't think it's suitable for a 27-footer, especially one weighing 6,400 pounds-and, he says, neither did

Specifications - Beneteau 265

LOA	26' 5"
LWL	24' 2"
Beam	9' 5"
Draft	4' 2"
Displacement	4,800 lbs.
Ballast	1,450 lbs.
Sail area	330 sq. ft.

most buyers of Catalina 27s over the last several years. (Among other problems, in a seaway an outboard prop tends to ventilate too much).

Still, Beneteau, with a 4,800-lb. boat, does offer an outboard version (base price $32,900 excluding engine, which is $5,150 below the inboard Beneteau price with engine) and recommends a 9.9-hp. outboard for those who wish to go this route. So far, few buyers have. Beyond the ventilating prop problem, the reason is mostly economic: By the time Beneteau buyers acquire the outboard engine and associated paraphernalia, the difference between inboard and outboard shrinks to around $3,500—and those who opt for the outboard miss the shore power option and electric hot water heater option which Beneteau throws in "free" with the inboard package.

The rigs of the two boats may appear quite similar at first glance, but upon close inspection a number of important differences emerge. The Beneteau features a seven-eighths rig with single spreaders, adjustable split backstay, mast stepped on deck with compression strut in the cabin, and shrouds tied into a force grid molded into the cabintop via a set of studs threaded into a patented configuration involving stemballs set into bronze plates. (We'd prefer a set of conventional—and more easily adjustable and replaceable—turnbuckles.) The mast is stepped on a hinge for lowering the spar at bridges, trailer ramps, or for maintenance, but Beneteau says use of the hinge is not recommended without side-sway preventers—currently available as an option in Europe, but not in the U.S.

The Beneteau's genoa sheets lead to cars riding on C-shaped aluminum tracks, which double as handrails, on the cabintop. It's not easy to grab the tracks/rails, which require feeding your fingers through a narrow slot molded into the coachroof. We'd rather see separate handrails. We'd also prefer to see the Beneteau's cockpit-mounted mainsheet traveler track moved forward onto the cabintop (as the Catalina is configured), so crew moving from cockpit to cabin don't have to dodge the mainsheet and car. But, unfortunately, moving the track forward isn't feasible because of the long companionway bridge deck, which reaches forward beyond the boom's midpoint.

The Catalina's masthead rig, even with double spreaders (permitting use of a lighter spar than the Beneteau), is more conventional. Although the Catalina's mast is shorter and its mainsail is smaller, the foretriangle height is two feet longer than the Beneteau's, resulting in more total sail area when setting a big genoa. The Catalina's rig design strives for simplicity (no backstay bridle adjustment, no line-adjusted genoa car position as on the Beneteau), and ease of use. Helping to make sailing the Catalina a no-hassle experience is an impressive array of standard equipment not seen on the Beneteau: A double-ended mainsheet, adjustable either at a cam cleat on the traveler car or at a cabintop stopper, where a winch can be used; a pair of two-speed Lewmar self-tailing #30s (compared to Beneteau's single speed #16s); a standard 135-percent genoa on a good-quality Hood single-line furler (compared to Beneteau's standard 100-percent jib and furler hardware available only as an option); a total of five cabintop stoppers (vs. three for the Beneteau; Dutchman mainsail flaking system; and single-line reefing (though the Catalina test boat did not have single-line reefing rigged).

Other features on deck also favor the Catalina. Working aft from the bow: The welded pulpit, like the stanchions, is 1-inch stainless steel tubing (vs. the Beneteau's 7/8-inch), has two horizontal rails (vs. one for the Beneteau) and four legs (three for the

Beneteau). There are twin anchor rollers at the stemhead (one on the Beneteau). Both boats have anchor lockers built into the forward deck, but the Beneteau's locker has a water tank fill cap in its bottom. This can make it extremely inconvenient to fill the tank when line and chain are piled over the cap. And the combination bow light is mounted directly behind and partly obscured by the center support of the pulpit.

Moving further aft, the Catalina's six stanchions are fitted with double lifelines and, being 24-3/4 inches off the deck, give a good measure of security. In contrast, the Beneteau has only four stanchions, less than 18 inches high, with single lifelines. The low lifelines are at "tripping height," and while the scale may be aesthetically pleasing, safety is compromised. If we were buying the Beneteau, we'd insist that she be retrofitted with taller stanchions.

The cockpits on both boats have comfortably high, canted coamings and angled seats. The Catalina's cockpit is noticeably roomier, due not only to the absence of a cockpit traveler, but also to the placement of the wheel way aft, with an athwartships helm seat 5 feet wide—big enough for three for cocktails at the mooring. On the Catalina, there's room for nine at the dock, as big a cockpit as could be desired in this size boat. And that doesn't include a pair of "observation seats" built into each corner of the pushpit.

In contrast, the Beneteau seats no more than seven at the dock, and that assumes that one passenger is seated atop the traveler and the tiller is swung up out of the way.

We have no objection to tillers—in fact we generally prefer them in this size boat—provided there's no noticeable drag in the rudder tube and that the forward end is a comfortable height over the sole. Unfortunately, the Beneteau failed both tests, even

with the height adjustment screw at the rudder head in the extreme "down" position.

The Catalina's 32-inch stainless steel destroyer wheel on a pedestal is an Edson, a brand we associate with high quality and reliability. The size and placement is good for steering from either a sitting or standing position; brake and compass binnacle (4-inch Danforth Constellation) are standard; pedestal-mounted brackets for additional instruments such as depth sounder and speedo are extra.

The Beneteau's compass is optional, mounted along with any other optional instruments on the cabinhouse bulkhead, a better position for crew viewing but not as good for the helmsman.

Both boats have swim platforms and stainless swing-down swim ladders. The Catalina easily wins the Ladder Sweepstakes with a four-step, 24-inch wide ladder with flat plastic treads, compared to the Beneteau's three-step, 8-1/2-inch wide ladder with treads only 1-1/4-inch wide, made by flattening the stainless tubing a bit.

The Catalina's ladder swings up to form the center part of the pushpit, a clever and neat-looking design. The Beneteau ropes off the transom area with a length of lifeline and a pelican hook.

Both swim platforms are molded into "sugar-scoop" transoms, and both are elevated 9 inches off the water, with a bit of transom projecting below. The bottom of the Catalina's transom misses the water by a couple of inches, but the Beneteau's, with a short horizontal lip extending aft below the platform, is slightly immersed and thus attracts sea life, evident

---

The Catalina's interior is brightened by the use of a two-layer Plexiglass skylight abaft the mast. The only real complaint we have is with the table, which has a troublesome lowering mechanism.

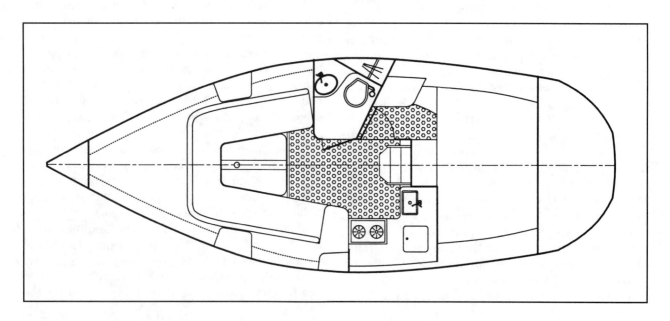

from the unsightly coating of saltwater slime on our test boat.

Construction

Both boats utilize external bolt-on lead keels, suitably thick fiberglass lay-up schedules, solid glass hulls and balsa-cored decks, and reasonably strong hull-deck connections. Both have highly engineered force grids molded into their hull liners, of particular note since the shrouds in both boats lead not to traditional chainplates but to intermediate tie rods, which in turn are joined to metal plates for the most part hidden behind interior liners. On both boats we would prefer better inspection ports to view these crucial joints.

On both boats, the pulpits and stanchions are fastened to the deck with a single large threaded stud, projecting down through the deck and secured with a large washer and nut. Although this design is somewhat non-traditional, it seems solid enough. Still, we question what will happen to the deck when someone falls against a stanchion; four through-bolts and large backing plates to distribute the load would be better.

Even more dubious are the two parts of the backstay bridle on the Beneteau which are simply fastened to straps welded to the bases of the pushpit, rather than to their own chainplates. Because of the extra forces involved, we'd worry about stress cracks eventually appearing around these bases.

Deck hardware (blocks, tracks, hatches, ports) on the Catalina is mostly made by Garhauer, Nibo, and Beckson, all vendors noted for producing decent-quality but low-cost equipment. On the Beneteau, Harken, Spinlock, and Lewmar are predominant. As already mentioned, both boats use Lewmar winches. We judged all branded hardware on both boats to be of acceptable quality.

Performance

We did our testing on the Manatee River off the pier of Massey Yachts in Palmetto, Florida. (Massey sells both Catalina and Beneteau). The test Catalina was the wing-keel version; the Beneteau had the standard rig. (A tall rig is optional.)

Both boats seemed quite stiff, well balanced, and very responsive to the helm. Both could be spun in more or less their own length. The day we sailed the Beneteau, it was blowing 15 knots steadily and 20 in gusts, and the 265 heeled not more than 25 degrees close-hauled with full sail. This impressed us. So did the Catalina, which was at least as stable on a breezier day (wind 20-25, occasional gusts to 30) with full sail, only burying the rail once in a particularly vicious wind burst. In short, we wouldn't hesitate to sail either boat in gusty weather.

Though hard to judge in such strong, shifting winds, we think the Beneteau had the edge in sailing speed, as her statistics would indicate. Under power, however, her smaller engine and prop (single-cylinder, 9-hp., 26-CID Volvo, 15 x 12 optional folding prop) was definitely not as effective upwind as the Catalina's (three-cylinder, 18-hp, 37-CID Perkins, two-blade 13 x 10 prop). The Catalina's Perkins also was smoother and quieter, despite the fact that its engine box (two removable clam-shells back to back, of fiberglass-foam sandwich construction) had no added insulation, while the Beneteau's plywood box was lined with soft foam. Engine and shaft log access was very good on the Beneteau, superb on the Catalina.

At the moment, PHRF for the Beneteau is 168. The Catalina's is not yet determined, but we would anticipate it will come in around the 195-205 range.

Interior

The interior layouts on the two boats are quite similar: large double berth aft, galley to port next to the companionway, head opposite the galley, U-shaped dining area around a smallish table supported by the mast compression post, and V-berth forward.

These overall similarities make the differences between the designs more obvious. For example, on the Catalina the entrance to the double aft is via a solid teak door, whereas on the Beneteau it is through a sliding curtain.

All berths on both boats have comfortable 4-inch cushions. The aft berth on the Beneteau measures 60" x 77", and you sleep parallel to the keel; the Catalina is slightly narrower at 57 inches wide, is 74 inches to 86 inches long depending on which side you're on, and you sleep athwartships. We wouldn't be inclined to sleep two in either aft berth, since the inside party not only doesn't have much vertical roll-over room due to incursion of the cockpit sole, but also must crawl over the outside party to get up.

Neither the Catalina nor the Beneteau forward berths have these problems. On the Beneteau, you can lower the table and set up the berth without undue commotion; but setting up the Catalina berth involves a lot of fussy positioning of the raised forward seat and locking it in place with a pair of hard-to-reach latches. We'd like to see Catalina re-study the process to make set-up easier.

The forward berth on the Beneteau measures 19 inches at the front, 76 inches at the back, and is 88 inches long. On the Catalina it's 10 inches at the front, 68 inches at the back, and 75 inches long. Tall folks will appreciate the larger Beneteau berth.

The Beneteau has the edge on locker space, with three separate hanging lockers (including one open-air unit in the head), and a liquor cabinet under what a Beneteau brochure describes as a nav station. In reality, there's not enough space to unroll even a small chart on the work surface presented, which is effectively cut in two by a fiddle across its middle. Still, the "nav station" top gives the galley slave some countertop space—space sadly lacking in the galley where it should be. The Catalina also suffers from lack of sufficient galley top working space.

The use of maintenance-hungry exterior wood has been completely eliminated on the Catalina, and minimized on the Beneteau except for the companionway drop slides (King StarBoard plastic on the Catalina, nicely varnished cherry-veneer plywood on the Beneteau).

Below, both boats use some wood to visually warm up the otherwise mostly white interior. The surface is totally fiberglass on the Catalina, but on the Beneteau, soft white foam-backed vinyl lines the upper halves of the hull sides. If this vinyl is anything like the stuff used on boats 15 or 20 years ago, the foam backing can be expected to dry out and crumble to powder eventually.

Catalina's use of wood is sparing (varnished teak doors and trim, teak dining table, small patch of maple and teak sole forward), while Beneteau's is lavish (varnished cherry bulkheads and trim, full teak sole). The wood is set off on both boats by neatly made upholstery on berths and settees, on the Catalina by a combination of Ultrasuede-like material and light patterned cotton fabrics, on the Beneteau by a practical and soft dark green velvet.

The Beneteau interior gives an impression of good craftsmanship, above-average but not consummately executed, and a dark though pleasantly airy cabin. On the Catalina, the impression is of a more basic, but much lighter and equally airy boat. The Catalina's lightness is helped by a skylight of milk-white Plexiglas (two layers thick) abaft the mast, and more area in the main cabin ports. For ventilation, the Catalina has six opening ports plus a forward hatch,

while the Beneteau has eight plus a forward hatch. Screens for the ports (but not for either the forward or main hatch) are standard on both the Catalina and the Beneteau. Neither boat has a roll-up sunshade over the forward hatch, which would be a nice touch.

The Bottom Line

To some extent, the choice between .. the Beneteau 265 and the Catalina 270 LE is a tradeoff between elegant French styling on the one hand, and no-nonsense American practicality on the other. (Of interest to "Buy America" advocates is the fact that both boats are built in the U.S., the Catalina in Woodland Hills, California, and the Beneteau in Marion, South Carolina.) <p2>The choice is also between the Beneteau's lighter hull with quicker acceleration, and the Catalina's equally maneuverable but heavier hull with greater load-carrying capacity and living space below.

All boats are compromises, and personal taste and prejudices do enter the picture. That said, we admit to a clear preference for the Catalina. We especially like the lightness and brightness of its interior, enhanced by numerous large ports and an overhead skylight. Most of all, we like the Catalina's greater value for the money—not just because the overall price is about 10 percent lower than a comparable Beneteau, but because of the better choice of standard items.

For example, note the differences between some of the Beneteau's items and the Catalina's: 9-hp. raw-water-cooled engine vs. 18-hp. freshwater-cooled;

The Beneteau's interior is quite similar to the Catalina's. One big difference is the aft cabin berth, which is oriented fore-and-aft on the Beneteau, athwartships on the Catalina.

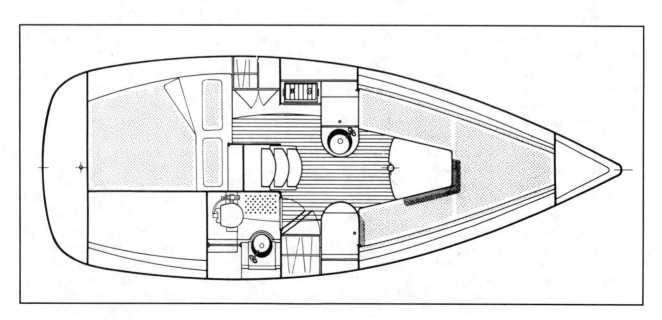

no engine tach or fuel gauge vs. both standard; 8.25-gallon fuel tank vs. 14 gallons; 16.25-gallon water tank vs. 26 gallons; holding tank 11.5 gallons vs. 18; single-speed #16 self-tailing Lewmars vs. two-speed #30 STs; a 1.6 gpm Shurno pressure water pump vs. a 2.8-gpm Shurno pump; a gimbaled two-burner non-pressure alcohol stove vs. a gimbaled two-burner LPG stove, and so on.

Now if Catalina would only install a good-size hanging locker, put in more working counter surface in the galley, make it easier to make up the forward berth....

The Hunter 27

The comparison between the Catalina 270LE and Beneteau First 265 was originally conducted in the summer of 1993. At the time, we were hoping to include the Hunter 27.

Unfortunately, Hunter Marine declined to let us test sail the boat, citing criticisms contained in an earlier review of its Hunter 23.5 water-ballast boat. Undaunted, we asked readers if any owners of Hunter 27s might be willing to let us inspect their boats and go sailing. A couple who keep their boat in Fairhaven, Massachusetts, responded, welcoming us to sail with them on Buzzards Bay. In early September of that year we spent a day with the father and son.

Since our test of the Hunter was conducted at a different time, under different conditions, we'll present it separately here.

The Hunter 27 is available in both inboard and outboard configurations. The inboard version of the Hunter 27 sold for about $35,000, essentially the same as the Catalina 270LE ($34,775) and somewhat less than the Beneteau 265 ($38,050). Like these two, the Hunter 27 has contemporary styling inside and out: scoop transom with swim platform, sloping cabin top, and an open interior plan with the head aft and a double berth under the cockpit.

Taken as a trio, these boats are similar enough in design, size and price to make good head-to-head comparisons.

Design

The Hunter 27, like the other two, has a modern underbody with fin keel and spade rudder. The keel is shoal (3' 6") with a bulb/wing configuration. A deep draft version isn't available.

The boat has a sharp entry and is very fine forward, while the boat's beam is carried quite far aft to provide interior volume for the aft berth and tank space under the cockpit.

Freeboard, interestingly, appears to be greater on the Hunter at the aft quarters than at the stemhead: we measured 40" versus 38" This compares with a more normal 32" aft versus 41" forward on the Catalina, and 32" versus 44" on the Beneteau. Under

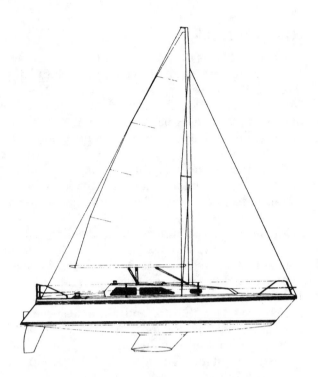

Specifications - Hunter 27

LOA	26' 7"
LWL	22' 5"
Beam	9' 0"
Draft	3' 6"
Displacement (inbd)	5,000 lbs.
Ballast	2,000 lbs.
Sail area	307 sq. ft.

sail, we sometimes had difficulty sighting the bow; we think the boat would look better with a lower stern and a higher bow, and that this would also keep the foredeck drier.

The waterline of the Hunter 27 is 22' 5", almost 2' shorter than the Beneteau and 1' 4" shorter than the Catalina; in many ways waterline is a more accurate measurement of a boat's size than length overall (LOA).

Displacement is 5,000 lbs., making it about the same as the Beneteau (4,800 lbs.) and considerably lighter than the Catalina (6,400 lbs.). Ballast is 2,000 lbs., same as the Catalina.

When comparing similar boats, it's instructive to look at weight without ballast (i.e., how much the fiberglass structure, engine, tankage and equipment weighs). The Catalina weighs in ex-ballast at 4,400 lbs.; the Beneteau at 3,350 lbs.; and the Hunter at an even 3,000 lbs., extremely light for a 27-foot cruising boat.

Rig and Deck

The Hunter 27 has a 7/8 rig with 1/4" upper shrouds and single lowers secured to the same chainplates; the spreaders are swept back. The 1/8" backstay is split to permit easy access through the pulpit gate to the swim platform. A backstay tensioner isn't provided, as on the Beneteau, but one could be added for not much money.

Standard sails by UK Sailmakers are a main with one set of reef points (including jiffy reefing hardware), and a 110-percent jib. According to the owners of the boat we sailed, the dealer had "thrown in" a Cruising Design jib furler at no cost. Feeling that the boat was underpowered with this sail, the owners bought a 150-percent genoa for the furler, saying it makes a big difference in light air.

Standard winches are self-tailing single-speed Barient #17s for the jib, and a single-speed #10 Barient on the cabin top for the halyards, compared to larger two-speed winches on the Catalina. Halyards are led aft through Garhauer clutches. A boom vang, with Schaefer blocks, is standard. The sheeting system for the main is a six-part mid-boom arrangement located over the seahood, which keeps it out of the cockpit. The tail is led through a cam cleat operable from the port side of the cockpit; we found it fairly easy to trim.

Edson wheel steering is standard, as seems to be the norm these days on boats of this length, though to some a tiller will seem more appropriate. The Beneteau has a tiller and the Catalina a 32" Edson wheel. A 3-1/2" Ritchie compass, smaller than on the Catalina and Beneteau, mounted on the pedestal is standard on the Hunter.

Other comments, working aft from the bow: It will be difficult to install a roller to handle ground tackle as the freshwater fill is located about as close behind the stem fitting as one could possibly place it. (This is because the forepeak is quite small and one wouldn't want the fill hose coming down next to the V-berth.) The anchor locker will take a lightweight anchor with a stock no longer than 21 inches; we consider this lunch hook size. (Both the Catalina and Beneteau have bigger lockers.) On the Hunter, a larger anchor must be carried aft in a locker or lashed to the pulpit.

Both bow and stern pulpits are made of 1" stainless steel and appear to be well made, though we prefer four-bolt bases to this baseless type that secures with a single nut under the deck (as do the Catalina's and Beneteau's). Stanchion height is 22", 4" higher than the Beneteau's, which we think are too low, but about 3" shorter than the Catalina's, which also have double lifelines for added security on deck.

The cockpit is T-shaped, which makes it easy to walk around the wheel, and isolates the helmsman from the crew. At anchor, the full-width helmsman's seat is a pleasant retreat.

The down-side of T-shaped cockpits is that the bench seats aren't long enough to lie down on, though one could make insertable shelves to bridge the gap between the benches and the helmsman's seat.

To use the swim platform, you undo the pelican hook gate, and lift out the center portion of the helmsman's seat and hang it on the stern pulpit. A four-step stainless steel swim ladder folds down into

The Hunter 27 has an open interior, with the head aft and a double berth under the cockpit. A lack of stowage space is its main drawback, in our opinion. We'd like to see a privacy curtain to separate the V-berth from the main cabin.

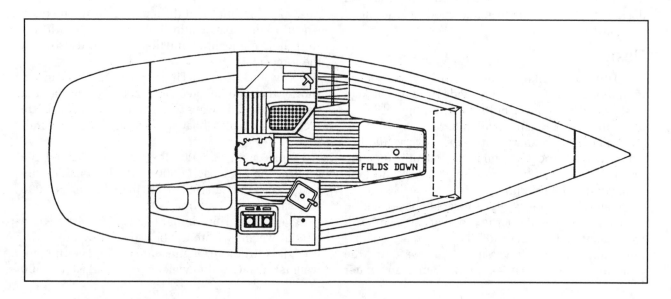

the water, making entry from the water pretty easy. We liked this arrangement.

Construction

Many boat hulls with reverse, scoop transoms must be laid up in two halves, then glassed together later. A good job of reinforcing this joint, filling and fairing, makes it unnoticeable. Some top-of-the-line boats, including the Hinckley Bermuda 40, are built this way (and not because they have scoop transoms). Hunter has taken a different approach for some years, instead incorporating the transom into the deck mold. But this leaves an unsightly joint running around the edge of the transom; it wouldn't look bad if the bedding compound wasn't visible.

The wing keel is external iron bolted to the hull with 5/8" stainless steel bolts. There are no visible floor timbers or a glass grid to distribute the load.

The bilge is very shallow, as is common on this sort of boat, but we think that some sort of sump should be provided as it doesn't take much water to overflow this small area. In fact, the owner of our boat said there were so many deck leaks from the stanchions (he said the starboard-side stanchions and pulpits had no bedding) that the factory-provided float switch on the electric bilge pump burned out the first season. They had additional difficulties keeping the bilge dry because there was no check valve in the bilge pump hose to keep water from falling back in once the pump was turned off; we don't necessarily expect a builder to provide the check valve, but it would be nice.

There is an inner liner or pan that forms the foundations of the furniture, and as is common, it makes inspection of the hull difficult in places. Thus we couldn't tell if or how well it was bonded to the hull.

Interior

Like the Catalina 270 LE and Beneteau 265, the Hunter 27 has no main bulkhead separating the V-berths from the main cabin. A privacy curtain is called for here, but none was provided on the Hunter. To give the V-berth its full length of 7', the athwartship dinette settee backrest is flipped up.

The berth is 55" wide (versus 68" on the Catalina and 76" on the Beneteau), and the narrowest of the three boats forward, too narrow for two sets of feet.

The U-shaped dinette is open and comfortable. The 36" x 24" table is reasonably sturdy, but only the starboard side leaf drops down, making access to the port settee a little clumsy. The port settee, by the way, at 5' 3", is intended only for kids. The starboard settee, at 6' 6", is fine for adults, though crew of all ages and sizes will have better shoulder room if the backrest cushions are removed.

In this plan, the head is moved aft to the port quarter; it's tight inside, but more than adequate for a 27-footer. There's a Par manual toilet, shower, molded fiberglass sink, and some stowage, though no wet locker as in the Beneteau's head.

Speaking of plumbing, the freshwater tank is located under the V-berth; water can be heated by shore power but not by the engine. The owner we sailed with criticized the lack of engine heating, adding that he felt misled by sales material.

The galley is again small but adequate, with a molded sink, two-burner Origo alcohol stove and a few stowage bins.

Aft, under the cockpit, is a athwartships double berth that is 47" wide (versus 57" on the Catalina and 60" on the Beneteau), and 81" long at the forward side by 67" long at the aft side. A fixed window in the hull and an opening portlight into the cockpit provide light and some ventilation. It would be tempting to criticize this arrangement, noting how the water heater could have been located here behind the engine (making it easy to provide hot water from the engine), and how sails and other gear could have found a home in commodious cockpit lockers. But this is a pretty comfortable berth, and it doesn't have to be made up each day, as is the case with convertible dinettes.

Interior finish is attractive. The overhead is textured fiberglass. The hull sides are foam-covered vinyl, which isn't particularly nice to the touch but fortunately there isn't much of it. There are teak slats (not really a "ceiling" in the proper sense of the word) on the hull sides forward, purely for decoration. Foam cushions are 4" thick (as the Catalina and Beneteau) and upholstered with a good-looking gray fabric.

The main detraction from the appearance of the interior is the lack of enclosed stowage, forcing one to use lots of string nets or just let stuff sit in the open. Owners may wish to add some teak trim here and there to hold charts and papers. Still, the cabins seemed cluttered. The reasons for this are clear: The Hunter has less beam than most of today's 27-footers; hence the settee backrests extend nearly to the hull in order to make the interior as spacious as possible; and because building drawers and cabinets is expensive, offering fewer of them helps keep the price down.

Performance

The day we went sailing, the winds began light, filling in as the day progressed, so that by mid-afternoon it was blowing 15-18, with occasional higher gusts.

The boat moved well in the light winds, making about 3 knots upwind in about 7-8-knot winds. She tracked fairly well and came about easily. As the wind increased, however, it was clear that a reefing the big mainsail was indicated. We tried luffing the main but on several occasions the boat rounded up uncontrollably, presumably because the rudder had stalled. We have been on a number of bigger boats that also do this, so we don't mean it as isolated criticism, but it is annoying, especially when there are boats available that don't round up like this, including both the Beneteau and Catalina.

Thinking we could continue to carry the full main off the wind, we bore off on a broad reach. However, the boat yawed quite a bit in mild seas, occasionally going into a big roll that seemed unwarranted. At that point, it was late in the day and we went in. The owners told us that they added a second reef to the main and that the boat handles much better with two reefs; they were mildly critical that just a single reef is standard.

We also felt the boat was a bit tender, both at the dock and underway. Though the 2,000 pounds of ballast seems like more than enough (the stiffer Beneteau carries just 1,450 lbs.), greater draft might help. Then again, it could have something to do with the amount or distribution of weight, or with hull shape (i.e., lack of form stability), but we saw neither the hull out of the water nor the architect's drawings, so are unable to comment on the exact causes.

Boat speed when reaching in a good breeze was 6 knots and we felt that on all points the Hunter 27 moves with appropriate speed.

Under power, the Yanmar single-cylinder 9-hp. diesel (half the power of the Catalina) knocks loudly, but moves the boat at hull speed, at least in calm winds and sea. It backs up straight, which is more than you can say for many other boats.

Conclusion

Our overall impression of the Hunter 27 is that it may be an adequate weekender for beginning sailors navigating in settled weather, though disquietingly skittish and tender. Both the Catalina and Beneteau handled better, and this weighs heavily against the Hunter, since sailing ability is what it's all about.

In terms of quality, we did note that the Hunter's joinerwork was better than in earlier years; still, there were a number of examples of sloppy workmanship. For example, the sea hood was improperly placed on the cabin top, so that stepping on it produced cracks in the corners. Neither did we particularly like some hardware choices: The bronze seacocks do not have flanges as specified by the ABYC, and the plastic Beckson portlights are not very substantial.

The price tag is essentially the same as the Catalina, but in almost every respect the Catalina emerges as the better boat and the better buy-stiffer, roomier, more of a "big boat" feel, more powerful engine, bigger winches, bigger standard jib, more opening ports, and a longer list of standard gear.

For these reasons, if we were looking to buy the Catalina 270LE, Beneteau 265 or Hunter 27, for cruising we'd still choose the Catalina because of its better space, stability and standard gear—or the Beneteau for its superior performance. **• PS**

Our test boat sailed well, though we found it a bit tender.

Five Midrange Racer/Cruisers

With $20,000 or so to spend, we go shopping for the best 30-footer we can find.

Sometimes the search for a good used boat begins simply with a budget and a rough idea of desired length. The next step is a perusal of the want ads in the local paper or regional shopper, and almost always the *Soundings* classifieds. There, among the thousands of listings you're likely to see the familiar names—Hunter, Pearson, Cal—as well as one-off racers, steel boats, and a smattering of foreign makes.

Because there are some good used-boat deals out there (industry analysts predict new and used prices will ascend once more), we decided to look at some middle-of-the-road family cruisers, suitable for weekending and occasional coastal cruising.

We chose the 29-30 foot range because that's about the point at which boats begin to look and feel like genuine cruisers, with standing headroom, inboard engines, full galleys and private heads. Because our "budget" is a modest $20,000 or so, we won't look much at anything more than 30 feet, beyond which boat prices seem to rise exponentially.

The budget also rules out some 30-footers, like the $75,000 Nonsuch 30 we saw listed this summer. Unexpected bargains aside, we begin our search realizing that how much we pay ultimately will be decided by a boat's size, original value, age, condition, and market reputation. Interestingly, because so many builders have gone out of business during the past 10 years, the value of "orphans" doesn't seem to have been adversely affected.

We also realize, particu-

larly in this size range, that there are so many builders and models we can't hope to cover them all. Hence our first shopping criterion: if you're at all concerned with resale value, stick with a well-known builder.

Columbia 8.7

The Columbia 8.7 was introduced in the late 1970s as one of the early models in the builder's new line of Alan Payne-designed "widebody supercruisers." Over the years, it was built under several company ownerships in several locations, from Virginia to Ontario, Canada. Although there are some differences, mostly in the choice of engine, the 8.7 has remained a comfortable cruiser with nothing startling about its performance, despite a lot of initial

Columbia made a big deal of the 8.7's wineglass transom, which it said reduced the quarter wave from a frothy wake to a quiet burble.

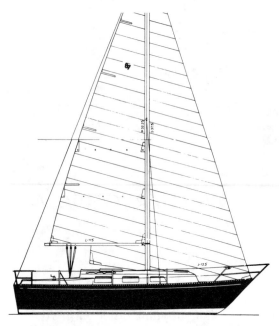

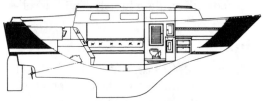

Specifications - Columbia 8.7

LOA	28' 7"
LWL	23' 2"
Beam	10'
Draft	4'8"
Displacement	8,500 lbs.
Ballast	3,500 lbs.
Sail area	424 sq. ft.
PHRF	200

clamor about the design.

Payne, the Aussie 12-Meter designer, was given wide latitude, and some good money, to come up with this innovative line, including the construction of models and test boats. He gave the 8.7 a straight sheer, a fairly flat bottom with firm midship bilges and a U-shaped bow. The rudder is located quite far aft and the prop is behind a skeg that fairs into the keel. And of course there is the distinctive wineglass shape from the stern view.

At 8,500 pounds with a modest sail plan, the boat is no *Gretel*, especially in light airs (the PHRF improves to 192 in windy northern California). But it is

stiff, as well as being nicely-balanced on all points of sail.

With a 10-foot beam, the 8.7 isn't more of a "widebody" than most of its contemporaries. Much of the interior space comes from carrying the beam aft and the relatively tall cabin, which accounts for the 6' 1" headroom below.

The teak-finished interior contains a small head, a well-equipped galley (with oven), and hanging locker with a three-drawer bureau; the lack of opening ports and vents on older models results in poor ventilation. Post-1984 models came with opening ports and Dorade vents.

• **Worth Checking**: Older models, with unanodized masts, should be checked for signs of corrosion; also the masthead shroud tangs that were factory-redone at some point; the two-piece rudder where delamination has been a problem; signs of water stains on the teak veneer under fixed ports; the integrity of the secondary bonding of the plywood Columbia used to beef up the uncored laminate hull.

• **Conclusion**: This is a well-built middle-of-the-road cruiser that offers good accommodations for its vintage. While not speedy, it's stable and makes a good coastal sailer for the family or beginner.

Though not necessarily an unsuccessful design, it never quite caught on—note the dramatic drop in resale values. Look for the later models with opening

The Gary Mull-designed Newport 30 could be considered a "value boat," but we think there are better boats available at the same price.

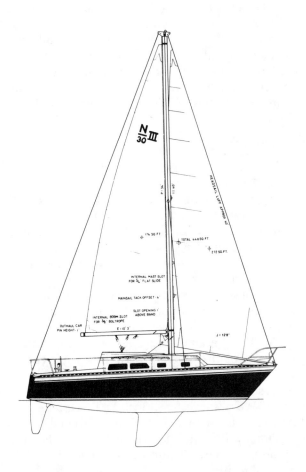

Specifications - Newport 30 (II/III)

LOA	30' 0"/30' 6"
LWL	25' 0"/26' 6"
Beam	10' 6"/10' 8"
Draft (deep)	4' 9"/5' 2"
Draft (shoal)	3' 11"/4' 0"
Displacement	8,000 lbs./8,500 lbs.
Ballast	2,600 lbs./NA
Sail area	419/425 sq. ft.
PHRF	180/170

ports and the higher-powered Yanmar 2QM15 diesel.

Newport 30 Phase II/MK III

The Newport 30, by Capital Yachts, was another of a slew of production cruisers introduced in the 1970s, when builders were modernizing their lines and attempting to build bigger-boat accommodations into smaller hulls.

This boat, in several versions, was one of the more successful in terms of sales, especially in southern California. Gary Mull, also an America's Cup designer, who died this past summer, designed the

original Newport circa 1971 for Capital Yachts and also the Phase II, debuting in 1976. The Mark III (we're not sure who modified it) came out in the mid-1980s. In all, more than 1,220 Newport 30s were produced. In all versions, the 30 was a relatively fast performer with good accommodations.

Owners report it as fairly stiff, but we have to wonder about the manufacturer's offer of "additional ballast," at $395, for the MK III. Satisfied owners cited value-for-price and the interior as main selling points.

The cockpit is roomy, but forward-sloping seats tend to collect rainwater and the scuppers are inadequate by most accounts. There's lots of headroom in the teak-trimmed interior below, 6'1" in Mull's version, 6'3" in the MK III.

Newport 30 owners reported lots of annoying problems, as well as horrendous dealer response. Quite a few later models also suffered from hull blistering. Additional complaints included inadequate wiring, poor ventilation, rudder stock and bolt failures, and poor to awful performance under power, especially with the undersized Universal Medalist 15.

• **Worth Checking**: Deck for signs of delamination, especially around the chainplates; through-hulls for substandard metal; signs of leaking at chain locker and chainplates.

• **Conclusion:** This is another average cruiser for a couple or small family, easily handled and stable. If we were tempted to buy a Newport 30, which we aren't, we'd look for a later Phase II version (or an unblistered MK III) that has been heavily upgraded by previous owners. Like the Columbia 8.7, resale values have plummeted; the good news in both cases is that you might pick one up at a bargain price.

Tartan 30

We liked the Tartan 30 when we first evaluated it, and we still like its value as a used boat today. Designed by Sparkman & Stephens, the 30 made its debut in 1971 and 750 were built before production ended in 1980.

Like most Tartans, including the new ones designed by the Tim Jackett team, the 30 was solidly built, offered good accommodations for its size and performed very well, especially to windward. Of the many 30s introduced during the 1970s, the Tartan compares favorably to the competition in just about every category.

Today, the 30 shows its age somewhat—and not just in the cosmetics of the gelcoat. Down below, things are a bit cramped within the 10-foot beam and storage is at a premium. Owners often find themselves using the V-berths (also cramped) for extra storage.

Two interior layouts illustrate the usual trade-

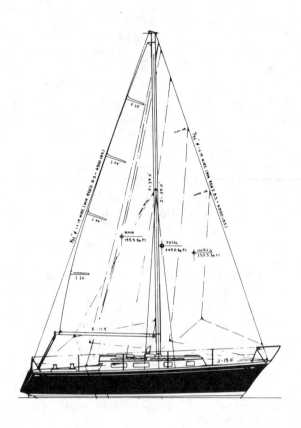

Specifications - Tartan 30

LOA	24' 3"
LWL	23' 2"
Beam	10'
Draft	4' 11"
Displacement	8,750 lbs.
Ballast	3,500 lbs.
Sail area	449 sq. ft.
PHRF	170

offs: The aft-galley plan eliminates one of the two quarter berths but leaves room for a settee berth to starboard, while the midship galley to starboard eliminates the settee but enhances cooking and permits a second quarter berth. All models suffer from off-center engine placement—in the way, under the saloon table.

• **Worth Checking**: Condition of the standard Atomic 4 (a new diesel's the best bet); mast step and butt for signs of corrosion; condition of teak cabin sole and main bulkhead tabbing; bilge area around keel for signs of a grounding or other abuse—loose timbers or keel bolts, misaligned engine shaft.

• **Conclusion**: Now 20 years old or more and selling for about its original retail price, the Tartan 30 represents staying power; that stability reflects the boat's successful blend of performance, sturdiness and undated styling. Many of the asking prices we saw seem too high; we'd be reluctant to spend more than $20,000 unless it had been repowered with a diesel.

Ericson 29

This 1970s Bruce King design has aged reasonably well. Our best guess is that about 500 were built between 1970 and 1979, with a 1974 modification that created a split cockpit to isolate the helmsman. Somewhat heavy for its length at 8,500 lbs., and with a relatively shallow modified full keel, the 29 needs lots of air to get moving. Some owners describe the boat as "solid," while others complain that it's tender; once again, we'd diagnose this as initial tenderness, that is, a boat that settles in at 15-20 degrees heel.

The Ericson 29 is no speedster off the wind, and some complain of its pointing ability, saying an early reduction in sail improves performance. At the same time, several owners complain of excessive weather helm. We'd suggest sail-testing in various conditions, playing with main and headsail combinations. Obviously, it can be made to move; in its day it won numerous races, including a Canadian Half-Ton championship.

The plethora of bunks make the interior of the Ericson 29 look like a crash pad. Not much attempt was made to hide the fiberglass pan.

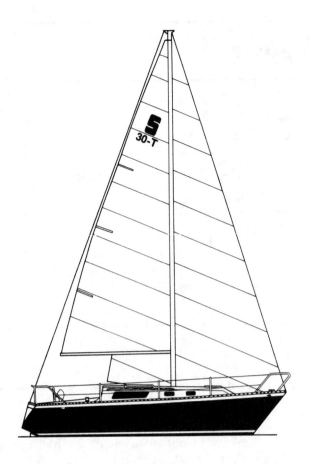

Specifications - Seidelmann 299/30T

LOA	29' 11"
LWL	24' 0"
Beam	11' 0"
Draft (deep)	5' 5"
Draft (shoal)	4' 2"
Displacement	8,000 lbs.
Ballast	3,600 lbs.
Sail area	420 sq. ft.
PHRF	170

Construction is solid, and most owners report no serious problems after 15 years or more of hard sailing. In fact, it's a remarkably complaint-free boat. One early problem, poor ventilation, was partially resolved during the makeover, with the addition of a skylight hatch. The interior, however, is bedeviled by Ericson's attempt to cram bunks onto almost every horizontal surface, sleeping six officially but giving the belowdecks the appearance of a crash pad. Since any boat this size will accommodate only four with any comfort, fewer bunks and more room for stowage, a chart table or a bigger head, would have been better. Engine access is poor on the port side,

which unfortunately contains the fuel system components.

• **Worth checking:** Exhaust and fuel tank for corrosion; whether a fuel/water separator, such as a Racor, has been installed; gate valves replaced by proper seacocks; condition of the wooden hatch.

• **Conclusion:** This is a good coastal cruiser, stable and easily sailed shorthanded, but not the best choice for those who crave speed or sail in predominantly light-air waters. Construction is average-plus; we've never liked fiberglass furniture foundations. The later models have a skylight hatch, but check out the divided cockpit first. Although Ericson is no longer in business (Pacific Seacraft is building some models), the name still carries recognition. Like the Tartan 30, the Ericson 29 has held its value pretty well, but again we think mid-20s is too much.

Seidelmann 299/30T

At this point, it's safe to say the name Seidelmann won't be associated with Tartan, Pearson or Sabre in the annals of nautical history. A one-design racer from Jersey, Bob Seidelmann was a sailmaker turned boatbuilder. His Berlin, New Jersey plant produced several models from the late 1970s to the late 1980s, including a 25, 29.5 and a 37.

In marketing (if little else), Seidelmann took a Hunter approach, providing a sailaway package that included sails, inboard diesel, dock lines, etc. for a modest price that ranged from $24,000 or so early on for the 299, to as high as $60,000 for the 30T in 1985. The builder advertised little and often sold factory-direct. At one time it was affiliated with powerboat builder Pacemaker.

The boats looked slick, offered considerable interior space and performed fairly well. But many owners (we got a four-page letter from one detailing defects) soon regretted their choice. One told us, "I was dumb."

A newer design than the others surveyed here, the 299 or 30T (a T-shaped cockpit and wheel appears to be the main difference) is an extremely beamy boat with narrow ends. Headroom is a generous 6' 5" in the main living area. Both models "sleep six in total comfort," according to company literature.

Seidelmanns apparently sail well in light airs, but tend to develop strong weather helm as the wind increases, even stalling, and need to be reefed early. A number of owners complained about tenderness; one said his portside water tank caused his boat to list.

Owner complaints were many—undersized fittings that broke or had to be replaced; peeling coatings on boom and keel, leaks from numerous sources, voids and blisters in the gelcoat; cracks in hull and deck.

One owner we spoke to, whose hull had cracked

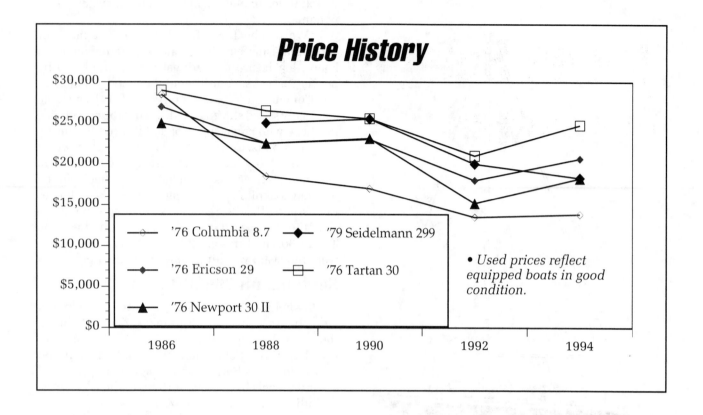

Price History

'76 Columbia 8.7   '79 Seidelmann 299

'76 Ericson 29   '76 Tartan 30

'76 Newport 30 II

• *Used prices reflect equipped boats in good condition.*

during its first winter lay-up, said you could see daylight from below through cracks in the deck. Once Seidelmann Yachts folded, the owner, now in the powerboat business, apparently declined to respond to complaints.

One positive note: Because it was introduced in '79, the 299 came standard with a diesel engine, whereas the others surveyed here were generally equipped with gasoline Atomic 4s.

• **Conclusion**: Seidelmanns make the point that a good value isn't necessarily a good boat. Although the cost of the 299/30T has dropped dramatically (note in "Price History" that the Seidelmann is three years newer than the others), we can't recommend either model. As a current owner told us, "We're stuck with ours."

The Bottom Line

Among the boats we looked at, the good points of the Tartan 30, plus the important fact that the manufacturer is still in business, makes us lean toward the Tartan 30. It's got the right mix of comfort and performance—like a newer Tartan, but within our budget. There are lots on the market, but many with too-high asking prices.

Other buyers, for their own reasons, might prefer the Ericson, which got high marks for quality from owners.

The Columbia 8.7 is built well enough, but has always looked a bit odd, then and now, which seems to have affected resale value.

The Newport seems a notch lower in quality despite attracting its share of buyers the first time around.

As for the Seidelmann 299/30T, our advice is to beat feet up the dock and keep looking.

Also worth considering are some of the early Dutch-built Contest 29s and 30s, which are a bit stodgy (especially the full-keel 29) but offer mahogany interiors with beautiful finish work; check the condition of the plywood engine access hatch, the chainplates and rigging—some owners have increased the sail plan to improve speed.

Nor should the better known makes be ignored. The Pearson 30, which defines the family cruiser of the 70s, is a good deal at between $15,000 and $17,000.

Some of the older O'Day and Hunter 30s are available at about $20,000, as is Bill Lapworth's Cal 2-29 and 2-30, the Yankee 30 and Ranger 29.

If you're more interested in a serious cruising boat, check out either the Alberg 30 and Pearson Wanderer, both well-built, full-keel designs that sell in the same price range as the fin-keelers mentioned here.

With any of the above boats, we'd favor one repowered with diesel, assuming, of course, that its price hasn't been jacked out of sight.   • **PS**

Three Semi-Custom Cruisers

The Alerion Sloop, Bristol Channel Cutter and Morris 40 cover the range from gentleman's daysailer to blue-water passagemaker. Each is of superior design and construction—it's nice to know you can still buy quality, but you'd better have deep pockets.

So often, we come away depressed from what has become a rite of autumn—the boat show. It's the same old story—nothing new under the sun. Oh, the giants like Catalina and Hunter may have squeezed in a 36 between their 35- and 37-foot models, or Beneteau may have some bizarre portlight design that catches your eye. But, you know the refrain: The more things change, the more things stay the same.

There's another reason why the anticipation with which we approach each new season soon falters: mediocre quality. As certainly as the leaves will fall, we will hear from friends and readers who after the show say they were appalled at some of the practices employed by boatbuilders: sloppy fiberglass and joiner work, non-marine grade parts, unsafe design elements and the like.

One might take this as a snipe at production methods, where cost cutting is the watchword, and that it is elitist to always demand better. We, like you, simply cannot afford top drawer. But still we like to look, and during the last year we've been aboard a handful of boats that just made us feel good to sit in the cockpit, a properly proportioned and contoured coaming supporting our aching back, running our finger over a tight mortise (no filler), and looking below to a cozy, well-appointed cabin, feeling drawn toward what designer Robert Perry calls the boy's cabin-in-the-woods (which we understand as a sort of primal approach-avoidance behavior: seeking, and taking a mysterious delight in, a safe haven in the danger zone).

Herewith are descriptions of three boats we'd be delighted to call our own, but due to financial constraints, probably never will.

The Alerion

Nathaniel Herreshoff, the famed "Wizard of Bristol,"

The high cockpit coamings of the Alerion make for comfortable and protected seating in blustery conditions.

Specifications - Alerion Sloop

LOA	26' 0"
LWL	21' 9"
Beam	7' 7"
Draft (board up/dn)	2' 5"/5' 2"
Displacement	6,000 lbs.
Ballast	3,480 lbs.
Sail area	383 sq. ft.

designed this 26-foot gentleman's daysailer in 1912. We believe he built two himself, one (which now resides at the Mystic Seaport Museum) that he sailed near his homes on Narragansett Bay and Bermuda, and another, Sadie, that lives at the St. Michael's Maritime Museum on Chesapeake Bay.

So the Alerion's history is a long one: Nathaniel's grandson Halsey designed a 25-foot fiberglass version for limited production, one of which was eventually bought by Alfred Sanford.

In 1978 Sanford's sons built a cold-molded wood version of the original Alerion on Nantucket (except that it was a half-foot beamier, to accommodate a modest interior, slightly shorter on the waterline, and had a small cutaway in the aft section of the

keel). They were beautifully made and the 20 sold are hard to come by on the used market. More recently, Carl Schumacher designed the 28-foot Alerion Express, which was first built by Holby Marine and now is built by TPI. The idea behind the Express was to combine the best elements of traditional looks with a modern "go fast" hull and appendages.

Which brings us to the latest incarnation of the Alerion, which is more or less faithful to Nathaniel Herreshoff's design (two differences: Capt. Nat's had a gunter rig, and, unlike this adaptation, did not have a balanced rudder).

It is built by Rumery's Boatyard in Biddeford, Maine, and "represented" by Kingman Yacht Brokerage in Cataumet, Massachusetts. The hull is constructed of vinylester resin with a Divinicell foam core; the deck is cored with balsa.

The house sides, coamings, toe rails, cockpit seats, cockpit and cabin soles, and louvered cabin doors are teak. The rudder post and hardware are bronze. The boat we saw had a Hall Spars aluminum mast (wood is optional) with Harken blocks, jiffy reefing, and a self-tending jib. Ballast is cast lead, internally positioned.

Rumery's intends to build just five or six a year, so there is a good deal of latitude in fitting out. Hull #1 has overnight accommodations that include a V-berth, small galley, navigation surface and reading chair. One may choose a varnished oak or spruce ceiling.

Optional is a Yanmar diesel (it seems almost sacrilegious to soil the bilge of this beauty with the oil that surely drips from an inboard).

We have two strong recollections of the Alerion. The first was in 1974, sailing Sadie on the Chesapeake Bay. The helm was effortless, and the hull seemed to move through the water with very little turbulence. She seemed not heavy, not light—just strong enough, and the proportions perfect. The second was perhaps 10 years later, on a rough day in Rhode Island Sound.

We were hammering along in our Pearson Triton and came upon Ron Barr (who owns the Armchair Sailor bookstore in Newport) and a friend, seated low in the deep cockpit, their heads as well protected as could be expected in a boat with such a low coachroof. Indeed, one is nothing if not comfortable in the cockpit of an Alerion. Priced at $52,500 with sails, you'd expect as much.

Contact- Kingman Yacht Brokerage, 1 Shipyard Lane, Cataumet, MA 02534; 508/563-7136.

The Bristol Channel Cutter

Lyle Hess today is an old man, losing his vision, which must be especially tough for one who likes to design boats, spending hours at the drafting table.

The Bristol Channel Cutter
LOD: 28' 0"
LWL: 26' 3"
Beam: 10' 1"
Draft: 4' 10"
Disp.: 14,000 lbs.
Ballast: 4,600 lbs.
Sail Area: 567 sq. ft.
Disp./Length: 346
SA/Disp.: 15.6

Specifications - Bristol Channel Cutter

LOD .... 28' 0"
LWL .... 26' 3"
Beam .... 10' 1"
Draft .... 4' 10"
Displacement .... 14,000 lbs.
Ballast .... 4,600 lbs.
Sail area .... 567 sq. ft.

But what an eye he had! Probably best known as the man who designed Lin and Larry Pardey's Seraffyn and Taleisin, Hess has also drawn several fiberglass production cruisers, including the 22-foot Falmouth Cutter and 28-foot Bristol Channel Cutter, or BCC for short.

The BCC, inspired by British work boats, is a heavy displacement cruising boat with a long waterline, short overhangs, full keel and big rudder. The cockpit, while small (it holds just 700 lbs. of water if filled) is quite comfortable, with generous backrests. The tiller does sweep much of its length, but is removable at anchor or when steered by a trim tab-type vane, as was fitted to Charles and Janet Smith's boat when we went aboard in Newport Harbor this

past summer.

Their's, called Freehand Steering, has a cloth vane attached to the backstay, which activates a trim tab hinged to the trailing edge of the rudder. This is a simple, very powerful type of mechanical self-steering.

Charles is 6' 6" tall. He told us he and his wife were looking for something larger than their Tanzer 22, a durable cruising boat in terms of both construction and aesthetic. They approached Roger Olson, one of the partners who bought the Sam L. Morse Co. in 1994. Roger had cruised a BCC for 13 years in the South Pacific and knows the boat intimately.

(He tells a funny story about working in the voluminous lazarette one day with the cover propped open. The boat moved, the tiller swung over and knocked the cover down, the hasp locking at the same time. He pounded until his girlfriend returned from shore and rescued him from his embarrassing yet serious plight. The hasps on all BCCs are now installed upside-down.)

In production since 1980, the details are much refined.

Back to Charles and his height problem. Olson arranged (for three grand) to lower the sole 1" and to cut off the coachroof of the cabin mold and raise the height 4" so Charles didn't have to wear a hard hat. They did an excellent job; it does not look at all ungainly.

The BCC is not a particularly fast boat, but performs very well for what she is. If you read Ferenc Maté's book, The World's Best Sailboats, he will tell you about a BCC that made the 3,150-mile passage from California to the Marquises in 22 days, averaging 5.8 knots, with a one-day run of 180 miles averaging 7-1/2 knots. That was Roger Olson, who, being a salesman now, will also advise you of these facts whether you're interested or not. Certainly they are noteworthy.

The hull is solid fiberglass with 3/4" bulkheads bonded on both sides to the hull; they even drill holes through the bulkhead so that the cured resin locks it in place.

Contributing to the appeal of the BCC is the scuttle hatch forward. This not only looks salty, but provides a secure deck area just abaft to work the mast. The drawback is the need to stoop when going forward from the saloon to the head, which is located under the hatch. The 8" bulwarks, bowsprit and bronze portlights continue the theme.

This is a go-anywhere boat, which, like the Alerion, is a piece of furniture (we'd varnish the raw interior teak pretty damn quick) that you hope your children will cherish when you pass on. The Smiths paid about $140,000 when all was said and done (radar, steering vane, sails, etc.). Base price is $122,500. The smaller Falmouth Cutter sells for $74,900.

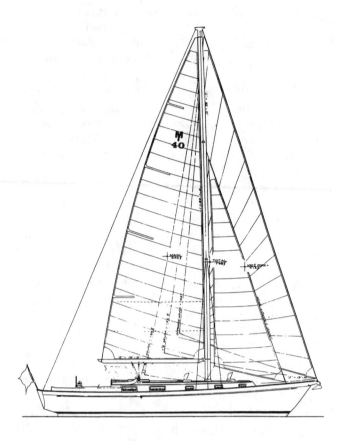

Specifications - Morris 40

LOA	40' 11"
LWL	32' 0"
Beam	12' 7"
Draft	5' 3"
Displacement	19,000 lbs.
Ballast	7,310 lbs.
Sail area	752 sq. ft.

Contact- Sam L. Morse Co., 1626 Placentia Ave., Costa Mesa, CA 92627; 714/645-1843.

The Morris 40

Tom Morris has been working the European market for some years now, principally Great Britain. In 1980, he licensed Victoria Marine to build his Frances 26 and Leigh 30 as the Victoria 26 and 30. Now he is licensed to build the Bowman 40 as the Morris 40. All are designed by Chuck Paine, a union too successful to mess with.

Paine says that he and Morris "Americanized" the Bowman for the U.S. market. This involved adding

11" to overall length, a bulb keel, taller rig and reduced weight. He calls the Morris 40 the "ultimate short-handed offshore yacht with sufficient speed for racing potential."

Morris eschews cored hull construction, but over time has felt the need to reduce the weight of a solid fiberglass hull. He now uses what he calls Rib-Core construction, which he says, "is engineered using longitudinal and transverse stiffeners encapsulated in the final inside laminate supported by the interior monocoque structure bonded to the hull and deck." This makes for a stiffer hull and a weight savings of 25%.

A cored hull, he estimates, would save an additional .9 lbs. per square foot of hull laminate. He makes up some of the difference with a few tricks such as using cored bulkheads. We think it's a very sound approach. We also like the fact that he uses all vinylester resin in the lay-up—more expensive, but with superior bonding and blister resistance properties. If you want to know more, read our review of the similarly constructed Morris 44 elsewhere in this book.

The low-profile coachroof provides excellent visibility for the helmsman, even without a humped seat. The side decks are wide and the foredeck easily worked. A custom weldment carries two anchors (we always anchor with two—a lightweight and a plow—a practice encouraged if they don't have to be untied or lifted out of a locker).

The engine is located under part of the galley, close to midships. Paine says this "further improves windward ability by reducing the mass moment of inertia of the yacht in pitching mode." (Chuck, where were you when we were attacked by readers for saying that keeping the ends light minimizes hobbyhorsing?).

The interior, of course, is exquisite, with much allowance for customization. It is essentially laid out for two couples (two double berths, two heads), though families could opt for single berths to separate the children.

The joinerwork is as good as any we've seen, here or abroad. Varnishing it will cost about $17,000, but having varnished the interiors of several boats ourselves, we are beginning to understand why it costs so much.

The Morris boats are, to our minds, a very successful combination of Paine's enduring style and Morris' quality construction; add the maximized performance obtained from the pared-away underbody and intelligent weight reductions and you get a boat that sails much quicker than it looks. The price sheet starts at $345,000, and the next slot in the production schedule is March 1996.

Contact- Morris Yachts, Clark Point Rd., Southwest Harbor, ME 04679; 207/244-5509. **• PS**

Buying Guide

-

Boats

Finding a Cheap Boat

Where to find salvages, repos, and auctions

Finding a bargain boat, if that's what you want, can be a matter of keeping your eyes open for opportunity. Last spring in our yard, we noticed that no one made an appearance at the O'Day 22 next door even as launch day approached. It turned out that the owner had conned the yard into hauling the boat without a deposit and simply disappeared. Could we have bought the boat for yard fees? You bet.

There's one big caveat here. The yard must have followed strict legal procedures in order to make a lawful sale. Since liens travel with a boat, not its owner, "You could be buying into a whole passel of troubles," says Dennis Nixon, a Rhode Island maritime lawyer. Many yards follow the quick route of filing a mechanic's lien, then obtaining a default judgment and holding a sale under the auspices of the state. This is above-board, but it doesn't erase any other liens and you may have difficulty in getting a state title. The safest route, Nixon said, is to buy through a U.S. Marshal's office; in this case, the yard has sued the boat and the marshal has cleared all liens and created a new title. "Never," Nixon said, "buy directly from a boat yard." Notices for both federal and state sales are posted in legal ads in the local newspaper of record.

Storm Bargains

Three summers ago, after Hurricane Bob, Joseph Migliore, an employee of the Rhode Island Department of Environmental Management, began calling insurance companies in hopes of finding a storm-damaged boat at a fraction of market value. Eventually, he was referred to a local salvage yard. After scouring over what he called "a great selection," he settled on a 1985 Hunter 31. The mast was gone, the rudder broken, and there was a six-foot hole on the port side. "It was beat up," Migliore said, "but it didn't sink. And the interior was in pretty good shape."

Migliore then spent close to 400 hours working on the boat. He spent an additional $15,000 for parts before renovations were complete. For Migliore, this was the perfect solution to moving up. "I couldn't have afforded a boat like that otherwise," he said.

Ernie Braatz, technical services director for BOAT/U.S., said BOAT/U.S. sold about 100 boats after Hurricane Hugo, another 75 following Andrew. In one case he handled, a Pennsylvania man got a bargain on a late-model O'Day that had been holed when Hurricane Gloria struck New England. "Three years later, it was a gorgeous boat, better than new," he said.

Braatz suggests going out and looking around after a major storm. "You have to get into the field, literally and figuratively, and poke around." BOAT/U.S. will hold its own regional auctions, usually one to two months after a storm.

But you don't necessarily have to wait for a hurricane. In one day alone last fall, Wentworth said he picked up three boats—two that went on the rocks and one that sank at its mooring. A call to insurance companies, or adjusters, should lead you to a salvage operation in your area.

Auctions

Or, how about those ads that promise to keep you informed of government auctions in your area at which, they promise, you can get "Vehicles Under $200!"—also sports cars, boats, RVs, etc.? We called one advertiser's toll-free number and got the spiel. For just $49.95, "fully refundable" if we weren't satisfied, we'd be on their mailing list for a year. Asked our location (Newport, Rhode Island), we were told, "There's government auctions there about once a week." Already something we didn't know. The annual fee was payable either by credit card or personal check. When we asked where to mail our check, the operator said, "Oh, you just give us your checking account information and we'll make the bank draft." No thanks.

There's no need to hire a middleman to get word of government auctions. Most government agencies in the auction business have their own public auction mailing lists, and an address when you can send a check or money order. U.S. Customs, which also handles boats for the Coast Guard, will send you a list of auctions, two to three weeks in advance of the sale, on a national basis, for $50 a year ($60 if you're out of the country), or, for $25, you can get either the west regional or east regional lists. They can be reached at EG&G Dynatrend, Attn. PAL, 2300 Clarendon Blvd., Suite 705, Arlington, VA 22201; 703/351-7887.

Finally, check the boat ads, especially newspapers and swappers. As with autos, there are a lot of motivated sellers out there. • **PS**

How Much Will $1 Buy?

New boat prices are up, but used prices are stable.

When buying a sailboat, many prospective buyers work from a fixed dollar amount, often a "no-more-than" figure. The question usually is: How much boat can I get for what I want to spend? It matters not whether the amount is $10,000 or $100,000.

Closely coupled with that limitation is the fact that for a given amount of money you can pick up a bigger old boat for far less money than you'll pay for a new one or a used boat only several years old.

For instance: For about $20,000, you can buy a new Precision 23 or J/22. For the same money, you can pick up a Pearson 35 or a Morgan 34—but they'll be about 20 years old.

To illustrate in greater detail, in 1990 *Practical Sailor* compiled (from thousands of advertisements and listings) a chart showing new and used boat prices, with the boats broken into five-year age groups. The chart clearly showed that, considered by the pound or by the foot, new boats carry a heavy premium and that the best buys were boats from 10 to 20 years old and 27 to 40 feet in length. This might be because so many boats in that size range were built in the late '70s and '80s, the halcyon days of sailboat production. In short, most segments of the used boat market still are glutted.

For 1994, we repeated the laborious exercise of scanning ads and listings, from all over the United States, and compiled a second edition of the 1990 chart shown on the following pages. The chart displays about 400 boats, cut down from the working chart because of space limitations. Five new boats, with sails and required equipment, are shown in each price category. We had space for seven boats in each used category. As before, we found too few expensive, old boats to fill some boxes.

It should be emphasized that the used boat prices shown are asking prices, not *selling* prices. Asking prices may be as much as 50 percent greater than the final selling prices.

Further, the asking prices are, with some exceptions, much higher than those listed in the BUC books we use to derive the price charts found in this book. The disparity in the price levels stems largely from the fact that ads and listings are *asking* prices while the BUC books supply *selling* prices based on actual transactions. Wishful sellers sometimes ask twice what a boat is worth. The average difference between "asking" and "selling" appears to be about 20 percent.

BUC's president, Walter J. Sullivan, said the sailboat market, severely battered in the last decade and recently pestered by an economy sweating about war, the banking crisis, a luxury tax and a national election, has shown a bit of a recovery this summer, especially in high-quality boats with good reputations.

"May, June and July were good months," he said. "August was not bad, either. Used boats are moving a bit better. I must emphasize that a boat's condition, equipment and location, which we factor in when compiling the BUC book data, are extremely important. And, the retail 'high' and 'low' must be considered as guides. A high-quality, 25-year-old boat that has been beautifully maintained and upgraded may be worth more than the 'high,' while a shabby, scruffy boat will fall below the 'low.'"

Indeed, it appears that some of the older fiberglass boats (those built in the early '60s) have ceased depreciating; in some instances, they seem to have increased in value.

Sullivan also said that because of the reduced numbers of boats produced in the last few years, it is difficult to find a good "young" used boat. Hence, the prices of some three- to five-year-old boats have increased.

"However," he said, "we're living in a complicated economic environment, and there's not yet a clear signal that anything significant is happening with boat prices."

Our new chart confirms Sullivan's considered judgment that nothing remarkable has happened to boat prices in the last three years.

Comparing our new chart with the prior one indicates clearly that new boat prices have increased 10 percent or more since 1990. Boatbuilders are stuck with increased costs and inflation.

However, the chart provides no trend or even a clue about what has happened to used boat prices in the last three years. For some boats the price appears to have remained the same. For others—usually desirable, high-quality, well-maintained boats like Hinckleys, Shannons and Com-Pacs—the price has gone up a bit. The bulk of them have merely moved down one price category on the chart because they

1994-95 Sailboat Prices: New & Used

Age	$5,000		$10,000		$20,000		$30,000		$40,000	
New	Com-Pac 16XL Catalina 16	6,988 6,500	MacGregor 26 Mariner 19 Beneteau 210 Catalina 22 Precision 18	10,990 9,795 14,500 9,500 8,560	Precision 23 Hunter 26 Nimble 20 J/22 Com-Pac 23D	15,900 18,850 18,000 18,750 23,995	Alerion Express 28 J/24 Seaward 25 Classic 26 Catalina 270	32,900 31,000 30,000 30,200 34,800	Nimble Kodiak 26 Precision 28 Com-Pac 27-2 F-24 Tri Beneteau 265	37,000 39,900 48,195 40,200 39,800
1-5 Yrs. Old	'92 West Wight Potter '87 Capri 18 '83 Freedom 21 '84 MacGregor 22	4,800 5,500 6,000 4,450	'88 Nimble 20 '88 Cal 22 '88 Beneteau 23 '89 Hunter 23 '89 Precision 23 '90 MacGregor 26 '89 Catalina 22	9,900 10,500 13,900 9,995 12,995 10,000 11,500	'88 Bayfield 25 '88 O'Day 27 '88 Olson 25 '88 J/24 '90 Capri 26 '89 J/27 '89 Marshall 19	22,000 18,500 18,000 24,950 23,900 21,900 19,500	'88 Com-Pac 27 '88 Pearson 27 '89 Catalina 27 '89 O'Day 285 '89 Com-Pac 29 '88 Beneteau 28	34,000 32,500 32,900 28,500 33,000 34,500	'88 Irwin 32 '88 Ericson 28 '89 Hunter 30 '91 Nimble 25 '91 Catalina 28	39,950 39,500 39,900 36,500 39,900
6-10 Yrs. Old	'79 San Juan 23 '81 Neptune 24 '80 J/24 '78 Pacific Dolphin 24 '81 Balboa 26 '78 Paceship 23	5,900 7,800 6,500 9,500 6,500 5,000	'87 J/22 '84 Hobie 33 '84 Watkins 25 '84 Catalina 25 '84 Com-Pac 23	11,900 13,900 9,500 9,000 8,400	'85 C&C 27 '84 Catalina 27 '83 Hunter 30 '83 Tanzer 27 '85 Gib'Sea 27 '84 Cape Dory 25	21,000 16,500 23,500 23,500 24,900 24,000	'84 Soverel 33 '84 J/29 '84 Catalina 30 '84 Pearson 303 '85 Irwin 34 '85 Hunter 31 '85 Cape Dory 28	29,500 25,700 30,500 35,000 32,000 32,500 30,000	83 Beneteau 35 '85 Bayfield 29 '84 Endeavour 33 '85 Hunter 34 '83 Catalina 38 '84 Tartan 3000 '83 Nonsuch 26	42,000 34,500 45,000 42,000 42,500 36,000 36,000
11-15 Yrs. Old	'74 Tanzer 22 '76 Chrysler 26 '74 Cal 25 '77 Ranger 23 '75 Ericson 23 '75 Catalina 22 '75 Balboa 23	4,500 5,200 5,250 5,500 5,790 3,500 3,800	'83 J/24 '78 Lancer 30 '80 Santa Cruz 27 '80 Cal 2/25 '82 Catalina 27 '82 Albin 28	12,000 12,950 12,500 9,000 14,500 14,750	'80 S2 28 '80 Irwin 30 '78 Catalina 30 '78 Santana 30 '82 Islander 28 '80 Bayfield 29 '79 Pearson 28	21,000 16,500 23,950 17,500 16,500 16,000 17,500	'81 Nicholson 33 '78 Ranger 33 '82 Morgan 32 '79 S2 9.2A '81 C&C 30 '82 Cape Dory 28 '78 Sabre 28	31,500 31,700 34,500 27,000 29,000 28,500 26,000	'80 O'Day 37 '78 Bristol 35.5 '78 Columbia 35 '81 Tartan 33 '80 Islander 32 '81 Niagara 31 '81 Southern Cross 31	39,500 43,500 43,500 44,000 45,000 41,900 44,950
16-20 Yrs. Old	'68 Sailmaster 26 '68 Columbia 28 '71 Cal 25 '71 Herreshoff 18 '69 Yankee Dolphin 24 '72 O'Day 22 '72 MacGregor 22	5,500 6,500 5,900 4,000 6,200 3,995 3,400	'76 Folkboat 26 '74 Tanzer 28 '74 Chance 30/30 '76 Catalina 27 '77 Pacific Seacraft 25 '74 Pearson 30 '74 Columbia 28	12,500 12,900 12,000 8,500 15,000 15,000 10,000	'75 Ranger 33 '76 Bristol 30 '79 Seafarer 30 '75 Cal 2-29 '76 Catalina 30 '73 Morgan 30 '76 Irwin 28	23,500 20,000 16,900 17,000 16,900 18,000 15,700	'75 Fales 32 '74 Seafarer 36 '76 Kenner Skipjack '75 Farr 36 '77 Ranger 33 '74 C&C 33 '76 Westerly 36	28,500 33,000 32,000 35,000 30,000 24,000 35,000	'77 Allied Seawind 32 '76 Fuji 32 '74 Irwin 37 '77 Sabre 34 '77 Downeaster 38 '76 Gulfstar 37 '78 Dufour 35	39,900 37,500 39,900 39,500 38,000 44,000 40,000
21-25 Yrs. Old	'67 Shark 24 '66 East Wind 24 '64 Columbia 26 '67 Pearson Ariel 26 '68 Coronado 25 '67 Columbia Sabre 32	4,250 6,400 6,000 6,000 6,900 7,000	'69 C&C 28 '68 Tartan 27 '71 Pearson 26 '69 Seafarer 26 '71 Irwin 23 '71 Morgan 27 '69 Columbia 28	9,990 12,500 8,000 8,000 8,500 7,800 13,000	'69 Cal-30 '70 Grampian 30 '72 Tartan 30 '68 C&C 31 '70 Ericson 29 '69 Pearson 35 '70 Morgan 34	16,900 15,900 18,500 18,000 21,500 25,000 16,500	'71 Contest 33 '71 Tartan 34 '70 Island Trader 37 '71 Dickerson 36 '72 Bristol 35 '69 Cheoy Lee 31 '71 Hughes 38	30,000 29,000 30,000 34,500 30,000 27,950 29,900	'73 Mariner 32 '72 C&C 39 '71 Cheoy Lee 36 '72 Allied Princess 36 '68 Tartan 34 '79 Downeaster 32	38,500 38,000 43,000 42,900 40,000 40,000
26 Yrs. or Older	'62 Stoutfella 28	6,800	'63 Seafarer 28 '66 Pearson Ariel 26 '65 Columbia 29 '64 Contest 25 '60 Pearson Triton 28	13,000 8,000 12,000 9,500 9,900	'67 Columbia 34 '66 Pearson 30 '65 Galaxy 32 '65 Pearson Vanguard 32 '66 Pearson Alberg 35	23,900 17,350 19,900 18,000 22,500	'66 Nicholson 32 '63 Stonington 42 '64 Bristol 32 '67 Seafarer 35 '66 Ericson 35 '53 Hinckley 36 '56 Cheoy Lee Lion	31,900 27,500 28,000 27,500 29,900 29,000 32,500	'67 Cal 36 '68 Bristol 29 '66 Morgan 34 '65 Cheoy Lee 35 '65 Allied Seabreeze 35 '37 Alden 36	35,500 35,500 45,000 36,000 39,000 38,500

are three years older.

The chart will not tell you whether a specific used boat you are considering is a good value. The BUC books (based on the old adage that something is worth only what someone is willing to pay) clearly emphasize that much depends on the boat's condition, equipment and location. Boats kept in fresh water in the northern half of the country continue to

$50,000		$75,000		$100,000		$150,000		$200,000+	
Beneteau 310	62,900	Catalina 36	72,000	Morgan 38	118,500	Tartan 372	148,300	J/40	240,000
F-27 Tri	60,600	Nimble 30	84,950	Gozzard 31	116,000	Valiant 37	165,000	Valiant 42	260,000
Tartan 28	62,750	C&C 30	81,000	Com-Pac 35	98,995	Cabo Rico 34	167,200	Endeavour 45	245,000
Hunter 30	52,000	Island Packet 27	73,500	F-31 Tri	95,700	Beneteau 400	139,800	Island Packet 35	199,000
Mariah 27	53,000	Sabre 30	87,500	Island Packet 29	98,950	C&C 40	155,000	Contest 46	360,000
'88 Nonsuch 30	59,000	'91 Hunter 35.5	73,200	'89 Catalina 42	118,500	'88 Sabre 42	169,900	'90 Tartan 412	187,500
'88 Pearson 31	52,000	'88 Irwin 38	61,000	'89 Morgan 41	118,000	'88 Tayana 42	139,500	'90 Nordic 45	297,000
'89 J/33	55,900	'88 J/35	79,900	'88 Beneteau 430	85,000	'88 J/40	175,000	'88 Beneteau	
'88 Frers 30	45,000	'88 Cheoy Lee 40	72,900	'88 CSY 44.5	120,000	'89 Morgan 44	160,000	First 51	250,000
'90 Hunter 31	46,000	'88 Island		'92 Crealock 34	116,000	'88 Jenneau 47	169,000	'89 CS 50	225,000
'90 Island		Packet 31	72,000	'89 Pearson 37	99,000	'89 Hylas 44	174,000	'90 Endeavour 52	389,000
Packet 27	49,900	'89 Beneteau 35	75,400	'92 Pacific		'89 Endeavour 42	129,900	'88 Irwin 54	274,000
'88 Nor'Sea 27	58,000	'89 Nonsuch Ultra	75,000	Seacraft 34	116,000			'91 Tayana 55	399,000
'85 Bayfield 36	55,000	'86 C&C 41	69,000	'83 Wauquiez 38	95,000	'87 Shannon 37	160,000	'83 Cherubini 48	300,000
'83 Moody 34	53,500	'84 Endeavour 40	75,000	'81 Freedom 44	116,000	'86 C&C 44	149,000	'83 Bristol 45.5	229,000
'84 Islander 36	59,500	'84 Nonsuch Ultra	70,000	'86 Nauticat 33	100,000	'85 Jenneau 45	139,900	'85 Hinckley	
'85 Ericson 32-3	47,000	'84 Morgan 45	79,500	'85 Gulfstar 45	117,500	'86 Beneteau 51	139,000	SW 51	499,000
'85 Tayana 37	60,000	'85 Hunter 40	79,000	'87 J/35	90,000	'85 Moorings 51	174,000	'85 Irwin 52	192,500
'84 Catalina 36	47,500	'84 O'Day/		'87 Hans		'84 Panda 38	149,500	'83 Mason 53	325,000
'86 Cape Dory 30	49,900	Jenneau 39	71,000	Christian 38T	125,000	'84 Whitby 42	137,500	'85 Tayana 55	315,000
		'86 Nauticat 33	79,500	'86 Baltic 35	125,000			'83 Swan 57	415,000
'82 Baba 30	55,000	'78 Swan 39R	75,000	'78 Shannon 38	110,000	'82 Hallberg		'74 Baltic 51	250,000
'82 Beneteau		'80 Bristol 40	78,000	'82 Tartan 42	109,500	Rassy 42	155,000	'78 Irwin 52	195,000
First 43	59,000	'79 Morgan 46	80,000	'81 Gale Force 33	95,000	'82 Island		'79 Bristol 45.5	185,000
'80 Freedom 35	50,000	'79 Pearson 424	85,000	'79 CSY 44PH	119,900	Trader 46	145,000	'78 Hinckley 49	299,000
'78 Westsail 32	55,000	'78 Cheoy Lee 41	75,000	'80 Cheoy Lee 41	89,900	'81 Hans		'82 Gulfstar 60	345,000
'80 Morgan 38	55,000	'81 Cabo Rico 38	80,000	'80 Fisher 37	125,000	Christian 43	150,000		
'81 Pearson 365	50,000	'79 Cal 39	67,500	'79 Gulfstar 43	83,900	'80 Tayana 42	125,500		
'81 Sea Sprite 34	60,000					'81 Pearson 530	185,000		
						'80 Valiant 40	165,000		
'75 Luders 33	45,000	'77 Valiant 40	65,000	80 Pearson 424	99,995	'76 Hinckley 43	159,000	'74 Alden Dolphin	189,000
'77 C&C 38	46,000	'76 Westsail 42	77,000	'73 Swan 44	116,500	'75 Gulfstar 50	126,500	'76 Nautical 56	395,000
'75 Columbia 45	54,900	'76 Gulfstar 43	75,000	'81 Morgan 46	95,000	'76 Morgan 51		'73 Swan 65	525,000
'73 Irwin 45	58,000	'76 Islander 41	85,000	'76 Cheoy Lee 48	110,000	Out Island	135,000	'76 Swan 50 MS	259,000
'75 Gulfstar 41	55,900	'73 Columbia 45	79,000	'76 Apache 41		'77 Irwin 52	149,900	'77 Hinckley	
'75 Rasmus 35	45,000	'75 Tartan 41	79,900	Catamaran	100,000	'77 Solaris 42		SW 51	255,000
'76 Allied		'72 Whitby 42	85,000	'75 Gulfstar 50	97,500	Catamaran	139,000	'73 Hinckley 53	325,000
Princess 36	45,000			'76 Tartan 42	100,000	'74 Alden			
						Dolphin 47	145,000		
'69 Cheoy Lee 36	48,000	'70 Morgan 42	72,500	'70 Hinckley 38	87,500	'72 Nicholson 48	118,000	'72 Hinckley B40	189,000
'70 Columbia 43	49,000	'72 Chance 44	69,000	'70 Hinckley B40	92,300	'71 Hinckley B40	129,500		
'70 Bristol 40	56,000	'70 Hinckley 35	64,500			'70 Concordia			
'67 Nicholson 45	55,000	'72 Swan 40	77,000			Cutter 45	167,000		
'70 Banjer 37	62,500					'71 Ericson 46	135,000		
'72 Alberg 37	47,000								
'72 Allied									
Seabreeze 35	52,500								
'64 Chinook 34	49,800	'64 Krogen 42	69,500	'66 Hinckley				'67 Hinckley 48	259,000
'66 Morgan 34	49,500	'67 Morgan 45	74,900	Pilot 35	79,000				
'63 Hinckley		'60 Little Harbor 36	64,500	'62 Lapworth 50	100,000				
SW 30	59,000								
'51 Concordia 39	59,000								
'60 Alden									
Challenger 38	49,000								

carry a premium, if they have been well-maintained and especially if they have been upgraded over the years.

At the least, the chart provides a handy reference for a reader who wants to narrow down the possibilities, to determine generally how much boat, new or used, he can expect to get for a budgeted amount of money.

• **PS**

Shopping for Financing

Banks may be tougher, but they can save you money.

Money for boat loans is relatively cheap as well as plentiful, but that doesn't mean it's easy to get. Banks and other lender, stung by their own loose lending practices of the 1980s and worried about the inherent equity of boats, are thoroughly checking both the would-be borrower's credit and the value and condition of the boats in question.

Some of this is the marine industry's own fault. Boat dealers, brokers and manufacturers for years perpetuated the myth that boats gain rather than lose value. That may have been true once, but no longer. Further, boat buyers, particularly sailboat buyers, were touted as superior credit risks, with an infinitesimal rate of default. That myth fell apart as boat owners, trapped in upside-down mortgages as the market bottomed and boat values plummeted, defaulted in droves in the late 1980s. A contributing factor was the inflation of a boat's true value by unscrupulous dealers (and customers) in order to obtain 100%, or even higher, financing during those anything-goes-days.

The good news is that interest rates are fairly low—about 8% for loans over $25,000 compared to 11%-12% just four years ago. Lenders are stricter about down payments, requiring 15% to 20% on new boats, 25% or more on used boats (BOAT/U.S. wants 30% on multihulls and houseboats).

In these times of low interest, most customers are choosing fixed rates at a slightly higher initial percentage on the premise that rates inevitably will be going up. Low variable rate "products" based on the prime rate are initially attractive, but predicting where your rate will be a few years down the road is a guessing game.

Some lenders won't lend below a minimum of $25,000, while others, such as BOAT/U.S., will make loans between $18,000-$25,000 at a rate of 10%. Lenders like the bigger loans because they prefer to work with boats that are documentable. While few lenders charge points or early payment penalties, many of the marine finance companies levy a hefty $400-$500 fee for a mandatory in-house documentation process. Surveys on used boats can run another $6-$10 a foot, but you often can choose your own surveyor. Some companies also charge a closing fee.

Banks

So what's the best route for obtaining a boat mortgage? One large brokerage house we spoke with suggested making your first trip to the bank. Banks might require a higher down payment, usually 20%, but that can work to your advantage.

"Boats really will depreciate no matter what you do with them," the broker said. "With a low down payment, if you want to sell, the principle isn't down enough—there's all that front-end interest."

In other words, instead of having equity at the time of the sale, you owe the bank.

Banks may limit your loan period to 10 years as opposed to the 15- or even 20-year terms allowed by marine lenders. Again, this can be a blessing.

Buyers often place too much emphasis on monthly payments rather than the overall cost of the loan, said Greg Proteau, executive director of the National Marine Bankers Association. Reducing your term by 40% or 50% can mean big savings, even at higher interest rates. Those who obtained loans at higher rates several years ago might want to refinance if they haven't already done so. Terms are usually the same as for new loans, including rate and minimum balance. Some firms report that about one-third of their current business is refinancing.

Banks also have more flexible ways to finance. Home equity loan rates usually are significantly lower than those offered through marine lenders. Equity loans or equity lines of credit can start as low as 7% (6% on a variable rate), but much of this is tax deductible if your boat doesn't qualify for a second home deduction.

One banker told us the variable rate, at 6% for one year, rising to about 8% after that, makes sense if a customer plans to sell or trade up in five years or so. Marine specialists are unanimous in saying that the average life of a boat loan is four to five years. Another advantage to borrowing on home equity is that there's no need to pay costly documentation fees or for a redundant survey.

Finally, banks may set fairly low maximums on boat loans ($49,999 in one case, or 25' or 5 tons), but they will spring for the smaller loan that the marine lenders won't touch. But, cautioned Proteau, because interest rates in general are so low, and because boats can depreciate rapidly, it doesn't make sense to take a big bite of equity out of your primary home.

Before you can get a loan, the bank (and other lenders) will conduct a fairly thorough credit search. Generally, they will want to see copies of your last two 1040 income tax returns, complete with schedules; self-employed persons will be asked for copies of their company's current balance sheet, income statement and tax returns; some will require a current pay stub.

One problem with banks mentioned to us by several brokers and dealers was their reliance on the BUC Used Boat Price Guide. The problem, they said, was that BUC recently has been undervaluing some boat models, being slow to recognize the upturn in the boat market that began about 12 months ago. As a result, banks were declining to finance the 80% of the boat's value some borrowers needed and deals were being lost.

Walter Sullivan, BUC president, defends the overall accuracy of his price guide, although he did acknowledge that prices had gone up after the publication of his 1992 edition. At any rate, the latest BUC editions are supposed to reflect the return of price stability to the boat market.

Marine Finance Companies

Familiarity with the ins and outs of boats is one reason marine lending specialists say you should seek them out for a loan. In a borderline situation, where a bank is equivocating, a recognized marine lender, such as Essex Credit, can "bring comfort to a deal that might not otherwise be done," said Proteau.

Marine lenders are essentially mortgage brokers, who obtain money from other sources and collect a fee for bringing in the business. A large firm, such as Essex, which does $10 to $15 million a month in boat loans, might use its own money to finance a purchase, make out a check to the seller, then sell off your loan to a third party just before closing. According to Alan Swimmer of Essex' home office in Connecticut, the sheer size of the company and the number of banks it deals with helps keep rates low.

Essex will pre-qualify buyers, checking out their income, debt and net worth.

"This tells us how much boat (a customer) can afford to buy," Swimmer said.

Once a boat is found, a more thorough financial search is conducted, basically to determine whether the customer can afford the down payment as well as the monthly terms. If Essex is satisfied, it will issue a credit commitment, which is basically a promise to close the loan. For new boats, the process can take three days, a week or so for used boats, which must undergo a lien search. Although many insurers don't require a survey until a boat is 10 years old, Essex wants one on all boats older than three years.

"It's cheap insurance," Swimmer says.

Some dealers or manufacturers may offer their own financing, touting quick approval and one-stop shopping; as with auto financing, this convenience is apt to cost you.

At last fall's Newport International Boat Show, we saw one couple get captivated by a 35-footer. Off they rushed to the nearest marine lender's booth to sign up for a loan. Chances are their thoughts were more on the boat than on getting the best financing deal by shopping around.

Conclusion

All the experts, including the lenders themselves, advise the customer to shop around, get all the options, read the fine print and then make a rational decision. Ideally, you'll do this long before you go boat shopping (lenders often will lock in a rate for 60 days).

Check first with your bank to determine the feasibility of a home equity loan as well as standard boat loan rates. Then compare their figures with those of a well-established marine lender, such as Essex and BOAT/U.S.

Like home mortgages, shopping for money deserves the same level of research, care and attention as choosing the boat itself. Fortunately, boat loans are easier to process, plus there are no points or closing costs. **• PS**

The Costs of Ownership

Okay, so you've bought it—now what?

This book is full of information about the going prices for boats of many sizes and types, but the money a boat costs to buy is only the beginning. The old adage about a boat being a hole in the water into which one throws money is as true now as it ever was. Between replacement of old, worn out gear (of particular interest to someone buying a used boat), insurance, slip or mooring fees, surveys, and the like, the actual cost of buying a used boat can add up to considerably more than the asking price.

How much any boat owner spends on his boat is dependent upon a lot of factors: type (and construction) of his boat, who does the work, the owner's degree of involvement, how the boat is used, the age and basic condition of the boat and her size and complexity. Not to mention where she's based—remember, everything costs more in Newport than it does in New London.

Certain generalities apply. Fiberglass boats cost less than boats made of other materials, especially wood. New boats are cheaper to maintain than older boats. Smaller boats are proportionately less expensive than larger boats. It takes more money to race than to cruise. Sailing experience saves money. The better built the boat, the lower the annual costs are relative to value.

To these simple generalities we might add another: compared to other endeavors and forms of equity, there is nothing economical about owning a boat.

A couple of these generalities seem to beg for explanation. First of all, smaller-sized boats owned by those who are experienced and handy mean than maintenance can be of the do-it-yourself variety. Boatyard labor rates are now routinely in excess of $30-$35 per hours and the help working on boats in those yards may be less qualified than the average boat owner. What these workers do have is time, equipment, and their choice of weather to work in. Many owners favor the argument that they can make more money doing their job than they can save by doing their own boat work. But invariably that choice runs up costs.

A second observation about the generalities is that they presuppose a boat owner maintains his boat in order to retain his equity. The more money he has invested in his boat, the more he is likely to be willing to spend to protect that investment. That is why better quality boats can take more money than lower quality craft. Yet quality does beget some savings; stapled drawer slides are apt to need repair before molded plastic drawers, for example.

The variable that is impossible to predict is the intangible personal taste of the boat owner, which is a direct determinant of owner involvement. Some owners are fussier than others.

There are three costs associated with boats: the initial purchase price (with or without financing charges), the annual cost of recurring maintenance that represents the basic cost of owning and using a boat, and, finally, the more or less optional expense of upgrading a boat.

So what items should be included in estimating these costs? Those we include are the following:

• **Insurance:** Premiums normally run about 2% of the value of the boat, and have risen precipitously in recent years; they can be considerably higher. This includes property and personal liability, and damage to the boat. The premium rate will depend on the experience of the owner, the geographical range the policy covers, the amount of time the boat is in commission, the extent of coverage, the amount of the deductible, the underwriters' evaluation of the degree of risk, and the probable cost of repairs. It usually does not pay to under-insure in order to reduce premium costs, but it may pay to increase the amount of the deductible, especially for an owner who does much of his own work or is savvy about contracting for work to be done. Remember, it pays to shop around for insurance. As a start, call one of the underwriters that specialize in boats, like Avemco.

• **Dockage or mooring:** Usually this is a figure related to length, but it may include yacht club dues, launch service or dinghy storage, trailer registration and insurance, and a number of other items apart from the fee for the boat herself. Be prepared, of course, to spend far more for a slip than for a mooring. The difference even for a small boat can be several hundred dollars, often putting a slip out of reach. Still, some marina managers are open to negotiation: we know a person who recently bought his first boat, and was able to negotiate the use of a slip for the first year at the mooring rate—thus saving several hun-

15 Ways to Keep Down the Annual Costs of Boat Ownership

• **Choose a boat with annual costs in mind.** For instance, darker colored topsides may be more attractive on a given boat, but they'll deteriorate faster. Also, remember that simple boats are cheaper to keep than complex ones, and can be just as much fun.

• **Develop a habit of regular routine maintenance.** This will not only make your gear last longer, it can keep you from having a real emergency on the water when a critical gilhickie lets go at the wrong moment.

• **Do the routine boat work yourself.** Why pay a worker of possibly dubious skill and questionable motivation a king's ransom to so simple a job?

• **Protect the boat during off-season storage.** Unstepping the mast and covering the boat will eventually save more than it costs.

• **Shop for price.** Take advantage of discounts, volume purchasing, group or co-op buying, used gear bargains, etc. Consider alternate sources for supplies—don't buy everything at a marine outfitters: a sponge is a sponge, and it costs a lot less at Wal-Mart than at a marine outfitters. Periodically compare boatyard and marina prices and insurance premiums.

• **Consider backyard storage:** There are obvious limits here, but if you can pull it off, you can save a bundle at the cost of considerable inconvenience.

• **Check your engine:** This includes the oil level (and changes!), water intake, exhaust, belts, etc.

• **Give a work order to the boatyard as early as possible:** Many owners wait until the last minute, producing a crunch at the boatyard. Get your instructions in early, and you may not only get better service, but save money as well.

• **Make use of winter evenings:** Many of the jobs that need doing can be done at home.

• **Set limits on the cost of work:** Give the boatyard a price limit and insist that they notify you if they exceed it. It pays here to be as familiar as you can with your equipment to avoid getting ripped off.

• **Insure the boat for its fair market value:** Also, set the deductible as high as you can stand to keep premium costs down.

• **Be on hand for mast stepping and unstepping:** Much of the cost here is for tasks you can perform yourself, like tuning the rig.

• **Protect your sails:** Keep your mainsail covered and your headsails below. Protect them from flogging, salt and abuse.

• **Plan major purchases and yard work in advance:** This can help you prepare your boat (and bank account) accordingly.

• **Know what your recurring costs are:** Set a budget and keep an eye on what you really spend on the boat. It's easy to let things slide, and you'll end up wondering where all the money went.

Finally, remember that using your boat won't lower the costs of her upkeep, but it sure will go a long way towards justifying them.

---

dred dollars. How the boat is kept can make a big difference in how much use it gets: you're far more likely to go for an evening sail after work if you don't have to row a dinghy out to a mooring to get at the boat.

• **Handling, storage and launching:** This is a figure that can vary widely. However, $15-$20 per foot is a fair starting point. If the boat is handled by a boatyard, it can make the owner's job easier by simply checking off those jobs the yard does for decommissioning: winterizing the engine and head, spar storage, battery charging, frame erection, etc. However, while checking them off is easy, writing a check to pay for them is not; you pay a lot for the convenience of having somebody else do the dirty work, and this can up your costs by fifty percent. If you have a boat that's small enough and the trucking distance is reasonable, backyard storage can be cheaper than boatyard storage.

• **Maintenance:** Also a widely varying figure depending on where supplies are purchased, whether routine maintenance work is done by the owner or is contracted for, and other variables. It is also a cost that can be affected by efforts to protect the boat, thereby reducing the amount of maintenance she requires. When estimating the cost of routine maintenance, do not forget the bill from the sailmaker for washing, checking, and repairing sails, travel expenses to and from a boatyard, and the cost of an engine tune-up—items easily overlooked in any flight from fiscal reality. Be sure to check the labor rates at the local boat yards before you decide to make a purchase. It's a good idea to set up a reserve fund to pay for items that you know are going to need replacing or refurbishing in the future: set aside a certain amount each month so that when it comes time to replace the sails or paint the bottom the money will be there. It can help to "rent" the boat from yourself: that is, figure out how much it should cost you to actually use the boat for a day, and put that much into your account every day you sail.

• **Taxes, fees, and the like:** Property taxes, mooring taxes, registration fees, rating certificate renewals, documentation renewal fees, etc. all have to be figured into any total, as does membership in a yacht club. Of course, these fees are different in different areas of the country, and in some areas certain one may not apply. Check with the state DOT and your local boat yard to get a handle on these costs.

• **Depreciation:** Ten years ago owners often saw their boats appreciating in value along with an inflationary economy. You'll note that many of the price charts in this book show a characteristic "hump," and almost all of the boats we've reviewed are steadily falling in value, in keeping with the continuing recession. However, the recession won't last forever (we hope), and historically boats tend to maintain their value over the long term. For those items such as electronics, outboard motors, sails, inflatable tenders and so forth that require periodic replacement, a 10-year or less depreciation schedule can be used. Few owners consider this as a real cost, but it can add up to between 3 and 5 percent of the value of the boat each year.

Obviously many boat owners have found ways—real or imagined—to shave the total annual expense of their boats.

One owner we know quoted us a very low figure for the upkeep of his 40-footer: he left out the cost of dockage because it was included in his condominium maintenance fee, making it a "household" rather than a "boating" expense.

Despite such ploys and self-deceptions, it still seems reasonable to believe that the recurring expenses of any boat over the size of a daysailer are likely to exceed 8-10% of the value of the boat. For owners who depend on boatyards to do their outfitting and use commercial facilities for dockage, the realistic total has to be closer to 15, even 20%, especially if gear depreciation is included.

There are, of course, other costs, such as the addition of gear and modification to the boat to increase her usefulness and, presumably, her value. These are not recurring costs *per se*, and they can be as high as your pockets are deep. • **PS**

Buying Guide
-
Gear

Ground Tackle

Overall winners in our tests were the Fortress, Danforth Hi-Tensile, and Delta.

During the last decade, there have been conducted a number of anchor tests, more than at any time in history. Some have been done by anchor makers and must be scrutinized most carefully, but many others have been managed independently and give more objective information than has been available before.

Unfortunately, none of the tests can be considered the final word on anchors. But taken all together, they do offer the boat owner good information that can be used as the basis for deciding which anchor to buy and what size is appropriate.

Heree take a look at the test information, supplemented by some trials of our own, and present what we think are the best conclusions possible, given the current state of knowledge on anchors.

The Tests:

We gathered together the results of the following tests:

The APAVE French Tests. These were conducted at the request of the makers of Britany anchors, by APAVE (the "Western Association of Steam and Electric Appliances"), an independent organization somewhat like Underwriters' Laboratories in this country. The test results were written up by Alain Connan of the Sailing School, but so far have not been published in an English translation. Don Bamford's book *Anchoring* has an adequate summary.

Tests by Robert A. Smith, NA. These were conducted in Oregon over a long period of time, using a Cascade 27 sailboat in the Columbia River. The test results have been published in Smith's book *Anchors: Selection and Use.* Danforth Standard and High-Tensile (lightweight types), CQR, Bruce, Northill, FOB, Benson, and Forfjord anchors were tested originally, and Smith's testing is on-going. He shared with us preliminary results of tests on the Danforth Plow, Delta, and Fortress anchors.

Navy Tests. The Naval Civil Engineering Laboratory in California has conducted a long series of tests over the years, primarily dealing with large anchors suitable for ships. Many of these tests were the basis for published information on Danforth anchors before the 1980s.

More recently, the Navy conducted tests in Chesapeake Bay (1987) and near Norfolk, Virginia (1989), as part of the Navy's Landing Craft Air Cushion (LCAC) program. The purpose of these tests, in general, was to compare newly available anchors—particularly the Danforth Deepset models and the Fortress aluminum anchors—to existing anchors used by the Navy.

Fortress Anchor Tests. As promotion for their recently introduced aluminum anchors, the Nav-X Corporation sponsored two tests, one in Florida and one in California. The tests, to measure holding power, were observed by a number of anchoring authorities and members of the press.

Bruce, CQR, Danforth Standard and Deepset models, Fortress, Sentinel (U.S. Anchor's Danforth-type anchor), and Delta anchors were tested for comparative holding power, through six pulls. Several other anchors—the Pekny (a Northill-type), Davis Sea Hook, Creative Marine's Max Anchor, Danforth Plow, and Plastimo Plow—also had one or two pull-tests done, but were not included in the regular cycle of tests. The results were published by the makers of Fortress anchors. The California tests were co-sponsored by West Marine Products and looked particularly at anchoring in soft mud. The results of those tests were also written up in a report by Chuck Hawley of West Marine.

Dutch Tests. A series of anchor tests were conducted for the Dutch *Watersport Journal* and published early in 1990. The tests were designed and supervised by Rob van den Haak of Vryhof Anchors, the Dutch manufacturer of anchors.

The tests were conducted in an "anchor box," a huge box filled with sand, with a layer of water on top. The sand was "re-packed" with a "vibrating needle" after each test, and the pull speed and setting procedures were virtually identical, to equalize the test environment for each anchor. These tests generally come closest to rigorous scientific procedure of any tests done.

Strength Tests. A series of tests were conducted by

BOAT/U.S. and *Cruising World* magazine. These tests did not evaluate holding power of the anchors at all but instead concentrated on the physical strength of the anchors. While interesting, the tests indicate that—with a few noteworthy exceptions—available anchors have breaking strengths greatly in excess of their holding power.

Danforth Tests. In 1988, Danforth conducted a series of three tests in San Francisco Bay, measuring the holding power of six anchors: two Danforth lightweight fluke anchors, two Danforth Plows, a Bruce, and a CQR. Weights varied from 13 to 35 pounds, and the anchors were tested in two different locations, one with a sand bottom and one with mud. Anchors were tested on short scope (2.5 to 1) as well as more normal scope (5 to 1). The results were published in *Cruising World*, in May, 1989.

Simpson-Lawrence Tests. Simpson-Lawrence, maker of the CQR plow, conducted tests in June, 1987, comparing their plow to a Danforth Standard, a Danforth Hi-Tensile, and a Bruce, all weighing between 20 and 25 pounds. The tests were conducted, according to the company, because recent tests (in which the CQR did not fare well) were unlike real anchoring situations. In addition to straight-line pull tests, a "veer" test was conducted in which the anchor was set and then the pull direction was changed 90 degrees and then 180 degrees, to evaluate resetting ability. Divers observed and photographed the anchors on the bottom. The results were summarized in the English magazine *Yachting Monthly* in 1988, and a shorter version reprinted a year and a half later in *Cruising World*.

RNLI Tests. In England, the Royal National Lifeboat Institution (RNLI) conducted a series of tests over the last decade, as part of their continuing examination of available anchors for equipping their lifeboats.

The principal tests were two trials, the first at Oban, where five 20-kg. anchors were compared in five "bottoms" over a five-day period, and the second at Weymouth, where five types of anchor—the fisherman, Danforth, Bruce, CQR, and Delta—were trialed in calm weather, and then later the fisherman and Delta were tested in rough weather. These tests followed some experiments done with miniature models of 10 different anchors in a "Model Anchor Tank" at the Hasler Admiralty Research Establishment.

Unlike most anchor tests, the RNLI lowered the anchors using a "running drop" with the boat drifting rapidly as might happen when they were executing a rescue. They also conducted tests using a more typical kind of yachtsman's drop, with the boat standing still or moving very slowly backwards. The results of the tests were printed in a technical paper, presented to a conference on "Surveillance, Pilot, and Rescue Craft for the 21st Century," early in 1990, and summarized last July in an English magazine, *Practical Boatowner*.

Checking The Tests

During the summer and fall of 1990, we performed a series of "checking tests," basically to see if we could replicate the findings of some of the tests, particularly findings that stood out as peculiar. We set and measured the resistance of a Fortress, a Danforth Deepset, a Bruce, an "old" Danforth Hi-Tensile, a "new" Danforth Hi-Tensile, and a Viking aluminum, and tried to evaluate their resetting ability. The tests were in two different bottoms—one sand and one mud—in Muskegon Lake, with a series of three pulls each. Later we repeated the pulls, adding to our tests a new Simpson-Lawrence Delta anchor, a new Max anchor from Creative Marine, an older Northill, and a "no-name" Danforth imitation.

This was all done following an eight-week cruise, in which we anchored 54 times, in a variety of bottoms, observing the characteristics of different types, frequently diving on the anchors to examine how they had set and frequently breaking them out by simulating big wind shifts. In setting the anchors, we observed the anchors' behavior from the dinghy when the water was sufficiently clear and shallow—about half the times. We "lived our tests," dragging anchor three times at night and often setting and resetting repeatedly to get a secure hold.

We also checked most of the available printed comments on anchors and anchoring, including such things as the American Boat and Yacht Council recommendations, and the recommendations of accepted authorities of both power and sail—such as Eric Hiscock, Donald Street, Elbert Maloney, Robert Ogg—and the anchoring books by Don Bamford, Brian Fagan, Alain Gree, Earl Hinz, Alain Peuch, and Robert Smith. We also surveyed all of the literature available from the anchor manufacturers.

The Trouble with Tests

The primary interests of the boat owner are the capability of the anchor 1) to be set easily, 2) to hold onto the bottom, 3) to reset following a wind or tide shift, 4) to be retrieved, and 5) to be stowed.

The primary interest of almost all of the tests has been number 2—the holding ability of the anchor. One test considered as a secondary matter number 3—the reset ability. The other capabilities are considered only in the most incidental way.

Our own trials demonstrated to us very clearly that there are differences in these other capabilities. Though we reached a few subjective conclusions about these other capabilities, it is to be hoped that more extensive studies can be undertaken, particularly with regard to setting and resetting.

However, there are problems even with the most studied capabilities—the holding power. Typically, in all the published tests, an anchor is set in the bottom two or three or six times, the anchor rode is pulled, and the point at which the anchor drags or breaks loose is measured, usually in pounds of force. Then an average figure for the pulls is calculated, and that number is listed as the holding power of the anchor.

If you look at the data rather than these simple conclusions, things are not quite so precise as published figures often appear. In the French tests, for example, the holding power of 26-pound Britany anchors (a lightweight-type) varied from 198 pounds to 2,028 pounds; a 22-pound Bruce varied from 165 pounds to 661 pounds, and a 25-pound CQR plow varied from 226 pounds to 1,102 pounds. All of these were in the same patch of water, with a bottom described as "uniform, good sand."

Similarly, in one of the Fortress tests, a Danforth Deepset's holding power in mud varied from 400 to 1,050 pounds; a Delta varied from 125 pounds to 625 pounds; and a Fortress from 525 to 1,325 pounds.

In our own tests, a new Danforth H-1500 with a nominal holding power of 1,500 pounds tested out all over the scale between 360 and 1,270 pounds, while a new Max anchor showed even greater variation—from 275 to well over 2,500 pounds, beyond our ability to measure.

Such gross variations are not at all unusual in holding-power tests; in fact they are quite typical. The most carefully controlled tests—those by the Dutch—intended at first to do a second pull to verify the first, planning on more only if the second tests varied by more than 10 percent from the first tests. As it developed, all anchors had to be tested on a third pull, and most on a fourth. The testers thought that the anchor rode was messing up the results and repeated some of the tests with a wire cable of small diameter rather than chain. Finally, they used figures for "mean" holding power in order to compare the anchors' abilities.

The science of statistics, of course, involves using lots of bad information to arrive at more accurate information. We spent considerable time plotting and trying to analyze all of the results from all of the different tests available—all to little avail. Below, we include a table which summarizes our findings, but we present the information with a great many cautions and qualifications, believing that accurate and defensible conclusions about usable holding power can be made only by imposing lots of subjective judgments on the available information. Among the qualifications are the following.

• Exactly what "holding" means is not at all clear or uniform in the tests. Many sailors think of anchors as simply sticking into the bottom and then remaining exactly in place until broken out. However, when anchors are actually observed under pull, it is clear that they all "move" through the bottom material. Some move more, some less, some "roll" or "dive" or "overturn" or "rear up," some "spiral" or "rotate," some "hobbyhorse," and so on. There seems to be no agreement on such terminology. An anchor might break one fluke out, for example, and the holding power (perhaps "resistance" would be a better term) will be cut in half. But the fluke begins to catch again, and holding power increases.

• Almost all measurements of tests are made "dead in line," yet holding power will vary significantly with the angle of pull, and an anchor will often show significantly different holding power immediately after resetting. On the other hand, changes in holding power often seem simply to be changes in the bottom consistency—what the texture of the mud or sand is.

Holding Power

Given all of the above qualifiers, we have attempted to rank the holding power of various anchor types, by size. The ranking is intended as a relative representation of holding power in good conditions, with an adequate scope and good bottom. The numbers are a simple arithmetical calculation from all the figures we collected. Comments on the individual anchors will appear in Part 2 of this article, and are intended to qualify the ranking.

The following list is from least holding power to greatest. The base number of 1 refers to the holding power of a traditional fisherman type (sometimes called a kedge or yachtsman's) anchor. A rating of 2 would indicate twice the holding power of a fisherman of the same size, a 3 would be three times the holding power of a fisherman, and so forth.

Anchor	Holding Power
Folding (grapnel)	0.6
Fisherman	1.0
Northill	1.1
CQR plow	2.4
Danforth plow	2.5
Bruce	2.5
Delta	2.7
Max (Creative Marine)	5.1
Danforth Standard	5.2
Danforth Deepset (Std)	5.2
Danforth Deepset (Hi-T)	5.4
Danforth Hi-Tensile	5.5
Fortress	5.6

The table represents anchors of approximately comparable physical size. If weight alone is considered (that is, if fluke size were ignored), the table would be almost exactly identical, except that the Fortress would have a considerably higher ranking—approximately 9.8—due to its aluminum construction.

Now we'll take a detailed look at individual anchor types and models.

Folding

The folding or grapnel-type anchor is useless for general anchoring purposes. If boaters know that they will have to anchor occasionally in rock, a folding grapnel might be worth considering for its compact stowage, but other anchor types are better even for that specialized situation.

Fisherman

The traditional fisherman or yachtsman's anchor is not commonly used as a primary anchor, but is nonetheless still worth considering.

The main problem with the fisherman is its small flukes. In order to achieve adequate holding power in typical sand, mud, or clay bottoms, very large-size anchors have to be carried. For example, a boat that might use a 35-pound CQR plow would have to carry a fisherman's anchor of over 100 pounds to get comparable holding in soft bottoms.

Not only is the weight a problem, but on boats without a long bowsprit the anchors are difficult to drop and bring back onboard without damaging the topsides, and they have to be disassembled to stow. Also, because the stock is perpendicular to the flukes and only one fluke is normally buried in the bottom, the anchor rode can easily be fouled on the stock or the exposed fluke after a wind or tide shift.

On the positive side, the fisherman anchor performs as well or better than a CQR, Bruce, or lightweight-type in pebble or "shingle" bottoms, and it can be used effectively in rock or coral where many other anchors do not work at all. Its weight can also be an advantage in penetrating thick seaweed.

In sizing, the traditional rule of thumb is two-pounds of anchor for every foot of waterline length (eg., a 60-pound anchor for a 30-foot waterline boat).

In this country, the Luke Storm anchor is a good representative of the type. All the other fishermen-type anchors we examined were oriental imports and varied considerably in quality and in fluke shape and size.

Northill

The sailor will have difficulty these days finding a Northill-type anchor to buy, though the Pekny is similar. Since its performance and characteristics are similar to the fisherman type and it offers no advantages, there seems little to recommend this type of anchor.

CQR

This plow-type anchor is made by Simpson-Lawrence, an English company, and the anchor is widely used in this country as well as in Europe. We suspect the ease of stowing it on a small bowsprit or bow roller is partly responsible for its popularity. All tests except those sponsored by the company indicate that its holding power is quite low relative to its weight. For reasons we cannot explain, the CQR does well in tests by the English, even those not sponsored by the manufacturer.

It is interesting to us that most tests of the CQR were done with shorter lengths of chain in the anchor rode than the 18-feet length that the company recommends. In our own cruising experience with a CQR, we were initially very disappointed in the anchor's performance, with only six feet of chain between the nylon rode and the anchor. After adding 12 more feet for a total of 18 feet of chain, it performed much better.

There are a number of claims for the CQR, both from the company and from dedicated users. One is that the pivoting shank of the CQR helps the anchor hold when the pull is not dead on. Another has to do with the structural integrity of the anchor, which also seems true.

Beyond these, it's hard to find any evidence in any of the tests for any other claims of superior performance by the CQR. In fact, the tests tend to make the anchor seem quite ordinary, with some peculiar habits of plowing through softer bottoms rather than burying deep, and twisting out of the bottom under strain or changing pull directions. Generally, the firmer the bottom, the better the anchor performs relative to the lightweight-type anchors; the softer the bottom, the worse the anchor performs relative to the lightweight types. Only in tests in gravelly bottoms does the CQR perform as well, and then not all the time.

It is often said that the CQR will reset better than other anchors after it has broken loose by a tide or wind shift. However, we tried a dozen resets at 90-degrees, comparing it with a Danforth Deepset, and could not conclude superiority for either anchor. Visually, the Danforth would carry a ball of bottom soil between its flukes, which seemed to impede resetting. On the other hand, the CQR often dragged along the bottom for quite a distance before beginning to dig in.

In spite of the mediocre showing of the tests, anecdotal reports from CQR users, including our *Practical Sailor* reader survey, generally indicate satisfaction with the anchor. It may be that the CQR performs adequately over a wide range of bottom conditions. Other anchors are much superior in specific bottoms, but overall the CQR proves satisfactory to these users.

Nonetheless, based on the tests and what we've experienced with the anchor, we would be hesitant to recommend the CQR to a new sailor. For choosing the correct size CQR, the company's recommendations on size are reliable, though a bit on the small side. If your boat is near one of the breakpoints, choose the larger anchor.

Danforth Plow

The Danforth plow is comparable to the CQR, and our thoughts on the CQR apply to it as well. Overall, tests show that the Danforth performs slightly better in terms of holding ability than the CQR. However, our judgment is that its construction is noticeably inferior to the CQR, particularly the pivot pin. For us, that makes it a toss-up with the CQR.

Delta

The Delta is a new plow-type design from Simpson-Lawrence. It bears a resemblance to the CQR but is one-piece with no pivoting hinge, and there are a number of other minor differences in design.

The tests done so far indicate that the Delta is somewhat superior in holding power to the CQR, though the limited testing at this point shows a wide range of results. Our own brief trials found it to be far better in mud but only slightly better in sand. Interestingly, in the reset tests we did, the Delta was noticeably the best at resetting once it had broken loose. In the RNLI tests, its performance was exceptional, showing greater holding power in clay and sand than even the Danforth.

The Delta is also a well-made anchor, and with a weighted plow tip it requires no assistance to drop smoothly from a bow roller. On the bottom, it tends to roll itself over into the dig-in position immediately, even with no pull on the anchor line. It also is easily retrieved over a bow roller, unlike the other plows which almost always require horsing the pivoting joint back on board.

Though there is very little experience with this anchor aboard actual boats thus far, we are impressed enough with it that we would recommend it over the CQR. In soft bottoms, it lacks the high holding power of the lightweight types, but it can be launched and retrieved easily over a bow-roller, and is a good choice for those sailors who demand that convenience.

The company's recommendations with regard to size are reasonable, though on the low side. If your boat is near a break-point, choose the next larger size.

Bruce

The Bruce is peculiar in that test results show its holding power to be low, yet users are almost universally pleased with the anchor's performance. Our own *Practical Sailor* survey showed that users had a more favorable opinion of the Bruce than of any other anchor, though it was also true that the Bruce owners didn't anchor as often as others.

Some tests show the Bruce to have significantly less holding power than a CQR; others show as much or significantly more. Unlike other anchors, it does not seem to be the bottom material that is the cause for the better or worse showing.

We have used the Bruce a number of times while cruising, but two middle-of-the-night fire drills caused by dragging led us to retire the anchor from regular use. Based on holding power tests, we think the company's recommendations on size are somewhat small.

It is often said that the Bruce sets more easily than other anchors and that it is better on shorter scope than other anchors. Tests do not indicate either of these claims to be true. We also found that its ability to reset after being tripped was about average.

On the positive side, the Bruce is physically a well-made anchor. And of course, it stows well on a bow roller and is launched and retrieved quite easily.

Based on tests results alone, we cannot recommend the Bruce strongly. However, owner reports are sufficiently positive that we cannot criticize the Bruce strongly either.

Max

The Max is a new anchor from Creative Marine, a company new on the anchor scene. In design, it is closest to the Bruce, though its flukes are much larger. The shank is also adjustable to three different settings, so that the angle between the shank and the flukes can be adjusted for different bottom conditions. As far as we know, the anchor has been tested only in San Francisco mud and in Michigan mud and sand, and there are no indications how it would perform in clay or less desirable bottoms.

The anchor we tested was one of the first off the production line. The anchor appears well made and should be as strong as the Delta and the Bruce.

When we talked to the company, they recommended a Model 20 as being comparably sized to the other anchors we were testing, such as the Delta 22 and the Danforth 20-H. But the 20 turned out to refer to inches rather than pounds. The anchor weighed 36 pounds, by far the heaviest we tested.

Its greater holding power, compared to the Bruce and the Delta, seems to come mostly from the great increase in fluke size. The flukes look like an enormous scoop shovel. In terms of holding power alone, the anchor seems to be worth considering, and the adjustability of the flukes means that the angle can be increased when you know you are anchoring in very soft mud.

On the negative side, the anchor is very awkward. Because of its big flukes, it would not fit in a bow roller that held a 35-pound CQR, and we are not sure what kind of arrangement would be necessary to make the anchor easy to launch and retrieve, except a long bowsprit.

In setting, we observed that the anchor performed much like the Bruce, normally lying on its side and then turning to dig in. The Max, though, frequently moved longer distances before it started to dig in. It's ability to reset also was similar to the Bruce.

Given the limited experience, we are hesitant to recommend the Max. It does generate much greater holding power in good bottoms, relative to similar anchors such as the Delta and Bruce, but its large flukes make storage, launch, and retrieval problematic. If that problem can be solved, the anchor is worth considering. It should be slightly better than the Bruce or Delta as an all-purpose anchor. At this point, few stores or catalogs carry it.

Danforth

The term "Danforth" is often used generically, but the more proper generic term is "lightweight type," indicating an anchor with long and relatively thin flukes that bury in the bottom, and with a round rod at the base of the flukes in place of a stock. Danforth is a brand name for the lightweight anchors now being manufactured by Rule Industries, Inc. The Danforths have been the most popular of the lightweight types, but a growing list of imitators has appeared.

For a number of years, the most popular Danforth models were the Standard and the Hi-Tensile. Five years ago, the company introduced a new line called the Deepset Standard and the Deepset Hi-Tensile, while maintaining the two original models, and last year it added a VSB (for "very soft bottom") version.

The Danforth became virtually a standard among the lightweights for good reason. Its light weight made it easy to handle and stow relative to other anchors, and its holding power was remarkably high in the right bottom conditions—soft clay, sand, or mud. Such bottoms are very typical of a majority of coastal anchorages where centuries of rain and run off have deposited layers of eroded soil for the anchor to dig into. On the negative side, the Danforth tests out as pretty useless in hard clay, gravel, or rock, and its light weight and broad flukes can actually become handicaps when weeds cover the bottom and the anchor must penetrate them in order to dig in.

The available tests seem to indicate that the old Danforth Hi-Tensile is the best of the lot—only tests sponsored by the manufacturer show that the newer Deepset models are superior.

According to company literature, the superior holding power of the Deepset models comes from the thinner, more-flexible shank. In the older models, a thicker shank, theoretically, keeps the anchor from penetrating the bottom as well. By thinning the shank, penetrating ability was greatly increased. This was demonstrated very well in large anchors, and it is puzzling why tests of the smaller, yacht-size anchors do not bear this out. Our own tests showed that an old (and well-used) 12-H was consistently as good as or better than the new Deepset Hi-Tensile T-3000, though the nominal holding power of the Deepset was triple that of the old 12-H.

Part of it may be that the thin shank of the Deepset could be effective but the thinness is offset by the shackle and chain that everyone carries with a Danforth. The Dutch tests demonstrated that the chain used for the rode decreased holding power, and that, when a thinner cable was substituted for the chain, holding power of the anchors was generally improved.

Impressed by the performance of the 12-H, we bought a new 20-H so that we could compare it with the Deepset T-3000, to which it was closer in size. When the new 20-H arrived we were shocked to discover that the design and construction had been changed significantly from that of the original 20-H. And, in fact, the holding power of the new 20-H proved more erratic in our tests, compared to the old 12-H.

In design, the new 20-H was noticeably different in that the stock is noticeably shorter than on older 20-Hs. Both the French and the Dutch tests suggest that the length of the stock is important to holding power, since one of the most common ways the lightweight-types break loose is by rotating or twisting out of the bottom. The French tests had shown that Britany anchors with rod-extenders held better than those with shorter rods.

We called Rule Industries and basically got a non-answer to our inquiry of why the stock had been shortened, though they did point out that it would make the anchor easier to handle on deck. We have also heard that boat manufacturers wanted it shortened to better fit in-deck anchor wells.

The welds were sloppy, the eyes for the shackle cut roughly and irregularly, and the finish poorer. When we examined them closely, we discovered what we consider a general quality-control problem. It was most significant, we think, in that the fluke angle, which is controlled by the way the head is welded on, varied as much as seven degrees in different anchors. This in itself may be enough to degrade performance.

On examining other tests, we found other comments critical of the newer Danforths. The Navy tests in 1989, for example, tried a Hi-Tensile anchor (H-3600) and "bent the flukes." They found the Deepset anchors they tested "structurally limited in their holding capacity." With the first T-6000 tested, "both the flukes and the stock were broken." The second T-6000 "failed at a weld between the crown and one of the flukes." The Navy found that the anchors "generally did not set quickly or easily."

The Navy also tested a Danforth T-7000. At the end of the first test (in which they got a maximum holding capacity of 2700 pounds) they said "the flukes were spread slightly and the stock was slightly bent." On the second test, "the anchor structurally failed under a 6,100-pound pull. The failure occurred at a weld between the crown and one of the flukes." They tried another T-7000 which held to only 4,300 pounds because "upon retrieval, the anchor's shank was found to be bent about 40 degrees to one side."

Granted, these were big anchors and the Navy doesn't mess around with light pulls. Yet the Fortress anchors in the same test withstood pulls more than double those on the Danforths and only suffered minor bending of the stock and shank.

Of the major-brand anchors in the BOAT/U.S.-*Cruising World* strength tests, only the Danforth S-1600 and the Danforth T-4000 deformed or broke at loads well below their nominal holding power. For the T-4000, for example, with a nominal holding power of 4,000 pounds, the test reported "At a load of 2,600 pounds, the welds holding the crown plate sheared off. Without the crown plate in place, the anchor opened to a full 180 degrees." Only the Danforth H-1500 (formerly the 20-H) exceeded its nominal holding power before breaking. It broke at over triple the holding power—5,250 pounds.

In the same vein, the Dutch tests found that the Danforth "flexed excessively," causing the angle between the shaft and the blades to change by eight degrees, depending on the pressure put on it. Their conclusion was that "the anchor's construction is average since the determining factor of the angle changes with big loads. The construction of the anchor does not match its holding power."

While we were finishing our own tests, we learned that West Marine Products had become sufficiently dissatisfied with the quality control of the Danforths they sell that they have begun production of their own lightweight anchors.

We've also received considerable anecdotal comment from readers on recent Danforth anchors, including numerous broken welds and a shank that had been broken in half during "moderate seas and 15- to 20-knot winds."

We enumerated these concerns to Rule Industries and received this response:

"Since the Deepset's introduction in 1986," general manager Gary Sable wrote to us, "the Deepsets have gone through a myriad of changes, in both design and manufacturing technology. The changes are still continuing. While some changes are visible, others are not. However, all changes represent improvements over previous Deepset anchors and are an integral part of the evolutionary progress that new products must undergo. One recent change was a major design improvement to the T-4000, T-6000, and T-7000 anchors to structurally strengthen them. The anchors currently in production are enormously superior to the ones tested by the Navy."

We hope the quality-control problems will be cleared up as the company claims, but we would recommend that buyers examine the Danforth anchors carefully before purchase. We would not buy one mail-order unless we were sure we could return it.

Given all these concerns, the tests nonetheless indicate that well-made Danforth Standard and Hi-Tensile anchors—both old and Deepset models—are excellent at holding in typical soft clay, sand, and mud, with significantly greater holding ability in those conditions than anchors like the plows or the Bruce.

The tests are also pretty clear that the Hi-Tensile models do consistently better than the Standard versions, enough to justify the higher cost. Probably the best of the lot is the older Hi-tensile model.

On the down side, the Danforths do not perform so well in coarse or hard bottoms. Only the British seem interested in testing in less than ideal conditions, and those tests indicate that anchors like the CQR, Bruce, or Delta are better in some situations.

As far as sizing is concerned, the situation with Danforth is different than with the other types since its holding power is so high. For our 36-foot boat, for example, a five-pound Hi-Tensile might be adequate for anchoring in winds to 30 knots, but we doubt if any 36-foot boat would want a five-pound anchor, for psychological reasons alone.

VSB (very soft bottom) models are similar to the other Danforths except that the angle between the shank and the fluke is much greater. The greater angle dramatically increases holding power in mud, as is shown both by the Fortress San Francisco tests and by the Dutch tests. The Dutch tests found the greatest holding at 50 degrees, a slightly larger angle than on either the VSB or the Fortress with the mud adaptor.

Though it has not been tested, the general feeling is that the large angles of the VSB and Fortress would put too great a strain on the anchors for anchoring in normal sand, clay, or hard mud bottoms. This means that the VSB is a specialty anchor. It definitely works well in these conditions, and one will have to decide whether it's worthwhile to carry an anchor for just this particular condition. Given the high holding power of the normal Danforths, it seems that in most instances they would hold boats adequately even in mud. In the Fortress mud tests in San Francisco, for example, a Danforth H-1800 (35-H) averaged 658 pounds holding, about enough to hold a 40-foot boat in 40 knots of wind. The VSB, by comparison, tested at enough holding power to hold the 40-foot boat to approximately 60 knots of wind.

Other Lightweight Types

The Danforth lookalikes that we have examined—from Crosby, U.S. Anchors, and Davis—appear to be closer in design to the Standard Danforths than the Hi-Tensile. We tried a U.S. Anchor, and the Fortress tests included a U.S. Anchor and a Davis, but we know of no other tests of these imitations. The tests suggest they perform like a Danforth Standard, but not enough has been done to draw definitive conclusions. In general, we believe the Danforth Hi-Tensiles will be a better bet, even though they are priced higher.

Fortress

The Fortress anchors are lightweight types made of aluminum by the Nav-X Corporation. They were introduced several years ago and have been promoted heavily. Old-timers will recognize the Fortress as being very much like the Viking aluminum anchors, similar in design and components, though the Fortress is somewhat better made and much better finished. The Vikings went out of production in the early 1980s.

For a given physical size, the Fortress' holding power is in the same range as the Danforths, some tests indicating slightly higher holding power, some slightly less. In our own tests, it measured well above all the other anchors except the old-style Danforth Hi-Tensile, to which it was just slightly above. We suspect its good performance is dependent in large part on the excellent construction, with the sharp, well-shaped blades and well-shaped shank making it superior to the roughly finished new Danforths.

All the tests indicate that the aluminum construction is sufficiently strong. The Navy bent the shanks, and the Dutch tests bent the cross rod at the bottom of the flukes. Both concluded that the construction was light, but sufficient. "Not adequate relative to the high holding power," said the Dutch report, "although test loads of the kind put on the anchor will seldom occur in actual use."

The company, of course, emphasizes the anchor's holding power relative to weight. In one sense this is fair, since the history of anchor design has involved trying to increase this ratio—the advance from a 500-pound stone to a seven-pound aluminum fabrication. And the aluminum anchors do easily outperform steel anchors of the same weight, so the bar graphs and tables produced by Fortress do look impressive. But in the yacht-size anchors, physical size is probably as important as weight, for stowage and handling purposes. For years we carried around a 33-pound Viking anchor disassembled. Put together, it was six-feet tall and four-feet wide, and the truth of the matter is that it was too big for us to handle, even though we could carry it boxed up under one arm.

We did use a Fortress extensively during a long cruise, and found its performance to be good once it was dug in. The shortcoming of the Fortress is in the difficulty of setting it. This shortcoming doesn't show up in any of the holding power tests, but it definitely showed up in our own tests.

With broad surface area in its flukes and its light weight, the Fortress will "plane" or "fly" when moving through the water. Naval architect Robert Smith found that, deployed off the stern of his boat in the Columbia River, a Fortress FX-7 on 25 feet of 3/8-inch line (no chain) "planed to the surface in 1.5 knots of current. With 20 feet of 3/16" chain," he says, "it planes at about three knots."

In trials, we found that with six feet of 1/4-inch chain we could get an FX-16 to plane to the surface at 2.7 knots. More importantly, at much slower drifting speeds we could easily get the Fortress to do a sort of quasi-plane, lifting off the bottom and then settling back as it twisted and turned in the water.

This characteristic often created problems in trying to set the anchor. First, in lowering the anchor, it would often twist and turn on the way down, settling in just about any direction. Observing the anchor through clear water, we frequently saw it bounce and jerk along the bottom in its quasi-plane, a tip digging in and starting to set. But then a pull at an odd angle would jerk it out and cause it to "fly" a few feet before settling like a nervous sparrow.

We eventually learned that, because of the light weight, a successful set demanded a straight, very slow pull, much more so than is required of the heavier Danforths. The problem occurred most often in windy conditions when the boat would start drifting backwards before the anchor could dig in. Success required that the anchor be put in the correct attitude on the bottom when the boat was dead stopped in the water.

The other problem with the Fortress is that we found the anchor much more problematic when there were weeds. We're not talking only thick weeds, which are a problem for all the lightweight types. With the Fortress we found that even small bits of weeds, which were no problem for a Danforth, presented setting problems. Several times we were able to observe the crown sinking into the weeds more than the flukes, so that the flukes were actually pointing upward rather than downward. In a phone call, the company recommended that we try setting the anchor on short scope—a good theory but erratic in practice.

It appears that the larger Fortresses might be less of a problem setting than the smaller ones, but we were not able to test this.

The Fortress can be assembled and disassembled, which in some instances might be worthwhile for stowage. One other feature is that you can purchase an optional "soft mud" crown for the anchor and substitute it for the regular crown. With the mud crown, the angle between the shank and the flukes is increased. With the mud crown, the Fortress tested well in the Fortress tests, close to the Danforth VSB. The "convertible" aspect of the Fortress may make it a better choice for those who might anchor in super soft bottoms.

The setting problem is a serious drawback to the Fortress anchors, but we nonetheless believe that they are a good anchor for the right bottoms. For sizing, the company's recommendations are good.

Conclusions

All the tests taken together prove the old saying that no single anchor is ideal for all conditions. We conclude that the Fortress and Danforth Hi-Tensile anchors (both the old version and Deepset) are the best bet for anchoring in softer bottoms and that the Delta is the best bet for anchoring in harder bottoms. As indicated, both the Fortress and Danforth have problems, but they are currently the best available of their types. We look forward to examining the West Marine lightweight-type anchors.

You continue to see published recommendations on carrying various sized anchors for a "lunch hook," "kedge," "overnight anchor," "working anchor," and so on—a carryover from the olden days when all anchors were fisherman types and excessively heavy. Given the light weight of modern anchors, those recommendations should be ignored, and all anchors should be sized as "working anchors." Long-distance cruisers will want to carry one larger "ulti-mate" anchor.

The company's recommendations on anchor chain, shackles, and nylon rope size can also be followed. We notice that many sailors choose oversize chain and nylon. This is not really desirable, as the larger diameter chain may hinder the anchor's setting ability and the larger nylon rode will stretch less than it should. Longer lengths of chain (as opposed to larger diameter) can be used, and will be desirable if you anticipate anchoring in coral or rocky areas where nylon can be chafed.

No one recommends that a boat carry a single anchor, but many boats do, particularly smaller sailboats which rarely spend a night at anchor. For those boats, a Danforth or Fortress is probably the best bet.

Larger boats and those that are anchored more frequently should carry at least two anchors, serious cruisers probably three. For anchoring in a variety of conditions, two different types of anchor are desirable. For someone buying new anchors, we think one should be a Delta and the other a Danforth or Fortress.

If we bought a used boat and it had a properly sized CQR or Bruce, we wouldn't go out and buy a Delta to replace it. Similarly, if the boat had an adequately sized Danforth Standard, we probably wouldn't replace it immediately with a Hi-Tensile, Deepset Hi-Tensile, or Fortress.

For a third anchor, we would recommend not duplicating another anchor, since all types work differently. If you carry a Delta and a Danforth Hi-Tensile, it would be better to get a Bruce or Fortress or Fisherman rather than another Delta or Danforth. Because a third anchor will probably be little used, an easily stowed anchor would be desirable—a disassembled Fortress or disassembled fisherman might be good choices.

It would be nice if there were one perfect anchor, but there isn't. And there is no indication that there ever will be.   • **PS**

Which Winch?

A look at four medium-sized winches shows that all are well-made, but Harken has the edge.

Because boat owners are keeping their boats longer or buying older boats, upgrading the equipment has become a paramount consideration. This is clearly indicated in our telephone conversations with readers. Winches are mentioned frequently and, because they are a major expenditure, most boat owners do careful research before buying.

For this report, we'll assume we're dealing with a 30-foot sailboat, give or take a couple of feet, with headsails not exceeding 400 square feet, for which we'd like to have a pair of the latest in two-speed, self-tailing winches.

Although they're costly, we chose two-speed, self-tailing models because they are marvelous modern workhorses.

There's about a five- to 10-percent loss of efficiency when self-tailing is added to a standard winch. However, the loss is more than balanced by the convenience. The only other disadvantage of a self-tailing winch is that when tacking it's difficult to throw off a jib sheet. No longer can you simply, with one vertical motion, free the sheet. It hangs up on the self-tailer arm. You literally must unwind the sheet.

The sizes of winches chosen was dictated by the power ratio needed to handle that 400-square-foot headsail on our hypothetical 30-footer. You need not do any calculations. Winch manufacturers routinely supply such data, and marine books and catalogs contain similar tables. All the recommendations are based on using a 10-inch handle. Those who like the ease and speed of an eight-inch handle must crank in a 20-percent power loss and buy a bigger winch to compensate for the loss.

Generally speaking, those buyers who can afford it are well advised to calculate their needs in primary winches and then move up one size. Especially is this so if one's muscles are not what they once were. We've never heard of anyone saying, "The winches are too *big*."

Another way of increasing the power of a winch is to use a 12-inch handle (or a two-handed model), but few indeed are the individuals who are comfortable with the two-foot turning circle. But if you're buying several winch handles, it might be wise to have one 12-incher for that unhappy time when you want to bring the anchor rode back to your biggest winch and crank yourself off a sandbank.

You can, of course, get very exotic and go for wide-body winches, three or even four speeds, with electric or hydraulic power or lightweight winches with plastic bearings and rare-metal parts. Winch manufacturers are extraordinarily accommodating, but they can dip into the very deepest reaches of your wallet. Besides, that's big-boat stuff. (The very macho gorillas on racing boats love to use eight-inch, two-handed handles. They get fast line retrieval with the small circle of the short handle, but the short handle subtracts from the very mechanical advantage a winch is designed to provide.)

Traditional sailors, a few of them, go for handsome bottom action winches from Murray. For cruising sailors, bottom action winches make considerable sense.

When taking the conventional approach to upgrading the winches on our theoretical boat, the choice nowadays is between Anderson (from Denmark), Lewmar (from England) and (from the U.S.) Barient and Harken. We'll not digress at this point to discuss who owns these labels. It's a tangled web.

We broke our evaluation into the following segments:

1. A line-pull test to measure the efficiency of each winch

2. A strip-down session to determine serviceability

3. A close examination of construction and appearance

The results of these three categories are shown as rankings on the chart.

The Line-Pull Test

What this test was designed to measure is the simple efficiency of each winch. Because we know that theoretical gear ratios are not the whole story, the question really is: For a given amount of effort exerted on the winch handle, how much pull is applied to the line?

For the line-pull test, we used a half-inch piece of Kevlar-cored braid. No test was made with minimum-sized line. The braid was firmly attached to an electronic load cell. To simulate the action of a jib sheet being trimmed, we used a single (for low loads) or double (for the high loads) length of half-inch, nylon-covered shock cord. This worked also to dampen (and provide increased accuracy of) the readings on the load cell as the line was trimmed.

To measure the force on the winch handle, we used (instead of winch handles) a torque wrench with a special fitting to fit the winch handle sockets. We made dozens of pulls, using torque wrench loads of 10, 15, 40 and 50 pounds. Because the torque wrench is longer than a 10-inch handle, the effort put forth by our trimmer was less than would be required with a handle.

The 10 and 15-pound pulls were, for the trimmer, easy work. The 40- and 50-pound pulls required close to what an average person would regard as maximum effort.

After obtaining a legal-sized sheet full of results, the numbers had to be adjusted for each winch's gear ratios. The four winches have different gear ratios (shown on the chart). This has some importance in a winch's power and line retrieval rate, something not always considered when buying winches.

For instance, the Anderson winch has the highest high gear ratio. At 1.3:1, it retrieves line faster than the other three. The Anderson also has the lowest low gear, 6:1, giving it the greatest theoretical mechanical advantage, but the slowest line retrieval rate. The Barient has gear ratios close to the Anderson. The Harken and Lewmar have more closely coupled gear ratios.

After all the necessary adjustments, our test numbers indicate that, over the entire range of low and heavy loads, Anderson and Harken are the most efficient winches. For the power exerted on the handles, more pull was exerted on the sheet.

The Lewmar was third and the Barient was fourth.

The rankings on the chart, derived from the 10-, 15-, 40- and 50-pound pulls, are shown in fractions to indicate the *amount* of difference between each winch. We regard it as significant.

There were some differences in efficiency between high and low loads. In the 10- and 15-pound loads—what one might experience when trimming a jib sheet in light to moderate air—the Harken ranked first, with Anderson second, Lewmar third and Barient fourth. At high loads, 40 and 50 pounds, as in trimming a sheet in strong winds, the Anderson proved the most powerful, with Barient second, Harken third and Lewmar fourth.

The data makes possible the following observations:

1. If you are *not* inclined to use winches to the absolute maximum of their power, the Harken offers the most efficiency.

2. When maximum power is required, such as sailing in hard air with a full genoa, the Anderson is best, with Barient second and Harken third.

3. With the best line retrieval rate in high gear and the most powerful low gear ratio, the Anderson may, for a cruising sailboat, offer the best combination of the unavoidable compromises.

Serviceability

Because they are such beautiful contrivances, winches thrive on good maintenance. Most of them are left in the open air. They accumulate salt and dirt, especially if they do not have drain holes.

To work properly and deliver the truly awesome power built into them, they deserve frequent cleaning and lubrication.

The ease with which they can be dismantled and reassembled has some importance. It's not nearly as paramount as in the days when stripping a winch sometimes meant a cockpit full of bearings. Good engineering has mercifully moved such a traumatic experience to the not-so-good-old-days category.

While it is true that after becoming familar with the task any modern winch can easily be stripped, cleaned and lubricated, we offer here some subjective views of these four winches. Our opinions are summarized with a numerical ranking on the chart.

To remove the drums, the Anderson and the Harken are the easiest. With an ordinary screw driver, remove three machine screws in the top of the Anderson and the drum lifts off cleanly. On the

Two-Speed, Self-Tailing Winch Comparison

Make	Model	Weight	Gear Ratio		Power Ratio		Drum Dia.
			High	Low	High	Low	
Anderson	40ST	10.8	1.3:1	6:1	8.5:1	39.5:1	3.0"
Barient	21-33ST C	13.4	1.7:1	5.4:1	10.6:1	33:1	3-9/32"
Harken	B32.2ST C	11.9	2.4:1	4.7:1	16:1	32:1	2-15/16"
Lewmar	30 C ST	14.4	2:1	4:1	15:1	30:1	2-7/8"

Harken, remove one big machine screw and the cylindrical socket for the handle and off comes the drum. With the Harken, two sets of sleeve bearings may be lifted off inadvertently. Until you get accustomed to looking for the sleeve bearings, it's possible that they could be dropped and lost.

The Barient requires a special tool (don't lose it, or buy an extra one) and an Allen wrench. As with the Harken, there are two sets of sleeve bearings plus a spacer to worry about.

The Lewmar has four Phillips-head machine screws, plus two locking "collets," and two sets of sleeve bearings. When replacing the Lewmar drum, there's a little trick to replacing the collets: The center spindle must be lifted ever so slightly to slide the collets in place. Once the drums are removed, the work has just begun.

If you just going to wash the innards with a proper solvent and regrease the gears, none of the winches are difficult to service.

Complete disassembly, for a more thorough cleaning or replacement of worn parts, is another matter. Lewmar and Harken are easy. At no time will you have more than one pin and three loose parts.

The Anderson requires that you pull the center spindle, at which time you'd better be paying attention. The Barient requires equal caution. The cast base must be dismantled with a hex wrench to get at the gears and pawls. Reassembling the loose parts requires a diagram and some practice.

If only cleaning and greasing is required, we'd rank Harken and Anderson as the easiest. For more serious service, Harken is the easiest, with Lewmar

---

Do-It-Yourself Calculations

For those who want to get involved in the mathematics, the theoretical power ratio of a winch is derived via this formula:

$$\text{Power Ratio} = \frac{2 \times \text{handle length}}{\text{diameter of drum}} \times \text{gear ratio}$$

For example, using a 10-inch handle (2 x 10 = 20) divided by a three-inch diameter drum (20 ÷ 3 = 6.66) times a 5:1 gear ratio (6.66 x 5 = 33.33), the power ratio would be 33:1.

Once the power ratio is known, you can calculate the pounds of pull on a sheet. For example, if you put 10 pounds of pressure on a winch handle in a winch with a 20:1 power ratio, you'd exert 200 pounds of pull on the sheet. That ignores friction. Because of friction, which can be measured but not calculated, the power ratio of a winch, especially when heavily loaded, must be downgraded. At the very high end of the load curve, friction will eat up nearly half of the power.

That's why winch manufacturers, who rigorously test and measure the actual power of their products, prefer that you follow their recommendations for your boat rather than do your own calculations. They don't want you to buy winches that are too small, and then be unhappy.

To determine the approximate sheet load on your headsails, the formula is:

$$\text{Load (Lbs.)} = SA \times V^2 \times .00431.$$

SA is sail area in square feet and V is apparent wind in knots. For example, a 400-square foot genoa times 15-knot winds would produce a load on the sheet of 388 pounds (400 x 225 x .00431 = 387.9). You'd have to apply about 20 pounds of force to the 20:1 winch to cope with the loads.

---

second, Barient third and Anderson fourth.

Construction and Appearance

As we learned in our earlier evaluation, materials and features may vary according to model. For example, the smaller Harken winches have two stainless steel pawls, the larger ones four. Therefore, it is important to remember that our observations and conclusions about these four particular models may not be true of other models manufactured by the same company.

We feel that all four winches are well-engineered and should provide years of trouble-free service with minimum maintenance. Drum materials available from the four manufacturers vary according to brand and model. You may be able to choose from aluminum, chrome-plated bronze, polished bronze and stainless steel. Because it is the lightest, aluminum is favored by most racers. Good chrome work is the most resistant to corrosion and will retain its shiny appearance for many years. Polished bronze will turn green where the line does not polish it, and while some may think the color is salty, it isn't very popular these days. Where

Line Size		Efficiency Rank			Servicability Rank		Construction & Appearance Rank
Min.	Max.	Overall	High Load	Low Load	Quick	Thorough	
3/8"	1/2"	2	1	2	2	3	2
5/16"	1/2"	3.33	2	4	3	4	3
3/8"	1/2"	1.66	3	1	1	1	1
3/8"	1/2"	3	4	3	4	2	4

weight isn't a concern, we like chrome-plated bronze. You'll certainly not want aluminum if someday you must use it with wire. Stainless is a nice combination of lighter weight and reasonable durability, though it probably won't weather as well as good chrome.

Inside the four winches we tested, all cages and gears are bronze alloys and appear to be of good quality. There are, however, subtle differences in construction, as well as different approaches to the self-tailing mechanism that are of some interest.

Harken

The Harken B32.2STC is a fine piece of engineering—simple, yet rugged and probably more friction-free than the other three. It is the only one with roller bearings on the center spindle where it revolves inside the metal cage. On the other three, the spindle surface mates directly with the turned cage surface. We're not sure how important this is, but it certainly must cost more and, one assumes, produces less friction.

Roller bearings are stainless steel set in nylon races. There is one drain hole in the bronze base, though it isn't very large. But one is better than none. The stainless steel spindle is of sufficiently large diameter and the general workmanship appears good.

As we have noted in previous evaluations of hardware, we suspect that many purchase decisions are based at least in part on style. And style, like beauty, lies in the eyes of the beholder. Harken, with its distinctive red line, contrasts nicely with the black anodized aluminum base of the drum (the rest of the drum is chrome-plated bronze). It's a minor matter, but we are not impressed with the stick-on name label, which we think will wear off in time. The name "Harken" and model number are, however, cast into the top ring.

The Harken winch is the only one of the four with a roller on the self-tailing arm, and it turns on ball bearings to boot. This is another example of Harken going an extra yard. The self-tailing jaws are of two materials: the grooved, stainless steel drum below and smooth black anodized aluminum above. We were told that Harken plans to add a grooved wave pattern to the top surface in early 1992, and change the narrowly spaced ribbing on the bottom to a crosshatched groove pattern, presumably to improve its grip on the line. The jaws may be adjusted for various size lines by pushing down the spring-loaded top plate and rotating it. Because the two jaw surfaces are essentially parallel (as opposed to V-shaped), the turn of line in the jaws stays in column with the turns on the drum below, which is important for even distribution of loads as well as shedding line at the same rate as it's drawn onto the drum. Spacers are available to adjust to a wider range of line sizes than those handled by the standard self-tailer.

The drum surface is the most abrasive of the four, which means it grips very well, but also will probably abrade line faster. Considering that the job of a winch is to grip line, this is probably a worthwhile trade-off: Would you rather replace line every so many years or have a winch that slips? We thought so.

Andersen

The Andersen 40ST is as handsome as the Harken, though decidedly different in appearance. Andersens are available only with stainless drums, and the quality of materials and workmanship appears to be excellent. The light weight of the cast stainless drum is significant and because stainless work hardens, it should show few signs of wear. A winch with a stainless drum probably won't be quite as light as an aluminum one, but should prove more durable. The Andersen 40ST is equally distinctive though we wish the stamping of the white name and model number on the black top ring seemed more permanent.

For some reason, the Andersen has stainless steel ball bearings on the top of the metal cage and stainless roller bearings on the bottom. These are smaller than the others, and there are fewer sets of races. Less surface area means less friction but higher loads. What is the right compromise? We're not sure. The excellent performance of the Andersen speaks for itself, but whether the bearings would wear faster is unclear to us.

There is a large drain hole in the base of the metal cage, considerably larger than that of the Harken. All castings are aluminum-bronze, which the company says is significantly stronger than the "ordinary bronze used in most other brands."

The self-tailing jaws are V-shaped with widely spaced "Power Ribs" to grip the line. It is the same pattern used on the drum, where the ribs are aligned vertically and spaced about an inch apart. Using braided line, we found the Andersen drum gripped line second best to Harken, though it undoubtedly would not abrade the line as much. It's a nice compromise.

Barient

The Barient 21-33ST C is physically the largest of the four evaluated. It has the smallest diameter spindle of the four, and a composite cage, a carefully-chosen plastic originally used to save weight in Barient's big racing boat models but later added (because it was eminently satisfactory) to all of the company's winches. Its roller bearings are Delrin. (Bigger Barients have bearing made of the more expensive Torlon.)

On this model, there is no drain hole in the base. The name and model are silk-screen etched on the top ring and though it initially looks attractive enough, it will wear off. We like a permanent name and model designation for easy, future ordering of parts.

The drum body has a needle-peened finish, which we found poor in gripping various types of line.

For this test, we bought this Barient 21-33ST C brand new from a discount catalog. In subsequent conversations with Barient, we learned that the top plate (with the black lettering) has been replaced with a thicker embossed version. That's a nice cosmetic improvement. A more important change, Barient said, is that the needle-peened drum has been replaced by 16-grit sandblasting, carefully chosen to permit line slippage at 35 pounds of pull. As Barient's spokesman said, to ease a sheet, the line is supposed to slip. The internal mechanism of this model Barient remains the same.

Barient, noted for meticulous customer service, quickly sent us the new model. Without the black lettering, it is better looking and, more importantly, the new drum surface is similar to that of the Harken.

Perhaps the point learned from our experience is that if you, in the near future, buy a Barient 21-33ST C, check first and make sure it's the new model.

The Barient's strongest feature is its patented self-tailing mechanism. The spring-loaded bottom jaw automatically adjusts to the appropriate line size. And, because the two jaw surfaces are essentially parallel, the turn of line in the self-tailer stays in column with the turns on the drum. Assuming the spring will last a long time, we like this feature a good deal. The Barient does have the advantage of holding the smallest diameter line of the four—5/16 inch. If you're inclined to use your primaries on light-air headsail sheets, this is a distinct advantage.

Lewmar

The Lewmar 30 C ST is the shortest yet heaviest of the four. The cage is bronze, the spindle is large diameter stainless steel, and the roller bearings are stainless. There is no drain hole in the base. It is a simple design and workmanship appears to be good.

Again admitting that style is a matter of personal preference, we like the Lewmar's look even though it isn't quite as distinctive as the Harken or Andersen. The self-tailing jaws are black anodized aluminum and the name and model are cast in—the most permanent and best looking job of the four.

The self-tailing jaws are V-shaped with widely spaced ribs. Like the Andersen, they are not adjustable. The drum has a needle-peened surface that, like the older-style Barients, gripped the line poorly when compared to the Harken and Andersen.

Conclusion

As we have tried to emphasize, we think these all are good quality winches. The average sailor, we believe, won't be disappointed by any of the four we tested. There are, however, differences in performance, design and price.

The Harken B32.2ST is our first choice for its overall power efficiency rating, serviceability and construction. The only reason we would not choose it would be if we felt we needed a higher second gear ratio or lower first gear ratio. The two are fairly close together (2.4:1 and 4.7:1). We think the adjustable self-tailer with essentially parallel jaw surfaces is superior to the V-shape as it develops less friction under load. The ball bearing self-tailer roller and roller bearings on the spindle are features not found on the other three.

It's difficult to choose bertween the Anderson and the Barient, Although quite different, both have very desirable features. We like the Anderson's light-weight stainless steel drum. Although stainless drums are available from other manufacturers, the Anderson drum is a gorgeous piece of metalwork. The ribs on the drum are a nice feature and they work, with less line abrasion than the sand-blasted drums on the Harken and new-model Barient. Another Anderson strong point is the large drain hole. If we wanted a high second gear ratio, Andersen's 6:1 would do the job well. It is by far the most expensive, however. We see the quality, but not enough to rank it above the Harken.

In its favor, the Barient 21-33ST is the lowest priced of the four and has that superb, patented, automatically adjustable self-tailing mechanism. Not only does its parallel jaw surfaces keep the line turns in column, it accommodates the widest range of line diameter. On the down side, the Barient has no drain hole and the poorest low-load efficiency of the four. We, unfortunately, are not able to make a judgment on Barient's claim that its composite spindle will wear better than bronze.

The Lewmar 30 C ST brings up the rear, despite being simply designed and ruggedly constructed. It suffers from its low efficiency ratings, slippery drum and lack of drain hole. And at discount it costs a few dollars more than the Barient.

Depending on how you use them and your own capabilities, the subtle differences in these four winches are important. Choose the one that provides the closest match and you'll not be unhappy with any one of the four. • **PS**

Winch Handles

An 11-way test we conducted in 1992 found Harken the finest, and Andersen the best value.

W hen we decided to test winch handles a couple of years ago, as is often true, it seemed doubtful initially that there was enough variety to make the effort worthwhile.

However, as we learned, there are considerable differences in design and in price among the handles offered by the major winch makers, Barient, Harken, Lewmar and Andersen.

In addition, there are handles made by independent companies, including several that because they float offer protection against further littering of the seafloor with winch handles. There must be down there, forever puzzling the creatures of the deep, thousands of Oh-my-God-there-goes-the-winch-handle tragedies.

No matter what size winches you have, there is one standard handle, a 10-inch lever that provides most of the needed mechanical advantage. Eight-inch handles, fast and handy, are favored by those with well-developed muscles to compensate for the 20-percent power loss. There also are 12-inch handles, which increase the leverage about 20 percent, but make for a difficult turning circle.

The basic 10-inch handle comes with a standard socket, which increases the odds of losing the handle overboard, or lock-in models, which have a simple trigger-operated dog to lock the handle in the winch socket. There also are push-button lock-in mechanisms, two-fisted grips, and even ratcheting handles if you like lots of clicking. There'd be a hue and cry if a 10-inch ratcheting handle went overboard. Even at discount, they cost a pair of hundred-dollar bills plus a couple of twenties.

Winch handles come in chromed bronze, which are heavy; stainless steel; plain or anodized aluminum for light weight; and the even lighter "composites." The good metal handles are forgings.

Because they are relatively simple, there's an inclination to view winch handles as unbreakable. We've never done so but we know of quite a few reports of broken handles. In every case, they have been aluminum handles. In some instances, minor injuries (sprains and the occasional nasty gash) have resulted. We can imagine worse injuries. At the very least, a broken winch handle probably would give you a jolt of some kind.

Luckily, because virtually all winches have the same size socket (11/16-inch or 17.5 mm), you can choose any winch handle you like. It's one of the few intelligent bits of international standardization in an industry in which many manufacturers take pride in being different and "better" than the next guy.

After reviewing the catalogs and brochures, we collected quite a few (but not all) of the winch handles, the standard brands from the major winch makers and some from independent manufacturers. We gave them a good work-out, a close examination and considered the widely different prices.

It proved difficult to make direct comparisons and develop rankings. However, some pronounced preferences did develop.

Some general conclusions:

1. It seems to us that on most of the handles the addition of the lock-in feature commands an unusual price premium. The addition of the lock-in mechanism, in most cases, nearly doubles the price of a given handle. For the work involved, the price differential appears extreme. However, for safety and convenience, lock-in handles enjoy a pronounced edge, especially on boats where more than one winch handle has taken a dive.

2. Plated bronze handles are very heavy compared with aluminum and plastic handles. The lightweight handles usually weigh half or a third as much as bronze. The use of stainless steel socket studs in drop-forged aluminum handles with lock-in heads undoubtedly increases the corrosion factor. It's a trade-off that involves personal choice.

3. The new floating handles, made of what the manufacturers call "composite" (because the term plastic still seems to carry a negative connotation), have a mountain to climb before they can be considered to have the strength of good metal handles. One of the composite handles (the Bernard) has a plainly stated load limit. The other, the Titan, is said to be immensely strong.

4. Quality winch handles have ball bearings to reduce friction. Cheap handles with plastic grips bearing on metal shafts bind when loaded. The friction defeats much of the efficiency so carefully designed into a good winch.

The accompanying chart displays the characteristics of the winch handles and our comments extracted from the following fuller observations.

Harken

Harken is a company that seems to give extraordinarily admirable attention to reducing friction. All Harken winch handles have circulating ball bearings. The grips spin freely on the shafts, at least when new. They seem almost friction-free.

In addition, the grips on Harken handles are the only ones with a matte finish, which makes gripping them much easier than the slick smooth grips of other makes. There are no mold marks on the grip.

The Harken grips also are longer than any others, by nearly a half inch, which makes them much more comfortable to use, especially for those with large hands.

The lock-in release trigger is plastic but has the same non-slip matte finish, a small but positive advantage.

The Harken handles, with the company's distinctive red stripe, are beautifully finished, which means that they not only are handsome but, as a practical matter, should resist corrosion better than those less finely finished.

Barient

Barient handles, both the chromed bronze and aluminum models, are nearly equal in finish to the Harkens.

Barient's strong point is a lock-in trigger mechanism that is all metal. The well-designed trigger is the sturdiest of all and has the smoothest, easiest movement. Like most of the others, the lock-in trigger is fastened with a roll pin.

The grip has a good shape but is a bit short. It has a very smooth surface, very slippery compared with the Harken, and the molding marks are very apparent. The Barient handles are the most expensive of the lot.

Andersen

The Andersen handle from Denmark is a stainless steel forging, well designed but, in execution, a bit crude, with grinding marks still visible and the finish definitely second-rate.

The socket stud is welded to the arm, again rather crudely (which may lead to some corrosion), and the grip is a two-cones-joined design that contains no bearings. The grip is, however, very comfortable and effective.

Peculiarly, the lock-in trigger works only in one direction, to the right, which might require a bit of digital orientation, especially for lefthanded individuals.

It is structurally a good, simple design. The lightness of the stainless steel (compared with plated bronze handles) is a definite plus. The handle probably is indestructible.

We don't like the finish work, the lack of bearings in the grip or the single-direction trigger on the lock-in mechanism.

Despite these shortcomings, the Andersen definitely warrants a "best buy" label simply because it is so very inexpensive. Available at discount for only $23, a third of the price of handles made by the other three major winch makers, the Andersen won't cause nearly as much pain if it disappears overboard.

Lewmar

As with its winches, Lewmar makes good, solid handles, but they have shortcomings.

In the grip, the metal bearings, contained in plastic races, are not very free-running. The grip is rather fat and has, in our opinion, a poor shape for good gripping. The lock-in trigger is plastic.

Compared with Harken and Barient, Lewmar's finish work is sub-standard, with many blemishes in the forging work, both in the bronze and the aluminum models we bought.

The plating on the bronze model is crude and the aluminum handle has on the underside of the head an unfinished edge sharp enough to do some damage to tender, wet hands.

The Lewmar handles cost about the same as Harkens, but do not appear, in design and workmanship, to be in the same league.

West Marine Products

From West Marine you can buy a cast stainless steel knock-off of a Barient handle. The little sticker identifies it as made in Taiwan.

The West Marine catalog states, "We're often skeptical of imported knock-offs of name brand products, but this is a truly excellent handle."

We don't think we agree.

The West Marine handle has a plastic grip with rather prominent mold-separation lines. The grip also seems to be off-center and doesn't rotate very freely. And the stainless casting has rather sharp edges and the lock-in trigger is too stiff.

As with too many knock-offs, it's not a very smooth piece of work. It appears to be drastically overbuilt and thus very heavy.

It probably will last forever, but for the money, we don't regard it as outstanding.

Sea-Dog

If you want a true "economy model," here's one that will give you not much pain if you drop it overboard.

Also from Taiwan, this grey-mottled cast aluminum handle looks cheap, feels cheap and is, in fact, only $15. The arm contains not much metal and the stiff, little plastic grip contains no bearings.

Unlike other aluminum handles, this one has an aluminum socket stud that won't take much wear. The square lock-in plate is off center, which makes it bind when being inserted or removed from the winch socket. And, like the Andersen handles, the trigger release works only in one direction, to the right.

To the West Marine catalog statement, "While it's not the same quality as its Barient or Lewmar cousins…," we say, "Amen." We cannot recommend this handle, even as a backup.

Titan

Because it is so very different, this one may be controversial. The material and appearance demands a leap of faith to regard the Titan handle as the equal of high-priced metal handles.

A colorful (available in red or green) floater, the Titan handle, engineered in Holland and manufactured in Australia, is made of glass-filled nylon with a tempered aluminum socket stud.

The U.S. marketer, D.B. Follansbee, said the handle has a breaking strength somewhere around 295 pounds, well beyond what can be exerted by an average human. A company spokesman said that in tests, using a hydraulic ram, the handle bent almost 45 degrees before the extruded 6061 T6 marine-grade aluminum drive shaft let go. The arm of the handle did not break.

Follansbee said it defies any human to break the Titan handle. When placed in the water, the Titan floats, handle up, but barely (see photo).

The grip, which could be a bit longer, contains no bearings and, at least when new, turns rather stiffly. The grip is shaped much like the design used by Barient and Lewmar.

The Titan handles truly deserves the sobriquet of "high tech." And, because of its very modest price, $24 at discount, it is an outstanding product that, as confidence builds in its "newness," may replace metal handles on all boats other than those whose owners feel that high price is the real badge of proper yachting.

Bernard Engraving

This is the other floating handle and we just don't know what to say.

Said to be made of reinforced Lexan, with a square aluminum socket stud, Bernard Engraving's handle is a shabby-looking thing to which is affixed a paper label that says:

"All warranties of fitness for purpose or merchantability EXPRESS or IMPLIED are EXCLUDED. The Bernard Floating Winch Handle is intended for MARINE USE ONLY under normal sailing conditions and shoiuld not be used in severe weather or for abnormal loads."

Defender Industries says in its catalog that the Bernard handle has a "safe workload of 80 pounds radial pull." You'd be at risk to use this handle beyond the stated limits.

At any price, it's not possible to visualize this handle aboard any boat whose owner has a high regard for safety and quality, let alone aesthetics.

The Bottom Line

Of the chromed bronze handles, our choice would be the beautiful 10-inch Harken. It is the closest to friction-free. It's fine finish work is pleasing. The long grip with the nice-feeling matte finish is superior to all the others.

As a best buy in a powerful metal handle, we'll take the Andersen. It has some shortcomings—a one-way trigger and poor finish—but for its very modest price, it cannot be ignored.

If what they say about strength and durability is true, which means that you must be able to accept a "high tech" approach in a very traditional tool, the floating handle from Titan has such immense appeal that it very well could be chosen for typical family sailing, at a very modest price, over all other winch handles. And, because the Titan is light weight, we'd choose it over any of the aluminum handles. • **PS**

Winch Handle Value Guide

Make	Size	Type	Price List/Discount	Material	Weight (Lbs.)	Comment
Barient	10"	Lock-in	$119/$83.50	Chromed bronze	2.5	High quality, but the most expensive
Harken	10"	Lock-in	$83/$70	Chromed bronze	2.4	Our top choice of the traditional handles
Lewmar	10"	Lock-in	$84/$71.50	Chromed bronze	2.75	Lewmar suffers only slightly by comparison
Andersen	10"	Lock-in	$55/$23	Stainless	0.9	Best buy in metal handles
West	10"	Lock-in	$90/$60	Stainless	2.4	An over-engineered, over-priced knockoff
Barient	8"	Std.	$45/$31.50	Aluminum	0.875	Probably the stongest aluminum construction
Harken	8"	Std.	$46.50/$40	Aluminum	0.625	Best of the aluminum 'shorties'
Lewmar	8"	Lock-in	$45/$32.40	Aluminum	0.75	Okay, but needs better-shaped grip
Seadog	8"	Lock-in	$22/$15	Aluminum	0.50	Economy that approaches the dangerous minimum
Titan	10"	Lock-in	NA/$24	Glass-filled nylon	0.50	If you like 'high tech,' this is the top choice
Bernard	10"	Std.	NA/$16.75	Reinforced Lexan	0.625	Don't even think of parking here

Inflatable Tenders

A sailboat might not be the only craft you buy. For many, some form of dinghy is necessary, as well.

While inflatable boats have been around for a long time (the first commercial model was introduced in 1934 to use up leftover dirigible fabric) they didn't become popular in the U.S. until the mid-1970s. Since then, their unique combination of features and characteristics has made inflatables a popular alternative to the hard dinghy.

The most obvious advantage of an inflatable is that it can be deflated when not in use, greatly reducing storage problems. They're also lightweight, which allows lively performance with small outboards; and extremely stable, making them easy and safe to board in a seaway, as well as providing ideal platforms for scuba divers. Inflatables have high-load capacities for their size, and provide a comfortable, if often wet, ride in rough water.

In 1991, we ran a Reader Survey on inflatables. Avon scored the highest "buy again" rating, as well as the lowest amount of trouble reported. At the bottom end were the economical Sea Eagle and Sevylor, which, the manufacturers pointed out, did not deserve to be compared in the same breath with more expensive models. Unresolved was the question of construction material—Hypalon versus PVC. To get a firmer handle on quality, performance and value, last summer we trucked 18 inflatables to the water, assembling, studying and testing each in a variety of conditions. Here's what we learned.

Variations on a Theme

Until the last few years, most inflatable boats sold as tenders or dinghies were designed primarily for rowing. Many of these had motor mounts, but the mount was less-than-rigidly connected to the hull. Hulls on boats of this type, variously described as "dinghies," "soft tails" and "round boats," were relatively flexible, which presented few problems at the low speeds the boats were capable of.

"Sport boats," the other basic alternative, are generally larger, have transom motor mounts integral with the boat, more rigid hulls, and air tubes that extend aft of the motor to provide buoyancy during acceleration. They are faster than dinghies, take larger engines and are alternatives to small runabouts.

The trend today appears to be away from the soft-tail dinghy, and towards the higher performance sport boat, even for owners who envision using them primarily as tenders. The sport boats are more expensive, but they're faster and handle better. When we asked manufacturers to identify their most popular boats in the 8-1/2- to 11-foot range, we found ourselves with only four round boats, as opposed to 14 sport boats.

What We Tested

To restrict this project to boats that would function well as tenders for a small cruising boat, we limited our choice to boats that fold up more or less completely, and, for now, elected not to include RIBs (Rigid Inflatable Boats).

We found ourselves with 18 boats, ranging in length from 8' 2" to 10' 7", and in price from $225 to $3,000, with 15 different brand names representing 10 different manufacturers. We included "house brands" from two major mail-order houses, West Marine Products and Boat/U.S., as well as two boats that double as sailboats, one of which triples as a lifeboat.

The objective was not simply to see which boat was "best." Inflatable boat design, like most marine design, consists of a number of trade-offs and compromises, with price being one of the major factors. We attempted to determine which boats would perform which tasks well, and what are the limitations of each boat.

Floors

We were struck by the variations in design and materials used in the boats tested.

One, the Sevylor Super Caravelle, was a "pure" inflatable, with an unreinforced PVC skin, multiple air chambers and no rigid pieces except for the motor mount and the oars. The Sea Eagle is similarly constructed, but adds a plywood floor, which provides firmer footing, though it doesn't exactly make the boat rigid. The Breeze 9, the only other boat that doesn't use nylon- or polyester-reinforced fabric, has a folding rigid polyethylene floor and a thick EVA inflatable bolster and seats; it provided a much more rigid hull than the other two.

Two boats, the Quicksilver 8' 6" Soft Tail and Boat/U.S.-distributed Seaworthy 8.3, have soft floors stiffened with transverse slats; longitudinal rigidity comes from the side air tubes. The Avon Roll-Up 2.85 and the Tinker Tramp carry this idea a step further. Both use abutting transverse slats to make a solid floor: The Tinker uses wide slats that are locked into place when the side tubes are inflated, while the Avon has narrower slats (something like a large roll-top desk) and uses both the side tubes and an inflatable keel to keep the floor rigid. All four boats are very easy to assemble, since all that's required is to unroll and inflate. The Avon and Tinker designs provide a much more rigid floor, with correspondingly higher performance due to less hull flexing.

The most popular floor-stiffening scheme, used on seven of the boats tested, involves the use of sectional wooden floorboards that fit nose-to-tail into the uninflated boat's bottom. They are pressed into place against the tension provided by the hull, and locked there using grooved aluminum, wood or plastic channels that fit over the edges of the floorboards, securing two sections.

This system provides a reasonably stiff floor, but is more difficult to assemble than the slatted floors, particularly on a small, pitching deck. The necessity for a number of small, easily dropped pieces doesn't help. Boats with sectional floorboards are best left inflated during the season, and towed or stored on davits, rather than deflated and stored between uses.

Two boats, the Calypso and Novurania, also use sectional floorboards, but these are not forced into place to hold them secure. Instead, these boats use a heavy two-section longitudinal beam, or keelson, as a sort of spine to support the floorboards and to provide a rigid structure. The two halves of the keelson are slipped into the ends of the hull, butted together at the center and pressed down to wedge them into the boat. A pair of bolts locks the whole thing into place, and the floorboards simply slip in on top of it.

This arrangement is heavy, but it's very secure and the keelson also gives shape to the boat's bottom. Like the sectional floorboard approach, it's not well suited to frequent assembly aboard.

Two boats, the Bombard A400 and the Zodiac Futura Jr. use an inflatable floor, which unlike those on the Sea Eagle and Sevylor, is extremely rigid. Instead of using a series of air chambers to make up the floor, these two boats use a through-stitched, double-walled design that is inflated to a relatively high pressure. Like the slatted-floor roll-up models, these inflated-floor designs are fairly easy to deflate and store, and simple to set up again. They are lightweight, but have the disadvantage of not providing a solid floor to which you can attach accessories.

Keels

One of the more annoying habits of inflatables is the tendency to steer poorly. This means you have to devote some care to holding a steady course. In a turn, a boat that tracks poorly will skid sideways, rather than carve a smooth, controlled path. Control of tracking is a matter of providing an effective shape to the boat's bottom.

Flat-bottomed inflatables track poorly, but this isn't too serious if you're only dealing with a small engine, pushing the boat at low speeds. Most of the boats that are capable of reaching higher speeds have some sort of keel. The Bombard A400 is an exception.

Most commonly, inflatables have an inflatable keel, consisting of an air chamber between the floorboards and the hull bottom. Inflation of the chamber shapes the bottom. The boats with keelson designs use the keelson to shape the boat's bottom. The Zodiac Futura, Jr. has a flat inflatable floor raised above the water to reduce wetted surface and an inflatable keel on the bottom of each air-tube to improve tracking.

You can have too much of a good thing when it comes to keels, however. A keel that is too deep makes it more difficult for a boat to come up on a plane. We found that some boats with deep-V keels in their forward sections had more difficulty getting up on a plane, sometimes nearly standing on end—an uncomfortable and unstable situation.

Materials—The Great Debate

There was a time when any self-respecting inflatable was made of a nylon fabric laminated to several layers of synthetic rubber, with an outer layer of a Du Pont-developed synthetic called Hypalon®. In the late 1950s, Zodiac, the largest manufacturer of inflatable boats, quit using Hypalon and introduced a PVC-coated fabric. The fight was on.

From a manufacturer's viewpoint, PVC has a very important advantage over Hypalon. Instead of requiring hand-gluing, it's possible to use automatic welding techniques that can transform inflatable boat manufacture from a cottage industry to true mass production.

From a consumer's viewpoint, things aren't quite so clear. Despite occasional reports of poor workmanship, Hypalon has developed a reputation for ruggedness and longevity. PVC fabrics, on the other hand, developed a reputation for premature failure, due largely to a run of problems during the early-to-mid 1980s.

Understanding of the situation is made more difficult by the fact that both PVC and Hypalon fabrics can vary tremendously in quality from fabricator to fabricator, even from batch to batch. To make matters more confusing, the durability of a boat is as much a function of the seams and joints as it is of the hull fabric.

We tried to evaluate the fabrics used in our test

boats by clamping a swatch of fabric in an airtight fixture that left a square of the fabric exposed. We then pressurized the gadget to the working pressure of the boat and dropped a weighted dart onto its surface to evaluate puncture resistance. We inflated another swatch, and dragged a weighted steel rasp across the fabric to see how well it resisted abrasion. And we exposed samples of each fabric to a collection of boat chemicals, fuels, antifreezes and oils to see how well each held up.

What we found was not definitive. There *were* slight differences in puncture and abrasion resistance, but we couldn't find any pattern. All the samples we tested, including unreinforced PVC, showed good abrasion resistance; all the reinforced fabrics showed good puncture resistance. PVC fabrics, however, were severely stiffened and discolored by overnight immersion in gasoline, so we are left with some concerns about spills and leaky hoses. On the other hand, we haven't encountered any reports of failures attributable to contact with gasoline. It seems to us that the way to deal with this problem is to wash off spills immediately, rather than to reject boats made of PVC-coated fabric.

As a side note, silicone compounds should never be used on PVC boats. A reader, Richard Schaefer of Glastonbury, Connecticut, told us he ruined his $2,000 Zodiac by "protecting" it with Armorall. We confirmed with Zodiac that silicone can cause separation of the seams.

The biggest question about PVC is whether it will stand up under severe sunlight for extended periods. We couldn't test for this, because of time constraints, so we contacted 20 inflatable-boat repair shops across the country. To minimize commercial bias, we restricted our survey to shops that either don't sell boats at all, or shops that sell both PVC and Hypalon® boats. We told each shop that replies would be treated confidentially. Each shop was asked the following question: "Making allowance for the fact that there are more PVC boats sold than Hypalon boats, have you encountered a disproportionate number of either type in the boats you repair?"

While responses varied, some patterns of responses did emerge. In the more northerly states, PVC boats and Hypalon boats seem to have comparable service records, at least for boats made since 1986 or so. In the south, most repair shops felt that Hypalon boats have better ultra-violet resistance than PVC boats, particularly in the Caribbean, where boats typically stay inflated all year and ultraviolet attack is strongest.

Our conclusion is that you can make good and bad boats out of PVC or Hypalon. If we were sailing in the tropics, we'd probably opt for Hypalon. If we tended to be careless about spilled fuel, or were cruising to remote areas (Hypalon is easier for do-it-yourself

repair) we'd do the same. But, for most people, especially those in more northern climates, we think that the choice of fabric is secondary to the quality of the boat. This opinion is supported by the warranties offered by the manufacturers: Except for Tinker, which offers a spectacular 10-year warranty on material and seams, and Avon, which offers 10 and 5 years on fabric and seams, respectively, all of the other boats made of reinforced fabric offer 5-year warranties on both fabric and seams regardless of construction material.

Load Ratings

Some boats we tested carry load ratings in pounds; some also specify the maximum number of people that can be carried. Inflatables, as a class, have extremely high load capacities (the boats we tested were rated for 700 to 1,140 pounds, and from three to five people), but most boats will perform much better if you keep well below the rated maximum. We found that putting more than three adults in any of these boats almost guarantees an uncomfortable ride and, if the skipper backs off too suddenly on the throttle, a very wet one. None of them have much in the way of freeboard.

Every boat we tested had at least two separate air chambers, and is capable of supporting its rated load with one main chamber deflated; they all have sufficient reserve buoyancy so that sinking one by accident is virtually impossible.

Engine Ratings

A few years ago, inflatables carried maximum horsepower ratings bordering on the suicidal. The industry, through a commendable self-policing policy, has brought engine ratings under much better control.

The boats we tested carry ratings from 3 to 15 horsepower. More to the point, several manufacturers are now issuing suggested engine ratings, which are lower and more reasonable than the maximum ratings. The Calypso we tested, for example, is rated at 15 horsepower, but the company recommends 8.

Speed and Planing

Today's inflatables tend to be a quick lot. The Zodiac Futura Jr., the fastest of the boats we tested, can reportedly approach 30 knots with a 9.9-hp. engine, and several of the other boats are almost as fast. Top speed *per se,* however, isn't really a vital consideration when you're dealing with a boat whose primary function is to ferry you back and forth to your boat. We found that all of the boats capable of planing provide exhilarating rides.

If you don't have any great distances to cover, the ability to plane isn't essential. A non-planing boat, however, is limited to a top speed of less than 5 knots, so if you have some open water to cover, a planing boat is definitely preferable. Unless we were financially strapped, or our needs were extremely modest, we wouldn't consider a non-planing model.

We tested all the boats to see if they'd plane with a minimal engine—3.3 horsepower—and one person aboard. We also checked each with a full load and the maximum rated size engine.

Accommodations

While most of the boats we tested come with seats of some sort, these are primarily for rowing. Most people perch themselves on one of the side tubes when under way. A more important aspect of design for comfort is the provision of handholds. Most boats have a grab line that extends around the outside of the outer tubes, though on some boats these do not extend far enough forward. A few boats are arranged so that oars are stored just where you want to sit, and the Tinker managed to locate a cleat that's part of its sailing package directly under the skipper's rear end.

The carrying handles on a few boats were much appreciated by our testers. Features such as bow dodgers and adequate hoisting and towing eyes are definite pluses. Another handy feature to look for is a tie-down for a fuel can.

Rowing

All of the boats, with two exceptions, were equipped with oarlocks and oars. All the boats could be rowed adequately, with the Breeze and the Tinker excelling in this category, but inflatables, as a class, are too light to be really good rowboats; weight, after all, provides momentum in between strokes. The Zodiac Futura Jr. and the Novurania Whitecap are equipped with paddles instead of oars, probably on the theory that they're essentially powerboats that would only be hand-propelled in an emergency, and too beamy to row well with the short oars that would stow conveniently. Rigid seats, we found, made rowing much more comfortable than did inflatable seats. And, when trying to get up on plane by yourself, with many small boats it's important to sit on the centerline. Some sort of seat is a necessity, even if it has to be purchased as an option.

Ease of Assembly

We noted how easy each boat was to assemble and inflate, as well as how many pump strokes each required. This depends on the design of the boat and the pump supplied, but since most people use the pump that comes with the boat, we think it's a fair comparison. Electric pumps, we found, are easier on the legs than foot pumps, but they aren't faster and don't provide adequate pressure to inflate most boats properly. You'll still need to use the foot pump for the final dozen or so strokes per chamber.

Once deflated, an inflatable has to be stored, which entails carrying it to the storage area. We noted both weight and stored size of each boat; when boats are stored in more than one package, we recorded the size of each.

On-The-Water Performance

We conducted our on-the-water tests at the Old Greenwich Yacht Club in Greenwich, Connecticut. Each boat was fitted with a small 3.3-hp. outboard for its first trials, then with an outboard that approximated its maximum rating, most often a 9.9-hp. We made runs in both calm harbor water as well as runs outside in small to moderate chop. First runs were made with one person, then with one and two passengers. Regardless of load ratings, at high speeds we don't think that any of these boats is really suitable for more than three people. Our "Overall Performance" ratings are based upon planing ability and high-speed handling. If high-performance operation isn't your main interest, you can ignore these ratings in favor of other, more specific characteristics.

While there were many similarities in handling among the 18 boats tested, we did find several noticeable differences: skidding due to absence of keel; boat standing up during acceleration due to short waterline and, possibly, excessive keels; and sluggish performance of "soft-tail" models with clamp-on motor brackets. Rigidity of the hull is an important factor in good high-speed performance; manufacturers achieve this through the use of large-diameter air tubes, higher air pressures made possible by reinforced hull materials, and/or rigid keelsons.

Most of the boats tested are capable of high speeds, especially those rated for 9.9-hp. and 15-hp. motors. In fact, all of the testers remarked that these boats can be dangerous, especially in the hands of an inexperienced person. Because these boats essentially sit on top of the water, at high speed the hull slaps across the water, and if one doesn't hold on tightly, it is easy to see how someone might be thrown into the water.

The situation is exacerbated by the boats' seating positions: You're generally perched on a side tube rather than sitting inside. A friend of ours has gruesome prop scars to prove such accidents are more than flukes. Before turning your teenager loose in such a powerful craft, we strongly recommend onboard instruction and specific rules, including the wearing of life jackets and obeying speed limits. Another surprising and unpleasant, if not actually unsafe, characteristic we noticed, was the tendency of many inflatables to submarine when slowing down too rapidly. What appears to happen is that because the flat bottom has so much drag, the hull is quickly overtaken by its own wake when depowered. Several times we soaked the forward-sitting passengers and on a couple of occasions actually swamped the boat until we learned to gradually depower, waiting for the stern wave to pass beneath before completely stopping. While none of the boats showed any tendency to sink, it made for a cold, wet experience.

Following are our individual remarks, listed in increasing order of discount price.

Sevylor Super Caravelle ($187)

The Super Caravelle is about the least-expensive inflatable you can buy that's usable outside of a swimming pool. It's made of unreinforced PVC, which limits the inflation pressure; as a result the boat is quite bendy. It has seven separate air chambers, which makes it safe, but also makes inflation a nuisance. That, plus the fact that the motor mount requires an undue amount of fiddling to install, makes assembly difficult.

Rowing and motoring were also poor, largely due to excessive hull flexing. When we turned up the throttle on a 3.3-hp. motor, the hull buckled so much we were afraid the motor would be dunked.

If all you need is an inflatable that will get you back and forth from your boat in a small anchorage, the Sevylor will do that job for the least money. If you're looking for higher speeds or exhilarating performance, you'll have to go up considerably in price.

Sea Eagle SE8H ($449)

Much of what we just said about the Sevylor applies to the Sea Eagle. While both are made of unreinforced PVC, the Sea Eagle felt a tad more secure underfoot because it has a two-piece plywood floor. Ease of assembly was poor.

As with the Sevylor, the Sea Eagle's performance problems seem directly attributable to its lack of rigidity, made worse by the donut shape which places the motor considerably outboard of the boat. Rowing performance was poor, and, like the Sevylor, the motor squats as throttle is applied, to the point it is nearly submerged in its own wake. It is more rigid than the Sevylor, but we don't think the difference is worth the extra cost.

Breeze 9 ($748)

The Breeze is very different from the others tested. It's technically an inflatable, but it features a rigid floor that folds in two lengthwise, plus inflatable airtubes and a fixed seat. The Breeze's air tubes are made of a thick non-reinforced EVA plastic. It sets up and deflates extremely easily, but folds to a long, fairly flat bundle that is best stored on-deck or lashed to a rail; it's too large for the lockers on most boats.

The unusual, almost double-ended design of the Breeze allows it to be rowed in both directions, which is convenient. Certainly it rows better than a conventional inflatable, but again it does not carry its way well because of light weight. It did not plane with the small outboard and did take some water over the bow in a chop; it's not rated for more than 4-hp.

The Breeze can be fitted with a sailing kit ($350) that converts it to a single-sail dinghy. Under sail it was reasonably quick and extremely stable, though the small leeboard allows too much leeway. Also, moving the leeboard from port to starboard is a pain and we invariably lost control for half a minute.

If you're not interested in high speed, and the option of sailing your dinghy is appealing, the Breeze is a good, rugged boat at a reasonable price.

Boat/U.S. Seaworthy 8.3 ($799)

The Seaworthy 8.3 is the lowest-price boat we tested with an integral transom. Like the Quicksilver 8.6, it has a slatted floor, which is extremely easy to set up or take down.

On-the-water performance wasn't particularly sporty. We blame the slatted floor for some of its problems. Planing was not possible for one person using either the 3.3-hp. or 6-hp. outboard (max. rating 5-hp.). The 8.3 rated average in most categories. We did notice that it was a bit wetter than other inflatables, perhaps due to its tube diameter and narrow beam.

Quicksilver 8.6 Soft Tail ($800)

Like the Sevylor and Sea Eagle, the Quicksilver 8.6 is a "soft-tail" design. Unlike them, it's made of a polyester-reinforced PVC that permits a higher inflation pressure and greater hull rigidity. It has a slatted floor, which lets you roll it up after deflating, without removing any pieces. The motor mount rolls up with the hull, making storage very easy.

Rowing performance was fair. With a 3.3-hp. outboard, the 8.6 would not plane with one person. With a larger 6-hp (max. rating 4-hp.) it still wouldn't plane, putting up a big wake as it plowed along. It helped convince us that donut-shaped inflatables, with clamp-on motor brackets, have some serious shortcomings compared to conventional transoms. Overall performance was below average. It's a step up from the less-rigid unreinforced PVC boats, but several steps below the integral-transom designs.

Quicksilver 8.9 Sport ($978)

The Quicksilver 8.9 is quicker than any of its less-expensive competitors. It uses a sectional-board floor and features an inflatable keel; ease of assembly was average.

While it will plane with one person and a 3.3-hp motor, it won't with three persons and a 9.9-hp. It's most obvious problem is the tendency to nearly stand straight up on its tail before settling onto a plane, even with crew weight shifted forward. We think this characteristic is potentially dangerous, particularly in high winds. It's certainly unnerving.

OMC Express 305 ($985)

The OMC Express 305 is a sectional-floorboard boat

with an inflatable keel. It comes in a bright white fabric, which stays cool, but shows dirt.

Rowing performance was below average and the oars are not captive. With both large and small outboards we noted some skidding in turns. It planed well with one person and a 3.3-hp outboard, but with the 9.9-hp. it would not plane with three testers aboard. The high bow helps keep passengers dry in

Value Guide: Inflatable Boats

Brand	Model	List	Discount	Compact Stowage	Floor	Keel	Material	Warranty (years) Material/ Seams	Max HP	Max Load (Lbs./No. persons)	# Chambers
Sevylor	Super Caravelle XR86GT	$225	$187	Y [3]	Soft	None	PVC	90 days	3.5	700/4	7
Sea Eagle	SE8H	$449	$449	Y [3]	Boards	None	PVC	1/1	3	950/4	5
Breeze	9	$748 [5]	$748	N[6]	Rigid, folding	Hull shape	EVA	5/[4]	4[2]	1000/5	3
Boat/U.S.	Seaworthy 8.3	N.A.	$799	Y	Roll-up slats	Inflatable	Hyp/Polyester	5/5	5	595/N.A.	2
Quicksilver	QSR 8' 6 Soft Tail	$899	$800	N	Roll-up slats	None	PVC/Polyester	5/5	4	770/3	2
Quicksilver	QSR 8'9 Sport	$1,099	$978	N	Boards	Inflatable	PVC/Polyester	5/5	10	1075/N.A.	3+keel
OMC	Express 305	$1,145	$985	N	Boards	Inflatable	PVC/Polyester	5/5	10	882/4	2+keel
West Marine	CS 10.2	$1,350	$995	N	Boards	Inflatable	PVC/Polyester	5/5	10	990/4	2+keel
Boat/U.S.	Seaworthy 9.2	N.A.	$999	N	Boards	Inflatable	Hyp/Polyester	5/5	8	965/N.A.	2+keel
Boat/U.S. Achilles	BA-96	N.A.	$1,195	N	Boards	Inflatable	Hyp/Polyester	5/5	8	970/N.A.	3+keel
Achilles	LS5-BU	$1,850	$1,250	N	Boards	Inflatable	PVC/Polyester	5/5	10	1140/4	3+keel
Bombard	AX400	$1,850	$1,310	Y	Inflatable	None	PVC/Polyester	5/5	8	925/4	2+floor
Calypso	C27	$1,695	$1,445	N	Keelson+Boards	Hard keelson	Hyp/Polyester	5/5	15 [1]	850/4	2
Zodiac	C310XS	N.A	$1,775	N	Boards	Inflatable	PVC/Polyester	5/5	10	1100/4	2+keel
Novurania	Whitecap 285	$2,100	$1,920	N	Keelson+Boards	Hard keelson	Hyp/Polyester	5/5	15	900/4	3
Avon	Roll-Away R285	$2,495	$1,948	Y	Roll-up slats	Inflatable	Hyp/Nylon	10/5	8	720/N.A.	2+keel
Tinker	Tramp	$2,280 [7]	$2,280	Y	Roll-up slats	None	Hyp/Nylon	10/10	4	882/4	4
Zodiac	Futura Jr. 0276	N.A.	$2,900	Y	Inflatable	2 Inflatable	PVC/Polyester	5/5	15	882/4	2+floor+keels

*Planing models only
Ratings: 1 poor, 2 fair, 3 average, 4 very good, 5 superior
[1] 8 HP recommended
[2] 2 HP recommended

[3] Motor mount detaches for storage
[4] Seamless construction
[5] Basic boat., without sailing kit. Sailing kit:$350
[6] Stores on deck or along rail in sailboard bracket

a chop. There are no forward lines for passengers to grab; we think that's a serious omission. Performance otherwise was average.

West Marine CS 10.2 ($995)

The West CS 10.2 is another sectional-floorboard design. The boat we received did not come with a seat, so that ease of rowing was poor; with a seat it would be average.

It planed with one person and a 3.3-hp engine, but planed only marginally with three aboard and a 9.9-hp. The West tended to lift its bow on hard acceleration, though not as much as the Quicksilver 8.9. It was average in dryness and comfort.

Boat/U.S. Seaworthy 9.2 ($999)

Unlike the 8.2, the 9.2 uses a sectional floorboard design, which improves high speed performance, but reduces the ease of assembly to only average. Like all sectional-floorboard designs, the Seaworthy 9.2 breaks down to a fairly large number of separate pieces, which can present problems, especially when working on the deck of a boat.

In general, on-the-water performance was similar to the 8.3. It too was a bit wet. Planing was not possible with the small outboard, but good with the 9.9, even with three people aboard. A minor complaint is that the metal outboard plate on the transom isn't positioned quite right to handle either an OMC or a Mercury 9.9-hp engine.

Performance rating: Fair

Boat/U.S. Achilles BA-96 ($1,195)

This sectional-floorboard model, while carrying the Achilles logo, is distributed only through Boat/U.S. Like all the sectional-floorboard designs, ease of setting up and deflation was average.

The BA-96, with one person aboard, was fairly easy to get up on plane, but with three persons it would not plane, even though we had a 9.9-hp., larger than the recommended 8-hp. Consequently, it created a big wake. And we found it a bit wet. With fewer passengers both Achilles models stayed on plane to very slow speeds, which we liked.

Achilles LS5-BU ($1,250)

The Achilles LS5-BU is another sectional-floorboard design, average in ease of assembly and disassembly.

Rowing performance was average. With a 3.3-hp. outboard, the

Stored Dimensions (inches)	Weight	Plane 3.3 hp (1 person)	Plane max. hp (3 persons)	Total Pump Strokes to Inflate	Ease of Assembly	Rowing	Dryness	Comfort	Handling*	Overall Performance
14-1/2 x 12 x 46	32.5	N	N	388	1	1	4	1	—	1
4 x 30 x 46 + 7 x 19 x 23	46.5	N	N	350	1	1	4	1	—	1
16 x 29 x 108	100.5	N	N	100	5	4	4	5	—	1
9 x 24 x 38	61.5	N	N	280	5	3	2	3	—	1
13 x 22 x 42	57	N	N	251	5	2	5	4	—	1
13 x 22 x 42	81.5	Y	N	575	3	3	4	5	3	1
13 x 20 x 38	69.5	Y	N	421	4	2	5	3	3	2
16 x 24 x 41	71.5	Y	Y (marginal)	547	3	2	2	3	4	3
8 x 24 x 39 + 6 x 22 x 34	96.5	N	Y	492	3	3	3	3	3	2
10 x 18 x 41 + 5 x 23 x 42	78.5	Y	N	407	3	3	2	3	4	2
12 x 21 x 45	88.5	Y	Y	573	3	3	3	3	3	3
14 x 20 x 38	45.5	Y	Y	620	5	2	2	3	2	2
10 x 20 x 40 + 5 x 22 x 35	101.5	Y	Y	260	3	3	5	5	5	5
15 x 22 x 46	90.5	Y	Y (marginal)	358	3	3	3	3	3	3
6 x 8 x 49+ 14 x 26 x 42+ 3 x 27 x 35	109.5	Y	Y	165	2	1 (paddles)	4	5	5	5
20 x 24 x 42	95.5	Y	Y	154	5	3	4	4	4	5
12 x 24 x 50	66.5	Y	Y	162	5	4	4	3	4	4
17 x 27 x 49	68.5	Y	Y	438	5	1 (paddles)	5	5	5	5

[7] Basic boat., without sailing or Lifeboat kit. Sailing kit: $700; Life raft kit: $907 ; Sea Anchor : $97
[8[Estimated. Manufacturer does not supply list prices.

LS5-BU was able to plane with one person, and with the larger 9.9-hp. it planed with three people, distinguishing it from some of the others. We did note that during acceleration the bow tended to rise higher than we liked, though not as badly as the Quicksilver. At high speed, in a chop, the floor-boards buckled and rattled.

Bombard AX 400 ($1,310)

Built by Zodiac, the Bombard A-400 dispenses with floorboards entirely, using a through-stitched double inflatable floor. This makes for light weight, compact storage and easy setup under adverse conditions. Unlike the inflated floor of the Sevylor, the Bombard's floor is inflated to a high pressure, providing a reasonably secure, if slippery, floor. The Bombard was excellent in terms of ease of inflation and deflation.

The Bombard lacks a keel, which severely affects its in-the-water performance. Rowing performance was below average. The oars are not captive. While the Bombard is fast and capable of planing with both small and large outboards, control was poor. In fact, at high speeds we felt it was quite skittish, even scary at times. This problem is exacerbated by the slippery floor. If it weren't for these problems, its "Overall Performance" rating would have been higher.

Calypso C27 ($1,445)

The Calypso, along with the Novurania, uses a two-piece bolt-together rigid keelson, or backbone, to support the floorboards. While this construction helps make for a very rigid boat, it also adds weight and complicates assembly and disassembly. The Calypso's commendable rigidity is enhanced by large-diameter air tubes.

The Calypso's keel gives it excellent control, and the large 17-inch diameter tubes make for a dry ride. It planed easily with all outboards. Rowing was slightly better than average, helped by a rigid, well-placed seat.

Overall, we found the Calypso to be a fine performer and, at a discount price of $1,445, we consider it a Best Buy.

Zodiac C310SX ($1,775)

Similar in appearance to the West CS 10.2, the Zodiac C 310SX was also average in ease of setting up and taking down.

On the water, this model rated average in most categories. It barely got up on a marginal plane with an operator and a 3.3-hp engine. With a 9.9-hp. it had difficulty planing with three persons. We noted some skidding, due to the lack of a keel, but handling was nevertheless satisfactory. The buoyant tube seat allows one to sit in the middle instead of on a tube, which can be important when motoring alone. For

1993, the C310X will be replaced by the YL310; design and performance should be similar to the C310SX.

Novurania White Cap 285 ($1,920)

The Novurania shares the Calypso's keelson-plus-floorboard design and large air tubes. It comes with a bow dodger and solid loops for attaching a hoist. Unlike most of the other inflatables, the Novurania is equipped with paddles instead of oars. This would seem to be an admission that inflatables don't row well and that an alternative approach might be better. Clearly you wouldn't want to paddle an inflatable very far, but for short distances you could make do.

Under power, the Novurania performed very well, though it did tend to skid a little on fast turns. It planed easily and handled well with one person and a 3.3-hp engine as well as three up and a 15-hp.

Overall performance was superior, and construction detailing was excellent.

Avon Roll-Away R285 ($1,948)

The Avon, along with the Breeze, shared the honors for fast and easy setup—we could get it out of its carrying bag and fully inflated in a shade over two minutes. This is due largely to its sectional floorboard design, which works something like a roll-top desk, and in part to a very good foot pump. When unrolled, the floorboard sections are locked into place by the boat's inflatable keel.

Rowing performance was average, but some of our testers didn't like the oar lock system, which does not hold the oars captive. Under power, the Avon tracked nicely and planed easily with one person using a 3.3 hp outboard. With the 9.9-hp operating at part throttle (max. rating 8 hp.) it was very fast, getting up on plane quickly and with the bow staying low. Control was very good except at top speeds, where we encountered some skidding.

Overall, a superior performer, and an excellent choice if you're going to inflate it and deflate it frequently.

Tinker Tramp ($2,280)

The Tinker Tramp is unusual in that it's designed to take a sailing kit ($700); there's a built-in centerboard trunk, built-in cleats and a pointy nose to help sailing performance. It also can be configured as a lifeboat kit with canopy, CO_2 inflation and drogue ($1,004)), which we didn't try to evaluate. The Tinker, like the Avon, has a roll-up floor and sets up only a trifle slower than the Avon.

Due to its unconventional design, including a fine bow, the Tinker rowed better than any of the other inflatables. It has wooden oars that are longer than the norm. It rated above average in all categories. It planed with one person and a 3.3-hp. motor; a 6-hp. was too heavy for the transom. Aside from the fact that the Tinker is clearly not a high-speed muscle boat—its maximum rating is for a 4-hp. engine—our only gripes are its narrow beam, which meant that the boat heeled a bit more than most of the others, and the fact that the centerboard trunk and cleats took away some usable space. These represent a trade-off with improved rowing and sailing performance. Performance was very good, given the Tinker's engine size limitation.

It is a surprisingly good sailer, tacking easily, though its light weight sometimes necessitates backwinding the jib to carry through.

Zodiac Futura Jr. O276 ($2,900)

The Futura Jr. uses a drop-stitched inflatable floor, similar to the Bombard, to eliminate floorboards. Unlike the flat-bottomed Bombard, however, the Futura Jr. elevates its flat floor between the air tubes, producing a tunnel effect, and has two inflatable keel tubes at the bottom of the air tubes for tracking and to further raise the floor.

Setup is very easy, although the large tubes require a lot of pumping. Unlike the Bombard, the Futura Jr.'s floor isn't slippery.

Like the Novurania, the Futura Jr. uses paddles instead of oars. Under power, the Futura Jr. has outstanding performance. It planed easily with one tester and a 3.3 hp; it planed easily with three up and a 9.9 or a 15 hp. Skidding was almost non-existent; we attributed the Futura's tracking characteristics to the double-keel. The elevated underbody leaves little wake.

Overall performance under power of the Futura Jr. was the best of the boats tested. This is high praise indeed, in light of the sparkling performances turned in by Calypso, Novurania and Avon.

Conclusions

If high-speed performance is your only requirement, our recommendations are clear: the Calypso C27, the Novurania Whitecap 2.85, the Avon Roll-Away R285 and the Zodiac Futura Jr. 0276 were the cream of the crop. For most people, however, there are other considerations.

While there are other considerations, including stowage size, ease of rowing and towing, the major factor for most people is price. The chart lists the boats in increasing order of average discount price. If your needs are minimal, and all you're looking for is an inflatable that will get you back and forth from your not-too-distant boat, it's hard to beat the Sevylor Super Caravelle at $187. While it doesn't measure up to more-expensive models in terms of performance, it's safe and cheap.

For a generally more versatile boat, the price goes

up. The Breeze 9 at $748, is a good, if unusual, boat, assuming planing performance isn't important. It's rugged, rows and motors well with a small outboard. While it doesn't fold up enough for locker storage, it can be set up and taken down quickly and easily for storage along a rail.

For a more conventional inflatable to operate at sub-planing speeds, the Boat/U.S. Seaworthy 8.3, at $799, has a slatted floor so that it rolls up for easy storage.

Until you get up to the $1,900-plus range, you won't find boats with the combination of compact storage and good high-speed planing capability. Of the boats that *don't* lend themselves to being stowed away in a locker, the West Marine CS 10.2 ($995) will plane with one person and a 3.3-hp., and the Achilles LS-5BU ($1,250) had reasonable overall performance. Our favorite in this category, however, is the Calypso C27 at $1,445. It had superior performance under power, was average in rowing capability and was generally well-made. Priced at $475 less than the next lowest-priced boat with comparable performance, we call the Calypso C27 a Best Buy.

The Novurania, a highly respected name among inflatable manufacturers, is similar in design to the Calypso. It discounts for $1,920, and is larger and roomier. Its motoring performance was superior, but it's not designed for rowing.

If you want compact storage *and* sparkling performance, the Avon Rollaway R285 and the Zodiac Futura Jr. 0276 offer both—at a price. The Avon discounts for $1,950; the Zodiac for $2,900. They're very different boats. The Avon is a well-made high-speed tender that rows adequately, motors very well and can be set up and taken down in a minimum of time with a minimum of effort. The Zodiac is essentially a high-performance sports boat that can't be rowed, but can be stored in a small space. The Zodiac is a faster boat than the Avon, but requires almost three times as many pump strokes to inflate.

The Avon is made of Hypalon and the Zodiac of PVC. As discussed in Part 1, if we were planning to cruise the tropics, where ultraviolet attack is more severe, we'd opt for Hypalon. It's also easier to repair in the field. For more casual use in the north, we don't think material is that important a consideration.

The pricey Tinker Tramp ($2,280) is an oddball in this company. What the Tinker does, it does extremely well. It rows better than any of the other boats we tested, planes easily with a 3.3-hp. motor, deflates, inflates and stores easily and is well-made. Its price tag, we feel, is out of line with the other boats if all you want is a tender. If you are interested in the sailing kit and/or the lifeboat kit, the versatile Tinker may well be a less-expensive alternative to buying a tender plus a life raft and/or sailing dinghy. • **PS**

Mainsheet Travelers

In a seven-model comparison, the least expensive traveler turned out to be one of the best.

With a mainsheet traveler, you can sheet to windward in light air to gain pointing ability; you can substitute the mainsheet for the vang upwind; and in heavy and puffy air, you can play the traveler car control rather than the mainsheet to power up or down without altering leech twist. As a consequence, performance-oriented sailors, given the choice, will invariably opt for a traveler rather than the triangular "Crosby" or "Lightning-type" mainsheet rig found on many older boats and a few new ones.

The attractions of the best modern traveler systems are hard to resist: Almost frictionless cars gliding on ball bearings, modular system components that let you lead mainsheet and control lines in virtually any configuration, installation that's so simple even a child can do it, and (at least for two of our test models) almost unbelievably low prices.

Test Procedure

Our test boat for this exercise, a 1968 Morgan 24, is designed to have a traveler located aft in the cockpit, rather than forward on the cabintop, which would call for heavier track because of the greater leverage that goes with midboom sheeting. Because the Morgan's tiller rises from the cockpit sole almost exactly under the boom end, and room is needed to swing the tiller up without interfering with the traveler track, we installed the test tracks 11 inches abaft the boom end, bridged across the cockpit footwell. This location places a sizable side load on the car, which, it turned out, is more easily handled by some car/track designs than others.

To avoid drilling too many holes in the fiberglass cockpit deck to mount our traveler tracks, we bolted a 2" x 4" board to the cockpit seats, and fastened each of the seven test units (and an eighth simple slide-on-a-T-track) in turn to the board. Only the ends were fastened, simulating a situation where the track would have to bridge across a 4-foot gap, such as an extra-wide cockpit footwell or a companionway.

All tests were conducted with the boat at rest and no mainsail hoisted. We shackled the main halyard to the outboard end of the boom to counteract the downward force of the sheet. Next, using a four-part mainsheet purchase, with the car centered on the track, we trimmed the sheet end to a tension of 50 pounds measured on a spring scale, giving approximately 200 pounds of upward force on the traveler car. Then, by using the spring scale on the car trimming line, we measured frictional car resistance (i.e. force to move the car) for each of the eight designs. It's worth noting that the vertical pull of the mainsheet was considerably more than 200 pounds when we read the trimming force, due to the geometry of the system (straight track, arced boom end path) with the car pulled almost all the way to one side. (It should also be mentioned that since the mainsail wasn't rigged, its side-pull was zero; close-hauled in a blow, a sizable force would be added to the one we measured.)

We also measured the vertical deflection of each track (except the plain T-track) under a 200-pound load with the car centered, cross-sectional dimensions of each track, and total weight of each rig.

Keeping these physical tests in mind, we evaluated each design's relative ease of assembly, installation, operation, and maintenance; its strength and durability; how well it could be adapted to special needs dictated by the configurations of individual boats; and its price.

Evaluations

Plain Slide on T-track

As a check to be sure that ball bearing cars are really necessary to ensure easy movement under load, we tested a 1967-vintage plastic Tuphblox T-track traveler system with a plain no-bearing car. Although it slid fairly well under light loads, it invariably began to bind when heavy pressure was imposed. A force of well over 50 pounds was needed to move the car when our 200-pound standard load was applied—more than triple the force needed for the worst of our modern bearing-equipped units.

Harken

Harken's heads-up product engineering, excellent workmanship, and consumer-oriented packaging all deserve high marks. In fact, we judged the Harken traveler best in every characteristic evaluated except price. And it had more useful features than any of its competitors except Schaefer, with which it was tied.

Installation, with clear printed instructions for assembling every component, was easy and quick. Mounting the track to existing holes in the boat was simple, thanks to the sliding "T-bolts" (actually hex-headed bolts with washers under the heads, riding in a T-shaped slot under the track).

Ease of operation and maintenance was also tops. The Torlon ball system worked superbly; the Harken traveler was the only system we tested in which *all* sheaves, as well as the car and the cam cleats, ride on low-friction balls. On the car, balls are exposed underneath, so hosing with fresh water now and then will keep salt and dirt from gumming up the works. Incidentally, Harken recommends a light lubricant such as LPS-1, WD-40 or dry silicone sprays for travelers (and Schaefer recommends Boeshield T-9); we didn't use any lubricants in our tests, however.

Strength of Harken's track was superior, with the smallest vertical deflection among the units tested. That's not surprising, given the 1-1/2-inch height of the Harken track cross-section—the tallest of the bunch.

Adaptability was also excellent. End sheaves can be stacked either one or two high, and blocks can be added easily to the car, if desired for varying levels of mechanical advantage. Control cams can be turned from approximately 35 degrees inboard to 15 degrees outboard to accommodate different deck layouts. And a unique (but expensive) "windward sheeting traveler car" accessory, which makes it possible to pull the car above the centerline without releasing the leeward control line, can be quickly bolted on.

One interesting sidelight: Consulting the Harken catalog, we discovered that the Harken 038 fiddle block needed for our test wasn't available in a standup model. When we called Harken to express our surprise, they opted to send us a prototype not yet released for production. They plan to have a production part available next fall, although they would supply the same prototype today to other customers if requested. Given this situation, we felt it was fair to give Harken credit for having a standup block available—and kudos for demonstrating quick response to customer needs.

Schaefer

Schaefer prides itself on designing products that are strong, durable, reliable, and easy to use; judging from our test traveler, that pride is justifiable. A case in point is its cam cleats. The color-coded cam bases can be useful as well as decorative. And the stainless steel cams are very strong and extremely corrosion resistant. By comparison, aluminum die castings tend to corrode and wear out faster, especially in a warm, salt-laden environment; plastic cams typi-cally wear even faster than aluminum (though Ronstan's new carbon fiber cams may prove to be the exception). Maintenance-wise, too, the Schaefer cams are well designed: hollow and open at the top so fresh water can be squirted in easily to flush away salt deposits and harbor grime. The open top also permits inspection of the edge of the cam spring, which is a stainless steel ribbon rather than the usual (and less durable) coiled wire.

Every unit tested except Schaefer and Ronstan had cars equipped with recirculating plastic balls in linear races. The Schaefer (and Ronstan) units used stainless steel balls in annular races, e.g. traditional ball bearings. This feature makes it relatively easy to remove the car for servicing (no loose balls to lose), and, judging from our test results, doesn't hurt performance (i.e. force required to move the Schaefer car was equal to or lower than every competitor's except Harken).

The Schaefer design had the best strength-to-weight ratio (tied with one competitor for lowest weight and with another for next-to-lowest deflection under load). The unit also scored well in our "Useful Features" and "Other Judgments" categories. Overall, with a list price 18 percent lower than Harken's, the Schaefer traveler may be the choice of many.

Garhauer I Track

Design of this unit is elegantly simple, with few parts and no worries about how it all goes together. On our test unit, everything worked just as it should, including the Torlon-ball-equipped car with Torlon balls bearing on both bottom and top flanges of the track. This design is especially good for angular loads such as those imposed in our test; the 11 pounds of force needed to move the traveler was well within the reasonable range.

Garhauer Double T

The main objection we had to this unit was its lack of a standup block. We liked the simplicity of design and good low-friction performance. And although we counted fewer useful features than any other traveler tested, to shoppers on a budget the Double T unit's very low price may more than compensate for its lack of frills.

Lewmar

The looks of this British brand's traveler, with its streamlined car, covered end sheaves, and smooth gray anodized finish, appealed to us. So did the T-bolt method of attaching track to the boat (which can help when you want to mount the unit on existing holes). But there were a number of things we didn't like about this rig. It isn't available with a standup fiddle block with integral cam cleat, though we were

Value Guide: Mainsheet Travelers

	Antal	Garhauer I	Garhauer Dbl. T	Harken	Lewmar	Ronstan	Schaefer
List prices							
48" track	$88	$150	$120	$89	$62	$75	$73
Car	$193	inc.	inc.	$114	$172	$103	$114
Block & Cam	$118	$50	$50	$88	$56	$60	$69
Ends & Cleats	$193	inc.	inc.	$200	$94	$114	$147
Total	$592	$200	$170	$489	$383	$352	$403
Tests							
Force to move car (lbs.)	12	11	10	8	9	18	9
Deflection of track (inches)	7/16	1/16	1/8	1/64	3/16	3/16	1/16
Useful Features Included							
Stand-up block w/ cam (5 pts.)	Yes	Yes	No	Yes	No	No	Yes
Mainsheet cam adjustable (3 pts.)	Yes	No	No	Yes	No	Yes	No
Sliding T-bolt on track (2 pts.)	No	No	No	Yes	Yes	No	No
Traveler cams adjustable (2 pts.)	No	No	No	Yes	Yes	Yes	No
Track bumpers (2 pts.)	Yes	Yes	Yes	No	Yes	Yes	No
U.S. threads (2 pts.)	No	Yes	Yes	Yes	No	No	Yes
Stainless cam cleats (2 pts.)	No	No	No	No	No	Yes*	Yes
Color-coded cam cleats (2 pts.)	No	No	No	No	No	No	No
Removable bail block (2 pts.)	Yes	Yes	Yes	Yes	Yes	No	Yes
Lightweight (2 pts.)	Yes	No	No	No	No	Yes	Yes
Total points	14	11	6	16	8	11	15
Other Judgments							
Relative strength (4 pts.)	1	4	3	4	2	2	4
Durability (4 pts.)	4	4	4	4	4	4	4
Workmanship (4 pts.)	3	3	3	4	4	4	4
Ease of maintenance (4 pts.)	4	3	3	4	4	3	4
Ease of assembly (3pts.)	2	3	3	3	2	3	3
Ease of installation (3 pts.)	2	2	2	3	2	2	2
Order/response time (3 pts.)	2	3	3	3	2	2	3
Total points	18	22	21	25	20	20	24
Overall Ratings							
List price	7	21	25	9	11	12	11
Car Friction	17	18	20	25	22	13	22
Useful Features	14	11	6	16	8	11	15
Other Judgments	18	22	21	25	20	20	24
Total Score**	**56**	**72**	**72**	**75**	**61**	**56**	**72**

Track Dimensions (height x width): Antal 25/32 x 1-1/32; Garhauer I 1-3/8 x 1-1/2; Garhauer Dbl. T 29/32 x 1-1/4; Harken 1-3/16 x 1-5/8; Lewmar 1-1/8 x 1-5/32; Ronstan 1-32 x 1-1/32; Schaefer 1-3/32 x 1-3/32.

* Face only

** Total Score represents the sum of individual scores of four attributes, each weighted equally: List Price, Friction and Deflection, Useful Features Included, and Other Judgments, each of which was graded on a scale of 0 (worst) to 25 (best). Thus, a score of 100 would be perfect. List Price scores were derived by assigning a top score (25) to the lowest-price unit, multiplying that score by that unit's price, and dividing the result by each other unit's price. Car Friction and Track Deflection was derived in the same way.

able to get a block with a cam cleat that didn't stand up, and another block without cam cleat that did. (We mounted both on the Lewmar track for our tests).

Then there was the difficulty in feeding the control line around the turning sheaves on both the car and the end fittings. The sheaves are hidden inside tunnels, so to reeve a line around them you must first fish a piece of bent wire through the tunnel and out again—a time-consuming nuisance. And we noted fewer useful features than most of the other units.

Overall we felt that the Lewmar traveler is satisfactory, but overshadowed by the units with more to offer, namely Harken, Schaefer, and Garhauer.

Antal

We had a problem with Antal in getting what we asked for. First the unit came with holes drilled in the wrong places. Then we found the end caps didn't fit properly. Eventually a unit with these problems corrected was air-freighted to us from Italy. Then we had to saw off the track to the 4-foot length we had originally specified, and drill and tap a hole to fit a metric-sized bolt. Altogether, we felt the hassle was more than many sailors would want to endure, especially when the list price was the highest in the group, and results in the friction test were only so-so.

Ronstan

Ronstan generally produces serviceable products; some, like their new turnbuckle with built-in adjustment scale, are quite clever. But we found their traveler's performance rather unimpressive.

In the force test, interference of the inside of the stainless steel bearing race caused the bearing to stop rolling and skid along the track when presented with a substantial angular load. The bearing even left a permanent silvery-white score mark in the aft upper inside corner of the black-anodized track as it skidded along. We're not sure, but we think the problem may have something to do with the sharp-edged shape of Ronstan's outer bearing race (compared to Schaefer's well-radiused edge, which performed near the top of the group). We've alerted Ronstan to the problem, and they are investigating.

The skidding car resulted in a trimming force of 18 pounds in our test—50-percent worse than the next competitor, and 125-percent worse than Harken. That, we think, is a sufficiently serious defect to judge this otherwise reasonably functional rig as unacceptable, at least for use when significant side loads are present.

The Bottom Line

In every category except price, the Harken traveler outshines the competition. There's no question that the Harken design is the target for other manufacturers, though so far no one has succeeded. The Harken engineering is too good, the customer service too responsive and on target, the product options too numerous and enticing.

Garhauer, however, has struck at the one big weakness in the Harken armor: Price. The two Garhauer test units may not have won the prize for beauty or clever design (though in our opinion they are quite adequate), and may have fewer useful features than the majority of the systems we looked at, but both are sturdy, serviceable units, with good enough performance to warrant serious consideration by the average sailor, whether or not he or she is on a tight budget.

Among the other units, the Schaefer rig comes closest to satisfying most typical needs, and (as with most or all of the other units) may be obtainable at prices significantly below list.　　　　• **PS**

Fiddle Blocks

Our look at fiddle blocks turns up Harken as the best buy. Avoid Lewmar and Garhauer.

This chapter is devoted to a look at fiddle blocks with swivel shackles, beckets and cam cleats. The size we selected would be suitable for about a 28-foot production sloop, either as part of a mainsheet system, or as a boom vang.

Because sheave diameter varies so widely among manufacturers, it was difficult to find comparable models. We used maximum line size (all are 1/2-inch, except one), breaking strength, and the manufacturers' recommendations to make our selection. Rated safe working loads (SWL) are typically half the breaking strength.

The safe working loads for these fiddle blocks range from 750 pounds to 2,000, though our bench tests cast doubt on the accuracy of some ratings. We asked Tripp Estabrook of Harken's Newport office to calculate the maximum vertical end boom load of a typical 28-footer. He chose the Tartan 28, and told us that load is 1,393 pounds. Using a four-part tackle, the maximum load per sheave would be one quarter, or about 348 pounds, well within the safe working load of all five blocks.

The five blocks chosen for this article are manu-factured by Antal, Garhauer, Harken, Lewmar and Schaefer. These are the same companies represented in our chapter on genoa lead blocks, with the exception of Harken, which does not at present make a conventional T-track lead block. As a substitute, we looked at its Italian-made Barbarossa line.

The Tests

Our criteria for evaluating fiddle blocks focused on three major characteristics: sheave friction, cam operation, and overall construction quality. Friction is difficult to measure without the right equipment and our remarks are based purely on our subjective feelings about the way each product operated. Cam performance, under normal sailing conditions, was much the same. We rigged each block on our test boat and in light air cleated and released the mainsheet to see how easy or difficult it was to pull the line into and out of the cam jaws. We then repeated the test in our shop with the blocks under much heavier loads—270 pounds. Under these heavy loads, the lines released from the cams only with great difficulty.

Also in our shop, we secured each block to a padeye on our test bench. With a load cell and come-a-long, we pulled a 3/8-inch line backwards through the cam, attempting to simulate what would happen in a flying jibe, where a shock load would be applied to the cam. Our objective was to compare the relative effectiveness of the cams to grip the line, and of the overall strength of the blocks' construction. These fiddle blocks all are designed to accomodate 1/2-inch line maximum, except for the Harken, which due to the width of its small sheave, is designed for 3/8-inch line. We tested with 3/8-inch line, which would have seemed to favor Harken, but as the results show, this wasn't necessarily the case.

Antal

Antal hardware is made in Italy and has a definite European look with its dull black anodized finish and clean design. Its gear has faired well in our other evaluations, especially its linestoppers, which were favored highly by BOC Challenge skippers in the

Fiddle Block Comparison Chart

Make	Model	List Price/ Discount Price	Line Size	Load (SWL/Breaking Strength in lbs.)	Cheeks	Sheaves	Straps
Antal	981.652	$106.20/N.A.	1/2"	1,700/3,400	AL	Mekton	AL
Garhauer	30-08-GB	$48/N.A.	1/2"	2,000/4,000	AL	AL	SS
Harken	038	$80.30/$70.65	3/8"	750/2,500	Delrin	AL	SS
Lewmar	9187	$54/$45.90	1/2"	1,350/2,700	Polycarbonate	Delrin	SS
Schaefer	22-55	$67/$56.95	1/2"	1,750/3,500	AL	Delrin	SS

1990-91 race.

Antal fiddle blocks are beautifully made of black anodized 3571 TA16 aluminum, both for the cheeks and straps. Their finish seems harder and more durable than some other anodizing we've seen. Many variations of the Antal blocks are available. We looked at two similar fiddle blocks, one with a composite fiber bearing and one without. Both have Delrin ball bearings to handle side loads. Mekton or aluminum sheaves are available, the latter carrying a higher safe working load rating. While we admired the fancier models, we stuck to the standard Series Two block without composite fiber bearing for purposes of this evaluation because its rated strength and price are more in line with the other four makes. Unfortunately, we were unable to test the cam on our bench as the only block in stock at the distributor's office had been sold.

Even without the composite fiber bearing, the large sheave of model #981.652 moves freely; the small block does not have ball bearings and turned with more difficulty. Tolerances are close, indicating precision machining. This means less noise and less friction. Ball bearings handle the side loads of the large sheave.

Both sheaves turn on stainless steel bolts insulated from the aluminum cheeks by nylon washers. The swivel can be locked in any 90-degree position by aligning a groove in the bottom with a ridge in a Mekton bushing/spacer on the top cheek bolt. A representative of the Antal distributor said this ridge cannot withstand high shock loads. The arms are adjustable to assure the correct lead from the large sheave to the cam.

While Antal makes its own cams, the U.S. distributor also represents the patented Servo Cleat from Germany. Euro Marine Trading told us they generally replace the Antal cams with Servo Cleats.

We are impressed with Antal hardware, but are well aware of the price differential. The fiddle we selected was twice the cost of several others, and the composite fiber model is twice as expensive as the Series Two. If you are equipping your entire boat with Antal hardware, you'll want an Antal fiddle block as well, just for consistency. But at its high price, we didn't feel it represented the best value or even necessarily the best performance.

Garhauer

As noted in the last issue, this California-based hardware manufacturer markets mostly to the OEM (original equipment manufacturer) market, which means it prefers selling to boatbuilders more than over-the-counter, after market sales to consumers. Garhauer supplies Catalina Yachts with hardware, as well as parts for upscale Alden Yachts and others.

The cheeks and sheaves of the 30-08-GB are gray anodized aluminum, the straps, arms and other fittings stainless steel. The arms are not adjustable. The sheaves turn on Delrin ball bearings, which surprised us, since this was the lowest priced block we tested. Ball bearing sheaves usually are found on the more expensive hardware. The sheaves turned freely, though there was noticeably more slop than in Antal's sheaves.

The bearings turn on hollow stainless steel tubes. The model we tested had a swivel snap shackle, unlike the others we tested, but as with all of the makes, different fittings are available.

The aluminum cam jaws didn't close quite properly; one side would hang up on the other because they were too close together. While cleating the line was fairly easy, the absence of a V-shape to the top teeth means you have to pull the line toward you more to get the line into the jaws. A pronounced V-shape, as with some other cams, allows you to simply pull the line down to cleat it.

In our pull test, the line slipped at 1,100 pounds, as much as any other fiddle tested. On inspection, however, the thin stainless steel arms had deformed, leaving the cam cockeyed. We concluded that there simply wasn't enough material in the arms to prevent distortion under high loads.

The Garhauer fiddle looks nice enough, but close inspection revealed several instances of sloppy work, such as loose tolerances and scoring in the cheeks around the rivets. Deformation of the cam arms indicates to us that they are under-engineered. The sizeable price differential we saw with the Garhauer genoa lead blocks doesn't exist with fiddle blocks. Perhaps this is due to the twin ball-bearing sheaves, which certainly add to cost. Though it is the lowest priced fiddle tested, we feel you can buy a better block for a few dollars more.

Harken

The Harken block is physically the largest of the five fiddles tested. Though other blocks tested had ball bearing sheaves, Harken's larger sheave diameters are necessary because the ball bearing movements

Bearings	Sheave Diameter	Weight	Cam Cleat Pull (lbs. at which line slipped)
Mekton/Delrin ball	2-1/2"/1-5/8"	15 oz.	NA
Delrin ball	2-1/4"/1-3/4"	15 oz.	1,100 (bent arms)
Delrin ball	3"/1-3/4"	20 oz.	1,100
Delrin bushing	2"/1-1/4"	13 oz.	600 (bent arms)
Delrin bushing	1-1/2"/1-1/2"	11 oz.	1,000

handle both side and radial loads. The design of the other makes of ball bearing sheaves use ball bearings just for side loads, relying on a hollow sleeve bearing for the radial loads. Because of the ball bearing movements, the Harken's safe working load rating is the lowest of the five; presumably, the Delrin bearings will crush before any other part fails. Despite its lower SWL rating, this is a superior design with noticeably less friction than the other four makes.

The #038 Harken fiddle block has Delrin cheeks or sideplates, solid aluminum sheaves, stainless steel straps and arms, and Cam-Matic cleats. The arms are adjustable. This patented cleat has Teflon-impregnated die-cast aluminum cams and baseplates with three rows of Delrin ball bearings inside. The teeth are rounded to minimize line chafe and there is a deep V-shape at the top to make pulling the line down into the cleat easy. Harken boasts that the Cam-Matic is the easiest cam to uncleat under load, and we agree.

In our pull tests, the Cam-Matic held to 1,100 pounds, then the line popped free. Earlier tests, with the cam slightly out of line with the sheave, caused the line to pop free at 850 pounds, so it is easy to see that adjustable arms are an important feature. Why the line popped free on the Cam-Matic, while on other cams it just started to slip through, is difficult to say. It is probably because of the rounded or "soft" cam teeth. There was no deformation of the arms, straps or cheeks.

Harken told us that the company has developed its strong belief in ball bearing sheaves to facilitate unloading rather than loading. For example, in light air when you want to push the boom out, the line runs more quickly and freely with ball bearing blocks.

The Harken fiddle is a big, almost gaudy block with its large arms and sideplates, both drilled with numerous holes in the name of weight savings. Styling, like beauty, lies in the eye of the beholder. Some people will love Harken's look, others will find the Antal more handsome. And we don't doubt for a minute that many purchases are based on looks. The red base and cam caps are Harken trademarks and make the line highly recognizable. Though priced higher than Lewmar, Schaefer and Garhauer, it costs less than Antal. It has the most features—two ball bearing sheaves, superior design, and the best cam cleat. We think it's the best fiddle block tested, and because the cost differential isn't great, it is therefore also the best value.

Schaefer

Curiously, the Schaefer 22-55 fiddle block was the smallest of the five tested. It's two identical sheaves measure just 1-1/2-inch in diameter, and the body is small. Yet it's safe working load rating of 1,750 pounds is about as high as any of the others tested. It is also available with ball bearing sheaves and a 1,000-pound SWL for just $8 more.

The cheeks are black anodized aluminum, the straps are stainless steel, and the sheaves are Delrin. The arms are very short, almost unnoticeable. The cam appears to sit on a shelf cut out of the cheeks, with the arms hidden inside and riveted. The cams have stainless steel bodies with a softer polymer top. They work well in operation, though we suspect the stainless steel teeth will abrade line faster than rounder or aluminum teeth. In our pull test, the cam held to 1,000 pounds. There was a slight deformation of the baseplate upon which the cams sit, but it was barely noticeable.

The Schaefer fiddle is well designed and well made. It has a very basic look to it; clearly the company has made no real effort to give it the sex appeal of the Antal or Harken, and that's fine with us. It's small size makes it easy to discount, but the truth is it performs well. We think it's a good product, but lacking some of Harken's features. We'd be inclined to buy Schaefer's ball bearing model for a few dollars more, if only to hear the satisfying rattle.

Lewmar

The Lewmar #9187 also is a small block, similar in size to the Schaefer. It does, however, have one large sheave (two inches) and one small sheave (1-1/4-inch). The cheeks are black polycarbonate, the sheaves Delrin, the straps and arms stainless steel, and the cams are patented Servo Cleats from Germany. These have stainless steel teeth molded into the polymer cams.

The Lewmar has a method of locking the pin in 90-degree positions that requires removing the shackle, pushing the pin in, and inserting a roll pin. It works, but we found it a bit tedious. On the other hand, it's not something you'd do very often.

In operation, the cleat works well. We liked the Servo Cleat, but don't rate it any better than Harken's Cam-Matic.

Our pull test showed the Lewmar's biggest weakness. At just 600 pounds, the line slipped and the thin stainless steel arms collapsed inward, pinching the large sheave.

The Lewmar was the biggest disappointment of the group, based on the company's generally good reputation for quality equipment.

This model, however, failed, in our opinion, to live up to its name. Despite being the second lowest priced fiddle tested, we see no reason to recommend it.

• PS

Boom Vangs

The Hall Quik Vang is the class act among the seven rigid boom vang systems we tested.

Being the largest moving part on deck, the boom of a sailboat has, as is ruefully known by every knot-headed sailor who ever stepped aboard, the potential to go in harm's way.

A boom can sweep across the horizon and smash a nose or shatter teeth. In its other ugly mood, bouncing wildly up and down when the mainsail is luffing or when the main halyard is released, it can drop squarely on a head or shoulder.

Both ways, people have been killed. It's been going on since the time of square riggers. The commonest exhortation on modern boats is, "Duck!"

The device that can eliminate at least some of the risk is called a rigid boom vang. It tames the boom in one of the two dangerous planes.

A rigid boom vang is, therefore, somewhat of a safety device, although we generally think of it as a way to control undesirable twist in the mainsail when reaching and running, and also to support the boom when parked or while reefing. Mainsail control on many boats is accomplished with a soft vang, an adjustable arrangement of line, shackles and blocks either permanently attached at the base of the mast or rigged at the rail as needed. The rigid vang does that, too, but, in its support function, it also replaces that snapping, whipping, befouling thing called a topping lift, which loves to chew up the ends of batten pockets.

In more exotic forms, the vang can be a hydraulic rod, for those who believe spending money is the key to success in racing, or can be a custom and costly semi-circular track as was seen on Twelve Meter boats during the heyday of the America's Cup.

What's Available

When we looked at rigid vangs in 1987, there were but three available. They were the Hall Quik Vang,

adjudged at that time to be the very best; the Voomwang Vang, an inadequate-for-the-task device which quickly disappeared from the market, and the Selden RodKick, which now in re-engineered and much-improved form is called the RodKicker. We'd also tested an Easykick, then imported by Merriman, but couldn't locate the distributor to retest.

The success of the rigid vang is indicated by the fact that, in addition to the Hall Quik Vang and the Selden RodKicker, we this time were able to gather up for testing five others, from Forespar, Sparcraft, Offshore Spars, Spinlock and LeFiell. And, in a future issue, we will take a look at a quite different device called the Boomkicker, from Seoladair, which is not really a vang but a boom support system.

Because some of these vangs have proper names, plus a manufacturer's name plus a distributor's name, we will, to avoid confusion, refer to them by their proper names as listed in the first column on the chart.

All seven rigid vangs come in at least several sizes. We chose those whose specifications fit *Practical Sailor's* test boat, a C & C 33. The prices on the chart are for those particular vangs. Larger ones would cost somewhat more, smaller ones less. Note also that some are priced with purchase tackle, but the mast and boom fittings always cost extra. If you already have a soft vang, it probably can be used on a rigid vang, if it has enough purchase to compress the spring.

Only of minor interest to you readers is the amount of effort required to figure out how to mount the fittings for seven vangs without riddling the boom and the base of the mast with two to three dozen holes. We solved the problem by using one mast fitting (Forespar's) and a length of track with a car on the boom.

Types of Vangs

There are basically two kinds of rigid boom vangs. There are vangs, generally rectangular in shape, with the purchase tackle or ratchet system rigged internally. There are vangs, usually round, with the purchase tackle mounted externally, although a basic internal purchase sometimes is part of the telescoping tube arrangement.

Because of the leverage exerted by a mainsail in a stiff breeze, selecting a vang for a given boat, and getting it mounted and working, requires some judgment. Taken to extremes, the result can be a broken boom, which on most boats is not a very strong structural beam. In fact, several of these rigid vangs contain in the instructions the warning that if you put a lot of weight on the end of the boom while it is supported by the vang, the boom may break.

We wonder, also, what would happen to a boom if one exercised the option (offered by several vang manufacturers) of taking the purchase up to 32:1.

A further categorization, when considering rigid boom vangs, is whether (to keep the boom from dropping or to cushion it) it has a fixed support, a spring, or a gas cylinder. Those who make vangs with springs say those with gas cylinders, whose cylinders are magnetic steel, corrode, leak gas and wear out. Manufacturers who use gas cylinders claim springs fatigue. To their credit, gas cylinders usually are easy to replace and are available in a wide variety of pressures, which may make it easier to fine tune the vang. However, because the springs used in vangs are hardened stainless steel that are rated for about a million compressions and on good vangs can be adjusted for tension, we'll give the nod to springs for most boats.

One further note: Because of the metal-to-metal connections at the mast and boom, there is virtually no way with a rigid vang to eliminate a certain amount of clicking noise made by the end fittings and clevis pins.

DX Index by Spinlock

Made in England by Spinlock, the DX Index comes in three sizes, with standard and high power options for all. It is the most unusual design, quite different from all the others.

It's a very clean, sleek, aerodynamic design, with a ratchet system and 8:1 purchase, all internal. The purchase can be increased to 32:1 with the attachment of external tackle.

The one we chose to test is a new model that can be switched via a button-operated show-red/show-green lever, from a free running mode to an auto-matic boom support. There's nothing on the DX Index to snag or foul errant lines.

This new model, which is very light, appears to be well-engineered and nicely finished. It can be disassembled via Allen screws. Getting used to its switchable automatic operation would take a bit of practice. It's difficult to estimate how well the internal ratchet system would withstand wear and the forces imposed by any rigid vang.

The DX Index is unique in that it uses no spring or gas cylinder to cushion the boom support function. You simply lift the boom to the desired location, switch from red to green on the switch, release the boom and the next ratchet tooth automatically engages.

With boom and mast fittings and Harken tackle (if you wanted more than the basic 8:1 purchase), the DX Index is very expensive, even at discount.

Bottom Line: In operation, the DX Index, with its "green-switch" free movement and its automatic "red-switch" boom support would be very handy, once the crew learned to use the switch. However, unlike spring or gas cylinder vangs, the DX Index would, if you expected the vang to provide a little support for the boom when running in light airs, require manual adjustment. Changing the switch also requires a bit of tension on the purchase system. It seems unnecessarily complicated. This expensive vang, radically different in principle from the rest, is not in our view preferable to better spring-action vangs.

Sparcraft Pneu Vang

Very ruggedly built, Sparcraft's Pneu Vang is simply two telescoping anodized aluminum tubes with big Delrin collars, sleeves and seals and aluminum end

Specs: Rigid Boom Vangs

Name	Manufacturer	Vang	Fittings	Tackle*	Total	Weight (lbs.)	Boom Support
DX Index	Spinlock (IMTRA)	$790	$237	Included 8:1 Purchase	$1,027	6	Rigid Ratchet
Pneu Vang	Sparcraft (IM)	$475	$205	$250	$930	11.5	Gas Cylinder
Offshore Vang	Offshore Spar	$645	$145	Included	$790	11.5	SS Spring
Quick Vang	Hall Spars	$770	$191	Included	$961	13.5	SS Spring
Rodkicker	Selden (Sailsystems)	$445	$115	$175	$735	9.4	Gas Cylinder
Yacht Rod	Forespar	$501	$187	$250	$938	13.6	SS Spring
Vari-Vang	LeFiell	$500	$185	$250	$935	10	Soft Spring

* For recommended Harken tackle

fittings. The boom-end fitting is riveted; the mast-end fitting is attached with stainless steel screws.

The Pneu Vang has a good, big aluminum sheave to carry the wire strop to attach the tackle, which is all external. The optional 12:1 or 24:1 purchase is applied by an external tackle made by Harken.

The boom support is a gas cylinder, which can be replaced by removing four screws from the big Delrin sleeve.

The mast fitting seems inordinately complicated compared with some of the others but the boom fitting is a simple two-piece welded stainless steel assembly.

Adding up the vang, the fittings and the 12:1 Harken tackle brings the list price to $930.

Bottom Line: We had some trouble with the Pneu Vang in that, despite the big sheave, the six-part Harken block and tackle rubbed against the big collar, binding the action as the tackle tried to get past the collar. Because of that and because this is a gas cylinder vang without a length adjustment (which means it would have to be very precisely mounted), we can't give the Pneu Vang very high marks.

Offshore Vang

The Offshore Vang made in Michigan by Offshore Spars is the same in principle as the Hall Quik Vang. It is two telescoping anodized aluminum tubes with 3:1 internal purchase and additional external purchase applied with the excellent Harken gear.

The Offshore Vang uses a heavy spring as a boom support and it has six (or seven in a larger model) length adjustment holes secured by a big fast pin (which fits in a nicely done stainless steel bushing).

The adjustment holes certainly make less critical the installation of the boom fitting and might be handy to accommodate mainsails with different leech measurements, to retrofit to existing fittings on the mast and boom and, most importantly, make it possible to lift the boom to clear a Bimini top or awning.

The fast pin also fixes one end of the spring within the large tube, which confers the slight advantage that the vang can be installed with either end up. The pin can snag lines, however.

Bottom Line: The Offshore Vang is a well-made, fully assembled piece of equipment that works very well with Harken tackle, which is supplied. Faulted only by the protruding fastpin used in the length adjustment holes, the Offshore Vang comes fairly close in quality and operation to the Hall Quik Vang. If you're looking to save money, this is the choice.

Hall Quik Vang

Designed right in the beginning, the Quik Vang appears to be unchanged from the one we tested five years ago.

It's a precision-made telescoping tube type with a unique feature: The spring tension is adjustable via two Allen head set screws. Adjusting the spring is not something you'd want to do often, but it's not difficult. As the spring fatigues, probably over a few years, the tension can be taken up. The adjustment feature also is handy if the leech of your main stretches a bit or you buy a new mainsail with a slightly different leech length.

The Quik Vang has Delrin slider sleeves and plugs along with closely machined, tapered aluminum end fittings. Hall supplies Harken tackle with a distinctive red take-up line. The telescoping tubes are hard anodized and all parts fit like no other vang in the group.

Hall makes a good scissoring mast fitting, but we liked the one made by Forespar because of its extra holes.

Plainly put, the Quik Vang clearly remains the standard by which all other conventional vangs with telescoping tubes and external tackle must be measured.

The Quik Vang comes in eight different sizes, the most of any vang on the market, with return pressures varying from 400 to 1,000 pounds.

Bottom Line: The Hall Quik Vang is supplied fully assembled and is easy to install. More importantly, the Quik Vang operates very smoothly. Its heavy Delrin plugs provide very friction-free, quiet adjustment. With its tapered, machined end fittings, it is, without doubt, the best quality vang on the

Warranty	Comments
2 Yrs.	Very sleek British design with ratchet mechanism and 8:1 internal purchase. Switchable from free to support mode.
1 Yr.	Rugged, simple gas cylinder design with a big collar that interferes with the purchase tackle. Length is not adjustable.
3 Yrs.	Well made with internal purchase and Harken external gear. Length is adjustable. Fairly close in quality to Quik Vang. Best buy.
3 Yrs.	The best. Comes fully assembled. Top quality. Spring operated with adjustable tension. Works very smoothly.
5 Yrs.	Very simple in concept. Easiest to dismantle, including access to gas cylinder. Light weight and moderately priced.
1 Yr.	A strong heavyweight spring vang. For those who intend to use existing purchase tackle, this is the best buy.
3 Yrs.	An odd design, with a soft spring, that won't support a drooping boom in a level position. Poor welds and magnetic roll pins.

market. Not outlandishly priced, it's the top choice.

Selden Rodkicker

The Rodkicker, imported from Sweden by Sailsystems, is another very simple vang. Rectangular in shape, the Rodkicker comes with a choice of soft or hard gas cylinders.

The gas cylinder is easy to replace because the Rodkicker sections have plastic end caps that remove by simply depressing two locking buttons. The end caps also serve as bushings and shock absorbers. In fact, the Rodkicker is the easiest vang to dismantle and reassemble, but it doesn't seem to us to be an important feature.

The dark gray end fittings are aluminum castings. They are fastened to the rectangular extrusions with rivets, which seems less desirable than machine screws, but at least the rivets are aluminum and avoids mating unlike metals.

The Rodkicker stands out (like the DX Index) because there's nothing to foul errant spinnaker lines or halyard coils. The mast fitting, if you elect to use it, is a trim, gray-anodized aluminum casting with a hefty stainless hinge pin.

We don't care for the "Selden Rodkicker" sticker applied to both sides of the vang, but it's a small point based on our observations that stickers are unsightly when the elements start eating them.

Bottom Line: Although simple in design, the Rodkicker is not very smooth operating. The use of plastic end caps and collar (which is intended also to be a shock absorber) make the fits between the telescoping sections quite sloppy. We like the five-year warranty but don't much admire the cast aluminum end fittings. It's the least expensive but, unless light weight is important, we can't recommend the Rodkicker over the Offshore Vang, which costs just $55 more. If you need or want a return action harder than what's available with coil springs, the Rodkicker with a super hard gas spring would be a viable option.

The Yacht Rod from Forespar

Forespar makes some outstanding sailboat gear but, peculiarly, it doesn't claim to make the best rigid vang. The company very honestly concedes that distinction to Hall Spars.

The Yacht Rod, a very simple design acquired in 1988 from the Canadian company called Yacht Tech, is aimed at cruisers and club racers who elect to refit their existing soft vangs to the rigid vang and save a couple of hundred bucks.

The Yacht Rod is a white anodized aluminum tube into which is inserted a polished stainless steel tube that rides on Nylatron bearings. The end fittings are machined aluminum. It is spring-cushioned.

The cable to which the tackle must be fitted is entirely external and requires attachment below the mast fitting; the purchase tackle is attached to the other end of the strop leading out of the vang. As supplied, it requires some assembly, including fitting and swaging the cable.

To its credit, the length of the Yacht Rod is adjustable. However, the adjustment is a crude affair, just four sets of holes in the tube through which is inserted a clevis pin, which because of its length, can be a line snagger. In that regard, it resembles the Offshore Vang.

Even more to Forespar's credit is its butterfly-shaped mast fitting. (The mast fittings with some vangs are solid affairs that may or may not fit your mast.) The Forespar fitting is scissor-hinged around the pivot pin to make mast fitting easier. A beefy, all-stainless assembly with a hefty price ($103), we elected to use it for all the vangs.

Bottom Line: The Yacht Rod is an honest effort by Forespar to offer a lower-priced vang with the features of the Hall Quik Vang. It works fairly well but lacks the fine workmanship of the Quik Vang. We'd rank it just below the lower-priced Offshore Vang, which it more closely resembles.

Vari-Vang by LeFiell

Here's another vang, on the market but two years, that is rather different from the others. It's a small diameter, thick-walled vang with heavy torpedo-shaped end fittings of machined aluminum, all anodized in a bluish gray shade.

A light spring, fine-tuned (like the Hall Quik Vang) with a sliding block fastened with two Allen screws, is used to lift the boom for light air support. Using a light spring means that when flattening the mainsail, you'll not be working against a 600-pound spring. The instructions state that the Vari-Vang is intended to "bottom out" with the spring fully compressed when the boom is at rest or the mainsail is being reefed.

Besides its light-weight spring action, what also is different about the Vari-Vang is that the pin-to-pin length can be adjusted up to 10 inches by loosening another Allen screw and twisting the large tube on an internal threaded rod. It's a handy feature, both for ease of mounting and for use with mainsails with different leech lengths.

A heavy tang to fasten the purchase tackle is welded on the mast-end fitting. The weld is very crude, as is the welding on the boom fitting.

A magnetic roll pin is used to attach the jaw fitting to the boom end of the vang and the blue-anodized aluminum sheave is held by a big magnetic roll pin, which also must function as a bearing. We don't like roll pins and readers often write about their bad experiences with them.

Bottom Line: If your boat has a boom whose aft

end is lower than the gooseneck while sailing, the Vari-Vang is not for you because with this vang the boom is intended to bottom out (fully compress the spring) while stowed. This means that you would have to stow the mast in the drooping position, with no possibility of lifting the aft end for cockpit convenience or to rig an awning. Because of this, and the poor welding and the use of roll pins, we don't recommend this vang.

Conclusion

A rigid boom vang, with the proper fittings and tackle, is an expensive retrofit item.

Part of the consideration may involve whether you already have an existing boom fitting (that will fit) and a good six-part soft boom vang that can be used to apply the necessary purchase. If so, you need only buy the rigid vang.

If this were the case, the sturdy Yacht Rod (with adjustable length and a spring mechanism) from Forespar, available at discount for about $350, is the best buy.

For a vang equipped with Harken Hexaratchet tackle, you might, if you're interested in saving $150, choose the Offshore Vang over the Hall Quik Vang. Still, the Quik Vang is the best.

Your decision should be based, at least in part, on how you use it. If you're a keen racer, the softer, more responsive coil-spring types allow you to play the vang more easily. In addition to the Quik Vang, you might even like the Vari-Vang, assuming performance is more important than a droopy boom. For cruisers with heavier displacement boats, who probably will hunker down on the boom only when sailing off the wind, the gas spring models will be satisfactory. An advantage of these, including the Rodkicker, is they can be fitted with high load springs to hold up heavy booms. Exchanging springs of different ratings is relatively simple, and the cost quite reasonable.   • **PS**

Rope Clutches

Lewmar's new Superlock rope clutch is the class of the field, outperforming Spinlock, Antal and Easylock

In the 15 or so years since rope clutches were first introduced, they've supplanted simple line stoppers as a better means of securing halyards, especially those led aft to the cockpit. But our tests show that some are a lot better than others.

A bank of linestoppers or rope clutches on the cabin top, lined up in front of one or two winches, means you don't need a winch and cleat for every halyard, as might be the case on the mast. After one halyard has been tensioned with the winch, and secured with the clutch, you can then remove the tail from the winch and proceed to raise another sail or a pole. Cleats, of course, don't work because you can't belay the line while it's wound around the winch.

Linestoppers and rope clutches are similar in that both grab the line by means of a toothed cam or compress it between two metal plates. The fundamental difference between stoppers and clutches is that the latter has a clutch mechanism, often employing a spring, to permit winching the line taut with the cam closed, and the gradual releasing of the line if you want to later ease or "bleed off" tension. In practice, we doubt you'd feel real comfortable easing halyard tension without the help of a winch to pay out line. Some clutches allow bleeding, some not at all, but even with the best the chances of letting the line go entirely are pretty good.

In 1987, we tested 11 different models of rope clutches. Our recommendation at the time was the Spinlock Express, made in England. Though some manufacturers have come and gone, we haven't noted much new in the world of rope clutches—until recently. Earlier this year Lewmar introduced its Superlock, proclaiming they had "re-invented the rope clutch." To evaluate their claims, we bench tested the Superlock, and five other models to compare performance.

The Tests

In addition to the Lewmar Superlock, we bought a Spinlock Express, Easylock Midi and Easylock Racing, and an Antal Master 12 Series. We also included a Schaefer EGR Halyard Stopper, only because it gave us a benchmark to compare results with our tests of five years ago; Schaefer no longer makes the EGR, though it may still be found in some discount catalogs, such as Defender Industries. Nor did we

Value Guide: Rope Clutches

Make/Model	Price (List/Discount)	Line Diameter	Ease of Bleeding (Rank)	Slippage (Before-After*)	Abrasion (Rank)
Lewmar Superlock	$57/$42.95 $75/$56	5/16"-3/8" 3/8"-7/16"	1	7/16"-7/16"	1
Antal Master 12	$85/$63.50 $86.80/$65.10	1/2"-9/16" 1/4"-1/2"	2	5/8"-1/2"	4
Spinlock Express	$114.25/$85.65 $54/$37.80	5/16"-5/8" 5/16"-7/16"	3	3/4"-7/16"	2
Easylock Midi	$88.75/$61.75 NA/$42	3/8"-9/16" 1/4"-9/16"	6	5/8"-3-1/4"	3
Schaefer 71-42	$78.54.75 $86.40/$60.50	to 3/8" to 1/2"	5	3/8"-9/16"	5
Easylock Racing	NA/$46	5/16"-1/2"	4	11/16"-13/16"	6

*Slippage was measured two ways, one with the line tensioned before closing the clutch, the other with the line tensioned

elect to include the Antal Junior and Senior, or the Forespar models, all of which produced above average line damage in our tests of five years ago. Our main objective was to see if the Lewmar Superlock is in fact superior to the popular Spinlock Express.

All models tested were singles, except the Superlock, which was a triple. Most clutches are available in single, double or triple configurations.

To test, we mounted the six clutches on a 2" x 6" board, and secured it to our test bench. A length of 3/8-inch braided line was led from our self-tailing winch and through the clutch to heavy shock cord secured to a padeye at the other end of the bench.

We tensioned the line to 600 pounds, five times with the clutch closed before tensioning, and five times with the clutch open (the clutch was then closed, the line released from the winch, and the clutch opened). We measured slippage (the amount the line slipped back through the clutch after the line was released from the winch; slippage of half an inch reduces the load by about 140 pounds), abrasion of the line, and ease of closing and releasing the clutch, particularly the ease of bleeding tension. As noted in the earlier report, slippage is generally greater when the clutch is closed before tensioning. We did, however, find some exceptions, particularly the Easylock Midi. In most instances, the differences in slippage (closing the clutch before or after tensioning) were not great. The results are shown in the accompanying table.

Antal Master 12 Series

Made in Italy, the Antal clutch is the smallest of the five models tested that are currently in production. As with all Antal hardware, materials are top quality, and the design is handsome. Also like most other Antal hardware we've tested (blocks, cams, etc.), performance is at or near the top.

The Antal housing is anodized aluminum, the handle is stainless steel, and the cam mechanism is stainless and bronze. The teeth in the cam compress the line against a series of teeth on the bottom of the rope alley. The unit is easy to install and easy to lead a line through. The flared stainless fittings at each end minimize abrasion, especially with unfair leads. We also found it easy to bleed line tension. While it ranked fourth in abrasion, there wasn't much difference between it and the Spinlock Express and Easylock Midi. In terms of slippage, it had the least, ranking it first.

Antal hardware often costs a premium, but in this instance, the cost of the 1/4"-1/2" model was in the same ballpark as Lewmar and Spinlock.

Bottom Line: We like the Antal for its nicely finished metal parts, small size and minimal slippage. As with most of the toothed cam clutches, abrasion is a concern. Overall, it's our second choice.

Easylock Midi

Made in Denmark, the Easylock Midi is the least expensive of the models tested. Construction is aluminum and stainless steel. The mechanism clamps the line between two corrugated steel plates.

In our tests, the Midi did not perform well. We found it impossible to ease tension; as the handle was released, the line blew out with a bang. No amount of care could control it.

Slippage was unpredictable, ranging from a very acceptable 5/8-inch to an unacceptable 3-1/4 inches. Abrasion was in the middle of the pack.

Bottom Line: While the price of the Easylock Midi is attractive, for $20 more you can have the best. The extra cost is well worth it. We wouldn't put the Midi on our boat.

Easylock Racing

Unlike the Easylock Midi, the Racing version uses a toothed aluminum cam and toothed base plate to grip the line. The housing also is aluminum. Compared to the Antal and Spinlock, the spring seems small. There is a fairlead provided that must be owner installed. We did not use it for our tests.

Operation of the Easylock Racing clutch takes a bit of getting used to. A button on the top engages the cam, indeed justifying the name Easylock. To release, however, you must pull the handle back and then push forward, in effect doubling the operation. It's not hard, just initially confusing. More serious, however, is that when releasing the line with your hand gripping the handle, your fingers may get crimped between it and the housing. Because it doesn't bleed tension easily, we found ourselves slapping the handle down with the palm of our hand to release the line. Under high loads, it gets scary.

The Easylock Racing was the only model tested which broke fibers after 10 repetitions, by far the worst performance. That, plus higher-than-average slippage forced us to rank the Easylock Racing last.

Bottom Line: Being easy to lock isn't as important as abrasion, slippage and release. Though the price is

Comments

Our first choice.

Easy to bleed. Easy to feed line through.

One mount screw difficult.

Cannot be eased.

No longer in production.

Easy to close, but must slap to release.

after closing the clutch.

again low, we can't recommend the Easylock Racing.

Lewmar Superlock

New this year, the British-made Superlock is indeed a better mousetrap. The housing is plastic and the mechanism is stainless steel. It grips by means of a patent pending "wavegrip" device that looks like five rings connected by side plates. As the handle is closed, the rings rotate to close the size of their opening. It can be likened to the domino effect. One obvious advantage is that a much greater surface area of the line is gripped than with a single cam.

Our tests demonstrate the advantages of the wavegrip design. The Lewmar Superlock ranked first in every category except slippage, where it came in just behind Antal, albeit by a mere 1/16 inch. Abrasion was almost non-existent and it was easy to bleed line tension. It is the largest of the models tested, but we don't reckon that's much of a factor.

Bottom Line: Priced in line with the Antal and Spinlock, the Lewmar Superlock is an easy first choice in rope clutches.

Schaefer EGR Halyard Stopper

As noted earlier, Schaefer no longer makes this model, though it does continue to manufacture its Spinnaker Halyard Stopper series.

We have included the data on the table for comparison purposes only. If you currently own Schaefer EGR stoppers, this will let you know how much you might expect to gain by upgrading to a different make.

Spinlock Express

Probably the most popular clutches in the world, we found the Express to be a decent performer. The body is plastic, the handle aluminum, and the clutch mechanism stainless steel. There are flared stainless fittings at both ends of the rope alley. The cam descends onto the line without rotating, by virtue of a well-thought-out design.

In our abrasion tests, the Spinlock Express showed only minute fraying of the cover threads. Slippage was a little more than the Lewmar Superlock and Antal Master. Bleeding tension was satisfactory. One of the mounting screws is difficult to place, but it's a job you'll only do once.

Bottom Line: The Spinlock Express, our top choice five years ago, still is a good piece of hardware. If it was priced lower than the Lewmar Superlock, we'd give it serious consideration.

Conclusion

Five years ago we noted that rope clutches were getting better, but still weren't perfect. The Lewmar Superlock represents the most significant improvement in that time. Based on our tests, especially for abrasion, we think the Superlock is a breakthrough that will save you the cost of replacing line every season or so. Often we expect to see such new products selling for prices much higher than the competition. Fortunately, that's not the case with the Superlock. It is an easy first choice.

Antal and Spinlock are good quality clutches, but toothed cams have certain liabilities that can't be overcome no matter how good the clutch mechanism and materials. The Easylock models were disappointing, especially the Racing model, which literally chewed our line to pieces. Unless Harken or Schaefer decides to put on their thinking caps and do Lewmar one better, the Superlock is, for the time being, the class of the field.   • **PS**

Chute Tamers

The addition of one of these devices to your rigging can take the intimidation out of spinnaker flying.

The spinnaker is the sail that makes landlubbers "Uhhh" and "Ahhh" but sailors know it's a devil to handle, hoist and douse. Just getting it up and drawing requires a lot of rigging of the pole, topping lift, downhaul, sheet, guy and halyard. Even a fully trained racing crew often gets something wrong.

For a cruising sailor, a mistake in the preparation can mean a rope burn cut instantaneously by a wayward halyard or sheet. The powerful spinnaker is so fraught with potential trouble that cruising sailors often forego the possibility of the dreaded spinnaker wrap, which can ruin a weekend cruise. Worse, if the sail has to be cut away from the forestay, it can wreck the summer cruise budget.

The spinnaker, by the way, is believed to have acquired its name from "spinxer," which is what the crew called the new-type sail aboard the British yacht *Sphinx* during a race in the Solent in the 1870s.

To check out the "store-bought" devices to manage the billowing beauty, we gathered up everything we could find. It isn't much.

On *PS One,* the magazine's C & C 33, we tried out the Kracor Spinnaker Gun, and two sleeve-type spinnaker tamers, one called a Chutescoop, the other an ATN. All three of these devices also work well on big headsails (whether called cruising spinnakers, MPSs, gennakers or whatever) not attached to the forestay.

Kracor Spinnaker Gun

The Kracor Spinnaker Gun is a molded plastic bucket, with a flared end and no bottom. Its utility is restricted to preparing a spinnaker for hoisting without breaking out prematurely. It's a giant step forward from the old laborious "rotten cotton" method of "stopping" a spinnaker. It also is an improvement on a piece of PVC pipe, which some racing crews have used for years.

To begin, one loads the small end of the Kracor with about 15 or 20 rubber bands. Then, working belowdecks with the loose spinnaker, the head of the sail is handed up through the companionway or a hatch to a crewmember on deck. The head of the sail is inserted in the wide end of the Kracor. While the crewmember below shakes out and aligns the tapes on the edge of the spinnaker, the helper on deck pulls the sail through the gun, stopping every three feet to roll a rubber band off the gun onto the sail. There are nice deep grooves on the gun to permit grabbing the rubber bands one at a time.

It might be done by one person. However, because of the desirability of keeping the tapes parallel, it is a job best done by two.

When finished, the spinnaker is neatly "tubed" in rubber bands, easy to bag or handle and ready for the attachment of the halyard and sheets.

When hoisted, the spinnaker hangs like a sausage until, by yanking the sheets, the sail initially breaks out first at the bottom, snapping rubber bands upward as it fills with wind. In the boat's wake will be a trail of broken rubber bands.

We found the Kracor Spinnaker Gun well-designed for its intended purpose and very easy to use. The spinnaker, hoisted in about 8-10 knots of wind (about the wind velocity in which a cruising sailor might use a chute), hung placidly until the sheet and guy were given a firm tug. Then the sail deployed smoothly, without ado.

The Kracor's liability is that it is somewhat bulky to store (it takes about a cubic foot). In addition, if cruising, one would need a goodly supply of #16 rubber bands. The Kracor comes in eight different sizes. It costs but $27.30, and is a cheap and easy way to preclude the premature deployment of a sail that can be dangerous.

The Chutescoop

Next, we thoroughly tested two sleeve-type devices. More versatile than the Kracor gun, the sleeves permit not only safe hoisting but also quick striking of the spinnaker...if all goes well. They also make storage easier, in that the "sausage" can be either folded into a sail bag or neatly rolled up and secured with a tie or two.

In principle, the two sleeves are exactly alike. Both are simple cloth tubes through which is led a control line to raise and lower the lower end of the tube to deploy the spinnaker. To set the sail, the lower end of the tube is pulled to the masthead (where it remains). To strike the sail, the sleeve is pulled down over the sail, compressing it in the tube as it is lowered. Then the sail can be lowered to the deck.

We first tried the Chutescoop made by the V.F. Shaw Co., Inc., of Bowie, Maryland. It's been on the market a good long time. The Chutescoop is a moderately complicated device that requires careful attention to the directions (which could be better done) and considerable care in executing them. It's best done at home on the living room floor. We rigged it aboard the boat and, to put it plainly, got confused several times. Backtracking and a bit of applied logic put it right.

The Chutescoop contains sewn-in stainless steel rings in the ends of the nylon tube. The bottom ring is, of course, larger than the top ring. Without these rings, the mouth would bind tightly and perhaps even roll and foul the sleeve in the sail cloth.

The Chutescoop requires a few adjustments at the top end. Basically, what must be done is adjust some lines so that the Chutescoop, when pulled in a bundle to the stop of the mast, has sufficient room to park itself without interfering with the full deployment of the spinnaker.

We had no trouble hoisting the Chutescoop, but when running the bottom ring up and down to free and then recapture the sail, it seemed somewhat catchy. Considerable force often was required on the control line. The dousing procedure begins easily when there is little spinnaker to force into the sleeve. But as the sleeve reaches the more voluminous portion of the spinnaker (about a third of the way down), the friction of the sail already in the sleeve plus the force needed to pull more sail into the sleeve makes for a lot of resistance.

We did not have the problem, but the instructions warn that the two small lines within the sleeve may twist and foul on the sail cloth. In fact, the two small lines inside the tube lead down through a few 2 1/2"-wide cloth straps inside the tube. If it happens, the instructions say to try running the sleeve up and down several times. If that doesn't free the jam, the whole thing must be lowered, worked free and repacked.

Further, the instructions say that it's best to have a Chutescoop 2-7 feet shorter than the bundled sail. This not only permits easier attachment of the sheet and guy, but also allows the guy to reach the spinnaker pole end fitting. Dropping the sail can be a problem if the pole is fully aback and the guy is cleated down.

(The company also makes what it calls a TurtleRoo, which is a bag in which to stow the Chutescoop. It has several pockets specifically designed for tying down the spinnaker head and clews. It's another $100 to $125 for the three available sizes.)

The Chutescoop comes in five sizes, ranging from 20 feet long ($95) to 44 feet long ($199). For our C & C 33, we bought from West Marine Products the 37-foot model.

ATN

The ATN, made by A.T.N., Inc., of Fort Lauderdale, Florida, is much better made than the Chutescoop.

To begin, it comes fully rigged. It has a small, tidy top closed by Velcro after simply running the head of the sail up through the tube and attaching it to a shackle on a strop, which is equipped with a swivel. The block for the control line is more substantial than that used on the Chutescoop.

More importantly, the control line, a single piece of high-quality braid, runs through a sleeve sewn to the outside of the tube. This means that the control line cannot foul the spinnaker within the tube, contained as it is in a separate channel. Most important of all, the bottom end of the ATN is a molded fiberglass flared oval securely attached to the sleeve.

We rigged the ATN in a tenth of the time needed for the Chutescoop, attached the halyard, ran it up the mast and set and snuffed the spinnaker a number of times with the greatest of ease. It was readily apparent that the separate channel for the control line, the larger block at the top of the tube and the smooth fiberglass oval at the bottom end all contribute to the very smooth operation of the ATN.

The man behind ATN is French sailor Etienne Griore, who broke a number of records in last summer's Europe 1 single-handed race from Plymouth England to Newport, Rhode Island. The ATN, he says, has been used by a number of BOC skippers. Surfing downwind in the Southern Ocean, with gale winds and huge breaking seas, it's no wonder they demand a strong, well-designed means of controlling their spinnakers.

The ATN costs $7.50 a foot in lengths less than 75 feet long and $9 a foot for lengths greater than 75 feet. That makes an ATN almost twice the cost of the Chutescoop. There is no question in our minds that the difference is worth it.   • **PS**

Buying Guide

-

Safety

Superb EPIRBs

These gadgets really can save your life. If you can afford it, go for one of the 406-MHz units.

Even with the best life raft, fully stocked with survival equipment, your chances of survival at sea are poor unless someone is looking for you. Marine VHF radios are only reliable to about 20 to 30 miles offshore. The range of portable VHFs is even less, though they can be of great use in hailing passing ships. High frequency (HF) SSB marine radios will carry much farther; however, they require well-engineered antennas and lots of power. Trying to use an SSB radio in a life raft would be a near impossibility. Your only choice for long-range communications after abandoning your boat is an EPIRB (Emergency Position Indicating Radio Beacon). this communication is only one-way. You won't know if anyone has heard your call for help, but the odds are someone will.

EPIRBs aren't only for offshore racing and cruising boats. We recommend that anyone venturing away from the immediate shoreline have one on board. Making a distress call on a VHF radio can often be a one-shot deal, or impossible if your batteries are dead. EPIRBs are automatic, they need only to be turned on. No channel selection or other operations are necessary. Even a young child can activate an EPIRB.

EPIRBs operate by transmitting a beacon signal on one or more predetermined frequencies. They are classified into several categories:

Class A EPIRBs: These are intended for use on commercial vessels, which are required to carry one. A Class A EPIRB is designed to float free of its mounting and activate automatically on contact with seawater.

Class B EPIRBs: These are generally less expensive than their Class A counterparts. Class B units operate on the same frequencies as Class A, but must be manually activated. They are usually supplied with a manually released mounting bracket, similar to those used for fire extinguishers. Class B units are not required to float, but flotation collars are available for most models that don't.

Class A and B EPIRBs continuously transmit a homing signal (a swept AM modulated tone) on boat 121.5 and 243 MHz. The 121.5 MHz frequency is used for international civil aviation emergencies. The 243 MHz frequency is the military aircraft "guard" channel. These two frequencies are routinely monitored by aircraft, especially when traveling on transoceanic routes. Monitoring is not mandatory, however.

Fortunately, the new COSPAS/SARSAT satellite system that monitors the 406 MHz EPIRBs also listens to the 121.5 and 243 MHz frequencies. this system is composed of both former Soviet (COSPAS) and American (SARSAT) satellites. When these satellites receive a signal, they relay to a ground station, an ultimately to the closest available rescue service. All of the models we tested were rated for satellite reception.

The major drawback of Class A and B units is their inability to identify the source of the signal. With a large number of units carried by both boats and aircraft, false alarms are common, and numerous cases have been reported of multiple EPIRB activations in the same geographical area. Rescuers, unfortunately, have no way to differentiate false alarms from actual emergencies. Thus, rescue can often be delayed for a considerable length of time, while authorities attempt to verify that a real emergency exists.

Class C EPIRBs: The Class C EPIRB is completely different from the Class A and B units. the Class C device operates by periodically transmitting a brief signal on VHF channel 16, along with a continuous homing signal on Channel 15. These are intended for use in coastal waters where Channel 16 is routinely monitored. In order to minimize interference, Class C models will turn off automatically after 24 hours of operation. If necessary, they can be manually reactivated.

The principle behind the Class C EPIRB makes sense. Commercial vessels and the U.S. Coast Guard are required to continually monitor channel 16. So theoretically, in coastal waters, someone should always be able to hear your distress beacon. in reality, because of their low output power, the signals from Class C EPIRBs are often masked by the heavy traffic of full-power radios on Channel 16. Unlike Channel 16, the 121.5/243 MHz an 406.025 MHz frequencies are never used for anything but emergency communications.

406 MHz EPIRBs: the 406 MHz EPIRB represents the latest technology for emergency signal transmission. In addition to a 121.5 MHz homing signal, these models also intermittently transmit a digitally coded identification signal on 406-025 MHz. This signal is unique for each individual EPIRB produced. After purchase, the new unit's owner is required to register his ID number with the COSPAS/SARSAT Mission Control Center that covers his intended sailing area.

Oddly, it is reported that only about 70 percent of these EPIRB are registered; some are presumably in the sales pipeline, but it appears that many owners, whether through ignorance or forgetfulness, are not registering them, thereby negating one of the most significant advantages of these more expensive safety devices. A postpaid registration card is provided with each new unit sold. The information supplied on the card is loaded into the worldwide COSPAS/SARSAT computer network, and can be accessed immediately in the event that the EPIRB is activated.

This system solves a major problem with the older, conventional EPIRBs. With those models, no indication is given of the type of vessel or aircraft in distress. The 406-MHz model tells authorities what they are looking for in advance of a search. Additionally, this allows rescue forces to attempt to contact the vessel's owner to determine if the EPIRB was accidentally activated. This can prevent a waste of resources on an unnecessary search-and-rescue mission. More than 90 percent of the signals monitored from Class A and B EPIRBs eventually prove to be false alarms, compared to less than five percent for 406-MHz EPIRBs, in part because a phone call can usually determine quickly if an emergency exists.

The satellites monitoring the 406-MHz frequency can store the particulars of an emergency signal, and postpone relaying it until the satellite is over a receiving station below. This gives the 406 MHz EPIRBs yet another advantage over 121.5 MHz units. the less expensive Class A and B units require "mutual visibility;" that is, the satellite must have both the source of the signal and the ground receiver in sight at the same time.

The 406-MHz EPIRBs are subdivided into Category I units, which include a float-free bracket and are automatically activated when released, and the somewhat less expensive Category II units, which must be manually released and activated. The mounting brackets supplied with the Category I models use a hydrostatic charge to release a cable or clamp that holds the EPIRB securely in its mount. These charges are calibrated to release at 2 to 4 meters under water. To minimize the chances of a false alarm, the Category I units are designed to be unaffected by rain or spray. A Category I EPIRB must be manually turned off if it is necessary to remove it from its bracket.

Test Procedure

Responding in part to complaints from Alaska fishermen, in 1989 the FCC tested all commercially available EPIRBs to determine if they met requirements for signal coherency, watertightness, shock resistance, and transmitter output. With the exception of some ACR models, virtually all failed. This sent manufacturers scrambling to redesign their units to comply with tougher standards, which had to be met before those units could again be sold. All eventually requalified.

Anxious to see if our collection of EPIRBs met those new standards, we tested each of the units in a radio-frequency (RF) shielded screen room (in order to avoid having search and rescue teams dispatched to our test location). Total power output of each unit was measure, along with the actual frequency on which each was transmitting.

Originally, we had planned to run each unit for a full 48 hours to test its rated ability to broadcast for this length of time, while monitoring the total output and actual frequency. However, several problems developed with this approach. First, we found that we were unable to reliably contain the signals during testing. Unfortunately, the shielded room provided to us was designed primarily to keep *out* unwanted interference, not contain signals. At one point, we monitored a signal from one of the EPIRBs over 500 feet away. This was too far, we felt, to insure that the signals would not be detected by the highly sensitive satellites. Therefore, we decided to not risk violating the federal laws that prohibit EPIRB transmissions except in emergencies.

Second, considering that all of our units had brand-new batteries and were being tested at room temperature, we calculated that their battery life should easily exceed 80 hours. Three or four days of continuously monitored testing was simply not practical, or necessary.

We considered removing each unit's battery and testing it on a "dummy load" that would draw the same amount of current. While this sounds simple, it actually is very difficult, especially with the 406-MHz models where current consumption is not constant over time. The 406-MHz units have strobe lights that draw high current during the charge cycle, and little current during the strobe flash. Moreover, the signal is not transmitted continuously. It is composed of periodic data bursts that occur at predetermined intervals. Current consumption is highest during these transmissions. In order to simulate actual operation, each of these functions would have to be simulated for each EPIRB tested.

All of the EPIRBs tested exceeded their rated specifications. And due to the extended life of lithium batteries, we have no doubt that all the units tested will operate for at least 40 hours. This rating takes cold temperatures and adverse conditions into account. In warm weather, all these units would probably operate for nearly a week. With the recommended replacement interval for an EPIRB battery equaling one-half of the battery's rated shelf life, this additional safety factor should ensure that it will operate long enough to effect a rescue. We concluded, therefore, that the difference between the units is primarily in their design and construction details.

406 MHz EPIRBs

The models tested were the Alden Satfind 406, the ACR RLB-23, Raytheon JQE-2A, Litton 948-01, and Litton 952-02.

Generally speaking, the 406-MHz models we tested were of noticeably better quality than the less expensive 121.5 MHz units. The construction of the Raytheon (made by JRC) and Alden units appeared to be especially durable. JRC's high level of experience with radio circuits was especially evident in the Raytheon's internal construction, although we found no fault with the Alden's construction, either. The Raytheon JQE-2A uses a more conventional spring-loaded antenna, while the Alden Satfind 406 uses a printed-circuit antenna that is sealed inside its waterproof housing. The Alden's large strobe light extends above the top of the unit, and its effectiveness is increased by the use of a Fresnel lens. the Raytheon's smaller strobe has a clear lens mounted directly on top of the unit. This could cause it to be more easily obscured in rough weather.

The plastic self-releasing mounts for the Alden Satfind seemed secure and provided adequate protection for the unit. Raytheon's stainless-steel mounting bracket is of an altogether different design, which uses a cable instead of a clamp assembly to retain the EPIRB. We believe it leaves the antenna and top of the unit exposed to potential damage.

The ACR RLB-23 is another well-made unit. Though it is somewhat larger, it closely resembles the company's other models in appearance. ACR's approach to designing a float-free bracket is distinctly different. Instead of a mounting bracket, ACR encloses the EPIRB in a fiberglass capsule, which affords superior protection to the unit. The design's only drawback is that heavy icing may effectively glue the capsule shut, delaying or preventing activation. ACR recommends periodic waxing of the case and frequent inspections if the threat of icing exists.

The fourth 406-MHz unit, the Litton 948-01, was formerly sold by Koden International as the Koden 948-01. Its circuit board was sandwiched between two pieces of styrene foam. The outside of the foam was sprayed with RF-reflective paint, and the foam halves were sealed with copper tape. Due to the fact that the copper tape must be replaced when the unit is refurbished, maintenance costs of this EPIRB necessarily increase. Accordingly, we would have preferred another construction method.

The Litton 952-02 is the only Category II 406 MHz EPIRB we were able to obtain for testing. We expected this model to be similar in design to the Litton 948-01. Fortunately, it was not. The 952-02 is of notably better construction, sturdily built and well designed. Flotation is provided by an external foam collar. The Litton 952-02 is less than half the size of the Category I units we tested, which makes it ideal for use aboard pleasure boats. Its simple design and lack of a complicated and expensive release mechanism make it considerably cheaper than the Category I models—by several hundred dollars. We believe it is a high-quality piece of equipment.

Bottom Line: Our first choices in 406-MHz EPIRBs are the Alden Satfind 406 and the ACR RLB-23. We believe their design gives them a slight edge over the Raytheon/JRC JQE-2A. Nevertheless, the Raytheon is also a top-quality unit, which we do not hesitate to recommend.

The Litton 952-02, the only Category II unit in this test, is recommended for applications where space is at a premium and automatic release is not required. The Litton 948-01's performance was acceptable in our ideal-condition testing. Litton engineers report success with the unit's polystyrene foam construction in terms of component support and thermal insulation. However, we don't prefer this type of construction because it increases maintenance costs.

121.5/243 MHz EPIRBs

ACR RLB-14 and RLB-20: These two models from ACR Electronics are similarly constructed. Each is enclosed in a tightly sealed plastic tube. A bottom plug in this tube unscrews to allow the battery to be replaced. The RLB-20 is a Class B unit, supplied with a fire-extinguisher-type bracket. The RLB-14 is a similar looking but slightly larger Class A transmitter including a float-free bracket.

Both units performed well in our tests, though we have some doubts about the RLB-14's float-free bracket. It does not hold the unit securely in place, and could be problematic on smaller high-performance boats that are subject to a great deal of motion in rough weather.

Bottom Line: Based on their performance, we recommend both the ACR RLB-14 and RLB-20 without reservation. Before purchasing the RLB-14, however, check out the bracket to be sure it is appropriate for use on your boat.

ACR RLB-21 Mini-B: This is a Class B unit intended for use as a man-overboard or life raft EPIRB. Its fully sealed case is about the size of a handheld VHF radio.

A Velcro patch is supplied for attaching it to a life jacket, which we feel is an excellent idea, particularly since it does not float without the optional flotation collar. The Mini-B must be returned to the manufacturer for battery replacement.

Bottom Line: The ACR Mini-B is a good-quality product intended as a back-up or "personal" EPIRB. We recommend it for its intended usage. For a primary EPIRB, however, we'd be inclined to spend an additional few dollars for the RLB-20.

Aquatronics Survivor 1: Like the Mini-B, the Survivor 1 is a smaller EPIRB designed as a backup or personal unit. Its sealed construction precludes repair or battery replacement except by the manufacturer. (We had to virtually destroy it to get a look inside.)

This model performed well and cost less than the ACR Mini-B. Our only complaint is that its BNC-type antenna connector could be prone to corrosion in a salt-water environment.

Bottom Line: The Aquatronics Survivor 1 is well made, but it is not repairable. Like the ACR Mini-B, we can only recommend it for its intended application as a personal EPIRB.

Guest 630A: The Guest is the least expensive model we tested. it is enclosed in a molded-plastic case with a screw-on top. It is the only model tested that has separate antennas for 121.5 and 243.0 MHz. The circuitry is not of the highest quality, in our opinion, but is rated satisfactory. No mounting bracket is supplied.

Bottom Line: We consider the Guest 630A to be acceptable for use on smaller boats for the peace of mind it offers at a reasonable price. We can't recommend it for use in the most severe environments.

ACR RLB-17: This is the only Class C unit we tested. It is similar in construction to ACR's other models, except for its telescoping antenna, which must be manually extended. (Fixed, flexible antennas are used on the other models.) The antenna is very fragile: we doubt it would take much of a beating.

The RLB-17 is the only unit that uses conventional batteries (eight C-cells). A fire-extinguisher-type bracket is included, along with a small strobe light that activates automatically in darkness.

Bottom Line: We are not entirely sold on the concept of the Class C EPIRB, and we are reluctant to recommend the RLB-17 because of its antenna. In any case, we would consider purchasing a Class C device only after having spent roughly the same amount on a good handheld radio.

Recommendations

The 406-MHz EPIRBs have significant advantages over the conventional units, though they are considerably more expensive—five to six times as costly. The additional expense would be justified for fishermen who run to the offshore canyons, and for cruisers exploring the out islands of the Bahamas or the Gulfs of California and Mexico.

Of the 406-MHz Category I units, we're most impressed with the Alden Satfind 406 and the ACR RLB-23. The Raytheon JQE-2A is also a recommended unit. The Category II Litton 952-02 is a good-quality, compact, and relatively inexpensive unit. It brings the power of 406 technology to a new level of affordability for sailor who have ambitions to voyage farther afield.

Of the conventional units, we recommend the RLB-20, though all of their EPIRBs are of excellent quality. If price is a big consideration, the inexpensive Guest 630A is also satisfactory. • **PS**

Life Rafts

Any raft is better than none, but we'll take the Givens and Switlik before the others.

Thanks to the wonders of modern technology—EPIRBs, VHF, helicopters and the like—if your boat sinks there's a reasonably good chance that help will be there before too long. The question is: will you? If your boat was equipped with a good life raft, the answer can well be yes.

A life raft isn't a magic charm that guarantees your survival if you have to abandon your boat. It is, rather, a last resort for the crew whose boat can no longer protect them. Or, as Greg Switlik of the Switlik Parachute Company, a major life raft manufacturer, pointed out, "A life raft won't save your life. It just provides a safe place for you to sit while you figure out how to save your own life." The most important thing to remember about life rafts is to get one. A life raft that isn't on board, ready to function, won't help save anybody's life. And, considering the very limited life expectancy of people in the water, even in the best PFDs, we feel that anyone who travels even short distances offshore without a life raft is either foolhardy or suicidal.

The Price of Safety

"You can't put a price on human life" is a statement that's been made so often that people often accept its truth without thinking. Sadly, it ain't so. The major factor that keeps most people from buying a life raft is its cost; as a consequence, raft manufacturers must make tradeoffs between quality and cost.

Unlike commercial and military vessels, recreational sailors are not legally required to carry a life raft. Nor are there generally applicable quality and performance standards for rafts, unless you are participating in racing events controlled by groups like the Offshore Racing Council (ORC), which requires life rafts and has specific design requirements.

As a result, the industry offers a baffling variety of life rafts, ranging from simple inflatable open platforms to highly sophisticated rafts that can help keep their occupants alive for extended periods of very bad weather. The range of capabilities is reflected by an extremely wide range of prices.

Even the most fundamental considerations, such as size, represent tradeoffs between cost and functionality. A six-man raft, for example, will typically have a floor area of 21 to 26 square feet. That's not very spacious. Even the largest of these is the equivalent of a circular-floor camping tent with a diameter slightly under 5' 9". Could manufacturers provide more room? Sure—but at the cost of pricing themselves out of a fiercely competitive market.

The Philosophies of Survival

It would be nice if we—or anybody else, for that matter—could give you an unequivocal answer to the question, "What life raft should I buy?" Or even to, "What's the best life raft?" These questions are much like the questions raised when you select a boat. The answer is: "It depends." Life raft design and construction, like yacht design and construction, is a matter of compromise.

Even if cost considerations could be ignored—and they obviously can't—the different conditions that a life raft may encounter, and the varied factors that add up to survival make it virtually impossible to define a single ideal life raft design.

Obviously, a life raft should be able to withstand tumultuous seas and rotten weather. It should keep you afloat and protected, even in conditions that have sunk your boat—an impressive task for less than a hundred pounds of fabric and synthetic rubber. Jim Givens, of Givens Ocean Survival Systems, Inc., flatly states," A life raft must be more seaworthy than the boat that carries it."

Less obviously, a life raft must provide conditions under which you can stay alive while awaiting rescue. This means providing an environment in which the raft's occupants can remain alive, alert and functional. It includes considerations of ventilation, warmth, adequate physical comfort, and useful activity, as well as water, food and medication.

Livability is a factor whose importance many people tend to minimize. The common feeling is that comfort is something you can do without in life-threatening situations. It's not so. In the words of the Alaska Marine Safety Education Association, "In a survival situation, the decisions you make will be more important than the equipment you carry." And prolonged bouts of thirst, seasickness, hypothermia, cramps and other results of overcrowded, underequipped living don't contribute to making sound decisions.

One of our staffers spent an exciting night in a life raft last September as part of a controlled test; even with Force 7 winds and eight-foot to 10-foot breaking seas, the major problems encountered on the raft were seasickness and overcrowding. A crowded life raft is an exceptionally difficult place in which to maneuver. An urgent need for someone to reach the canopy opening can make for major upheavals, considerable discomfort and feelings of extreme irritation and hostility by the raft's other occupants. On one raft, five of the six occupants were seasick, one sufficiently so that it was necessary to effect a premature "rescue."

Similar experiences are not uncommon. In 1985, Fred Edwards, in *Yachting* magazine, reported that three out of five experienced sailors became seasick within two minutes of entering a test life raft in moderate seas.

One became so dehydrated and electrolyte-depleted that he had to be removed from the raft after 45 minutes. A recent in-the-water test conducted by West Marine Products had to be aborted because of excessive seasickness among the rafts' occupants.

It's difficult enough to make a life raft that can handle worst-case seas adequately. It's just as difficult to make a raft that's livable for long periods of time. Combining the two is a monumental task; combining the two while staying within a tight budget is a virtual impossibility. Something has to give.

Types of Rafts

The two broadest categories of life rafts are coastal and offshore models. There aren't hard and fast definitions, but generally an offshore raft will feature two flotation tubes, stacked one over the other, a closable canopy supported by inflatable arch tubes, and a kit of survival gear that includes food, water and pyrotechnic signaling devices. A coastal raft may use a single flotation tube, a canopy that lacks support arches and a much more limited survival kit, generally not including food or water.

Coastal life rafts represent an attempt on the part of the manufacturers to provide a lower cost raft for people who aren't likely to encounter severe weather conditions and who aren't apt to have a prolonged stay in a raft. They are less expensive and occupy a bit less deck space.

Coastal rafts, with one notable exception, are not approved by the ORC; the single-tube arrangement that is typical with these rafts lacks the redundancy that is felt to be necessary. An exception to the ORC regulations is the Switlik Coastal Raft, which uses a unique "sock" arrangement within its single tube to keep the entire tube inflated if punctured.

The Rafts We Tested

For this test, we rounded up a total of eight life rafts, representing five major manufacturers. Three—from Avon, Plastimo and Switlik— were coastal rafts; the other five—from Avon, Givens, Plastimo, Switlik and Zodiac—were offshore models. We tried to get six-man rafts in each case, but were only able to obtain Avon's offshore raft in its four-man version and Zodiac's in its eight-man size.

The rafts were deployed in a sheltered basin in Rhode Island and key features—flotation tubes, boarding systems, canopies and the like—were carefully inspected and compared. This process actually began with the aforementioned Chesapeake excursion, an experience that gave us a real-world opportunity to assess important features and lifesaving criteria that could be applied to our independent evaluations. In addition to visual inspections, we tried to flip each raft in order to assess capsize resistance, discovering that some rafts turn over easier than others.

Flotation tubes

The Avon Coastline and the Switlik Coastal use a single flotation tube. The Avon's tube is split into two separate chambers. If either is punctured, the other retains its air. Either chamber carries enough air to support the raft's rated load, although a puncture will collapse the canopy support.

The Switlik takes another approach. Inside the large-diameter single tube are a pair of sleeves, with one end sealed, that divide the tube into two sections. If the tube is punctured, air pressure from the intact half forces the sleevesinto the punctured section. The result is that the sleeves form an air-tight liner for the damaged tube; the entire tube remains inflated, although at a lower pressure. As with the Avon, the remaining air is sufficient to support the raft's rated load. Unlike the Avon, however, you can then use the hand pump provided to reinflate the tube to its normal buoyancy and pressure. The Switlik's canopy tubes are independent of the flotation tubes, so that a puncture has no effect on the canopy.

The two-tube rafts achieve redundancy by having the two tubes inflate independently, from the same cylinder. Redundancy is an important consideration, not only in case of puncture, but in case of a malfunction in the inflation system. This last is not as rare an occurrence as one might think. In our tests, one raft, the Plastimo Coastal, failed completely to inflate when we pulled the triggering lanyard. About 10 minutes later, its top tube inflated, but the bottom tube never did. We've spoken to several life raft specialists, who told us that a failure rate of 10 percent was not surprising.

Size

Life raft manufacturers rate their rafts in terms of capacity: four-man, six-man, eight-man, etc. We find, however, that a six-man raft will provide usable accommodations for four, at most; an eight-man raft is best suited for no more than five or six. As a general rule, if you load up a raft with more than 60 to 70 percent of its rated capacity, you'll provide an iron-clad guarantee of extreme discomfort. At the same time, too few persons in a large raft with limited stability could become unstable in rough conditions.

The actual design of the raft can affect the usable seating area. The Switlik Coastal Raft, for example, is shaped like a rounded rectangle (or a squared egg.) It's length provides considerably more leg room within its 24 square feet than do pentagonal or round shapes of the same area.

Canopies

The shape of the canopy supports also has a definite effect upon seating comfort in an enclosed life raft. Tent-shaped canopies, where the canopy walls slant in sharply toward a top horizontal tube, tend to force occupants to sit in a tiring, hunched-forward position. The Zodiac 8, with a fairly tall canopy, provided a better seating position than did the lower-profile Avon Coastline. The Plastimo and Avon offshore raft canopies were judged to fall between the other two tent-shaped models in terms of comfort.

The Switlik Coastal Life Raft uses two arched tubes to support the canopy. These tubes are almost vertical at their bases, and the arched canopy that they support provides a good deal more usable room inside the canopy than does a more-conventional tent-type canopy. Unlike the other rafts, the canopy support tubes of the Switlik Coastal do not inflate automatically with the buoyancy tubes; the raft in-flates with the canopy furled, and the arches must be inflated afterward, using a hand pump or an optional separate CO_2 inflator.

The Givens and the Switlik Search and Rescue rafts have self-inflating, curved canopy supports. The Givens inflates with the canopy up and the hatch closed (although easily openable with a push); the Switlik inflates with the canopy furled. The latter arrangement offers both advantages and disadvantages: it simplifies entering the raft, particularly from the water. On the other hand, the raft's occupants get no protection from breaking waves until the canopy is erected. With both of these rafts, the arched canopy tubes provide considerably more seating comfort and usable space than you might expect from their rather limited floor areas—20.9 and 21.6 square feet respectively.

The Plastimo coastal raft has no canopy supports. You crawl under a flat cover if you need weather protection—an uncomfortable arrangement that we don't find all that appealing.

Hatches and Ports

A canopy, when it's closed, can provide needed protection from the elements. When that protection isn't needed, though, a closed canopy presents several serious problems. The lack of a fixed visual reference, in combination with a life raft's inevitable motion, exacerbates the seasickness problem.

It is very desirable for the raft's occupants to able to see outside the raft as much as possible. A collection of survivors in a small volume such as a life raft generates a surprisingly large amount of body heat. While this may be welcome in cold weather, it can rapidly create dangerous overheating conditions in temperate or hot weather. There's not much room

Life Raft Data Sheet

Offshore Models Tested

Make	Persons	Tubes	Material	Ballast	Capsize Resistance	Floor Area (sq. ft.)	Canopy Type
Avon	4	2	Neoprene/nylon	Icelandic	Good	16	Tent
Givens	6	2	Neoprene/nylon	Toroidal/hemispheric	Excellent	20.9	Tripod arch
Plastimo	6	2	Vinyl/polyester	Icelandic	Fair	25.8	Tent
Switlik	6	2	Urethane/nylon	Toroidal	Very good	21.6	T-shaped arch
Zodiac	8	2	Vinyl/PVC	Weighted bags	Poor (2)	32.8	Tent

Coastal Models Tested

Make	Persons	Tubes	Material	Ballast	Capsize Resistance	Floor Area (sq. ft.)	Canopy Type
Avon	6	1	Neoprene/nylon	Icelandic	Good	24	Tent
Plastimo	6	1	Vinyl/polyester	Icelandic	(1)	25.8	Unsupported
Switlik	6	1	Urethane/nylon	Icelandic	Good	24	2 arches

[1] Did not inflate when triggered. 10 minutes later, one tube inflated.

[2] Small, unweighted ballast bags did not open by themselves; plastic stuck together.

for carrying water on a life raft, and excessive perspiration—or seasickness—can lead to fatal dehydration in a short time. The obvious solution is to provide adequate ventilation.

There's also a very real need to provide the raft's occupants with relatively easy access to the outside air, for purposes of elimination and, all too often, vomiting. A small hatch in the canopy of a crowded raft can make such access difficult and slow. Lastly, a closed canopy makes it impossible for a lookout to see if any vessels or aircraft are in the vicinity. A canopy with a small hatch isn't much better, even when that hatch is open.

The design of the hatches on the rafts we tested reflect the manufacturers' differing philosophies of survival. Avon and Givens, for example, opt for a relatively small opening with a sleeved porthole opposite it. This arrangement emphasizes protection against water intrusion in rough seas. Avon uses a triangular opening. Givens has a somewhat larger square one. On both rafts, visibility is limited.

Plastimo's offshore raft and the one Zodiac we tested make provision for opening one full side of their tent-shaped canopies. The Zodiac supplements this with a zippered slit in the opposite wall. Both rafts provided good ventilation and reasonable visibility. On both rafts, however, when the zipper was fully open, we had difficulty reassembling the two sections and starting the zipper.

Switlik has chosen a tack completely opposite to that taken by Avon and Givens. On both Switlik rafts, the canopy can be completely furled, if desired, or adjusted to provide varied degrees of protection. On the offshore Search and Rescue model, the arched canopy supports stay up at all times. A furlable canopy is secured to the raft at one edge; the canopy

can be unrolled over the supports to any degree desired. In the fully closed position, there's a modestly sized conventional hatch that can be closed completely.

The Switlik Coastal Raft offers even greater versatility in terms of canopy configuration. There's a furlable top, two in-dependently furlable sides, and two end sections that are permanently attached to the arched canopy supports that can be "furled" by deflating the support tubes. As a result, it's a fairly simple matter to choose a canopy configuration to suit your needs: ends only, ends and top with one or more open sides, ends and sides with open top and so on. Visibility is excellent.

It's even possible to drop one support and the top and leave what Switlik calls a "sail-away configuration." Considering the hull design of a life raft, we don't think too much of the idea. Even if you were to collapse the ballast pockets, as suggested, by "drawing them tight…," you wouldn't have much of a hull for the 10-square foot "sail" to push. And, in most cases, you'd be best off deploying a sea anchor and not trying to sail; rescuers will be looking for you where the boat was supposed to be. Nevertheless, some survivors, such as Steve Callahan (as recounted in his book *Adrift*), after realizing that help wasn't coming, have successfully accelerated the speed of their rafts toward land.

Boarding

To make any use of your life raft at all, you must first get aboard it. And this can be a bigger problem than most people realize, particularly at night in a rough sea. If you're boarding the raft directly from your boat, the technique is to jump onto the raft's canopy, rather than trying to jump into the small moving target that is presented by the raft's hatch. Canopies are soft, tough, resilient and easier to hit. Once you're on the canopy, it's usually fairly easy to find the entrance hatch in the canopy—the canopy support tubes will pop up again once your weight is removed. The two Switlik rafts deploy without the canopy in place, so you can just jump directly into the raft. We're not convinced this is easier than jumping onto the canopy, but it may make some people feel more comfortable about jumping.

If you can't enter the raft directly from your boat, but must do it from the water, the problem becomes a more serious one. All the rafts have provisions for climbing aboard, but some are distinctly better than others.

All the rafts have webbing or rope lifelines around the perimeter. The Avon Coastline simply lengthens two sections of this lifeline to provide a sort of "boarding ladder." We found that this arrangement, together with a paucity of handholds inside the raft, made for difficult boarding.

Boarding Type	Ease	Visibility	Rain Catchment
Web ladder	Good	Fair	Very good
Web ladder	Very good	Fair	Excellent
2 loops w/rung	Good	Good	None
Platform	Very good	Excellent	Excellent
Web ladder	Good	Very Good	None
Web loops	Poor	Fair	Very good
2 loops w/rung	(1)	Excellent	None
Web ladder	Very good	Excellent	None

The two Plastimo rafts are easier to board. They also use a pair of extended lifeline loops as ladders, but use a short section of garden hose as a rung stiffener. This helps, as does a more-conveniently located grab rope.

The Avon offshore raft and the Zodiac have multi-rung "rope" ladders made of webbing. This works well, but not quite as well the double-width webbing ladders used on the Givens, and the Switlik coastal raft. The ease of boarding either of these rafts is enhanced by well-located grab straps. We particularly liked the Givens arrangement, which consists of a ladder-like network of webbing that extends from the hatchway to the center of the raft, and can be detached and tucked out of the way when not needed.

The Switlik Search and Rescue replaces the boarding ladder with a self-inflating boarding platform. We found this design, which will be found on more rafts in the future due to impending U.S.C.G. regulations, a mixed blessing. While there was no problem in getting aboard the raft from the platform, it wasn't that easy to climb onto the platform itself. It's surface is slippery, and we would have welcomed more handholds. We judged this raft's ease of boarding only "good." On the other hand, the platform provides some welcome extra space if the weather is fair. On the Chesapeake Bay test mentioned above, the only member of one raft's six-person crew that did not become seasick spent the night in a survival suit on the raft's boarding platform.

Stability

This factor is the biggest bone of contention among life raft manufacturers. Life rafts achieve stability through the use of water-filled ballast bags. Until a decade ago, most rafts depended upon a few small bags. Spurred by the tragedy of the Fastnet Race of 1979 , there was a series of tests conducted by agencies of the United States, United Kingdom and Icelandic governments. The findings of these tests were that more effective ballasting was required, a position that Givens pioneered in the middle 1960's, with his patented Toroidal/Hemispheric ballast chamber.

There was a flurry of redesigning among the raft makers, and several different designs emerged. The three basic designs are: the Givens system, a toroidal chamber integral with a hemispherical bag that fills with water and hangs beneath the raft's floor; the Switlik Toroidal Stability Device, a doughnut-shaped water-filled bag that hangs below the bottom inflation tube; and the so-called Icelandic system that has several large bags attached to the underside of the raft around its perimeter containing weights to help open the bags so they can fill with water.

There has been, and will undoubtedly continue to be, a continuing argument about the effectiveness of these different systems. We certainly can't provide the last word in this argument, but we did try to evaluate each raft's stability in the calm water we were dealing with.

The Zodiac we tested was, by far, the easiest of the rafts to capsize. One man was able to accomplish this, with no difficulty, by standing on one inflation tube and pulling on the opposite edge of the raft. When we examined the Zodiac's ballasting system, we were not at all surprised to find that it consisted of several small, unweighted plastic bags. Even after 20 minutes in the water, these did not fill with water.

We judged the capsize resistance of the two Avon rafts to be fair; one man could capsize either raft, but he had to work a bit to do it. Righting was easy. Both Avons use three Icelandic-type ballast bags. The Plastimos' resistance to capsizing and ease of righting were comparable to the Avon models.

The Switlik Coastal was considerably more difficult to capsize than were the other rafts that used an Icelandic-type system. This was undoubtedly due to the large size of the bags.

Righting was also simple, aided by the highly legible instructions printed on the underside of the life raft. We judged the Switlik Coastal's resistance to capsize as good.

The Switlik Search and Rescue, with its toroidal chamber, resisted capsize even better. Two testers, working hard, could not induce a capsize. After some experimentation, we finally were able to turn the raft over by piling three persons against one of the canopy walls, tipping the raft to about 45 degrees, and then simulating the effect of a strong wind by having another person push on the raft's upper edge. When the raft was tilted to about 90 degrees, it finally went over. Righting, since the ballasting toroid was drained when the raft went over, was again easy. We judged the capsize resistance of this raft to be very good.

The Givens raft defied all our efforts to capsize it. We subjected it to the same tests as we did the Switlik, and it resisted capsize even at an estimated angle of 110 degrees. We even tried capsizing it with its lower flotation tube deflated, three persons leaning on the canopy from inside the raft and two others pushing from a dock. The raft did not go over, even at angles in excess of 90 degrees. We judged it's resistance to capsize to be excellent.

What isn't clear is the practical difference between the capsize resistance of these rafts. Our tests were meaningful but hardly realistic. The opportunity to test rafts in an actual hurricane wasn't available, even if we were willing to try it. Elaborate Coast Guard tank tests of the three principal ballasting systems—hemispheric chamber, toroidal doughnut and ballast bag—indicate all three resist capsize in a breaking sea to some extent. Coast Guard slow-motion videotapes reveal, however, that the hemispheric chamber and toroidal doughnut offer greater stability in addition to capsize resistance. Stability of any of the design is enhanced by the use of a substantial drogue.

Miscellaneous Features

Most of the rafts can be supplied in either a valise pack, for stowage belowdecks, or in a hard canister, which is deck mounted. The canister is a safer arrangement, as you may not have the time or opportunity to drag a 50- to 100-pound pack up from below while your boat sinks. The valise is useful if you lack deck space for a canister or must frequently move the raft from one boat to another. Among the hard canisters, only the glass-reinforced ones supplied by Switlik and Givens were judged rugged enough to take the beating that a piece of on-deck equipment must endure. The others are made of unreinforced molded plastic, and can easily crack. The Zodiac and Plastimo rafts are vacuum-packed in a plastic bag within the valise or canister. This seems to be a good idea, because neither the valises nor canisters are absolutely watertight.

With the sole exception of the Zodiac, which comes with a double inflatable floor, all of the other rafts have a single-layer floor design, at least in their plain-vanilla models. A double floor is an option, typically raising the raft's price by several hundred dollars to more than a thousand. It is, we feel, an option that's sufficiently important to be considered essential. Normal skin temperature is in the mid-to-high 80s and even fairly warm water can pull a lot of heat from your body in a very short time. Our testers complained about cold bottoms after only a few minutes in the rafts. The Zodiac's double bottom made a very easily noticed, and much appreciated difference.

Some of the rafts, as noted in the Data Sheet, have provisions for collecting rainwater. This is a helpful feature, but we were surprised to note that only the Givens and the Switlik Search and Rescue rafts come with a container in which this water can be stored.

Survival equipment

No two rafts seem to provide the same level of survival equipment, though all have such items as paddles (of dubious value), a bailer, seasickness pills, a knife, a flashlight and a throwable rescue quoit, attached to some polypropylene line. Offshore rafts often, but not always, include flares (an inadequate number), water (a marginal amount), and food. In any case, it behooves the purchaser of a life raft to obtain and pack a waterproof, floating abandon-ship pack with the items the raft manufacturer omitted for reasons of space and cost.

Probably the four basic additions we'd make to the gear supplied with any life raft are a handheld VHF radio in a waterproof case, a watermaker (preferably a reverse-osmosis water desalinator such as the Survivor 35, as opposed to a solar still), additional pyrotechnic signaling devices and an EPIRB. You'd also want to pack any medication that you or your crew normally take. Less obvious items are warm clothing, a more complete first-aid kit, a decent fishing line (the ones that many provide are awful) a package of plastic garbage bags (useful for all sorts of things) and a deck of waterproof playing cards.

Recommendations

The Plastimo Coastal's failure to inflate, even if it was a fluke, makes us nervous. And we don't trust the skimpy ballasting of the Zodiac. Still, most of the life rafts we looked at are capable of saving your life under the conditions most frequently encountered.

Based on our testing, we deem the Avon Coastline and the Plastimo coastal raft to be clearly less competent rafts than their offshore siblings. They probably shouldn't be considered unless it's a choice between one of them and no raft at all.

Although we think that the Avon and the Plastimo offshore rafts are good, serviceable rafts, we didn't care for the limited ventilation and visibility we encountered on the Avon nor the difficulty we had in working the Plastimo's zipper.

For most people, sailing in waters in which hurricanes and high breaking seas are rare, we like the Switlik Coastal Raft. It's more stable than the Avon or Plastimo coastal models, and is by far the most livable raft we looked at, in terms of seating comfort, ventilation and visibility.

If, on the other hand, we were setting out for an extended ocean cruise, our major concern would be rough seas and foul weather. Our choice under those circumstances would be the Givens, although we recognize we'd be giving up the Switlik Search and Rescue's superior ventilation and comfort. • **PS**

Inflatable PFDs

We tested a dozen models, with and without safety harnesses. Some were impressive.

The lifejackets we tested for this report are all inflatable-only types. Widely used in Europe and England, they are relative newcomers to the U.S. recreational boating scene.

Inflatable lifejackets are less bulky than their inherently buoyant counterparts; inflated, they provide greater flotation. On the downside, inflatables require significantly more maintenance and care in storage than do non-inflatables. Inflatable-only lifejackets are not U.S. Coast Guard approved for recreational boating. If you use one, you'll still have to purchase and carry U.S.C.G.-approved PFDs.

We obtained a dozen different models from seven different manufacturers, and evaluated them for in-the-water performance, as well as comfort, wearability, convenience and details of construction.

We tested Crewfit, Mustang, Sospenders, Techvest, Switlik, Survival Products and Norvik devices. Four models—from Crewfit, Sospenders, Switlik and Norvik—incorporate safety harnesses, while one Mustang product is an inflatable float coat.

What Sets Them Off

All the jackets use one or more CO_2 cartridges to inflate the bladder, with oral inflation as a back-up. CO_2 gas is released from the cartridges(s) either automatically—when a sensor is immersed in water—or manually, when the wearer pulls a tag (or tags) attached to the release mechanism. The jackets that employ automatic inflation also use pull tags as a secondary trigger.

The automatic triggering devices use a piece of water-degradable material to hold back a spring-loaded needle; when the trigger is immersed, the spring releases, allowing the needle to puncture the seal on the CO_2 cylinder. On the manually operated triggers, jerking the release tag pulls a small lever that forces the needle through the seal.

Inflation, with all the automatic triggers we tested, is extremely rapid, requiring three to four seconds after the lifejacket wearer hits the water. This is about the same time required for manual operation. All the jackets we tested are reusable once you replace the CO_2 cartridge and, for automatic models, the water-sensing element.

How We Tested Them

For our in-the-water evaluations, we used a short, bulky male of the type that has little problem in floating and one "sinker"—a tall, slender male who normally requires effort to stay afloat. Each tester put on each PFD (including a conventional Type I and a conventional Type III for comparison purposes.) Each tester then fell into a swimming pool.

We noted how long it took for each jacket to inflate and bring the tester up to the surface, how well each rolled an "unconscious" tester over from a face-down position, and made judgments of the stability of the face-up position. We also noted such factors as ease of manual inflation (if the automatic inflator failed or if the jacket was a non-automatic type) and ease of oral inflation (in case everything else failed.) Each tester commented on comfort, both inflated and uninflated, ease of adjustment and other convenience factors.

After use, each jacket was deflated, dried, and repacked, noting any difficulties encountered. Lastly, we went over each jacket with a critical eye, looking for possible defects in design and making judgments on the overall quality of each model's construction.

To see if a heavy rain or spray will trigger the automatic inflation device, one of our intrepid testers donned each jacket and shivered in a New England breeze while an assistant sprayed him with a garden hose.

We also tested the water-sensing portions of the automatic-inflation models for storage stability under adverse conditions. We stored samples for one week at 150°F and 95-percent-plus relative humidity, and then checked them out to see if they still worked. No automatic inflation device failed either of these tests.

Finally, we asked a number of staffers, associates and friends to try on each jacket, so that we could identify less-obvious problems with instructions, ease of adjustment and fit. Here's what we found.

Sospenders 1-38A (without safety harness) and Sospenders 1-38-AH (with safety harness)

These are the automatic-inflation adult-sized versions of Sporting Lives Inc.'s, inflatable lifejacket, with and without safety harness.

We found both Sospenders to be easy to put on—you slip into one just as you'd put on a suit vest—and easy to adjust for our testers' varying physiques. The harness model's interlocking buckle arrangement is undeniably solid, but some testers complained that it wasn't easy to close.

None of the PFDs tested is really unnoticeable while you're wearing it, but Sospenders comes very close. Both models fit nicely over the chest and feature a curved fitted collar section that doesn't chafe the neck. In our judgment, Sospenders, harness or no, represents the most comfortable—at least before inflation.

When inflated, we found Sospenders a bit less comfortable, due to bunching up of the cover around the neck, but this is a minor complaint. Oral inflation is easy.

Repacking Sospenders is, unfortunately, not easy, despite some new and extensively revised instructions supplied by the manufacturer. The bladder is only tenuously connected to the cover, and it's necessary to completely and thoroughly deflate the bladder (by depressing the check valve and squeezing out the air) before you can start folding the bladder while you are tucking a cover that always seems to be in the wrong orientation.

Crewsaver Crewfit Automatic and Crewfit Automatic with Harness

The British-made Crewfit Automatic Gas model has heavy gauge 1-1/2 inch-wide nylon straps for both the back and chest straps, as well as a double buckle arrangement that avoids the dangling tail of an adjustment strap.

The Crewfit's cover is made of a rugged, closely woven nylon.

It was easy to put on and adjust. Uninflated, it lay flatter against the chest than did any of the other PFDs except for the Techvest.

In the water, it's hard to fault the Crewfit's performance or comfort. The bright-yellow bladder is fastened to the cover along its entire edge, so when the bladder inflates, there is little bunching of cover material.

Manual inflation was easy. The oral inflation tube is equipped with a check valve. We like Crewfit's provision for easy deflation: If you remove the cap from the oral inflation tube and put it back upside down, it holds the check valve in the open position.

Repacking the Crewfit is quick and easy. The Crewfit consists of an inflatable bladder that is firmly attached to its cover for almost its entire length. This construction eliminates any problems in positioning the bladder against the cover when repacking, and makes an otherwise onerous job simple.

A secondary, but useful feature of the Crewfit automatic inflation system is that an automatic model can be converted to a manual one by simply unscrewing the automatic actuator and storing it in a safe (and dry) place. This means that the Crewfit can be used as an emergency flotation device under circumstances that call for you to be in in the water when automatic inflation is undesirable. The Crewfit's automatic actuator, unlike the bobbin used on the other automatic-inflation models, does not require periodic replacement. The most impressive feature of the Crewfit is its quality of construction. The bladder, for example, is made of 30-percent thicker material than that used on most other PFD's we tested. All seams are heat sealed and bound with tape, rather than just sealed. All straps are well stitched and firmly attached.

Techvest

Survival Technologies' Techvest, a new arrival on the market, has obviously been inspired by the Crewfit, so much so that a detailed description of the Techvest would merely echo much of what we said in the previous section.

The Techvest's most interesting design difference from the Crewfit lies in the angle at which a wearer is supported in the water. While most lifejacket manufacturers try to achieve an angle of approximately 45 degrees, Survival Technologies believes that a more-vertical orientation is desirable, since it keeps the head higher out of the water. Exact measurements are difficult, but the Techvest appeared to support a body in the water at an angle of 50-55 degrees, rather than the 45 degrees we encountered with the other products tested.

Survival Technologies has taken a positive step towards encouraging regular maintenance of an automatic PFD—purchasers who send in a registration card will receive a free replacement activator bobbin every nine months for a period of 54 months. CO2 cartridges are plastic-coated to prevent corrosion.

The Techvest's quality of construction appears to meet the high standards we encountered in the Crewfit, except for its lighter-gauge bladder material.

Norvik 30pu Lifejacket (with and without harness)

Compared to the shawl-type PFDs described above, the Norvik's closed ring design is somewhat more obtrusive when worn uninflated, and a bit more secure-feeling when inflated in the water. The Norvik's cover is a bright-orange, closely woven nylon.

The Norvik Lifejacket with safety harness uses essentially the same flotation gear, but attaches it to a substantial—and totally baffling—tangle of webbing. When we sorted it all out, we found a single 1-inch back strap, a pair of 2-inch-wide shoulder straps and a 2-inch-wide chest strap, with a single D-ring and a stainless steel tongue-and-slot interlocking closure. None of our testers found that sorting out and donning this PFD to be a simple task. Seven of the nine who tried gave up in disgust. The jacket's instructions were of little help—they were printed in Norwegian.

Our testers found that the Norvik's ring design pressed against their necks uncomfortably during long-term wearing evaluations; otherwise, we found the non-harness model easy to wear.

Repacking the Norvik PFDs is easier than the Sospenders, but not as easy as the Crewfit and Techvest. Rearming is similar to that of Sospenders and Techvest.

The Mustang Inflatable Collar

The Mustang Inflatable Collar, while still an inflatable lifejacket with about 35 pounds of flotation, differs noticeably from Sospenders, Crewfit, Techvest and Norvik in design. The Mustang is a zip-front, backless collared vest; there's no safety-harness-equipped model available. We were unable to obtain an automatic-inflation model, but the manufacturer informs us that they achieve automatic inflation with the same Halkey-Roberts valve used by Sospenders and Techvest.

To put on the Mustang, open the zipper, slip the whole thing over your head, close the zipper and fasten the strap. Uninflated, the Mustang is quite comfortable, a feeling that's helped by its light weight.

Our testers preferred the less-confined feel of the Crew-fit and Sospenders in our longer-term tests.

The only problem we encountered with the uninflated Mustang was its propensity to snag on a variety of objects. This was due to gaps in the Mustang's closure: unlike the other models we tested, which use long continuous strips of Velcro to keep the cover in place, the Mustang employs a series of small Velcro patches spaced along the openings.

Our testers noted that if they adjusted the Mustang's strap for a comfortably snug fit when the device was uninflated, it became uncomfortably tight once it inflated. In-the-water adjustment was required. Once adjusted, we found that the Mustang's vest configuration provided an exceptionally secure feeling in the water. Oral inflation wasn't particularly convenient—Mustang's inflation tube doesn't use a check valve, but has a valve that requires you to press in on the tip while you blow into it. Our testers found this inconvenient even in a calm pool.

Repacking the Mustang was little better than repacking Sospenders. Once the bladder is deflated (through the same annoying press-to-open valve at the end of the oral inflation tube), it wasn't difficult to position, but folding it and closing the cover over it was—the little Velcro patches kept popping open.

Switlik Helicopter Crew Vest and Fastnet Crew Vest (with harness)

These vests are serious pieces of life-saving equipment. The Helicopter Crew Vest consists of a nylon mesh vest with a heavy-duty zipper closure.

Inflatable PFD Data Sheet

Rank	Model	Price Vest/Rearm Kit	Type	Inflation Manual/Auto/Oral	Cartridges (# and capacity)	Weight (ounces)
Non-Harness Models						
1 (tie)	Crewfit Automatic	$199.95/$19.95	Shawl	M/A/O	1 x 33 gm.	28
1 (tie)	Survival Technologies Techvest	$159.95/$11.75	Shawl	M/A/O	1 x 33 gm. (1)	24
2	Sospenders 1-38A	$169.95/$14.95	Shawl	M/A/O	1 x 38 gm.	23
3	Norvik 30pu Automatic	$180/$14	Ring	M/A/O	1 x 29 gm.	26
4	Mustang Inflatable Collar	$199.95/$25.99	Vest	M/A/O	1 x 33 gm.	20
5	Switlik Helicopter Crew Vest	$225/$3.80	Vest	M/O	2 x 18 gm.	42
6	Mustang Inflatable Bomber Jacket MIJ145	$239.99/$7.99	Jacket	M//O	1 x 33 gm.	46
7	Survival Products Inflatable Life Vest	39.75	Vest	M/O	2 x 18 gm.	21
Harness Models						
1	Switlik Fastnet Crew Vest	$295/$3.80	Vest	M/O	2 x 18 gm.	54
2 (tie)	Crewfit Automatic	$245/$19.95	Shawl	M/A/O	1 x 33 gm.	34
2 (tie)	Sospenders 1-38AH	$214/$14.95	Shawl	M/A/O	1 x 38 gm.	37
3	Norvik 30pu Automatic	$280/$14	Ring	M/A/O	1 x 29 gm.	53

(1) Rust-resistant coating on cartridge
(2) Distributror says present shipments include patches of reflective tape for user application
(3) Two separate chambers; first tube location is excellent, second is poor, being blocked by bladder
(4) Adjustment may be inadequate for small sizes

The Fastnet Crew Vest is similar in design to the Helicopter Crew Vest except for the presence of a harness of 1-3/4-inch-wide webbing sewn onto the vest and a pair of steel D-rings instead of the plastic buckle.

Switlik's background in aircraft and military safety equipment shows in a number of ways, from the extremely detailed manuals supplied to the extra flaps of cover cloth that help avoid damage to the inflatable bladders. The seams are sealed and bound.

Nowhere does this background show up more clearly than in the use of two independent bladders, providing at least 17.5 pounds of flotation even if one cell fails completely.

Switlik doesn't make an automatic-inflation model; when we asked why, we were told that Switlik doesn't feel that automatic inflators have the degree of reliability that Switlik requires.

One penalty for this commendable degree of care is extra weight (see chart). Another penalty is bulk. While still much less bulky than any non-inflatable, the Switlik vests take up enough space on the wearer's upper chest to make it doubtful if a casual recreational boater would consider wearing one on a regular basis.

In the water, the two Switlik vests were the most secure-feeling. The uppermost bladder pops up around your jaw and cheeks, and holds you well out of the water. This is a feeling that is apt to be appreciated in high seas, but is constraining if the waves are less intimidating.

Oral inflation of a Switlik isn't easy. Since there are two separate bladders, there must be two independent oral inflation tubes. The first one that you can reach is conveniently mounted on the jacket's left side, and is protected by a restraining patch; the valve is an easy-to-use check valve. Once you inflate the first bladder, though, the inflation tube for the second bladder pops up in a position that's very difficult to reach.

The Helicopter Crew Vest has a shoulder-mounted light with a water-activated battery; the Fastnet Crew Vest doesn't.

Survival Products
Inflatable Life Vest

The Survival Products vest has several appealing features. It sells for $39.75. And it's in-the-water performance is as good as any of the jackets we tested. That's the good news. The bad news is the it isn't really suitable for use as a PFD, in our opinion.

This vest looks and behaves like the inflatables that are stowed under the seats in commercial airliners. It consists of two independently inflatable bright yellow bladders with no protective covers. The bladders are fastened together at the bottom to form a ring that goes over your head and is secured with a 1-inch-wide web strap and plastic snap buckle. There is a light, powered by a water-activated battery, attached.

The Survival Products would work in conditions where you always had enough advance disaster warning to put on a PFD immediately before hitting the water. Accidents at sea, unfortunately, don't

Whistle	Light	Pocket	Reflectors	Ease of Oral Inflation Location	Valve	Ease of Adjustment	Comfort (uninflated)	Security in water	Ease of Repacking
Yes	No	No	No (2)	Good	Excellent	Good	Very good	Very good	Excellent
Yes	No	No	Yes	Good	Excellent	Excellent	Very good	Very good	Excellent
Yes	No	Yes	Yes	Excellent	Excellent	Very good	Excellent	Very good	Good
Yes	No	No	No	Good	Fair	Excellent	Good	Excellent	Fair
Yes	No	No	Yes	Good	Fair	Excellent	Very good	Excellent	Fair
Yes	Yes	Yes	Yes	(3)	Excellent	Good	Good	Excellent	Good
Yes	No	Yes	No	Good	Fair	(9)	Excellent (7)	Very good	Excellent
No	Yes	No	No	(3)	Excellent	Excellent	Poor	Excellent	(8)
Yes	No	Yes	Yes	(3)	Excellent	Good	Good (6)	Excellent	Good
Yes	No	No	No (2)	Good	Excellent	Good	Very good (4)	Very good	Excellent
Yes	No	Yes	Yes	Excellent	Excellent	Very good	Excellent	Very good	Good
Yes	No	No	No	Good	Fair	Poor	Good (5)	Excellent	Fair

(5) Very confusing assembly to put on
(6) Some women may object to strap position
(7) Excellent, but restricted to use in cool weather; jacket is quite warm
(8) No repacking required
(9) No size adjustment. Purchase by size

work that way. A life jacket is effective only if worn. If you tried to wear this vest all the time, its unprotected bladders would be continually exposed to abrasion and the risk of puncture. We can't recommend the Survival Products vest at any price.

Mustang Bomber Jacket MIJ145

This is an inflatable float coat. It has a manual valve/cartridge with pull tag and an oral inflation tube concealed under a decorative nylon panel, and a bladder concealed between the outer shell and the lining.

The MIJ145 is a comfortable jacket, and, in the water, an effective lifejacket. We were a bit surprised at how secure it felt, since there are no provisions for adjusting the fit short of purchasing a different-size jacket. But the full jacket configuration kept our testers and the bladders in place quite well, even when the jacket was several sizes too large. A nice feature of this jacket is it's hypothermia protection; our testers noted how much less chilled they became after extended submersion.

The MIJ145, unfortunately, isn't available with automatic operation and suffers from the same awkward press-and-blow oral inflation tube. Otherwise, we had few complaints about its performance or construction.

The Mustang Bomber Jacket isn't a replacement for one of the other inflatable PFDs during the warmer portion of the boating season. In cooler weather, though, it can be a comfortable and effective article of life-saving gear.

Recommendations

In considering the advantages and disadvantages of these 12 PFDs, it's easy to get so wrapped up in comparisons that you forget a basic point: All devices, execept the Survival Products vest with unprotected bladder, are much more comfortable to wear than even the lightest-duty U.S.C.G.-approved PFD, and provide much more protection. What we're discussing here is differences among a group of very good lifejackets.

Non-Harness Inflatable PFDs: The most recent U.S.C.G. figures show that 90 percent of those who drowned were not wearing PFDs. Hopefully, less-bulky and more-comfortable PFDs will encourage more people to wear them. Our major consideration, once we were sure that the PFDs did an adequate job of keeping you afloat, was wearability. And, because there's no guarantee that a person going overboard will be conscious and won't panic enough so that purposeful activity is impossible, we prefer PFDs with automatic inflation.

Of the non-harness models, we like the Crewfit and its virtual clone, the Techvest, best. While lacking some of the niceties of Sospenders, we were extremely impressed with the well-thought-out design, very high quality of construction and ease of repacking. The Crewfit uses a heavier-gauge bladder material than the Techvest, but otherwise it appears comparable.

The Sospenders was an extremely close third to Crewfit and Techvest in our judgment. We liked the way the uninflated Sospenders felt even after an extended period of time, and we liked the attention to safety details: pocket, whistle, reflective tape. The Sospenders' brilliant orange bladder is likely to be a bit more visible than the yellow used by Crewfit and Mustang. We didn't like Sospenders' more-difficult repacking procedure—it's possible that a lot of practice will make this less of a nuisance, but we think that it's enough trouble to discourage users from conducting necessary periodic checks.

The Norvik, although a bit more secure-feeling in rough water than the first three, was downrated because it was less comfortable than the first three when uninflated. Otherwise, it performed quite well.

The Mustang Inflatable Collar feels great inflated in the water, not so great uninflated out of water. Its awkward repacking procedure helped keep it from a higher rating.

The Switlik Helicopter Vest is extremely well made, and provides the maximum in flotation security of all the non-harness PFDs we tested; it's also the least likely to be worn on a regular basis and can't be bought with an automatic inflation system. Consequently it's at the bottom of our ratings for everyday use.

The Mustang Inflatable Bomber Jacket isn't really for everyday use, but it makes an excellent supplementary device for chilly days and nights.

The Survival Products, we think, is a poor choice for any sailor.

Harness/Inflatable PFD Combinations: Blue-water sailors (we like to think) are more aware of the need for effective lifejackets than are their coastal cousins. As a consequence, our major concerns in rating harness-equipped PFDs were (assuming adequate wearability): flotation security, quality of construction and general ruggedness.

The Switlik Fastnet Crew Vest is our first choice. It's not cheap ($295), it's not light (54 ounces), but it's certainly solid. We liked the double bladder system both in terms of redundancy and support in the water, we found that the mesh vest fit securely without the need for excessive strap-tightening and we liked the heavy-duty cover and the pockets.

The Crewfit Automatic with Harness and the Sospenders 1-38AH were effectively tied for second place: we liked the Crewfit's finish and ease of packing, but we preferred the Sospenders double D-ring/steel buckle arrangement. Neither had the rock-solid feel of the Switlik in the water, but both performed very well and should give satisfactory service under the worst conditions.

The Norvik pu30 with safety harness was an extremely frustrating jacket to use: it's very difficult to put on. Once it's on, it performed quite well, but the agony of trying to sort out the tangle of black webbing was enough for us to rank it dead-last choice among the harness-equipped models.

Conclusions

Putting aside considerations of how well they behave on the high seas (very well, as a matter of fact), we look on these devices as the only PFDs that are comfortable enough to be worn on a regular basis. Regardless of how reliable a non-inflatable may be, the one you're not wearing won't do any good. • **PS**